D0160617

A SALUTATION
TO LINCOLN KIRSTEIN

Although Lincoln Kirstein occasionally refers to himself as "little me," he has been a driving figure in the humanities since the nineteen twenties, when he initiated an avant-garde literary review and helped produce exhibitions of new art as an undergraduate at Harvard. His writings on the arts frequently are inflammatory but usually they prove definitive, both because of his ability to say what he means in evocative prose of distinction and because of the probing research he has undertaken to connect apparently diverse strands of narrative.

Lincoln Kirstein inhabits a lonely, rarefied position, both on account of his style and his encyclopedic, pioneer understanding of the arts and of society. As I have followed his inspirations and his sermons since 1935, I have been edified every time he opened both barrels, critical or historical. He has revealed vistas with charged energy. For more than six decades he has been both a scholar and an active banner-bearer for theatrical dance as a major art form, collaborating with a pantheon of contemporary artists including Igor Stravinsky, Pavel Tchelitchew, Paul Cadmus, and Virgil Thomson.

The writing of Lincoln Kirstein is ripe, full of meaning, metaphor, and symbols far beyond the surfaces of the particular subject. *Dance: A Short History* is an enduring phoenix that has gone through thousands of impressions in five incarnations and is still serving neophytes and all of us who need to have our imagination stimulated. As I salute Lincoln Kirstein, I commend this book to the twenty-first century. It is a classic!

Baird Hastings
Musician and author of
Choreographers and Composers
June 1994

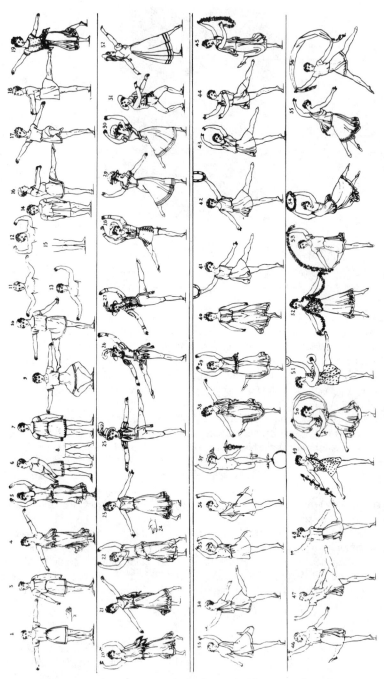

From "The Code of Terpsichore" by Carlo Blasis: London 1830.

DANCE

A Short History
of Classic Theatrical Dancing

LINCOLN KIRSTEIN

* * *

Anniversary Edition

With an appreciation by Nancy Reynolds

A DANCE HORIZONS BOOK
Princeton Book Company,
Publishers

This is an unabridged republication of the
original edition, first published in 1935,
by G. P. Putnam's Sons, New York, and reissued
in 1942, by Garden City Publishing Co., Inc.,
New York, under the title *The Book Of The Dance,*
to which an additional chapter was added.

ISBN 87127-019-6

Library of Congress Card Number 70-77179

Printed in the United States of America

Anniversary Edition, 1987

Princeton Book Company, Publishers
P.O. Box 57
Pennington, NJ 08534

Cover Illustration
Courtesy Bibliothèque Nationale, Paris

AN APPRECIATION

Originally published in 1935, *Dance*—the first comprehensive dance history in English—remains the most widely read introduction to the rich and varied chronicle of how man has moved to music in theatrical presentations through the centuries. In more than 50 years, it has not been superseded, although its author would be the first to argue that his book is not—and cannot be—complete. The text, once briefly updated, stops in 1942; one will find nothing here of the great Greek cycle of Martha Graham, the reductive masterpieces of George Balanchine, or the sometimes hermetic mindset that informs postmodernism.

The years since its publication have seen both a remarkable explosion in dance activity and the stretching of conceptual boundaries as to the very nature of the art. Moreover, dance scholarship, virtually nonexistent when Kirstein wrote, has become a respected academic discipline; scholarly monographs, archives devoted to dance subjects, and the age of video have brought to light exciting primary material not available to the historian of the 1930s. One has only to consult the bibliography of Kirstein's own brilliant *Movement and Metaphor* to be aware of the vastly increased resources for students of dance history.

What has not been superseded is the book's quality of thought and powers of synthesis. Educated in the time-honored tradition of classical humanism—Latin, Greek, literature, art—Kirstein brought to his dance history investigations a knowledge of Western culture enflamed by a love affair with the stage. Dance is presented as more than a series of productions or a sequence of movements; politics, the arts, and society are as much a part of his narrative as the steps that were performed. In range of thought and sweep of statement he is the first—and, so far, perhaps, the only—great generalist in the field. It is safe to say that the dance world has not produced a more fearless, erudite and impassioned spokesman.

Dance is a *tour de force* of a young man not yet 30, and it was by no means the author's sole undertaking at the time. In addition to many nondance activities, he had already written a long scholarly article on Diaghilev and a monograph on Fokine; collaborated with Romola Nijinsky on her biography of her husband (a task that required as much emergency hand-holding as it did research and writing); brought George Balanchine to America; and made possible the world premiere of the eternal *Serenade*. In the year the book was published, the first Balanchine-Kirstein company made its professional debut in New York. Ahead lay the pioneering dance history journal, *Dance Index;* the founding of the Dance Archives; and the long flowering of Kirstein's "life tutelage" under Balanchine, the creation of a living Balanchine laboratory, the New York City Ballet.

One must not look to Kirstein, in this book or elsewhere, for unbiased observations. He has been scathing on the subject of modernism, in art as well as dance. Academic classicism, as manfested in the ballet, is the cornerstone of his artistic universe. In the original forward to *Dance* he wrote: "Ballet will be presented as a basic, skeletal training on which our best theatrical dancing depends, from which it has stemmed, in which it constantly revives itself." And there were deeper implications. *"La danse,"* he was fond of saying (using ballet's original language, perhaps for heightened effect), *"c'est une question morale."* A decision about life. "What I love about the ballet is not that it looks pretty. it's the method in it. Ballet is about how to behave."

Nancy Reynolds

FOREWORD

No history of the origins and development of stage-dancing exists in English. Such a work would fill volumes without achieving completeness. Not only should all phases be covered under such headings as 'Dance and Music,' 'Dance and Costume,' 'Dance and Theater,' 'The Dancer's Social Position,' but each of these would be subdivided into books treating Italy, France, Scandinavia, Germany, England, Spain and Russia. At least a third of such a series would be occupied with Near and Far East, Africa, Islam, etc. It would be a life task, not for one person, but for a staff of devoted encyclopædists.

This book outlines some forms of theatrical dancing in the Western Hemisphere. *Ballet* will be presented as a basic, skeletal training on which our best theatrical dancing depends, from which it has stemmed, in which it constantly revives itself. Ballet, as a form, is as important as the invention of perspective in painting or the symphony in music; that is, a major contribution of Western culture. India, China, Japan and Java have had little or no effect on European dancing, except in recent sporadic pastiches, and are hence hardly mentioned, except here, in hopes that some informed historian may give us a comprehensive hand-book to this great manifestation of Eastern civilization.

In recent years there has been a rebirth of interest in dancing, not only as spectacle or pretext for brilliant shows, but in dancing for its own sake, and in dancing as a means for social expression. This brief history will attempt to show a few of the vicissitudes dancing has withstood, how it developed its forms to survive economic, religious and moral changes, how a residual element has persisted in a supple, continuous line which is the great tradition of theatrical dancing, and which ceases to be traditional (in the good sense) as soon as it stagnates, or stops absorbing those many elements, which, at first, may appear to be the reverse of traditional. No central or unifying theory of recurrent manifestations in the dancer's art will be attempted in this necessarily brief work. Such theories do exist, and even here there will be enough documentation to support a good deal of speculation. Theatrical dancing, besides being an art, is an exact science and a rigorous craft. The forms it has employed for the last two hundred years under the general term of 'ballet-dancing' have produced a considerable body of practical and theoretical writing defending certain standards and opposing experimental intrusions. No attempt will be made here to compete with these in a technical discussion of ballet. That requires class-rooms; bars and mirrors alone.

Theatrical dancing is a visual and personal art. It is supported by music, but music in this book will be less emphasized than, for example, the development of the stage floor, or of costume design, or of the economic and social background surrounding particular performances, mainly because in monographs on great musicians such as Lully, Rameau, Gluck or Tchaikovsky, the musical element has been completely treated, with the aid of musical comparison and example. Pictures are the best part. They show actual dancers as their audience saw them; not in movement, alas, but in essential style. As for personalities, one could make another kind of history entirely out of dancers' biographies. Here, the gossip is chosen to show the quality of an epoch with dancers in it, rather than to give color which abounds anyway.

This work has no claim to completeness or originality. In it no original research has been involved, merely a considerable reading of available bibliography in three languages and a fourth in translation. Europeans will quickly recognize sources the names of which are given in notes at the back. Conclusions of the best authorities on ancient dances have been accepted without question, although obvious disagreements are always the author's. For contemporary dancing it is the author speaking entirely, he having been fortunate enough to have seen, or to have talked with many of its creators and performers. Wherever possible, source documents have been quoted. At the end of the book will be found acknowledgments, an outline of important dates, a selected bibliography and suggestions for its use. There is also a list of gramophone records illustrating important dances.

CONTENTS

DANCE

CHAPTER I

Origins: Definitions: Primitive Dances

Under the stress of joy, Man makes words. These words are not enough; he prolongs them. The prolonged words are not enough; he modulates them. The modulated words are not enough, and without even perceiving it, his hands make gestures and his feet start to move.

(From the Chinese)

THE ENGLISH word *dance* is close to the French *danse*, which in turn is supposed to derive from the ancient high German *danson*, to stretch or drag. This meaning, 'to stretch,' is important to hold in mind. *Danson* becomes in Middle-English, *daunce*, or less frequently *dawnce*; in Swiss and Dutch, *dans*; in Danish, *dands*; in Portuguese, *dança*; in Spanish and Italian, *danza*; in German, by the modification of Grimm's law, *Tanz*. *Danson* and *Tanz* have in common *an*, a root-combination of letters which are present in the original Sanskrit *tan*, which meant tension, stretching. In Greece it is *teinein*, to stretch; in Latin many of our words stem from the verb, *teneo*: notably, and probably directly: tension, intense, tenuous, etc. The Lithuanian is *dinsan* or *thinsan*.

It is apparent, therefore, that the idea of tension, from the very beginning, has been foremost in people's minds when they have thought about dancing seriously enough to invent or adapt word-sounds for it.

In all parts of the world, regardless of climate or other outside influence, there is a striking similarity in *all* of the earlier manifestations of human activity, whether it be in Canada, Java, South Africa, Greece, Tahiti, or Tierra del Fuego. Without any palpable mutual contact or intercourse, certain rites or habits of custom can be continually recognized as spontaneously correspondent. Normal human vigor seems to express itself emotionally through the medium of dance with an instinctive exuberance almost identically formulated. Obviously, there are differences in accompaniment of music and costume, governed by geography and accidental historical considerations. But, aside from these, and the nomenclature, there is an astounding likeness, even in small matters, in all primitive cultures.

Not only is a study of primitive dancing compulsory for a comprehension of the origins of dramatic art, but a constant recollection of its many categories, forms and uses continually classifies occasions for dancing right down to our own day. We may have lost the original significance of a date in our calendar or the source of its rite, but it always exists beneath if we lay bare a thin surface. In ancient Greece, spring festivals were the occasion for choral competitions; the clash of Roman sword dances reëchoed to symbolic fights in the contest of the new year and the old. The Christian Mass reiterated the ritual drama of dismembered Osiris, a tribal scape-goat. The Twelfth-

Night Masquerades in London's Inns of Court have a complete ancient magical precedent of mummery or disguising, while modern American negro spiritual singing, and 'sanctified' dancing presuppose not only a Congo heritage but are parallel to the transports of Bacchic Mænads, the mediæval Italian flagellants who sang their *Laudi,* and the mad dancers of Northern Europe whose mania attended the Black Plague.

The subject matter of primitive, or source dances is the seasons of man's life, the seasons of vegetation, and the seasons of the tribe's development or mythic history. By the seasons of man, one means the occasions of his birth and entrance into his tribe, the occasion of his coming-of-age, the marking of adolescence when he becomes a marriageable hunter, the occasion of his marriage, when he commences to increase his tribe, and the occasion of his death, when he quits his tribe. These human seasons have their correspondence in the solar wheel; spring, or planting time, compassed by the equinox; summer, the growing season, stamped by one solstice which we know as Midsummer's Night or the Eve of Saint John; autumn, the harvest; then winter, the dead season which has in its other solstice, sleep, and the rebirth of the sun. Tribal history itself furnishes many occasions for dance and song, not only the current events of the tribe, everyday life of necessary huntings or plantings, but the whole epos of a memorable past; old wars, old victories, old miracles; the worship of the ancestor Totem. Death dances were also connected with the ritual around fresh-dug graves, when the killed young tribesman met in the clouds, the fathers of his father.

Within these grand divisions two convenient subsections suggest themselves,—those dances which originate in social aims, and those which have a magic or religious purpose. There are birth dances of family and tribal congratulation, initiation dances which instruct new tribal members into cult-secrets and sexual information, marriage dances of sexual selection and property endowment, war dances and dances of welcome to strangers, or testimony of good fellowship. No hard or fast separation from magico-religious rites can be asserted, but there is an obvious difference between such functions, and those which involve dance worship of the tribe's deity, Sun, Moon, Fire or River, Snake or Lion which gave the tribe its seed. Definitely utilitarian dances involving mimicry and magic are more dramatic, more concentrated than the others. Food, fish or game are desired. Or rain is needed. Or floods must be dried up. Then dance for it. A warrior is sick. Dance the demons out of him. A man dies. Dance to lay his ghost and protect his survivors from possible threats of his wandering shade. As Ruth Benedict says of the American Zuni, in 'Patterns of Culture':

> The Dance, like their ritual poetry, is a monotonous compulsion of natural forces by reiteration. The tireless pounding of their feet draws together the mist in the sky and heaps it into the piled rain clouds. It forces out the rain upon the earth. They are bent not at all upon an ecstatic experience, but upon so thorough-going an identification with Nature that the forces of Nature will

swing to their purposes. This intent dictates the form and spirit of Pueblo dances. There is nothing wild about them. It is the cumulative force of the rhythm, the perfection of forty men moving as one, that makes them effective.

Since death and disease are believed due to magical or supernatural reasons, those persons who have supernatural control are used to combat them. Hence magicians in using dances as medicine can be considered the first choreographers. As a magical operation, dancing is important for the attainment of desirable ends of every conceivable kind. From dancing benefit comes to both individual dancer and dancing group. Strength is generated, inculcated and a harmonious dynamism is set up towards a definite aim. Hence, in earlier times, dance was an absolute expression of the whole human being, since tribal members were completely religious.

D. H. Lawrence writes of a group dance, in 'Mornings in Mexico':

All the men sing in unison, as they move with the soft, yet heavy bird tread which is the whole of the dance, with bodies bent a little forward, shoulders and heads loose and heavy, feet powerful but soft, the men tread the rhythm into the center of the earth. The drums keep up the pulsating heartbeat and for hours, hours, it goes on.

Even before there was definite, separated accompaniment, primitive people could not help being conscious of the sound of their feet tapping the earth. Dancers, in themselves, created a percussive accompaniment, and it was but a short step from clapping palms together, or on their thighs or bellies, to the slapping on an animal's skin, stretched between squatting knees or over a frame. Melody, the line of tune, whether imitation of wild bird notes or a vocalized projection of ordinary speech, is subsequent ornament on the initial skeleton of rhythmic beats. 'Keeping in time' is a necessity in dance and the essence of music for it not only states the interval of the rhythm but it enables one to remember it. Percussive ordinance aids a solo dancer, but is an integral part of communal dance, providing a monitory signal, and a control of the group cadence which can be accelerated or relaxed with the intention of the dance's leader.

In natural, unfettered societies, the whole body, not merely parts of it, participates in this language, but our civilizing education in the conventions of respectful politeness teaches us not to point, not to laugh too loud, not to leap for joy, not to embrace in streets. Our demonstrative idiom has been withered from the time when kings in Israel tore their hair, wept aloud, beating their breasts or throwing themselves on the ground, or when King Charlemagne tore his beard for wrath at news of Roncevaux. The effect of this withering is most apparent in modern social dances and their practically static positions and movements.

When people seek to repress emotions too strong for expression, they adopt certain familiar gestures to explain conveniently what otherwise could not be risked to words. Signals for Yes and No, are much the same all over the globe, but there are tribes in Thibet and Africa, among whom nodding the head means No, turning it from side to side, Yes. The bending of one individual before another is universally accepted as a mark of respect, signifying both self-abasement before superior power and willingness to assume a comparatively defenseless position before the superior's mercy. A hand rubbed on the belly means hunger. Covering or uncovering the head, hat-tipping from the visor-raising of medieval helmets, nose-rubbing in mutual affection, handclasp, all are part of a visualized mimic telegraphy, but not of necessarily imitative gesture. Mimicry is another department of the dance; however highly developed, it is, nevertheless, secondarily developed.

Then there are movements of a more or less useful nature, which become regularized for efficiency, and by repetition methodized and professional; the swing of sowers and wood-choppers, bend and sweep of brick-layers or masons, heave and haul of sailors on tilted decks, the shift of weight from shoulder to shoulder of blacksmiths or miners. These actions, continuously repeated, tend to become, with alternations of strong and weak muscular reaction, infinitely precise, subtle, ingenious and quick; the movements, for example, of the fingers of cigar-makers, brain-surgeons or ivory-carvers, each possessing beauty in their mechanic proficiency. Fragmentary patterns in the physical acts of workmen, traffic-signals of policemen, the wind-up of a baseball pitcher, piston-legs of a Nurmi, arms of Koussevitsky, have qualities of dance about them, although it is snobbish and inaccurate to consider them, which is frequently done, 'as beautiful as a dancer's.'

There are also the gestures wholly separate from the instinctive, useful or acrobatic, which are neither linked to the physical world which conditions them, nor are direct reactions from exterior stimuli. These gestures are the manifest language of our interior lives, bodily signals of states of mind, our bodies being the most delicate and frankest instruments of all our action, cerebral as well as physical. These signals have ideographic significance. When seen by the eyes of those whom we interest, our thoughts and feelings are quite clear, even without words. These gestures have been called 'plastic epiphenomena,' or border activities of our moral lives. Like many physiological, functional gestures, a great number of psychological ones are spontaneous. Hops and leaps of children, or grown-ups in primitive society; spasmodic movements like fist-clenchings, lip-bitings, accelerated breath in anger, a large vocabulary of suggestive caress, tenderness, hostility or beckoning,—these are acts of which every one makes use, without having to be instructed by others, or even by observing others.

From the point of view of actual technique, primitive dancers have not a great deal to offer either in methodology or structure for our theatre. The ends for which they dance are entirely different from ours. Nevertheless, physiologically, as ritual health, they are fascinating. It is obvious how highly developed are the pelvic, visceral and gluteal regions of primitive people. The movement of the belly is a great aid toward digestion. Exercises of the female pelvis ease birth. The general physical condition of a constant dancer is apt to be excellent, and excellence in competitive dancing is an index of sexual vigor aiding in the choice of a well-developed, durable mate. All individualistic physical considerations are important but definitely secondary to the communal needs. Their results are frequently gratifying, but they are by no means the initial impulse behind tribal dances, which many popularizers would have us believe are merely sexual games or amorous pastimes. Primitive dances are, first of all, useful to the tribe as a whole for the large reason of its tribal survival and continuation.

Seeing films or hearing phonograph records of primitive dances and music is infinitely more valuable than reading descriptions of them, however detailed, which in print merely register as variations of shuffling, hopping, handclapping, howling, swaying, and a missionary's assurance that they were 'indecent,' 'barbaric,' 'graceful' or 'repetitious,' which in all likelihood they were.

Even in its most advanced stages primitive dancing is still definitely itself: that is, *primitive:* repetitious, limited, unconscious, and however beautiful or novel, an extremely retardative and closed expression in comparison to the able use of the dances of cultures with progressive technique.

When, in the Western Hemisphere, architecture and dance proceed together, consciously developing in complement to each other, certain forms of theatrical dancing result, which are the subjects of this book, forms of dancing devised to interest an audience placed in specific physical conditions so they may be receptive to the performance of trained executants.

CHAPTER II

Ritual Myth and Drama-Dance of Egypt

AMONG primitive people, magical dances were the first methods for dealing with the unknown, and as such, were the earlier manifestations of both science, religion, and forms which were more immediately impressive, of poetry, drama, and their combined use. Imitation of animal movements by dancers is recognized all over the world. In early stages of the history of hunting tribes these simple ceremonies were probably purely descriptive. By the employment of sympathetic magic, by flapping arms like wings, raising feet like a bear's paw, the food supply would be increased. But later the cult grew into an animal worship. Tribal ancestors were believed to return to their old homes in the guise of animals, an efficient way to preserve some animals from extinction by totem *tabu*. This belief also served as a rudimentary externalization of the hunter's admiration for stealth, grace and courage inherent in animal energy. Tribal clans took as their badge ancestral bear, wolf or buffalo, and in return for propitiatory behavior, the spirits residing in the beasts interested themselves in their clan's welfare and continuation. With the periodic repetition of these songs and dances two important features emerge: the more or less conscious codification of ritual; the creation of position of priest-dancer, who, responsible for the correct maintenance of rites, wields great power. In most primitive society there is an imperative necessity for the identical rehearsal of ceremonies. Strict accuracy of detail, careful repetition of all the various elements are believed to be essential to the success of the rite. And it was, of course, a convenient loophole for the witch-doctors when rain wouldn't fall, or when game continued scarce, to show their people that the guilt lay in their faulty performance. In the Bear dances of the Kwakiutl Indians of Vancouver Island,

> All dancers who made mistakes in their performances must always fall down, as if dead, and the Bear impersonators fell upon them and tore them to pieces. Sometimes this was a pretense, but, according to the traditional teaching for certain errors there was no mitigation of the penalty.*

Just as the essence of magic is faith in some secret sympathetic link, so ritual, or the methodology of achieving magical results, consists in the *doing* of what is wanted to *be done*. When warriors return from a victorious foray, they reënact their success in a mimic dance, for the benefit of those who stayed at home. From a particular victory this easily tends to become a generalized war game, which not only commemorates that one particular triumphant day, but which is important to practice before the next expedition or battle to insure success. The dance becomes a wishful prayer, a wishful prophecy which, when courage, boldness and cunning are needed, rehearses these virtues in imitation,

* *Patterns of Culture,* by Ruth Benedict. Houghton Mifflin Co. Boston. 1934.

keeping a battle technique fresh in mind and body for that near moment when its use will be actual.

The phenomenon of periodicity regulates the repetition of rituals. Every one is conscious of the pulse under his left breast. Mornings follow nights, and, compassed by sun and moon, the day's phrase in seven given numbers. The return of the wheeling seasons regulates the presence or absence of food-supply. The exact dates are regulated by geographical features of the land itself, and its place on the globe. In the South Seas dancing men await the hour of the Monsoon; in Egypt, the minute of the Nile's flooding.

In the extremely complex, highly organized patterns of Egyptian civilization we can see ritual in a high form, becoming a fine art separate from the belief which was the source of its arising. Not only can parallels be taken from the Egyptian cult to match subsequent degenerations in Greece and Rome, but an understanding of how they treated their resurrection myth and how they produced it as a dramatic act-of-faith will prepare us for striking similarities with ancient Greece, Rome, and early Christianity in the origins of their dramatic dance. In a homogeneous culture, which suffered, until its precipitate decline, from so few exterior influences that each at its inception is at once apparent, we can find a rich mine of documentation and vital testimony. Every factor, from the prompting geographical necessity, the historic myth, the tribal deification, the ritual honors and supplication, the priest-ordained laws for repetition, and finally the myth, become mass dance-dramas, is clearly displayed.

The whole life of Egypt was based, and to a great extent still depends on the annual inundation of the river Nile. The country is a virtual desert, served by the flowing vitality of waters which split it. The river is controlled by an elaborate, ingenious system of dams, locks and irrigation-canals, regulating the floods by distributing a yearly renewal of fertile mud washed down its bed from the equatorial lakes and mountains of Abyssinia. The rise of the river is watched by the entire population with great concern. If it should become too high and run wild, or if it should be too low to enter the canals, a year's famine results. The Nile starts to swell in June. It is in flood-tide by the end of July or start of August. High-water mark passes in September, and with luck, by then the whole countryside is submerged. The river starts to recede in October, and by late December or mid-January it is back in its ancient bed. With summer's approach Egypt is parched, dry, deadened with acrid layers of desert dust. From mid-April to mid-June the brown country gasps for a new Nile. The necessity for a resurrection legend, or body of belief in human survival is obvious. If it had not expressed itself in the particular form of the Osiris myth, it must have created a similar one. The reality of the Osiris legend is literally reflected in the yearly existence of the Egyptian people.

Without trying to determine a human kingly prototype for Osiris in Egypt's remote past, let us know his story in its developed form as Plutarch collected it from various sources which in his lifetime were not yet dead. Osiris means 'Many-Eyed,' which is used as the sun's name in many old cultures. He was the bastard of the Sea God and the Earth Goddess. When the Sun God, Ra, found out his wife had tricked him, he cursed her issue, vowing it would be born in no-month and no-year. But the Earth Goddess had another lover, Thoth, who, playing checkers with the Moon, won from her the seventy-second part of every day. Combining out of these parts five whole days, Thoth added them to the three hundred and sixty of the Egyptian year. This is the mythical origin of the supplementary time needed to reconcile the Lunar with the Solar calendar. On these five days, considered as entirely outside recorded time, the Sun's curse had no strength. Osiris was born on the first day. At his birth a loud voice proclaimed the coming of the Lord of All. On the second day his mother bore Horus, on the third his brother-adversary Set, the fourth, his sister-wife Isis.

As King, Osiris redeemed the Egyptians from barbarism, gave them laws and named them gods. Isis, his sister-wife, to whom Plato attributed the invention of singing and dancing, discovered wheat and barley, and Osiris introduced the cultivation of cereals, inducing the people to stop eating men and start eating corn. Osiris first gathered fruit and grew vines for grapes. He lent the rule of Egypt to his wife and traveled over the world's face, spreading everywhere agriculture and civilization. Returning in triumph, he was adored as god. But his brother, tainted with the Sun God's curse, and seventy-two companions representing the cheated year, plotted against him. By a trick Set took his measure, had a coffin made to fit it, and in jest, contrived to place him in it. This he shut, sealed, and flung into the Nile. Isis, hearing, mourned, and through many involved adventures, sought her beloved's body. But Set, hunting a wild boar by moonlight found the coffin, and cut the corpse into fourteen parts. Isis discovered each in turn, separately buried them as she found them, so that he might be worshiped in many places. However, his penis had been devoured by the Nile fish. She made an image of it, instead, and buried that. The Sun God now took pity on bereaved Isis and when the parts of the dead god were reassembled, all the usual burial ceremonies were observed. Isis fanned the dead clay with her wings and Osiris was resurrected, and from then on ruled as King in the world of death, where he is Lord of Time, judge of death, consigner to life everlasting or hell's reward.

In Osiris as their symbol, Egyptians saw the promise of eternity and believed with literal confidence that they too would inherit eternal life if their surviving friends or families dealt with them as Osiris had been used by Isis. The ritual ceremonies at death were observed with a most scientific, fanatical strictness, copying the ones which jackal-headed Anubis and Horus had performed over the dead god. At every human burial was reënacted the divine mystery of mourning friends attending the torn relics. By spells, offerings and manipulation the wrapped corpse was reanimated. The mummy of each dead man was Osiris, and from the time of Middle Kingdom on (ca. 2300 B.C.) it became the custom to address the corpse as Osiris Insert-His-Name. The professional mourners acted his two sisters, Isis and Nepthys; Anubis, Horus and all of the rest of the holy hierarchy. There was a national industry of funeral trades; tomb-making, decorating, furnishing, embalming. There were classes of professional mourners equipped with alabaster bottles to contain their purchased tears which were buried together with the mummy's celestial furniture; singers of funeral hymns, and dancers for funeral feasts.

Two chief cities were associated with the Osirian cult, Busiris, in lower Egypt, which enshrined his backbone, and Abydos in upper Egypt, reliquary of the divine head. From about the year 2400 B.C., Abydos, previously an obscure village, became the Holy Sepulcher of the kingdom, and every pious subject longed to rest near his god's grave. As in all these mortuary affairs, the economic consideration was important; those who were not rich enough to afford propinqual burial had their remains piloted past the spot before reburial in their native land, or had cenotaphs or memorials raised nearby to share, in sympathy, the god's reflected glory.

A festival for Isis was celebrated when the Nile started to rise. It was believed that the wife-sister was mourning for her loss, and her tears falling fast flooded the river. Osiris, as god of corn, was mourned in midsummer. The harvest past, the fields lay barren, the river was dry mud, life itself static. A signal for the river-rising was given from heaven. Sirius, clearest of fixed stars, which they named Sothis, appeared in the eastern dawn, nearing the time of the summer solstice, just when the river slowly commenced to swell. Sothis was the star of Isis. Its apparition marked the start of the Holy Year, and the first work of great importance was cutting the dams, which up till now had checked the pregnant Nile. August released the waters. In November there was enough subsidence for sowing. In March and April wheat, barley and sorghum could be reaped. After the dam-breaking, the next great observance was the committal of seed to the soil. It was a mournful November ritual, shrouded with preventive and protective magical fear. The Egyptian harvest was not in autumn as is ours and most European and Mediterranean peoples, but in the three spring months. The harvest, though really an occasion for joyful thanksgiving, was marked with show of grief by the precautionary conventions of the Egyptian literalists, in order to give no offense to the god deprived of his fruit. The farmer, in cutting the first gilded sheaf, was severing the body of the corn-god and trampling it to bits under the hooves of his cattle on his threshing floor. A melancholy hymn of apologetic invocation, which the Greeks knew as the *Maneros*, propitiated ever-suffering Osiris.

On the night of the memorial of his divine passion, there was a festival of nocturnal illumination observed throughout the kingdom, whose oil-lamps commemorated not only dead Osiris, but all the ghostly company who lived with him from all time, for all time. It was All Souls' Night which has been anciently observed with us in the form of All Hallow's Even, and which remnants of disguising have descended to us with all sense of the magic mummery forgotten. The purpose of the ceremonies, detailed by Plutarch, were to represent in dramatic form, with the agency of dance, music, song and pageantry, the search for the god's dead body, its joyful discovery and assembly, followed by its resurrection. With shaven heads the celebrants annually mourned a buried idol, slashing their breasts, opening old wounds, until after the several days they professed to find the mangled pieces.

The rites lasted eighteen days, and set forth the nature of Osiris in his triple aspect as dead, dismembered, and finally reconstituted by the union of scattered limbs. Small images of the god were molded of sand or vegetable earth and corn, to which incense was sometimes added; his face was painted yellow and his cheek-bones green. These images were cast in a mold of pure gold, which represented the god in the form of a mummy, with the white crown of Egypt on his head. The festival opened with a ceremony of plowing and sowing. Two black cows were yoked to the plow, which was made of tamarisk wood, while the share was of black copper. A boy scattered the seed. One end of the field was sown with barley, the other with spelt, and the middle with flax. During the operation the chief celebrant recited the ritual chapter of 'the sowing of the fields.' On the tenth day, at the eighth hour, the images of Osiris, attended by thirty-four images of deities, performed a mysterious voyage in thirty-four tiny boats made of papyrus, which were illuminated by three hundred and sixty-five lights. On the twelfth day, after sunset, the effigy of Osiris in a coffin of mulberry wood was laid in the grave, and at the ninth hour of the night the effigy which had been made and deposited the year before was removed and placed upon boughs of sycamore. Lastly, on the eighteenth day, they repaired to the holy sepulcher. Entering the vault by the western door, they laid the coffined effigy of the god reverently on a bed of sand in the chamber. So they left him to his rest, and departed from the sepulcher by the eastern door. Thus ended the ceremonies in the month of Khoiak.*

Osiris as a preëminent type of resurrection god, was the hero of a real mystery-play, or tragedy annually produced at Abydos. In this purely ritual drama we can recognize the three essential ingredients of Greek popular tragedy which by the time it was written, some thousand years later, would, in spite of religious and moral significances, be pretty well secularized. There is for Osiris an *agon,* or contest with his enemy-brother Set; there is his *pathos* of suffering: defeat, death and dismembering: there is his *anagnorisis,* or recognition. Similarly were celebrated in Babylon the rites of Dumuz-i-absu or Tamuz 'true-son-of-the-waters.' The midsummer ceremonies of gored Adonis echo the fading of the year's flower. In Syria the cults of Tammuz and Attis can be considered as purely ritual features rather than as ritual become art. But in Egypt and Greece the rituals of Osiris and Dionysos are represented as much or more in art as they are in ritual.

Art is not an imitation of nature. It arose from the breaking down and intensification of religious essences by magical methods for desirable ends, just as in chemistry certain substances must be split up for a new gas. It involved

* *The Golden Bough,* by Sir James George Frazer. The Macmillan Company. New York. 1930. Page 375.

synthesis, intensification and repetition of observation. A rite, as something done for a purpose, had no intention of imitating, competing with or imposing on nature. A rite was an aid in deriving strength from nature and frequently sympathetic mimicry was employed. In ritual dances or dramas, the priest, leader, chief-actor, or first-dancer becomes in his person as god or hero, the personification or personalization of the entire enacted legend. The ritual is expressed *en masse* by the dancing group, but the first-dancer is used as a focus, with which every other dancer can identify himself and gain emotional tension. The Pharaoh could represent the incarnation of Osiris. This human mortality would be fused with his god's divine immortality. The emotion of a nation could be polarized for religious and political reasons on the personal drama of a first-dancer. Dancing is a constant reminder of life and death, in its various aspects as rite, tragedy, or mass. In Egypt this periodic festival framed with dancing-praise not an *immortal,* but a *perennial* god. This aspect of divinity was perhaps more attractive to a people constantly at the mercy of opposing seasons than the Christ, who, once resurrected, was never to die again.

An inscription of one I-Kher-Nefert, an official of the King, Usertsen III (ca. 2400 B.C.) has left us a record of the annual mystery performed at Abydos. I-Kher-Nefert seems to have been responsible for the organization of the spectacles; and tells us of the rôles which he himself took.

> I performed the coming forth of Ap-uat when he set out to defend his father; I drove back the enemy from the Neshmet boat; I overthrew the foes of Osiris; I performed the 'Great Coming-Forth'; I followed the god in his footsteps; I made the boat of the god to move and Thoth....I caused Osiris to set out in the Boat, which bore his beauty. I made the hearts of the dwellers in the East to expand with joy, and caused gladness to be in the dwellers in the West, when they saw the beauty as it landed at Abydos, bringing Osiris Khenti-Amenti, the Lord of Abydos, to his palace.

As with dancing, music and religion in ancient Egypt were interdependent, though in all likelihood the cults modified and controlled music, which was primarily an accessory. The Egyptians had wind, stringed and percussive instruments as well as bone and clay whistles, harps and buzzers. Bands of female singing dancers were attached to temples for the constant honor of its god. The royal houses possessed troupes of entertainers which could serve on secular as well as sacred occasions. Slaves were taught dancing as well as music, to be domestic entertainers; and much later there was a class of professional performers who had no link with either private life or public ceremony.

However, as far back as the first Dynasty (ca. 3000 B.C.) a wooden relief of the King Semti shows dancing as plastic prayer. The King's pose would show him moving rhythmically to simple instrumental music or hand-clapping. An official of the King Assa (fourth dynasty, ca. 2400 B.C.) brought from the land of Punt a pygmy dancer who 'knew the dance of his god' and was believed to have come from the spirit-world. Negro midgets were prized as buffoons and grotesque dancers. There is a fine ivory statuette of a dancing pygmy in the Metropolitan Museum of New York City, dated ca. 1950 B.C. The little creature, clapping his hands to mark time, was part of a toy which danced if its strings were pulled. Wall reliefs at Gizeh of the Empire (ca. 1580–1150 B.C.) show girls posturing with tambourines, clacking castanets curved and carved to form conventionalized fingers. Although Egyptians were fond of buffoonery and gesticulation, they had no public shows of pure amusement like our theater, nor were there pantomimic exhibitions, accompanied by scenic representations. The nobles of later epochs forbade their children to learn dancing. Professional dancers and acrobats were enjoyed largely in private social-entertainments. In Roman times, there was public dancing at banquets in pleasure gardens at Canopus and Alexandria by night and day, involving big crowds and considerable license.

Important religious festivals did, nevertheless, use dancers who had at least a degree of preparatory training. The goddess Hathor, who is frequently represented with the attributes of Isis, the sister-wife of Osiris, presided over the dance. Pharaoh, in his capacity as son of Hathor, is often seen, jingling a sistrum before her, while her priests are represented as dancing and clattering castanets. At all her festivals dancing was an indispensable feature. The god Bes was originally a dancing figure from the Sudan, and is depicted as performing grotesque dances before the young Sun-God. Eventually he, too, became a patron of dance and music. At Thebes and in other places, on Hathor's annual festival, her priestesses after the conclusion of the temple services and parades, marched in the streets, and accompanied by male priests of the cult, stopped at the houses of the people and bestowed Hathor's blessing by singing and dancing, holding out the necklace-emblems of the goddess to be touched for the sake of fertility.

One Athotus was considered the inventor of dancing. He is said to have observed that music used to accompany sacrifices naturally precipitated the body into motions. He took the occasion to reduce the movement of the feet to a proportional measure, which was already dance, as we think of it. The Egyptian clergy, with their obsession for ceremonial, were naturally conscious of the carriage of their bodies, as an attribute of majesty. What is often translated from hieroglyphs by the word 'dancing' would perhaps read more accurately if understood as meaning 'bearing' or 'posture.' There is, for example, an inscription preserved detailing how a newly appointed minister of state should, on his reception, greet the king: He should enter the Audience Chamber dancing, so that from his gestures, poses and mimicry could be seen devotion, loyalty, grace, tenderness and energy. The king would reply to the minister with a different 'dance' and the levée would terminate with a procession of court functionaries, priests and musicians. The etiquette of living was scarcely less important in Egypt than the rules for dying and being buried. There was the universal persuasion, here far more highly ornamented than among savage tribes, but of an identical nature, that the exterior *form* of observance directly represented the *essence* of the truth involved. Court and clergy developed the magical formulæ to such a degree that many ceremonies were fantastic nonsense and ritual degenerated into a kind of sacred blackmail which the priests exercised over the people, corresponding to the descent of the control of power from the three social classes. At first it was only kings who knew the name of the secret of life, but this was shared later with the priests, to become their property until at last, by a similar involuntary surrender, the whole people had it.

Among the most important of their festivals, and one which contains survivals of ancient fertility rituals, were the ceremonies in honor of the consecration of the bull Apis. The sacrificial animal itself was chosen with considerable care by the priests. Its very conception was already a miracle, for it could only be fertilized by a shaft of moonlight. Also, at its birth, certain unmistakable signs showed its divine selection; entirely black, save for a triangular white patch on its forehead and another on its right flank, representing the crescent moon in the black night. The conformation of the hairs on its back represented an eagle, and under its tongue must be found a knot of skin in the form of a scarab. There were numerous other qualifications which had to be fulfilled and no doubt the priests knew well enough how to simulate the symbols.

After the official pronouncements, the bull Apis received as its home a specially constructed stable-temple, facing east. For four months he lived there fed on milk. He was presumably attended by forty nude virgins to please his eyes, and then when he had grown up a little, the priests, profiting by a renewal of the moon, had him transported on a special gilded barge to Memphis where he was greeted with music, dances and the shouts of the people. He was conducted in pomp to the Apeum, his home. Here his servants performed secret dances, retailing the adventures of the god of whom the bull Apis was the living image.

In their dance parades inside and outside the temple, the priests acted out the adventures and benefactions of Osiris in pantomime: his mysterious birth, the games of his childhood, his love of his sister. The birth-events of other divinities were also memorialized. The male priests in special dress, etc., represented Osiris and his companions, while the girls were Isis and hers. The spectacle closed with a violent finale which represented the conquest of India.

Perhaps the most ingenious of all their dances of which we have any record is their so-called Astronomic, or Dance of Stars. This is rather a special form of sacred rite, showing the whole cosmic order rather than praising any particular divinity. It was exclusively performed by the priest class, in temple precincts, without an audience. The dance was scientifically designed, perhaps the original choreographic plan being given by astronomer-priests who could also plot the path of Sothis and thereby regulate the cutting of the Dikes. In this science the Egyptians were considerably informed. Ranged around a fixed altar which represented the sun, priests clad in scintillating clothes made signs for the Zodiac with their hands, while turning rhythmically from east to west, following the course of the planets. After each circle the dancers froze into immobility to represent the constancy of their earth. By combining mimicry and plastic movement the priests made legible the harmonies of the astral system and the laws of the universe. Plato thought it must have been invented by a god for its ingenuity was entirely divine. Although he heard of it in a comparatively late period in Egyptian history he seems to have had fairly close contact with its observance. One of the reasons that we have no exact records of any of these dances, except by accidental report or occasional murals, is the secrecy with which the clergy zealously guarded their patterns to increase their mystery, transmitting their rules only by word of mouth.

Although most important to the cults, dancing also had not a wholly minor position in private life. Professional entertainers for dinner-parties were known in remote antiquity. Among the common people, who usually imitated the nobles, there was dancing too, but more in the nature of burlesque. Later, it would be by no means rare to find in big towns like Thebes, Memphis or Alexandria, small roving troupes of mimes or acrobats who gave impromptu shows in public-squares to the clash of cymbals and tambourines, taking voluntary offerings from passers-by. In the art of pure dance (or, rather, as we should understand it, in the craft of spectacular dance) there seems to have been in later epochs a more or less highly developed system of set steps and gesture, used in ceremonial, continually encountered in wall-paintings and low-reliefs.

There are hieroglyph names for dance-figures or positions which, without describing what they actually looked like in motion, give a hint at least of their categorical variety. There is the making of the figure called the 'calf,' 'the-successful-capture-of-the-boat,' 'the-leading-along-of-an-animal,' 'the-fair-capture (or rape)-of-the-beauty,' 'the-taking-of-gold' and 'the-colonnade.' Their acrobatic positions remind us strongly of our own contemporary vaudeville adagio, where two men hurl a woman through the air, or support her in sustained poses by her extended or bent-back arms and legs. What seems to have been an actual *pirouette,* a turn on one foot with the other raised, is portrayed at Beni-Hassan in a relief at least thirty-five hundred years old. Another similar figure seems either to be starting or finishing a step we call *'entrechat,'* where the feet cross and beat in the air. If reconstructions from static posture have any value at all, it seems likely that many of the feminine dances were slow, to vocal or instrumental accompaniment, emphasizing with aid of the tight, transparent and pleated costumes, the plasticity and moulded muscular roundness of arms, breasts and bellies. There seem to have been soloists, *pas de deux, de trois,* with a choral background, as well as whole corps of semi-gymnastic dancers, who tumbled, somersaulted and made bridges with their backs like our circus tumblers. Indeed the position of 'the bridge' becomes a kind of ideogram for the meaning: acrobatic-dance. Sometimes this position of hands and feet on the ground, with navel pointing to the zenith, is considered a symbol of the over-arching sky of night; at others, a single pose in a panto-mimic expression of the wind swaying back the reeds of the Nile. We shall find 'the bridge' in Greek and Roman acrobats and in that mediæval Salomé who tumbles for Herod on the portal of Rouen Cathedral. Whether or not it is a carver's convention, or a formula for the actual gesture employed, several dance figures indicate a consecutive pattern; two figures, for example, often men, advancing or retreating towards or from each other, mirroring each other's gesture, not identically, but in reverse. The dancers accompanied them-selves or their team-mates with double-flutes, guitars and cymbals, or clapped their hands to mark the measure. Two reliefs show women executing the 'splits' like the *grand écart* of the Moulin Rouge.

The hands, in these reliefs, are never cut with spread fingers, but are por-trayed, conventionally at least, like flexible fins. There were sleight-of-hand tricks at private parties, juggling with full and empty wine-goblets; feats of balance involving high degree of muscular control, stomach-dances probably not unlike those still to be seen in Cairo. Others walked on their hands and carried objects on their flat upturned naked soles. It would be hard to differ-entiate, as two classes, professional dancers and acrobats. They were inter-changeable. There were also, if later, satiric mimes who could parody the mannerisms of unpopular priests or potentates, though these were usually proscribed. Although they had nothing which we would know as theatre, their official ceremonies were contrived with the greatest theatricality. The dancers employed must have passed through a certain training, by means, if nothing else, of the ritual repetition. When attempting to reconstruct Egyptian dances it is important to remember that, as in Greek vase-paintings, the silhouette of the 'significant-profile' was an accepted plastic limitation, since rules for perspective and foreshortening on a flat plane had not been discovered. The flat, abrupt, single-plane *Egyptian* dances we find in revues and motion-pictures would not be recognized, even remotely, by their models. If their great sculpture is any clue to their feeling for mass in air, they must have used all the three-dimensional possibilities of the human body admirably in space. The fact that male dancers are always painted red and women white or pale yellow, is less conventional when we remember that the men spent all day in the fields under the bronzing sun, but their women were left inside shady houses.

Osiris as dancer is not one of his chief identities, although his earlier fol-lowers knew him as dancing, as did the first Christians recognize the dance of Jesus. Dionysos was more of a dancer, even if it was a wild rout he led. And although he does not directly affect our history in any way, it may not be useless to recall that Siva, the Indian creator, danced. He is the completest type of gods who dance, and most primal divinities do. Siva Natarja is the Lord of Dancers and King of Actors. His theater is our cosmos. In the multiformity of his steps, he is both dancer and audience. Whatever the remote ethnic origins of Siva's dance were, it has come to represent the clearest symbol of the activity of a creative god. The image of his rhythmic play is understood as the source of all cosmic motion, action and tension. The purpose of his dance is to release the innumerable souls of mankind from the snare of illusion. The theater of his dance and the center of the universe is within the human heart. He danced the world into being and his dance keeps it alive.

Egyptian dances may have affected the early artists of Greece, or at least Crete, from sailors across the Mediterranean; Osiris quite possibly had more than accidental likenesses to Dionysos. But Egypt is primarily interesting to us as the first great culture which used the magic habits of tribal civilizations for the control of a great homogeneous nation. The system and method of this control exhausted their magical virtues by the inertia inherent in meaningless repetition after the first sources had been long forgotten; but the structure, as art, survived, and is among the foundations of western spectacle.

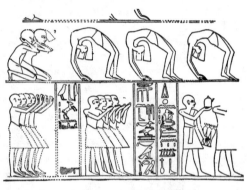

ACROBATS   *Deir-el-Bahri*

CHAPTER III

The Origins of Greek Tragedy: Dance and Theatre

THE myths of Egyptian Osiris and Grecian Dionysos are strikingly alike, though definitely independent, and the structure of ritual and ceremonial attending each cult are similar expressions of the mimic death and revival of earth's vegetation. Dionysos did not become the god of Greece's great period of tragedy until many generations had fused their contributions of diverse local myths and practices into a single godhead. Dionysos himself was a relatively late semi-oriental importation into Greek legend, but once he becomes entirely atticized he will contain all the previous indigenous characteristics. To know Dionysos in a complete form enables us later to retrace our steps to the foundations of those tragic games of which he was the patron.

There are numerous theories as to his origin. Some find him already among the Chaldees, a tribe of Akkadians descended from an Aryan race of Hindu-Brahmans. The Chaldees were astrologers in Babylon and their nomad tribes brought the concept of Bacchos-Dionysos west from India. The name Dionysos can be read as God-from-Nysa, a mountainous region between Egypt and Phœnicia, known also as the Sinai of Moses. Osiris was also said to have been raised in Nysa. Later, heretical Christians will say Christ's secret name is Bacchos; his body and blood, like the Greek vine-god's, is bread and wine. In the play of Euripides, Dionysos came to Thebes, had known all Asia and was the son of Zeus and Semele, a mortal maiden. The god was seized from his mother's womb, hidden in his father's thigh until he was safe to issue, which he did, being thus twice-born. He was later torn limb from limb, and the pomegranate sprang from his spattered blood, as anemones from gored Adonis. He descended into hell, was resurrected and became divine. In the Cretan myth he is the bastard of Zeus (like Osiris, of the sun). Going abroad, Zeus ceded his throne to the youthful Dionysos, but knowing that Juno, his wife, hated the boy, he entrusted him to the care of guards. These, by her aid, lured him with mirrors into ambush, where her satellites, the Titans, cut him limb from limb, boiled his body with herbs and ate it. His sister had saved his heart and showed it to returning Zeus, who slew the Titans, and made an image for the heart, enclosing it in a shrine.

Under the name of Zagreus he is 'the-hornéd.' He is also a goat; on occasion a bull. As Bromios, he is clamor-king, the-thunderer. In early epochs (Homer takes little notice of him except to speak of his hailing from Thrace) he has a black beard, is long-haired, and in one hand holds the thyrsus-branch, a spring-sign. His ever-greening crown shows him master not only of grapes, but of all green plants. A huge phallos is often carried before him proclaiming his generative gifts. Later Bacchos becomes younger and younger, ending up in Hellenistic times as an androgynous, beardless boy. His wild rites seemed at first excessive to the Greeks, but once introduced, spread like wildfire.

It was once widely believed that tragedy was the exclusive invention of Dorian Greeks, and their choral odes, entirely in praise of Dionysos, a vegetation and survival god, were the immediate ancestors of Æschylos. But it has subsequently been shown that in a more exact sense, tragedy sprang from totemistic homage paid to local dead tribal chiefs all over Greece, and these chiefs, later forgotten as individual identities, had their myths and rites preëmpted for social, political and religious convenience under the name of the new god, Dionysos. We remember the magic powers held by totems of animal and human progenitors, and how in order to secure peace, prosperity or new life, propitiatory dance-games are offered the old-dead with the new-dead. So it was with hero-tombs in many sections of Greece, whose local protectors would be eventually confused with the universal name of Bacchos-Dionysos.

One of the most interesting as well as oldest of ritualistic hymns which were the ancestors of Greek dance-drama has been found at Palaikastro, on the island of Crete, and is quoted and explained in Jane Harrison's 'Themis.' It is a song of the Kouretes, young men just come to maturity, whose legendary ancestors were the nursery-guards of infant Dionysos. First, he is invoked by titles of 'wet-and-gleaming.' He is wished for; he is expected. He is hailed as Kouros, *the* 'young man' at the head of his *daimones* or companions. Here we have already a hero and his chorus whom we shall later recognize as Bacchos with troupes of Mænads and satyrs. The god when young needs an escort. When mature, he is free to wander alone. After the introductory invocation there is a statement of the myth: the babe, taken from his mother is tended by the Kouretes, who dance over him an armed protective dance. Then the child is hidden, killed, dismembered by Titans; finally, reappears, revitalized. Here we have elements of drama we remember from Abydos: the contest (here an armed dance); the mimic death; the reappearance as god. The sword-dance of the Kouretes will be found again as the Spartan and Roman pyrrhic, in mediæval tournaments, in the Morris-Dances of England. The swords, whether sharp steel or dull wood, are always summer against winter; night against day; life against death.

The rites and myths of Zagreus-Dionysos take on a familiar significance if we see in this adolescent god, a corn- or year-divinity. The *Kouroi* are young men already initiated into tribal practice, who steal youths from their mothers to teach them communal secrets. They pretend they shall suffer death in order to harden them, then restore them as full-grown members of the tribe. Pantomimic dancing is at the root of all mysteries and it is very important to comprehend the *protagonists,* the sufferers, or competitors in these mysteries not as 'religious figures' or 'spiritual types' but as residuals of *social* customs. These Kouroi are not sophisticated literary abstractions, but primitive realities. The whole body of religious belief in early forms is social and collective. Primitive faiths are not individualistic. The ritual dance-act, a functional, simple, useful action, is earlier than any theological idea of divinity.

Aristotle himself asserted that Greek tragedy arose from the *Dithyrambos,* the ritual spring song of birth, or rebirth, or of the *twice-born.* The weak baby Dionysos, snatched from his mother, Semele, was tested in fire and cleansed in water to strengthen and reanimate him. The father-(mother)-god cries out. The babe is born anew from its father. This birth is not a *real* birth, but a *mimic* birth, and *the* type of all mimetic rites. At spring fertility festivals, the Dithyramb, supposedly imported from Phrygia, was chanted, describing the nativity and adventures of Dionysos; how the Mænads, or wild-women, nursed the holy child until it was old enough for full-grown men to take it away for rearing. The song was accompanied by a flute and by expressive mimetic gesture. A *company* of people, singing the Dithyramb, rejoicing in phallos-bearing processions, were a *Komos.* Hence, the word comedy. Each band had usually one leader who declaimed monologues, and soon dialogues with his companions, and here we have choros and chorosleader. The rite, or thing (understood as sacred thing) that was *done* is termed *Dromenon.* The collective presented utterance had become a collective representation. From the magic of doing what was wanted to be done, from the sacrifices to the year that it should be fruitful, the puberty rites of primitive tribes, the propitiation of totem tombs, we have no longer mere ritual but artificed *drama.*

Tension, the root, name-essence of dance, finds its relief in an expression arising from exciting movement. Its relaxation is both physical and psychological. This violent dance, this essential *doing* is the source of drama. The highest emotional tension is best induced by doing together a thing felt socially. Indians derive great communal strength from all-night dances. *Dromena* are not merely things done, however intensely or collectively, but things repeatedly done, prophetically done, enacted, represented, in commemoration or in anticipation.

At the end of the seventh century, or the beginning of the sixth, Aristotle tells us that a poet, Arion, imposed order on the Dithyramb, fixed as choros at fifty, established in addition to the single stanza or strophe, the antistrophe; displaced the sober Dorian mode with a more passionate Phrygian, combining pipe and strings. Verses were spoken between the singing. The Dithyramb was not inspired by a single bard, but was the choral-dance song of a company. Masks, a common governing rhythm, exciting words, color, are all used to intensify the collective emotion. The feeling thus communally generated is far stronger than any individual emotion. The group's emotional enthusiasm and nervous physical discharge are a seed-bed for the invention of myth, the bacillus-culture of godhead. Gods emerge from their uttered, formulated, exteriorized desire as definite personifications, Osiris, Dionysos or Christ.

Yet no matter how electric group emotion may be, it can never create a personality without some nucleus of mythical fact, or without the agency of a leader. The choros always has a leader, a spokesman, or chief-dancer. The choros makes him its proxy, and then withdraws, at least from the actual responsibility of command. Its attitude gradually becomes thoughtful, though respectful. The collective tension is broken. The choros is now an audience, at first sympathetic; later, critical. In this slow process of separation, from a religious point of view the choros becomes worshipers of that god it has created, and from a theatrical point of view, they are the spectators of a play. At this strategic point we have the first definite vision of a frame which will encompass theatrical dancing as understood in our own contemporary meaning.

The Dithyramb gradually split into two chief artistic forms, the first purely choral, later known as the Dithyrambic, for which Lasus, born ca. 548, established contests where the odes of Simonides and Pindar were sung by cyclical choirs to the accompaniment of a flute. The other, a dramatic form, comprised tragedy (*tragedeos,* or sacrificial goat-song); and comedy, or chant of a reveling company. Satyrs, the original goat-footed companions of Thracian Bacchos, were superseded by ordinary farmers in the choros of Dionysos Dithyrambos, the twice-born. The Dorian arrangement of strict statement and response was abandoned, and the newer, looser metric permitted a growth of rhetorical speech, interesting in its own right.

One can derive some idea of the nature of the dances performed at these early celebrations, from the Askolia (*askos,* wine-skin). This amusement, more a game than a dance, was customary for the second day of the Rural Dionysia. Naked boys hopped on one leg upon a full-filled wine bladder which had been greased. Considerable skill was necessary to enable them to keep their balance, and crowds would surround them, laughing at their comic postures. But there are poetic fragments which mention their gracefulness and elegance.

At the beginning of the sixth century, Thespis, described by Aristotle as 'a dancer,' was born in Icaria, a center of the Dionysian cult. By 'dancer,' we understand he probably taught the bacchic choros. He is traditionally conceded to have introduced theatrical tragedy, as we think of it, into Athens. His theatre is supposed to have been the open end of a cart which could be wheeled from place to place. The actor's face was painted, and in time this make-up would turn into a mask. His innovation consisted of introducing a single actor, separate from the choros. Thus greater prominence was given to interludes and spoken conversation. He broke sharply with tradition, which heretofore limited the subject matter specifically to the exploits of Dionysos, by introducing legends of other gods and heroes in personified rôles. This laid him open to charges by Solon, the law-giver, of blasphemy for presenting divinities in the flesh, but the device was too interesting to be suppressed. By the use of the complex mythology there was opportunity for unfolding dramatic action, which in the Dithyramb was so elementary as to have been almost negligible. The single actor, by the use of masks, took all the rôles of humorous characters.

In Greece, no matter how distinct from its ritual sources it might become, the theatre was intimately connected at all times with festivals of Dionysos. Participation in the dramatic seasons was a religious exercise, not merely an amusement. The plays were only performed at annual spring festivals, during which time other affairs were set aside. The compositions of the plays were in the nature of contests for which an honorary prize, a vase or a wreath, was awarded. The Greeks had a passion for competition, not only in theatrical games but in music and sports as well. Part of the extraordinary fertility of the Greek poets, only a fraction of whose effort has been preserved for us, is due to the warmth and interest in these competitions. At first the plays were produced only by amateurs as voluntary improvised amplifications of the Bacchic chorales.

The most important of the several festivals was that of the City Dionysia, the feast of Dionysos Eleutheros. The poet who won here could gain no greater prize. It was celebrated on five days at the end of March, close to the spring equinox, when the seas were again navigable after winter winds, and the streets of Athens would be full of visitors from the provincial leagues. Foreign emissaries came especially for the tragic games, which were regulated by the state under a delegated officer charged with each particular festival. On him lay the responsibility of selecting competing dramatists; at first three, and later five. On him lay the choice of actors, the distribution of rôles and the preparation of the plays, but generally he would appoint or have chosen a special *choregos* or choros leader for detailed tasks.

On the first day there was a grand Dionysiac parade, which, exhibiting the god's image, left it standing in his theatre. The tragic, comic and satiric contests were followed by lyric competitions in the Dithyramb. These choirs of fifty members were selected from the ten main tribes and a victory for a choros meant triumph for its tribe. Our first date for a competition, virtually the first definite record of a theatrical performance in history, is the year 535 B.C., two thousand four hundred and seventy years ago. The populace had an intense interest in the theater. There were no books then, nor films for a wide audience. No one was satiated by going to see a play at dawn, watching tetralogies of independent or related subjects till sundown. Besides, it only happened once a year.

The expenses for rehearsing and producing the plays were imposed by the state on rich citizens, in rotation. Maintenance of the stage was a civic function and duty. This expense was not small. Besides training the actors, the choregos or his agents must provide rehearsal rooms for the choros, chosen from the general citizenry. He must costume them, arrange for music, and whatever machinery was called for. The audience met in the theater around break of day, well provided with food which was consumed during the tedious parts and intermissions. Herald trumpeters announced the commencement of the performance.

Originally the Greek theatre was little more than wooden bleachers surrounding a stamped-down earthen circle, rimmed with stone. This circle can easily be recognized as the place of the dithyramb, the *orchestra* or dancing-floor, based on threshing-floors which were rimmed to keep the grain in. At harvest time dance figures easily followed the form of the circular rim or cut it in quadrants. In time (ca. 500 B.C.), temporary bleachers, *theatron* or seeing-place were replaced by stone, carved from convenient cup-shaped hills, with the seats placed away from the sun. The Dionysian Theatre in Athens seated twenty thousand people. A booth or *skene* was erected for changing the actors' clothes. Originally open, the auditoria grew later to be closed by the necessary buildings opposite the seats, grouped in an architectural unit, faced with a decorative background or 'scene.' The leader of the dithyramb would mount on a rude altar, or simply a table, the better to conduct his choros, and a stone stage floor would later, in Roman times, be raised so that the actors could more easily be seen. As time went on various innovations of costume (thick-soled shoes and masks); of scenery (painted side-scenes; elevators for gods to rise and descend); and of movement (gesture and choral dance) combined to make the shows theatrically efficient and spectacular.

Before we can clearly understand the place of dance (*orchesis*) in Greek plays or the nature of its movement and gesture, at least a rudimentary background in literary history is important, to show us how each dramatist used and developed his choros or dancing-choir. Æschylos, born in 525 at Eleusis, a town famous for dramatized mysteries of the vegetation cult of Demeter, expanded the Thespian monodrama and gave it the form by which it would be known. He stressed the importance of a second actor for purposes of more vivid narration, so the chief *antagonists* were actually brought face to face. His grand triptych made from the legends of Troy and the house of Atreus demonstrates the catastrophe incurred by transgression, not only on the instigator of the evil, but on the sinner's heirs. In the 'Agamemnon,' a returning victor is murdered by his adulterous wife. In the 'Chœphori,' her son avenges his father by slaying his mother. In the 'Eumenides,' the matricide is pursued by relentless furies. Æschylos trained his own choros himself, creating dance-patterns and gestures. To him is attributed the invention of the tragic choral uniform, a black tunic and mantle as well as the introduction of properties, swords, wands, and scepters which may have been modeled on ritual implements. He had painted snakes in the hair of his masked Furies and created a sensation by such hideous realism. In the early plays the choros was all important, but from the fifth century on, its part dwindled, and finally would be no more than an attendant band. But even with the advent of actors, and surely in Æschylos, they are prominent, and indeed most of the dramatic interest, as in 'The Suppliant Women' or 'The Furies,' surrounds their emotions.

Sophocles, who lived from 497 to 406, had a thorough education in music and dance. As a choir-boy he danced in the triumph, after the defeat of the Persians. A century had elapsed since Thespis died, and Sophocles synthesized earlier innovations and introduced a third actor. The long contest between actors and chorus was now really at an end; the actors had won. The chorus now witnessed the action, no longer participated. They follow the story, the interludes give them a chance to moralize on past or coming events, and they afford the principal performers a breathing space. Sophocles was the first to use the full possibilities of three separate actors on the stage at once. He also abandoned the trilogic form which earlier competitions had demanded, humanized the tragic situations, making those elements personal which had been previously rather morally abstract or religious. He gave a considerable impetus to painted scenery which was set in portable panels against three- or four-sided revolving drums on both sides of the stage. He increased the choros, which in the days of the dithyramb had been fifty, but was now only twelve, to fifteen singing dancers.

With Euripides (ca. 480–ca. 406) the choros as an active member of the tragic cast almost disappears. In his youth he had been cup-bearer to a guild of dancers, a painter and an athlete. His imagination, of all the Greek dramatists, strikes us as nearest ours. He had a more cosmopolitan, less insular idea of the world than his predecessors. His situations are not far from our own romantic drama; a passion for spectacular realism and poetic immediacy. He felt the choros an encumbrance which hindered the swift, implacable crises of his action, and excluded them from actual participation, although they remained for choral interludes, often as doddering old men too feeble to take part, chanting odes almost irrelevant to the play, though having their own beauty, not unlike the highly conventionalized choral background of nineteenth century Italian opera. Plato, at a not much later date, complained that in the old days dancing was superb but all the choros did now was to bawl, with no attempt at gesture or movement.

But in the 'Bacchæ,' Euripides' last great play, perhaps the last and surely among the greatest of all Greek tragedies, there is a startling reassemblage and reëmployment of the choros, almost as if it were summoned for a magnificent farewell before its ultimate dismissal. Not only is the play remarkable for its employment of the choros but also for a recapitulation of all literary elements which had contributed to construct Greek tragedy, and of all ethnic and ritual factors upon which the literature was based. The 'Bacchæ' was written expressly for production in Macedon where the Bacchic cults were deep-seated and popularly felt. It was not, however, produced until after its author's death, being first played in Athens ca. 405. Partly on account of the possibilities it offered for spectacular display, with the presence of the violent dancing choir, it was long a popular piece. Euripides rarely named his plays from their chorus and then only if the action rendered them more memorable than the protagonists themselves.

A bare outline of the story tells the tragedy of King Pentheus, a personification of the Greek concept of *hubris,* that insensate self-reliance or vain pride which goes before a fall. To Pentheus' kingdom comes a stranger with a band of devotees. The god Bacchos-Dionysos and his Bacchants, mænads or possessed women, are neither recognized as god nor even as strangers worthy of hospitality, but only as blasphemers endangering the kingdom. Pentheus is warned, but in spite of warning, imprisons the god, threatens his followers, while even old nobles of his court have put on leopard skins, taken the thyrsos in their hands to try to recapture on the mountains, the essence of life and youth which the god promises. God founders his puny prison, and with terrible cunning reappears before Pentheus, still unknown to him as god, induces him to put aside his male attire, to disguise himself as a girl, that he himself may go up into the hills and spy on the profane rites. The effeminized king is seduced into a circle of Bacchants. Suddenly the loud voice of Bacchos betrays the intruder, and the wild women tear him to pieces. His own mother Agave returns in triumph with her son's head, believing it to be a lion's she has slain in the frenzy. God now appears in his obvious godhead, claims homage and disenchants the world. It is a conclusive statement that the power of fertility which gives life to nature cannot be denied by men without provoking their nemesis.

Again we recognize the structure used in the Osiris mystery. In 'The Bacchæ' there is a long *agon,* or contest of the Year spirit against its enemy, light against willful darkness which will not recognize it. The sequence of Pentheus' and Dionysos' encounters is, in the play, divided by choral hymns and dances, which give the names of the god, his history and power, his swift vengeance. The *pathos* is the ritual, sacrificial death of the doubting King. Adonis, Osiris and Dionysos (who in an old myth is identified with Pentheus as one person) is torn to pieces; but in Greek drama there was a sensible convention of never showing an act of horror on the stage, since visual presentation is inevitably less impressive than the idea itself. Hence they evolved the institution of the *messenger.* 'News comes' that the god is dead. The corpse is often displayed afterwards, covered, on a bier. The *Threnos* or choral dance and song of lamentation defines for the audience the clash and contrast of emotion; the death of the old and its remorse opposed to the birth of the new and its joy. In 'The Bacchæ' there is an elaborate threnos with the god-maddened women in hunters' triumph collecting fragments of the body which they have split. Finally there is the inevitable *Anagnorisis,* the discovery of the slain and mutilated year-Daimon. Dionysos is at once killer and his kill. The choros' homage to the reality of his continuous truth is followed by the *Theophany,* or advent of the god as god, resurrected in apotheosis, the ultimate statement of his power and glory.

The author of this study was fortunate enough to see a performance of 'The Bacchæ' directed by Eva Sikelianos, who founded the new theater in the open air at Athens, and who produced the 'Prometheus' at Delphi in 1927.

She strives, not for a strictly archeological reconstruction, but for an essential revivification of the ancient text. The setting was a flat green playing-field.* In front of some four hundred seats, like baseball-bleachers, a large whitened circle lay, in the center of which was a small triangular altar. Overhead, an enormous sky, with June thunderheads pushing on towards late afternoon. The audience had to walk across a river, some quarter of a mile away from town. They were removed into another atmosphere from the start. Barely seated, one caught a glimpse of nodding leaves and shifting heads, far off across the bridge. A trumpet blew two phrases in the antique modes preserved by the Greek Orthodox Church, and the flash of a purple dress preceded the column of Bacchants. Headed by Dionysos, fifty girls in clothes that for the first time to many made Greek sculpture alive, swept up and over the plain. Over their tunics were slung dappled panther skins. In their hands they brandished wands bound with oak-leaves, the badge of their cult. While the last seats were being occupied, as it must have been in the Athenian theater, the God commenced to speak.

Eva Sikelianos wove the hundred-odd costumes herself; it took her five months and she knows how the thick threads hang up and down, the thin threads across. Her tunics sag in their own weight, not chiffon but light solid stuff, chiseled by sun and air, holding the shape of breast and thigh, and also the shape of the material. Off-white, eggshell, light tan, the chorus of girls, their hair caught in ivy, were a throbbing background for the rash king, unholy in red, with his fringe of beard shaved when he traded his manhood for his curiosity, and the blond winey god, remote and bathed in purple.

The most impressive part of the play was the large choros. Divided into five choirs the girls danced and sang the action simultaneously. Their thin voices were untrained and lost to the wind. With the Greeks there was time to train them and a *skene* to reflect their sound, like a preacher's sounding board. Two silver flutes were accurate though not satisfactory. Nevertheless when the choral-leader, a girl with red hair and a real fury, crashed her brass cymbals and leapt into the circle, followed by her companions in antiphonal singing and miming, an atmosphere was evoked that was as ancient and pungent as the charred smoke of incense from the altar. The gestures were not from Isadora Duncan, but closer, if one needs modern precedent, to Nijinsky's invention of an archaic plastic, in the 'Afternoon of a Faun.'

At the end, one saw, nearly a half a mile away, the tricked Queen with her women, their arms suddenly flung up like a wave, approaching the city and leaping around her son's head. The large perspective in the late afternoon sunlight, with all the ruffling accidents of cloud, light and wind, gave tremendous significance to the mysterious fatality of the site. Our deadly separation of audience and actors was lost. For two hours, without a break, on hard seats, without applause, the spectacle was felt with close attention. It was ritual drama, danced tragedy, in the original and best sense of the word, a

* Northampton, Massachusetts. 1934.

choreodrama. In the 'Prometheus,' the setting sun glittered on the fire-bringer's chains, as his effigy revolved on a constructed mountain. In the 'Trojan Women' the Greek torches would flare into Priam's house as dusk fell on the audience, scattering fiery fragments on the marble steps.

Poetry, music, dancing were to the Greeks inseparably imagined, but poetry, for the dramatists, was the ruler. Music was an accompaniment and dancing was seldom introduced merely as spectacle. Plato said that *orchesis,* dancing, "was the instinctive desire to explain words by gestures of the entire body"; and Aristotle, that dancing "was an imitation of actions, characters and passions by means of postures and rhythmical movements." Theatrical dancing was always combined with song, to explain or intensify the words. Song in verse and dance, as arts, had developed together. The terms in the science of poetic metric referred to dance steps. The smallest division of a verse was called a 'foot'; two feet were 'basic' or a stepping. The *arsis* and *thesis,* the alternate stress of the voice in singing or declamation originally indicated the position of the feet, up or down. By the study of *music,* the gift of the Muses, the Greeks meant training in song or melody, dancing and verse. It was the fiber of their education, and illustrated in harmonious unity both ethical relations and moral principles. Aristotle thought music had a power to form character, and was not to be enjoyed only for the pleasure it incidentally gave. However simple it may have been in mechanical resources, Greek music had a close relation to emotional conditions.

From very remote times dancing was generally popular among the Greek lands for the health it gave, for the social sympathy it induced. From ancient social, educational and religious dances a strong influence descended to the more sophisticated, artificial dances for the theater. Without understanding both, one cannot have a clear appreciation of either. Historically speaking, there is ancient testimony to the existence of dancing both in poetry, painting and sculpture. At Palaiokastro, in Crete, the source of the Kouroi hymn, have been found terra-cotta groups of figures dancing in circles dating from the sixteenth and fifteenth centuries before Christ. Besides these rather static figures there are frescoes of dancing ladies in the so-called Palace of Minos; Sappho referred to the Cretan islanders as clever dancers. These antique references, not in themselves necessarily important, do show that Greek dancing was not simply of one late period, and that the well-known reliefs of dancers of the epoch of Phidias, or more often of Roman times, which mean 'Greek-dancing' to too many contemporary dancers, had a long and prolific ancestry.

In the Homeric epic, which dates from the eleventh to the tenth century, there are references to dancing in the Iliad, and the religious element is by no means foremost. This dance is a kind of social game.

> Also with great skill he made a dancing-floor, like that which Deadolos had done in broad Knossos for blonde Ariadne. These youths and maidens worth many oxen were dancing, holding each other's hands by the wrist. Of these

some wore delicate linen dresses, and others golden swords hanging from silver belts. At one time they moved rapidly in a circle with cunning feet, right easily, just as when a potter, seated, tries the wheel fitted to the hand to see whether it runs; at another time they moved rapidly in file. And a great crowd stood round the charming dance, enjoying the spectacle; and amongst them a divine bard sang to the cithara; and two tumblers, when he began his song, whirled about in the middle.

But it is particularly in the Odyssey in connection with the story of Nausicaa, that Homer gives us vivid pictures of early dances. The young princess asks permission of her father Alcinous, to launder clothes for her dowry. Two of her brothers already have wives, and three others "are always wanting clothes newly washed when they go out to dances." After their laundering is finished the princess and her girls lunch. Then

the food having satisfied their appetites the hand-maids and their young mistress next threw off their scarves and turned to playing with a ball. The white fore-arms of Nausicaa, leading the chorus, beat time for this ball-dance. She moved among them, as arrow-loving Artemis goes down the mountain-steeps . . . for that she bears her head so high, and her brows, and moves carelessly notable among them all where all are beautiful, even so did this chaste maiden outshine her maids.

Here wandering Odysseus found her and she brought him back to her father's house, and there Alcinous gave him a feast in order to impress the stranger with his country's

surpassing goodness in seamanship and running and dancing and singing. . . . At the word of Alcinous his herald ran to find the polished lyre in the palace. Other nine men stood up, the elect and appointed stewards of the crowd, whose duty was to set the stage. They leveled the dancing ground, making its ring neat and wide. The herald arrived with the minstrel's singing lyre. Demodocus advanced into the cleared space. About him grouped boys in their first blush of life and skillful at dancing, who footed it rhythmically on the prepared floor. Odysseus watched their flying feet and wondered. . . . (After the minstrel's song of the love of Aphrodite and Ares.) . . . Then Alcinous ordered Halias and Laodamas to dance, by themselves, for never did any one dare join himself with them. They took in their hands the fine ball, purple-dyed, which knowing Polybus had made them, and played. The first, bending his body right back, would hurl the ball towards the shadowy crowds: while the other in his turn would spring high into the air and catch it gracefully before his feet touched ground. Then, after they had made full trial of tossing the ball high, they began passing it back and forth between them, all the while they danced upon the fruitful earth. The other young men stood by the dancing ring and beat time. Loudly their din went up. And great Odysseus turned to Alcinous, saying, 'My Lord Alcinous, ruler of rulers, you did assure that your dancers were the best: and now it is proved true: this sight is marvelous.'

And at the end of his many adventures when it is finally granted to Odysseus to take his wife in their own bed, below, "Telemachus and the herdsmen, staying their feet from the dance and staying the women, so that all slept in the darkling halls." *

The civilization of Mycenæ was heir to the primitive culture of Crete, and the Peloponnesus became famous for its dancing, which was usually a votive rite or a gymnastic or military drill. The armed Pyrrhic was taught to all Spartan males from the age of five, and conserved its educational character for the longest time. In Attica from a remote period regular dance competitions existed. But it was in the fifth century that dancing, which had been slowly accreting various local elements and maturing for the previous two hundred years, came, with architecture and drama, into its greatest perfection, comparing not in the importance of specific dances or dancers but as an esthetic force to the odes of Pindar, the drama of Æschylos, Phidias' sculpture and the painting of Polygnotus.

Towards the end of the fourth century, the choros of simple citizenry passed out of fashion; dancing, more and more, became the province of professionals. The mimetic element, present from the beginning, now became increasingly predominant; so much so, indeed, that the dance itself tended to disappear in the refinements of pantomime. In fact, certain forms of pantomime or dumb-show were not unknown in antique epochs, whether as banquet interludes or, as in the Delphic mysteries, where an antique religious mime represented the contest and victory of Apollo over Python. But pantomime as such is a separate art and we must wait for Roman times to investigate it fully.

All Greek dancing developed from the communal form of choral dance. There may have been solo dancing and *pas de deux,* but if so, they were secondary. Most frequently, the choros would move cyclically or circularly in its *orchestra* or dancing-floor, but there were also the theatrical choros which marched in rectangular ranks or files. Both forms are shown in the existing monuments as variable, and to be combined.

In the tragic dance, where mimicry was important, they moved without touching each other, to be free for gesture. Greek dancing was not based on the relationship of the sexes, hence the most ancient may have been exclusively male or female. Later, they would attribute the innovation of a reunion of the sexes to Dædalus, their creator, or to Theseus, who led first a boy, then a girl out of the Labyrinth. The inference might be that these dances had not always existed. On most early vases, when men and women are shown dancing together, they are usually separated. Later on when there were *pas de deux,* the partners rarely touched, not from any sexual prohibition but because mimicry was the chief aim in such dancing, and each dancer wished his maxi-

* *The Odyssey*—Col. T. E. Lawrence's translation. Oxford University Press. New York. 1934.

mum freedom. This freedom was never lost, except willfully, when in the choros, they gained the greatest emphasis by mass motion, moving in unison, like singing in unison.

It is convenient to think in two technical categories when investigating Greek dancing; the *movements* or large orbit of action, and *gestures,* which involved specialized expressive mimicry. In general Greek dancing was more active if less precise, less restricted to the feet alone, than the nineteenth century ballet. Socrates refers to the wholeness of the body's use. It had a vital connection with gymnastics, and in the palæstra, to the music of a flute, children went through harmoniously designed exercises, while in the gymnasia, the naked *epheboi* (newly matured men) and athletes used more strenuous calisthenics. A child's first dancing-teacher would be his first physical-instructor, and these masters were more highly regarded than mere dancing-masters, since they were the standard of all that was excellent for training models for the public contests. In the palæstra and gymnasia males learned the Pyrrhic and the Chieronomic, in the specific *gymnic* (naked) sense of the word. They were the correct preparation for the execution of battle motions. Plato, in his 'Laws' considered the dance with its combat-drill as having no other purpose but physical well-being, agility and personal beauty. However, between simple gymnastics and dance itself, a division was quick to appear. The cultivation of the body was not considered, as we too often think of it, entirely as 'physical culture.' It involved, as well, cultivation of the imagination, and to movement as exercise was added expressiveness.

This new element, the quality of dance as dance, might already be inherent in gymnastic motions by the indication of a fast or slow rhythm, and since they were, after all, executed to produce a desired effect. But Greek dancing was to become far more intensely imitative or representational of objective nature. The athletic *chieronomia* consisted almost entirely of mechanic repetition of poses useful for war, a limited exercise no more expressive than foundation lessons in boxing, tennis, or fencing. However, the word *chieronomia* came to mean all rhythmic gestures of the arms, hands and fingers which would be an essential part of miming, and also, the earliest means of musical regulation for what would later develop into the science of orchestral conducting by a fluent use of arms and fingers. The formal, vital aspect of a god or a man could be plastically constructed by a succession of suggestive poses, lyrically designed up to the climax of one sustained attitude. For contrast, a quiet position corresponded to a musical silence, emphasizing the final meaning of the series, holding the attention of the audience in its culmination; *chieronomia* was the simulacra of action of people or ideas expressing a mobile equivalent of the words of hymns which accompanied the dancing. Phyrinicos said dancing provided him with as many figures as the waves of the sea or the breath of storms. Telestes, who designed the action for the 'Seven Against Thebes' was renowned for having invented a *chieronomia* so telling that one believed one actually saw the spoken words.

The positions of the arms and feet in Greek theatrical dancing are considered by its two best historians, Maurice Emmanuel and Louis Séchan, as remarkably similar to classic Franco-Italo-Russo-Austro-Anglican ballet. Exactly how similar, no one can say, although the comparison is a convenient device, if for no other reason than to understand the chief differences, which may, after all, be more in degree than kind. In Greece, theatrical performances were given but once yearly, and except for rehearsals of single performances there could have been little chance for that repetition of movement which tends toward clean precision and technical ingenuity, the hall-marks of ballet. The Greek dance had far more freedom or looseness than ours and hence an impression of greater spontaneity. But on vases and reliefs we do recognize familiar positions—the so-called *attitude,* shared by Giovanni da Bologna's 'Mercury,'—the whole system of diagonal harmony or lateral opposition, the Italian baroque principle of *contraposto,* the French *croisé.* There was nothing academic or rigid about the Greek theatrical dance although it must have presupposed some sort of training by useful exercises.

Movements of the arms were lively, stylized towards an artificial visual symbolism for the purpose of being legible to an audience at some distance from the performers, the principle of all good theatrical movement. They seemed to have a predilection for steps involving turns, which they executed not scientifically, as in our multiple *pirouette,* but rather 'naturally,' letting the air catch the swirling folds of their costumes. Their technique was undeveloped, and may have been frequently more vital than much of our dance, though this was relatively accidental. Obversely, some of their intention must have been lost on the spectators since they had no exact method of determining the effects. Much was left to the fantasy and initiative of individual choral members. Within broad limits, they behaved according to the demands of the dramatic situation. Certain gestures, understood as the basic theme, admitted personal variants or amplifications,—the arms raised in supplication, or the sinuous feline pose of panther-girls, a supple figuration appropriate to 'The Bacchæ,' punctuated by padding soles of their feet.

The nomenclature of the dances is so elaborate as to be wholly confusing. The antique authority, Meursius, gives some two hundred among them. The Tray of Sacrifice, the Tongs, Blossoms, Mortar, Kneading-Trough (from the quality of the movement involved), Flight, Boisterousness, Spilling the Meal, etc. A large number must refer only to steps or figures. Even so too many exist to be usefully listed here. They were often called after their legendary inventor or the locale of their origin, like the various musical modes. It is impossible to classify in any way the value of these dances from a geographical point of view. Attica absorbed the contributions of all the Dorian tribes, and her rôle was to develop and perfect the various dances. With politics, so it is usually with dancing. In the wars against the Persians, Spartan soldiers, trained in the Pyrrhic dance, had of all the Greeks, the superior armed forces. The Peloponnesian League headed by Sparta, was an entirely defensive alliance. So it remained, and so Lacedæmonian dancing remained, with no internal or external conditions to urge it into forms of expansion resulting from empire or imperial complexity. But Athens, as captain of the Ionian League, was forced by pressing economic exigencies to convert her power into empire, and thus drew into her dance the native forms of various multiple species used by her allies and subjects. One might oppose a large category of Cretan or Laconic types to the semi-barbaric bacchic forms of Thrace and the northern mountains. The oriental influences from Asia Minor, violent, effeminized, often orgiastic, were at odds with the virile Apollonian measures of the lower Archipelago itself. All the local types and their subdivisions of war, social, gymnic or ritual dances could be easily drawn on for theatrical use. Plato, in the seventh book of his 'Laws,' however, considered there should be but two possible classes out of many,—the serious war dances, against other less functional, and hence more frivolous practices, and those pacific dances which were devout. He proscribes the use of comic or buffoon dances, if not for the theater, at least for private citizens in his ideal state.

Dances involving the use of weapons are to be found among all primitive societies. These were anciently known in Greece, and if they had a preparative, educational function in the classic periods, they must surely have had, as among all other cultures, some remote magical arising. To dance before battle gives strength, rehearses thrusts and parries. The clash of bronze also drives away evil spirits. We are familiar with the Cretan Kuretes. An armed dance of the Amazons of Artemis at Ephesus, female counterparts to the Kouroi, may have sprung from an ancient tribal protective ceremony. Armed dances at funerals frighten away influences which disturb the heroes' sleep. A dance of triumph was not only exultation, but also a purge of the souls of dead enemies from the surrounding air.

The Pyrrhic, in the fifth century, was taught entirely as an aid to military education, a public state-regulated institution. Music and valor were allied. It was wholly different from the religious armed dance, from which it may have sprung, and with which it is often confused, even by ancient writers. It received its name either from *Pyrrhos,* the son of Achilles who performed it first after his victory over Eurypylos, or from Achilles himself, celebrating rites at the *pyre* of Patroclos. The war dance was called the *red,* from the vermilion tunics or blood-simulating stains which the Plateans, and above all, the Spartans, used. The word for fire is also *red,* recalling as well crematory games. It flourished in Athens in the sixth century, in the epoch of Peisistratus, that tyrant who codified the Homeric fragments and for purposes of centralizing his own power, moved the primarily rural, popular god Dionysos into the town. It was continually danced at the Panathenaic festivals. It could be accompanied by struck chords, the alert flute, or by a lively song of the dancing fighters. A warlike-pantomime, it linked battle formations, phalanx on the march, charging over ditches, retreating in good order, pairing off for single-combat. Indeed it sometimes was danced as a solo, like shadow-boxing, against an imaginary adversary, and called *skiamachia* or *monomachia* (shadow-fight or single-fight). Apuleius, the Roman, writing after 160 A.D., describes the Pyrrhic as then danced by young boys and girls in shining raiment, with eloquent rhythmic steps. . . .

> In order due they moved through graceful figures, now sweeping round in full circle, now linked in slanting line, now massed in squares or breaking away from the throng into separate groups.

In 'The Golden Ass' it is used as an entirely theatrical prelude to a ballet-pantomime and even in Sparta the spectacular effect on its watchers must have been calculated. Executed *en masse,* it became a popular ornament to Spartan town festivals at the feast of their Dioscuri founders; in Athens at the great and small Panathenaic. As with drama, rich citizens were charged with its preparation and each of the ten tribes was represented by a Pyrrhic troupe. Everywhere (except in Sparta) it soon changed its nature, and from the reign of Alexander of Macedon its bellicose connotation was lost. It fell under Bacchic influence, and swords turned into torches and thyrsi, clashing in celebration of the victory of the god in India over Pentheus, his enemy. It came to mean a lascivious circus dance to Roman Christians and in a thousand years or more the Scots and North Saxons came to dance something not far from its source-forms, and it becomes identified with aspects of English Morris-dancing.

An athletic dance of rather a different kind was the *Gymnopedia.* It used as choros, men, young men (*epheboi*), and children, directed by palm-crowned dancers, singing the pæan, chiefly in honor of Pythian Apollo, whose shrine was in Sparta's Agora. Sung and danced in memory of the fallen at Thermopylæ, its cult may have been the occasion for the celebrated cantata, preserved by Plutarch, on the three ages of man.

> *Old Men:* We've been already, young and brave. . . .
> *Young Men:* We are; draw nigh; you'll see it well.
> *Children:* One day we will be: braver than both.

Spectacular dances were not always first performed consciously in theaters, but often in temple precincts and in the stadia. Among well-known Spartan forms, the *Gymnopedia* was particularly revered. It was preëminently the show which exalted the soul of the stiff old town. No reprimand was so severe as exclusion from its participation. The greatest care was taken with its preparation and performance. There is the incident in Xenophon, when a messenger brings tidings of the defeat at Leuctra, arriving on the last day of the ceremonies, at that very moment when the men's choros went out before the audience; then the city-fathers, keeping the catastrophe to themselves, let the solemn games continue, and only proclaimed it by adding to these holy dead, already cherished in the city's memory, the names of the newly slain. Such parade marches, to the sharp cadence of a hymn, might be theatrically transformed for the entrance of such a king as returning Agamemnon.

In the large group of entirely pacific dances, known under the general head of *Emmelia,* there were those appropriate to purely devotional ends; mimetic, corporal, plastic prayers or sacraments, like the processional hymns of Homer. The *Hyporchemia* was a dramatized hymn from Crete, danced by two choirs, of immobile singers and silent dancers. The song was carried now by one voice, perhaps the composer's, now by a section of the choir which stayed quiet, or executed simple motions, while the rest consecrated themselves entirely to dances, illustrating the hymn. It differed from the pæan where every one sang and danced at once, and was much more vivacious and expressive. The *Geranos* (stork or crane) came from Delos. It was based on the story of Theseus who saved the Cretan hecatomb of youths and virgins from the labyrinth. It was held in the month of Hecatombeon, of sacrifice, in mid-July. Probably once a nocturnal fertilization ceremony, girls and boys led each other by the hands, imitating with the carriage of their heads, necks and flapping arms the V-shaped flight of birds. Then there were dances which used veils as a chief feature, with deft manipulation of woven materials in the air, disturbed by the moving bodies of the dancers. Cloth covered the whole body, even the head (except the face) and hands. Such dances are familiar in oriental and Islamic countries. In Greece they may have come from the cult of the fertility goddess Demeter or Persephone, shrouded in mourning for her lost summer. The best exemplification of these dances are the popular Tanagra fired-clay figurines, which give a vivid idea of skillful dress-play. In the minds of the ancients they also may have had a significance which eludes us, imitating the sudden apparition of gods, veiled in mist or night,—revelation and disappearance. Some orgiastic dancers tossed veils, and these feminine symbols were used by men in the female impersonations of Dionysiac theatrical dancing, which is exemplified by the transvestation of Pentheus in 'The Bacchæ.' Another branch of *Emmelia* which has been popularized in architectural sculpture was the *Karyatid,* once annually performed at the feast of Artemis Karyatis, *the* female dancer of the gods, at Karyai on the Laconian-Arcadian border. These may have started with the girls bearing flower-baskets on their heads. Their uniform is always a short tunic. They took quick, brief steps, moving as much as nature would permit on their tiptoes. This may have been affected by the upright carriage of the backbone necessary to balance their burdens. There were no leaps or jumps, and the dancers seemed to glide along the ground. They are conventionally represented actually on the tips of their toes, but more realistically on the high half-toe. They flowed in continuous chains, arms high to support the baskets. In architecture, as on the 'Porch of the Maidens' they become static pillars.

Distinct from the war-dance, yet so much more violent than any of the *Emmelia* as to be really separate from both, were a considerable number of orgiastic measures, basically oriental or at least alien to native Greece. The noble, stately eurythmic measure of the *Emmelia,* the dignified Spartan and Attic processionals seem characteristically Hellenic while the Dionysiac routs were replete with alien influence. Bacchos personified not only wine, but every vital secret in nature, and his votaries obeyed him in mad explosions of extreme exuberance, an ecstatic eclipse of individuality, in which by passionate, self-indulgent relief they would lose their simple identity and merge in a group-consciousness with the God's pervading influences.

These phenomena need not seem so remote to us for in North America there are several more or less familiar parallels to the *orgia* of Dionysos. In 1870, the cult of the Ghost Dance swept the West. It was a Round, danced in a tense, monotonous rhythm, till all the participants, one after the other, sank stiff to the earth. During the induced trance, the Indians saw visions of their reconquest of the continent from the white man; while the exhausted ones lay motionless, the rest danced on eventually to join them. Some tribes of Northern Mexico danced themselves into frothy frenzies on their stone altars. "For the American Indians as a whole, and including those of Mexico, were passionately Dionysian. They valued the violent experience, all means by which human beings may break through the usual sensory routine, and to all such experiences they attributed the highest value."

Lucian, a late Greek, describes the Dionysiac threat:

> For they had heard strange reports from their spies concerning his army: that his phalanx and bodies of troops consisted of mad and raging women, crowned with ivy, clad in fawn-skins, carrying short spears, not of iron, but also made of ivy; they bore small shields, which gave forth a booming noise if one so much as touched them—for their drums resembled shields. There were also, it was said, a few rustic youths among men, naked, dancing the Kordax, having tails and horns.

Once introduced, these excesses were popular, and indeed there were a few precedents in Greece herself for them—notably in cults of the ancient vegetation goddess, the Artemis of Ephesus. The religion of the Phrygian earth-mother-of-all, Cybele, and her servant Corybantes, was not popular until the fifth century, but when it had so become, wild casting of arms and legs, convulsive, tearing turns, barbarous shrieks and crashing cymbals spread like wild-fire, fusing with similar rites of Thracian Dionysos. As an oriental effeminizing innovation it would always remain suspect, to be censured by such outraged puritans as Demosthenes. But a succession of public disasters, and the disintegration of the old religion caused a general demoralization in whose anarchic atmosphere the orgiasts had fertile possibilities. Cybele's young lover was Attis, who perished mutilated in an excess brought on by the goddess' jealousy. Adonis, Osiris, Dionysos himself, now Attis, had no effect on the established state religion, but their rites were practiced in *private,* which corrupted the whole fabric of Athenian state belief. The foreign rites were locally adapted and the foamy-lipped, mad-eyed, seizing hysteria finds its most perfect artistic definition in 'The Bacchæ.' As for the technique of the orgiastic dance, insomuch as it can be reconstructed from Greek monuments (and these have been considerably imitated and readapted by late Græco-Roman artists) it seems to have consisted of three or four dizzy turns on the half-toe, a small bound, alternations of the feet, turns, and successive leaps. The head was tossed back in an extremity of tension, a position impossible to maintain for long except in an advanced stage of nervous tautness or pathological spasm. There was a wild sweep of thrashing arms, sudden thrusting supplication or invocation, the torso twisted, rush forward, quick arrest and dip; then a wave-like resumption to an almost inevitable dénouement in physical collapse: 'Mænad, Thyiad, Phoibad, Lyssad,—mad, rushing, inspired, raging one.' These dances were considerably more varied than monotonous Persian or Arabian dervish-dances which produce a similar exhaustion. Indeed they were not specifically aimed to produce delirious transport; these conditions were rather the result of an induced state of mind. Satyrs and sileni of the comic and satiric choros could also practice such violent dances, but they would probably accustom themselves to a broken, trotting, horsy beat. Angular movements of their arms, hunched heads and stamping goatish feet were more petulant and brutish, faunish, and neither insane nor drunken.

In contrast to the circular dithyrambic choros, from which the tragic choros evolved, when the singing-dancers finally entered the theater, it was in a rectangular form. In the early Æschylean 'Suppliant Woman,' for the purpose of the story of the fifty daughters of Danaos, the number of the choros was the same as the old dithyrambic choir, but afterwards the choros of tragedy and satyr play seems to have been composed of fifteen members with three files of five persons, or five of three. In the comedies a similar set-up numbered twenty-four, the choros, entering in silence or led by a flautist, could present itself in ranks, advancing in an order wider than deep, but more often in the reverse, deeper than wide, which was more suited to a defile. As the choros was almost always present during the action, entering from the right, the left file was the most observed by the spectators, and for this reason its most attractive members were placed in front. In the middle, in the third row, was the acknowledged place of the choir-leader.

Theatrical dancing was divided into three chief categories after the three dramatic types: the grave *Emmelia,* for tragedy; harmonious, unbroken, close to the religious *Emmelia;* the lively *Kordax,* for comedy; and the lewd *Sikinnis,* for satyr-plays, whose members wore pink drawers or skirts for attachable horse-hair tails and phalloi. These three specific types did not preclude the use or combination of usage of other dance forms which might be called for by nature of the action.

Too often our idea of ancient drama is more influenced by French seventeenth century imitations of Roman tragedy, than by Greek relics themselves. Even in its most developed epoch, its authors never lost sight of a lyric-dance origin, devoting much thought and emphasis to a synthesis of song, movement and verse. In the 'Suppliant Women,' the earliest preserved play of Æschylos, the principal character, as such, is the band of Danaos' daughters.

And in 'The Bacchæ,' the last of Euripides', the Bacchants are equally, if otherwise, indispensable.

The choral entrance or *Parados* consisted of a simple processional apparition in full view of all, though in the 'Eumenides' the choros dashed furiously in, and the 'Birds' of Aristophanes entered one after another to have their plumage described in turn. The most important dances of all were those of the *Stasima,* the three or four lyric interludes where the chief actors having left the scene or were quiet, the choros *stayed* in the dancing-place to perform. Their movements were usually sober, often more plastic attitudes accompanying song than what we would consider dance. Movement varied to the metric of song, recitative, or conversation. It is difficult to allocate their parts. Sometimes they moved and spoke in groups, at others responding singly. They were frequently on familiar terms with the actors, particularly in comedy.

No comparisons of our contemporary theater with the Greek serve to clarify our understanding of the Greek. It is true both are spectacular in essence. The shows are framed by the *theatron,* a place for seeing; although the proscenium frame itself will not really appear until the Renaissance. Here the similarity ends. There was no surprise in Greek tragedy. The prologue explains conclusively what will be shown. The main deed, the killing, always happens off-stage. There are continual scenes of long, wrangling dialogues. The climax is not a finale. The action, unified in time and place, always happens on the last day before, or the day of the catastrophe, a kind of continual atmosphere of doomsday pervading all the verse. In their theater there was much less division between the audience and the actors. Choros linked actors and audience by being audience when watching the main actors, and actors when they thought aloud for the audience. The audience surrounded them, sitting on three sides of the dancing-place. In the dithyramb, audience and actors were one. Later they were mutually dependent, but definitely separate. This was the transition from joining in the action, and watching the action. Now the dance is not only danced, but watched. There was perhaps a loss of emotional immediacy and intensity, but a growth of the spectacular.

The music was simple, severe, subordinate to verse and action. All choirs sang in unison. The melody was fitted to the words, as in the Bach Mass. There were no harmonics. Each note corresponded to a syllable, and the audience could hear the choros with great distinctness, since they were trained to articulate precisely and throw their voices in speaking poetry, which was, after all, the prime element. The accompanying strings or flute used the melody's identical tune. In lyrical, as opposed to dramatic verse, there was a tendency for the flute to overpower the voices. The modes took their names from the places of their geographical origin and had the differences of, say, Irish, Swiss or Spanish folk-music. The Dorian and Myxolydian were proper to tragedy in general. Æschylos favored the severe Ionic. Sophocles used the semi-oriental Phrygian, and Euripides was ridiculed by Aristophanes for it. Sometimes a few notes of incidental music were inserted to emphasize a choral introduction, or finale, or to point off the speech of the chief actors, like the struck chords before a Mozart aria.

The Greeks had few musical instruments, but they are the same three types we now possess: strings, wood-wind and tympani. Among the last were not only drums, but cymbals, timbrels, tambourines and castanets, and these were not always favorably regarded, since as percussive importations they were used for new and suspect orgiastic rites. The most common flutes were a series of seven or nine graduated hollow reeds bound together by wax or thongs, which we call 'Pan-pipes'; the double flute or *auloi* (the medieval shawm or hautboy) each having a vibrant reed at the mouth like our clarinet; and the trumpet which was of metal, for use in battle, as ritual signal or as a call for attention in mass gatherings. Sometimes, in the fifth century at least, boys generally learned to play the flute; but one could not sing and play at once, so the practice was fairly well taken over by professional choral accompanists who were employed in the theater, at games, and to lead soldiers on the march. The lyre, originally two animal horns inserted into a tortoise-shell sounding-box, to which four or seven strings were pegged, was held in the left hand, and its player, with a plectrum in his right, modulated or silenced the chords with the free fingers of his left. From the lyre descends guitar, mandolin, zither and all viols. Pipes were the first musical implements to be developed by technical virtuosi, who in the latter part of the fifth century created the cross-flute (our flute), from which emerged pipe-organ and the symphony of wood, lead and brass down to our saxophone.

Even taking into consideration all peculiarities of the ideology of their plays, notions of what were theatrically effective or permissible, the frugality of the presentation and the simplicity of the music, the single element that must strike modern dramatic artists as most original and most different from our own conceptions the institution of the Greek choros as a singing and dancing unit. Not only was it a plastic background, but also a fluent means of inducing atmospheric changes, a kind of barometer of action which created its own weather. Particularly in Sophocles, before the declaration of catastrophe, the choros is permitted considerable gayety, the better to contrast with imminent gloom. Often, in the course of the most tensely pathetic scenes, the choros entered into direct colloquy with the protagonist, and its speech or song alternated with his words. This was *Kommoi* or communion. As a dramatic device we will again encounter it in the drama of the Christian passion where the choros is its responsive *schola cantorum*. In 'The Bacchae' there are indications for mimetic play between Pentheus, Dionysos, choral leader and chorus. The movements and attitudes of the heroic characters were stylized from habit so they would be legible, prefiguring Roman dramatic pantomime.

The history of the comic choros is parallel to the tragic. Here dancing is less important, while miming and buffoonery are more. A special and important feature of the comic chorus was the *parabasis,* where the members threw off their rôles as dramatis personae, and apostrophized the public directly in their own name or their poet's. Choral movements were more brusque and sharp. The *Parados* or entrance-dance was frequently in the agitated trochaic beat; no steady processional, but in the 'Acharnians,' a race; in the 'Knights' a battle-charge; in the 'Birds,' a succession of daft pirouettes; in 'Lysistrata,' a mock combat. The *Exodos* of comedies was not brief and perfunctory as in the tragedies, but almost always a rout or buffoon's game. Aristophanes had a tendency to make his exodos a separate amusing or facetious piece with grotesque dances, almost in the nature of a terminal ballet, without vocal accompaniment. The *Kordax* was the name of that dance always associated in Roman and Christian times with the lewdest aspects of comic dance, and of these there were no lack; obscene jesting with great leather phalloi or horse-hair tails strapped front and back, their performance was later considered a real dementia. There was a good deal of leering verse, suggestive hip-rolling, nose-thumbing, thumb-biting, chest forward, buttocks thrust out, kilt-flouncings and outrageous parodies of the ordinary movements of familiar popular or social dances. The mimic actor-dancers of the comedy burlesques are the descendants of fabulous half-animal creatures who snuffled, stamped, laughed and gambolled with Thracian Bacchos. Horse-hooved and goat-footed they remained, sinewy reminders of the fertility of animal life. There were also masked and painted demons with sacks for bellies and flapping genitalia. The *Sikinnis* was the type-dance of satyr-plays of which only one example remains in the 'Cyclops' of Euripides, an episode of the one-eyed giant in the Odyssey. The name and origin of the *Sikinnis* are equally vague; the satyr-plays followed the tragedies; perhaps a remnant of early Bacchic worship. There were tragic figures among fools and dancing clowns, insomuch as they parodied incidents from the preceding tragedy. The satyr-dances were not so much comic-relief, as a religious hangover, when the tragedy itself had lost its significance as a ritual act. As a dance, the *Sikinnis* accompanied the liveliest choral parts of the satyr-plays, and were characterized by an alacrity often noted in ancient sources to parallel the pyrrhic.

It is impossible here to more than mention the complex systems of Greek metric and the development of prosody which was the underlying rhythmic indication of both dance and music.* The imitative and tragic dances adopted the iambic; in all the odes, the song was sustained by rhythmic movement strictly linked to the articulation of triad, strophe, antistrophe and epode, keeping an interior time to the syllabic beat of syncopated or regular phrasing.

The dances in private life for personal recreation or social amusement probably had less direct influence on stage-dancing than the public religious or civic forms. But since they did exist it would not be unlikely to assume that for various purposes they found their way into the drama, either as solo adaptations, or perhaps most frequently in the comedies, as satirical pantomimic comment on the behavior of men and women in the privacy of their homes.

* See notes at the back for names of source-books referring to Greek metric.

Wedding dances are frequently mentioned by Euripides and they are anciently referred to in Homer. Called *Epithalamia,* they were performed in honor of Hymen, the marriage god. By torchlight, young friends of the bride and groom would hymn them to their marriage chamber, and once abed, they would return for a final dance and serenade. The custom inspired many beautiful verses, and two thousand years later, masques of the Italian, French and English renaissance.

Funeral dances, we know, are also connected with survival rites and ancestor worship. In Greece they had become, perhaps under Egyptian influence, rather stereotyped and conventionalized. The hands are shown clasped in stylized attitudes of noble grief. Perhaps the remote and independent prototypes of mediæval dances of death, or *danse macabre,* they are more popularly represented in tombs that the Greek colonists painted in Sicily and Magna Græcia. Entertainments at feasts included many acrobatic features we have already seen in Egypt; there were dances by invited guests and others by professional entertainers who tumbled, juggled, walked on ropes, on their hands, executed rapid flip-flops, with such dangerous variations as performing neat somersaults between upright knives. There were also miniature interludes of monodrama or monomime, in the same relation to drama as chamber-music would be to a full orchestra.

Among the popular social dances, there were those inspired by various labors, flower-dances celebrating the year's first fruits and blossoms, play-dances, such as the *Hormos,* or collar, a circular round of alternating boys and girls, similar to our old-fashioned 'ladies' chain.' Many of these dances can hardly be differentiated from games. There was, in the later periods, from the fifth century on, a sharp demarcation between amateur and professional,— the citizen who participated in civic and religious observances,—or danced at dinner parties, and the stage-dancer or banquet-entertainer, who were often hard to distinguish from courtesans. These were accustomed to dance naked at feasts from remote antiquity. Certain of them banded themselves together, under a kind of ballet-master, and could be had for hire, either placing themselves at the disposition of a choregos, who may have been preparing plays for the annual season, or else performing in public as they found the chance. The dancing-masters of the palæstra, however, who were originally poets as well, held honorable positions, and the daughters of the best Lacedæmonian families, were expected to dance the Karyai. At the age of sixty, Socrates is supposed to have been taught some new dances by Aspasia, who as a *hetaira,* may also have been a professional dancer: "Am I," he asked, "to be blamed for reducing the corpulence of my body by a little dancing?"

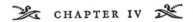

CHAPTER IV

The Roman Theater: Pantomime and Imperial Spectacle

THE gamut of Roman dancing offers us a complete contrast to everything Greek, although a basic part of Roman theatre was seriously influenced by ideas from Attica herself, and from Hellenic colonists in Sicily or Magna Græcia. Dance, as the Greeks understood it, and to a great extent as we understand it, held little meaning for Romans, but they were responsible for several contiguous forms which have had serious, if only subsequent effect on the mutations of theatrical dancing.

The history of our modern stage-dance can be interpreted as a triangular contest between dancing proper, expressive mimicry and spectacular decoration in costume or scenery. One or the other of these elements, during the last two hundred years, seems always ascendant, and it has been the task of great reformers, Noverre, Vigano, Richard Wagner or Fokine to reassert the necessity for a synthesis. The Greeks, as far as we can tell, and as we would like to believe, in order to have at least one perfect point of reference, may have managed by a happy series of circumstances to achieve the equilibrium of song or verse, dance and expressiveness. They were limited by technical poverties and insular boundaries, but this was their good fortune. In Rome, with the growing obsession of imperialist world-domination, all limits disappeared. An audience by no means trained or concentrated as the Greek, set a low common denominator for public tastes. Instead of attempting to conserve those factors necessary for a lyric dance-drama, Romans were quick to over-emphasize each element in turn, with main accent on mime and spectacle. Dancing was practically eliminated, and through little fault of its own would receive such a bad reputation in company with other excesses, that it could not reëmerge in a form worthy of its past honorable name for a thousand years.

We study the history of the Roman stage to show, not a connection with dance, but a separation from it. Aside from indigenous marriage rites, secular or religious feasts of aborigines in the Italian peninsula, with whatever aspects of theater they shared in common with drama-dances of any primitive society, their first theatrical representations were probably arranged by Greek colonials who remembered seasons of the great Dionysia. These starts fell on naturally fertile ground. Of all Mediterranean races, the Italians remain manually the most demonstrative. Their hands, shoulders, their whole bodies coincide with their tongues to make their meanings more intensely vivid. A number of local elements were fertilized by an already formulated Greek drama which can be briefly noticed. The inherent Latin gift for the assumption of a rôle was characteristically employed by composers of wedding-verses in Southern Etruria, who would sing, chant or shout scurrilous and witty descriptions of ceremonies, as nuptial serenades, with appropriate invocations to the gods of fruitfulness and love. They were called *Fescennine* (*fascinum* equals Greek: *phallos*). Although they turned into a complex literary form they never merged into dramas, as did the dithyramb. There were also players from Istria who had been imported to Rome at the foundation of 'scenic games' in 364 B.C. when the Consuls considered it necessary to propitiate the gods with theatrical entertainment, and distract a populace harassed by plague. These Etruscan dancers and pantomimists, whose speech even seemed alien to the Romans, had not been out of touch with Greek settlers, and became so well-known that as *istriones* they are remembered for the name attached to all histrionic art. Their performances gave impetus to the popularization of the *saturæ* (from *goat*-skin shepherd's cloaks), farcical after-pieces of a rustic origin, independently parallel to Greek satyr-plays. The *scenici* or *mimi,* specifically imitative actors, had their beginnings with the springs of the art itself. Their name may have replaced the older, *planipedes,* flat-foot or bare-foot buffoons among slaves and poor farmers. These mimes not only parodied the everyday life of a difficult existence, but in their versions enacted vulgar adaptations of the lives of gods and heroes. Their bawdy farces were at first performed alone, then as epilogues to the official dramatic games, and again, under the Empire, reasserted themselves, mostly preserving elements which were specifically pantomimic or in dumb-show.

The *mimi* also drew considerably from an important genre of Latin play. These were the so-called Atellan Fables, satirical comedies of small-town life, full of definite, recognizable characters. These have counterparts not only in previous comic types of Aristophanes and later Greek comedians from which they were also borrowed, but centuries later in Venetian and French farces of the seventeenth and eighteenth centuries, and our own contemporary satires of Broadway or the Boulevards. Historians have made much of a consecutive tradition for all comic plays. Indeed there is much to support theories of absolutely unbroken descent. It is also a simple fact that domestic situations involving conflicts of married life, of contrast between city, suburbs and the farm are as comical and pitiful in Syracuse, New York, as they were in Græco-Roman Syracuse. In *Fabulæ Atellanæ* (from the town of Atella in the Campagna) we find Pappus (or Papa), the heavy father;—Maccus, an ass-eared glutton, a white-washed country-bumpkin, hunchbacked, with big nose and skull, the prototype of Punch; Bucco, a puffy gossip,—and such others as the wily Cheat, the boasting Soldier, the grasping Whore, the Doctor-Charlatan, the effeminate Young-Man. They may be more real to us if we compare them to our equivalents of farce or comic-strip; the difficult *Mother-in-Law,* the put-upon *Father* who has his sentimental triumph before the third-act curtain in spite of seeming silliness, the *Son-in-Law-to-be* whom Father privately encourages when his beautiful but fickle *Daughter* prefers the slick *City-Fellow,* or if in the city, the smooth *Foreigner.* The plots of the Atellanæ were simple. The dialogue was improvised by actors as they went along. Plenty of slap-stick relief and broad local allusions with the names of local characters inserted drew ready laughter. For a short time they assumed a literary formulization but were wholly absorbed into pantomime under the Emperors. Plots recounting the abuses of demagogues and official corruption were often popular, but adultery and love were the most popular themes. After Nero murdered his mother, one Datus, an actor of the *Atellanæ,* accompanied a speech starting 'Hail Father, Hail Mother,' with the gestures of a man drinking from a cup, and thrashing about in water; this referred to the poisoning of Claudius, the drowning of Agrippina. Nero only banished him from the country.

The origin of the academic Roman stage had its occasion in 240 B.C., when, after victory in the first Punic War, public games were held with especial glory, after the precedent of Macedonia and Greece. The writer of both the comedy and the tragedy performed then was one Livius Andronicus, a freed slave of Hellenized Tarentum, the city famous for its Dionysiac celebrations. He was traditionally believed to have once lost his voice and hence invented the art of mime. His models were late Attic playwrights. The choros, as such, had little place. The dialogue was broken up by *cantica,* songs of a young boy, stood up in front of a player on the *tibia* (flute), while a single mime interpreted his lines by gesticulation. Actors took their parts very seriously. Quintilian reports seeing them leave the stage in tears after a particularly pathetic scene. The style of their declamation was patterned on normal speech, but was no servile copy. Precision and grandeur were added. Gesture, predominantly of hands and arms, followed a preordained canon. Senatorial orators were instructed by actors in order to gain more powerful effects. Plutarch analyzed the Dance (movement) in three sections. *Motion,* a blanket term; *Posture,* a dancer-actor's attitude at the moment of an arrested pause in motion; *Indication,* a gesture whereby some external object, the heavens or earth, was pointed out. Roman dramatic literature degenerated into sophisticated, derivative dilettantism. Romans loved a full stage, noise and color. They were enchanted with Pompey who equipped the return of Agamemnon in the 'Clytemnestra' with six hundred superbly laden mules. Since the theater proper was an inadequate place for semi-military spectacle which they grew more and more to demand, it was replaced by the Circus and the Arena. This change was encouraged by censorious puritans of the conservative Republic who promoted the martial allure of gladiatorial combat as against the softness of the stage,—sensing quite early an electioneering facility held by controlling the games whose popularity was proverbial. Juvenal's *mot,* summing up the desires of the people, *Bread and circuses,* was no negligible half-truth to the Senate.

The Roman theatrum made several amplifications of the Greek *theatron* (place for seeing) which tells us directly little or nothing of its effect on Roman dancing. But this we must keep in mind for fifteen hundred years until Renaissance architects, in attempting to reconstruct the Roman stage from archeological sources, will provide a frame for our stage-dancing. This frame, however unlike its original, would be, nevertheless, our standard for the next half thousand years.

In Rome, as far as theatrical history extends, in spite of the perfunctory attitude by which Consuls voted games to propitiate the divinities, theatre was always theatre. Greeks were by nature participants, if not actually actors. Romans were always spectators. The Senate, perhaps because it was jealous of any amusements except the circus-games which it could control and exploit, for a long time prevented the erection of permanent stone scenes. The first lasting theatre at Rome was erected by Cornelius Pompey in 55 b.c., but even here the *scena,* or performer's portion, was wood. It had some eighteen thousand seats. Seventy-seven years later, in the reign of Tiberius, this house was burnt—and he completely rebuilt it in stone, though he hated the circus-shows.

The Romans, since they understood better than the Greeks the constructional advantages of key-stone arch and concrete vaulting, could bank seats upon such level ground as the Field of Mars, while the Greeks usually had to make the best of semi-circular hillsides. Roman auditoria were absolute semi-circles, and stage-buildings were integrated with them, making the whole fabric for the first time an entity. The stage platform was not more than five feet high, but far deeper than the Greek, and backed by an elaborate *episkenion* or frontal stage-scene, embellished with decorative architectural fantasy, broken entablatures or rosettes in recessive vaults supported by ornate pilasters and free-standing columns which held nothing but fancifully vegetated Corinthian capitals. The Greeks knew such a permanently busy décor would compete with the performers to their disadvantage, but Romans were not troubled by such logic. Indeed, performers seem almost to have been a rather minor consideration, compared to the splendors of the buildings' physical appurtenances, huge painted awnings to keep sun from their eyes, flower-water squirted about to cool them off, the regulated claques of applauders. There is much in the crassness and technical ingenuity of Roman civilization to remind us of our own. Nowhere is the parallel so upsetting as between their big, comparatively unloved theaters, and our own monstrous movie palaces with every miracle of exotic decorative allusion. We have 'Egyptian,' 'Spanish,' 'Gothic,' 'Renaissance,' etc., while the Romans had only Greek, and besides air-conditioning, acoustics, long range projection, velvet comfort, conventionalized courtesy, all for the presentation of films, and mostly what films!

A secondary reason for the decline of Roman dramatic literature, and exclusion of any possibility of dance-drama comparable to Greek, which if not in actual breadth or nobility, might have at least resulted in a brilliant dance-satire (if not Euripides, then Petronious),—was the social-position of actors, mimes and dancers. Originally, poets hired their own troupes, training and performing with them, but later permanent companies composed of south Italian or Greek slaves, once owned by rich nobles, were rented out to the theatrical managers. As slaves, these wretched half-starved, insecure artists could be bullied or flogged at will, which they frequently were, or even killed by a master's or a rentor's word. There were some, who by the quality of their art were freed and achieved intimacy with the Emperor, which we shall see was not an undiluted blessing. But such exceptions did little to improve the status of thousands of professional or semi-professional mimes who neither had nor could ever hope to have, civil rights. Their miserable condition contributed to the unattractiveness of the stage as a profession. But had the patrician fathers really desired it, or the populace preferred it to games or big shows, the situation could have been altered.

What dancing there was in Rome surviving in records of paint, stone or verse, is of a preponderantly religious, or at least ritual nature, and when stage-dancing was designed for use either as dramatic interlude or a part of circus-shows, its form must have been somewhat determined by remnants of ceremonial usage. The Etruscans, one of three folk who created the Latin race, were of obscure origin leaving a meager history. They seem to have become a conquering nation before the start of the sixth century B.C.; were obsessed by the animal sacrifice, the inspection of entrails to prognosticate future events. This habit Romans later made spectacular, but without the pretext of prophecy.

They were masters of the double flute, and strictly observed a predetermined order in their dance-steps as a functional rite, which might lose its virtue if incorrectly repeated. Their goddess Menvra (Roman, Minerva), was the patroness of music, flutes and horns. Etruscan nobles did not take part in their games, and for funeral-dances supported a class of professionals who were of the same caste as flute-players, acrobats, or the best-looking slaves. There are very full tomb murals extant at Corneto, with vivid presentations of a *crotalisteria,* a female dancer with bells and flexible clappers or *crotali,* with which, as *première danseuse,* she marks her time. A male dancer and his partner (*saltator* and *saltatrix*) are paired, accompanied by a flautist (*subulo*). It was these people who were borrowed as famous dancers for the first known spectacles, to appease their neighbor's gods.

One of the most ancient of Roman dances was Ariadne's Dance, or the 'Troy-Game,' of Grecian origin, which we have had already in quotation from the Iliad, and which Virgil attached to the legend of Theseus. Its pattern is scratched on a Pompeian wall, with an inscription: 'Labyrinth: here dwelt Minotaur,' and it is found frequently as a design in mosaic pavements, with hero and bull-headed monster standing in the center. Later on the *Ludus Troiæ* was an equestrian sham-battle, revived as a brilliant game for young knights by Augustus. It is vividly described in the fifth book of Virgil's Æneid. Another early Roman dance was *Bellicrepa,* supposedly invented by the city-founder Romulus, to commemorate the Rape of the Sabine Women, and in essence was a survival of marriage-by-capture rites. Dancing as a whole played much less of a part in both national and private lives of the Romans, than the Spartans or Athenians. Cicero, who is said to have had a bad physique, formulated the Republican attitude against dancing (that feature of the theater which was most Greek), in one of his celebrated speeches:

> Cato calls Lucius Murena a dancer. If this be imputed to him truly, it is the reproach of a violent accuser; but if falsely, it is the abuse of a scurrilous railer. Wherefore, as you are a person of such influence, you ought not, O Marcus Cato, to pick up abusive expressions out of the streets, or out of some quarrel of buffoons; but ought not rashly to call a consul of the Roman people a dancer; but to consider with what other vices besides, that man must be tainted to whom that can with truth be imputed. For no man, one may almost say, ever dances when sober, unless perhaps he be a madman; nor in solitude, nor in a moderate and sober party; dancing is the last companion of prolonged feasting, of luxurious situation, and of many refinements.

These infuriating and priggish phrases form one of the best examples of a vicious element of moral dishonesty which makes the parallel between Romans and too many modern peoples frightening. The so-called early Roman fathers, infected with that will to power which resulted in Rome's fall, found it convenient to make of Greece a nationalist butt, having appropriated as much Hellenic culture as they could stomach. It is true, however, the Athens of Cicero's day had sadly degenerated from the time of Pericles, and was filled with a mongrel population of dilute natives, Levantines and other less virile people. Later on Rome would be infested with innumerable oriental religions, of Attis, Isis, Osiris, Serapis and Mithras, brought into Rome for the convenience of worshipers who were alien to the empire's capital. Dancing was often their distinguishing mark and at least some of the popularity for native Romans in these cults may have derived from their ritual dances. This feature was conveniently sensational and always attracted the wrath of puritan chauvinists.* Seneca spoke of the malady of having a dancing teacher in every patrician house.

An artificial step of measured solemnity was affected by votaries of Juno, who, halting in the Forum, sang her praises, dancing a simple round. Other processional dances accompanied the lustral, or purification ceremonies, in which a circular figure was described, within whose radius no evil influence could act. Another was done by the Arval Fraternity on the occasion of Ambarvalia, a feast of Ceres. The Brothers of the Ploughed Fields, on the second of a three-day rite, in a special thrice-repeated three-step (*tripudium*), led around pigs, rams or bulls for sacrifice to Mars, formerly a vegetation, not a war god. February celebrated the Lupercalia, once the occasion on which Julius Cæsar was thrice offered and thrice refused a crown. It may have been connected with a memorial to that she-wolf (*Lupa*) who suckled Romulus and Remus, but seems rather to be named for its *Luperci* (ones aproned in goatskins), who raced around the Palatine, worshiping Pan, thrashing thongs

---

* Apulieus, in *The Golden Ass* (VIII, 27, 28) gives a full description of a Syrian flagellant's dance.

cut from sacrificed goats. In March and October were held holy processions of the Salii, whose ritual occupied three weeks. Led off by trumpets, equipped in full-battle armor they paraded the capital; at every shrine and temple they halted, and directed by two captains, performed a solemn pyrrhic in three measures, singing their own accompaniment.

> The *Salii,* the priests of Mars, twelve in number, were instituted by Numa. Their dress was an embroidered tunic, bound with a girdle ornamented with brass. They wore on their head a conical cap, of a considerable height; carried a sword by their side; in their right hand a spear or rod, and in their left, one of the *Ancilia,* or shields of Mars. On solemn occasions, they used to go to the Capitol, through the forum and other public parts of the city, dancing and singing sacred songs, said to have been composed by Numa; which, in the time of Horace, could hardly be understood by any one, even the priests themselves. The most solemn procession of the *Salii* was on the first of March, in commemoration of the time when the sacred shield was believed to have fallen from heaven, in the reign of Numa. After their procession, they had a splendid entertainment, the luxury of which was proverbial.*

The Roman word for dance, *saltio,* is perhaps falsely confused with these *salii.* There was an Arcadian, one Salius, held responsible for first instructing the Romans in dancing. The pacific, semi-historic king, Numa Pompilius, supposedly initiated this order with twelve youths of noble birth, who, shirted in purple and buckled into ceremonial arms, beat time with short swords on sacred shields. In late Roman sculpture they are confused with the Kuretes, the dancing nurses of Cretan Zeus. The Salii also honored Saturn, god of the sown-seed, leaping (*saltatio*) high into the air, so that by inductive magic they caused corn and other cereals to wax tall. There were numerous colleges of such dancing priests all over the peninsula, whose ritual was useful for fertility. A late Roman historian, Varro, says in connection with the Salii: "The meaning of dancing at religious rites is that our ancestors felt that no part of the body should be debarred from religious experience." One might add that the ancestors, if he means the original farmers of the seven hills, or even the Etruscans, probably derived such an idea from the Greeks. Another such cult, but entirely feminine, was connected with the worship of Bona Dea or Great Mother, whose secret rites no man knew, and when the fiend Caligula presumed to participate in her ceremonies he honestly scandalized people whose capacity for scandal was exhausted. The great feast of Saturnalia, observed on the seventeenth of December, has not left us any particular descriptions of dances, but it is perhaps important to record here, because when Roman Christians would appropriate its season for Christ's Mass it would, through ensuing centuries, be occasion for many dramatic dances. Saturn's festival lasted a week. On the day, gifts of wax tapers (our Christmas candles), presents and dolls (survivals of human-sacrifice) were exchanged. At this time, all distinctions of class were nominally, in many cases actually, set aside.

* *The Lives of the Twelve Cæsars,* Suetonius.

Masters and slaves ate together. Supposedly instituted by Romulus at the winter solstice, it was a season for universal license, drunkenness, dancing in the streets; the only days in the year when bondsmen had freedom of speech.

There were also secular dances, none of which strike us as having any particular claims to national innovation when we remember Greece. In fact, a great deal of our idea of Greek dancing, at least in sculpture, comes from Græco-Roman or pure Roman illustration. To be sure, Italians must have made variants of their own, and with a constant influx of captives from Cordoba, the Teutoberg forests, Nubian deserts and Scottish hills, Roman games adorned themselves with exotic tribal dances. But these were adornments, prized for their barbaric strangeness, testifying to the remote confines of Imperium Romanum, rather than for the dance-movements themselves. What a Roman connoisseur of the Empire found good in dancing is shown in 'The Golden Ass':

> Only the other day, at Athens in front of the Painted Porch with these two eyes of mine I saw a mountebank on horseback swallow a sharp sword point foremost, and again, for the offer of a few pence, thrust a hunting-spear, its death-dealing point downwards, right into his very vitals! And, look you, above the lance-head, where the shaft of the inverted lance rose from his open jaws towards his crown, there stood up a pretty girlish-looking boy who danced so nimbly with many a tortuous bending of his body that he seemed to have neither bone nor muscle. All we who stood by marveled. You might have likened him to some splendid snake twining with slippery coils about the staff that the god of healing bears, all rough with knots where the twigs had been lopped away.

The Romans were consistent in nothing but possibly their legal codes, and their attitude about dancing is no exception. As a whole they liked to see it, though they would allow themselves to be shocked if it was openly performed by too skillful amateurs or society-women. Sallust wrote of Sempronia: "She played and danced more gracefully than a respectable woman should."

Later on in his wonderful book Apuleius gives us an enchanting description of that type of dance-entertainment called by the Romans 'dance-fables,' but which can only be accurately translated by our word *ballet*. This term has been hesitatingly employed here though other historians and translators are less shy, labeling the Astral dance of Egypt, the Spartan Pyrrhic and the Roman Troy-Game equally as ballets. *Ballet* in this essay is used in a very specific sense as a form appearing first only in the Italian Renaissance; but the spectacle that Apulieus saw, or at least that he described, even though it has no connection with the later form, is pure ballet. Libretti for such dance-drama were composed by poets like Lucan, and Apulieus must have had some practical experience to have written of them as he did.

Preceded by the Pyrrhic elsewhere quoted, and by other sportive dances, the 'great curtain fell away, the lesser curtains were drawn back, and the stage was arrayed before our eyes.' There is too much to quote entirely, but here is enough to show how strikingly close the performance of nineteen hundred years ago resembles, for example, Fokine's *Daphnis et Chloé* or *Narcisse,* Ben Jonson's and Inigo Jones' Masques, and the ballets of Lully, Rameau, and even Noverre. Stage-machinery, color, even music in dance-suites, combining the several harmonic modes, and the succession of *entrances,* or grouped dancers; all are identical:

> Juno was followed by Castor and Pollux, whose heads were covered with oval helmets with stars set bright upon their crests. And Castor and Pollux also were no more than youthful actors. This maiden came forward to the rippling music of the Ionian flute, and with quiet and unaffected gesture and stately movement of the head promised the herdsman that if he awarded her the prize of loveliness she would make him king over all Asia. But she whom her array of armor showed to be Minerva was escorted by two boys, the armor bearers that go with the goddess of battle, Terror and Fear, dancing fiercely with naked swords. And behind her a flute-player sounded the warlike Dorian mode, mingling deep booming notes with shrill blasts that rang like a trumpet call, and he danced with nimble strength. With restless head and eyes in whose glance were threats, with swift and nervous gesticulation and fiery mien, she showed to Paris that if he accorded her the victory in beauty's battle, he should by her aid be made brave and glorious with the trophies of war.

But it was not in such dances that Rome made a lasting contribution to theatrical tradition, but rather in instituting pantomime as a form in itself. There is some confusion over the word, which, by itself, derives from Greek *mimeomai,* to counterfeit. The noun *mime,* its plural *mimi,* are some-times used to signify performers of exclusively obscene shows. This usage is late, favored by Christians. *Pantos* means 'all' and 'pantomime' was a more general term for the mute interpretive art. Both 'pantomime' and 'dancing' were referred to by Latin and Roman Christians as *Saltatio,* and 'saltation' is employed down through the eighteenth century by critics and historians of France and England.

The appearance of the phenomenon of imitation in animals and chil-dren is early and universal. It may be secondary to the instinct for rhythm, but at least in its aspect of unconscious play or recreation, it precedes dancing itself. Most primate animals and many birds imitate their wild neighbors, and it is obvious how quickly children ape the inflection of a nurse or parent's voice. In primitive social mimic dances, by their magic power of attracting the beasts imitated, are inextricably involved with totemism, the protection of a tribe by its animal-ancestors. These may be pleased by repetition of dances or motions which they once did in this world. The origin of costume, aside from that purely protective against the weather, is linked to mimicry, for the addition of fur or feathers increases the similarity of dancer to model.

In Rome, given a race gifted with a deep sense of mimicry, a strong love of shows, and a theatre disintegrating because its components of dance and song were never understood in necessary fusion with plot and dialogue, the development and popularity of pantomime was logical. But there is another and very real reason for the supremacy of the pantomimi. The tragic drama, as such, persisted into comparatively late times, as a pet luxury for intellectual snobs, but its audience was small. The great audience, the vast, roaring heterogeneous mob, diffuse and monstrous, who existed beneath the Roman rule, spoke not merely Latin, but mainly Syrian, Egyptian, Iberian, Gallic, Teutonic, Greek and Algerian. The language of the pantomimi was a universal tongue. It made no difference with what accent an actor's fingers, hands, arms or body spoke at Orange, Aspendus or Athens. Eyes read plainly what ears could not possibly understand. Then also, both Consuls and Emperors used the theater as an efficient means of placation or distraction, and it was important to have as many seats, in as huge houses as possible, to affect the greatest numbers. In spite of the science of acoustics which taught them to bury hollow jars in stage floors and walls to transmit sound, audiences in all great theatres could see further than they could hear. Part of the value of masks, aside from their impersonalization, their intensification of an actor's rôle over and above the actor's identity, was their large-cut features which carried more clearly across stage, orchestra and into the audience.

The pantomimic dance-drama became an independent expression under Cæsar Augustus, about 22 B.C. The two most famous rivals who brought their art to an unsurpassed perfection were Pylades, a Cilician, and Bathyllus, an Alexandrian. The Emperor once took the former to task for his incredible jealousy: and the mime replied, "It is your luck, Cæsar, that the mob concerns itself with *us*." The new form was predominantly tragic. Its libretti were derived from literary tragedy. The unity of place was kept; the action consecutive. A choros, as well as chanting the text to be mimed, may also have sung in intervals to allow the dancers to change their costume and masks. It was in the year 22 that Pylades introduced a choir, instead of a single vocal accompanist, and an enriched orchestra in place of simple flutes. Pantomimes were famous for their robe, or cloak dances, which rather remind us of Loie Fuller's skirt dancers. They used the cloak as a kind of Protean mask for the whole body. It could be draped, or rearrayed or tied up, to imitate in motion 'a swan's tail, the hair of Venus, the scourge of Furies' and so on.

In Ludwig Friedländer's 'Roman Life and Manners,' perhaps the single fullest compendium of information on the subject, he explains that:

The pantomimic dance was not a dance in the modern acceptation; it consisted in expressive and rhythmic movements of head and hand, natural movements of the body, bendings and turns and even leaps. Nomius the Syrian, a rival of Pylades and Bathyllus, was censured for the slow movements of his hands, while his feet stirred too fast. Galen says that the strenuous exertions of dancers, the high leaps, quick turns, cowerings, and jerks, contraction and stretching out of the legs, like all violent exercise, strengthen the body. But such motions took place after the pantomimic dance proper, according to Nonnus, whose Silenus leaps up on one foot and then on both, stands on his right foot, and lifts his left up to his breast and shoulder, bends it round his back up to his neck, whirls round, bent over backwards, so fast that his head seems to circle on the ground. But this does not take place until he has concluded his clever pantomimic display with the hands.

Incessant training and careful diet, especially abstention from rich food, secured the pantomimes full command of their bodies, and a pliability, elasticity and readiness, by means of which every movement could be graceful, elegant and effeminate. These qualities made them especially successful in feminine rôles, in which they almost lost their sex. Apuleius says of his step-son's father-in-law, whom he reproaches for vice and lust of all kinds, that he was so pliable in his youth, as pantomime, that he seemed to have no thews and sinews, but his acting was untrained and inartistic. In the lewd scenes, which were the spice of this drama, seductive grace combined with luxury and shamelessness knew no limits. When Bathyllus, a beautiful boy, was dancing Leda, the most impudent actress of mimes felt like a mere country novice on seeing such mastership in the art of refined sensuality.

We are fortunate in having a complete portrait of the Roman mime in his full flower from a dialogue on Pantomime, preserved in the works of a Greek satirist, Lucian of Samosata, who lived roughly from one hundred and twenty to one hundred and eighty years after the birth of Christ. He was a witty, imaginative writer; observant, learned and realistic. He started as a sculptor's apprentice, but learned rhetoric instead, made a living by composing speeches, traveled widely, living later in Egypt. His essay on the Roman mimic-stage is labeled *Orchesis,* an adaptation from the Greek *orcheisthai,* a word for the whole art of dance, by which he specifically meant pantomime. It is cast in the form of a dialogue between two friends, one of whom, Crato, hates the stage and will have none of it,—the other Lycinus, who by his insistent, overwhelming exposition of its long history and power, convinces him of his error. It is good to read in full. Better than any other document, it tells us the real quality of the Roman pantomime.

Crato wants to know how any one can

> sit still and listen to the sound of a flute, and watch the antics of an effeminate creature got up in soft raiment to sing lascivious songs and mimic the passions of prehistoric strumpets to the accompaniment of twanging string and shrilling pipe and clattering heel?

The mimes had accompanists shod with iron soles to beat time for them. Crato would not

> show my long beard and white hairs amid that throng of women and lunatics [the audience]; and clap and yell in unseemly rapture over the vile contortions of an abandoned buffoon.*

Lycinus defends the merits of the art:

* *The Works of Lucian of Samosata,* Vol. II, p. 241. Oxford University Press.

Of the manner in which it combines profit with amusement; instructing, informing, perfecting the intelligence of the beholder; training his eyes to lovely sights, filling his ears with noble sounds, revealing a beauty in which body and soul alike have their share.

He explains how the art of dancing originated with Eros, the love-god who created all; how the heavenly bodies, in their orbits, danced. Perhaps Lucian had heard of the astral ballet of the Egyptians. He mentions the Kuretes, Homer's respect for the dance, Sparta's Pyrrhic, dancing in India, Ethiopia, and the Salii, themselves. His information is a precious conglomeration of personal observation, hearsay, reading, even the permissible amplification of a poet's fancy. One thing, however, is clear. Lucian loved the dance. He compares dance-pantomime with tragedy, comedy and those occasional performances on flute and lyre, which have a snobbish prestige, to show the superiority of mime.

> In forming our estimate of tragedy [and Lucian the Greek, must refer chiefly to performances of Latin plays], let us first consider its externals—the hideous, appalling spectacle that the actor presents. His high boots raise him up out of all proportion; his head is hidden under an enormous mask; his huge mouth gapes upon the audience as if he would swallow them; to say nothing of the chest-pads and stomach-pads with which he contrives to give himself an artificial corpulence, lest his deficiency in this respect should emphasize his disproportionate height. And in the middle of it all is the actor, shouting away, now high, now low,—*chanting* his iambics as often as not; could anything be more revolting than this sing-song recitation of tragic woes? The actor is a mouthpiece: that is his sole responsibility;—the poet has seen to the rest, ages since.
>
> On the other hand, I need not tell you how decent, how seemly, is the dancer's attire; any one who is not blind can see that for himself. His very mask is elegant, and well adapted to his part; there is no gaping here; the lips are closed, for the dancer has plenty of other voices at his service. In old days, dancer and singer were one: but the violent exercise caused shortness of breath; the song suffered for it, and it was found advisable to have the singing done independently.
>
> I am chiefly concerned with pointing out the profit and pleasure to be derived from modern Pantomime, which did not begin to take its present admirable form in ancient days, but only in the time of Augustus, or thereabouts. In those earlier times we have but the beginnings of the art; the tree is taking root; the flower and the fruit have reached their perfection only in our own day, and it is with these that I have to do.

He finally arrives at the function of the pantomime—

> What must be his qualifications? what his previous training? what his studies? what his subsidiary accomplishments? You will find that his is no easy profession, nor lightly to be undertaken; requiring as it does the highest standard of culture in all its branches, and involving a knowledge not of music only, but of rhythm and meter, and above all of your beloved philosophy.

There is a long section on the subject-matter of which a pantomimic dancer should avail himself—the world's whole history from chaos to Egyptian Cleopatra. In this, he includes myths of all gods and legends of all heroes, in Greece, Rome and Egypt.

Lycinus then recounts the experience of the cynic Demetrius, who had inveighed against pantomime exactly in the terms of Crato's own objections:

The pantomime, he said, was a mere appendage to flute and pipe and beating feet; he added nothing to the action; his gesticulations were aimless nonsense; there was no meaning in them; people were hoodwinked by the silken robes and handsome mask, by the fluting and piping and the fine voices, which served to set off what in itself was nothing. The leading pantomime of the day—this was in Nero's reign—was apparently a man of no mean intelligence; unsurpassed, in fact, in wideness of range and in grace of execution. Nothing, I think, could be more reasonable than the request he made of Demetrius, which was, to reserve his decision till he had witnessed his performance, which he undertook to go through without the assistance of flute or song. He was as good as his word. The time-beaters, the flutes, even the chorus, were ordered to preserve a strict silence; and the pantomime, left to his own resources, represented the loves of Ares and Aphrodite, the tell-tale Sun, the craft of Hephæstus, his capture of the two lovers in the net, the surrounding Gods, each in his turn, the blushes of Aphrodite, the embarrassment of Ares, his entreaties,—in fact the whole story. Demetrius was ravished at the spectacle; nor could there be higher praise than that with which he rewarded the performer. 'Man,' he shrieked at the top of his voice, 'this is not seeing, but hearing and seeing, both: 'tis as if your hands were tongues!' ...

The pantomime is above all things an actor: that is his first aim, in the pursuit of which (as I have observed) he resembles the orator, and especially the composer of 'declamations,' whose success, as the pantomime knows, depends like his own upon verisimilitude, upon the adaptation of language to character: prince or tyrannicide, pauper or farmer, each must be shown with the peculiarities that belong to him. I must give you the comment of another foreigner on this subject. Seeing five masks laid ready—that being the number of parts in the piece—and only one pantomime, he asked who were going to play the other parts. He was informed that the whole piece would be performed by a single actor. 'Your humble servant, sir,' cries our foreigner to the artist, 'I observe that you have but one body: it had escaped me, that you possessed several souls.' ...

Other entertainments of eye or ear are but manifestations of a single art: 'tis flute or lyre or song; 'tis moving tragedy or laughable comedy. The pantomime is all-embracing in the variety of his equipment: flute and pipe, beating foot and clashing cymbal, melodious recitative, choral harmony. Other arts call out only one half of a man's powers—the bodily or the mental: as a physical exercise: there is a meaning in his movements; every gesture has its significance; and therein lies his chief excellence. The enlightened Lesbonax of Mytilene called pantomimes 'manual philosophers,' and used to frequent the theater, in the conviction that he came out of it a better man than he went in....

All professions hold out some object, either of utility or of pleasure: Pantomime is the only one that secures both these objects; now the utility that is combined with pleasure is doubled in value. Who would choose to look on at a couple of young fellows spilling their blood in a boxing-match, or wrestling in the dust, when he may see the same subject represented by the pantomime, with the additional advantages of safety and elegance, and with far greater pleasure to the spectator? The vigorous movements of the pantomime—turn and twist, bend and spring—afford at once a gratifying spectacle to the beholder and a wholesome training to the performer; I maintain that no gymnastic exercise is its equal for beauty and for the uniform development of the physical powers,—of agility, suppleness, and elasticity, as of solid strength....

I now propose to sketch out the mental and physical qualifications necessary for a first-rate pantomime. Most of the former, indeed, I have already mentioned: he must have memory, sensibility, shrewdness, rapidity of conception, tact, and judgment; further, he must be a critic of poetry and song, capable of discerning good music and rejecting bad. For his body, I think I may take the Canon of Polyclitus as my model. He must be perfectly proportioned: neither immoderately tall nor dwarfishly short; not too fleshy (a most unpromising quality in one of his profession) nor cadaverously thin....Another essential for the pantomime is ease of movement. His frame must be at once supple and well-knit, to meet the opposite requirements of agility and firmness....

Lycinus admits, however, that:

Pantomimes cannot all be artists; there are plenty of ignorant performers, who bungle their work terribly. Some cannot adapt themselves to their music; they are literally "out of tune"; rhythm says one thing, their feet another....

And he gives an alarming example of the excesses in which an inartistic mime may indulge:

In most respects a capable, nay, an admirable performer, some strange fatality ran him a-ground upon this reef of over-enthusiasm. He was acting the madness of Ajax, just after he has been worsted by Odysseus; and so lost control of himself, that one might have been excused for thinking his madness was something more than feigned. He tore the clothes from the back of one of the iron-shod time-beaters, snatched a flute from the player's hands, and brought it down in such a trenchant sort upon the head of Odysseus, who was standing by enjoying his triumph, that, had not his cap held good, borne the weight of the blow, poor Odysseus must have fallen a victim to histrionic frenzy. The whole house ran mad for company, leaping, yelling, tearing their clothes. For the illiterate riff-raff, who knew not good from bad, and had no idea of decency, regarded it as a supreme piece of acting: and the more intelligent part of the audience, realizing how things stood, concealed their disgust, and instead of reproaching the actor's folly by silence, smothered it under their plaudits; they saw only too clearly that it was not Ajax but the pantomime who was mad.

Lucian was perhaps criticizing the distressing aptitude of the great Roman audience to prize grosser and more sensational aspects of realism as the height of artistic perfection, a tendency which let them be titillated only by the spilling of simulated or actual blood, as if liquid gore was the true shine of tragedy, a taste indulged to the hilt only in the circus. The contribution of circus-games to the history of stage-dancing is remoter than pantomime. But we frequently hear in deprecation of contemporary or recent dance-drama, that it is too circus-like, too spectacular. The first time this criticism leveled itself fairly was in Rome.

Roman public games, even to the last, had that perfunctory link to religion, with which first Consuls, and then Emperors found convenient to mask their personal intention, although the mob was too absorbed in the spectacle to care much under whose auspices it was held. However, for the sake of formality, at the start of each civil year games were vowed to the gods for the common weal. These expenses were incurred at the public debt. The taxes of whole provinces were easily squandered on them. On the colonnade of a stable in Palatium is portrayed an imperial sideshow. A rope-dancer in buskins, dances on almost invisible wires: a climber edges up a wall away from a bear he has tormented. Bears act a comedy. A hundred trumpeters toot in chorus. Manilius mentions rope-dancers and jugglers, some hovering in mid-air, while others leaped to the ground from a tower, soaring through fire, like a fish in space. Animal trainers succeeded in schooling beasts in tricks against their natural habits. Boys danced on the backs of wild bulls, reared; were paired with horses to perform in pools; sea-lions greeted the populace by turning towards them, and barked answers to their given names. Such murderous careerists as Sulla were little less than artists in politic manipulation of the circus, and at no cost to themselves. In the year 93 B.C., as Prætor, he exhibited one hundred wild lions in the arena, loosed and shot by archers specially imported by King Bocchus, his friend. An old senatorial decree which prohibited the importation of African beasts was conveniently repealed for the occasion. Sulla was a typical republican politician, who by his tacit campaigning with the games set the scale for more magnificent fiendishness in the later Cæsars. Of him, Plutarch tells us:

> he had so strong a natural love of buffoonery, that when he was still young, and of no repute, he spent his time and indulged himself among mimi and jesters; and when he was at the head of the State, he daily got together from the scena and the theater the lewdest persons, with whom he would drink and enter into a contest of coarse witticisms.... Towards the end of his life Roscius the comedian, Sorix the chief mimus, and Metrobius (with whom he was long attached in his youth) and who played women's parts in men's dress, enjoyed his favor.

The dramas of the Greeks demonstrated punishments of proud or godless men as horrible—but that horror, whether it was the blinding of Œdipus or the fate of Orestes, never intruded as only a bloody sight. The Romans were too unimaginative to accept a messenger's report of disaster, however impressively he may have been set in dramatic relief by the questions and movement of a trained choros. They wanted literally to see and hear the antagonists knife each other. Virgil bade other nations devote themselves to science or the arts, but *tu regere imperio populos, Romane, memento*—Remember, Roman, thou shalt rule the world! Their spectacularization of cruelty was merely a visible, dramatized action of their instinct for hatred, their gluttony for power. The worst thing about vice is its demand for repetition, the necessity for increasing a dose to produce any excitement. Hence the staggering proportions of Roman games. It is not by accident that a lictor's *fasces* or bundled whipping-rods, lashed round the headsman's ax, is the fascist symbol.

The Circus Maximus could hold at one time three hundred and fifty thousand spectators. As a multiple political-club, lounge, social rendezvous, betting-ring and amusement-park, the great circuses all over the Roman imperial world were an extremely important social factor. For those who wish to reconstruct their chariot-races or the vari-colored factions, gladiatorial combats of condemned prisoners or captives of war, sea-fights with slave-manned galleys in carefully flooded ditches, there is a mass of absorbing document. The last refuge of a profligate was the gladiatorial school. The aristocracy rarely was forced to perform in public. However, Cæsarism, whose chief policy was the mob's pleasure, did not regret the humiliation of nobles as another spurious example of their aims toward the destruction of classes.

To learn the game's value as entertainment to a civilized human, one need only read Pliny, a sensitive writer of the epoch, who says the circus was so boring in pointless repetition of fights and fights that he couldn't imagine how any one could support its tedium twice. That Pliny should find the sight of death by delicate torture merely continuously boring, rather than, for example, sickening, is an index of the period. The Greek attitude towards spectacular tragedy is defined in Aristotle's 'Ethics.' Neither the killing of a criminal, nor the accidental death of an innocent man provides tragic pleasure. The killing is no misfortune in the eyes of the audience. There is no ethical problem involved. His pleasure is only the moral satisfaction of seeing justice. The death of the innocent is so senseless and unjust as to be merely hateful.

But here we are particularly occupied with dancing, and the chief importance of the games to the dance was the bad name which one incurred by association with the other. How bad a name can only be understood by feeling the righteous horror with which Augustine and Tertullian anathematized them. We may feel these antique churchmen were stupidly, even perhaps hypocritically censorious and blame them for attacks which withered dramatic art as a medium of free expression. We shall learn of the Christian Church's direction of the dramatic instinct in the next chapter, but we have not only Augustine and Tertullian as prosecutors, but such typical Romans as Seneca or Suetonius.

In a letter * the former ironically asks,

* Seneca: *Seventh Epistle.*

What use is protection or training? These things only postpone death. In the morning men are killed by lions and bears, at midday they are killed by the spectators. The killer is sent out to be killed, and the victorious fighter is kept back for another murder. "But," you will say, "one of them was a bandit." What of it? "He murdered a man." Then he deserves to be killed; but *you,* you wretch, what crime have you committed to make you deserve to see such a sight? "Strike him, flog him, burn him! Why does he shrink from the blade? Why does he strike so timidly? Why does he die so grudgingly?" This is an interval in the show—we must have some throat-cutting as an ent'racte.

As for the matter of stage-dancers, with the advent of Caligula, we may understand a bit more of what Augustine would mean:

He also zealously applied himself to the practice of several other arts of different kinds, such as fencing, charioteering, singing and dancing. In the first of these, he practiced with the weapons used in war; and drove the chariot in circuses built in several places. He was so extremely fond of singing and dancing, that he could not refrain in the theater from singing with the tragedians, and imitating the gestures of the actors, either by way of applause or correction. A night exhibition which he had ordered the day he was slain, was thought to be intended for no other reason, than to take the opportunity afforded by the licentiousness of the season, to make his first appearance upon the stage. Sometimes, also, he danced in the night. Summoning once to the palatium, in the second watch of the night, three men of consular rank, who feared the words from the message, he placed them on the proscenium of the stage, and then suddenly came bursting out, with a loud noise of flutes and castanets, dressed in a mantle and tunic reaching down to his heels. Having danced out a song, he retired. Yet he who had acquired such dexterity in other exercises, never learnt to swim.

Those for whom he once conceived a regard, he favored even to madness. He used to kiss Mnester, the pantomimic actor, publicly in the theater; and if any person made the least noise while he was dancing, he would order him to be dragged from his seat, and scourged him with his own hand.

Towards the end of his life Caligula was plagued with certain sanguinary premonitions. Psychiatrists tell us he was suffering from dementia præcox, but the diagnosis is recent; Suetonius continues:

Whilst he was at sacrifice, he was bespattered with the blood of a flamingo. And Mnester, the pantomimic actor, performed in a play, which the tragedian Meoptolemus had formerly acted at the games in which Philip, the King of Macedon, was slain. And in a piece called Laureolus, in which the principal actor, running out in a hurry, and falling, vomited blood, several of the inferior actors vying with each other to give the best specimen of their art, made the whole stage flow with blood.

Caligula's successor, able, stammering Claudius, also had a considerable affection for the stage:

He took great pleasure in seeing men engage with wild beasts, and the combatants who appeared on the stage at noon. He would therefore come to the theatre by break of day, and at noon, dismissing the people to dinner, continued sitting himself; and besides those who were devoted to that sanguinary fate, he would match others with the beasts, upon slight or sudden occasions; as, for instance, the carpenters and their assistants, and people of that sort, if a machine, or any piece of work in which they had been employed about the theatre did not answer the purpose for which it had been intended. To this desperate kind of encounter he forced one of his nomenclators, even encumbered as he was by wearing the toga.

As a youth Nero gained much credit by his firmness in the equestrian Troy-Game. His mother being banished, he then lived with his aunt Lepida, in a very poor way, under the care of two tutors, one a dancing-master, the other a barber. During his reign he visited some rather spectacular punishments "on the Christians, a sort of people who held a new and impious superstition."

Tacitus tells us that many of them

> were dressed in the skins of wild beasts, and exposed to be torn to pieces by dogs in the public games, that they were crucified, or condemned to be burnt; and at nightfall served in place of lamps to lighten the darkness, Nero's own gardens being used for the spectacle.

Nero, who at his own murder regretted the artist perishing in him, fancied himself as a singer and inflicted himself on impatient audiences all over Italy. To make sure of his reception,

> he chose young men of the equestrian order, and about five thousand robust young fellows from the common people, on purpose to learn various kinds of applause, called *bombi, imbrices* and *testæ,* which they were to practice in his favor, whenever he performed. They were divided into several parties, and were remarkable for their fine heads of hair, were extremely well dressed, with rings upon their left hands. The leaders of these bands had salaries of forty thousand sesterces allowed them.

The name *bombi* was derived from the humming of bees,—a confused din made either by hands or mouth; *imbrices,* from rattling of rain or hail on tile roofs; *testæ,* from the smashing of terra-cotta jars. The last two were made by beating on hollow vessels placed in the auditoria for the purpose. People were instructed to give applause with skill, and there were *Laudicena,* or praisemasters had for hire by actors, poets and god-Emperors. Here we have the clearest proof of the quality of Rome's theatricalization. Instead of a spontaneous audience following a contrived performance, a spontaneous actor directs contrived applause.

CHAPTER V

The Roman Christian Church: Its Spectacular Elements

Oh infatuated men, what is this blindness, or rather madness, which possesses you? How is it that while, as we hear, even the Eastern nations are bewailing your ruin, and while powerful states in the most remote parts of the earth are mourning your fall as a public calamity, ye yourselves, should be crowding to the theatres, should be pouring into them and filling them; and, in short, be playing a madder part now than ever before? This was the foul plague spot, this the wreck of virtue and honor that Scipio sought to preserve you from, when he prohibited the construction of theaters; this was his reason for desiring that you might still have an enemy to fear, seeing as he did how easily prosperity would corrupt and destroy you.*

THUS, not more than fifteen years after Alaric had sacked Rome, Saint Augustine tried to reason with the City and Empire of Rome proposing a new empire, The City of God.

For Rome was falling and falling fast, and still the arenas were full and churches were not. Hell's mouth yawned. The late Romans drugged themselves with games. Three thousand dancing-girls were allowed to remain in the starving city, while scholars were driven away. Although invaders infested the once invincible town, its people still flocked to the games. And Augustine, with that insight which would make his monument an encyclopedia for the Dark Ages and the one philosophy of history the Middle Ages knew, concentrated all his energy on denunciations of the shows. It was not as a Puritan that he had felt in his youth the attractions of the theater. He admits,

> the scenic spectacles enraptured me. In my time I had a violent passion for them, which were full of the images of my miseries and of the amorous flames of fire which devoured me.

He had seen his agreeable young friend Alypius, suddenly transformed from a sensitive student of Roman law into a sadist, at the gladiatorial combats.

> For so soon as he saw the blood, he at the very instant drunk down a kind of savageness; nor did he turn away his head, but fixed his eyes upon it, drinking up unawares the very Furies themselves; being much taken with the barbarousness of the sword-fight, and was drunk again with that blood-thirsty joy.†

Just as many historians today insist the nature of our capitalist crisis is purely economic, so Augustine, but with greater reason for his limits, believed Rome was crumbling from wholly moral poison. Games, shows, dances, were visible gangrene in the Imperial body. And he, and following him his

---

* Augustine: *The City of God*. Book I: 33 and 32. Dod's translation.
† St. Augustine: *Confessions*—VII-8.

church, though not for three hundred years would the ban be complete, anathematized, without exception, the symptoms, the obvious stench of Roman virulence, among them, dance. There would be no more theatrical dancing for nearly a thousand years, a long time for the cessation of a form which through the cultures of Greece and Rome had achieved such a high degree of formal development. We shall see how the instinct towards dancing expressed itself in other channels. This is fascinating history and remarkable testimony to the sturdiness of its prompting human necessity. But as far as any actual innovation, technical development, or even conservation of tradition, the period from the years 300 to 1300 A.D. is a virtual blank, should we limit ourselves strictly to facts relevant to the dance in theaters, which we cannot possibly afford to do.

Rome fell for innumerable reasons inherent in her instinctive philosophy of property acquisition. In the wide swamps of a policy of imperial sadism there are many parallels to terrify even people today, who presume dancing is some special sanctuary where politics cannot intrude. To understand the nature of theatrical dancing we must know enough of conditions surrounding it, shedding upon it those colors to which it of all the arts, except possibly music, is most susceptible. Rome perished because she had overextended herself; the organization of communications and arms for which she is so famous was superimposed rather than organic. Satisfactorily tense enough when her conquering drive was on its long crushing rise, Imperium Romanum was no plan for maintenance, for consolidating far-flung positions once they had been violently achieved. The scenic games, under the Republic a real power for centralized placation, became with the Empire a huge, dangerous and necessary adjunct to the throne, whose monstrous abuses were in direct proportion to their unwieldy influence, and by which the Emperors came to be governed as much as they governed. Their expense exhausted provinces not only of money but of animal-life. Their actual sights had a moral effect which has only been possible to hint at here. The scenic games surely contributed to Rome's catastrophe, but to a far less degree than the religion held by their first frank opponents. In the games, the Christians seized an immediate vicious example of all they opposed. The general situation was too livid to make us marvel much that they did not stop to pick out of the welter that part of theatrical-dancing which might have been worth saving, even if lilies actually existed on such a dung-heap. Besides, Christians had seen their friends and fathers martyred in amphitheaters where their agony was merely a prelude to, or an incident in, the shows.

That the church Fathers would honestly have denied any desire to employ consciously a trace of taint from Roman spectacle we have no reason to doubt. But what they could in all good faith damn on one plane of consciousness, they absorbed, for future use, on another. Church history is full of the courageous and violent denunciations that the early Fathers launched against the shows. At first their complaints were pure rhetoric, but with the advent of

Christian Emperors, they began to carry weight. As early as 300 a council at Elvira decided no person in any way connected with circus or pantomime could be baptized. In 398 at the council of Carthage a rule was established excommunicating anyone who attended the theater on holy days. As Alardyce Nicoll writes, in his exhaustive work on the period, had this been actually enforced

> half of Christendom, including a section of the clergy, would have been out of communion with the church.... From East to West, in Constantinople, in Antiocha, in Alexandria, in Rome, the mimic drama flourished, uniting together old pagans and new Christians in the one common enjoyment of pure secularism.*

It was, as we can well understand, necessary for Holy Church to compete with the mimes on their own ground. This could be done without endangering her conscience, as long as her own priests were quick to suspect each other of imperial practice, and condemn creators of forms which seemed either too near pagan wickedness or too entertaining for their own sake. Such quarrels were part of the famous controversy between the Arians and the Athanasians. Athanasius charged Arius with willfully copying an infamous Alexandrian playwright, in his work on Liturgy called after the Greek comic muse, 'Thalia.' He alleged that his 'Thalia' not only included dramatic hymns but also an actual program of pantomimic dances commemorating the crucifixion. Unfortunately little remains of Arian documents to enable us to determine the degree of their corruption. The triumphant Athanasians not only issued an 'Anti-Thalia' but destroyed whatever Arian manuscripts they found. The 'Thalia' was so popular that even its opponents recognized the attractions inherent in the liturgical embellishments it proposed, and from the fourth century, particularly in the Eastern Empire, possibilities for a frankly religious theater were considered.

But such an institution was rendered virtually impossible, by the attitude of the mimes themselves. They were a byword for lewdness, symbol of so much, in no matter how purified a form, the church opposed. It was difficult to make allies of actors who outrageously parodied the very usages of the Christian liturgy. Saint Gregory of Nazianzus, in the fourth century, bemoaned the fact that "nothing on the stage was more pleasing to auditors and spectators than the comic Christian." In our contemporary burlesque and vaudeville we have the comic Jew, always good for a laugh by virtue of his hook-nose and derby hat. Romans had roared at broad parodies of the country lout, the provincial rustic as well as the loves of Venus and Mars or the rites of Bona Dea. Now ecclesiastical debates of solemn churchmen seemed equally preposterous, and the ceremonial of the church, amusing rigmarole. For example, in one play, a mimic-fool is made ready for baptism, undressed and robed in white. To him approach a funny priest, a slapstick bishop, exorcist

* *Masks, Mimes and Miracles*, pp. 136-138. Harcourt, Brace & Co. New York.

and acolytes, made droll with ritual symbols turned into phalloi, reminding us of Athenian satyr-plays. The burlesque climax is where the would-be Christian is dumped into a tub of lukewarm water.

There was also the story of the mime Philemon, under Diocletian, in the year 287, who had been hired by a frightened Christian to take his place, in a disguise, and celebrate those pagan rites, which the poor deacon's conscience, if not his courage prevented his fulfilling. But when Philemon came before the inquisition he said in a loud voice: "I am a Christian; I will not sacrifice." As he affirmed this, he raised his hood so that all could see it was no timid deacon but Philemon, the popular stage-star. The court roared, and because of his reputation was prepared to let the whole thing drop as a bold joke. But Philemon said again: "I am a Christian; I will not sacrifice." The prefect, furious, realized he was facing a convert and asked the people if he should not be doomed to instant death. They unanimously cried out to save their favorite. But Philemon was unmoved. Again the officer pleaded with him. He said the audience in the theater would be miserable if he did not recant, that their grief would be unbearable if they would have to see him crucified. But the mime was obdurate and went to his death joyfully, amid the spectators' mourning, and became a martyr and saint of the Roman Catholic Church.

There could be no truce between theater and church. After the Lombard invasion of 568 there is rare mention of shows or games in Rome. For some two or three hundred years later there are records of them in the Eastern Empire. The mimi, as individuals, existed in wandering parties, large or small—but the day of Roman spectacular entertainment was over forever.

In the year 791, the English priest Alcuin wrote warnings to a friend that "the man who brings actors and mimes and dancers to his house knows not what a bevy of unclean spirits follow them." He counseled the Bishop of Lindisfarne that it was "better to feed the poor from your table than actors," which would prove that not all clergymen were as uncharitable to artists as an English follower of Augustine.

This all may seem very far from dance, nor yet shall we find any dancing in the Church's great innovation, its Mass. Nor is it strange that this Mass, which found itself forced to exile other forms of previous ritual observance should have excluded the dance as well. But when we look into it more closely we shall discover that while not exactly strange, neither is it entirely simple or logical.

Dating from about the year 160 A.D. there exists in a Gnostic romance known as the Acts of John, a remarkable hymn, quoted in the Catholic Dictionary as being known to Augustine. It describes an incident of the last or Lord's Supper, where Christ, taking leave of his disciples, instituted the custom of Holy Communion, the symbolic basis of the Roman Christian Religion and the source of the Catholic Mass. But here, instead of the breaking of bread and sipping of wine testifying to the oneness of Christ's body and blood, we have dancing.

Before Jesus was taken by the Jews and unbelievers who hold to Satan's Law, he gathered us altogether and said: Before I am delivered over to them, let us sing a hymn to the Father. We will then go to them, together. Then he asked us to form a circle: we took each by the hand, he being in the middle and said: Amen: Follow me; and he commenced the hymn.

Jesus: Glory be to the Father! (*and we who were encircling him responded*): Amen.

Jesus: Glory to thee—the word. Glory to thee—the grace.

Disciples: Amen (Thus let it be)

Jesus: Glory to thee—the Holy Ghost—praise be to thy glory.

Disciples: Amen

Jesus: We praise thee, Father—we render thanks to thee, light where no shadows dwell.

Disciples: Amen

Jesus: Of that unto which we render thee thanks I speak—to be saved is my desire and I desire to save.

Disciples: Amen

Jesus: To be delivered is my desire and I desire to deliver.

Disciples: Amen

Jesus: To be blessed is my desire, and I wish to bless.

Disciples: Amen

Jesus: To be born is my desire, and I wish to engender.

Disciples: Amen

Jesus: To be nourished is my desire, and I wish to nourish.

Disciples: Amen

Jesus: To hear is my desire, and I wish to be heard.

Disciples: Amen

Jesus: To understand is my desire, with all my intelligence.

Disciples: Amen

Jesus: To be cleansed is my desire, and I wish to cleanse.

Disciples: Amen

Jesus: Forgiveness is our *choregos* (dance-leader)—to sing is my desire, let us dance together.

Disciples: Amen

Jesus: I wish to be grieved for, weep you all.

Disciples: Amen

Jesus: I am your light, ye who see me. I am the gate, ye who enter.

Disciples: (*The twelve now dance*)

Jesus: Those who do not dance will not comprehend what shall befall.

Disciples: Amen

Jesus: Then all of you join my dance. You who dance, see what I have accomplished.

Gods who dance are not exactly rare, as we have seen, but this Gnostic Christ, resembling far more Siva than Dionysos, is, as far as the present writer has discovered, the unique mention of Jesus as a dancer. The Christian Bible is not, like the Koran, a homogeneous work, but rather a compilation or selection of many books, which were chosen through centuries of controversy, political convenience or literary taste. The so-called Apocryphal Acts of the Apostles from one of which the above service is taken, were frequently absurd, irrelevant inventions, and outlawed from an accredited place in the sacred compendium for many good reasons.

Gnosticism was close to Catholicism in many respects, but laid most of the emphasis of salvation on *gnosis* (knowledge), an understanding of esoteric information possessed by them alone, and compounded of conglomerate beliefs, predominantly oriental. Had its elements been sufficiently popular to have insured its expansion, dancing might not have slept so long. Inclusion in church ceremony might have revitalized dance in the lay world.

There were dozens of such groups later to be outlawed as heretical, like the eccentric Asiatics who danced with women, remembering the triumph of Israel after the Red Sea passage, and those of the Sect of the Unbended-Knee, whose members prayed standing, tossing their arms about according to prescribed rules for expelling evil spirits from the surrounding air. And far from Syria, in the primeval German forests, freshly converted Teuton warriors would sing battle-songs to their new hero, a Christ as blond as Balder. In some Roman churches, youths and girls partook of love-feasts; chanted love-glees called *agape* and were quickly suppressed.

In passing it is only fair to mention a few instances of dancing in Christian churches. The Abbot Meletius, an Englishman, upon the advice of the first Gregory, permitted dancing in his churches up to 604. The nature of the dancing is obscure. The existence of edicts against mixed dancing in cemeteries does not show that the dances themselves were in any way connected with the liturgy. The Jesuit father, Menèstrier, whose history of dancing published in 1683, is full of valuable data about his own time, as well as of curious tales of earlier, tells of seeing in certain Paris churches the senior canon leading choir-boys in a round-dance during the singing of the psalm. The Paris Liturgy reads '*Le chanoine ballera au premier psaume*': 'The canon will dance to the first psalm.' Such dancing could scarcely be called ritual, probably as much physical activity was involved as with the gnostics. Scaliger said the first Roman bishops were called *præsuls* and they led a sacred 'dance' around altars at festivals. Theodosius says that Christians of Antioch 'danced' in church and in front of martyrs' tombs. In some mediæval cathedrals, awnings were hung before the west door, over a place called *Ballatoria* or *Choraria* (dancing-pavement). Without discussing the exact contemporary connotation of the verb, *baller,* we may assume that the movements were sufficiently timid or restricted to preclude either their offending the celebrants, exciting the participants, or in any real sense enriching the Missal. *Los Seises,* the dancing youths of the Cathedral of Seville, whose annual performance on the feasts of Corpus Christi and the Immaculate Conception was connected with the ancient Mozarabic rite, are often described as ritual dancers, though their dance was really an independent votive act, peculiar to the towns of Seville and Toledo.

But the heirs of Saint Paul had plenty of reasons for preferring a more static formula when they created Christian ritual. Although he was an oriental, or at least a Jew, Paul had been born in Tarsus, a city predominantly Greek in culture. His strong contacts with Stoic philosophy would naturally make him suspicious of the semi-oriental survival or vegetation cults which abounded in Asia Minor and from which Gnosticism unquestionably derived. Pauline Christianity was but one of the Christian parties which were then battling for mastery, but it was far more durable than the ephemeral orientalism of the Gnostics who soon degenerated by virtue of their very differences from his practical and popular salesmanship. In his first epistle to the Corinthians (4:9) Saint Paul established scriptural authority for all opprobrious connotations in the words 'theaters,' and 'spectacles,' to which his followers could triumphantly point, for the next thousand years.

> For I think that God hath set forth us the apostles last, as it were appointed to death: for we are made a *spectacle* unto the world, and to angels and to men.

Although Hebrew ritual dancing had only a very indirect or negative effect in creating the Christian Mass and a remote literary influence on subsequent dances in theaters which emerged from the Cathedrals, nevertheless, because of the numerous biblical references to dancing, and the vast influence of the Bible in the Middle Ages, it might be well, in passing, to mention a few.

The Jews have given rise to misconceptions about themselves by an insistence on their isolation, or uniqueness. The nation as a whole was for many centuries neither better nor worse than other tribes which lived as their friends or enemies in Palestine. Their ancient customs and tribal ceremonies were similar to those of primitive peoples whom we have already cursorily examined. Their dances fit into the same categories of the seasons of men and the calendar that were shared by Australians, Egyptians and Cretans; except that Jews were Semites, dwelling in another part of the earth. For a people who make so many references to dancing in their literature, it may seem strange that there is no provision for it in the Mosaic code, which scrupulously regulates all other ritual matters. However, dancing, unlike their religion, was not by that time, a primarily moral, hygienic, legislative or theological matter. Some Christian writers, perhaps to give precedence to the absence of dancing in their own church, suggest that Jews frowned on the practice, but this is not true. The Hebrews were reformers, insomuch as they did their best to purge from their ceremonies those elements popular among the gentiles which seemed barbarous or idolatrous, but they would not have been so vain as to attempt the suppression of dancing, that instinctive expression shared alike by both Jew and gentile, with all the other folk of the world. Although there are no early rabbinical texts fixing the postures for solemnities, or correct methods for singing, neither song nor dance is ever disparaged.

The Hebrew word roots for 'dance' suggest 'play,' 'laughter,' 'whirling,' 'rotation,' 'writhing' and 'twisting' (as in a woman's labor pains, a very Semitic ideogram); 'sporting,' 'merry-making,' and 'dancing' itself. There are associational meanings of 'skipping,' 'going-around' (in a circle), 'leaping-over' and 'celebrating-a-feast.' From the Old Testament itself, we have the sacred processional of 'King David and all the house of Israel dancing before Jehovah with all their might.' In the Hebrew he is said to 'rotate with-all-his-might,' 'to jump,' 'whirl-around' and 'skip.' In the last two Psalms of David, the prophet exhorts his people to "praise His name in the dance," "praise him with the timbrel and the dance"; Moses came down from Sinai and found the Israelites praising the golden calf with dances. The idol, not the method of its praise, was sacrilegious. There was a famous torch dance, held at the feast of Succoth or Tabernacles. On the second day of the festival, in the women's court of the temple, dances and processions took place, accompanied by hymns. Because the participants carried palm-branches, such a traveler as Plutarch would be inclined to confuse them with the thyrsi of the rites of Dionysos, and, should a careful Christian and inadequate anthropologist like Augustine read of it, it would further convince him of the evils of oriental dancing in church. After the passage of the Red Sea "Miriam, the prophetess, the sister of Aaron, took a timbrel in her hand; and all the women went out after her with timbrels and with dances." There was dancing for use in the marriage ritual:

> Return, return O Shulammite;
> Return, return, that we may look upon thee.
> Why will ye look upon the Shulammite,
> As upon the dance of Mahanaïm?

This refers to a sword-dance of ancient origin; a weapon is flashed and brandished by the bride symbolizing her defense against all suitors but her chosen spouse. It is still customary among the Jews of the Sephardim, for mourners to walk seven times around a laid-out body, during which seven short supplications are intoned, each ending with the words, "And continually may he *walk* in the land of life, and may his soul *rest* in the land of life."

Although Paul converted among many congregations where he had recently preached as a Rabbi, orthodox Jews were not calculated to receive his new religion with open arms. Nor did they. And so, balked on the one hand by the anti-ecclesiastical satires of the late Roman mimes, and on the other by the orthodox Rabbis, Pauline Christians of the first five hundred years of their Lord's era invented a new service, based neither on the ritual esthetics of the Romans among whose descendants they were to work and triumph, nor upon the body of Jewish ideology from which they drew their arising. The creation of the *form* of the Mass, (here nothing need be said about ancient sources of its *ideas* of sacred-supper, its doctrines of mediation or transubstantiation,) was in its ultimate synthesis, if not in its component parts, the very original contribution of the Roman Catholic Church. Thus it is, almost but not quite, as if here, on the brink of investigating the source of forms for administering the Eucharist, that we commence our study of modern stage-dancing.

Just as we traced the roots of Greek tragedy from mysteries of a perennial earth-god, we see mirrored in the Mass so much that has its beginning, not in Greece which exhausted itself in Græco-Roman games, to undergo a thousand years later a merely literary revival, but in Christian Rome, under the patronage of an ecclesiastical empire whose life will flow in the channels ancient Romans laid for their ruin. In this sense, but in all honesty, in only this sense, can our history be read as a continuous stream. We must not forget that like architecture, music, poetry, painting and sculpture, dancing, which had enjoyed as high a development as any of these arts, would for nearly a thousand years be virtually dormant.

From the first, the Christian church was treated as a subversive movement, which in every way it was, from the point of view of the Roman State. A radical superstition, its members were likely to be thrown to lions, or to flare as torches for an Emperor's night. In more ways than one the early Christian Church resembles the Communist party in Czarist Russia. Its meetings were literally held underground, in cellars and burial-caves. In the beginning there were no cathedrals. Mass was said, the vessels were set out on tables or on the stone tombs of those martyrs whose bodies could be rescued from the Arena. Recollect that the worship of Dionysos fused with dances around ancestral tombs. The tomb-top was the *mensa,* on whose surface a sacred-supper (sacrament) was set. Among early ornaments were a *sepulchrum,* or altar-cavity, which could both hold relics of a martyr and remind congregations of Christ's deposition and resurrection after his martyrdom. The *ciborium* was a canopy over the altar,—the *predella* a platform on which the celebrants or officiating priest could stand.

When the church was strong enough to come up out of the catacombs there was no sacred Roman edifice, already erected, which could simply have its gods removed to permit the new faith to enter. Roman temples to individual gods were not, in most cases, large, and were usually smallish buildings constructed entirely to enshrine particular statues and votive gifts. But there was, however, a type of secular building, of which numerous examples existed, moderately well-adapted for holy theaters. They were the Roman Basilica, or Law Courts; long, rectangular halls, either barrel-vaulted or roofed with a coffered ceiling supported by monolithic columns in two or more long aisles down the length of the room. The very forms of the Roman law had dramatic structure in their procedure. Sir Henry Maine, in his 'Ancient Law' says, "An ancient conveyance (contract) was not written but acted." By their very parlance, lawyers or parties to agreements, enacted the priority and actual meaning of their promises. He quotes the comedian Plautus to show how "effectually the attention of the person meditating the promise must have been arrested by the question, and how ample was the opportunity for withdrawal from an improvident undertaking." Naturally the architecture of the law-courts was efficiently designed to frame the drama of its law.

The clergy would come to seat themselves in the, frequently, semi-circular apse, hooded by a mosaic half-dome where the judges had sat, in front of a table-altar-tomb facing their congregations, from whom they were separated by the *cancelli,* or lattice, which had been the attorneys' bar. In Eastern Greek Catholic Churches this chancel would develop into an *Ikonostasis,* or three-doored holy picture-screen, into whose central portal priests would enter to perform the mysteries secretly from their audiences. It has been ingeniously suggested that this arises from that ancient convention of the Greeks which arranged the actual scene of tragedies off-stage, so that the Christian ikon becomes a kind of invisible *deus ex machina.* But the development of the Greek church is another story and has only a very indirect bearing on theatrical-dancing through ancestral connections with Russia.

In the Western Church, the high-altar was moved to the east end of the church, with space in front for deacons and sub-deacons. Between this and the nave proper was a choir, with seats banked on either side for the respond-ing clergy. Later sanctuary and choir were known as the chancel (*cancelli*), and would be divided from the main body of the congregation by an arch, or steps, or pierced screen, or all three.

The development of *theatra,* of seeing-places is inextricably connected with *dromena,* things done in them. As the liturgy developed, symbolism accreted, forms amplified, and by the thirteenth century, with a special em-phasis on the cult of the Virgin, cathedrals will have become the great but-tressed buildings we all know, though also by that time their influence on any dancing which interests us will have passed. Transepts on either side are laid out, and the whole fabric becomes its founder's sign,—a Cross. Many altars to His many saints displace Christ's single tomb. Aisles around nave and choir (ambulatories) permit the passage of bannered processions.

Although the altar-platform was raised to afford the congregation greater legibility, and although the Mass itself grew more and more decorative, we must not easily assume that basilicas were sacred opera-houses, or the Mass was a holy pantomime. In both architecture and act there is much of the spectacular, but let us determine exactly how much of the theatrical.

To be sure there is an officiating priest, with whom one could make false analogies, likening him to the single actors of early Greek tragedy. There is a chorus, which on occasion he addresses and which formally responds. There are definite preordained movements and postures for the participants, and those actions necessary for transferring candles, books, censers, and other ritual implements. Groups and individuals come into contact with one another and separate. There is an introduction, a climax and a finale to the ceremony. Wherein, then, is this not holy drama?

As Karl Young demonstrates in his 'Drama of the Medieval Church,' one must not confuse dramatic externals with genuine drama. A play is a narrative action in which the chief factor is not forms of speech or movement, but the *impersonation* by actors, of characters who create a narrated situation. In the Mass there are numerous atmospheric effects achieved by the combination of sound, movement, poetry, color and even odor. But neither do the celebrants attempt to resemble or impersonate anyone but themselves, nor does architecture or accessories attempt to depict any place or quality of locale other than contained in church precincts.

> The impossibility of there being impersonation in the liturgy of the Eucharist arises from the fact that since the early Christian centuries this rite has been regarded as a true sacrifice.

That is, when the priest blesses the wine and wafer it becomes, is transubstantiated into, the very blood and body of Christ Jesus himself.

> The central act is designed not to represent or portray or merely commemorate the crucifixion, but actually to repeat it. What takes place at the altar is not an esthetic picture of a happening in the past, but a genuine renewal of it. Just as Christ sacrificed himself on the Cross, so in the mass He is present invisibly, and sacrifices Himself again. The consecrated elements *are* Christ, and through the words and acts of the celebrant, Christ accomplishes His own immolation, being Himself, in reality, both the victim and the priest. The celebrant remains merely the celebrant, and does not undertake to play the part of his Lord. He is only the instrument through which Christ acts. As Peter was Christ's rock, and as Pope was Christ's vicar on earth, so is the first actor of the mass only the instrument through which Christ acts.
> The mass, then, has never been a drama, nor did it ever directly give rise to drama. The dramatic features of this service, along with those of the Canonical Office (the eight daily celebrations) and the symbolizing of virtually every sentence, gesture and physical accompaniment—these phenomena may have contributed suggestions as to the possibility of inventing drama, and may, indirectly, have encouraged it; but the liturgy itself, in its ordinary observances, remained always mere worship.

Perhaps it may seem here that a great deal of attention has been devoted to forms remotely connected with stage-dancing, that it would have been better simply to proclaim the absence of any dancing in the thousand years between Roman pantomime and Renaissance ballet. But dancing, particularly theatrical dancing, is not an isolated phenomenon. It depends, as does its name, on theater, and in order to understand forms it will take when it again emerges as dance, we must be content to follow theatrical history wherever, no matter how far afield, it may lead us. There are veins of that ore in the Missal which will be used later as links in forging our final chain. Then we shall need not only each of several elements but all elements in their correct proportions and relations to each other.

It is, to be sure, the indirect contribution of the Mass with which we are occupied, but even so, we must at least be familiar with its outline to understand the principles of regularized metaphor, its orderly ranks of references, symbols powerfully to affect poetry, music, costume, architecture and their combination towards a real theater which will raise its stages outside cathedrals. The element of gesture, as such, is slighter because it was not until the thirteenth century elaboration of the Mass that the Host was more decoratively elevated with the amplification of arm motions. By that time mimes would have returned again, fools as dancing devils, accompanied by dancing acrobats and dancing-masters.

The Mass is based on Christ's passion. It is called Eucharist or Thanksgiving, since its celebration *gives thanks* for bread and wine. The word Mass (Latin—*Missa*) comes from that part of the older service when the children and unbaptized (catchumens) are *dismissed*. It is a *communion* (Greek—*Kommonia*) to show the fellowship between Christ and his faithful. It is called the 'Lord's Supper' because he instituted it. It is a sacrament, or holy meal, because those material elements comprising it are consecrated. It is a *mystery* since only those who are rightfully initiated into it, may partake of it. It is a true sacrifice, as we have been told above, since it is a rehearsal of Christ's passion.

Saint Paul intended that all faithful should regularly hold religious meetings to partake of the Lord's Supper, but some came early and ate all the provender. The poor were left hungry and the rich got drunk. There was more factionalism than brotherhood. So he directed when they came together they should wait for one another, that their meal should not be the private dinner-party of rich Dives, but a communal meal shared by the whole flock.

Instead of presenting a skeleton or norm of that Mass, which from the ninth century has been only slightly changed, it is perhaps better to outline the first recorded ordinance of a Roman Mass. It may have less splendor of celebration than those at Chartres or Paris four hundred years later, but its five main parts are the same, and in this more stripped condition subsequent spectacular adornments can be more easily applied.

At this time (ca. 730) Rome had seven ecclesiastical districts, each with deacon, sub-deacon and acolytes, each with its own week day for the rotational celebration of high ecclesiastical ceremonies. There are minute regulations for the assemblage and marshalling of the procession which meets a pontiff, which robes him and escorts him to his throne.

Once at the sacristy, he does not leave it until the *introit* (entrance) is heard from the choir already in the church. He goes in to stand at the altar before the *gloria* (to the Father, Son and Holy Ghost). After the *kyrie eleison* (a Greek survival—"God have mercy") has been sung as many times as he indicates, he himself begins *gloria in excelsis,* in which the choir joins him. During the singing he faces east: at its finish, he turns for a moment to bless, and proceeds to the *oratio* (or collect; i.e., the faithful are gathered *"Quam collectum dicunt"*). This finished all seat themselves in order while the sub-deacon ascends the ambo to read the day's Epistle. After he has done, the cantor with his book ascends and gives out the *responsum*. The deacon then silently kisses the pontiff's feet, and is blessed. Preceded by acolytes with lit tapers and sub-deacons burning incense, he ascends the ambo where he reads the gospel. At the close, with the words *"Pax tibi"* (may you have peace), the pontiff after another *oratio*, descends to the senatorium (an imperial Roman survival) accompanied by certain of the inferior clergy, and receives in order the oblations, or offerings (of wine) from the nobles. The arch-deacon who follows takes the liquor from each separate vessel and pours all into one. Similar oblations are received from the other ranks and classes present, including women. This done, the celebrants wash their hands, the offerings in the meanwhile being set out by the sub-deacons on the altar, and water, supplied by the choir-leader, is mixed with the wine, while the choir (*schola cantorum*) has been singing the *offertorium*. When all is ready, the pontiff stops them, and enters upon the *preface*, the sub-deacons responding. At the Angel's Hymn (*Sanctus, Sanctus, Sanctus*) all kneel, and continue kneeling, except the pontiff, who rises alone and begins the *canon*, or consecration. At the words "*Per quem haec omnia*" the arch-deacon lifts the cup with the offerings, and at "*Pax domini sit semper vobiscum*" he gives the peace (*pax tibi*) to the clergy in their order, and to the laity. The pontiff then breaks a particle from consecrated bread and lays it upon the altar; the rest he puts on a plate held by the deacon. It is then distributed while the *Agnus Dei* (Lamb of God who takest away the world's sin) is sung. The pontiff, in communicating, puts the particle into the cup, making the mixture of bread and wine which is Christ's body and blood, and those present communicate in their order. As the pontiff descends into the senatorium to give the communion, the choir begins the *antiphon*, continues with the *Psalm* until all have finished. The sign is given for the *gloria*. They cease, and the celebrant, facing east, offers the *oratio ad complendum*, which being terminated, the arch-deacon says to the congregation: "*Ite, missa est*"—"go, you are dismissed," and they answer, "To God, the thanks."

In time the Mass would be altered, until in its present form it supports an astonishing exuberance of minute detail, each tiny point related to a central truth of the religion.

The bishop, clad in his sacred vestments, at the end of the procession, emerging from the sacristy and advancing to the altar, represents Christ, the expected of the nations, emerging from the virgin's womb and entering the world even as the Spouse from His secret chamber. The seven lights borne before him on the chief festivals are the seven gifts of the Holy Spirit descending upon the head of Christ. The two acolytes preceding him signify the law and the prophets, shown in Moses and Elias who appeared with Christ on Mount Tabor. The four who bear the canopy are the four evangelists, declaring the Gospel. The bishop takes his seat and lays aside his mitre. He is silent, as was Christ during His early years....*

In the cathedral the font is placed near the west door to signify by the gate of baptism one enters Christ's fold. The raised choir, separated from the church by a screen, will show the body of the fabric as church militant; the choir, the church, triumphant in heaven. The altar is east, for Christ is the

* H. O. Taylor: *The Medieval Mind:* Vol. II, p. 103 (paraphrase of Durandus: *Rationale divinorum officiorum*). The Macmillan Co. New York.

Sun of Righteousness and rose in Easter dawn. In the ninth century when the papacy had assumed the power of the Cæsars, they also saw fit to robe themselves in a manner fitting their dominion. They took from Roman civil dress the ordinary cut of tunic and mantle and adapted it to their use. To a large extent, with later additions, the dress, like the Mass itself, remains the same. There were five liturgical colors—white being most common, signifying the Lamb's pure fleece, appropriate for all feasts except the Passion; red was for martyr's blood and Christ's agony; green was the special verdant Sundays between Epiphany and Septuagesima; violet, the Advent, Intercession, penitential Masses, and a purple stole, or scarf, was worn at extreme unction; black is the mortal hue of death and Good Friday.

More and more the church would become a splendid court and an imperial household. Its magnificent ministers, champions of Christ, capped with *amice* or helmet (sign also of the tongue's discipline), and armored in a pure white *alb,* breastplate for spiritual warriors, created a fitting frame for their celebrations. And there was the cultivation of Gregorian singing, which, in its way, was as functional as the building, color, or action, since its specific purpose was to set off the meaning of the verses. Once, Augustine had said,

> Yea, very fierce am I sometimes, in the desire of having the melody of all pleasant music, to which David's Psalter is so often sung, banished both from mine own ears, and out of the whole church too—and the safer way it seems unto me, which I remember to have been often told me of Athanasius a Bishop of Alexandria, who caused the reader of the Psalm to sound it forth with so little warbling of the voice, as that it was nearer to speaking, than to singing. Notwithstanding, so often as I call to mind the tears I shed at the hearing of thy church songs, in the beginning of my recovered faith, yea, and at this very time, whenas I am moved not with the singing, but with the thing sung (when namely they are set off with a clear voice and suitable modulation), I then acknowledge the great good use of this institution.*

Every contributing factor was arranged so that the people could share audibly, visibly, in a voluntary ritual. The process of amplifying the Mass would grow so quickly into a florid gloss on a simple skeleton that an Augustinian tone will have to be taken by such a one of his successors as Saint Bernard of Clairvaux (died 1153). He castigates the celebrants of the mass rather than the splendor of its celebration, but the theatricalization of the one affected the manners of the other:

> Woe unto this generation, for its leaven of the Pharisees which is hypocrisy! ...today, foul rottenness crawls through the whole body of the church... ministers of Christ, they serve anti-Christ. They go clothed in good things of the Lord and render him no honor. Hence that *eclat* of the courtesan which you daily see, that theatric garb, that regal state.†

* *Confessions—X—33.*
† *Sermo in Cantica—33* par. 15 (quoted in H. O. Taylor's *The Medieval Mind*).

But however free we decide the church may be from strictly defined theatricals, and it will take more study than has been summarily placed here to convince one of it with any ultimate understanding, the theater, not inside but outside the church—the theater exhausted, outlawed, weak and dispersed, was, nevertheless, still alive. These surviving remnants would shortly benefit from the lively inner splendors of the cathedral, after which the dance-drama we once knew would reëmerge. Closest to church were the plays performed from an early date with its sanction, plays which would become famous as the mystery and miracle plays of the twelfth century.

Although Christmas is perhaps to us the most attractive of Christian festivals, and will later serve French and English courtiers with many occasions for balls which are relevant to this history, the celebration of Easter is a much more profound dramatization of fundamental religious tenets. The underlying reason for its ability continually to touch the hearts and minds of believers is familiar to anyone who has heard of Osiris. For Jesus, like the Egyptian, had a mortal existence, contested the world's authority for evil, was sacrificed to redeem His people and came again, like Osiris, to balance souls in the eternal shadow, though Christ sits not alone, but on His Father's right, to judge the quick and the dead. At Abydos so it was at Jerusalem, and after Jerusalem, at Rome. The acts of Christ—being taken down (deposed) from the Cross of His agony, His being placed in a mortal's tomb, the tomb watched by His friends and enemies and found to be, miraculously, void—these are the vital symbols of a church whose whole sovereignty depends on the doctrine of mortal death and immortal resurrection. Hence, for the Easter service certain special ceremonial offices were devised as amplifications of ordinary liturgy, to emphasize at the year's climacteric, the God who made the year clean.

Starting as a simple processional, even as early as the seventh century, the service came to involve not only the ordinary altar as tomb, but to have special ornamental tombs constructed for this purpose. Host and Cross were symbolically wrapped in winding-vestments, buried or covered, and night watched the relics. Then, with due observance, the symbol would be elevated and the resurrection was made a fact, accomplished as vivid reminder for those who kept vigil in the churches, as the Maries had waited before the Saviour's sepulcher. In some places there were carved stone *sepulchra,* a dummy for burial, grave-sheets for wrapping it, and a slab to seal the tomb. But all that was spoken or sung was the Mass or office of the particular day of the year. There is still no impersonation, but dramatic factors in the symbolism are considerably intensified.

Step by step, ritual facts prompt liturgical practice into elastic and more decorative forms. Within the church, engendered by accumulations of its religious energy, symbols teem and must have more and more channels for expression. Still inside the liturgy, a swelling body of poetry, song and accomplished deeds will interact until suddenly, almost as if it were spontaneously, we have liturgical drama.

We are told that after Christ had died and been buried, after He had risen, He then descended into hell, to choose from those already in limbo, which should be released into heaven, or which consigned forever to a lower hell. In medieval literature this was known as the "Harrowing of Hell," and in the pictorial and plastic arts we often see a gaping monster's mouth, barbed with teeth, from which Christ leads His chosen. The realization of this symbolic myth found its place in natural chronological order following Deposition and Elevation. Only here, the words, used themselves, though a familiar psalm of the Jewish church, had a peculiarly dramatic, or rather operatic, significance.

Its performance at Bamberg * is particularly full.

Before the beginning of the observance the lay congregation is allowed to gather at the sepulcher, there to be joined by a procession of the clergy from the sacristy. After the reciting of two psalms and of several familiar liturgical forms, the sepulcher is opened, and the Host and Cross are censed, sprinkled and elevated into general view. Then both objects are carried through the cemetery outside the church, the chorus singing the antiphon *Cum Rex Gloriæ*. When the procession reaches the first portal of the church, two priests, carrying an especially large crucifix, strike the door with the shaft three times, singing *Tollite Portas*. †

"Lift up your heads, O ye gates; and be ye lift up, ye everlasting doors; and the King of Glory shall come in."

And a person, inside the church with only the *voice* of Satan asks, "Who is this King of Glory?"

Chorus (outside): "The Lord strong and mighty, the Lord mighty in battle."

However, the portals remain shut, the procession continues, and repeats the dialogue at the second door, and again at the third.

"Lift up your heads, O ye gates; even lift them up, ye everlasting doors; and the King of Glory shall come in."

"Who is this King of Glory?"

"The Lord of hosts, *He* is the King of Glory."

Against such a King, the King of Hell must bow; the doors yield. The procession enters the building, marching towards the choir. Even now, we have not seen an impersonated Devil. We have only heard his voice.

The Bible itself, even with its treasure of Hebrew poetry and Christian narrative, was not, if strictly quoted, very full of many such fortunate questions and answers. Instinctively, the priests widened the dramatic possibilities of a given legend, yet preserved the semblance of strict holding to the given word. Tropes were invented. Tropus (Greek: *tropos*) refers to the melody to

* Young: *The Drama of the Medieval Church*—I-176 *seq.*
† The last four verses of the 24th Psalm.

which a verse is sung, but it came to signify the words themselves, words which were embellishments, or interpolations in sacred texts. We have heard the words of the priest, *Ite, missa est;* go, you are dismissed; the people respond: To God, the thanks.

> Into these two brief and adequate utterances, a zealous monk of St. Gall interpolated some sixteen words of his own, in the form of the following trope:
> Priest: Ite *nunc in pace, spiritus sanctus super vos sit, iam* missa est.
> People: Deo *semper laudes agite, in corde gloriam et* gratias.*

A path is now free for comparatively liberal decoration, soon adaptation and even rearrangement of set old texts. Not only is the sense of praise emphasized by baroque figuration, but the increased number of syllables gives a chance for amplified musical vocalization.

From the same remarkable monastery of Saint Gall has been preserved a prose trope of the tenth century, whose last word introduces the word: *resurrexi*—"He is risen," of the Easter Mass.

> *Interrogatio:* Question—*Quem queritis in sepulchro, Christicole?* Whom do you seek in the sepulcher, O Christian women?
> *Responsio:* Answer—*Iesum Nazereum crucifixum, O caelicolae.* Jesus of Nazareth, crucified, O heavenly ones.
> *Non est hic: Surrexit sicut praedixerat.* He is not here: He has arisen even as he foretold. *Ite, nuntiate quia surrexit de sepulchro.* Go, announce that He is arisen from the sepulcher.
> *RESURREXIT!*

And we still can hear the choir of women and angels, shouting HE IS RISEN!

Although the embellishment does not in any way offend or dilute the text, nevertheless, in germ, we have drama. The angels are not nuns, but angelic messengers: the women are not "lay-sisters" but Maries at the tomb. With freedom permitted by the insertion of tropes, with an increasingly frank realization by the clergy that the more theatrical the exposition of their religion the stronger its attraction and hold on members, real drama at last arrived in the medieval church. One might almost echo its resurrection chorus, applying it not only to its god, but to the spirit of theatrical-dancing, which has also been in limbo.

Around the eternal recrudescence of spring, ritual and art ceaselessly polarize, and at Easter-tide the Catholic Church recradles all her ancient composite traditions to garland the festival in her own way. Certain portions of the New Testament almost shine out in self-illuminated script, demanding a repetition, a re-creation of the story.

> Now there stood by the Cross of Jesus His mother, and His mother's sister, Mary the wife of Cleophas, and Mary Magdalene. When Jesus therefore saw

* *The Drama in the Medieval Church:* I—178.

His mother, and the disciple (John) standing by, whom He loved, He saith unto His mother, Woman, behold thy son! Then saith He to the disciple, Behold thy mother! And from that hour that disciple took her unto his own home.

It is Jesus alone here who speaks. Mary, in stoic silence, merely stands. *"Stabat Mater,"* and as a woman and as a mother, she must have wept to see her son where he was. By the twelfth century a great cult of the Virgin Mother would have grown, and for this cult splendid cathedrals with their glass, cut-stone and ritual glory would be raised.

No need to say that the gospel of Jesus was addressed to the heart as well as to the mind; and for times to come the Saviour on the Cross and at its foot the weeping mother were to rouse floods of tears over human sin, which caused the divine sacrifice.

We remember the tears of Isis which started the Nile to swell. Even in the fifth century Augustine expatiates in touching rhetoric on the plaining tears of Mary; and some seven hundred years later there are religious plays called *Planctus Mariæ,* or in German, *Marienklage,* which would not only give voice to the silent mother's grief, but also motion to actors and speech to the stage. There is one *Planctus* from the Italian town of Cividale del Friuli which is particularly interesting to us. On vellum, initialed in color, the black script clear and sturdy, we see between words and music on their staves, interlinear indications in red, or *rubrics* specifying the action.

Magdalen speaks:	O brothers!	(*Here turns herself to the men with arms held out*)
	And sisters!	(*Here to the women*)
	Where is my hope?	(*Here beats her breast*)
	Where is my consola-tion?	(*Here raises her hands*)
	Where is my whole salvation?	(*Here inclines her head, casts herself at Christ's feet*)
	O master mine?	
Virgin speaks:	O sorrow!	(*Here points to Christ with open hands*)
	Deep sorrow!	
	Why, why indeed	(*Here points to Christ with open hands*)
	Dear Son	
	Hangest thou thus	
	Thou who art life	(*Here beats her breast*)
	And hast forever been?	

Then speaks disciple John (*here, with arms extended points to Christ*); the third Mary follows, later both Mary Virgin and Mary Magdalen speak together. The indications for movement of head and arms, of the whole body, are as plain to us in their stylized rigidity as Gothic carvings which show coarse grain in the cut wood. Brusque, the anguish angular and abrupt, stripped to an icy formula of grief, here is no extraneous decoration or pretty quaintness. It is rude but it is tragic, and the tragedy comes as much from the virgin's wrung hands, from her signing to her pendant son, from the thump of her fists on her breast, as from her chanted *O dolor! Proh dolor!* As much, but no more, for we have again, even if in an undeveloped form, that equilibrium between gesture, music, verse and meaning which creates the atmosphere most nourishing to a future for theatrical dancing. Just as the gestures were of an hieratical simplicity, of a quality whose action would remind its spectators more of the movements of the Mass than of wandering jugglers, so the color, the costumes fitted holy subjects based on holy writ. The Maries were veiled and wore such church-wear as surplice, cope, dalmatic, orphery or alb. They were either in white or liturgical colors; Magdalen probably in red. They sometimes carried boxes or painted vases for the spice and burial ointments. Angels sat at the tomb-door, in white, gilt-crowned. In some places they held candles or lit lamps, and a palm or corn-ear symbolizing the resurrection. The actors were clergy, holy-sisters, choir-boys. The play was more chanted to music than spoken in a stage-voice. Later saints would hold symbols of their martyrdom or power—Peter his keys, Stephen his stones, Lawrence his gridiron.

By 1250 liturgical elements would have ceased to influence the form of the plays. All manner of purely secular ideas and incidents gradually crept in, making a complete separation of church and stage only a matter of time. Each biblical fact, bare enough in gospel, admitted not only a symbolic religious interpretation, but a human, every-day significance as well, creating figures, which would have been normally remote and incomprehensible, into men as touching and familiar as one's neighbor, miller, clerk or farmer. French shepherds in leathern smocks would hail a cut-out gilded star hung from a beam, and bear fresh vegetables or baby lambs to the crib of Christ. At a later date, Melchior, Caspar and Balthasar, clad like kings of Orient, brought more expensive toys. The three Maries, no longer stiff figures in a pieta, would purchase their perfumes from a stall, conveniently set up just outside the sepulcher. King Herod would roar and stamp when the news comes of another king in Israel. Instead of being spoken in various accents of Latin which priests derived from Roman contacts, they talked what we call old-English, old French, or medieval German. Everyday speech replaced the sacred tongue. From their initial position at the altar's east-end, the plays were moved out onto the broad west porches, hooded with great gables of carved saints in glory, and Christ showing His wounded hands, from the tympanum. Cathedrals were not empty at Matins, but their doors were packed for miracle plays. The church, in her half-conscious sanction of the rise of the vulgar theater was electioneering perhaps better than she knew. The same dangers which Augustine feared from the profane games of Rome, reared up again to plague deacons of Rouen and Winchester. However sacred their origins, plays were shows, and it was not long before the ordained clergy was prohibited from participating in them, some four centuries later. The body of Molière was not permitted holy ground. And even in Milan today, the ballet-girls of the Scala Theater are not permitted confessional and must seek charitable nuns to shrive them. But it was too late to prohibit a lay-stage now. Not the mass itself could compete with the Corpus Christi spectacles produced by a gold-beaters' guild or a society of master-tailors. The theater, a revitalized universally popular theater, delighted itself and its spectators by closeness to the life of the world at large, based on a conveniently legible structure of church fact and fancy which everybody, in every class, everywhere, immediately recognized.

From altar to portal to church-square or market-place was the path of the plays. Stages were erected, high enough for people standing to see clearly. The seeing-place here was not localized as in Athens or even as within the church. Nor was the stage. There were numerous platforms, which, taken as a consecutive cycle, told the whole story; or there would be a single scaffolding with a composite simultaneous background on "mansions," of practicable sets ranging from yawning Hell's maw at the right, by quick steps past Limbo, Gethsemane garden, the Mount of Olives, the sepulchers and finally The Golden Gate. The placing of this scenery was regulated by the corresponding features in the church itself. The set for the Resurrection (altar) would be to the left (north) of the audience, opposite Hell to the hot South.

But dancing—what about the dancing? As we know from acquaintance with Augustine and Alcuin, dancing is the Devil's business. Appropriately enough, the Devil is the first-dancer of the middle ages. Those other social dances which in medieval times were to set the floor for renaissance court-balls will be described in another place. But as for dancing in the theater, that was the fiend's unique province. Occasionally he might permit his legitimate daughter Salomé to turn a few somersaults, as shown on the porch at Rouen, and infrequently the angels, if in solemn processional, could risk an emulation of David's dancing chorus, but these are exceptions.

We have met the Devil in church once before, as deacon, or as devil-voice, when in the rôle of type-skeptic, he demanded "Who is the King of Glory?" The principle of pure good needs the mask of pure evil. The Devil more than filled this bill. Rapidly he became one of the liveliest, most appreciated of the *personæ*, whether he prompted Adam, snatched sinners off to Limbo, or sulked when his offer of the cities of the world failed. The Devil's antics and dances were proverbial. In a Cain-and-Abel playlet, Cain, a grasping, miserly farmer, will give no tithes to his god: he says,

> Ya; Daunce in ye devil way, dresse ye downe,
> For I wille wyrke euen as I will.

In the Bible itself, the Devil as a person, in the rare instances when he is described, is treated as a serious menace. But on the medieval stage he was always a horrid comic, frequently introduced again and again not only as comic-relief, but for the sake of his own buffoonery and tricks. The Devil, or Lucifer, Beelzebub, Satan, with such lackeys and hell-fellows as Amon, Baal, Mammon, Moloch, and some German devils called Hellhound, Womansrage, Vicebag, Looking-glass and Goatbeard not only betrayed Adam and urged Judas to do the same for his master, but were on hand to urge him to hang himself, to give Herod the notion of massacring the Innocents, to turn Magdalen into a loose woman.

The Devil wore a furry skin, not unlike a satyr's. His wiry snake's tail was barbed, his face was blackened, horned or masked. In the Garden of Eden he is an adder with the fair face of a virgin.

> Then the Figure (God) must depart to the church and Adam and Eve walk about in Paradise in honest delight. Meanwhile the demons are to run about the stage, with suitable gestures, approaching the Paradise from time to time and pointing out the forbidden fruit to Eve, as though persuading her to eat it. Then the Devil is to come and address Adam.... In the last scene, ... Then shall come the Devil and three or four devils with him, carrying in their hands chains and iron fetters, which they shall put on the necks of Adam and Eve. And some shall push and others pull them to Hell; and hard by Hell shall be other devils ready to meet them, who shall hold high revel (*tripudium:* Latin for triple-step of Sallic priests) at their fall. And certain other devils shall point them out as they come, and shall snatch them up and carry them into Hell; and there shall make a great smoke arise, and call aloud to each other with glee in their Hell, and clash their pots and kettles, that they may be heard without. And after a little delay the devils shall come out and run about the stage; but some shall remain in Hell.*

Interludes in the plays were relieved by minstrel music and as many as forty musicians at a time were employed at Bristol. There were also dances by "vyces" (vices or devils) who amused the spectators before and after the show itself. Belial is, in a morality play, to have gunpowder burning in pipes in his hands, ears and other convenient parts of his body. *Anima,* the soul, in a play called 'Mind, Will and Understanding' has small demons chasing in and out from underneath her petticoats.

> In the Domesday scene at Coventry the 'savyd' and 'dampnyd' souls were distinguished by their white or black color. The hell mouth was provided with fire, a windlass, and a barrel for the earthquake—Lucifer goes down to Hell 'apareled fowle with fyre about him' and the plain is filled with 'every degre of devylls of lether and spirytis on Cordis.' Lucifer becomes "a fyre serpent made with a virgyn face & yolowe heare upon her head."

*From Adam, The Benedictbeuren Christmas Play: E. K. Chambers: *The Medieval Stage,* Vol. II, p. 80.

This Devil is by no means an isolated phenomenon. We shall meet him again, under a form with which we have already a cursory acquaintance, that mischievous fool of the Roman comedy, the *stupidus* or *stultus,* whose Greek cousins had goat-hoofs. Neither Punch nor Harlequin will remember that their lineal great-grandfathers roared down the aisles of Nôtre Dame on the Feast of Fools, or that their great-grand uncles, spitting flannel flames, dashed among the burghers of German market towns, seizing their terrified children to be delivered to King Herod, who massacred them with a brushful of red paint.

THE DANCE OF DEATH   *Nuremberg Chronicle:* 1491

CHAPTER VI

The Mediæval Dance

IT may seem that the development of stage-dancing is more accurately a record of the survival of an instinct towards the dance, which only at intervals of five hundred or a thousand years actually flowers into forms worthy of serious attention on purely esthetic grounds. And yet the more we study, this surviving, this persistence against odds is what genuinely absorbs us. Such culminations as 'The Bacchæ,' the Catholic Mass, the ballets of Noverre and Vigano, *Les Sylphides,* or 'The Rites of Spring' are spectacles to be felt actually in seeing, in participation. But they are rare,—how rare it is difficult for most of us to remember, since the history of ballet in the last three hundred years is so richly documented, and so thinly in the three thousand before. Naturally we have a right to prefer what we have seen to what has merely been described to us. Our history teachers, in their haste, show us only highlights, the towering monuments. We acquire a habit of assuming that unique masterpieces are immediately related, logically capping each other. But between a Bacchæ and a *Marienklage,* between the pantomime of Pylades and the pantomime of Grimaldi, between a Saint George's mumming and 'A Masque of Blackness,' are networks of tenuous but indestructible threads, which, bound by innumerable ties of tradition, time and accident, set off the first-rate monuments in their truthful remoteness, their frank perspective.

The empty theaters of Orleans and Epidauros bleached in the sun, but the ideas of Aristotle were not entirely lost to the conquerors of Hellas. The tragedies of Seneca were written, read, yet not played; the Coliseum served as a quarry for building another Rome, and pillars of the imperial forums supported the basilica of St. Lawrence Without the Walls. We have seen how the church made her Mass, entirely independent of the mimes, and how mimes reëmerged from the very pages of the missal. But it was not entirely to the Roman Christian Church that the survival of theatrical-dancing, sometimes following the reëstablishment of theaters, sometimes preceding them, would be entrusted. The Church provided one path for survival, but only one, however indispensable, of several.

It was not long before the shows which, moving out onto the cathedral porches, transferring themselves into church-squares or market-places, had accumulated such a repertory that it could be divided into three important, distinct, if related categories. The *mystery* plays treated only of orthodox scriptural events, a general huge topic of world redemption through Christ's sacrifice, with picturesque tableaux from Old and New Testament. The *miracle* plays were a secondary, if not always distinguishable, addition. They told legends of the saints which increased from century to century with the facts of new martyrdoms and an identification of real people with scriptural precedent. The *morality* plays were a still later innovation, and though teaching and illustrating truths familiar to church-goers by homely allegorical personifications of virtues, vices, and qualities, they were the most purely secularized of the three. By the thirteenth century, France, England and Germany had a thriving interest in such spectacles and Devils, Salomés and Follies were dancing on their platforms.

But already in the tenth century, there exists a dramatic phenomenon, not only combining the features of mystery, miracle and morality, but illustrating other important threads: the dwindling legacy of the classic Roman stage. It persisted not only from the Italian peninsula but also from Byzantium, where shows which survived for a longer time were as magnificent as in Milan or Rome itself. Hrotsvitha, "the loud-voice of Gandersheim," was a young German gentlewoman, who, at the age of twenty, or a little older, entered a nunnery (ca. 955). She received an excellent education, for her abbess, Geberga, was the highly intelligent niece of the Emperor Otto. Under the Saxon supremacy, such convents, being close to the Imperial Court, were havens for noblewomen. When Geberga died, she was succeeded by Princess Sophia, a worldly half-Byzantine girl who had been a nun with Hrotsvitha, and who brought her into vital contact with the Empire of the East. Her plays form a curious reference which is not impressive in itself until understood as a focus packed with cross-influence. For a practicing dramatist, Hrotsvitha had no audience, no stage; not even readers. Her plays seem to have been written to be acted. Only one actual performance is recorded and that, two hundred years after her death. No mediæval writer mentions them; they were published complete for the first time only in 1501, with Albrecht Dürer's illustrations. Why then, if they were neither known by her contemporaries nor produced by her followers, are they, as plays without dancing, significant to us?

In the first place, although mediæval scholars often thought that Roman comedies were monologues, to be declaimed by a single mime, and hence far more literary than dramatic in their appeal, and although the church had brought every weapon in her arsenal to bear against the Roman stage, a persistent thread of pure classic tradition *did* remain. This thread, however tenuous, stretches from Terence straight back to Aristophanes and Greek satyr-plays of goat-foot dances. Hrotsvitha, in the library of Gandersheim, had found a manuscript of Terence, and blushingly admitted she was seduced by his enchanting style to read his salacious plots. Hence, with a practicality which the Fathers would have commended, she utilized Roman dramatic forms, not in slavish imitation of their profanity, but rather to frame worthier legends of the inviolable chastity of Christian virgins, by that very instrument which the pagans provided. Far more than an accidental imitator of Terence, she was valuable as a link to the Byzantine Theater.

Byzantium not only conserved the traditions of Euripides in a purer form far longer than Rome, but also attempted to christianize the stage without destroying it, and met with considerable success some centuries before Hrotsvitha. Constantinople, the capital of an Emperor who persuaded every important Roman family he could find to migrate there, had not only classic comedy and tragedy, pantomime-ballet, but also Theodora, its harlot-dancer-lion-taming Empress, its vaudeville, its theatrical sensations and claques and every parallel to ancient and modern theatrical excitements. We can only permit ourselves to be occupied with traces of Byzantium present in a Saxon poetess. For Hrotsvitha, although one might imagine her nearer the soil of Terence than the land of Hellas, took all of her six plots from the hagiography of the Greek church. Not only that, but Hrotsvitha had never seen a play, for there had been none in the west for centuries, nor had she even read a description of a stage, unless by an unlikely chance there was a manuscript of the Roman architect Vitruvius in Gandersheim's library. Nevertheless her plays bear performance as written, and her *Gallicanus* was presented often in the twelfth century at Alderspach. Where did she get her practical notions of dramaturgy? Probably through conversations with her new abbess and old school-fellow, the Princess Sophia, who had seen plays in the Greek Byzantium of her youth, and who was constantly traveling back and forth between eastern court and western cloister.

In the comic-tragedy, or tragic farce of *Dulcitius,* three virgins were secretly wooed at night by a seducer. But as soon as he came into their house he succumbed to a laughable delusion that pots and cooking-vessels were the chaste damsels and he emerged in the morning to appear before his officers of the guard, with sooty face and dirty clothes. His lieutenant, Sisinnius, is ordered to avenge his captain, and is led a roaming dance through hill and dale, which reminds us of Ariel's foolery in 'The Tempest' and Puck's tricks with the Athenian lovers. In *Sapientia* (wisdom), Hrotsvitha dramatizes a fable from the time of Diocletian's last great persecution of the Christians. Sapientia was the mother of three beautiful daughters, Faith, Hope and Charity, who learned from their parent to be as good as she. After they were killed and dismembered by the Emperor's order, their holy mother collected their remains, buried them five miles outside Rome and herself perished forty days later. This allegorical parable is presented in a dramatic narrative and prophetically anticipates the Italian and English morality masques of four centuries later.

Men, in the middle ages, imagined and sensed indirectly. A chain of thought in a mediæval mind was inclined to run as often from symbol to symbol as from fact to fact. Those manifestations of ideas, whether in verse, stone or paint, which bear another secret, figurative reference, a more profound connotation than their obvious, visible form, are allegories. We have seen how many meanings were appliquéed to the basic structure of the Mass. It was only natural for a nun like Hrotsvitha to write in symbolic shorthand. It became second nature to carvers on churches, poets of hymns, designers of stained glass windows, and, as well, arrangers of the libretti in plays, ballets and opera, from the tenth century, down into the high renaissance.

The best historian of the epoch's spirit tells us unforgettably that it

> seemed to rely on everything except its sin-crushed self, and trusted everything except its senses; which in the actual looked for the ideal, in the concrete saw the symbol, in the earthly church beheld the heavenly, and in fleshly joys discerned the devil's lures; which lived in the unreconciled opposition between the lust and vain-glory of earth and the attainment of salvation; which felt life's terror and its pitifulness, and its eternal hope; around which waved concrete infinitudes, and over which flamed the terror of darkness and the judgment day.*

If there is any single symbol which represents in instantaneous flash a lyric concept of mediæval emotion it is the so-called Dance of Death. So-called, because in its most influential expressions it is not a dance, but a poem or a picture; and yet dance, for us, because of its origin, its associations, and because we shall frequently employ it as a touchstone to the medieval mentality. We have seen how, inside the Church and outside her doors dramatic essences were nourished, by Mass, miracle-play, and even from some salvaged mutations of the Roman stage. There remain two other important channels; the dramatic ritual-games arising from vegetation or survival ceremonies among indigenous folk, and the inventions of such individual artists as troubadour, jongleur or minstrel. Between morality-play and folk-rite stands the Dance of Death, with hands in both directions.

It was not the idea of death as peace, death as a blessed release, death as a dignified end to man's labor that obsessed the mediæval brain. To the man of the middle ages death was a graveyard ghoul, a chilling spectral horror, a death frightening now only to listeners of ghost stories or children whistling past cemeteries. *"Dies iræ, dies illa,"* on that day, dread day of wrath, as the great chant rolled, graves belched up their burdens, and King Christ would come a second time to judge the quick and dead. "What is man . . . but a stynkynge slyme, and after that a sake ful of donge, and at the laste mete to wormes?" From their stone perch dismal preachers terrorized their congregations, pointing to the displayed skulls and bones of their departed.

Orcagna, or perhaps the brothers Lorenzetti, painted such a sermon in the Pisan Cloister.

> In those piles of the promiscuous and abandoned dead, those fiends and angels poised in mid-air struggling for souls, those blind and mutilated beggars vainly besieging Death with prayers and imprecations for deliverance, while she descends in her robe of woven wire to mow down with her scythe the knights and ladies in their garden of delight; again in those horses snuffing

* H. O. Taylor—*The Medieval Mind:* Vol. I, p. 13. The Macmillan Co. New York.

at the open graves, those countesses and princes face to face with skeletons, those serpents coiling round the flesh of what was once fair youth or maid, those multitudes of guilty men and women trembling beneath the trump of the archangel—tearing their cheeks, their hair, their breasts in agony, because they see Hell through the prison-bars and hear the raging of its fiends, and feel the clasp upon their wrists and ankles of clawed hairy demon hands.*

The term *Danse Macabre* refers to the *Danse des Morts,* the *Totentanz,* and English Dance of Death. Macabre or Macabrée is a curious adjective. It may come from the name of Saint Macarius, an Egyptian hermit. Three live young men arrive at his cell and he shows them three open coffins containing three corpses. Thus it is shown in the cited fresco of the Pisan Campo Santo. More likely it comes from an Arabic word *Maqbara* (plural, *Maqábir*), a tomb. There are only two Dances of Death in Spain, and since both are copies of the French, it is unlikely, though possible, that the knightly companions of Du Guesclin brought the word back from Moorish Spain in 1366. Some derive it from the English: *make-break* or the Italian: *macheria,* a mural or wall. Perhaps the most plausible origin of the word connects it with the Biblical Maccabees, followers of Judas Macchabeus. There is a story, whose authenticity is doubtful, but typical of others similar, that among many Scotchmen who overran Paris in 1424 was one MacCaber, a kind of wizard who lived in a tower, thin as a skeleton. He is said to have instituted a kind of churchly procession which took place in a cemetery, where a figure representing death invited all comers to a round.

It seems likely that French verses inspired wall-paintings, which in turn were imitated by dancers, but since, as is the case of other like phenomena, when an idea pervades the air, it explodes into spontaneous expression everywhere, and one cannot fix any absolute priority. In the black-letter rhymes every human type in medieval society was given a verse and a woodcut portrait, from Pope to Emperor to Cardinal to King to Prince, Archbishop, Baron, Lady, Squire, Abbot, Prior, Lawyer, Bailiff, Astronomer, Deacon, Merchant, Monk, Physician, Minstrel, finally down to the Laboring Man. In printed versions, the dance is more of a parade; each type marches forward according to his rank, not eagerly, but solemnly, reluctantly: only Death dances a grotesque step, asking questions of all men and pointing to the inevitability of his triumph. Death, in a poem before 1480, says to the minstrel (*Mynstralle* or *Mimus*):

> O thow minstral: that cannest so note & pipe
> Unto folkes: for to do plesaunce
> By the right honde anoon I shal the gripe
> With these others: to go up-on my daunce
> There is no scape: nowther a-voydaunce

*J. A. Symonds: *The Renaissance in Italy* (Modern Library Edition), Vol. I, p. 680,

> On no side: to contrarie my sentence
> For yn musik: be crafte & accordaunce
> Who maister is: show his science.

and the minstrel answers:

> This new daunce: is to me so straunge
> Wonder dyuerse: and parsyngli contrarie
> The dredful fotyng: doth so oft chaunge
> And the mesures: so ofte sithes varie
> Whiche now to me: is no thyng necessarie
> If hit were so: that I might asterte
> But many a man: if I shall not tarie
> Oft daunceth: but no thynge of herte.*

The original *danse macabrée* showed only men. Its leader, Death, was not a personification of mortality but the living human shown as he would soon find himself. Its earliest extant wall painting is Swiss, and was executed in 1312 at Klingenthal in Little Basel, but the most famous example was French, ca. 1424, in the charnel cloisters of the Paris church of the Holy Innocents. Many mediæval churchyards would be decorated with similar frescoes, in Lübeck, Dresden, Lucerne, in London's Old Saint Paul's and in the church Shakespeare knew in Stratford-on-Avon. Remember the hideous doubts of Juliet before she took the sleeping-draught:

> Alack, alack, is it not like that I
> So early waking, what with loathsome smells
> And shrieks like mandrakes' torn out of the earth,
> That living mortals hearing them run mad:
> O, if I wake, shall I not be distraught,
> Environed with all these hideous fears?
> And madly play with my forefathers' joints. †

There are three independent ideas in the Dance of Death, not the least of which is its satirical or ironic context. Before Death, all men whether they be great kings or poor laborers are equal. In feudal Europe this equality, almost an idea of revenge on the rich, contributed enormously to the popularity of the parable. Secondly, there is the conception of living people confronted with their dead images, a development of a thirteenth century French poem, 'The Three Quick and the Three Dead.' A trio of young nobles were hawking in a wood when they stumbled on three corpses, who lectured them on human vanity. Finally there was the connection with actual miming and dancing.

In 1373, the Black Death, a bubonic plague, swept Europe. No town was free from terrible sights and sounds of a ravage which no prayer could

---

* Daunce of Death. Ellsmere MS. LXIII-LXIV (Florence Warren: *The Dance of Death,* pp. 60, 62.)
† Act IV, Scene iv.

stay. Single graves were too small. Infants and young girls, men in their life's prime, sickened and smoldered with unthinkable maladies. With the disease, ideas of the Dance of Death spread as a universal fable. Wakes for the dead took on an insane gayety. There was a game of some Slavonic origin, where guests took each other by pairs, dancing merrily, laughing and singing. Suddenly, on a shrill note, the music ceased. Silence and immobility fell on the company. Then a sober, sad melody was piped, which grew into a funeral march. One of the young men sank to the ground, playing dead. The girls and women danced around him, in graceful parody of mourning gestures. At the same time they sang an hilarious dirge, then one after the other, bent over the dead man and kissed him back to life, till a general round-dance concluded the first half. The second part was the same, except boys mourned a young girl. The kissing part was naturally popular, and no one worried about the transmission of plague germs from mouth to mouth. Theocritus described a Sicilian Grecian kissing contest in memory of a dead hero.

> About his tomb, so surely as spring comes round, your children vie in a kissing-match, and who so sweetliest presses lip upon lip, returns laden with garlands to his mother.

Mediæval games were less pretty. In Hungary, for example, at wakes, one of the mourners lay down with a handkerchief over his face. Bagpipers struck up a dance of death. Then men and women, half singing, half wailing, crossed his hands on his chest, trussed him up, turned him over, played tricks with him, even set him on his legs and made him dance. The mock corpse was entirely limp, his arms sagged, his head lolled. Once indeed, God punished such foolery and when they went to rouse the player, he was dead indeed. Perhaps he had already contracted plague from the nearby body.

In one of the English miracle-plays of the Coventry cycle, the 'Slaughter of the Innocents,' a 'Dethe, Goddys Messangere,' steps in to slay King Herod. In the time of John Chrysostom, one of the popular celebrations of the Eastern Church during the festival of the Kalends of January (New Year's), was a mock-funeral of the old year, and incidentally of all the dead.

As early as 1285, in Scotland there was an entertainment at Jedburgh Abbey. To celebrate the nuptials of Alexander the Third, and Joleta, daughter of the Comte de Dreux, Death, in his skeleton, joined maskers who danced before the King and Queen. The presence of Death on a marriage-night may have been a practical joke, a political hint, or merely an admonitory reminder. The Scotch poet, William Dunbar, who is familiar to lovers of English poetry for his 'Lament for the Makirs' (*Timor Mortis Conturbat Me*), wrote in 1507 a 'Dance of the Seven Deadly Sins.' [*] It was a satirical description of the masked ball given in that year at Edinburgh's court, on the day before Fastern's Eve, and combines the Dance of Death with a morality-masque. The Dance of Death would become, in the Renaissance,

[*] William Dunbar: Scottish Text Society. Vol. I, p. lvii; Vol. II, pp. 116, 119.

more elegant and sophisticated, and reappears again and again as a motif in love-poetry, on dagger-handles, mantel-pieces, tapestries and in Elizabethan tragedy.

The most magnificent Dance of Death effloresced at the Tuscan Court, when, in 1507, the painter Piero di Cosimo, designed a macabre masque for the Duke of Florence. The city was surrounded by sieges and imminent disaster; it was exquisitely tense, heedless, insecure, in imminent physical danger. It is worth reading Vasari's notice of this pageant which perfectly illustrates sophisticated embellishments upon a remote activity of the folk.

The triumphal car was covered with black cloth, and was of vast size; it had skeletons and white crosses painted upon its surface, and was drawn by buffaloes, all of which were totally black: within the car stood the colossal figure of Death, bearing the scythe in his hand; while around him were covered tombs, which opened at all the places where the procession halted, while those who formed it, chanted lugubrious songs, when certain figures stole forth, clothed in black cloth, on whose vestments the bones of a skeleton were depicted in white; the arms, breast, ribs and legs, namely, all which gleamed horribly forth on the black beneath. At a certain distance appeared figures bearing torches, and wearing masks presenting the face of a death's head both before and behind; these heads of death as well as the skeleton necks beneath them, also exhibited to view, were not only painted with the utmost fidelity to nature, but had besides a frightful expression which was horrible to behold. At the sound of a wailing summons, sent forth with a hollow moan from trumpets of muffled yet inexorable clangor, the figures of the dead raised themselves half out of their tombs and seating their skeleton forms thereon, they sang the following words, now so much extolled and admired, to music of the most plaintive and melancholy character. Before and after the car rode a train of the dead on horses, carefully selected from the most wretched and meager animals that could be found: the caparisons of those worn, half-dying beasts were black, covered with white crosses; each was conducted by four attendants, clothed in the vestments of the grave; these last-mentioned figures, bearing black torches and a large black standard, covered with crosses, bones, and death's heads. While this train proceeded on its way, each sang, with a trembling voice, and all in dismal unison, that psalm of David called the *Miserere*.

There are innumerable graphic representations of the mediæval dance of death, which gives us an unparalleled completeness of documentation for costume, manners, and science of the period. The clothes are suited each to that type who is the representative of his station in life, and in successive engravings one can trace the development of sleeves, shoes, hats, or gloves. Engravers were unkind as Death itself, and spared neither fat bishop, foppish squire, lecherous housewife, or wise doctor gazing at his urine-glass. In the beginning, Death is shown as a rotting cadaver, his flapping belly full of intestinal snakes. Not until the Renaissance had destroyed superstitions against anatomical research was Death shown as a correctly articulated bony skeleton.

One of the strangest side-lights on mediæval dancing, and a phenomenon intimately connected with those pestilences of which the Black Death was most famous, is the so-called *Danseomanie,* or dancing-mania, which flared up in a dozen places, all over the European continent, from the eleventh to the fourteenth century. There is a legend that

> on Christmas night, 1013, a Parisian priest named Robert could not chant his Mass in peace, because he was bothered by the singing and dancing of carolers, eighteen young men and fifteen young girls who clamored in the cemetery outside. He told them to hush up and go away, but they only laughed at him and sang louder. So he cursed these bad Christians, saying, "May God make you all sing and dance, the whole year through without missing one single day." And so it was they danced all night and all day, every day and every night. No one had ever seen such frenzy or such sadness, as they pounded the tombs of the dead. At the end of a year, Herbert, Bishop of Cologne, came to absolve them. As soon as the couples, joined together for twelve months, were permitted to separate, three of the girls, one of whom was the priest's daughter, fell down dead. The others slept for three days and three nights.

There is a similar story told of German dancers who were cursed at Kolbigk in 1021. The legend is of Frankish origin and was later exploited by the low-Saxons. The writer in the great Nuremberg world-chronicle of 1493, who signs himself Othbert the Sinner, writes that a girl's arm fell off into her partner's fingers, but she danced right on; that in spite of hunger, thirst, rain or shine, on they danced; that their sole-leather wore out and their clothes unravelled but they danced on; that the ground underfoot was treaded into a deep hole, but still they danced. At the year's end, the priest, (here of St. Magnus) undid them.

It must have been some form of pathological aberration, or group-hysteria of whole villages at a time, forcing them to dance until they fell. It does not seem so remote from us if we recall our "Dance Marathons," which have been held in such public places as Madison Square Garden, where couples jog on, pummeling each other to keep awake, for weeks at a stretch. To be sure the dancers of the middle-ages competed for no prize. But in 1237 a band of German children danced from Erfurt to Arnstadt; many of them died on the way, and the survivors suffered for the rest of their lives from nervous disorders, or tremblings like St. Guy's or St. Vitus' dance. In 1278, a crazy or perhaps drunken company of dancers danced down the bridge at Marburg; the bridge fell, and all were drowned. In 1347 a troop of men and women danced on to Aix-la-Chapelle, continuing into Belgium and the Low Countries. At Metz there were five hundred maniacs, and only a little further on, eleven hundred. A priest came out and tried to break the spell, but failed. In the course of dancing, the people suffered from hallucinations of extreme joy or deep melancholy, accompanied by violent aversions to the color red, and to long curved shoes in the style known as *la poulaine.* Needless to say, one can hardly rely on the absolute truth of such suspiciously repetitious reports which seldom seem to come from eye-witnesses. For example, at Utrecht in 1493, dancers on a bridge failed to do honor to the sacrament, which a passing priest was carrying to an extreme unction and in the collapse of its arch two hundred people drowned. Churches and cemeteries were often the scenes of these excesses, which frequently degenerated into orgies. In 1374, the year after the Black Death, the Chorisants, a sect believed by contemporaries to be under diabolic influence, arose in Flanders and on the Rhine and Moselle.

> It being that the people began to dance and rush about; they formed groups of three and danced in one place for half a day, and while dancing they fell to the ground and allowed others to trample on their bodies. By this they believed that they could cure themselves of illness. And they walked from one town to another and collected money from the people, wherever they could procure any. And this was carried on to such an extent that in the town of Cologne alone more than five hundred dancers were to be found. And it was a swindle, undertaken for the purpose of obtaining money, and that a number of them both women and men might be tempted to unchastity and succumb to it.*

But it was by no means all a fraud, and in Italy such mania was thought to have been induced by the bite of tarantula spiders. Later, the origin of their folk-dance, the tarantella, was attributed to therapeutic measures for curing the bite by making the person dance madly, since if he remained still the venom would kill him. Mediæval women frequently passed through psychological crises, melancholia, or elation, preceding holy festivals, and on the Saint's Day were cured at Mass. The first physician who attempted to treat dansomania scientifically was the great Doctor Paracelsus, who died in Salzburg in 1541. He sensibly protested against the use of charms, and divided the disease into three aspects, *chorea imaginativa* (auto-suggestion or self-hypnosis), *chorea lasciva* (sexual excitement, to be cured by a plunge in cold water), and *chorea naturalis,* which was simply hysterical laughter.

The Dance of Death, besides its important connections with historic events, social customs and the Church, had genuine links with those vegetation ceremonies which are not so much traditional as ubiquitous and perennial. One could hardly say the games of Provençal or English May Day had a Greek or Roman ancestry, any more than one can assume the Roman Pyrrhic is a direct source of Nordic sword-dances. In every instance the year's weather and its influence on a particular soil whose crops it affects determines the nature of ritual forms. Inevitable and striking similarities tend to fuse and often a false descent is suggested. Nevertheless, separate from both the shattered literary heritage of Roman civilization and attempts to revive it, from the church that replaced it, and from individual artists who were active in spite of church domination, a living body of ritual belief, a real religion of the folk, farmers, poor city-workers, small merchants

* The Nuremberg Chronicle: 1493.

and villeins, existed well into the Renaissance and we must look into it for
the sources of much of the later developments which by the end of the
sixteenth century will absorb us; in particular the seasonal *Magi* or May
plays in Florence, the New Year masques and May Day dances of England
and France.

The advent of Christianity by no means completely displaced either Druid
cults or the religion of Thor or Wotan. Catholic priests prevailed upon the
Celts and Saxons to give up their more cruel forms of human sacrifice, but
they did not attempt, wisely enough, to root out all the harmless nature
superstitions, and these persisted, often only to be repeated as good-luck
charms, with all realization of their tribal function or ritual use lost, or
else as infrequent rustic amusements which were simple relaxations in the
difficult lives of the people. As Sir E. K. Chambers explains:

> It was of the customs themselves that the people were tenacious, not of their
> meaning, so far as there was still a meaning, attached to them, or of the names
> which their priests had been wont to invoke. Leave them but their familiar
> revels, and the ritual so indissolubly bound up with their hopes of fertility
> for their flocks and crops, they would not stick upon the explicit consciousness
> that they drank or danced in the might of Eostre or of Freyr. And in time,
> as the Christian interpretation of life became an everyday thing, it passed out
> of sight that the customs had been ritual at all.

The spirit of fertilization persisted in May games. Before daybreak
peasants would go into the forests, cut big hawthorn boughs and carry them
with other May-greens into village streets to decorate their houses. A pole,
festooned with wreaths and hung with ribbons, was the erect symbol of
new growth. Boys, with branches tied all around them, hopped onto lawns
like bouncing bushes. They were called 'Jack i' the Green.' There were
May Kings and May Queens as well, the center of the dance-games or
plays. At Midsummer's Night, or St. John's Eve, a night, in which, as
Shakespeare has shown, strange happenings are not rare, there were fire
festivals, when peasants to make their crops grow would drive cattle through
a bonfire and leap over the flames, symbols of cleansed power. There was
scarcely a rustic holiday without some sort of garlanded procession, usually
followed by *quêtes,* or requests. Children, or originally grown-ups, felt entitled to take up collections of eggs, cakes or small coins. Carollers on Christmas Eve would serenade a house and expect at least a warming drink. Little
boys and girls in America, sometimes on Halloween, more often in big cities
on the national Thanksgiving Day still feel free to mask themselves, shoot
off cap-pistols and ask for pennies. The Easter egg-rolling on the White
House Lawn is a similar survival, and even the New England Puritans
went out to gather arbutus or Mayflowers. Most of us know, through Hawthorne's tale, of the regrettable ceremonies on May Day 1628, performed by
godless Morton of Quincy's Merrymount. Bradford, the historian, wrote,

They set up a Maypole, drinking and dancing about it many days together, inviting the Indian women for their consorts, dancing and frisking togeather like so many fairies or furies rather.

Endicott made short work of such profanity. This must be one of the earliest, if not the earliest, mention of dancing by the English in America. A Maypole was set up again in Charlestown, Massachusetts, in 1689, and promptly hacked down.

Dancing was a very important adjunct to all folk festivals, and gave the Church considerable trouble. Upon important Saints' Days, which were superimposed upon the local gods, just as Dionysos had preëmpted earlier divinities, whole choirs of women entered the cathedral precincts with lewd *cantica* and *ballationes*. In 1338, the chapter of Wells Cathedral forbade *chorea* and other *ludi* (games) within the church grounds, not so much on account of their pagan scurrility as on account of the damage done to cathedral properties and furniture. Singing and dancing were inseparable, and the most frequently mentioned name of a dance is the *carole,* which we have still as a popular Christmas ballad or carol.

Originally the carole was a Provençal dance-song particular to May, but spread by traveling minstrels, it came to be sung and danced the whole year through at fairs, on Saints' Days, at midnight vigils and Christmas-tide. The churchmen openly may have condemned it, but nevertheless, the rhythm of its meter found its way into their devotional verse. From the middle of the twelfth century one sees pictures of it from Spain to Norway. It was particularly popular in Sweden, where it is first mentioned in 1260 as having been performed at a princely wedding, and there is a fresco of it in the Danish Cathedral of Orselev from about the year 1380. Numerous young Danes who were studying at the University of Paris saw it in the square before the Church of Our-Lady-of-the-Carole, and joined the dancers. The dance itself was a kind of processional. The dancers turned from right to left, in marching steps, beating one foot against the other. The choral-leader, or first-dancer, sported a glove, a nosegay or a flowery chaplet, a cup or a May-branch (the Dionysian Thyrsos), or at night a torch, and led his company in a rapid advance. In Germany, the Minnesingers knew it as *Springtanz* or *Espringale,* and filled it with small leaps and hops. In a simple prelude the leader would invoke nature, and other carollers took up a refrain. Its poetry had the sweet clean atmosphere of espaliered arbors, fresh leaf-shoots and the budding year. The choruses were full of roulades and sounds made with the tongue and lips, a vocalized yodelling, or onomatopoetic imitation of instrumental accompaniment: bagpipe, flute, drum, rebec or psaltery. Giovanni Boccaccio, writing about 1350, relates how, on the very first day of that country house-party which was to be the scene of his *Decameron,* where a company of young people had gone to escape the plague:

Breakfast done, the tables were removed, and the Queen (or elected story-leader) bade fetch instruments of music; for all, ladies and young men alike, knew how to tread a measure, and some of them played and sang with great skill; so, at her command Dioneo, (that is, Boccaccio himself) having taken a lute, and Fiammetta a viol, they struck up a dance in sweet concert; and the servants being dismissed to their repast, the queen, attended by the other ladies and the two young men, led off a stately carole.

In the Town Hall at Siena, Pietro Lorenzetti pictures such a dance, of young girls clad in parti-colored, heraldic, embroidered robes, with ribbons in their hair, hands linked, and to the accompaniment of a singer who strikes a tambourine, they pass through a kind of London-Bridge. In a detail of Fra Angelico's 'Last Judgment' in the Florentine Monastery of Saint Mark, a heavenly carole is trod on holy ground studded with such starry blossoms as only this angelic master could conceive. Enchanted monks alternate with haloed beauties, lead off a winged saint who draws on a carolling candidate for eternal life. At the end of the chain an angel invites a blessed monk from whose tonsure gilt rays spike out, to join the celestial dance. Perhaps Angelico knew the recommendation of Saint Basil, who urged his faithful to practice dancing as much as possible upon earth, since it was the principal occupation of angels in heaven.

M. de Montaiglon, in his *Doctrinal des Filles,* urges the young ladies to step it modestly.

Fille, quant serez en *Karolle*	Lass, when you dance *Karolle,*
Dansez gentiment par mesure	Dance it neatly, measured tread
Car, quant fille se demesure	For, when lassie leaps too wild
Tel la voit la tient pour folle.	Such that see her hold her mad.

Before 1372 Geoffrey Chaucer had turned the *Roman de la Rose* into English verse. The original author was one Guillaume de Loris, writing about 1237, and in his dream Sir Mirth, Gladness, Courtesy, Cupid, Frankness, such qualities one after another are imagined in a fanciful garden of love, dancing the Carole.

> Then mightest thou caroles seen,
> And folk ther daunce and mery been,
> And make many a fair tourning
> Upon the grene gras springing.
> Ther mightest thou see these floutours, (*flautists*)
> Minstrales, and eek jogelours,
> That wel to singe did her peyne (*did carefully*)
> Somme songe songes of Loreyne.
> For in Loreyen his notes be
> Ful swetter than in this contree.
> Ther was many a timbestere (*female tambourine-player*)
> And saylours (*dancers who leap*): that I dar well sweare
> Couthe (*knew*) hir craft ful parfitly.
> The timbres (*tambourines*) up ful stilly (*skilfully*)
> They caste, and hente (*caught*) ful ofte

Upon a finger faire and softe,
That they ne fayled never-mo.
Ful fetis (*neat*) damiselles two,
Right yonge, and fulle of semlihede,
In Kirtles, and non other wede, (*dress*)
And faire tressed every tresse,
Had mirthe doon, for his noblesse,
Amidde the carole for to daunce;
But her-of lyth (*her litheness*) no remembraunce,
How that they daunced queyntly.
That oon wolde come al prively
Agayn that other: and whan they were
Togidre (*together*) almost, they threwe y-fare (*out*)
Hir mouthes so, that through hir play
It semed as they kiste alway;
To dauncen wel coude they the gyse; (*manner*)
What shulde I more to you devyse?
No bede (*offer*) I never thennes go,
Whyles that I saw hem daunce so.

Watching the progress of the carole, (which seems also to have elements of a French kissing-game perhaps from Lorraine) the poet is observed by Courtesy.

"What do ye there, beau Sire?" quod she
Come her, and if it lyke you
To dauncen, daunceth with us now."
And I, withoute tarying,
Wente into the caroling.

And so each dances, and in the simple, precise tapestry filled with clothes, qualities and manners of ideal lady and type cavalier one gets a very clear notion of a social dance, which was at the same time a processional display, a verdant pageant of mediæval dancers.

Parallel to May Day, the sign of spring's arrival, is another folk-custom known as 'The Carrying-out of Winter' or the 'Expulsion of Death.' Its forms are familiar to us. Often, on the fourth Sunday in Lent (in Germany, *Todten-Sonntag*), a straw doll is made, or a beech-bough or birch-twig puppet of rags or such. This is Winter-Death. He is treated with every expression of hatred and fear and a procession of the folk bear him well beyond the town limits where he is burned, or buried or drowned. Even today, we burn in effigy unpopular political figures. In Florence, the dummy of an old woman was hung on a ladder. In the middle of Lent there was a ceremony of sawing her through. Stuffings of nuts and dried fruit fell into the square where crowds scrambled for them. In South Germany there is a leafy fool, similar to the May-Day Jack-i'-the-green. As a 'wild man' he suffers a mock-death, and then another boy, dressed to parody the village doctor, pretending to bleed him brings him back to life. In French Dauphiné there was a variation on this death-and-survival game, when the leaf-lad lies dead on the ground, and is revived by a girl's kiss. There is a similar Russian custom. Recall the Sleeping Beauty in the Enchanted Wood, the subject of Marius Petipa's greatest ballet.

At this seasonal change there are many mock-battles, sometimes no more than a conversation between summer and winter, at others a rough football game, where the ball was once a head of winter-death or a slain enemy. Wandering mediæval minstrels were well known for their juggling tricks with swords, and we recall the mock-combat of the Spartan Pyrrhic and the Roman Troy-Game. In 1350, in Nuremberg, there was a folk-game using a Sword-Dance, and from that day onward it has, under numerous forms and mutations, constantly recurred at Shrovetide or Yule, and the revels at nuptials, royal entries, and births of kingly heirs.

There is a description of the 'figuir' (figure), of a Shetland Island sword dance, transcribed around 1788, but it unquestionably refers to a form which is ancient, typical of many others of a Nordic nature.

> The six stand in rank with their swords reclining on their shoulders. The Master (Saint George) dances, and then strikes the sword of James of Spain, who follows George, then dances, strikes the sword of Dennis, who follows behind James. In like manner the rest—the music playing—swords as before. After the six are brought out of rank, they and the Master form a circle, and hold the swords point and hilt. The circle is danced round twice. The whole, headed by the Master, pass under the swords held in a vaulted manner. They jump over the swords. This naturally places the swords across, which they disentangle by passing under their right sword. They take up the seven swords, and form a circle, in which they dance around, (and so on, until at the end,) after several other evolutions, they throw themselves into a circle, with their arms across the breast. They afterwards form such figures as to form a shield of their swords, and the shield (a star of David) is so compact that the Master and his knights dance alternately with this shield upon their heads. It is then laid down upon the floor. Each knight lays hold of their former points and hilts with their hands across, which disentangle by figuirs (figures) directly contrary to those that formed the shield. This finishes the ballet.

The Scotch sword-dance is usually a solo. The characteristic thing about its English variant is the presence of two buffoon-characters, mock-king and queen, which are also found in Italy, Germany and Bohemia. There is a fool, or Tommy, who sports a fox-skin and a fox-tail, and a Bessy, who is a man dressed as a girl. They are accompanied by a set of other *personae,* differing according to the country. There is a Yorkshire version which has Thomas, the clown-fool, his son Tom, a Captain Brown, Obadiah Trim, a tailor; a foppish Knight; Love-Ale, a vintner; and Bridget (Bessy), the clown's wife. At Christmas time the dancers come. The clown indicates a circle with his flat wooden sword, and calls on the others for little verses, which generally result in a quarrel where one of the grotesques is killed, in order to be revived. At the collection, the fool is bursar. Sometimes local celebrities are replaced by the seven champions of Christendom, St. George for England, St. James for Spain, St. Denys for France, St. David for Wales, St. Patrick for Ireland, St. Anthony for Italy and St. Andrew for Scotland. A dance from the Harz Mountains employs the five kinds of England, Saxony, Poland, Denmark and Moorland, Hans, a serving-boy, and one Schnortison, treasurer for the *quête*.

Similar to the sword-dance and far more famous is the Morris, whose chief badge is the bells on knees and ankles of its dancers. It is ancient and was frequently, but not always, performed at May games, being particularly popular in the sixteenth and seventeenth centuries, especially in the south of England.

The legendary source of the Morris, Morrice, Morrisk or Morisco traces its importation into England by John of Gaunt, who went on an embassy from Edward the Third to Moorish Spain, but very similar folk-plays were performed in Normandy and probably in England itself long before that. Nevertheless it is not until about the time of Henry the Seventh that records appear testifying to its popularity at parochial festivals. Early historians connect it not only to the Roman Floralia (purely a May festival), but to Provençal and Florentine *Magi* or May games.

The dancers, then, carry bells and often wave kerchiefs. Sometimes their faces are blackened, or among their number is one Blackamoor, his presence explaining perhaps the persistence of the name. But far more likely such sooty faces depend on a tradition even older than Moors in Granada, from that epoch when Saxon or Celtic tribesmen smeared their faces from the holy-ashes of a sacrificial fire. Later, May-Day would be the particular property of chimney-sweeps. Much further on, characters from the legend of Robin Hood, Maid Marian, Little John and Friar Tuck would be identified with the Morris, as well as a hobby-horse and a dragon, who would be killed by Saint George of Cappadocia or England, and restored to life by a Doctor. Maid Marian was sometimes Mother Eve, a shepherdess, or the Fool's wife. The Blackamoor would be Beelzebub or even Mahomet. With the arrival of these characters, their speeches and requests, the element of dancing retires into the background, and literary drama evolves.

Aside from its ethnic and ritual significance, the Morris was also interesting from a choreographic point of view, and is still widely performed in England and America by the good offices of Folk Dancing Societies, stemming from researches of the late Cecil Sharp. The figures are extremely ingenious and elaborate. There is little use of the whole body; the arms only wave handkerchiefs; a kind of jog-trot is always maintained, but the feet, jingling bells, carry the dancers in an orderly maze of complex steps, changing and replacing each other in delightful precision. Such a dance is naturally more fun to do than to watch, but the Morris would later become a spectacular court-dance during the renaissance, known in Italy as the *Matacino,* in France and England as *Danse des Bouffons* or Matachins. It would be performed theatrically in such Elizabethan dramas as 'The Two Noble Kinsmen,' where it was a reproduction of one of the anti-masques in Beaumont's 'Masque of the Inner Temple.'

A curious variation of the Morris was danced in 1599 by William Kemp, a famous comedian. He jogged with his bells, from London to Norwich, and in the broadside he issued after his marathon, a woodcut shows him in shirt, collar and hat, very like portraits of Shakespeare, in whose 'Romeo and Juliet' he achieved a great success as Peter, the lovable page. He is accompanied by a man with a drum and pipe. His apologia was as much "to refute the lying ballads put forth concerning this exploit, as to testify his gratitude for the favours he had received during his gambols." In Marston's play, 'The Scourge of Villanie,' Kemp's jig is referred to, neither as a song nor a ballad, but as a theatrical-dance:

> A hall! a hall!
> Roome for the spheres; the orbs celestial
> Will daunce Kempe's jigge!

Kemp said of himself that he "spent his life in mad jigges," and the music of his longest one, or, at least, a Morris bearing his name, exists.

The contribution made by the Church and by the folk, however indispensable as background and as source-material, is an indirect continuation of the tradition of theatrical dancing, and in a strict sense, secondary to the creations of individual professional dancers who, though dispersed as a class at the fall of Rome by ecclesiastical edict, nevertheless persisted as individual artists, in all corners of Europe. And, accidentally or consciously, these often forlorn and always insecure wanderers, would do much to create and develop not only a new poetic metric for a reborn narrative and dramatic literature, but a new musical style as well; and most important, for our purposes, they would lay foundations for our techniques of theatrical-dancing.

By the fourth century, there were rules that clergy officiating at weddings and christenings must, without fail, quit the room before actors came in. Such private engagements were about the only means of support for the outlawed *scenici.* Exiled from theaters, they were still popular at private dinner-parties, or rural festivals or merry-makings before taverns in city streets, or wherever they could attract the fragments of their old audience. Hardship and a new economic system in emergence changed the whole nature of their repertory and performance.

In particular, the *pantomimi* suffered. Their highly developed and subtle medium of expression, so dependent on all the ancient surroundings of stage and imperial society, however corrupt it may have become, was nevertheless a fine art. There was little place for it in Gothic civilization. Some of these dispossessed actor-dancers were perhaps the ancestors of the Italian *Mattacini,* buffoon-dancers of the early renaissance. The *mimi*, as such, had always a larger appeal to the mass-audience, though they were now reduced from their once exalted position, and competed for a pittance with acrobats, tight-rope walkers and down-at-the-heel gladiators, who, often as not, would turn into animal-trainers, making tame bears dance or dogs jig on their hind legs. They used their wits as best they could, even to the extent of learning flip-flops and cartwheels, and memorizing interminable narratives which so pleased the German and English barbarians.

> Nevertheless, in essentials they remained the same; still jesters and buffoons, still irrepressible, still obscene. In little companies of two or three, they padded the hoof along the roads, traveling from gathering to gathering, making their own welcome in castle or tavern, or if need were, sleeping in some grange or beneath a wayside in the white moonlight. They were, in fact, absorbed into that vast body of Nomad entertainers on whom so much of the gayety of the middle ages depended. They became *ioculatores, jougleurs,* minstrels.*

The land *par excellence* of the minstrel was Provence, that once rich Roman province which still boasts its circuses and theaters at Nîmes, Arles, Orange and Marseilles. Not only did it preserve valuable relics of Latin culture, but it was also a transfer station of Moorish civilizations both in Spanish Granada, the Mediterranean islands, and Saracen capitals as far East as Constantinople and even Bagdad and Persia.

Islamic gifts to the western mediæval science, astronomy, mathematics, and anatomy are more or less appreciated. They also had a somewhat more obscure effect on poetry, music, and, since most of Provençal songs were to be danced, upon dancing. The successive crusades precipitated an exchange of influences between Orient and Occident, but even aside from the crusades, there were peaceful infiltrations of minstrelsy from beyond the Pyrenees, along the adjoining sea-coast. The Moors not only prized singing and instrumental music in the peace of the harem, but also as an epic reminder and incitement to bravery in battle. Nevertheless, the transcriber of the Koran, we may be surprised to discover, considered music much as did Saint Augustine. The prophet insisted that it must be kept in check. "Your prayers," he told the faithful at Mecca, "will end only in piping or hand-clapping if music forms a part of them." From a similar attitude the Islamic plastic arts do not portray human-figures but only foliage, or infrequently, animal-life. "Music and singing," said Mahomet, "cause hypocrisy to grow in the heart, as water makes the corn grow." There was no music in mosques, no bells tolled in minarets; the Muezzin called with his own far-carrying voice, the hours of prayer. Banished from natural alliance with religion, the Mohammedans enjoyed music as an illicit indulgence, like wine, which they were also forbidden. They developed a number of virtuoso instruments, the most popular of which was the lute, in its many forms. An Arabian grammarian wrote:

* Sir E. K. Chambers—*The Medieval Stage:* Vol. I, p. 25.

In the days of ignorance, before Mahomet came, shepherds watching sheep in the desert were wont to while away the night by answering one another on their flutes, with which they poured out alternate melodies, one flute responding to the other.

And later, though still before the Hejira, two flutes were displaced by two singing voices, which answered each other singing questions and answers of a poem. We have already seen how parallelism, the statement and response of the Hymn of David which demanded who is the King of Glory?, had in it a germ of dance-drama. Similarly, Moors in Spain had a form of minstrelsy which was a dialogue, a *contention,* of two points of view or of two testimonies to some fact, dealing generally with love. Both the poems of Theocritus and the Eclogues of Virgil employed conversations between spring and winter. In Provence there was the *Tenzon,* a kind of verbal tournament which turned into rhetorical exercises, not into drama, but was at least an element of the atmosphere from which other dance-songs emerged.

Provence with its intense, shifting *mistral* currents, its craggy towering volcanic rocks, perfect for a castle perch, has a curious position not only geographically but also historically and socially, as well. The extraordinary energy of its creative period, the curiously sensitive intense though minor quality of its verse, much of which seems so attractive to contemporary readers, the elaboration of its manners and ideas and the sudden terrible collapse of its civilization, is a puzzling and absorbing problem. Favored by mild weather, small isolated communities gathered around over-lords. Gothic invasions had ceased. Aside from incidental feudal robbery, there was, after a long nightmare of barbarian chaos, comparative security. But no urban society, and what must have been a really oppressive boredom, was relieved by the welcome amusements of wandering minstrels. It is perhaps hard for us to realize, with the immediate accessibility of all forms of entertainment, what it would be like for a whole world to have nothing really resembling it for five hundred years. Suddenly, after the year 1033, when the Millennium, after Christ's birth and death had passed and earth was still whole underfoot without Doomsday's arrival, there was leisure for something other than starving, fighting, escaping, or, for the luckier ones, securing a thin existence.

The entertainers were as frequently castle lords and ladies as wandering artists. There is some misunderstanding in their terminology; if we define the words, the categories will be clear. The Latin word *minister* means 'inferior,' hence personal attendant. The *ministeriales* of the late Empire were personal appointees of Emperors. By the end of the thirteenth century, the diminutive *ministrallus* or French *menestral* achieves a special sense of household *ioculator.* An *ioculator* could be both a *mime* (Roman actor) or *scôp* (Germanic folk-singer). *Ioculator* becomes the French *jongleur,* and *ioca* is *jeu* (game), the same as Latin *Ludus.* In Provençal there is the *joglar* which Chaucer knew as *jogelour* and we, as 'juggler.' By 1273, the last of the troubadours, Guiraut de Riquier of Narbonne, found it necessary in a verse letter to Alfonso the

Learnéd of Castile, to clear up all confusions by which poets, singers and every sort of entertainer were indiscriminately lumped together. Most important are *doctors de trobar* (French *trouver,* to find or invent), or *trobaires,* the (usually) noble composers of verse and music; the troubadours themselves. The *joglars* were, properly speaking, their instrumentalists, their accompanists or executants. Lowest of all were *bufos,* entertainers of the lower-classes, who could not be considered as *joglars* at all. The Provençal *trobaire* would become French and Norman-English *trouvère.*

Troubadours were aristocratic composers, travelling in considerable style from castle to castle, often with a whole train of *joglars* and serving-men; in such style on occasion, that the only way they could recoup their bankrupt coffers was to enlist in a crusade. The troubadour was expected to arrange fêtes at castles he visited, and they regarded him as an arbiter of taste in the vicinity. Some troubadours, because of their expenses, even sank into the class of *joglar.*

Although it is an entirely different time and society, we can perhaps understand more clearly the importance of Provençal dance-song, if we remember without a strict comparison, the dithyrambic contest, that gave rise to much of the formal structure of Greek tragedy. Both in Provençe and Attica there is an atmosphere of greening seasons, a vocal and physical expression of spring-freshets and the way men feel in April and May. The Dithyramb was the hymn of the springtide of antique culture. The *Mairoles* or May songs of the troubadours announced a renewal of that culture, heralding an imminent renaissance, the fabric of modern civilization.

The *chansons de danse,* or dancing songs, were written for a Provençal stringed instrument known as *viele,* a type of viol as an accompaniment to the *estampie.* The name of the dance comes from the participle of the *estamper,* to strike or stamp the foot. Old German is *stamfon;* modern: *stampfen.* The chief characteristic of this dance seems to have been an accentual tap on every third beat. The troubadour, Rambaut de Vaqueiras, wrote a famous *estampida* which was sung to strings, called *Kalenda Maia,* or First of May.

> Neither May dawn, nor beech-bud, nor bird-song, nor gladioli, can touch my heart, fair one, till I spy your quick messenger arrive, bringing love's comfort from you to me, till I am at your feet, till I can see my jealous foe struck by the lightning of your wrath.

Here, as in early Greece, music, poetry and dance united, and here also a protagonist is introduced, the principal singer, either gentleman or lady, and his chorus. This convention necessitated a definite allocation of the various musical parts. The importance of solos over their choral background naturally led to mimed or danced scenes called *baleries.* The English word 'ballad,' in its earliest sense can be taken as close to this. Solomon's 'Songs of Songs' which is a dramatic lyric, was known as the 'Ballad of Ballads.' There were *rondeau,* round-dances, similar to those used for May-poles, and combinations of all the various forms. There is, for example, *Bele Ælis,* a great favorite in the thirteenth century, which is indeed a little opera-ballet, with choruses like rubrics indicating the action.

Chorus: *By morn arose fair-shaped Ælis*

She: Know you what says Nightingale?
He says love dies of lovers false.

Chorus: *Nightingale says true.*
But I tell you he is mad
Who wants to part from love....

She: And since I have good love
I'll gather violets
Under green bough.
Who loves for sake of love
Must gather violets.

Chorus: *Fair is her adorning, fairer still her robing*

He: You heard the Nightingale aright:
Who loves not true, betrays true love.

Chorus: *Cursed be the betrayer,*
He who feels its pain
Is well rewarded by it....

He: And since I've loved aright
I have my lady own;
Fair and most fair....

Chorus: *She took water in a golden jug*

She: Nightingale tells us in his tongue
Lover, love; joy through your days....

Chorus: *She bathed her mouth and eyes and face ...*

He: Well was he born who is a loyal friend
Nightingale promises paradise to him.

And at its end the two dancers sing, together with the chorus. These aristocratic pastimes seem more like children's games to us. Their innocence is less simple when we recall Cabestanh, whose heart was served up to his lady in a dish, or mad Piere Vidal, whose passion for his lady was such that he literally took her name, Louve (*lupa*), clothing himself in a wolf's pelt to be worried by hounds in a hunt.

There was also the *reverdie,* a special spring-dance song appropriate to May Day; the *pastourelles* or 'songs of the shepherdess; the *alba* or dawn-songs, a beautifully conventionalized love lyric which cursed dawn which came so soon to part the lovers.

Yet Provence was not to have a great dance-drama; indeed Provence was to have no theater at all, though long after she had been absorbed into united

France her melodies and metric provided measures, under very different names, for later dances.

But the Middle Ages had other entertainers beside the troubadours. In Rome we recall the Saturnalia, when on New Year's Day all class distinctions were dropped, while master and slave danced and drank at a common feast. Similarly, with Christians on the day of Circumcision, the eighth after Christ's birth, symbol of his first blood shed, there were extraordinary demonstrations in cathedrals.

> Priests and clerks may be seen wearing masks and monstrous visages at the hours of office. They dance in the choir dressed as women, panders or minstrels. They sing wanton songs. They eat black puddings at the hour of the altar while the celebrant is saying mass. They play at dice there. They cense with stinking smoke from the soles of old shoes. They run and leap through the church, without a blush at their own shame. Finally they drive about the town and its theaters in shabby traps and carts; and rouse the laughter of their fellows and the bystanders in infamous performances, with indecent gestures and verses scurrilous and unchaste.

Thus, in 1445, Eustache de Menil, dean of the faculty of theology at the University of Paris, addressed the bishops and chapters of France on the abuses of the *Fête des Fous*. He denies that such games are relics of antiquity. They are devices of the Devil, the toils of original sin. But the Feast of Fools at Rheims, in 1490, was occasion for a satirical onslaught by vicars and choir-boys on the fashion of hoods worn by the *bourgeoises*. This led to anti-ecclesiastical reprisals. In a sense, the Feast of Fools was a safety-valve by which once a year people felt free of the sacred system, and in unrepressed and sacrilegious parody, exhausted themselves of stored-up boredom and rancor against the liturgy, its class of celebrants and everything for which it stood. It was a rare holiday for the lay clergy against their superiors, and was paid for by levies on its watchers. In our news-reels we constantly see newsboys, caddies or Wall Street runners who are made Mayors for a day as sheepish symbols of equality. At the Feast of the Ass, a live donkey or a priest disguised as one, or a man on a hobby-horse (as in the Morris-Dance) was dressed in vestments and put through a mock Mass.

The mediæval Fool, in parti-colored red and yellow clothes, his ass-ear hood, cox-combed wattles (perhaps relics of ancient animal-sacrifice), his bells and bladder-bauble, symbol of the world's folly, is that jester, tolerated in noble homes no matter how cruel his jokes, how biting his remarks about his keepers. Sometimes he hid under the protection of insanity. The Middle Ages, like many savage tribes today, thought madness holy. Sometimes a madman would be dwarfed or hunchbacked, and the little monsters gave illusions of mercy and tolerance to brutal or infantile masters. The dancing-Fool and Death, the Dancer are not far apart. The idea that the whole topsy-turvy world was mad; that no one, no matter how rich or wise was wholly sane has parallels in the cheery concept of the tomb's ultimate equality.

The Church, naturally, held an unfriendly attitude towards fools and minstrels. Its canon law wrote strict ordinances against them, though in actual practice the law was seldom enforced. They enjoyed enormous popularity among courtiers, town merchants and peasantry, but their hard life was scarcely relieved by a promise of eternal damnation assured by the church to all of their profession. Nevertheless, infrequently, to be sure, minstrels had not only friends at court, but at church as well. One of the most superb of all mediæval characters, Francis of Assisi, who in his youth had known troubadour life to his fill, called his order of Minorites, *Ioculatores Domini,* Minstrels of our Master. Religious words would be more and more set to their secular, popular tunes.

During the reigns of the Angevin and Plantagenet Kings the minstrels were ubiquitous. They wandered at their will from castle to castle, and in time from borough to borough, sure of their ready welcome alike in the village tavern, the guildhall, and the Baron's keep. They sang and jested in the market-places, stopping cunningly at a critical moment in the performance, to gather their harvest of small coins from the bystanders. In the great castles, while lords and ladies supped or sat around the fire, it was theirs to while away many a long bookless evening with courtly *geste* or witty sally. At wedding or betrothal, baptism or knight dubbing, treaty or tournament, their presence was indispensable. The greater festivities saw them literally in their hundreds, and rich was their reward in money and in jewels, in costly garments, and in broad acres. They were licensed vagabonds, with free right of entry into the presence-chambers of the land. You might know them from afar by their coats of many colors, gaudier than any knight might respectably wear, by the instruments upon their backs and those of their servants, and by the shaven faces, close-clipped hair and flat shoes proper to their profession. This hen-speckle appearance, together with the privilege of easy access, made the minstrel's dress a favorite disguise in ages when disguise was often imperative.*

The earliest English poem is 'Widsith,' the far-traveler. Though amplified and edited by Christian Englishmen, it is in essence a heathen narrative, the autobiographical epic of a wandering *gleóman,* dating from around 400 A. D. The gleemen, scalds or *scóps,* were bards and harpers, common to most Nordic communities.

The Saxon words for dance were *hoppan, saltian* or *stellan,* to leap; and *tombian* or *tomban,* in an acrobatic connotation. Piers Plowman could "neither saylen ne saute" (French: *sauter:* leap). In Ardgar's oration to Dunstan, the minstrels are said 'to fling and dance.' There is preserved an odd tale of Gaimar, how in 978, King Edward was murdered by his stepmother. She paid a dancing dwarf to lure the young King alone to her chamber, and he, fascinated by the dancer's tricks, fell into her trap. The gleómen themselves were not dancers, but their heirs were.

Disguised as a harper, Alfred the Great is supposed to have eluded the

* E. K. Chamber: *The Medieval Stage,* Vol. I, p. 44.

Danish invaders. The specifically Anglo-Saxon gleómen disappear after the Conquest, but they do not cease to sing. They hide, and from secret coverts, in field and fen, are ralliers of nationalist sentiment, English chanters of the songs of Hereward the Wake against the Norman French, in whose train the trouvères are coming to displace them. Three hundred years later, these native minstrels will do much to establish the supremacy of the English language. But the Norman trouvère were really the conquerors, and they brought to Britain all the diverse traditions of Italy, Provence and Moorish Spain. The minstrel of the Digby manuscript, (*Les Deux Menèstriers*) in the Bodleian Library at Oxford boasts:

> I can play the lute, the violin, the pipe, the bagpipe, the syrinx, the harp, the gigue, the gittern, the symphony, the psaltery, the organistrum, the regals, the tabor and the rote. I can sing a song well, and make tales and fables. I can tell a story against any man. I can make love verses to please young ladies, and can play the gallant for them if necessary. Then I can throw knives into the air, and catch them without cutting my fingers. I can do dodges with string, most extraordinary and amusing. I can balance chairs and make tables dance. I can throw a somersault, and walk on my head.

There is a tenth century Saxon codex which shows one gleeman juggling three balls and three knives to the music of a viol. Taillefer, the minstrel of William the Conqueror's army, amazed the English at Senlac. He begged leave to strike the first Norman blow; his request granted, he dashed in front of his host, hurled a lance three times in the air, caught it by the handle; did the same with a sword, singing the while a *geste* of Charles the Great, Roland, Oliver and the vassals who died at Roncevals. Later minstrels were not only masters of sleight-of-hand, of music and verse, but dancing masters as well.

> I remember to have seen Martin Baraton, an aged minstrel of Orleans, who was accustomed to play upon the tambourine at weddings, and on other occasions of festivity. His instrument was silver, decorated with small plates of the same metal, on which were engraved the arms of those he had taught to dance.*

There was also a type of minstrel known as *tregetour*, (sometimes *prestigiatore*) or conjuror. His tricks were deemed possible only on account of an understanding between *tregetour* and the Foul Fiend. With the aid of rude glass lenses and a candle they could construct a simple magic lantern. Chaucer in his Frankeleyn's Tale, describes one making wild deer appear; falconers on a river bank displayed their hawks pursuing and slaying herons, and knights jousted on a plain.

> Tho (*then*) saugh he knightes justing in a playn;
> And after this, he did him swich plesaunce,
> That he him shewed his lady on a daunce

*Fauchet: *Origine de la Langue et Poesie Francoise:* 1-7-72.

> On-which him-self he daunced, as him thoughte.
> And when this maister, that this magik wroughte,
> Saugh it was time, he clapte his handes two,
> And farewel! al our revel was ago.

The *tregetour* was popular enough to warrant him a place in a Dance of Death. In a poem written about 1430, John Lydgate, a famous organizer of mummery, places an actual person in his *Daunce de Macabre*.†

> Maister John Rykell, sometime tregitoure
> Of noble Henry Kynge of Englande,
> And of Fraunce the myghty conqueroure,
> For all the sleightes and turnings of thyne honde,
> Thou must come nere this daunce to understonde.

And the mortal minstrel is forced to confess "Lygarde de Mayne (ledger-demain) now helpeth me right nought."

Women dancers or glee-maidens were also tumblers, tomblesteres or tombesteres, from Saxon, *tomban*. Salomé is frequently shown on her hands, her seven veils reduced to a single flying night-dress; "When the daughter of Herodyas was in comyn, and had tomblyde and pleside Harowde." A pious French writer of the thirteenth century attributes John Baptist's death to the "well-skilled tumbling and cheating tricks" of that dancing-girl. There were dances involving a blindfolded man who would pass back and forth between eggs laid on the ground, without breaking them. This was alternated with a sword-dance where knives, their handles stuck in earth, blades up, were missed by nimble feet. There were also slack-rope walking and dancing, and dancers used stilts as well. There is hardly a one of these semi-acrobatic dances which did not have an antique precedent. Remember the tumblers and the accompanying bard in the Iliad; even to stilt-dancers who in Greece wore pink skin-tights, and were called *gypones*. There was considerable skill at the command of the minstrel-dancer, of a somewhat grotesque sort to be sure, but nevertheless of a definitely spectacular and theatrical nature.

> A party of gleemen and glee-maidens came to the village, leading a pair of dancing bears with them. As soon as the gleemen touched the strings, the bears reared themselves up to dance, and marked the time with their feet, springing very high at times, and often feinting to come to blows with one another, and doing other antics while the music lasted. Then the bears would dance with the glee-maidens, who sang the song of the dance with most melodious voices; and the bears would dance with them, putting their great paws in their pretty hands, and footing step by step and quite correctly the measure of the dance, growling contentedly the while.*

* A Latin verse quoted in J. F. Rowbotham's *Troubadours and Courts of Love.*
† Harleian MS. 116.

CHAPTER VII

Feudal Pageantry and Danced Disguisings

THOUGH the Church bore little love for the theater, and none for dancing, nevertheless a lovable theater had grown from under cathedral shadows, and dances were a part of it, nourished more from dramatic expression in folk-games, peasant dances, and Provençal music than from liturgy. Though we may have been able to discover many individual elements in mediæval dancing which are still useful to us, they have been only as a distinct, separate source. There is a complex tradition present, but no form which combines to frame it and transform it into a shape in which we can recognize dance-drama or ballet. After all is said, the Mass *is* the great medieval dramatic work, and the semi-religious theater of the people, putting religious features to its uses, borrowing and embroidering on May-games and fertility rites, would never evolve one work which can still be performed with anything but antiquarian pleasure. But in the end of the Middle Ages, wholly outside the Church, there were forms which would be far more influential on subsequent developments in the dance than Mass or miracle play. These were ceremonials inherent in the structure of feudalism itself.

Feudalism was a fighting organism. In all tribal communities, coming-of-age ceremonies, marking the arrival of a young man's strength to aid his tribe, were elaborate and important. Feudalism built up a remarkable body of visible formulæ relating to the facts of knighthood and the philosophy of chivalry. The eighth century wars against the Saracen demonstrated the need for a large, mobile body of horse troops. The badge of a member of the military class was a strong war-horse, *cavallus* or *cheval:* hence chevalier and chivalry. By the twelfth century, knighthood was an order, in general the property of the nobility, but nevertheless an order into which no one, be he prince, count or petty baron, could be born. He must be admitted into it, after training and careful preparation. The ceremonies of investiture, of 'dubbing' (*adoubement*) in their elaboration took on religious and dedicatory significance. In these ceremonies, costume, color, music, even dancing had their place.

The colleges for admittance into chivalry were in the everyday atmosphere of any feudal castle or court. A well-born child, from constant attendance on his elders, would absorb from boyhood into adolescence an orderly education in moral and physical discipline which would prepare him to be a knight, passing from one grade of servitude up into another, until ultimately he could bear his own sword. As a page, he entered service at about the age of eight, acting as constant personal aide both of his master and his mistress. He waited at table, held spare dogs or hawks for the hunt, amused his lady in her garden, cared for his lord in camp. Merely by constant association with the castle personnel, monks, serving-women, squires and serfs, he picked up a rugged education in religion, the arts and crafts of love, war, the chase and even perhaps a little book-reading, or the playing of a stringed instrument. When he was past fifteen he became automatically a squire, though there were only minor differences in his manner of living. Perhaps now he not only waited at table, but carved and served the dishes. He helped to clear the great hall for dancing or minstrelsy, and joined in the entertainment as well. He spent more and more time at athletic sport and military exercise. He swam, ran, leaped, learned to bear the weight of armor standing and riding, tilted at the quintain and used the broadsword. Soon he became a shield-bearer, an actual aide-de-camp, helping his lord to horse, succoring him if unhorsed, guarding his pennon in tournament and battle, and practically, by deeds, inuring himself to the hard life he would ultimately follow. Finally the time came for his actual admittance into the order of Knighthood. Sometimes, as a conspicuous mark of trust or merit, he would be dubbed on the battlefield, before or after the fight. His lord or general, uttering a formula of initiation, struck him, kneeling, three times with the flat of his sword and bade him rise. But at home, under less pressing conditions, the rites were less simple.

Although in Feudal Europe the ceremony was surrounded by a deliberate and sophisticated gravity, consciously elaborated from generations of accreted form and symbolism, there is no part of the induction which differs largely from initiation ceremonies of native Africans, Australians or American Indians of our North and Southwest.

On the evening before the rite itself, the candidate submitted himself to the care of two esquires. These might be friends of an older age or his affectionate teachers in this post of honor, not unlike the best man at a wedding. Under the direction of these two guards a barber-surgeon shaved the youth, and clipped his hair. Then they led him to his room where a bath had been prepared, hung with linens and tapestry, during which he was formally advised as to the precepts of the chivalric order. Then they poured some of the bath-water over his shoulders, signed his left shoulder with the cross, and retired. He was then escorted from his bath to a barely set-out bed, where he stayed till he was dry, whereupon he was clad in a white shirt and a coarse russet monkish habit. Then his two elder preceptors returned and led him to the chapel, the younger esquires, not yet his age, going before them. In the chapel he was left alone to pray the whole night through, with perhaps a very few companions to watch his arms at the altar. He commended himself to God, the Blessed Virgin, and his own lady, hoping he might become a true knight. At dawn the chaplain confessed him, and he went to Mass, offering a taper and a coin stuck to it,—the candle to the glory of God, the money to him who should make him knight. After this he went back to bed where he stayed, until roused by friends and minstrels. They dressed him in special clothes, and then mounted horses to ride to the ceremonial hall. His future squire rode bareheaded before him, bearing his sword by its point, in its scabbard; his spurs hanging from its hilt. When everything was ready and all the people gathered together, the prince or lord who was to bestow knighthood, came into the hall. He heard the candidacy proposed, had the lad's spurs strapped on by his groomsman, fixed the sword himself and then, the boy kneeling, struck him on the neck or back, saying, "Be thou a good knight." Rising, he kissed him and every one went into the chapel to the sound of music, where the new chevalier dedicated his ungirded sword to the church. As he came out into the sunlight, the master-cook was waiting with a carving knife, and claimed the gilt spurs as his fee. He said to the young man who once had pilfered his pantry: "If you do aught against your vows, I'll hack the spurs from your heels."

The actual girding of the sword, the gift of the defensive and offensive weapon, was the climax of the rite, and the blow was the formal finish. At first we find in the twelfth century the blow as a resounding fisty thwack on the bare neck, which must be borne unflinchingly, a blow symbolically received and *not* returned. By the time of Elizabeth, the accolade was but a bare tap on the velvet shoulder.

Dancing was a part of the chivalric amenities. Dancing in pairs was not widely popular, however, until about the beginning of the fifteenth century. The earlier dances were round, with perhaps one knight leading a lady in either hand, and stepping around the room in measures not unlike the polonaise, with an alternate marked beat, to their own vocal or stringed accompaniment.

The posturing must have been extremely gradual and gentle, for Heinrich der Teichner, who died in 1375, says that during some dances it was possible to balance a full glass of wine on the head and not spill a drop. Two centuries later, Montaigne, who arranged a ball in the Italian town of Lucca, offered prizes for dancing to both the ladies and to their partners. He writes that there was a lady who danced with a full bowl of water on her head, and did not spill a drop. Such tricks are known, merely from daily work-habits among contemporary Egyptians, Moroccans and other Africans. But as court dance, the lady must have had practice, and had watched the peasants balance oil-jars on their heads.

There were boisterous dances as well where the dancers even limped in time, as well as hopped and skipped. In the *Hoppelvogel*, bird-hops, the *Firlefanz*, fiddle-faddle, and *Krummen Reihen* (crooked rows), the German ladies shrieked, while their cavaliers yelled back. There were also such panto-mimic dances as described in the *Ruodlieb* of the first half of the eleventh century, when a young man parodied the flight of a falcon, his lady the pursued swallow. Early German Gothic dancing was habitually performed in rows or circles. When the personal physical contact of dancing in pairs came in, there was the same sort of scandal which rocked Europe at the entrance of the waltz six hundred years later. The town council of Ulm at once prohibited the public performance of paired dances. Then the noblemen in the free cities of the Holy Roman Empire, built themselves private ballrooms. The first of which we have record is Frankfort-am-Main in 1350. The knight, Leo von

Rozmital, was asked to a great party by the nuns of the towns of Neuss. "They knew all the best dances," he wrote, "and I may say that I have never seen so many beautiful women in a convent."

In the famous *Mittleälterliche Hausbuch,* an enchanting folio of pen-drawings of German medieval social life, made around 1480, the fifth planet Venus exercises a benign influence on children born under her. Verses say, They shall be cheerful here on earth, sometimes rich and sometimes poor, dancing, kissing, roving,—they have fair bodies and pretty mouths: *Tanczen, helfen Kussen und Rawmen, ir leip ist schon, ein hubschen munt.*

In passing we might consider another holy German lady who danced. She was a mystic sister, Mechtild of Magdeburg. She died in a Cistercian cloister in 1277, leaving records of her experience of divine love, called 'The Flowing Light of God.' In it, the Soul, clad in a shift of humility, covers it with the white robe of chastity and repairs to the forest. Here nightingales chant oneness with God. She tries to follow in a holy *dance,* or less symbolically, she strives to *imitate* the deeds of the prophets, the Virgin's chaste meekness, the virtues of Christ, and His pious Saints. Then the Youth comes, saying: "Maiden, thou hast danced holily, even as my Saints."

> *Soul:* I cannot dance unless thou leadest. If thou wouldst have me spring aloft, sing thou: and I will spring,—into love, and from love to knowledge, and from knowledge to ecstasy, above all human sense.
>
> *Youth:* Maiden, thy dance of praise is well performed. Since now thou art tired, thou shalt have thy will with the Virgin's Son. Come to the brown shades at Midday, to the couch of love, and there shalt thou cool thyself with him.
>
> *Soul:* (to her guardians, the senses): I am tired with the dance; leave me, for I must go where I may cool myself.

A popular function intimately connected with chivalry, and which will ordain much of the form of entry in the French Renaissance *ballet de cour,* is the *tournament.* This form of elaborate mock-combat derived its name, many of its participants thought, from the *Ludus Troiæ,* the Troy-game, which we knew in Rome as an equestrian Pyrrhic. The derivation is probably false. More likely it comes simply from the French *tourner,* referring either to the rapid turning of the horses, or the turning of the quintain-dummy, a practice exercise. At first perhaps a real trial of arms, to the very death, the tournament developed through various stages into a ritualized show of competitive skill, until by the middle of the fifteenth century its chief attraction was luxurious pageantry. Tournaments are supposed to have been held in the eastern Roman Empire, under the Emperor Emanuel Comminus at the siege of Constantinople; under the first German Henry, who died in 936; in Norman France before the conquest of England.

These dangerous games, in time, forced the codification of certain laws to prevent unnecessary injury to knights-at-arms, as well as to crowds of people who thronged the jousting-places. Around 1292, a 'Statute of Arms for

Tournaments,' decided "At the request of the earls and barons and of the knighthood of England," that pointed swords, sharp daggers, clubs and studded maces were prohibited. Only delegated squires, bearing their lord's arms were to raise up an unhorsed knight. Any non-delegated squire who performed this act was to lose his arms and horse and be jailed for three years. Disputes were to be settled by a court of honor, with a jury of earls and princes.

> Oyez; Oyez (*ouir:* hear). Be it known, lords, knights and esquires, Ladies and Gentlewomen; you are hereby acquainted, that a superb achievement at arms, and a grand and noble tournament will be held in the parade of Norrais, King at Arms.*

Thus runs a formula for announcement, and here are the regulations:

> The two barons on whose parts the tournament is undertaken, shall be at their pavilions two days before the commencement of the sports, when each of them shall cause his arms to be attached to his pavilion, and set up his banner in the front of his parade; and all those who wish to be admitted as combatants on either side, must in like manner set up their arms and banners before the parades allotted to them. Upon the evening of the same day they shall show themselves in their stations, and expose their helmets to view of the windows of their pavilions; and then 'they may depart to make merry, dance and live well.' On the morrow the champions shall be at their parades by the hour of ten in the morning, to await the commands of the lord of the parade, and the governor, who are the speakers of the tournament; at this meeting the prizes of honor shall be determined. †

The King-at-Arms, or the umpire, stands in the middle of the field. The minstrels, or heralds of the two contenders, emblazoned with their masters' coats-of-arms, sound an overture. In Greece, there were sacred heralds for the Eleusinian mysteries, and trumpeters at the public games who announced names of competitors and victors, as well as heralds at law-courts and in the theaters. After the shock of arms, the cheering, the bearing-away and the proclamation of the victor, there was banqueting, and afterwards, dancing.

The elaborate courtesies paid to women at the tournaments by the respective opponents, scarves tied around armored elbows, the roses in helmet visors are well known. The adoration of women in the Middle Ages, starting simply enough in the mutual attraction of the sexes, underwent a fantastic and mystical progress. In Provence originated a sort of amorous tournament, the Court of Love, which spread in various forms up into the North, particularly into Burgundy. In one sense, the Courts of Love were an amplification of the poetic form of the *tenzon,* that embryonic opera-drama-dance, shared alike by Hebrews, Arabs and Troubadours. Guillaume de Poitiers said, "If you propose to me a game of love, I am not so foolish but that I shall choose

* Harleian MS. No. 69.
† *The Sports and Pastimes of the People of England,* by Joseph Strutt, p. 207.

the best side of the trial," and in a contention between two troubadours Giraut says: "I shall conquer you, provided that the *Court* is loyal and honest. I send my tenzon to Pierrefeu, where the beautiful lady holds a court of information." And Peyronet replies, "I choose as my court of judgment the honorable castle of Signe."

The Courts of Love arbitrated over various highly dialectical arguments on the nature of passion, deciding between competing troubadours whether to champion an individual lady, all the ladies of a district or merely an abstract debatable question. The judges were noble dames, wives or widows of feudal lords, who were accustomed to the neat points involved by long familiarity with troubadour verse. There were some thirty-one absolute laws in the code of Love which constituted a basis of reference for decision; as example:

1. Marriage (alone) cannot be pleaded as an excuse for refusing to love.
2. No one can really love two people at the same time.
7. If one of two lovers dies, love must be foresworn for two years by the survivor, and
31. Nothing prevents one lady being loved by two gentlemen, or one gentleman by two ladies.

On the 29th of April, 1174, the Countess of Champagne presided over a Court of Love on the following case: "Can real love exist between married people?" It was decided that it could not. At the end of a sitting of the court the winning poet was crowned and the day's sport ended in a banquet and ball. Just as in the more sanguinary tourneys, gradually the interest centered more and more on the spectacle, less and less on the bloodshed, so we shall find the form and debates of the Courts of Love reappearing in the libretti of Italian and French opera and ballet, and in English pageants and masques.

The Court of Love, like the Dance of Death, seems to have been the source of far more literary and pictorial works than in actual observances indicated by their titles. The original, of which the 'Romaunt of the Rose' is a translation by Chaucer, is a case in point. Nevertheless, in both cases, the literature reflects on an independent actuality. Fantasy alone prompted neither. An antique French poem, mentioned by W. A. Neilson,* includes a very vivid description of allegorical action within an architectural frame, so clear in fact that it could be transferred to tapestry or ballroom merely with the aid of weavers, musicians or dancers.

In *Florence et Blancheflor* or *Le Jugement d'Amour,* a fantastic dwelling is indicated, even more fanciful than Ovid's palace of Apollo. The Latin poet was extremely influential through all these manifestations.

The walls are not of stone, but of roses and other flowers, and the grounds are fenced in with Cupid's bows. No 'vilain' can pass the gates: all must bear the seal of love. On arriving, the damsels dismount under a pine, and two

* *The Origins and Sources of the Court of Love:* 36.

birds come down from the trees and lead them to the palace. When the God of Love sees them he leaps from his bed, salutes them courteously, and, taking them by the hand, seats them beside himself and asks their needs. Blancheflor states the case, and the King (he was a god a moment before) assembles his barons to decide the question. When the court, which consists of birds (cf. Aristophanes), has assembled, the King lays the question before them. The side of the knight is taken by Sire Esperviers, Sire Faucons, and the Gais (Jay); that of the clerk, by Dame Kalandre, Dame Aloe, and the Rossignox. The jay thinks the clerk's business is to pray for souls, and the knight's to love ladies. The nightingale offers to fight in support of the clerk's claim, and the parrot accepts the challenge. After a fight in which the armor consists of rose-petal helmets and the like, the nightingale wins, and the parrot yields up his sword, confessing that the clerk is valiant, and more courteous than any other.

However, the influence of the literary Courts of Love did create a type of entertainment leading towards dance-drama. In 1474, King René of Anjou instituted the *Jeux de la Fête-Dieu* at Aix in Provence, to replace the extreme licentiousness of the Feast of Fools, which he had been forced to suppress, a kind of ambulant spectacle. On the Monday of Pentecost, the people met after Mass to elect a *Prince d'Amour,* an *Abbé de la Jeunesse,* and a *Roi de la Bazoche.* The games themselves were farces taken from scripture: 'The great game of Devil's, in which red and black demons baited Herod, the visit of Sheba to Solomon, and so on; but it is important for us to understand here, that however much these might seem to be like the earlier plays, there was no dialogue, only dumb-show, pantomiming and dancing.

The tournament was really a public spectacle and became a show of very definitely conscious and contrived character, to impress the people, or display the wealth of their lords. The pageant, although similar, only occasionally or incidentally involved the element of a dramatized contest.

Pageant is connected with the Latin *pango,* and signified something compacted together, or else from *pagina,* a plank, applied to wood-staging in the early miracle plays. In our time it has taken on a rather special use, limited to narrative spectacles arranged for special historic commemoration. But there is a contemporary survival very much like the medieval pageant. In various American cities on New Year's Day, on Thanksgiving Day, or in the South, where Catholic traditions are strong, in Lent, there are great parades with decorated cars, or floats, sometimes in a related series, sometimes merely independent advertisements for various commercial houses. In the French and English miracle plays, the small individual stationary settings for Herod's house or the gates of Hell were sometimes known as 'pageants.' With the rise of trade guilds, the various artisans and tradesman's companies contrived representations, like allegorical plays. But instead of being set in one place, to be seen one after the other, the living-pictures were put on wagons, and to the accompaniment of dancers, singers, and costumed drovers, were dragged through towns. All the influences from church symbolism, folk-beliefs, spectacular tournaments and the individual devices of minstrel and juggler were present in these ambulant spectacles. The pageant cars themselves were elaborate affairs, battlemented perhaps, with towers teeming with three or four of a Saracen army, while the Christian host of half a dozen made threatening gestures up at the paynim.

These processions were used by the Church on Saints' Days as votive parades, the various guilds offering up portable miracles. In time, certain parts of the bible-story would seem to take on a particular appropriateness to one guild or another. Each company had a patron saint and their martyrdoms were full of picturesque material. But we are interested only in pageants which formed part of the entrances of Rulers into their towns, or on their visits to friendly capitals for marriages, coronations or embassies. The earlier examples speak merely of a 'riding' forth, a cavalcade, headed by the mayor and his corporation, who, appareled in their Sunday best, gold chains of office around their sabled shoulders, ride out to the gates of their town, and ceremoniously escort the visitor back into the town-hall for a welcoming banquet. Often, subjects would accompany the chevaliers, leading a more or less arranged carole to the place where loyal speeches were exchanged and presents of gold ewers and platters were given, before decorated balconies or on raised and flower-hung platforms.

The first recorded London pageant, with 'devices and marvels,' was held in 1236 to celebrate the marriage of Henry the Third to Eleanor of Provence. Though this is only a date and no description remains, the subsequent chronicling of European pageantry is crowded with splendors. In 1377 at the crowning of Richard the Second, a great castle was erected at Cheapside. On its four turrets, white damsels scattered gilt leaves onto the King's head and dropped gilded coins on him and his horse, offering wine from the pipes of a fountain secreted in the structure. When Henry the Fifth returned from his great victory at Agincourt in 1415, Cheapside Cross was covered again, by a palace, painted to be white marble, green and red jasper, out of whose door swarmed a bevy of virgins, who with dance, tambourine and songs of 'Nowell, Nowell,' reminded the populace of David's return after his triumph over Goliath. The cry 'Noel, Noel,' was also raised by the French as a shout of loyalty, as opposed to the 'Vive Bourgogne!' (Long live Burgundy). The Noel was also a Christmas dancing-song, much favored among the peasantry, and fused with the Carole.

In 1432 was held a lovely dumb-show in London at the return from his coronation of Henry VI and his French wife Catherine, as King and Queen of France and England. At the foot of London Bridge was a *pagina* of two antelopes supporting the arms of Lilies and Lions. On the bridge itself reared a superb 'fabric,' framing Nature, Grace, and Fortune, who dowered the passing royalty with gifts. To the right were the seven celestial virtues, who, signifying the bounty of the Holy Ghost, released seven white doves. To the left, seven terrestrial virgins offered the regalia. Then the entire choir of fourteen, clapping their hands, and breaking into *tripudia* (dance), sang welcome hymns. The term *pageant,* appeared first in connection with this show, which fifty years later was in universal use. It was perhaps borrowed from the allegorical dramas. The actual structure of the pageants themselves, precursors of the set scenery for Renaissance ballet, arose naturally out of the special adornments which hid the familiar architecture of city gates or bridges. As the tradition of the pageants strengthened they drew on to themselves, as do all forms of expression, elements from the people. Morris-dancers would ride out with the processions. The church provided Virgins and Vices; literature, both popular and classical, contributed Minerva and Mary, Star of the Sea, to ornament the same portal of an early sixteenth century French welcome. Such foreign curiosities as the Courts of Love inspired ladies disguised as the Amorous Qualities who scattered a conqueror's path with rose-leaves, or crowned him king of Love as well as King of France.

Dramatization by no means stopped in the streets. The paraders would naturally terminate their welcome with food, and it was merely an extension of compliments to continue pageantry into the cuisine. One of the earliest modern amateur theatricals occurred at Treviso in Italy in 1214. A made castle was defended by two hundred beautifully dressed society ladies. They hurled violets, roses and lilies of the valley, but were overpowered by fruit, small cakes, spiced tarts and flagons of perfume by storming chevaliers. The surrender was solemnized by a banquet and dance.

It has been seriously proposed that opera-ballet arose from table-decoration. Surely the curiosities and fantasy of the feasting boards contributed much to it. In Burgundy there was an elaborate ceremony at the entrance of the roasted peacock, its feathers preserved by the miracles of a culinary taxidermists. The fowl was borne in on a golden tray, with a whole cortège of ladies and pages, to the sound of drums and horns. The roast was set before the guest of honor, who must swear an oath upon its breast. This *voeu du paon,* or peacock-vow, enjoined its carver to enter on some special exploit. The skilful carving of the bird was in itself a drama. The table-appointments at the Burgundian Court under Duke Philip the Good reached an apogee of ingenuity. The ornaments were of such grandeur that the guests could hardly discover where the food left off and the entertainment began. Banquets were used sometimes to initiate a new crusade, a military alliance or merely to rejoice in the birth of an heir. In one monstrous pastry, an orchestra of twenty-eight musicians was concealed; a sixty-foot whale from whose hinged jaws tritons and sirens issued to dance a quadrille, swam in on wheels.

A very important festivity occurred in 1377 when the Commons of the City of London paid a complimentary visit to King Richard the Second. The first English masking of which we have record, it combines features of mumming and disguising, both important elements in the form of ballet.

In the fifteenth century courtiers were entertained by sophisticated

Morisco dancing in combination with a form of play called *Momerie* or mummery, another example of the chivalric prettification of a folk-custom growing out of remote ritualistic origins. It consisted usually of a company of maskers who came into their friends' and neighbors' houses to play a dice-game called 'Mumchance.' The word *'mummer'* may have some connection with the onomatopoetic mumble, mutter, mute, to murmur indistinctly, or to keep still when questioned; but it is more likely, without going deeply into its vastly elaborate etymology, that it refers to the German *mumme* or face-mask.*
The Greek word *mommo* means mask. The phenomenon of *disguising,* the essence of which is to have a masked visage, had, in the Middle Ages and Renaissance a very special significance. To us it may merely mean 'dressing-up,' but in the days of tournaments, a fully armed knight could be known only by his shield. Many, for personal reasons, like the disinherited knight in 'Ivanhoe,' masked their escutcheons, and contested unknown to the spectators. It was usually a formal compliment for two opponents to raise the vizards of their helmets that they might get a look at each other. Tipping our hats to ladies today is a survival of this custom. In Feudal Europe it was often a convenience and even a necessity to travel incognito, so when masquers entered a hall in fantastic disguise, although the aim of their visit was, in all probability, a good-humored courtesy, there was the almost unconsciously felt atmosphere of mystery and even danger which still makes masked balls exciting. Romeo and his friend, in disguise, could penetrate into a hostile house. In their masks they were made wholly welcome. Bare-faced they were enemies. In Carnival time, a remnant of the Saturnalia, and linked to the Feast of Fools, whole towns would mask, and liberties taken on these occasions were counted outside the reckoning of the rest of the calendar.

'Disguising' as such is related to mumming, but here not the face alone but the whole body is masked. The source of disguising among primitive peoples is pure magic. Tribesmen clothe themselves in leaves of a green tree, or in skins of slain strong animals. The beast's head is skinned and worn on his head, a living mask. In sophisticated societies the magic may be lost, but it somehow unconsciously lingers as a good-luck charm. Myth and literature supply the dresses for the disguise. Before the year 1330, at Norman tournaments, the nine worthies of Christendom, as well as Amor, god of Love, had made their entrance. Twenty years before that, at Stepney in England, there was a mystic *Rex de Vertbois,* King of the Greenwood, which at once suggests a link with the village 'jacks i' the green.' Masquerading was by no means limited to the aristocracy; by 1334 there were laws in London forbidding the citizens at Christmas time to go about the streets with a false face or visor. Entertainments at festal times of the year spontaneously or at least unconsciously, or traditionally, suggested themselves. Groups of friends would form a related and disguised company. Perhaps knowledge of their arrival

* This material on mumming is borrowed from Enid Welsford's remarkable and exhaustive book *The Court Masque.* Published by The Macmillan Co.

would precede them, and though surprise was simulated, they would be greeted by hot food and drink after their songs and dancing. The masquers, often borrowing the characters from the Morris, would tread a measure, and then invite their hosts or spectators to join. Just as there was a vague boundary between food and the scenery in which it was set, so here merges distinctions between dance, dancers and disguisers. The popular folk-dances of the people would be brought into the court ballroom by peasant maskers, to whom carnival gave license; or often the lords and ladies would parody the peasantry.

This transitional period of the late Middle Ages is extremely important to us because of incipient trends soon to emerge. Church, folk and minstrel, in a tangle of cross-current and similar expression, pour forth a great fountain of creative exuberance, which under the alchemy of an imminent Renaissance, will receive the ultimate channels by which we acknowledge them today. Any idea that the Middle Ages were some gray or brownish time, languishing in an historic limbo for the verdant sprouts of the Italian spring to revive Antiquity, has of course passed away. The Middle Ages themselves were very much a Renaissance. Both Charles the Great and Otto the First considered themselves revivers of the Western Roman Empire, not founders of a new one, but direct successors of the Cæsars. The Middle Ages saw a rebirth of early Roman ideas of the related Empires. Instead of *Imperium Romanum,* feudal loyalties knit the fabric close, perhaps not so close as the centralized administration of the highly organized imperial order, but nevertheless, sufficiently in contact with its parts to spread evenly, notions of knighthood and doctrines of the Church, while it gave to all western Europe artificed forms of masked entertainments, no longer loud tourneys at arms, rude morality plays or rustic mock-fights, which cradled opera, tragedy and ballet for Italy, England, France and Russia.

One Masque, which in ornament and inventions is but a minor example of mediæval mummery, has nevertheless, because of an accident, a peculiarly vivid atmosphere. Subsequently famous in miniature, tapestry and verse, frequently attributed to other people and other places, it has always appealed to imaginations like Poe's, Scott's and Hoffman's, and indeed holds the essence of Gothic Masquerade. This was the masque of the Wildmen of the Forest, or Wodehouses, or *Bal des Ardents,* the Burner's Ball. Green-men, wildmen, moors, foresters, leafy-devils were very frequent characters in court Moriscos. In 1393, a young knight married one of the French Queen's gentlewomen and the feast was made at court. A Norman squire, says Froissart,

> advised to make some pastime. . . . He devised six coats made of linen cloth covered with pitch, and thereon flax like hair, and had them ready in a chamber: the king put on one of them . . . and the squire himself had on the sixth: and when they were thus arrayed in these said coats and sewed fast in them, they seemed like wodehouses full of hair from top of the head to the sole of the foot. . . . (The king commanded all the varlets holding torches to stand

by the walls, and all the dancers to avoid contact with the wild men, but) ...
Soon after the Duke of Orleans entered into the hall, accompanied with four
knights and six torches, and knew nothing of the King's commandment for
the torches nor of the mummery that was coming thither, but thought to
behold the dancing and began himself to dance. Therewith the king, with
the five others, came in: They were so disguised in flax that no man knew
them: five of them were fastened one to another; the king was loose and
went before to lead the devise. When they entered into the hall every man
took so great heed to them that they forgot the torches. The king departed
from his company and went to the ladies to sport with them as youth required,
and so passed by the Queen and came to the Duchess of Berry, who took and
held him by the arm to know who he was, but the king would not show his
name. Then the duchess said: 'Ye shall not escape me till I know your name.'
In the mean season great mischief fell on the other, and by reason of the Duke
of Orleans: howbeit, it was by ignorance and against his will, for if he had
considered before the mischief fell, he would not have done as he did for
all the good in the world: but he was so desirous to know what personages
the five were that danced, he put one of his torches that his servants held so
near that the heat of the fire entered into the flax (wherein if fire take there
is no remedy) and suddenly was on a bright flame, and so each of them set
fire on other. The pitch was so fastened to the linen cloth and their shirts
so dry and fine and so joining to their flesh that they began to burn and to
cry for help. None durst come near them; they that did, burnt their hands by
reason of the pitch. One of them, called Nantouillet, advised him how the
buttery was thereby; he fled thither and cast himself into a vessel full of water,
wherein they rinsed pots which saved him, or else he had been dead as the
others were, yet he was sore hurt with the fire.... A piteous noise there was
in the hall. The Duchess of Berry delivered the king from that peril, for she
did cast over him the train of her gown and covered him from the fire ...
the bastard of Foix, who was all on a fire, cried ever with a loud voice: 'Save
the king, save the king!' Thus was the king saved: it was happy for him that
he went from his company, for else he had been dead without remedy. This
great mischief fell thus about midnight in the hall of Saint Pol in Paris, where
there was two burnt to death in the place, and other two, the bastard of Foix
and the earl of Joigny, borne to their lodgings and died within two days after
in great misery and pain. Thus the feast of this marriage brake up in heaviness; howbeit, there was no remedy; the fault was only in the Duke of
Orleans, and yet he thought none evil when he put down the torch.

Here was a masque of death, indeed. A marriage of young aristocrats,
graced by the royal presence, full of wedding excitement; the usual appre-
hension that nothing would go amiss in the arrangements of the day or its
entertainment. Then the entrance of mummers; a delicious chill of mysterious fright at their appearance; their rude shagginess under the flickering
braziers. And then, wild-fire, which at first must almost have seemed another
trick, a new conceit; the shrieks, smashed pots in the pantry, the shattered
wedding-night. On February 7, 1570, at a masquerade which took place at the

Castle of Waldenburg, Count Georg and Count Eberhard von Hohenlohe, similarly disguised as wild-men in tow-shirts, were accidentally lit by a torch and burned to death.

We have seen how foundations have been laid for scenery, and, by inference, for future costume, verse, and music which would once again join in a dance-drama. But as for dancing itself, very little has been said. It is almost impossible to discuss the dances without the aid of a musical instrument, or quotation, and even then we can hardly be sure of the sounds since the notation with which we are confronted is so complex, and admits of so many interpretive variations. But nevertheless, let us examine, at least in passing, the work of an Italian dancing-master which is typical of several early Renaissance technical treatises, and which has the advantage for our easier comprehension of the masterly scientific and scholarly treatment of Dr. Otto Kinkeldey of Cornell.

Nothing is known of the life of Guglielmo Ebreo, or as we know him, William the Jew of Pesaro. He seems to have been born before 1440. Lorenzo the Magnificent was born in 1448, and was famous for the composition of his dances. The complex and extremely refined figuration of the upper classes wholly separate from country-dances, were defined for the Italians by such men as the poet of Piacenza called Antonio Cornazano who lived, roughly, from 1431 to the end of the century. A certain Domenechino, from Piacenza and Ferrara, seems to have been the master of both our William and Cornazano. He taught dancing to the house of Sforza. Several flattering references in contemporary verses prove that the Jew was highly considered in his profession. Like that of most of his colleagues his work commences with a theoretical section, defining the dance, describing steps and movements. In places it is extremely obscure, but it is one of the first known examples of choreographic technique of which the modern world has any record, and hence is a monument from which descends the brilliant pedagogy of contemporary ballet. William was not indicating dances for the stage or for professional dancers, but for courtly balls, held by amateurs. Nevertheless, these people were on show, not only before their partners but in the contrived entertainments, masquings, moriscoes and disguisings of which court life was replete. His precision strives for elegance, the elegance tends toward a conventionalization which once given a raised and localized stage becomes immediately theatrical. However, the dancing-place of William's pupils was at best a polished stone or wooden floor in ballrooms of the early Renaissance.

Dancing is an action, showing outwardly the spiritual movements which must agree with those measures and perfect concords of harmony which, through our hearing and with earthly joy, descend into one intellect, there to produce sweet movements which, being thus imprisoned, as it were, in defiance of nature, endeavor to escape and reveal themselves through movement. Which movement of this sweetness and melody, shown outwardly (when we dance) with our person, proves itself to be united and in accord with the singing and with that harmony which proceeds from the sweet and harmonious song or from the measured sound we are listening to.

Of music he makes a distinction between the instrumental accompaniment of strings and horns, and the dance-song, which we know from Provence.

> The art of dancing is for generous hearts that love it, and for gentle spirits that have a heaven-sent inclination for it rather than an accidental disposition, a most amiable matter, entirely different from and mortally inimical to the vicious and artless common people who frequently, with corrupt spirits and depraved minds, turn it from a liberal art and virtuous science, into a vile adulterous affair, and who more often in their dishonest concupiscence under the guise of modesty, make the dance a procuress, through whom they are able to arrive stealthily at the satisfaction of their desires.

Perhaps this is a tactful bow in the direction of those among the aristocracy who are still shy of the dance, sharing Augustine's general attitude towards its seductions. Then William defines six primary requisites for a dancer, without which no one can hope to dance. In the first place, *misuro,* measure: the ability to keep time, in the musical sense of rhythm and proportion. In the Paris manuscript of his work, done about 1463, a youth in a tabard jacket edged with ermine superciliously leads two ladies, with equally raised eyebrows, and a seated harper accompanies them. Second: *Memoria:* 'merely means that you must recollect the steps that you have to make in the things you undertake to dance.' Third: *Partire del terreno:* that is, one's sense of the ground or space in which one dances. It is necessary to observe the physical limits of the chamber or ballroom. Fourth: *Aiere:* an obscure term, connected with airiness and dexterity, but more particularly it seems to indicate a "certain swaying and upward movement of the body with the corresponding settling down." Fifth: *Maniera:* linked to *Aiere,* having to do with the adaptation of the body to the movement of the feet.

> When one performs a single or a double step he should turn his body, so long as the movement lasts, towards the same side as the foot which performs the step, and the act should be adorned and shaded with the movement called *maniera.*

Whatever that means; no doubt some subtlety of style or manner obvious to the dancers of the time. It is not easy to indicate the quality of physical movement in words. And finally: *Movemento corporeo:* carriage, a vague injunction to move gracefully.

There are directions for the beginner, whether or not he knows a given dance well enough to try it.

> Let the dancer try a measure or two against the musical time. If he carries it through, it will afford him much pleasure, will sharpen his intellect, and make him attentive to the music ... for everything is known and better understood by its contrary.

The music for the dance is based on four principal voices, corresponding to earth, air, fire and water, elements comprising the human body. In proper equilibrium, the quartet fills the hearer's ears with such sweetness

> So that they ofttimes stand still and listen. For they are constrained by this sweetness and melody to make some bodily movement, some external demonstration that shows what they feel within. The dance is derived from this melody, as an act demonstrative of its own nature. Without the harmony and consonance the art of dancing would *be* nothing and could *do* nothing.

By the middle of the fifteenth century, dancing received considerable new impetus from an infiltration of country dances. These were a good deal more lively and vigorous because of their rural origin, than the grave and temperate measures we still see in Burgundian tapestries and Norman miniatures, where dancers seem almost to disdain both the dance and each other. In an early English dramatic interlude of the 'Four Elements' there is reference to people

> That shall both daunce and spring,
> And torne clean above the grounde
> With fryscas and with gambaudes rounde,
> That all the hall shall ryng.

Hence for general deportment, the Jew of Pesaro advises young ladies to be modest, gentle, dignified but sure.

> Her glance should not be proud nor wayward, gazing here and there as many do. Let her, for the most part, keep her eyes, with decency, on the ground; not however, as some do, with her head sunk on her bosom, but straight up, corresponding to the body, as nature teaches almost of herself....And then at the end of the dance, when her partner leaves her, let her, facing him squarely, with a sweet regard, make a decent and respectful curtsey in answer to his.

Antonio Cornazano, William, the Jew of Pesaro's contemporary, gives four general categories of type dances or dance-measures. The *Piva* consists of double steps only, animated and hurried by the quickness of the tempo. The *Saltarello* (little leap) is the most jocund. Spaniards call it *alta danza,* the high-dance, meaning that the feet frequently leave the floor. The *Quaternaria* is a German saltarello, consisting of two steps and a reprise with a beat between. But the queen of all dance measures is the *Bassa Danza,* the low dance, dignified, steady, yet active and slower than any of the others. The dancers stepped to the beat, pacing the measure with very slight raising of the feet, low off the ground. As *basse danse* it will be familiar to us in France in the fifteenth and sixteenth centuries. In Germany it is *Hofdantz* (court-dance), and the eighteenth century *menuet* is its lineal descendant.

The dances bear more or less fanciful or poetic titles such as Mignotta, Cupid, Fair Flower, Little Lion, Ring, and so on. Generally speaking, in all of the treatises, the dances fall into two sections; the low dance and the *balli*. The *balli* were livelier, with the feet raised high and quick from the ground, perfectly termed *saltarello, Springdantz* or *Huptauf*.

> The Composers exercised great ingenuity in making their combinations, the dances varying greatly in length, from just a few lines to a whole page or more of descriptive text. Occasionally a few of the livelier *saltarello* or *piva* steps are inserted, by way of variety, in a *bassa danza;* but on the whole the difference is carefully observed. As a rule the headings indicate whether the dance is to be executed by two or three or four persons. Some even go as far as six or eight. Likewise we are informed whether, in the case of more than two or three, the dancers are arranged in couples or in lines, as in the country dance or lancers. Sometimes we also find directions that the partners are to hold hands.*

To give at least a rough idea of the complexity of the directions for the dances, as well as their technical jargon and the differences between the two chief types, we can read the beginnings of a *bassa danza* called *Piatosa*, and a *balli* called *Colonese;* the first is for one couple.

> First, two simple steps and a double, commencing with the left foot; then they make a *represa* (never clearly explained), and the man makes two *continenze* (balance, or shift from side to side). During the time of the *continenze* the lady goes from the under hand of the man with two simple steps, beginning with the left foot. Then they take hands and make two *riprese,* one on the left foot, the other on the right, and then make two *continenze*. And all that has been said is done a second time, until the man returns to his place. Then they make a *riverenza* (curtsey, or bow involving foot movements) on the left foot and then two bars of *saltarello,* beginning with the left foot, and the man curtsies on the left foot.

There is as much again of this dance's description, which we are assured is a fairly short one. The *balli,* below, is for six dancers, three men and three women.

> First, sixteen bars of *saltarello*. Then they stand still, and the rear couple goes forward with two single and four double steps, crossing through the other couples so that the rear couple finds itself in front, with the lady at the upper hand of the man. While the rear couple does this, the middle couple makes a round turn in two simple and one double step, beginning with the left foot, that is, taking right hands, both of them. Then in the same time they also go around with two simple and a double step taking left hands and starting with the right foot. There they curtsey. Then the middle couples do what the rear couple did, with two single and four double steps. And while that couple goes back, the couple now in the middle keeps making turns with two single and one double step, as was said, until the ladies are all in their places as they stood at first. Then all stand for one bar (and so on and on).

* *A Jewish Dancing Master of the Renaissance: Guglielmo Ebreo,* by Otto Kinkeldey: A. S. Friedus Memorial Volume, page 346.

Antonio Cornazano brags that in his youth he needed only to have a dance explained to him once, or even to see it performed once, to enable him to repeat it on the spot, without a hitch. Perhaps he could, but we can easily understand why William of Pesaro stressed *memoria* as one of the dancer's prime qualifications.

MORRIS DANCE   *Burgkmair (or Dürer)*

CHAPTER VIII

Renaissance Foundations for Court Ballet

MASS, mummery and minstrel, source, form and means by which the Middle Ages developed their approach to theatrical dancing have been considered till now with only an indirect glance towards Italy. Until that fortunate day when a method of writing history is discovered whereby it can be demonstrated in simultaneous chronology, rather than by the necessarily confusing and mutually exclusive sequence of chapter after chapter, we must run the risk of assuming that while there was great activity in France, England and Germany, nothing was going on in Italy. No assumption could be farther from truth. The peninsula, for reasons of its predominantly urban culture, its conflicts of Commune and Church, was not susceptible in nearly the same degree as the North to feudal chivalry. Italy was to use feudal pageantry as a literary decoration, and as plastic embroidery well into the Renaissance, but the source of this sophistication in a large measure would be Provence, France and England. The Italian miracle plays, or what under their various names corresponded to the shows before cathedrals at Paris, York or Coventry, were rare in the early Middle Ages. A striking exception was the dramatic services from the town of Cividale del Friuli, which with rubrics for mimed action we have observed in its *Planctus Mariæ*. When the miracle plays came to the South, the element of the grotesque, the charm of the homely commonplace which put dancing devils and biblical clowns on the same pageant, were almost absent. Although a line of demarcation between the mediæval and the new learning was dimmer in Italy than anywhere else, it is not so much the Middle Ages which must occupy us there as the Renaissance, which was to effervesce in Italy while France, England and Germany were still Gothic.

Inasmuch as Roman civilization, successor to Greek, had actually inhabited the soil of Italy, and since Italy exists in time, one can only limit the sources of its Renaissance to the Cæsars, and treat the long gap between as a gradual evolution or becoming,—back to something approaching the ancient influence; though in every way the new was to be from the direction of creative art and science, immeasurably superior.

The mediæval phenomenon which most interests us in Italy is religious revivalism, which, though not unknown in other countries, took a different form among the Umbrian hills, and which, still as hysteria, but as organized hysteria, was to provide an important channel for the birth, or rather the revival of dancing in theaters. The very air of Europe in the twelfth and thirteenth centuries breathed a lively bacteria of pathology. The Church supplied, to be sure, a structure of solid reference which one might think would have checked psychological aberration; but the Church, or at least its doctrines, had become so inherent, so instinctive in the people that any logical control was more accidental than not. Churchmen practiced all sorts of emotional and incitatory methods on populations only too susceptible to frenzies, to accomplish even less epochal manœuvres than the Crusades. Europe's was settled with vast floating crowds of deracinated peoples. Their recent ancestors had swept the continent in the wake of the Gothic invasions, and instincts for vague immigration still chafed their feet. The Crusades distributed thousands of unfortunate fanatics on the unfriendly sands of Palestine. European cities had become inured to the constant sight of penitents with fixed eyes and running sores, fakir-beggars in holy mania or pitiful disheveled women possessed by the singing insanity of the Holy Ghost. A great unorganized, but very pressing Dance of Death was a daily spectacle in every town, which, if it had not yet been plague-visited was temporarily only lucky.

After an epoch of anarchic devotions which poured the psychic energies of thousands into the air, the Church, sensibly alarmed at indiscriminate passion, set up its great shrines. The relics of St. Thomas of Canterbury, of Saint James of Campostella, of Saint Peter at Rome, acted both as localized safety-valves, and as definitions of emotion which would lead to drama. For example, in January, 1448, Fra Roberto de Lecce, a twenty-two year old Franciscan, already so famous that a crowd of fifteen thousand packed the Piazza of Perugia to hear him preach, mounting the stone pulpit which gave onto the square, by merely raising a crucifix moved the mob to tears; their sobbing and murmuring, shouting *Jesu Misericordia,* lasted half an hour. On Good Friday he spoke again to the assembled citizens. When the moment came for the Elevation of the Cross

> there issued forth from San Lorenzo Eliseo di Christoforo, a barber of the quarter of Sant' Angelo, like a naked Christ with the cross on his shoulder, and the crown of thorns upon his head, and his flesh seemed to be bruised as when Christ was scourged.

Naturally, the people were shattered. They groaned, shouting aloud *Misericordia,* and Fra Roberto created monks at once from among the converts.* This incident, however, is comparatively late. More violent events had occurred for two hundred years. The Chronicles of Pisa describe for us:

> In the year 1260, when Italy was defiled by many horrible crimes, a sudden and new perturbation seized at first upon the folk of Perugia, next upon the Romans, and lastly on the population of all Italy, who, stung by the fear of God, went forth processionally, gentle and base-born, old and young, together, through the city streets and squares, naked save for a waistband round their loins, holding a whip of leather in their hands, with tears and groans, scourging their shoulders till the blood flowed down. Not by day alone, but through the night in the intense cold of winter, with lighted torches they roamed by hundreds, by thousands, by tens of thousands through the churches, and flung themselves down before the altars, led by priests with

* Symonds: *The Renaissance in Italy.* Vol. I, p. 311 (Modern Library Edition).

crosses and banners. The same happened in all villages and hamlets, so that the fields and mountains resounded with the cries of sinners calling upon God. All instruments of music and songs of love were hushed; only the dismal wail of penitents was heard in town and country.

This intensity seemed to spring from the same Umbrian hills where Saint Francis commenced a joyful practice of his moderate minstrelsy. But these *Battuti,* the flagellants, did not belong to any order. They were the conglomerate population of whole districts. No focus for their praise, no Crusade to raise, no relics for homage. They were not of one class but of all classes; not of one town, but of all towns touched by the mania. Doomsday, a sense of sin cultivated to a fine point of advanced paranoia, a desire for immersion in an anonymous group-guilt where the individual would perhaps escape a measure of punishment assured for all, lashed on the delirious people. Florence barred her gates to them; the Milanese Tyrants of the Towers set up six hundred gibbets as a threat. The southern states were only spared the epidemic by Manfred, who threw a military cordon across his boundaries.

After a time, the crisis of emotion passed. This hysteria and self-hypnosis of a group inevitably reminds us of the Bacchantes and Thracian devotees of a spring-God whose badges were torn limbs of goats and trees, whose transports produced a frenzy knowing only the discipline of hymns; and later, the definition of dance-drama. After the public demonstrations of the Italian crowds had ceased to a considerable degree, there were numerous private remainders from the activity of the *Battuti.*

Brotherhoods among the laity were consolidated, in Umbria, in Tuscany, everywhere. They knew themselves as the *Disciplinati di Gesu Cristo.* They planned to persist in the ascetic practices of the Flagellants, but by less violent means. They whipped themselves, more as a formula than as self-indulgence. Their orders were open to the whole people and complemented without conflict the institutions of the Church. From their inception they were much occupied with hymns, sung not in priestly Latin, but in the vulgar Italian dialects. The songs, devoted to the Passion of their Lord, surpassed by their directness and intensity in expressing fierce emotion, all previous singers of Catholicism. Gradually, the importance of their hymns began to signify to the public their whole meaning. No longer were they Battuti or Disciplinati, but *Laudesi:* no longer the Beaten, or the Disciplined, but the Praise-Givers.

Unquestionably the greatest of these givers of praise was Jacopone da Todi, who shares every degree of the flagellants' obsession, from vague psychic or physically organic arising to a pure transport into an etherealized, spiritual glee. He came of a noble family of Todi, took his degree as doctor of laws and practiced shrewdly, not only making his living by his learning, but by those contemporary tricks which did not always serve justice first. His wife was his fair and richly clothed companion at many balls and gatherings. One day at a noble ball, so a contemporary tells us,

While she was dancing and taking pleasure with the rest, an accident occurred, fit to move the greatest pity. For the platform whereupon the party were assembled, fell in and was broken to pieces, causing grievous injury to those who stood upon it. She was so hurt in the fall that she lost the power of speech, and in a few hours after died. Jacopo, who by God's mercy was not there, no sooner heard the sad news of his wife than he ran to the place. He found her on the point of death, and sought, as is usual in those cases, to unlace her; but she, though she could not speak, offered resistance to her husband's unlacing her. However, he used force and overcame her, and unlaced and carried her to his house. There, when she had died, he unclothed her with his own hands, and found that underneath those costly robes and next to her naked flesh she wore a hair-shirt of the roughest texture.

In fact the Franciscan vision had been given to her, and unbeknownst to her friends, family, or her husband, she underwent all the usages of extreme asceticism. The effect on Jacopone was violent. To describe his grief as madness would be understatement. He sold everything which he had possessed, stripped himself naked, wore a donkey-harness. Once he came into a party of his former companions naked, smeared with turpentine, to which feathers clung. He consecrated himself to being a fool for the sake of Christ. At the end of ten years of methodical madness, he joined the lowest of the Franciscan order and wrote a great deal of the world's most magnificent religious poetry. In English it has no equal, except possibly in the verse of Crashaw or Gerard Manley Hopkins, though by the nineteenth century there is little left of the stupendous violence, the wild lightning-like discharge of the eleventh. Not only Christ's agony but love for Jesus made him smolder with incredible delights.

> He ran in a fury of love, and under the impression that he was embracing and clasping Jesus Christ, would fling his arms about a tree.

But he was also a shrewd political observer and for his insight into the corruptions of the papacy, Boniface the Eighth imprisoned him, which only served to inspire his writing of more wonderful verse. But to us he is interesting for a different reason. From his devotions, in the form of dialogues, a whole type of popular religious drama and pantomime was to evolve. The dramatic forms of these holy plays would be taken over part and parcel by Renaissance designers of secular spectacle, and two centuries later the soul of Jacopone, through the lyrics of Girolamo Savonarola, would attempt to replace the pagan hymns of Lorenzo di Medici's profane triumphs, the *Trionfi* that owed much to the *Laudi;* the *Trionfi* that lent more to the ballets of Florence and Paris.

Jacopone wrote a kind of *Planctus Mariæ*. The gospel facts were perennially electric to such conductors. A messenger informs the lady of Paradise that her son has been arrested. She goes, aided by Magdalen, to Pilate's court of law. A chorus of Jews shout

> Crucify! Crucify!
> Who would be King, must die.
> He spurns the Senate by
> Our laws, as these attest.
> We'll see if, stanch of state,
> He can abide this fate
> Die shall he at the gate
> And Barab be redressed.*

Christ is taken to Golgotha, and before the weeping Marys, suffers. Even those who are not fortunate enough to grasp completely the original Italian, can even by a glance at the repetition of '*figlio*' (son), gain at least an idea of the rapt, concentrated ferocity of grief. Such words literally clamor for bodily movement, not so much as an accompaniment, but to make them physically tolerable.

> *O figlio, figlio, figlio*
> *Figlio, amoroso figlio,*
> *Figlio, chi dà consiglio*
> *Al cor mio angustiatio!*
> *Figlio, occhi giocondi,*
> *Figlio, co' non rispondi?*
> *Figlio, perchè t'ascondi*
> *Dal petto o' se' lattato?*

They display the cross to her, his mother. In excruciating detail, they describe the driving of the nails. She cries out, and the son comforts her; bids John take her. The end is swelling elation, a staggering expression of grief surpassed, and in the final vision Mary sees herself nailed on to her son's body, by his own nails.

In Symonds' great work 'The Renaissance in Italy,' † he describes a Good Friday in Umbria, where the essential atmosphere of the early Italian theater was revealed to him. In his description there is also inference as to the part music played, a very important part, significant to us as a later governor of the sub-structure in dancing-melody.

> The psalms were sung on that occasion to a monotonous rhythm of melodiously simple outline by three solo voices in turn; soprano, tenor and bass. At the ending of each psalm a candle before the high-altar was extinguished, until all light and hope and spiritual life went out for the damned soul. The soprano, who sustained the part of pathos, had the fullness of a powerful man's chest and larynx, with the pitch of a woman's and the timbre of a boy's voice. He seemed able to do what he chose in prolonging and sustaining notes, with wonderful effects of *crescendo* and *diminuendo*, passing from the wildest and most piercing *forte* to the tenderest *pianissimo*. He was hidden in the organ-loft: and as he sang, the organist sustained his cry with long-drawn

* Symonds' translation.
† Vol. II, p. 479.

shuddering chords and deep groans of the diapason. The whole church throbbed with the vibrations of the rising, falling melody; and the emotional thrill was as though Christ's or Mary's soul were speaking through the darkness to our hearts.

That early *Planctus* of Cividale del Friuli was a very rigid expression, in comparison to the emergent religious theater which stemmed from the *Laudi,* and there is a remote, but not very impressive connection between the two. For although the *Planctus* indicated movement, the emotional intensity of the later verses elevated the whole nature of the performance into an entirely different dramatic plane. Given the impetus of Jacopone da Todi, the evolution of the Italian religious spectacle was swift. Already in 1223 there were cribs in Umbrian churches, representing Christ's manger at Bethlehem. Jacopone, who died about 1306, had written a Christmas Carol, to be sung before such cribs or *presepe.* In the Arena chapel at Padua, Giotto painted a fresco illustrating a portion of the hymn. The arrangement of the simple, monumental figures may very easily have been prompted by dumb-shows he had seen enacted.

In its dramatic formulation, the Hymns-of-Praise were called *Divozione,* beginning in the middle of the fourteenth century. Composed in various stanzaic forms they generally told the story of the Passion, since the singers of the *Laudi* were obsessed with the spectacle of Christ's physical suffering as the key to salvation. Eventually, however, they did utilize a larger subject-matter. A Laud for the Advent displayed the Apocalypse of St. John the Divine bringing in the Anti-Christ, no mean undertaking even for our films. A company inventory of the year 1339, from the Perugian Confraternity of Saint Dominic includes

> Wings and crowns for sixty-eight angels, masks for devils, a star for the magi, a crimson robe for Christ, black veils for the Maries, two lay figures of thieves (for the crucifixion), a dove to symbolize the Holy Ghost, a coat of mail for Longinus.

No date can be set upon which the *Laudesi* quit their churches and started to act out *Divozione* in the squares. A Passion play is supposed to have been performed in the Roman Coliseum in 1260. By 1375 the practice had become wide-spread in the Church, of giving holy plays with an illustrative sermon, rather like a lecture with lantern-slides. The actors were called the *Chorus.* The preacher, the *Choregus.* That term was last encountered in the gnostic Hymn to Jesus, where Christ the dancer filled that rôle at the Last Supper.

These *Divozione* bridge the gap from the *Laudi* of the thirteenth to the *Sacra Rappresentazione* of the fifteenth century, and in the fifteenth century we are on the brink of ballet. The Sacred Representations were the consummation of Italian religious drama, especially beautiful in Florence. The Renaissance in Italy was not, as in other European countries, a national expression, but rather the individual creative gift of separate city-communities or individual artists. The Florentine sacred drama was active in its best epoch from about 1470 to 1520; but here we are interested only in the earliest descriptions.

In spite of exceptions in Pisa, Padua, Borgo San Sepolcro and Venice, Florence and the Italian Renaissance are synonymous. If the significance of the Renaissance can be summed up in a word, we may call it an 'intellectual' rebirth, and Florence was preëminently the intellectual Italian town. When Boniface the Eighth accepted the homage of the ambassadors of Christendom at the Papal Jubilee of 1300, he noticed that every one was a Florentine citizen. He is said to have remarked that 'the Florentines form the fifth element.' They were first in poetry, law, scholarship, philosophy, science, and the plastic arts of painting and sculpture. Their contribution to dramatic spectacle was the first in Italy.

The greatest festival held in the Tuscan capital was the midsummer feast of Saint John. Matteo Palmieri in his chronicle describes the festival of 1454 in such a way that in it we recognize all the earmarks of shows, which Florentine artists and engineers, because of their technical priority, would be hired to spread over Europe, two, three and four hundreds years afterwards.

> On the 22nd day of June the Cross of Santa Maria del Fiore moved first, with all the clergy and children, and behind them seven singing men. Then the companies of James the woolshearer and Nofri the shoe-maker, with some thirty boys in white and angels. Thirdly, the Tower (*edifizio*) of Saint Michael, whereupon stood God the father in a cloud (*Nuvola*); and on the piazza, before the Signoria, they gave the show (*rappresentazione*) of the Battle of the Angels, when Lucifer was cast out of heaven.

The Tower is a scenic ancestor which we saw in another form on London Bridge when Henry the Fifth returned from Agincourt. The *Nuvola* is a very Florentine innovation and will be seen in ballet, opera and masque, ubiquitously, for centuries after. The *Nuvola* provided a practical arrangement for applying a slice of heaven to earth. Such Italian late-renaissance engineer-designers as the brothers Parigi, Torelli, and Bibiena were to instruct the French and above all the Englishman, Inigo Jones, how to create Paradises, which became an almost indispensable background for court ballet.

Vasari says that the inventor of the *Nuvola* was Filippo Brunelleschi, the great architect. Scarcely inventor, for as we have seen there had been for a long time pendent stars coming out of church-roof heavens. Nevertheless Brunelleschi gave them a new magnificence. On Saint John's Day the Piazza before the Duomo was covered with a wide azure awning sown with the golden Lilies of the city and called a 'Heaven.'

> Beneath it were the clouds, or Nuvole, exhibited by various civic guilds. They were constructed of substantial wooden frames, supporting an almond-shaped aureole, which was thickly covered with wood, and surrounded with lights

and cherub faces. Inside it sat the person who represented the Saint....
Lower down, projected branches made of iron, bearing children dressed like
angels, and secured by waistbands....The woodwork and the wires were
hidden from sight by wool and cloth, plentifully sprinkled with tinsel stars.
The whole moved slowly on the backs of bearers concealed beneath the
frame.

Brunelleschi may indeed have ordered the arrangement of the floats on
classic models. He was an indefatigable archeologist, and could easily have
seen the sense of adapting the form of Roman triumphs to Christian spectacle.
The highest honor the antique Roman senate could bestow on a victorious
general was to vote him a 'triumph.' The celebration consisted of a grand
parade, forming at the Campus Martius, beyond the city walls, which passed
through the city streets up onto the Capitol. The houses were garlanded and
the marchers were acclaimed with shouts of 'Io Triumphe.' On a series of
chariots the weapons, spoils and families of the conquered were displayed,
culminating in a great chair upon which the empurpled general, attended by
troops and choirs, sat crowned in glory.

The tower, or *Edifizio* in the Saint John's Day *Sacra Rappresentazione,*
was mounted on a car, similar to the ancient war-cars. The Italians had a
predilection for such chariots. One of the most famous of the forms which it
took was the *Caroccio,* a symbol of the Communes or free towns. In 1037
Heribert, archbishop of Pavia, in the first war for communal liberty invented
a great car, dragged by oxen, upon which were set the arms and banners of
the Commune, with an altar for the priests. Around this standard the burghers
rallied for their independence, comforted by the presence and sanction of
the Church.

The parades which had been sacred cyclical representations of Bible history were turned by the pagan alchemy of the Renaissance into *Trionfi.*
Already in 1326, the conqueror Castruccio Castracane had entered Lucca in a
spectacular show which was founded, as he thought, on the triumph of the
Cæsars.

For us it is perhaps difficult to recapture the Renaissance passion for
Antiquity. It is something much more complex than any mere parvenu pleasure in building a Greek temple to house a swimming-pool or post-office, or a
Gothic chapel for a dining-room or movie-theater, as we do today. We have
suffered no Middle Ages, no era of absolute ecclesiastical domination. We
have not known statements of iron dogma which precluded any discussion
of scientific possibility. We are free from the universal idea of indivisible, centralized authority which the Church realized and required. We never knew the
ingenuities of scholasticism, which took all the intellectual curiosity and energy
of five hundred years and turned it to an expansive fabric of remote dialectic
and hair-splitting epistemology.

At the beginning of the twelfth century an entirely new historical feeling
arose. The past took on an immediacy after its relegation to a thousand years

of limbo. Historians were moved by the ruins of the Coliseum to imagine vaguely the possibility of Rome revived. There was an unresolved synthesis between the triumphant empire of the Church, and the faded empire of East and West. Rienzi, the hero of Wagner's opera, called himself knight and tribune of the Senate and People of Rome, as had the first Julius. On August 15, 1347, celebrating his 'election' to the tribunate, he assumed six crowns of classic foliage: ivy, myrtle, laurel, oak, olive and silver-gilt. His shields were honored with the keys of Saint Peter and S.P.Q.R.; *Senatus Populusque Romanus*. His senatorial baton was capped not with a Cæsarian Eagle, but with a gilded orb and crucifix, enclosing a saint's relic.

The great papal libraries were founded. Archeology, the quest for the antique, became a great business. Manuscripts of the classics which had survived Gothic invasions and the abuses the Church had put them to in making new pages or bindings from the vellum of Roman copies of Euripides and Terence, were prized more than gold bullion. If Greece and Rome could not be actually resurrected in Florence and Rome, at least Romans and Florentines, by the acquisition of ancient relics, books, sculpture, architectural fragments, and law, would hope to make Florence and Rome as close to the past as possible. Boccaccio wrote that "Sulmona mourns because she holds not Ovid's dust; and Parma is happy since Cassius lies within her walls." The rebellious town of Arpino received an amnesty because the orator Cicero had once been a citizen of the same place. One of the most splendid gifts Venice could send to Alfonso of Naples was a leg-bone, attributed to Livy.

Hence, it was with something like relief that people in the streets of Florence at Carnival time saw the triumphs of Lorenzo di Medici, not as parables of Jesus but as metamorphoses of Ovid. Needless to say there was a good deal more precedence for dancing in the literature of pagan Antiquity than in holy writ. The Florentines had always been dancers. The Carole in Tuscany was the inspiration for charming *Ballate,* or dancing-songs by Dante, Boccaccio and many minor poets. Very often the well-turned rhymes of the literary men would descend into the street and become popular songs, known by apprentices and spinner's girls. Later, these rhymes, vulgarized and danceable would be taken up by such noble verse masters as the Medici to be recoined as *Canzon a Ballo* or dancing-songs. Boys and young girls met in squares and arcades, while a youth with a high voice accompanied himself with a stringed instrument, or minstrels sang part-songs and dancers joined the refrain, as in Provence.

In fact Provence was directly connected with the Medicean *Trionfi.* The poet Petrarch, who was perhaps the earliest Renaissance figure to raise the idea of self-culture, of acquired information to a literal ideal, had spent a considerable time in Avignon and all along the Troubadour coast. Also, Raimbaut de Vaquieros, whose poem the *Carros* or War-Cars, an allegory of courtly virtue, served Petrarch as a model for his own vastly influential *Trionfo d'Amore,* had been in Italy from 1179 to 1182. Petrarch's Triumphs include not only those of Love, but also of Time, of Fame, of Holiness, of Chastity and, to be sure, of Death. His Ovidian verses with their allusions to such famous lovers as Jason, Venus, Cæsar, Hercules, as well as Guinevere, Tristan, Iseult and Lancelot, were virtual libretti for triumphal processions. The idea of the Triumph of Something, usually Love, but frequently of Time or Death is an expression of the mediæval formulatory instinct which by allegory and personification also created the morality plays and the Dance of Death.

Lorenzo di Medici is famous as a poet of *Canti Carnaschiali* or Carnival Songs. The custom of the Florentine Carnival was ancient. Perhaps the word has a Christian origin, it meaning *carne vale,* 'farewell flesh' (at the start of Lent); or from *currus navalis,* the ship-car wheeled in on a pageant or procession, similar to the sacred ships that Isis sent down the Nile with candles to search for Osiris. In Florence, people roamed the streets, masked, singing satirical ballads. Lorenzo saw a wonderful chance to please and impress the people; he caused the very best artist possible to design chariots, and the most skillful engineers to execute their divers ingenuities. He himself wrote the triumphal lyrics based on the form of antique odes. There was a distinction between the *Trionfi,* the mythological or allegorical masques, and the *Carri,* which bore symbols of crafts and trades before which choirs would chant, not imitations of the Latin, but obscene rhymes about everyday Florentine life. Il Lasca, the early historian of Medicean paradings, writes that it was their custom

> To go forth after dinner, and often they lasted till three or four hours into the night, with a multitude of masked men on horseback following, richly dressed, exceeding sometimes three hundred in number, and as many on foot with lighted torches. Thus they traversed the city, singing to the accompaniment of music arranged for four, eight, twelve or even fifteen voices, supported by various instruments.

The Medicean pageants, following the inventions of Lorenzo, always bowed toward the direction of classical Antiquity, but there was an element of pure fantasy bred from the folk which is an odd strain, and which we shall encounter again when the Medicis, become French, will patronize in the Louvre and at Fontainebleau the *ballet de cour.* In the anthologies of carnival songs we find Masques of Scholars, Frog-Catchers, Furies, Old Men and Young Wives, Devils, Jews, Tortoise-Shell Cats, Nuns Escaped from Convents, Young Men Who Have Lost Their Fathers, and Perfumers.

The Renaissance Triumph was, in the fifteenth and sixteenth centuries, very much an out-of-door spectacle which was to influence greatly the indoor theatricals of the seventeenth and eighteenth. After that, all tincture of Florence and the Medici passed; a loss in many ways, not only because of their grandeur, but also because of the fine talents involved. The Triumph was an expression of its time in a balance of verse, music and to a less degree, dance. But its essence, even to excess, was its display. Before dancing finally moves within doors, let us recall a famous triumph, which has always appealed to lovers of the past as the lyrical definition of its epoch.

In 1513, the Casa Medici was honoring in its native city, Giovanni, the head of the house, who had recently been elected Pope. His brother Giuliano, Duc de Nemours, was the captain of a club of noble young men, which had as name-sign the Diamond, testifying to the constancy of his family. He decided that the Diamond should produce a worthy spectacle. Lorenzo, Duke of Urbino, and titular chief of the Medici, headed a rival society called *Il Broncone;* a withered spray of laurel, putting forth green leaves. It was to the competition of such aristocrats that at least a portion of Renaissance ingenuity was due. Giuliano hired the classicist Dazzi, to devise after the Roman mode a program of three cars. A good architect supervised the construction, and Pontormo, a very interesting painter, conceived decorations. On the first chariot rode fair boys; on the second, strong youths; on the third, honorable old men. Dazzi may have read in Plutarch the already quoted description of the Spartan Pyrrhic cantata.

Lorenzo applied to Nardi, historian of the city and translator of Livy, for a libretto suitable to the Laurel Branch, and was given a pageant of seven cars typifying the golden age, each with descriptive verses: In the first, Saturn and Janus, guarded by six shepherds, naked and muscular, on unharnessed horses; in the second, Numa Pompilius, the city-founder, surrounded by ancient pontiffs; in the third, Titus Manlius, consul of the First Punic War, symbol of the Empire's initial conquest; in the fifth, Augustus and twelve laurel-crowned bards, their horses winged like Pegasus; in the sixth, Trajan the Just, with Lawyers. The seventh car held the world. Pontormo designed upon it a dead knight, in rusty armor, from whose cleft plates sprang a living boy, naked and entirely gilded. This proved the end of the Age of Iron, the Dawn of the Age of Gold; Feudalism fading into the New Learning: "The world's great epoch now begins: the Golden Age returns."

The little golden boy died of his gilt, his father receiving ten soldi. Lorenzo and Giuliano were both to perish before their time: now they muse at each other from marble seats Michelangelo cut for them in the Sacristy of San Lorenzo.

Although the renowned banquet of Duke Philip of Burgundy, in 1454, that dinner party of the peacock vow, antedated several of the Italian dinners, its confusion of chivalric fragments and classic symbols, its unwieldy carts and burlesque tricks is more a Gothic than a new manifestation. The Italian banquets were to have a feature shared also by the French, which would regulate the convention of the so-called 'entries' in ballet. This was the appearance at intervals in the feasting of a series of groups of disguised dancers. The French word is *entremets,* which has come to mean the sweetmeats served to terminate a meal. The word is derived from low-Latin *intromissum,* the third or middle course of a banquet. The original Latin, of course, is "something inserted into something else." The Italian was *intromesso,* and shortly became *tramesso*. When the dancers of the feast hall had been transferred to the ballroom, and from ballrooms to theaters, they were known as *Intermedio, Intermezzo,* and were danced interludes in classic comedies, or tragedies, preludes and epilogues to operas, before they themselves achieved the dignity of becoming separate acts or entries, in ballet.

One of the commonest forms of entremet was the Morisco, in Italy called *Brando,* and different from the English dance. The most important feature of the Morris was the involved ground patterns which its dancers followed; though in Italy there was little figuration. The *Brando* was given far more to pantomiming, to dramatic gesture.

At a Sienese ball held in 1465, there descended out of a great golden wolf, a morisco of twelve, one of them clad as a nun, who danced to songs. Cardinal Pietro Riario, whose uncle was Sixtus the Fourth, gave a fine dinner in 1473. A King of the Feast had been elected, who entered the hall attended by a hundred and more torches. After the food there was a 'worthy morisco,' or a mimed and danced action. In came a Turkish Ambassador, complaining of the crowning of a Macedonian King, which he predicted would lead to war. Then entered a troop of Turks, captured by Crusaders. After a little sermonizing they were converted and sang "Long live the faith of Christ Jesus; also the Pope and Cardinal San Sisto." Later a triumph-car was displayed in the cortile, out of which, one after the other, issued morris-dancers. On the morrow, the Turk and the Macedonian King met in mock-battle, after which the Macedonian led the Saracen a captive through Rome.

In the same year, the same cardinal feasted Leonora of Aragon, promised bride of Ercole d'Este, the great Duke of Ferrara. The boards were piled high with eatables modeled to illustrate Greek fables. At the end of the eating, eight pairs of well-known antique lovers danced. Hercules fought 'a lovely skirmish' with eight centaurs, who came to rape the nymphs. The banquet closed with a dumb-show of Bacchus and Ariadne.

The apogee of these arrangements for eating and dancing occurred in Milan in 1489, and has been sometimes referred to as the 'first' Ballet. More truthfully, it was a banquet-ball, but all the entremets were related to one another in a consistent pattern, and the fête was designed as an artistic entity, though the dramatic action was fragmentary, and any expression of emotion merely a literary device for seemly display.

Gian Galeazzo, Duke of Milan, was given a banquet at the town of Tortona, when he passed through with his new wife, Isabella of Aragon, by an aristocratic amateur, one Bergonzio di Botta, a specialist in fancy-cooking and fancy-dancing.

When the Duke and Isabella walked into the banquet hall, from an opposite door entered Jason, with his Argonauts. By pantomime and to the sound of war-like music they expressed their virile pleasure in the Ducal presence, left a Golden Fleece (a roast, gilded lamb) before the pair, and retired. Mercury arrived, and in recitative, told of the craft by which he stole a calf from

Admetus. Three quadrilles terminated his entry. Diana and her nymphs were succeeded by a litter upon which the stag Actaeon sat. She told them that this youth, as a hart, was glad to be eaten by one so fair as Isabella. A symphony of strings announced Orpheus. The Thracian lyre for the first time since the loss of Eurydice was struck with joy, discovering such bliss as the Duke's, the Duchess'. A brusque note broke his song; it was Theseus, Atalanta and the Calydonian hunt. Their wild boar, duly slain, was offered the Duke to carve. There was a course of fowl, disguised as Isis, throned on a car drawn by peacocks, followed by nymphs supporting platters of birds cooked in their feathers. Hebe poured her divine nectar. Arcadian shepherds, Vertumnus and Pomona brought fruits. The Imperial epicure Apicius, represented by his ghost, gave all the fantasy of gourmandise known to antique Rome. Then a spectacle of sea gods; the Lombard Rivers offered up their fish-foods, dancing suitable figures. And so it went, entry after entry, until it terminated with a Bacchic rout.

If these marvels are tedious to read of in cold print, think of what they must have been like to see: four or five hours of them at a stretch, and food and drink between. Aside from expenses involved, for costumes and scenery were beautifully finished as useful objects, how can one explain the plethora of inventions? Why was not every guest nodding with boredom half-way through the meal? How could they go on and on marveling and compli-menting each other on the fantasies, the ingenuities? We forget the epoch. Men of the Renaissance were not satiated as we are. On the contrary, they were starved for wonders, craving splendor. They had incredible energies for war, for lust, for hate, for building and for sensory enjoyment. They were not tired by centuries of repetitious spectacle. Their perceptions were sharpened to experiment. Every new dinner was a competitive innovation. Ennui was an unknown self-indulgence. Their sensitivity to the beauty of surfaces, to the texture of woven stuffs, to apparitions of adorned bodies was unappeasable. They had few standards of comparative judgment. Uncritical in the extreme, their curiosity had a health and vibrance perhaps since unknown. Their whole beings were unclogged for their free, sweeping appetites in spectacle and sound.

This is by no means to infer that however boring they may seem to us, these displays were not beautiful. Leonardo da Vinci, with his heart-break-ing prodigality of talent, devoted weeks to preparations for masques. A Milanese Duke heard of him as a child, because of his musical virtuosity. This bastard of a notary and country-girl had fingers so strong he could twist iron rings, so delicate he could pluck magic chords from a lute which he himself had fashioned; the lute an equestrian head in beaten-silver, its acoustics deter-mined by a system he had himself discovered.

When Gian Galeazzo finally arrived at Milan, still hungry after the feast of Botta, he was greeted by another extravaganza designed by Leonardo. It was *Il Paradiso,* a gorgeous heaven, an unbelievable improvement on the wood and wool of Brunelleschi's cloud-effects. Da Vinci's was a swimming paradise studded with seven planets, mounted with men dressed as the poets had described. Jove from his celestial seat commanded each orb in turn to descend and give in his name homage to the Duchess. In Naples, the Court of Aragon; in Ferrara, the Este; in Florence, the Medici were patrons of entertainments which may have been equaled, if on a crasser scale, in Imperial Rome but surely never since.

Incidental amusements of banquet-balls by no means inhibited the development of independent theater. If anything, they accelerated it. Ercole d'Este put on comedies of Plautus and Terence at an enormous cost of academic research and hard cash. But this gesture towards erudition, the satisfaction of immersion into the antique, resulted in a literary drama which was sterile, snobbish, of little interest to us. In 1502 Lucrezia Borgia came to Ferrara as Alfonso d'Este's wife. Ercole made a theater on antique models. From Rome, Siena, Mantua and Ferrara itself he gathered a troupe of one hundred and ten actors. For five nights the fête lasted, and on each night another Latin comedy, unproduced for nearly a thousand years, was performed with minute care. But even Ercole knew how restive his fashionable audience would become. The farces were relieved by a welcome series of *intermedii.*

There were moriscoes of Roman gladiators, of shepherd-satyrs, of Moors with lit candles between their teeth, of goat-feet dancing to music from a mechanical toy hidden within the head of an ass, of farmers performing the labors of the calendar. One entry was introduced by a girl riding on a chariot led by a unicorn. Upon it, several personages bound to a tree-trunk, and four lute players, sat under boughs. The captives, unchained by the girl, stepped down from the car and danced, while the stringed accompaniment sang lovely songs. The last play, on the fifth night, was the *Casina* of Plautus. The audience must have been very much like contemporary devotees of Bayreuth and Salzburg, eager but not unflagging in their interest. Inattention has never been wholly the fault of the audience. Human eyes and ears can only stand so much. Spectators who knew no Latin, and cared little for all this revivalism must have been chiefly amused by the numerous dances, although they were largely in the nature of a sop. After the *Casina* there was a

> dance of savages contending for the possession of a beautiful woman. Suddenly the God of Love appeared, accompanied by musicians, and set her free. Hereupon the spectators discovered a great globe which suddenly split in halves and began to give forth beautiful strains. In conclusion, twelve Swiss armed with halberds and wearing their national colors entered, and executed an artistic dance, fencing the while.*

The word *Balletti,* diminutive for *Ballo,* a dance, is used to refer to dances performed in a ballroom. In the beginning, *balletti,* as a term, had no special theatrical meaning, but meant merely performances of danced figures, not unlike a developed English Morris, which was greatly in vogue among high

*Enid Welsford: *The Court Masque,* p. 89: quotation from Gregorovius.

life of Milan. Not until after Marie de Medici had established the Italians in France did it acquire a specifically dramatic significance.

Nevertheless, in the Renaissance, we have, if only as *intermedii,* dancing in theaters. The development of buildings for housing actors and dancers, though primarily intended for actors, exerted a great influence on the arrangement of dances. Such influence may not have been consciously felt for a century, and then more in France than in Italy. But the source of all this growth came from Italian Renaissance architects and painters. As far back as 1452 Alberti had made a theater for that Pope Nicolas the Fifth who formed a nucleus for the Vatican Library. But it was not until 1484 that an edition of the works of the Roman builder, Vitruvius, was first issued. For two hundred years or more every European architect was to pay tribute, directly or indirectly, to this record of Greek and Roman staging. The place for sitting, the banking of seats, arrangements for entering or leaving the auditoria, were based on antique models; but the hemicycle of seats no longer formed the exterior façade. Four walls enclosed the whole building in a rectangle, and the house was roofed. However, contemporary Renaissance painters introduced an important feature to the revived stage, the principle of aerial perspective. To give the illusion on a single plane that one object is in front of another in space, requires the practice of certain practical graphic laws. These laws were extended to the usages of a raised stage, where the illusion desired was not to be on a single plane, but on a very restricted area, which must give an appearance of indefinitely extensive space. The Italian painters, who never worked in a single medium, but were also engineers, anatomists, sculptors and dress-designers, had been absorbed by problems of perspective since Brunelleschi. They sought not only the discovery of sight-lines focused on the vanishing point, but also means by which atmosphere could be made to mantle hard edges of forms which, ever since the rigid convention of Italo-Byzantine artists, had been so raw. Research had brought remarkable results, and the greatest masters never felt it beneath them to paint stage-decoration. In the beginning, these were not necessarily always in perspective. Mantegna's superb series of panels depicting the triumph of Julius Cæsar, now at Hampton Court, were probably intended as side wings in the Mantuan performances of Plautus of 1484. There is a description * of stage decor in the same town, in 1501.

> The shape was rectangular, longer than it was wide: the two sides opposite one another had each eight architraves with columns harmonizing with and proportioned to the breadth and height of the said arches: the bases and capitals were most imposing, the whole giving the impression of a permanent antique building, full of beauty; the arches with flowers in relief formed a wonderful perspective; the width of each was about six feet; the height proportionate. Within the scene were cloths of gold and some shrubs, as the

* Alardyce Nicoll: *The Development of the Theatre,* p. 87.

scenes required; one of the sides was decorated with six panels of the triumph of Cæsar by the famous Mantegna.

In the year 1513, the great comedy of Bernardo Dovizio was produced at Urbino, before a distinguished audience. His play, 'Calandra,' which charmed its spectators by adapting Boccaccio's prose style to the stage, was no longer the accustomed, tedious Latin pastiche, but perhaps the first contemporary treatment of the times in which it was produced, and if not wholly free from the pressure of Plautus, indicating, nevertheless, the future direction of Italian comedy.

> The scene was made to resemble a very lovely city with streets, palaces, churches, towers, real streets, and everything *in relief,* but assisted by beautiful painting and clever perspective.

The scenery was actually built in three dimensions, but its distances were elongated by tricks of deceptive sight-lines, blending tones into the painted shadows. During the 'Calandra,' there was performed an advanced type of Morisco, and it is described in a letter of the great 'Courtier,' Balthazar Castiglione.

> The intromese were as follows: the first was a Moresca of Jason ... who came in dancing, dressed as a warrior of antiquity, and in a series of rhythmic movements yoked the fire-breathing bulls, plowed the ground and sowed the dragon's teeth, which quickly sprang up as armed men, who danced a proud moresca. The second intermezzo consisted of the car of Venus, drawn by doves and accompanied by cupids who danced a moresca beating time with their lighted torches. Other cars of Neptune and Juno, other dances of Moresche and brandi followed; and at the end of the comedy appeared the god of Love.

In Enid Welsford's book on the Court Masque, in which so much of this material is aptly illuminated, are linked English Morris and Italian Morisco.

> The Italian dancers, for instance, wear bells, they often fight a mock-battle. The Cupids brandishing their torches, Vulcan and his Cyclops beating time with their hammers, are not so very far removed, after all, from the villagers beating time with their sticks in 'Bean-setting' or 'Rigs-O-Marlowe.'

Castiglione, whose symposia of society, written between 1508 and 1516 has left us a picture of Rennaisance life as it best might have been, was an acute observer of dancing. We remember, how, at the start of his *Decameron,* Boccaccio's guests danced the Carole. Similarly, in Urbino, after the first evening's talk as to the nature of the true courtier,

> My lady Duchess desired Madonna Margarita and Madonna Costanza Fregosea to dance. Whereupon Barletti, a very charming musician and excellent dancer, who always kept the whole court in good humor, began to play upon his instruments; and joining hands, the ladies danced first a *basset* and then a *roegarze,* with consummate grace and to the great delight of those who saw them.

The *basse* dance we already know from the Jew of Pesaro. The *Roegarze* must be typical of many folk or country-dances, which, observed among the peasantry were, with their tunes, adapted to court use. This particular dance was French in origin, the *Rouergoise,* deriving from the town of Rouergue, an old French province, southwest of Lyons. Castiglione provides us with the perfect Renaissance standard for dancing-behavior. The elegance, the mutual consideration, the precision looks a long way forward into French dancing history.

> Thus you see how the exhibition of art and study so intense destroys the grace in everything. Which of you is there who does not laugh when our friend messer Pierpaolo dances in his peculiar way, with those capers of his,—legs stiff to the toe and head motionless, as if he were a stick, and with such intentness that he actually seems to be counting the steps? What eye so blind as not to see in this the ungracefulness of affectation,—and in many men and women who are here present, the grace of that nonchalant ease (for in the case of bodily movements many call it thus), showing by word or laugh or gesture that they have no care and are thinking more of everything else than of that, to make the onlooker think they can hardly go amiss?
>
> Messer Bernard Bibbiena here said, without waiting:
>
> Now at last our friend messer Roberto has found some one to praise the manner of his dancing, as all the rest of you seem to value it lightly; because if this merit consists in nonchalance, and in appearing to take no heed and to be thinking more of everything else than of what you are doing, messer Roberto in dancing has no peer on earth; for to show plainly that he is not thinking about it, he often lets the cloak drop from his shoulders and the slippers from his feet, and still goes on dancing without picking up either the one or the other.

Castiglione gives us the distinction between the semi-professional dancer, dancing-masters, and aristocrats who dance only for their pleasure:

> There are certain other exercises that can be practiced in public and in private, like dancing; and in this I think the Courtier ought to have a care, for when dancing in the presence of many and in a place full of people, it seems to me that he should preserve a certain dignity, albeit tempered with a lithe and airy grace of movement; and although he may feel himself to be very nimble and a master of time and measure, let him not attempt those agilities of foot and double steps which we find very becoming in our friend Barletti, but which perhaps would be little suited to a gentleman. Yet in a room privately, as we are now, I think he may try both, and may dance morris-dances and brawls; but not in public unless he be masked, when it is not displeasing even though he be recognized by all.

Dancing was an every-day adjunct to court life in all European Renaissance palaces. Queen Elizabeth is supposed to have made Sir Christopher Hatton her Lord Chancellor, not because of his particular wisdom in the law, but because "he wore green bows on his shoes and danced the pavane to perfection." The English were famous as fine performers. In 1592, Balthasar

Paumgartner wrote his wife from Frankfort-on-the-Main, describing some he had seen, "the most accomplished at leaping and dancing that I have ever heard of or seen." Dancing in Germany, extremely popular at all festivities, though not theatrical, retained for a long time its Gothic exuberance. Couples snatched at each other, screamed and shouted. Men tossed their partners high off the floor, and there were the usual church-inspired ordinances against 'shameless twirling.' In Max von Boehn's entertaining 'Modes and Manners' we find:

> Andreas Osiander wrote to Hieronymas Besola at Nuremburg in 1550 that all the couples who had danced together at his daughter's wedding had been fined, and great was the indignation of Bartholomaus Sastrow when he was penalized by the Greifswald magistrate for similar conduct at his own nuptials.

Town-councils issued various rules such as: both men and women must be decently dressed; that is, no man might dance in breeches and doublet without a coat; women and girls must not be whirled or thrown about. Mutual claspings were frowned on. Strangely enough, the Reformation instigator himself by no means shared these views. Martin Luther wrote, "I always loved music; whoso hath skill in this art, the same is of good kind and fitted to all things." In 1540, he said at table, "Dances have been instituted and permitted in order that courtesy may be learned in company and to encourage friendship and acquaintance among young men and girls." Burton, the Anatomist of Melancholy, quotes another great Reformation authority:

> If he is truly touched with the loadstone of love, he must learn to sing and dance and play upon some instrument, for as Erasmus hath it: *Musicam docet amor et poesin.*

But as is often the case, the followers were not as gracious as the founder. Protestant clergy quickly took up a grim tone towards dancing. Melanchthon himself was severely reprimanded for loving it. Melchior Ambach, a Frankfort preacher, said it was sinful because unfounded on the Bible. He could not have looked very far. Most Church irritation was political, directed against the balls of the nobility. The traveler, Montaigne, describes a party in Augsburg in 1580:

> The gentleman took the lady's hand, kissed it, and placed his hand on her shoulder; he then clasped her securely, holding her so close that they were cheek to cheek. The lady placed a hand on his shoulder, and in this way they circled round the room. The menfolk have their own seats quite apart from those of the ladies, and apparently do not care to mix with them.

Hans von Schweinichen, a knight of Silesia, visited the same town five years before:

> It is the custom for ... two persons, who wear red robes and long white sleeves, to dance the figure first. Whenever they turn, the other dancers must turn too; and when they embrace each other the young men may embrace

the damsels with whom they are dancing. The young men often bribe them to do so frequently, and many a hug may be had for half a thaler.

But such dancing, popular in Germany, would have horrified the Italians by its boorishness. Not until the eighteenth century did Germany make a contribution to stage-dancing; and only then, by the indirect appropriation of Bavarian folk-dances, which after considerable variation and refinement, emerged as the waltz.

France was neither ignorant of Italian dances in the early part of the sixteenth century, nor poor in pageantry of her own devising. Francis the First in 1520 arranged his Field of Cloth of Gold, on a broad plain close to Calais, for a long time a standard of magnificence. By meeting Henry the Eighth on conquered territory, Francis showed he wished the English as his friends. Two hundred thousand livres subsidized silk weavers in Touraine and carpenters in Picardy. Innumerable tents were to be raised, and Francis ordered his of gold cloth, crowned with gilt apples, a gilded Saint Michel to cap it all. In addition, he built a Roman theater of wood.

Cardinal Wolsey insisted upon an equivalent British magnificence. The English amazed every one by their ingenuity. They had built a grand casemented castle at home, to be shipped to France in sections, where it was quickly set up. Covered with canvas, a marbleized court, arras on the walls and dazzling chandeliers, the fountains spouted wine in its court. After the meeting, the castle was sent back to England. The poet, Joachim du Bellay, said nothing was lost but the expenses of the return freight.

But no matter how tasteful or talented were the Parisians, they needed the inbred gifts of Florentines and Milanese to create their ballet. And Florence, too, needed France. For after the *Trionfi,* the *Intermedii,* the archeological revivals, the launching of their own popular comedy, dancing in Italy will not occupy us again to any marked degree until the early nineteenth century. As soon as the stamens of the Fleur de Lys are pollenized by the Lilies of Florence, the history of European stage-dancing is French, and remains so, until Salvatore Vigano and Carlo Blasis recapture it for thirty years, before the ultimate Russian supremacy.

Catherine de Medici was an only child of a pageant-loving Lorenzo, Duke of Urbino, and his young French wife, a member of the house of Bourbon. She was the last member of the older and greater branch of a house which had included the most influential men of Florence. From birth, an orphan, she was raised by relations to be an exceptionally well-educated princess, not in literature alone, but in philosophy, music and the dance. Her youth, due to her unique position, was full of constant threats and lively danger. This violence merely steeled the remarkable personality she shared with the line of Cosimo, Pater Patriæ and Magnificent Lorenzo.

Catherine embarked from Porto Venese, on the gulf of Spezia, to become the bride of Henri, duc d'Orléans. Her arrival was, in itself, a nautical *trionfo.*

The fleet as it approached the harbor of Marseilles was a picturesque sight; it consisted of sixty ships, that conveying Catherine having sails of purple cloth embroidered with gold, and being followed by that bearing the Pope, which was covered with a tent of cloth of gold, the deck being carpeted with crimson satin. On landing, a procession of unusual splendor took place through the city; it was headed by a white horse with white trappings, bearing the host, and led by two equerries also dressed in white. Then followed the Pope, conveyed in his chair borne on men's shoulders, and succeeded by a long procession of bishops and cardinals on horseback, wearing their robes; and lastly Catherine herself, dressed in a robe of gold brocade, and riding by the side of her uncle-in-law, John Stuart, Duke of Albany, who had married her mother's sister, Anne. From every balcony hung costly draperies of velvet and embroidery, while across the streets were festooned countless garlands of the deep-colored damask roses of Provence mingled with the lilies of France.*

Symbolic entrance in more ways than one, combining powers and homages of England, Provence, France and Italy, four strains of the first importance in the creation of the new ballet. When Francis the First died, Catherine was Queen of France. The French aristocrats hated her not only for an alien, but for the Italian bourgeoise of distinctly plebeian ancestry, which she was. Naturally enough they accused her of poisoning the Dauphin in order to attain his throne. But when the charges were investigated, with the usual torture, it was discovered that neither Catherine nor Charles the Fifth of Spain were guilty, but "The Dauphine, who was of a sickly constitution, died of having drunk too freely of cold water after over-heating himself at tennis, and not of poison at all." This, merely to indicate Catherine's existence at the French Court was calculated to make her draw as much as possible upon the culture of the land of her birth, which with an onslaught of more frightful happenings, she increasingly did. Her own gloomy husband did little except flaunt in her face his mysterious mistress, Diane de Poictiers. Nine years married, she was childless. Only the sudden birth of an heir saved her from divorce.

In 1547, her husband became Henry the Second. For Catherine there were a dozen tragic years during which she was forced to watch a man whom she secretly adored, under the complete domination of that eternally young Diana whom Goujon cut in marble, making love to a stag. Cultivating a dignified policy of unprotesting self-discipline, she raised her family well, and became a Frenchwoman. On the 25th of April, 1558, her eldest boy, Francis, was married to Mary, Queen of Scots. They were both fifteen years old. The nuptials were performed with true Medicean brilliance. In the evening, a great ball at the Palais des Tournelles, with 'masques and mummeries' in the Palais de Justice.†

The children of the Dukes of Guise and Aumale rode on artificial horses caparisoned with gold and silver trappings and drawing coaches filled with

*G. F. Young: *The Medici,* Modern Library Edition, pp. 395, 415.
†Ibid. p. 415.

gorgeously dressed pilgrims. These were followed by six ships covered with crimson velvet, and imitating as they moved the rolling motion of the sea, in the foremost of which embarked the king and the young bride, in the next the Dauphin and Catherine, in the third the Duke of Lorraine and the Princess Claude, and so on, the ships then sailing round the great hall, 'which was illuminated as much by the blaze of jewels worn by the company as by the torches and cressets.'

For the next year, two more royal marriages; more splendor terminating in an actual tournament. Premonitions and warnings could not dissuade the king. After several courses, Montgomery, captain of his guard, by a hideous mischance pierced the sovereign through an eye; Henry died after ten days of agony. From that day Catherine never took off her weeds. She was forty. In the next three decades of her life she was to administer France and powerfully affect the world. It is difficult, even considering the late Middle Ages and early Renaissance, monstrosities of despots like Ezzolino da Romano, or the Borgia horror, to imagine a bloodier time than this period of religious war and party decimation. Italy seems somehow remoter, almost as if lives lost there were sacrificed inevitably to a tremendous rebirth the land was undergoing. The French terror is more immediate, the courage more constant, the emotions more contemporary, the violence more refined and frightening. Its tragedy is less grotesque, less bestial. The protagonists are not so much historic figures as men we should like to have known. It was heart-break gayety, a green-arbor atmosphere of gardens at Fontainebleau and fountains of late Paris afternoons. But the shed blood was blood enough, even wiped off marble floors, and in this sweet and bloody air, the *Ballet de Cour* evolved.

Balls at this French court interest us mainly in relation to their effect on the seventeenth century, which culminate in the founding of the Royal Academy of Music and Dancing, the source of the influence of Lully and Rameau, the world's standard for two hundred and fifty years. But as we read faded descriptions of the dancing, we cannot forget that every ball could be pretext for a plot. Politics plucked the strings of lutes, designed collars and crowns, arranged the order of dances. Catherine was implicated in innumerable poisonings, assassinations by steel and magic, of most of which she was entirely innocent. The theater for the crimes, since there were no special stages, was grand salons in Paris, Fontainebleau, Blois, Chenonceaux, or wherever her court progressed.

The Queen-Mother loved dancing. Her mourning did not keep her from the ballroom. Brantôme, a valuable documentor of the period on its amorous as well as on many other sides, tells in his "Lives of the Gallant Ladies": *

> At court we have seen some delightful ballets played by our Queens, and in especial by the Queen Mother; yet we courtiers would commonly cast our eyes only on the feet and legs of the ladies taking part, and take the greatest

* Translated by H. M. 1924, Vol. I, p. 220.

pleasure in watching the dainty play of their legs, twinkling and frisking their little feet more bewitchingly than anything in the world; for their petticoats and robes were much shorter than usual, though not so short as those of the Nymph's (Diane de Poictiers) nor so high as some would have liked. Nevertheless our eyes were always lowered a little, and most of all when they danced the quick step, which in making the skirts fly out would always reveal something pleasant to see—whereat I have seen many to lose their heads with delight.

When both Catholics and Protestants had lost their commanders, Catherine was able to arrange a treaty in March, 1563. It was the end of the first religious war. She was so happy she 'danced for joy' and proclaimed peace by the Edict of Amboise. She could not know seven more wars were yet to come. She immediately took her children, Charles the Ninth, Henry duc d'Anjou, François, Duc d'Alencon, his wife, and the Prince de Conde, the Duc de Guise and Henry of Navarre down to Chenonceaux, where at the great house a week full of celebrations was enjoyed.

She was granted a respite from war if not from plotting, for a few peaceful years. Wisely she kept away from Paris, the storm-center of dissension, taking her fourteen-year-old son, the King of France, on a two-year tour of the southern provinces. Her train included eight hundred people, their servants, coachmen, guards and so on. Her progress was interrupted by a series of shows testifying to the loyalty of the natives. At Macon, the Queen-Mother was called upon to act as peacemaker in peace-time. A fierce sectarian situation was caused by her arrival. Should Protestant children be permitted to walk beside Catholics in the welcoming processions?

They reached Bayonne in June of 1565. Although ostensibly a meeting of the Queen-Mother with her daughter Elizabeth of Spain, Philip the Second did not neglect to send his Duke of Alva, scourge of Holland. He came primed with his Catholic Majesty's moderate requests: to exclude Protestants from all public office, to prohibit Protestant services, to expel from France all Protestant ministers. The Huguenots, with something less than reason, always maintained this was the secret origin of Saint Bartholemew's seven years ahead. Margaret, the Queen who was to succeed Catherine, in a letter to Brantôme, writes memories of Bayonne:

Nature seemed to have made ready the ballroom with her own hand, for there, right in the heart of the island, (off from the city), stood a great oval meadow girt with giant trees, in the shadow of which the Queen-Mother had great niches placed all around and in each niche a table laid for twelve.... The crossing from Bayonne to the island was accomplished in richly decorated gondolas and canoes, around which sported tritons and sea-gods blowing horns and warbling sweet songs. On either side of the landing place the shepherds and shepherdesses (the banquet waiters) footed the appropriate dances of their province; those of Poitou danced to the strains of the shawm, those of Burgundy and Champagne to the small oboe, the fiddle and the tabor;

the Provencals executed their *volta* with tympani, the Bretons indulged in the *passe-pieds* and the merry brawl (*bransle*); . . . Then the nymphs climbed down and danced a ballet, the perfect beauty of which so angered envious fortune that a violent storm arose with thunder and rain. The confusion in getting back by boat that night caused as much fun next morning as had the festivity itself.

But Catherine had time for work as well. She completed the main fabric of the huge Palace of the Louvre and was the first sovereign to sleep there. She employed Philibert de l'Orme to commence the construction of the Tuilleries. She made improvements in many of the Châteaux of Touraine, and she patronized the *Pleiade,* a semi-official academy of poets of greater and lesser fame, immortal from the work of Pierre Ronsard, Joachim du Bellay, and particularly to us, of Jean Antoine de Baïf.

Baïf was born in 1532, and in 1570 he obtained from Charles the Ninth letters patent permitting him to found an Academy of Saint Cecilia: Academy, because that was the Athenian term for such an institution; Saint Cecilia, since she was the Christian protectress of music. His academy though dissolved some years later, established the precedent for future institutions under such patronage and exerted, during its own life, a great influence not only over music for church, but also of the chamber, and for the ballroom.

Music is so important in its relation to dance that one hesitates to speak of it here as a mere side-issue. Threads that bind its rhythm to the bodies of dancers since the beginning are no less divergent or confusing than those of dancing forms. When we play contemporary arrangements of Provençal music, for example, it seems weak and sad. A piano is no instrument for such melody. Our voices cannot recapture the modulation of throats freshened by distant and southern airs. Similarly, the Valois tunes are faded, monotonous, if magical. It is useless to attempt to recapture a charm which was even more inherent in *performance* than in musical structure. But we must know enough of this structure to indicate the split between ballet and opera, when the fork comes.

The singing of madrigals was extremely popular throughout the Renaissance everywhere, although we may be inclined to think of it as peculiar to England. Part-songs were developed more for an interest in vocal harmonics for which they served as pretext, than either for melody or words, both of which were accessories. A considerable scientific energy was exhausted on formalizing the madrigal. In Palestrina's great musical revolution, he opened up, among other things, a possibility for dramatic diction, the whole mechanics of opera. Although his work was largely ecclesiastical, its effect was universal. He had a French pupil, one Goudimel, later slain on Bartholemew's, who wished to revitalize the entire repertory of Mass, cantata and madrigal. His contemporary, Clément Janequin, an independent, courageous composer, worked by himself, publishing in 1544 twenty-four musical inventions. They were experimental descriptive pieces; the 'War,' the 'Swallow,' 'Jealousy,' the 'Song of Birds,' the 'Battle of Marignan,' the 'Taking of Boulogne.' These musical forces, combining a lively, if largely mistaken, effort to revive antique Greek poetic metric, with the work being done on the other side of the Alps, would result in the songs and symphonies which were to accompany the *Ballets de Cour.*

Italian musical history was already so full we can scarcely hint at it. The Company of the Gonfalon as far back as 1264 had presented an oratorio of the Passion, which was in essence, dramatic. Around 1450, the composer Beverini, already author of a 'Conversion of Saint Paul' composed 'Darius,' half-opera, half-heroic tragedy, in three acts. Supposedly requiring some fourteen changes of decorations, it was equipped in the Renaissance fashion with elephants, mountains and palaces.

There was also Poliziano's pastoral of 'Orpheo,' given in 1471 with considerable music, and in such Milanese fêtes as Bergonzio de la Botta's, the instrumental accompaniment was large, related and important. In 1503, a Venetian, Petrucci, invented the process whereby musical notation could be printed from type. This enormously accelerated the interchange of creative influences, which had previously been handicapped by the slavery of copyists. While Janequin was writing his bird-notes in Paris, Saint Philip Neri was organizing Italian holy spectacles, very much in the nature of sacred operas, although called, after the Order of their instigator, *Oratorios.* France and Italy are braided together until the end of the century, when the French, with their preference for the masquerade, chose the route of theatrical dancing; while the Italians, with natural predilection take to theatrical singing.

Already in 1558, Jodelle, arranger of court fêtes, had invented a consecutive spectacle whereby, in frank imitation of the *trionfi,* Orpheus praised Henry the Second, on his entry into Paris. The French loved masquerading not for any inherent interest in disguised parades, but as pretext for divertissements, amusing, ingenious or fantastic interludes. Burgundian tournaments were famous for the conceits of costumed suites of their contestants. Feudal forms celebrated the entry of Catherine into Paris, and were the background of her husband's death. In the sixteenth century nobles frequently ruined themselves by competitive extravagance which, compared to the antique literary revivals in Italy, strikes us as mediæval. However, a very French feature was the conclusion of the entertainments with the distribution of gallant verses by the masquers to the invited guests. This custom was a remnant or rather a Renaissance adaptation of an older custom of presenting gifts, demands for which we remember in the English medieval sword- and morris-dances.

The history of different forms which processions, masquerades and silken tournaments took under the regency of Catherine is so complex and has been chronicled so admirably by Le Cerf, Prunières and Welsford, that only a bare outline will be given here. It is a history as interesting and as devious as the creation of that atmosphere in pre-Elizabethan England, which was the seed-bed for Shakespeare. The *Ballet de Cour* had no Shakespeare, but it received a form, as did English tragedy, which shadowed its descendants well into the seventeenth century.

In this book no attempt can be made to give instances of the first time a specific Italian feature is used at the French court, or the innovation of a new variant on previous native forms. This is less important to the enthusiast than to the scholar. Perhaps a more vivid idea of the progression may be obtained by alliance with politics.

In 1572, Catherine's attempts to achieve another peace in the bloody business seemed again to be crowned with success. Five hundred Protestants, headed by Henry of Navarre, arrived in Paris, where Admiral Coligny, the young Prince de Condé, and a great crowd of Protestants gathered for the wedding of Princess Marguerite and Henry, which was, ostensibly, to bury the past and cement the party interests. The subject of the ballets (the term was universally used now), the mimed and sung scenes, the *intermedes à la Italienne,* have a sinister significance.

It is 'The Defense of Paradise': who arranged the partition of the rôles? The Catholic King of France and his brothers defend Heaven; the Protestant King of Navarre and his friends guard Hell. On the right of the salon in the Louvre, is Paradise, guarded by three armed knights: Charles the Ninth, the Duc d'Anjou, the Duc d'Alençon. At the left, Hell, with devils and tortures. We recall the miracle play settings at Valenciennes. Between Heaven and Hell a river flows upon which Charon paddles his barge. Behind Paradise, the Elysian fields, in the form of a lovely garden of artificed trees and brilliant gilding. In the sky, glows the Zodiac, seven planets and stars. The Knights, commanded by Navarre, attack Heaven. The fight, calculated in advance, left the victory to Charles the Ninth, and his assailants were thrown back to Hell, which swallowed them. Then Mercury and Cupid descended from Heaven upon a giant rooster. Estienne le Roi, a famous singer, chanted the rôle of the messenger-god. Finishing his tempered harangue, addressed to the heavenly knights, he mounted skywards again, leaving them with Love to seek the favors of twelve nymphs. After another interminable ballet, victors and (clearly) vanquished joined each other in Paradise. The conclusion was a pyramidal fountain of gun-powder which was set off in the middle of the hall, an eruption and a finale. Yet it was not until 1830 that the Comte de Salvandy, at a fête given by the Duke of Orleans to the King of Naples first spoke of dancing on the edge of a volcano.

The 'Paradise' occurred on the 18th of August. Four days later, Admiral Coligny, walking home from the Louvre, was fired at by a retainer of the Duc de Guise. He was hurt in the hand and arm. The King and Queen Mother, expressing the greatest concern, sent their great surgeon Ambrose Paré. On Saint Bartholemew's, six days later, came the massacre.

Such a spectacle as 'The Defense of Paradise' held under such auspices must have been rehearsed not once, but several times. What background for a ballet! Men, who had just left killing each other, courteously, in the toils of music alone, combined for a short while in pretensions of mutual honors. That they both loved dancing was no simulation. That they hated each other could have been no secret. Yet there they were, reconciled in a common show. We can picture Catherine, whose practical interest in these matters was intense, inspecting preparations, observing the erection of Heavenly Gates, the Jaws of Hell. Perhaps as she passed through the salon, she saw one of the Protestants who that night would play a Demon. Perhaps she had known him in the old days, or in a previous armistice. Perhaps he would be summoned for a moment, and for a moment relinquishing his fealty to Navarre, kneel and kiss the hand of the Medici, rise and leave her to resume the rehearsal.

'The Defense of Paradise' is a show without particular significance in the long history of ballet. The massacre of Saint Bartholemew is but a well-known outrage in wars which, on both sides, held worse. But the junction of the two is a precious convergence of incident, an example of a work of art tragic in essence and in action, a definition of the epoch in which it is set.

We have now come to the end of a long prelude, a prelude which started in attempt to understand the very origins of the word for dance. We have had dealings with the gods; Osiris, Dionysos, Jesus. We have known a dance-drama achieved in ritual as the summit of artistic form. We have watched that form disintegrate with an empire, and revive with a new religion. We have found elements which were not new to Greece, newly used in Provence and Italy, for fusion in France. In the gestation of wars and religious hate, in the savage, sane cruelty of Italians and French,—music, painting and dancing have not been either apart from bloodshed or distant from each other. The combination which we are about to be given is the court ballet; the history we are about to give is that of modern stage-dancing.

ENTRY OF HENRI II INTO ROUEN 1550

❧ CHAPTER IX ❧

The BALLET COMIQUE *and the* BALLET DE COUR

WHILE the Valois were having balls and masquerades designed and danced we have scarce reason to suppose they were constantly aware of their political or artistic significance. Each masking had a political as well as a purely social function. The particular occasion for the party determined the form in which the dances were arranged. But to the designers political intrigue was no more significant than their allowance of gold-leaf, the number of viols, or their budget for scenery. While participating in their entertainments they were occupied with the mechanical ingenuities as much as with the ceaseless conspiracies which webbed France. Sometimes, to be sure, plots of ballets coincided with plots for thrones, but such was the vitality of the Renaissance, that instead of one suffering by the other, ballet would even profit, if for no other reason, by masking suspicions of murder. In a way, the ballets were created consciously, by poets, musicians and painters, to be performed absent-mindedly by courtiers who loved them, not as relaxation, or anodyne, but as enchantment, the peculiar magic of living in a lyric counterpart of personal lives which were predominantly tragic.

When Polish ambassadors arrived to offer their country's crown to Henri Duc d'Anjou (later, the third of his name to be king of France), his mother entertained them at a grand spectacle in the Tuilleries in a hall erected for the occasion. One of the reasons for the fragmentary development of both drama and opera was the absence of permanent theaters. Not only did all maskings have to be rehearsed, but each time, unless a ballroom could be adapted for their use, a house must be raised to give their audience shelter. Paris skies were not so clear as those of Florence. Brantôme writes of the Polish fête of 1573:

> And all about was an infinity of torches; she (Catherine) presented the most beautiful ballet that was ever on earth,...which was composed of sixteen ladies and young girls...they were set upon a great silvered rock in niches ...representing the sixteen provinces of France, with the most melodious music imaginable, and after the rock had made a parade-tour of the room... all came to step down from the rock and being formed into a little battalion of bizarre invention, viols to the number of some thirty sounding pleasantly forth an *air de danse,* they came forward to step to the tune of the viols and in perfect time, without ever getting out of step, approached unto and stopped themselves a little before their majesties, and then danced their ballet, so fantastically conceived, and by so many turnings, *contours et detours,* interlacings and confusings, encounters and arrests, in which not one lady ever failed to turn in her place nor in her rank, so well that every one was amazed by such confusion and such a disorder never ceasing from a superior order, for these ladies had solid judgment and good memory and had been so well

rehearsed; and this bizarre ballet went on for less than an hour, which being finished, all the ladies, representing the said provinces, were presented to the King, to the Queen, to the King of Poland, to Monsieur, his brother, to the King and Queen of Navarre and the other lords of France and Poland, each gave to the other a golden plaque, big as the palm of one's hand, well enameled and nicely worked upon which were engraved the fruits and specialties of each province, in which each was fertile: Provence, lemons and oranges; Champagne, wheat (not yet the wine); Burgundy, wines; Guyenne, warriors ...and mark you well that all these inventions came from no other shop nor other wit than the Queen's (Catherine).

This has been called the prototype of the *Ballet Comique de la Reine,* which was the first modern integrated theatrical dance-drama. But rather, *Le Ballet des Polonais* marked the fashion, and the triumph, in France, of figured-dancing. The chief interest of the maskers was not silvered rock, nor costumes, nor music, elements which we have long known, but the complexity of the step's figuration. The dancers were masked, but d'Aubigne noticed:

The Nymphs descended, to dance a ballet twice; first masqued and then without masks. The Poles marveled at the orderly confusions, the well-formed numbers of the ballet, the different musics and said the dance of France was impossible to equal by all the kings of the earth.

The greatest single influence on the *Ballet Comique* was the Academy of Baïf, which, though it may not have directly invented the ballet, was nevertheless responsible for its synthesis, because of the theories it held on the antique, the researches of its members into the past. The views of the *Pleiade,* the starry crown of poets, had a profound effect on musical form and substance. As we have indicated, up until about 1550, there was little relationship between verses sung and the tunes sustaining them. Before then, the prime interest was vocalization, or more descriptively, onomatopœia. The poet Clément Marot, for example, had scarcely any interest in a marriage of his words to his lute strings. But the following generation of Pierre Ronsard very much did, and insisted upon animating the poem by its music. Thus, the *Pleiade* precipitated an end of madrigals. They were no less possessed by the antique than the Italians; Orpheus was their eternal, literal symbol. Verse must be linked to his lyre-strings. During this period, famous composers were really less significant than everyday lutanists or singing-teachers, who tried to dislocate words and phrases of sung poems as little as possible. Since it is necessary to educate and affect the large public if ideas are to have any lasting power, Baïf and Thibaut de Courville sought royal patronage for the foundation of an influential Academy of Music and Poetry. Baïf, in the formulation of the Academy, hoped to achieve a great literary and musical reformation by the practice of measured verse *à l'antique*. Many contemporary poets, perhaps more Italian than French, had applied the metrics of Horace and Sappho to their rhymes, but no one had yet proposed a method for the ideal union of music and words, the secret of which only ancients were believed to know. In Baïf's Academy, instrumentalists learned to respect the laws of prosody, their tunes coinciding with rhythms in metrical verse in such a way as to make possible dramatic *recitative* to which the Franco-Italian Lully was to give perfect expression a hundred years later.

In Paris, as in Florence, poets, musicians and humanists attempted to discover the riddle of the antique *Melopeia,* or euphonious verse. But while Italians, chiefly as actors, searched for a renewed lyric declamation which would permit them to chant poetic tragedies on the stage, French reformers mainly thought of conforming music to the strict exigencies of a given prosody. This is one reason why a new form of melodrama could not emerge from such literal application of humanist ideas, and why the humanists had such difficulty, both in France and Italy, confused as they were by antique longings, to create living work.

Baïf and his academicians hoped to present plays in measured verse, based on ancient canons. But the religious wars, breaking out again, put an end to their plans. This was not an unalleviated disaster. Such slavery to Greek and Roman metric might have pleased its producers, scarcely a large public. They had no future. On the other hand, the *ideas* of the Academy, interpreted, reunderstood and practiced by musicians and choreographers who followed, liberated as they were from pedantic prejudice, creating lively works rather than historic pastiche, precipitated the invention of the *Ballet de Cour.*

Baïf was too intelligent and too curious not to interest himself in the researches of Italian dancing-masters. The French conquest of Milan had had an important effect on their dancing. Just as Florence, Ferrara and Mantua were sources of court masque and pastoral opera, so Milan cradled the choreographers of Italy. There was Pompeo Diobono, a famous teacher, and among others the theoretician, Cesare Negri, whom the Marechal de Brissac, Piedmont's conqueror, took back with him to France in 1554. With him came ideas of figured dancing, which culminated in such exercises as the ball to the Polish Embassy. Due to Medici connections, there were numerous other Italians at court, hence a lively vogue of Italianate dancing hitherto seldom seen. In came the *Brando,* which was, we have seen, a theatricalized morisco permitting mimicry, and the *Balleto.* These were not like *Corrente* or *Gagliarde,* subject to fixed forms; choreographers were free to invent without limit, new evolutions, keeping within the indicated rhythms.

Hence, Baïf having been raised in an atmosphere of the ascendancy of figured-dances quickly realized what could be borrowed for his own purposes. He was haunted by the ideals of 'The Bacchæ,' and what he could reconstruct of the combination of tragic choros and tragic action. Soon, he formulated a plan of choreographic reform, inevitable and necessary complement to the revolution of music and poetry, which he had also undertaken. Musicians would be free to give a looser melodic line to their composition and could liberally employ harmonies which pleased them, although they must strictly conform to metrical regulations of the poetry.

Dancing must follow the same principle. Already, dancers had quite naturally arranged steps to be en rapport with instrumental cadences. There was a close link between the length of steps, and duration of notes. Baïf realized the possibility of translating into plastic form varied rhythms of a vastly complex Greek prosody, of placing in harmonious balance gestures and foot-movements with those songs which the dancers would, at the same time, sing, and with violins which accompanied them. Thus would be achieved an equilibrium of song, verse and dance, lost since Euripides.

Whether or not Baïf invented this idea, or borrowed it from the Milanese, lineal descendants of William, the Jew of Pesaro, is an academic question. Numerous Italian dancing-masters, Florentine, rather than Milanese, were in Paris from the time of Francis the First. One of the most famous was Fabritio Caroso, active much later, around 1590. His *Ballo del Fiore* was carefully measured into dactyls and spondees, but in actuality, these terms of almost sacred pedantry had little significance. The rhythms are, to us, surprisingly banal. Their patterns, painstakingly described in antique phraseology, are only *contre danse de salon,* ordinary ballroom figures. Which influence was prior is not important. French and Italians combined to provide the Academy with its choreographic reform.

After the massacre of Saint Bartholomew's there was scarcely an important fête for ten years. Baïf's Academy, deprived of its royal subsidy, was discontinued. It had enjoyed the active collaboration of the king and many musicians of his chamber orchestra and of his chapel. Thus, the ideas it fostered toward a dramatic synthesis of music, verse and dance, continued to simmer in the minds of many people close to court. It was inevitable that they would reappear, almost as a vindication, in the first real *Ballet de Cour.*

The word *first* is advisedly used. While no single man can be held responsible either for Italian *opera* or French *Ballet de Cour,* since all component factors had for a hundred years been in the air, nevertheless the 'Circe' of 1581, for many reasons of historic accident, can safely be labeled the 'first' ballet, as we still read the term. It takes a man of considerable energy, if not of genius, to assimilate the labors of his predecessors for fifteen years, welding them into a coherence which, while not in its parts, is, nevertheless in its whole effect, original.

Such a man was Baldassarino da Belgiojoso, who gallicized his name to Balthasar de Beaujoyeulx. He had come to France as a violinist in the band imported by the conqueror de Brissac around 1555, perhaps in the very troupe of which Pompeo Diobono, the dancing-master, was also a member. He was an excellent musician, a clever courtier, a man of ingenious wit and pleasing imagination. His ballet was in no way a profound work, but rather a clever adaptation to the French taste of humanistic or Italian Renaissance theories on antique drama. Using the only means for scenographic realization which had served choreographers of royal masquerades for twenty years, Beau-joyeulx created a work in its most essential sense original, by putting to practical use the esthetic formulated by the Academy of Baïf.

Beaujoyeulx, Baïf, the Milanese figured-dance and the parlous state of the Valois court were the sources of the *Ballet Comique de la Reine;* an Italian turned French, a Frenchman immersed in Italianate humanism, a milieu under the influences of its dominant personality, the Franco-Italian Queen-Mother. There was, however, one other feature in the new ballet which we have not encountered before, but which in many adaptations we shall find again and again down to our own time: the Pastoral. The Pastoral was a Renaissance revival which enjoyed considerable popularity in the sixteenth century, in its nature quite different from comedy or tragedy.

We remember the *intermedii,* lyric or choreographic interpolations into longer plays. The pastoral was a kind of swollen interlude but of special atmosphere. Its characters were costumed as rustics, bucolic peasants, happy farmers or wise shepherds. Sometimes there would be a chorus of satyrs, wood-nymphs, or rural gods of fountains, rivers or grottos. There was an enormous vogue of the Latin eclogue, imitations of Virgil, usually broken up into leisurely dialogue, in which, as in Provençal *tenzon,* Winter would argue with Spring; Summer with Autumn. Real courtiers were confused with imaginary farm-folk. The verses were often bare-faced pretexts for official flattery. The culmination of this genre resulted in Tasso's *Aminta* of 1573, which was more than an occasional interlude in a court show. It drew upon their Arca-dian atmosphere to produce something which parallels in the *Aminta's* rela-tion to future opera, Beaujoyeulx' 'Circe' and its effect on subsequent ballet.

The central idea of Tasso is in a series of emotional, and basically, social conflicts. He opposes the reality of the world of scheming, murder and career-ing (his Italian Court), to an Arcadian paradise of security, pleasure and love. The green earth is contrasted with the bloody State: the laws of feudal loyalty to the law of the Courts of Love; the behavior of gods and shepherds to the manners of Renaissance princes.

Tasso was in France in 1571, and Baïf had traveled in Italy. The *Aminta* was produced by a famous Italian company of actor-dancers, the *Comici Gelosi,* and a short time afterwards they performed in Paris. If he had not actually seen *Aminta,* Beaujoyeulx must have read it, as its popularity was unexhausted after many editions and translations into every European tongue. It bred many imitations of which the *Ballet Comique* was but one. Indeed, perhaps at first, he was thinking to produce merely an Italian pastoral, but little by little the idea came to him to have all three elements, the painting, verse and music, compete equally. The dance is not specifically mentioned by him, but it is implicit in his description.

Its immediate occasioning was the marriage arranged between Anne, Duc de Joyeuse and Mlle. de Vaudemont, the Queen's sister. Beaujoyeulx, among many others, was commissioned to invent parts for the festivities, the like of which had not been seen in many years. He actually quit the Court in order to think more at his ease, and on his emergence presented plans, at once accepted. In his introduction to a beautiful printed edition of the *Ballet Comique,* completely ignoring the terrible state of the country, its author indulges himself in a pretty piece of sophisticated Apologia for his use of the term *Comique.* By usual Renaissance standards the tragic mode, with a final catastrophe, would have been considered more suitable to such an august occasion. He explains the change in courtly esthetic on grounds of seemly joy, but what he dared not write was that Catherine de Medici, with something more than superstition, believed 'tragedies' brought bad luck.

La Chesnaye, the king's Almoner, wrote the verses. The Sieur de Beaulieu, a relative of the Queen, composed charming music, while the King put at Beaujoyeulx's disposal musicians from his Privy Chamber. Jacques Patin, upon the Queen's word, designed costumes and scenery. The decor, strangely enough was not on an Italian model, made no use of perspective; but in the old-fashioned Gothic taste used dispersed practicable sets all around the great hall of the Petit Bourbon, very like the individual backgrounds for miracle-plays. An enormous amount of money was spent on it. The King avowedly wished to astonish Europe by its magnificence, and Catherine wrote a letter deploring the late arrival of some alien envoys who could not arrive in time to see it.

Comique, we have understood, "for the lovely, tranquil and happy conclusion by which it ends, by the quality of the personages involved who are almost all gods and goddesses, or other heroic persons," and *Ballet,* because it was, as its creator continues, "a geometrical arrangement of numerous people dancing together under a diverse harmony of many instruments." There is little doubt that theoreticians of the seventeenth century believed this ballet, however diluted, was nevertheless an exact image of the tragic choros of ancient Greece.

Le Ballet Comique de la Reine Louise was presented on Sunday, the fifteenth of October, 1581. Its fame had preceded it. Not only was the hall packed, but people blocked entrances on the outside in trying to get in. Archers of the King's Guard had orders to admit no one except of known importance. There were between nine and ten thousand in the assembly. The royal family sat beneath a canopy at one end of the room. The audience was ranged around the walls, some on the floor, more in raised tribunes. The main floor surface was for performers. On the King's right was constructed the Arbor of Pan, with a grotto flanked by illuminated trees. On his left, was the Golden Vault, a niche for musicians, framed by clouds, similar to the Italian *nuvole,* lighted within. At the extreme end of the hall were the garden and castle of Circe, the enchantress, with passages on both sides for entrances of dancers and cars, supporting personages in the manner of the Italian *Trionfi.*

After the overture, at a little past ten in the evening, a gentleman came fleeing out of Circe's palace, terrified, into the center of the hall. He was the Sieur de la Roche, gentleman-in-waiting to the Queen-Mother. He was clothed in cloth of silver covered with shiny stones. He wiped his forehead, seeming much moved. He caught his breath, and addressed verses to the King. This interminable rhymed tirade, *Harangue du Gentilhomme Fugitif,* was a kind of prologue. Opening with a few philosophical remarks on vanity and the hope of happiness, he then begged the King of Peace and Abundance whether or not he had seen Circe, that enchantress who, having transformed him into a lion, then softened, and restored him to mortal form. If so, would the gracious lord please save him? He had scarcely finished when Circe herself appeared to sing: 'The Complaint of Circe having lost a Gentleman': She regrets having given him back his mortal shape, and angrily retires into her garden. Now comes the *Premier Intermède,* a procession of sirens and tritons singing together, 'having their tails *retroussées* upon their arms, made in scales of gold and burnished silver.' The singers in the Golden Vault respond to them while they march around the hall, announcing the arrival of a float like a fountain, bearing Thetis and Glaucus in the midst of the Nereids. On gilded steps at the base of the elaborate jet, in plastic groups were arranged Naiads, chief dancers of the evening. La Princess de Lorraine, les Duchesses de Mersœur, de Guise, de Nevers, d'Aumale, etc., etc. Behind the chariot comes a choir of eight Tritons. The parade halts; after some polite exchange of verse between Glaucus and Thetis, the *corps de ballet* of Naiads step down and start their *premiére entrée de ballet.*

They were preceded by two ranks of five violinists each, in white satin embroidered in gold, with aigrets. Behind the strings, a dozen pages, six and six; then the Naiads who took their stations during the first part of an orchestral overture. In the second, they turned toward the King and executed the figures of their dance. They started in three lines with the Queen as their focus; three, in the rear; then six, in the middle, then three before Her Majesty. There were twelve separate geometric figures in this first entry, but unfortunately, its author did not see fit to leave any record of them. At the very moment when the last figure had unrolled itself, Circe, in a fury, issued from her garden, and struck the nymphs with her magic wand. They were ranged in two lines *en croisant.* And that is the only indication left to us of an actual choreography.

Now came the *Entrée de Mercure;* the gods' messenger, descending in a cloud, was the Sieur du Pont, Gentleman of the King's Bed Chamber, "Dressed in Spanish satin incarnadine, with gold passementery; hat with gilded wings; cape of violet cloth of gold; in his hand, the Caduceus." He declaimed a philosophical speech, full of flattering innuendo, sprinkled the enchanted Naiads with a holy herb, released them to continue their ballet, which was followed by the *Deuxieme Intermède,* an Entry of Satyrs, eight of them, conducted by the Lord of Saint-Laurens. This enfilade gave 'great pleasure by the new and gay music' which accompanied it. Their costumes, of which an excellent engraving is extant, testifies to an exact archeological observance of Græco-Roman cups and sarcophagi. These satyrs toured the hall, singing, and after each of their couplets, the choir in the Golden Vault responded; upon which rolled in another car, the Entry of the Dryad Wood. This was a chariot, imitating a small forest, in which sat four pastoral virgins. Observing this greenery come towards them, Satyrs joined Dryads and there was more singing. Then the soliloquy of the Nymph Opis, followed by the Discourse of the Nymph Opis to the God Pan, who was summoned to rescue the Naiads from their witch. A third *Intermède* was heralded by an entry of the Four Virtues, in long robes, charged with gold stars, two playing lutes, two singing. Then came the Entry of the Car of Pallas, drawn by a monstrous serpent. The goddess asked the aid of Jupiter, who came down from heaven as *Deus ex Machina,*

> on an eagle to the sound of joyous chanting from *la voute dorèe*. Pan came out of his bower, heading a troop of satyrs armed with sticks. All together, divinities and lesser spirits made a grand assault on the palace. Circe defied them, but in vain. Jupiter struck the enchantress with a thunderbolt and led her captive before the King (of France), to whom at the same time he presented his two children Minerva and Mercury. The Dryads danced for joy and brought the disenchanted Naiads out of the palace, and then all the nymphs together danced a *grand ballet* or great figured dance.*

All the dancers of the ballet then came, two by two, into the middle of the hall; the first couple, the Queen and the Princesse de Lorraine. There were fifteen figures, "after each of which they turned their faces toward the King." This was only an overture to the big ballet of forty geometrical passages "accurate and considered in their diameter, some square, some round, in various forms; in triangles within a smaller square." Afterwards, the dancers presented specially conceived personal emblems in the form of symbolic medals to the great personages present. The Queen offered the King a *Dauphin* (coin) with the words: *Delphinus ut Delphinum rependat:* "I give you a Dauphin that I may receive a Dauphin (an heir)." There were others of a witty or paradoxical nature, reminding us of the ritual relic of give and take in the English mumchance of the Middle Ages. The evening concluded with social dances, those in ballet-costume now dancing with those in court-dress. The show lasted, as far as we can judge, somewhat over five hours.

The verses sung were full of the moral ideology of the new learning and suggested to the erudite artists who collaborated in their performance, an allegorical meaning wholly lost on us. Circe, the bad fairy, was the spirit of Evil, to whom was opposed an influence for good, the Nymphs, made up of heat and humidity, natural forces. The four who gathered herbs were the elements: earth, air, fire and water, components of physical matter. Circe changed them into monsters by that necessary corruption, involving the re-

* Enid Welsford: *The Court Masque,* p. 108. The Macmillan Company.

newal of all nature. Ulysses, the great traveler, the Wandering Jew of antiquity, is both *le gentilhomme fugitif,* Time which none can stop, and the Soul which cannot be affected. Circe is the path of the year around the sun, who keeps Ulysses a year in her toils, and by him has their children, the Four Seasons. And so on, with cross references which accrete meaning in imaginations fattened on the rich food of scholasticism and mythology.

The single innovation of the *Ballet Comique de la Reine* consists in a *unification* of separate elements; tournament, masquerade and pastoral, which separately had long been familiar to Florence, Ferrara and France itself. Its effect was great. Beaujoyeulx was flooded with complimentary sonnets. The libretto was published in a charming edition, and imitations of it were produced all over the continent, even in Italy, to which it owed so much. But in France, an immediate succession was blighted. It had cost, we are told, three million six hundred thousand francs, a king's ransom indeed. And aside from its artistic repercussions it caused grave political crises as well. Hearing of the fame of its lavishness, in 1582 the Swiss ambassadors were outraged that they had not been paid large debts due them for the almost sacred services of their royal guard. The outlay had also a bad effect on the ordinary citizenry who were not at all enjoying the Elysian pleasures of the Golden Vault. France was generally bankrupt and the great majority of people were violently restless, exploited on the one hand by royal taxation, on the other by whichever side, Protestant or Catholic, claimed them in the wars. If small causes give impetus to great results one might almost say the *Ballet Comique* dealt a final blow to the personal authority of Henry the Third. Nothing approaching its scale of grandeur followed for years to come. Then it was not French but English audiences who were dazzled.

Seven years after the production of the first ballet, appeared a book which was to have even a wider effect and which remains the most important record of sixteenth century dancing in existence. This was 'Orchesographie' of Thoinot Arbeau: (*orchesis,* dance: *graphos,* writing). The author's name was an anagrammatic pen-name for Jehan Tabourot, a canon of Langres. Born in Dijon in 1519, the son of Etienne Tabourot, a king's counsellor, little is known of him except that he was a Catholic priest. His only other surviving work dealt primarily with astronomy and mathematics, a good background for anyone occupied as he was with the geometry of dancing. His book, published in 1588, is a great advance over the rudimentary attempts of the Jew of Pesaro, or even Caroso. He is far more able to make clear technical complications and his musical notation can be, with our learned contemporary editing, easily read with some assurance that we are hearing the sounds that he set down.

The form of his treatise reminds us forcibly of Lucian's dialogue on Pantomime, for in it Arbeau himself and a beginner called Capriol converse on the nature of dancing. In their conversation is his exposition. He commences with a historico-mythological basis for dancing in antiquity, very much as Lucian did, and then proceeds to tabulate every conceivable variety of drum-rhythm, the basis of all rhythmic measure and the substructure of the dance, to the number of eighty odd, and similarly demonstrates the fife. He then explains a simple system of dance notation, whereby, for example, he explains the *Basse Danse,* which we recall from Pesaro:

R b   ss   d R d R b   ss   d d d   R d R b   ss   d R b c

means *revérénce* (a bow); B means *Branle* (a type of step emerging from the Carole); ss means two *simples* (single-steps); d means *double* (step), and so on.

The book is reprinted in Cyril Beaumont's admirable series * and is recommended to any one interested enough in the technique of music and dancing to spend a rewarding day on it. But for us, here, interested particularly in stage-dancing, 'Orchesography' offers us those dance-rhythms and dance-steps, which in origin, ballroom measures, nevertheless later become ballet posture and movement in the seventeenth and eighteenth centuries.

Apart from dance-tunes which were often dance-songs, there was little, if any, instrumental music before 1550. The development of musical form eventually resulting in the symphony is largely conditioned by inventions of dancing-masters. There was a great deal of vocal dance-music. Again and again down through Mozart, orchestral suites, not written for dancing, but specifically for concert or serenade will bear the names of many of Arbeau's dances. English *Ballet,* a variant of the French, was a term applied to short pieces of a well-defined rhythmical nature, suited to dancing. The dance itself, was always linked with, if not actually responsible for, the measured tune or line of melody, as distinct from the melodic phrases of contrapuntal music where each separate voice has an equal importance. For, in dancing, a single singing or instrumental voice must lead, imposing its metrical continuum on the design of steps. As Ezra Pound writes in relation to poetry:

> Music begins to atrophy when it departs too far from the dance; poetry begins to atrophy when it gets too far from music; but this must not be taken as implying that all good music is dance music or all poetry lyrical. Bach and Mozart are never too far from physical movement.

In the 'Orchesography,' young Capriol who takes a lively pleasure in sword-play and tennis, which have made him a good comrade for young men, says he knows nothing of dancing, and hence cannot please young ladies on whom, it seems to him, the reputation of an eligible young man depends. Arbeau is sixty-nine—too old to dance, but he will instruct the youth if he has patience. To make the categories clear, he compares contemporary dances with the antique. We know, from Greece, all these historic names, and probably have a far clearer idea of their nature than the Canon of Langres. Nevertheless, the very invocation of the ancient terms lent prestige to his instruction.

In the class of the grave 'Emmelia' were Pavannes and Basse dances. The

---

* *Orchesography:* by Thoinot Arbeau: Translated by Cyril W. Beaumont. Published by Cyril W. Beaumont. London.

latter we have seen in Italy, a measure of queenly gravity; feet close to the floor. The Pavanne, Pavin, Panicin or by whatever other variants one recognizes it, derives its name from either the town of Padua or *Pavo* (French *paon*) a peacock, from the manner in which ladies swept their long trains or from one of its figures, where the dancers are arranged in a circle in the manner of a peacock spreading its tail. Pavannes were set in duple or quadruple time and generally followed by a Galliard, a sprightly dance in triple time, the tune of which was sometimes, but not always, a rhythmic transformation of the preceding tune. Italians knew their Gaillards as *saltarelli*: and it is said to have originated in the Campagna where it was known as Romanesca. It once had five steps, and hence was called *cinq-pas,* or in English sink-apace, or passymeasure (*Passamezzo*). The Pavanne was popular all over Europe. Italy, France and Spain claim it as a national dance. There was the French term *'en se pavenant'* which means 'strutting like a peacock,' or more technically, 'to step, as in Pavannes.' Spain assures us it was invented by the conquistador Fernando Cortez. Arbeau gives a famous Pavanne tune, *Belle qui tiens ma vie,* a tragic, deliberate melody which commands gracious sobriety and noble carriage. The English composer, Peter Warlock, has somewhat elaborately orchestrated six of the more danceable tunes in his 'Capriol Suite.' But the recording gives a good idea of the atmosphere of sixteenth century dancing.

Under the heading of 'Kordax,' which we recall was a Greek dance of doubtful decency, are placed *gaillards, tordions, voltas, courantes, gavottes* and *branles.*

> At the commencement of the gaillard you must presuppose that the dancer, holding the damsel by the hand, makes the *revérénce* at the moment when the musicians begin to play; the *revérénce* done, he assumes a goodly modest attitude. To perform the *revérénce* you will keep the left foot firmly on the ground and, bending the right knee, carry the point of the toe a little to the rear of the left foot, at the same time doffing your bonnet or hat and saluting your damsel and the company as you see in this picture.
>
> When the *revérénce* has been performed, straighten the body and replace your bonnet; then, drawing back your right foot, bring and keep the two feet together (*pieds joints*). This is considered to be a correct position when the two feet are so disposed that one is on the right of the other, as you see in the picture below, the toes in a straight line, so that the body is equally balanced on the two feet.

Arbeau defines the principle of feet apart (*pieds larges*), the weight equally divided on both. In fact, here is the foundation for the five absolute positions of the *danse d'école,* the ballet footing, necessary and practical today as they were three hundred years ago, and which he first diagrammed and established as rudimentary.

Tordion was a gaillarde danced keeping the feet close to the ground. *Volta* means turning. Its origin seems to have been Provençal, and troubadours called the turning or dividing accent of sonnets, the *volta. Courante (courir:* French:

to run) had, supposedly an Italian origin (*corrente:* stream). It consisted of brief advances and retreats, with flexible smooth knee-movements. It was also known as courant and corranto.

> In my young days there was a kind of game and ballet arranged to the *Courante.* For three young men would choose three girls, and having placed themselves in a row, the first dancer would lead his damsel to the end of the room, when he would return alone to his companions. The second would do the same, then the third, so that the three girls were left by themselves at one end of the room and three young men at the other. And when the third had returned, the first, gamboling and making all manner of amorous glances, pulling his hose tight and setting his shirt straight, went to claim his damsel, who refused his arm and turned her back upon him; then, seeing the young man had returned to his place, she pretended to be in despair. The two others did the same. At last all three went together to claim their respective damsels, and kneeling on the ground, begged this boon with clasped hands, when the damsels fell into their arms and all danced the *Courante* pell-mell.

There were any number of Branles (French: *branler:* shake) linked to the satyr-dance or 'Sikinnis.' They were also known as 'Brawls'; hence our word for rough-house. Older people danced *Branles Doubles* or *Simples;* young marrieds, *Branles Gais,* while youths and maidens the Burgundy Branles, which were from side to side in double-time, like the others, only faster.

Arbeau then lists a series of branles specifically adapted to miming and ballets. There is a Maltese Branle:

> *Arbeau:* Some knights of Malta devised a ballet for a court masquerade where there was an equal number of ladies and gentlemen, dressed in the Turkish fashion, who danced a *Branle* in a round with certain gestures and twistings of the body, which they called *Branle de Malte.* It is about forty years ago (ca. 1540) since this dance was first performed in France. The air and movements are in slow duple time, as you see in this tabulation (cited below).
> *Capriol:* Perhaps the inhabitants of Malta customarily practice this dance, so that it is not a ballet devised for a special occasion.
> *Arbeau:* I cannot believe that it is other than a ballet, because it is danced with certain gestures, mimings and expressions of the features which have persisted during all the time it has been in use.

The 'Washerwoman,' danced in duple time, was so named because those who danced it clapped their hands, and sounded like the wooden bats with which the launderers of the Seine-Bank slap their wash.

> I shall place among the mimed *Branles,* the *Branle des Hermites,* which is called so because gestures are made in it similar to those which hermits make when they greet some one. I believe that it derived from some masquerade of former days, in which were young men dressed like hermits. I advise you not to disguise yourself in such garments, nor to counterfeit the faces of monks,

because their clothes and persons should be respected. On this occasion I will pass it over.

There speaks Jehan Tabourot, the priest of Langres. Also he cites a Branle of Torches, of Puppets, of Horses and a Branle which is nothing more than the English country dance known as Shepherds Hey. In French it is *Branle de la Haye*. When we read terms like courante, gagliarde and gavotte, we must remember that in Arbeau's sixteenth century, there are only the names to connect them with dances similarly termed in the seventeenth and eighteenth. His *gavotte,* for example, was a collection of several branles arranged in sequence by musicians, wholly otherwise than those written by Bach, or Händel. As for the *Morisques:*

> In my young days, at supper-time in good society, I have seen a daubed and blackened little boy, his forehead bound with a white or yellow scarf, who, with bells on his legs, danced the *Morisques* and, walking the length of the room, made a kind of passage. Then, retracing his steps, he returned to the place where he began and made another new passage, and continued thus, making various passages very agreeable to the onlookers.

The jigging Morris-step of Kemp and the English is replaced here by indications for a more accentuated heel-and-toe. In the description of *Canaries,* one might almost believe Arbeau's historical sense is troubled by vague articulations of an anthropological instinct. When he refers to 'savages' he would mean either Moors or even Indians from Peru or Virginia. Columbus had been dead almost a century, and the vogue for the 'noble savage,' in its cradle, had not yet developed into the absolute passion it became in the seventeenth and eighteenth centuries, when not only Lully, but Rameau and all their imitators would employ plots full of Incas and Iroquois (often more Chinese than Indian) but feathered at least. *Canaries* was a definitely spectacular dance.

> Some say that this dance comes from the Canary Isles, and that it is regularly practiced there. Others, whose opinion I should prefer to share, hold that it is derived from a ballet composed for a masquerade in which the dancers were dressed as kings and queens of Mauretania, or rather, like savages, with plumes dyed in various colors. This is the manner of dancing the *Canaries.* A young man takes a damsel and dancing with her to the phrases of a suitable air, conducts her to the end of the room. This done, he returns to the place where he began, gazing at the damsel the while. He then goes towards her again, making certain passages, and, this done, he returns as before. Then the damsel comes and does the same in front of him, and afterwards returns to the place where she was; and both continue these goings and comings as many times as the diversity of passages affords them the means. And note that these passages are lively, yet strange and fantastic, resembling in large measure the dances of savages.

Les Bouffons or *Mattachins,* Arbeau connects with the Pyrrhic danced by the twelve Salic priests of Rome, and also with Cretan Kuretes. It is a sophisticated sword dance, circular in form and very popular on the French and English stage in the late sixteenth and early seventeenth centuries.

> The dancers are dressed in small corselets with ribbons on their shoulders and below their belt (the latter set off by a fringe of taffetas at the waist), morions of gilded card-board, the arms bare, bells on the legs, the sword in the right hand and the buckler in the left. These danced, with clashings of their swords and bucklers, to an air in duple time peculiar to this dance. To understand it one must know that several different gestures are made. One of these is called *feinte,* when the dancer jumps on both feet holding his sword without touching anything with it. The second is termed *estocade,* when the dancer draws back his arm and thrusts the point of his sword forward to strike that of his companion.

And at the end of all his notation, his music, his quaint fancy and careful direction, his pupil, young Capriol, like the well-brought up boy he is (we can imagine, cap in hand, perhaps with a *revérence*), says

> M. Arbeau, I thank you for the trouble you have taken in teaching me to dance. And Arbeau answers:
> I should like to have been able to make the result equal to the wealth of my sincere affection for you. In the future I hope to give you the airs and movements of several ballets and masquerades which have taken place in this town. We will deal with these in a second treatise as soon as we have leisure to do so. However, practice these dances carefully and you will become a fit companion of the planets, which dance of their own nature, and of those Nymphs whom Marcus Varro said he had seen in Lydia come out of a pool and dance to the sound of flutes, and then return to their pool. And when you have danced with your mistress you will return to the great pool of your studies and gain profit from it, as I pray God give you grace to do.

The historic significance of Arbeau's 'Orchesography,' a French treatise using Italian models in an assimilated French expression, and of the *Ballet Comique de la Reine,* a work conceived by a Franco-Italian poet, French painters and French musicians, performed not by trained Italian virtuosi, but by professional or semi-professionals, is enormous. By these two achievements alone, France assumed a direction which up to then Italy had monopolized. The great merit of the *Ballet Comique* was its idea of establishing a logical, less haphazard ordering of all its elements. The notion of a consecutive plot unifying the action may be flagrantly violated later, but the violations are understood as outside the progress of formal ballet, which will be, in spite of retards, predominantly French. Both French ballet and its twin, French opera, about to be born, were, in essence, free from alien influence. Anticipating Monteverdi's *Orpheo* (Mantua: 1608), often considered the first recognizable music-drama in the terms of Wagner, it preceded by eight years Shakespeare's 'Tempest,' a great innovation in another kind and spirit.

We have been speaking of the *historic* significance of the *Ballet Comique,* its place in the record from a perspective of three hundred and fifty years. Its immediate influence was small. After 'Circe,' superior in every way to the ballets *à grand spectacle* which had preceded it, one might have hoped that its qualities would produce a new genre to be fully developed at the French Court. But a strong reaction set in. It was only followed by masquerades in the old style. The formulization of ballet returned to Italy to be developed there on parallel lines of a more musical emphasis, and would return fifty years later in a type perfected under the patronage of Cardinal Mazarin and the creative genius of another Florentine, Lully. Political disasters, royal poverty and general misery precluded any repetition of Beaujoyeulx's extravagance. To Mazarin would fall the distinction of introducing the perfected Italian opera into France.

If ballets *à grand spectacle* were not to reappear then how did the tradition descend? Although its lavishness was arrested with a subsequent decline in theatricality, the masquerade in high society received a great impetus, and became the vogue in the early years of Henry the Fourth's reign. People would appear abruptly at balls in fantastic or romantic disguises, to dance ordinary social dances. Very quickly, under the influence of ideas still in the air, from the triumph of the *dramatic* elements in the *Ballet Comique,* private maskings were transformed. Ballet itself presupposed the expensive collaboration of poetry, painting, elaborate costuming and choreography which such a finance minister as the economical Sully would not tolerate. Hence the masquerade was combined with the ballet to produce an inexpensive spectacle, destitute of dramatic interest, without expression, but agreeable enough, and known as the hybrid *ballet-mascarade.* They took little time to prepare and disguises were chosen entirely by the caprice of participants: Moors, monkeys, Indians, Jews or birds. Only a ballroom was necessary, without decor. Violins formed the first entry, oddly dressed and masked. Perhaps their masks and clothes would be stuck on backwards, so upon entering they seemed to be playing their strings from behind. Then pages appeared carrying torches, and arranged themselves around the dancing-floor. The first quadrille appears, bows, dances, retires; is followed by a second, and so on, for as many as there are. For finale, all maskers unite, in a *grand ballet.* After the mummery was over, masks were doffed, and they all danced branles, courantes and gagliardes till break of day. Sometimes even, there would be no dancing in the *ballet-mascarade,* but only pantomime or acrobatic tricks, human pyramids and somersaulting.

These grotesque and ingenious disguisings were particularly suited to ballrooms, but around 1605, there was a parallel form evolved known to Prunières as the *ballet-comique.* This was for performance specifically in constructed theaters, and was occupied not with fantasies of millers, chess-players, sailors, wrestlers, usurers or animals, but with pastoral and mythological subjects. It was the source of the *ballet à entrée*. There may seem to be an elaboration of terms, for types of spectacle not far apart. That they are close is true, but in no way are they identical and each has its place in an ultimate defining with which Lully will be busy.

It is very difficult, and perhaps unnecessary to indicate in detail the transitional period between 1600 and 1615, or definitely to state where the spoken words of the *recits, harangues* or declamations gave way to singing, or *ballets mélodramatiques,* for court entertainments obeyed no tradition or formula. Nevertheless, there was evolution, and an increasing predilection for mythology at least served the purpose of providing plots, which however involved, were nevertheless, related, and a pretext for consecutive, *dramatic* action. *Ballet-mascarade* need not keep us, if we only gain an idea of the exact part dancing played in it, for this element will have important parallels in the English Masques of Inigo Jones and Ben Jonson, of a slightly later date, although in *Le Ballet de la foire de Saint-Germain* there is no connection between the two parts. To use Enid Welsford's *précis* of this type *ballet-mascarade:*

The ballet began with the entrance of a small boy heralding the advent of the Miracle of the Fair of St. Germain:

> "C'est une homasse
> Qui surpasse
> Les effects du genre humain."

Then a midwife entered and danced a ballet around the hall, after which there came in a huge wooden figure representing a fat woman decorated with combs, drums, mirrors, and other fairings of the kind. The midwife then proceeded to draw various sets of dancers out of the wooden figure: four astrologers who danced a ballet, presented an almanack to the ladies in the audience, and retired; then four painters who pretended to paint in rhythm; then four operateurs (i.e., pedlars) who, as they danced, distributed to the ladies phials of scent and some very coarsely worded recipes. Finally came four pickpockets who pretended to draw the teeth of the pedlars *"et au mesme instant leur couppoient la bourse."* After all these had left the stage Mercury entered with his lute and announced the subject of the main masquerade, which was to be the triumph of constant over inconstant love. First inconstant love entered with eight Knights and performed a lively ballet, then constant love followed with another eight Knights, who danced a more stately entry, and then both troupes combined to dance the grand ballet, which consisted of a series of figures imitating mock combats, until at last *"l'Amour constant triomphe de l'Amour volage."*

The history of music and the history of dancing for the whole century overlap. The *ballet mélodramatique* logically points toward opera rather than ballet, just as the English Masque will develop into singing more than dancing. But during the period when forms are assuming their final shape, dancing plays a large part in all these shows and cannot be ignored. An Italian poet, Ottavio Rinuccini, having observed the *Ballet Comique* in France, put the idea into production both in Mantua and in Florence, after the Paris production of 1581. We have seen that Beaujoyeulx was not fortunate in his successors in the French Court. Nevertheless Rinuccini, working with the great composer Monteverde, supervised entertainments at the Court of Mantua in 1608, which were to have important repercussions in both France and England. It was for the marriage of Francesco Gonzaga, Duke of Mantua, and the Infanta Margherita of Savoy.

> At the end of the third act, the main scene of the comedy displayed a prospect of shadowy grottos full of dread nocturnal creatures. Out of this gloomy place, Night, summoned by Mercury, arose on starry chariot, while behind her there issued out of the cave Dreams and Phantasms on little clouds resembling a dense smoke. On the cloud nearest to the chariot of Night were Morfeo Forbetore and Fantaso who sang. Still Night soared upwards, the sky darkening and the moon and stars appearing as she rose, the Fates appeared riding on a cloud, Jove entered on his chariot, and Aurora dawned gradually and the air was lit up by a sudden comet.

Here, finally, is the accomplished scenic transformation of cloud effects which since the time of Filippo Brunelleschi's *Nuvole* for the Blessed Virgin, had been more and more ingeniously contrived by the Florentine architects. These stage effects were introduced into France by the engineer Francini, and the vogue for clouds (*gloires*) almost overshadowed interest in singing and dancing. The theme of the above Mantuan *intermedio,* the imminence and approach of Night, her passage until dawn, will be a favorite theme in all European entertainments through the century.

In France, the abandonment of related dialogues and speeches had temporarily turned the course of ballet away from danced music-drama. It was necessary for music to come back with a new Italian importance for its reintegration. In 1610, the *Ballet de Monseigneur le duc de Vendosme* was remembered as 'Alcine,' first of the genre of *ballet mélodramatique.* It adroitly combined the burlesque entry of the *ballet-mascarade* with the related noble entries of the more theatrical *ballet comique.*

> The curtain, opening, discovered a decor representing a forest. A curious person emerged. It was "Messire Gobbemagne, grand gonfalonier of the Isle of Monkeys," followed by three violins "dressed as Turks who danced and played." Gobbemagne drew from the wood two torch-bearing pages disguised as green-snails, who did monkey-tricks in cadence. Then one after the other, all the violins and all the torchbearers thus entered into the hall. The violins mounted on to their stand, and the green snails, having danced bizarrely, retired. After this burlesque prologue, the action began: the enchantress Alcine came out of the forest, sounding a lute.... Alcine came before the King's throne and sang verses in which she was followed by her chorus of nymphs, who took up the last verse of each rhyme.*

* Henry Prunières: *Le Ballet de Cour Avant Lully.*

'Alcine' had many analogies to opera. Music more and more occupied an impressive place. The action would perhaps be varied in the conceits of detail but the *idea,* had not changed at all. In 1617 was given the *Délivrance de Renaud.* This was the final type of *ballet mélodramatique* and superior to the general run of the ballets of this epoch. It is reprinted in full, with music and decorations in Prunières' monumental volume and is certainly the best ballet since Beaujoyeulx, thirty-six years earlier. The young King Louis Thirteenth danced several entries, side by side with his favorite, the Duc de Luynes, who had charge of the court entertainments, and who played the rôle of Renaud. The mise-en-scène was Italianate. A stage erected at one end of the hall, was connected with it by two gently inclined planes. On either side, two green bosquets divided the orchestra and the singers. Before the curtain, they heard the couplets of a tender choir.

> After the overture, the scene unfolded. Upon a bed of soft turf, at the foot of a hill planted with trees, Renaud (the Italian Rinaldo of the epics), surrounded by the spirits who guarded him. These demons, superbly clad, danced a long time, then went with Renaud into a grotto, cut in the mountain-side. The knights followed, dancing upon a trumpet's tune and tried to force their way into the grotto, but then as if by magic (Francini, the engineer) the scene changed. It represented the enchanted gardens of Armida, adorned with jetting fountains. The knights, armed with magic wands, stopped, in touching them, the various waters. Suddenly a nymph, unclad and disheveled, threw herself from under the fountains and in a musical recitative, begged them to leave Rinaldo and Armida in peace.*

The action was consecutive, coherently demonstrated by pantomime and sung words, and as for a plot, it only served as a pretext for danced entries, noble or buffoon, terminated by the familiar *grand ballet* executed by all the masquers. Towards 1620, the *Ballet de Cour* constituted a definite dramatic genre, half-way between the opera and *ballet-mascarade.* It perfectly satisfied the French love for expressive dance and for theatricality. Rational, voluptuous, recalling all the magnificence of the past, it flattered eye, ear and mind. One might almost imagine that under these conditions, French ballet had achieved a definitive form, and that for, at least the remainder of the century, poets, musicians and dancers would be inspired to surpass works we have mentioned, but this was not true. The decadence of the genre started immediately. There was a swift regression of *all* dramatic interest. Visibly, the *ballet de cour* declined towards lyrics and choreography, as it deprived itself of coherent expressiveness.

A recapitulation in this maze of crosscuts may be helpful. The chief forms, which issued from the masquerade, are simplified by Prunières in three groups. There is the *ballet comique,* with declaimed scenes, *ballet mélodramatique,* with sung recitative and a predominantly musical interest, and the original *ballet-mascarade,*—varied court spectacles of linked entries with a theatrical

* Henry Prunières: *Le Ballet de Cour Avant Lully,* p. 117.

character. Melodrama triumphed for ten years with subjects drawn from pastoral and romance as big shows given only once a year. Masquerades were far more popular in private and princely houses. They enriched themselves at the expense of the passing melodrama, and began to include sung scenes.

What resulted, in emergence, out of all these, Prunières calls the *Ballet de Cour Classique* or the *ballet à entrée*. And indeed, the classic ballet is the ballet of entries, which will be presented to great musicians at the end of the seventeenth and all of the eighteenth centuries, for their excellent use. It would be composed of several sections, related by one idea. Each section maintained the general structure of the *ballet-mascarade*, an opening recital (verse or song) followed by a succession of groups. At the conclusion, a choir announced the arrival of the united *grand ballet*. From 1625, for thirty years, up to the coming of Lully, the *Ballet de Cour* would take neither pastoral nor tragi-comic plots, thereby precluding any strong dramatic interest. The music was also weak, losing its theatrical interest. In 1632, ballets were shown, not to invited court guests alone, but to any one who could pay the price of admission.

It is not easy to discover the causes for abandoning the tradition of the *ballets comiques*, in themselves perhaps not works of genius, but which could have easily developed into them, since most of the elements necessary were there in correct proportion. Probably the chances of a pastoral ballet were ruined by the revival of the classic (antique) theater. In this epoch, tragedy, comedy and pastoral did not constitute well-defined types but continually overlapped. Towards 1625, however, comedy and tragedy commenced to submit to the Aristotelian unities of time, place and action, revived by the Florentine Academies. In France this coincided with a rationalist esthetic stemming from the philosophy of Descartes. Order, logic, reason were found to be desirable, and soon indispensable. Then the *ballet de cour,* forsaking the direction of its inspirers in Baïf's Academy, took a position on the margin of the stage which tragedy and comedy would henceforth reclaim for themselves. By a strange contradiction, from the very day ballet definitely renounced dramatic subjects, their librettists undertook to apply some of those rules which determined the classic drama.

> The ballets are dumb comedies and must be similarly divided into acts and scenes. The recitations separate the acts and the entries of dancers from the scenes. The number of acts however was extremely variable. M. de Saint-Hubert tells us "a grand ballet, or what we call a ballet royal is ordinarily composed of thirty entries. A fair ballet, of at least twenty, and a little ballet of ten or twelve. It is not necessary to submit oneself to this ruling, but to the subject, which will oblige one to augment or diminish them." *

All agree upon that. Everything depends on the subject. And it was the subjects which were the chief difficulty; it was the lack of subject that precipi-

* Prunières, *op. cit.,* 131.

tated the decline of the court ballet and sends us across the channel for any development in dancing which will keep us from marking time until the Academy of Lully. The imagination of the librettists seemed to be exhausted by the constant enchantment of Tasso and Ariosto, the allegorical or patriotic flatteries, the reiteration of metamorphoses *à l'antique*. Vocal music is increasingly reduced, and it will be long before it will give to the *ballet à entrée* an appearance of even a small opera. Luckily for the dance, the fertile influence of Italian opera, which does not stand still, imported by the Ministry of Mazarin, reawakens and stimulates the creative imagination of the French, and sets them again on the progressive road towards music-drama, even though it would be very like the old *ballet mélodramatique*.

In England, with more direct pressure from Italy than France, the principles of the *ballet comique* approached something like fruition. Imported there, upon a soil already prepared with feudal pageantry and court disguisings, at the end of the sixteenth century it was quickly to produce work approaching the quality of masterpiece. The masques of Jonson and Milton became a kind of verse-comedy, where plots ingeniously motivated possible entrances for dancers. Both verse and decoration, if not the music, were superior in beauty, coherence and actual sense to anything yet achieved in France or Italy.

FIGURES FROM ARBEAU'S 'ORCHESOGRAPHY'   1588

CHAPTER X

The English Court Masque and the Academy of Lully

ENGLAND was preoccupied with Wars of the Roses which were scarcely favorable for court shows, and while Burgundy was making itself the center of Europe's chivalrous pageantry, English disguisings confined themselves to intermittent balls in private castles. When Henry the Seventh came to the throne, however, a lively interest was shown in Court Revels. The word 'Revel' (French, *reveiller,* to awaken) is used by that distinguished British historian, Enid Welsford, as a group-term to include entremet, masque, ballet, intermedio and the tourney-games all over Europe, but it has a particularly English significance, referring to court entertainments under the Tudors, Elizabeth and the Stuarts. Henry had suffered exile in France, and there had close acquaintance with Paris, moriscoes and masquerades. He brought some of these customs into his own palace, and on two occasions, troupes of French players appeared in London. The Christmas Revels, due to the joyful season of Christ's Birthtide, were particularly favored, and to the ancient post of Lord of Misrule (a King in the Feast of Fools) was added a Master of the Revels, around 1545. The Christmas games were of remote antiquity. We are left remnants in our Carols, which were dancing-songs, showing the name of provençal Carole, combined with French Noël. Here is a little dance drama in carol form, from the reign of Henry the Sixth, which introduces Holly, a green-girt lad, and Ivy, his leafy partner:

> Holy stand in the halle,
> Fayre to behold;
> Ivy stond wythout the dore
> She ys ful sore a-cold

> *Nay, Ivy, Nay*
> *Hyt shal not be, I wys;*
> *Let Holy hafe the Maystery*
> *As the maner* (custom) *is.*

> Holy and hys mery men,
> They dawnsen and they syng;
> Ivy and hur maydenys
> They wepyn and they wryng.

> *Nay, Ivy, Nay....*

On one side, in the blaze of the Yule log Holly-men with a gilded and garlanded pole; on the other, Ivy with her maidens; each side taunting the other; then maybe tugging for 'prisoners.' 'Ivy-girls,' too, used to be burned by companies of boys, and Holly-boys by girls—all yawping and yodeling at the sport, Jacks and Jills i' the Green.

With the accession of Henry the Eighth, court revels took on an almost Burgundian splendor. In his great love for magnificent tournaments, Wolsey abetted him. Though actually a Renaissance figure, Henry fancied himself much more the valiant knight than Apollo or Bacchos. Perhaps the long feuds between York and Lancaster had prevented English Gothic pageantry from an earlier expression, so when it finally flowered, it assumed at once many antique Italian features. 'The Kyng beyng lusty, young, and couragious, greatly delited in feats of chyvalrie.' In 1510, the year after his coronation, a 'joust' was held at Westminster in honor of the Queen's churching, or safe recovery from confinement. Enid Welsford, in 'The Court Masque,' says:

> The challengers were the King and three others, calling themselves *"Cure loial, Bon voloire, Bonespoir, Valiaunt desire,"* and collectively *"Les quater Chivalers de la forrest salvigne."* The most noteworthy thing about the tournament was the elaborate pageant which brought the challengers into the hall. This pageant was made like a forest, with rocks and hills and dales, and a golden castle in the midst of it. It was drawn by a golden antelope ridden by two ladies and led in by "certayne men appareiled like wilde men, or woodhouses, their bodies, heddes, faces, handes, and legges, covered with grene Silke flosshed...." When the pageant had come to a standstill in front of the Queen the six foresters who were seated on it blew their horns and "then the devise or pageant opened on all sydes, and out issued the foresaied foure knyghtes...."

The Tournament under the Tudors quickly became a combination of pageantic jousting and court-disguisings, already familiar to us, and naturally took on the significance of political morality plays or interludes, from the events which framed them. In 1518 a marriage agreement between Lady Mary Tudor and the French Dauphin was honored with revels, often imitated in future entertainment.

A coherent dramatic element which steadily increased can be noticed in these revels as early as 1501. There were speeches and singing, but what pleased most was decoration, costume's color and dancing. The Tudors furthered the sophistication of English Folk customs and made Royal Progresses out of the First of May. Although they involved Morris Dancers, and the native figures of Robin Hood, Maid Marian and Friar Tuck, there was little specifically national about them. There were May games in Tuscany and the Ile de France, and while the able, centralized Tudor rule was conducive to an establishment of conditions which would healthily nourish national drama, to a degree Italy never enjoyed, the development seems to have been natural rather than induced. In spite of his preference for knighthood's flower Henry wanted England to have her full measure of European Humanism and the Florentine Renaissance. So, in 1512, he produced the innovation of the Italian 'masquerie,' an entertainment whose notoriety had already preceded its arrival, and which satisfactorily 'scandalized' the court.

> On the daie of the Epiphanie at night, the kyng with xi. other wer disguised, after the maner of Italie, called a maske, *a thyng not seen afore in Englande,* thei were appareled in garmentes long and brode, wrought all with gold, with visers and cappes of gold, and after the banket doen, these Maskers came in, with sixe gentlemen disguised in silke bearyng staffe torches, and desired the ladies to daunce, some were content, and some that knewe the fashion of it refused, because it was not a thyng commonly seen. And after thei daunced and commoned together, as the fashion of the Maskes is, thei toke their leave and departed, and so did the Quene, and all the ladies.

This passage in Hall's 'Chronicles of the Reign,' has been the source of much scholarly contention, as to the extent of the scandal, as to whether or not it was the *first* masking. But as Enid Welsford sensibly concludes, all misunderstanding vanishes "once it is realized that it was the *masquerie* (not a new kind of dramatic entertainment, but a notorious social custom from Italy)."

Elizabeth was very much her father's heir in her love of magnificence, but her use of the exchequer was more limited than his. During her reign it was often necessary to brush up costumes and decorations for old masques, with a little tactful regilding, or neat patching in the velvets if moths had got at them. The Italian masquerie, once introduced, was extremely popular. Used frequently at royal arrivals, celebrations, and loyal pretexts, for its brave show of dresses and dances, it flourished also in the great Elizabethan Manors, whose lords regaled the Queen on her private jaunts into the countryside. In 1600, Rowland Whyte writes to Sir Robert Sidney:

> There is to be a memorable maske of eight ladies. They have a straunge dawnce newly invented.... Those eight dawnce to the musiq Apollo bringes; and there is a fine speach that makes mention of a ninth, much to her honor and praise. After the wedding, he writes again: "After supper the masks came in, as I writ in my last; and delicate it was to see eight ladies so pretily and richly attired, Mrs Fetton leade; and after they had donne all their own ceremonies, these eight ladies maskers chose eight ladies more to dawnce the measures. Mrs Fetton went to the Queen, and woed her to dawnce. Her Majesty asked what she was? *Affection,* she said. *Affection,* said the Queen, is false. Yet her Majestie rose and dawnced.

If one had been a Frenchman or an Italian visiting the late Elizabethan Court, its Revels would probably have seemed awkward and unrefined. While Beaujoyeulx was striving to flatter equally the eye, the ear, the mind,—the English were lucky if their predominantly literary and dramatic conceits achieved even a partial synthesis with their pretty clothes, negligible music and rather accidental dancing. That the Queen loved the social-dances is proven continually in accounts of the epoch. The German traveler, Von Wedell, saw a ball around 1585.

> Then a dance was begun. Men and women linked hands as in Germany. The men donned their hats or bonnets, although otherwise no one, however ex-

alted his rank, may put on his hat in the Queen's chamber, whether she be present or not. The dancers danced behind one another as in Germany, and all the dancers, ladies and gentlemen, wore gloves. Though the dance at first sight seemed to be of German nature, it was no German dance, for they made a few steps forward and then back again. Finally they separated. The couples changed among one another but at the right moment each dancer returned to his or her partner. While dancing they very often courtesied to one another and every time the men bowed before their lady partners they doffed their hats. Slender and beautiful were the women who took part in this dance and magnificently robed. This dance was danced only by the most eminent who were no longer very young. But when it was over the young men laid aside their rapiers and cloaks, and clad in doublet and hose invited the ladies to dance. They danced the galliard and the Queen meanwhile conversed with those who had danced. The dancing over, the Queen waved her hand to those present and retired to her chamber.... But as long as the dancing lasted, she summoned young and old and spoke continuously. All of them ... knelt before her. She chatted and jested most amiably with them, and pointing with her finger at the face of one Master or Captain Rall told him that there was smut on it. She also offered to wipe it off with her handkerchief but he anticipating her removed it himself.

In 1594, occurred a very important event which was to determine the subsequent history of the English Masque, and indicate that direction which facilitated a fruition of its loveliest ideas. The gentlemen of Gray's Inn, after a suspension of their traditional King-game for four years, decided to revive it. There was a particularly elaborate coronation of a Fool-King, or as he was called 'The Prince of Purpoole.' These Twelfth-Night Revels also included an imitation of a classic Roman farce, but the stage was so crowded with people not much acting could be done, except dancing and a Comedy of Errors (*'like to Plautus his Menechmus'*). Next day, a mock trial and inquisitions held over the causes of the previous 'Night of Errors,' by the members of Gray's Inn, 'for the Recovery of our lost honor.' The show they finally gave is not particularly impressive in symbolism or fancy, but it is very important insomuch as its final *masque* was not merely an adornment. Rather, the whole course of the previous revels was designed deliberately to build up to it. We have now, a combination of 'the Masque in the show, and the Masque with presenters and speeches'; in other words, the ultimate formula for the English Masque under the Jacobean and Stuart dominance. What was now lacking was only taste in its adorning, the talent of poets and the creation of pure dancing in anti-masques.

For Shrovetide, the Queen was received by the Gray's Inn Masque of 'Proteus and the Adamantine Rock.' It included a prologue of song and speech, the masqued entry, the masque dances, the *revels* proper (a more important general dance or ballet), the final speech and chorus, uniting all the performers, the whole being linked by a mild plot with expressive gestures. It was the normal form to be exploited by Ben Jonson and his collaborators, but was it specifically English? How is it different from the syntheses achieved in the *Ballet Comique de la Reine,* or of sung spectacles at the Tuscan Court? In all these matters Welsford is the complete answer.

> Both in the French ballet and the English masque, however varied the forms of entertainment might be, there was one constant factor: the raison d'être of the whole performance was the arrival of noble personages disguised and masqued to dance a specially prepared dance. They might dance other dances as well, either all together or in groups, but there was one special dance in which they all took part which was the center of the whole thing, and that dance was known in France as *le grand ballet,* in England as the main or grand masque dance. The chief features of the costume of the noble masquers were also very similar in the two countries. An important difference must, however, be mentioned. In France *le grand ballet* was a grand finale. In England it almost always occupied a more or less central position, and was followed by *revels* (i.e., ordinary ballroom dancing between masquers and audience) and by the final dramatic business of speech or song or both, and perhaps a final dance of the masquers, known as the 'going off,' or 'the last dance.'

The Stuart Queens were foreign and few economical considerations hindered them from lavish outlays which would make the Jacobean Masque in every way the equal of French and Florentine. Anne of Denmark and Henrietta Maria of France thought that masquings were efficient as political propaganda, reflecting the power of their acquired thrones and the richness of their realms. They could not know how imminent was Oliver Cromwell. The extravagance of the Stuarts was not, however, pure good luck, even for such a side-issue as the Masque, for mere money is not able to command richness in fine verse, clear plots, or good acting so much as elaborate machinery, showy scenery and magnificent clothes. Ben Jonson valiantly strove to preserve the dramatic integrity of the English Masque against the purely decorative corruptions of a foreign invasion, but he failed. In 1603 he became official poet for the Revels. He wrote an enchanted pastoral, or *Satyre,* full of the fairy kingdom of Midsummer's Night, Queene Mab, Oberon and Puck. The Twelfth Night masque of 1605 started a great collaboration between Ben Jonson and the architect, Inigo Jones, a partnership of two individual and complementary talents which raised a basically ephemeral and trivial form of art, to something approaching an independent grandeur seen nowhere else in Europe.

At the expense of the Earl of Arundel, Jones had traveled in Italy. He borrowed from the fine engravings of Jacques Callot, the French engraver who has wonderfully preserved for us some of the finest *intermedii* settings by the Parigi and other Italian engineers. He took what he wished from the Tuscan fêtes, observed the devices of Stefano della Bella's Roman shows, and at the Danish Court had an opportunity to show what he could create, in a practical sense. He made admirable use of the Vitruvian principles reedited by Serlio, the great pupil of Baldassare Peruzzi who had been an innovator in scenic perspective. A genius like Palladio did not so much influence Inigo Jones, as to fertilize his native talent and render it capable of reintegrating in England the full glory of the late Italian Renaissance. Permanent theaters were being built, in France and in Italy, with elaborate mechanisms for shifting scenery and clever devices for lights and reflectors. Most important of all, the proscenium arch was finally a fact, framing the stage as a picture. From now on, in its best uses, the scenery was a fringe in a revelatory frame, enhancing the atmosphere in which the performers danced. The line between audience and actors was no longer equivocal. Before, the dancers of a ballet were nearly indistinguishable both in dress, dancing, and dancing-place, from their spectators. From now on, all discussion of stage-dancing refers to dancing in theaters. The contribution of the ballroom will be felt, but its influence comes in over the footlights. To Inigo Jones, the English masque was a lovely pretext for accomplishing scenic marvels. To Jonson, a poet-dramatist, it held possibilities for formal dramatic employment, using color and music but not depending on tricks alone. Before their inevitable quarrel, fine work was to be seen.

Queen Anne expressed a desire to appear, with her train, as black-a-moors, and from the whim, Jones' first court-masque arose. There were no changes of scene, but all decor was localized at the far end of the hall. Never again would there be Gothic dispersed scenic arrangements, as in the Golden Vault, the Forest of Pan, the Palace of Circe, of the *Ballet Comique de la Reine*. The scene in perspective, the contrived sea-waves, were Italianate devices, and Jonson's libretto showed traces of a study of recent Florentine festivities. The plot of the Masque of Blackness related how:

Niger, accompanied by his daughters and their attendants, has arrived together with Oceanus at the Court of England. He explains to Oceanus that his daughters have fallen into a profound despair on hearing of the superior beauty of nymphs living in other parts of the world, and have been wandering, in obedience to a vision, in quest of a land 'whose termination (of the Greek) sounds tania,' where they hope to get cured of their blackness. At this point in the action the Moon goddess reveals herself, and explains that she has now come to announce that her prophecy has been fulfilled, in that the daughters of Niger have arrived at *Britania,* a land governed by 'bright Sol' (i.e. King James).

> Whose beams shine day and night, and are of force
> To blanch an Æthiop and revive a corse.

First, for the scene, was drawn a *landt-schap* (landscape) consisting of small woods, and here and there a void place filled with huntings; which falling, an artificial sea was seen to shoot forth, as if it flowed to the land, raised with waves which seemed to move, and in some places the billow to break, as imitating that orderly disorder which is common in nature. In front of this sea were placed six tritons, in moving and sprightly actions, their upper parts human, save that their hairs were blue, as partaking of the sea-color: their disinent parts fish, mounted above their heads, and all varied in disposition. ...Behind these a pair of sea-maids, for song, were as conspicuously seated; between which two great sea-horses, as big as the life, put forth themselves ...upon their backs Oceanus and Niger were advanced....These induced the masquers, which were twelve nymphs, negroes, and the daughters of Niger; attended by so many of the Oceaniæ, which were their light-bearers. The masquers were placed in a great concave shell, like mother of pearl, curiously made to move on those waters and rise with the billow; the top thereof was stuck with cheveron of lights, which indented to the proportion of the shell, strook a glorious beam upon them as they were seated one above another: so that they were all seen, but in an extravagant order. On sides of the shell did swim six huge sea-monsters, varied in their shapes and dispositions, bearing on their backs the twelve torch-bearers, who were planted there in several graces....

These thus presented, the scene behind seemed a vast sea, and united with this that flowed forth from the termination, or horizon of which (being the level of the state, which was placed at the upper end of the hall) was drawn by the lines of prospective, the whole work shooting downwards from the eye; which decorum made it more conspicuous, and caught the eye afar off with a wandering beauty.

The English Masque, had, among other important effects, an influence on the rhythm and pacing of several of Shakespeare's loveliest portions. But there is no space here to hint at such fascinating literary relations or to attempt to paraphrase the Masque as a moth-like, fantastic but vital reflection of its elusive and tragic time, or as a cradle for English Opera and Henry Purcell. We must limit ourselves to theatrical dancing, and from now on fairly strictly. The greatest contribution in form, though in form only and not in technique, that Masque made to ballet was its so-called Anti-Masque.

Dancing in the Masque was along the same lines, if inserted differently, as in *Ballets-de-Cour*. There were Moriscoes, or since it is England, a theatricalized Morris, as well as English social dances—amplified with more showy adaptation of Milanese or Franco-Italian figures. In Jones' and Jonson's Masque of 1608 "The Hue and Cry after Cupid," the episode of Venus and Amor is treated as a rudimentary antimasque. The Love God is attended by

twelve boys, most antickly attired, that represented the Sports, and pretty Lightnesses that accompany Love, under the titles of Joci and Risus.... Wherewith they fell into a subtle capricious dance, to as odd a music, each of them bearing two torches, and nodding with their antic faces, with other variety of ridiculous gesture, which gave much occasion of mirth and delight to the spectators.

In 1609, the Anti-Masque is officially announced; in the Preface to "A celebration of honorable and true Fame, bred out of Virtue," Jonson explains to the Queen:

And because Her Majesty (best knowing that a principal part of life in these spectacles lay in their variety) had commanded me to think on some dance, or show, that might precede hers, and have the place of a foil, or false masque: It was careful to decline, not only from others, but mine own steps in that kind, since the last year, I had an *antimasque* of boys; and therefore now devised that twelve women, in the habit of hags or witches, sustaining the persons of Ignorance, Suspicion, Credulity, &c., the opposites to good Fame, should fill that part, not as a masque, but a spectacle of strangeness, producing multiplicity of gesture, and not unaptly sorting with the current and whole fall of the device.

The idea of the Anti-Masque, if not its name, is familiar enough if we recall the French entertainment of three years before, *Le Ballet de la Foire de Saint-Germain.* In 1613, Princess Elizabeth was engaged to the Prince Palatine, and the dances of the Anti-Masques, presented by the Inns of Court, were a very important feature. Francis Beaumont, the partner of Fletcher, conceived one of the arrangements and now, instead of a single ballet-entry (for in essence it is only that), there are two.

The Statues enter.... At their coming, the music changed from violins to hautboys, cornets, &c. and the air of the music was utterly turned into a soft tune, with drawing notes, excellently expressing their natures; and the measure likewise was fitted into the same, and the Statues placed in such several postures, sometimes all together in the center of the Dance, and sometimes in the four utmost angles, as was very graceful, besides the novelty. And so concluded the First Anti-Masque....

The Second Anti-Masque rusheth in, they dance their measure, and as rudely depart; consisting of a Pedant; May Lord, May Lady; Serving-man, Chambermaid; a Country Clown or Shepherd, Country Wench; an Host, Hostess; a He-baboon, She-baboon; a He-fool, She-fool, ushering them in; all these persons appareled to the life, the men issuing out of one side of the boscage, and the women from the other. The music was extremely well-fitted, having such a spirit of country jollity as can hardly be imagined; but the perpetual laughter and applause was above the music. The Dance likewise was of the same strain; and the dancers, or rather actors, expressed every one their part so naturally and aptly, as when a man's eye was caught with the one, and then passed on to the other, he could not satisfy himself which did best. It pleased his Majesty to call for it again at the end, as he did likewise for the First Anti-Masque, but one of the Statues by that time was undressed.

The future of the Masque under the latter part of the Jacobean period and under the Stuarts does not directly concern us. There is, to be sure, a deal of dancing, but to all historical purposes, it is a repetition of what has already been described, set differently perhaps, with greater or less taste or ingenuity, but basically the same. Nor, as some have said, did Cromwell and his Revolution destroy English music or dancing, any more than destroying the Royal Principle, when they beheaded Charles the Martyr.

Great Oliver himself danced till five in the morning at one of his daughter's wedding. It was only "lascivious" dancing that the Catechism of the Westminster Assembly (1643-7) opposed. Indeed, there were decided touches of puritanical priggishness in the French "Orchesographie" of 1588. Biblical precedent was constantly invoked in favor of dancing; in Ecclesiastes, for example, the famous citation that among all other times there is "a time to dance"; and that Miriam danced in triumph; although this elicited a pat Presbyterian reply: *Aye, but not wi' a pairtner*. There was even a Masque, under the Commonwealth performed in honor of a Portuguese embassy in 1653, "Cupid and Death," by the poet Shirley with music by Matthew Locke and Christopher Gibbons. In "The Puritans and Music," Percy Scholes' complete work on the period, a great deal of information testifies to the lively interest of the Revolution in continuing the traditions of Jones and Jonson. Milton's "Comus," although written before civil war, is more a verse-morality than a show for dancing, but there were dances in it of which engravings of the "final ballet" exist. It was performed at Ludlow Castle in 1634 with music by Harry Lawes.

In 1651, the second year of the Puritan supremacy, John Playford published "The English Dancing Master: or, Plaine and easie rules for the Dancing of Country Dances, with the tunes to each dance." In this anthology of one hundred and four dances, we have a very popular repository, not of theatrical dance, which is our chief interest, but of those social dances, which were to be performed for two hundred years afterwards among the English-speaking people on both sides of the Atlantic. And even today the mountain-folk of Kentucky and Virginia, and the county-folk of Cornwall and Wales repeat much the same figures as those collected by Playford. Sometimes, of course, these dances would be adapted to the stage, but one could hardly suggest Playford's volume as any parallel to Rameau's or Arbeau's.

In fact the English, except for their Anti-Masque, have always kept aside from the main course in the development of theatrical dancing. They contributed various national- or country-dances to choreographers who have wished to use them. The 'final' dances in their Restoration Comedy were an acknowledged and almost compulsory institution, and did not disappear until after 1750. During the eighteenth century French ballet was constantly coming across the channel, and we shall see that the actor Garrick called Noverre "The Shakespeare of the Dance." But there have been very few (if any) great English dancers, and only recently has a contemporary national ballet been able to hold audiences which have always been more than eager to acclaim French or Russian dancers. Without either native dancers or choreographers it is not surprising there has been little British blood in the veins of modern ballet, although in the last few years there is evidence that the situation is finally changing.

This history has cursorily examined the progress of theatrical dancing in Italy, France and England up to about 1650. The scope of such a work, limited by the covers of a single volume, is pitifully meager, even with the comparatively thin documentation which we are given up to this date. The remaining time, from 1650 to 1935, is very richly recorded, far too richly for one book. Hence, in order to maintain something more than an arbitrary selection, though at the risk of a lack of completeness, we shall have to reconcile ourselves to following a system, which if it has no other value, at least keeps our history proportional, balancing chief elements in their cross currents. Borrowed from Ezra Pound's "A. B. C. of Reading," and there referring to literature alone, those categories can be used to deal with any form of creative work.

First, we shall deal with those artists or artistic events, which are the first coherent examples of a particular expression; that is *innovation* (Noverre: Vigano). Second, we shall examine those *significant works* which, although they are not of initial importance, are produced in a healthy period of culture, by men who either found new processes or used them in a more masterly way than their inventors, and in spite of, or on account of their being influenced by the first, call for attention by their independent excellences (Ballets of Rameau and Petipa). Third, *dilutions,* or weak imitations of the first two, which serve to throw the more important examples into a proper relief (French and Italian ballets of the late nineteenth century). Fourth, the starters of *crazes,* or fads, of isolated movements which, having only a temporary influence, nevertheless do affect the large tradition, either directly or by reforms implicit in a reaction against them. (Isadora Duncan: Mary Wigman.)

The French *ballet de cour* had been declining into a static low level of repetitious fantasy, but with the advent of Mazarin at the death of Richelieu, France again becomes interesting. Giulio Mazarini, the son of a Sicilian, had been well educated in arms, gallantry and law to that point, where as Papal Nuncio at Paris, he had been invited to enter the service of France and in 1643 became Prime Minister. This post he held during the Queen-Mother's Regency in the minority of Louis Fourteenth. He was by no means as skilful in his management of French foreign policy as Richelieu, but he knew how to please Anne of Austria, and there is a well-known myth that he was really the sire of the Sun King.

To please the Queen, he invited from Parma an Italian engineer, Jacomo Torelli, *le grand sorcier,* to supervise new productions of Italian opera. Mazarin had reason enough to prefer a form of entertainment particular to the land of his birth, aside from his love of music, for his nepotism, his extravagance and his alienation of both bourgeoisie and nobility caused the invention of an extraordinary number of ballets and court-satires launched against his person and family. The subjects of these ballets were bizarre and trivial, but the allusions were too gross to be ignored. He could more easily control the subject matter of native Italian opera, and also it had a prestige, not entirely divorced from the snobbish acclaim in which French connoisseurs always held alien work.

Around 1580, and considerably after the Academy of Baïf, some Florentine gentlemen formed a similar *Camerata* of poets, nobles, artists, scholars and musicians, who, tired of the exhaustion of their given musical and dramatic forms, sought for a revivification in the chanted declamation of Greek tragedy. Their efforts resulted in more than archeology, precipitating the operatic device of *recitatif,* and *aria,* with their harmonic accompaniment. The old ring-around madrigals disappeared, as they had in France under similar pressure. Lyric pieces took on more body and expression and gave an added impetus to the work of Monteverdi and Cavalli. The former's 'Orfeo,' first presented in 1606 was the point of departure of our lyric drama, in terms of modern orchestration. Mazarin called Francesco Cavalli to the French Court, and his 'Xerxes' had a profound effect on Lully. The word 'opera,' though it only means 'works,' now took on a significance formerly held by 'tragedy-with-music.'

At Carnival time, from 1645 to 1647, Mazarin consecutively produced Italian opera for the Parisians. The *Orfeo* of Luigi Rossi, mounted in 1647 at the Palais Royal at a cost of 400,000 livres, created an extraordinary impression, more because of Torelli's amazing *ingegni,* than for any other reason. Although the dancing and singing were supposed to be excellent, the performance lasted over six hours, inducing no small degree of ennui among the spectators, who preferred the easy diversion of *ballets à entrées.* The Queen however adored opera, or at least she wished to please Mazarin for his pains, and though most of the court could not understand a word of Italian, they felt the need of showing as much enthusiasm as possible.

Paris had already been equipped with three more or less permanent public theaters, but none were as efficient as several in Italy, stemming from Palladio's historic *Teatro Olimpico* at Vicenza. So, in 1659 Gasparo Vigarini was summoned from Modena to build a luxurious auditorium in the Tuilleries, furnished with all the latest mechanical conveniences. France was primed, after her stages had been set by the Italians, for a national French opera, just as the *Ballet-de-Cour* had needed the impetus of Florence to precipitate 'Circe.' Belgiojoso had become Beaujoyeulx. Now all that was needed was the transformation, in a strikingly similar metamorphosis, of Giovanni Baptista Lulli to Jean Baptiste Lully.

He was always known as *Le Florentin.* There, in the great town on the Arno he was born, a miller's son. Louise d'Orléans, *la grande mademoiselle* Montpensier, cousin of Louis Fourteenth, had asked another cousin to bring back from a tour, one small Italian who could have conversations with her. In 1642, at the age of fourteen, Lully was presented and forthwith became her *garçon de chambre.* He soon had not only a great reputation as a violin virtuoso, but as a *baladin* or dancer with professional technique. In 1653, only three months after taking leave of Mademoiselle, partly at least on account of the disturbances of the Fronde, he appeared in five rôles of the *Ballet de la Nuit,* which is said to have lasted for thirteen hours. This ballet of night recalls the 'Masque of Blackness.' Displaying only incidents that occur after sundown, it blended by a device typical of the time, myth and reality, with one entry of the loves of Venus and Endymion, another of a nocturnal fight between soldiers and robbers. The actual extent of Lully's collaboration at this early date is unknown, except that he danced and immediately found favor with the King. He was appointed officially a composer of instrumental music, collaborating regularly with other court musicians, frequently dancing in entries side by side with Louis, who had made his debut in 1653 in the ballet of *Cassandre,* and whom Lully continually amused. His agility and mimicry were generally admired, and he struck up a genuine intimacy with his sovereign by which he was not slow to profit. During all this time he was not only virtuoso as dancer and violinist, but he became a brilliant musical technician, directing an orchestra of twenty-four strings. His reputation was universal. His songs were sung in the salons of the Louvre, and in the streets and markets of all France. He became in 1661, a citizen of France, and superintendent of the King's music.

Mazarin died, and in his passing the Italians lost their last patron. In 1662, on the stage of Vigarini's beautiful new theater was presented the *Ercole Amante* of Cavalli. In spite of a fine score, the music did not please, largely due to the incredible elaboration of the mise en scène. The clatter of huge machines for the *gloires* which descended from the skies, bearing one hundred and fifty singers and dancers drowned out the melodies. As if that were not enough, a political cabal, many said headed by Lully himself, was launched against this Italian opera which included the Florentine's own *entrées.* As a recently naturalized Frenchman, taking his cue from the great Minister Colbert, who bore no love for the aliens, Lully completely changed his tactics. He had for a long time used only French texts for his tunes, and would increasingly foster native talent, cleverly exiling his own compatriots without their ever being able more than to suspect his duplicity. Lully, in addition to being a great artist was an inspired entrepreneur, a ruthless, direct adventurer who had little remorse at whatever disagreeable steps helped him to secure his desired ends. A clever foreigner in an unfriendly milieu, he had plenty of opportunity to develop a method for the consolidation of his increasingly secure position.

A wretched poet called Perrin, whose improvidence was constantly landing him in debtors' prison, was obsessed with one idea. He was determined to elevate French opera to a place above the whole world's. A mediocre poet, his industry and persistence were unique. In 1659 he had written, while jailed, the book for a "Bacchus and Ariadne" with music by Cambert, the court organist. He insisted that it was the *first* French pastoral, as if it were a question of life or death. He loathed Italian opera. It was "merely a caprice of musicians apt enough at their art, but entirely ignorant of verse; ill-conceived and worse performed." Their *récitatif* he thought insupportable psalmody. He was overjoyed when the *Ercole Amante* failed. He probably tried to enlist Lully's aid in the cause of national opera, but the Florentine considered him too inconsequential for any collaboration; besides, his colleagues were Molière and Benserade.

Lully's enemies said he insisted opera could not be supported in France. It was not as simple as that. While Perrin and Cambert put on their pastorals, which were no more than concerts in costume, Lully in ballets and in lyric comedies or tragedies multiplied scenes in the dramatic manner. It was rather that Lully did not believe the Parisian public could sustain an interest in sung plays. As Prunières explains, the tepid reception given to good work, such as Cavalli's, convinced him that France was too taken with 'rationalist' ideas to accept operatic convention. But La Bruyère, a Frenchman of the French, defended that symbol of opera: *La Machine.*

> It is only to cultivate bad taste to say that the Machine is a childish amusement, fit only for puppets. It augments, embellishes the fiction, sustains in the spectacles, that sweet illusion which is the theater's whole pleasure, wherever it can still create the marvelous. There is no necessity of lights, or floats or change of scene in the *Bérénice* or *Penelope* (of Racine or Corneille); there are, in the opera (ballet), and the virtue of that show is to hold mind, eyes, the ears in an equal enchantment.

Perrin, with his *idée fixe,* far less intelligent, in no way as talented, saw more clearly than Lully though it did him personally little enough good.

Perrin had ideas for a French Academy of Music and Poetry, based on Italian models, rather than on those of Baïf. Having gained two years' respite from his creditors he ingratiated himself with Colbert, gathered together a company of singers, and finally, in partnership with Cambert, received letters patent permitting him to found a national opera. Although he made constant reference to the precedent of Italy, there had never been an *Accademia* which gave permanent opera. His *Privilège du Roi* authorized Perrin to undertake large expenses "for stages, machines, decorations, costumes and other necessaries." It forbade officers of the Royal Suite from entry without payment, and no one for twelve years could present opera in France without Perrin's permission.

The idea of an Academy is extremely important in the foundation of any national artistic tradition. In the beginning, a genuine aid and rallying point for creative energy, it often disintegrates into rigid bureaucracy. Then, its standards are useful only insomuch as they precipitate against official rigidity, all youthful violence and ambition of talents, which usurping its authority, cause envy, contempt and reform. A good Academy is not by any means an anomaly, although recently there has been not much proof of this view. Wisely used, or even conservatively used, Academies provide a solid basis, if only for practical technical information. However uncreative in itself, it is indispensable as an instrument in the hands of imaginative craftsmen. Whether or not Perrin consciously saw three centuries ahead to the present dreary *Académie Nationale de la Musique et de la Danse,* we shall never know, nor is it important that had he seen it he would have found little pleasure in the fruition of his great idea. The principle of an Academy, as such, was established in France, and would be increasingly imitated all over Europe. In the eighteenth century, Russia, picking the flower of French ideas, after all their experimental birth pangs, would establish Academies which ever since have been the pride of the world.

Poor Perrin! His opera was a success but he received not one sou, and Colbert, with the prerogative of princes, soon presented Lully with his privilege. No doubt this rankled doubly sore, since the Florentine was amazed at the success of native opera, and Colbert granted him monopoly not only for a dozen years, but for the duration of his life. After Molière's death, the King summarily gave Lully the great comedy hall of the Palais Royal for his ballets, a perfect theater, where Torelli's machines, constructed for 1647, were still in good working condition by 1673.

Lully was a wholly remarkable man whose talent for composition was no less than his capacity for establishing his results with an unqualified success. He so perfectly understood public taste, so skillfully manipulated the materials which he was given, that tragedy-in-music, which he defined, would remain without an important change, even in spite of Rameau, until the arrival of Christoph Willibald Gluck, a century later.

At least a part of the secret of his triumph was his adroit management of the King, by no means a simple problem. But Louis, like Nero, fancied himself as a dancer, and from performing with Lully in countless *entrées,* fell into the habit of treating him as a boon companion. The familiarity which he enjoyed at the King's pleasure never ceased to astonish the courtiers. What was the fascination of this ugly, mobile man, his clothes carelessly dusted with snuff, grimacing like a monkey, never afraid of annihilating his own personality in brilliant mimicry? Lully entertained the King, who was not a fool, and who prized amusement highly, since in many instances it was by the very distractions of amusement that he governed. Lully was valuable as an organizer of court fêtes, but above all, in his music he reflected and immortalized the rays of the reign, the virtues of *Le Roi Soleil.* The King chose the subjects and Lully would sing them to him, even before rehearsal, as they were written. Preparations at Versailles or Saint-Germain were always under the King's eye.

Louis Quatorze may have been framed in ample baroque scrolls, but he had the bold look of a Renaissance prince and his gestures, which made him point out of his portraits to his possessions or in to his proper person, were magnificent. Like the vast triumphal canvasses of Charles le Brun, the wide vistas of Le Nôtre's gardens; the heroic alexandrines of Racine or Corneille, Lully celebrated the glorious epoch of imperial French expansion; its arms, as well as its arts. He may have been a miller's son, but his manners were no parvenu's. He was at ease with every one whether it was his least important violin or the King himself. And aside from everything else, Lully wittily and subtly abetted his monarch's private life. In his *Proserpine* he gave to Ceres (Madame de Montespan), in the words of Mercury excellent, sobering advice. In his *Isis,* persecuted by Royal Juno, all Paris recognized the unlucky Comtesse de Ludes as butt of the Montespan's jealousy. Lully was envious, proud, capricious, extremely hardworking. Few artists of his quality have been able to enjoy such immediate popularity.

Although it is Lully's effect on the dance that primarily interests us, this is inseparable from his innovations as a composer of opera. As a dancer, and a celebrated one, he understood from first-hand experience, basic problems of ballet-music. His dance-tunes were closely constructed, gracefully precise, with free-flowing melody, sustained by simple counterpoint. He had a natural Florentine gayety, continuous harmony, a strong line surely indicated and nothing senselessly complicated by rhetorical decoration. Lully was an important revolutionist against unnecessary ornament and played a master part in the evolution of ballet-music and opera. When he came to France, a single ballet score was an amalgam of perfunctory pieces from all the court composers. Lully insisted on a personally coherent work, at least as far as each important element of ballet went, which for him was the music. One, not four or five costume-designers; one, not a half-dozen poets and painters would be employed. He influenced the whole genre of ballet according to his views, to be no longer a suite of dances related by tenuous plots, but rather mimed plays, or a succession of dramatic scenes linked by a single unifying subject, taken from fable or fantasy free of the restrictions of one time or a single place.

While Lully had dictatorial notions as to the importance of his *Académie Royale,* while he insisted an orchestral score be the work of a single composer, we cannot imagine he was a man with whom it was difficult to work. Rather, under his influence, French music-drama, finding its own special form, achieved a synthesis far nearer the antique, than had ever the naïve academicians of Baïf. Lully's eager collaborators were the greatest artists of his time, the decorator Bérain, the dancer Beauchamps, the poets Benserade, Racine, Corneille and Molière. But it is with Molière alone that their partnership resulted in an important contribution to theatrical dancing, in their evolution of the *Comédie-Ballet.*

It is all clearly explained in the preface to *Les Fâcheux.* Molière's connection with ballet was accidental, although, sooner or later it was inevitable for Jean Baptiste Poquelin and Jean Baptiste Lully to work together. In 1661, while preparing the play, he had intended that it should be entirely separate from the usual ballet. However, there were few good dancers available, and it was decided to insert their *entrées* between the acts, to give them enough time to change their costumes. Molière was primarily a dramatist. Not wishing to break his plot, he related the dancing to speeches, merging dance, music and witty words into a whole; a combination, which as he wrote

> is new to our stage, but one might find authority for it in antiquity; and, as everybody was pleased with it, it may serve as a suggestion for other performances which can be worked out more at leisure.

Les Fâcheux was produced in the noble gardens of Vaux-le-Vicomte, the magnificent palace of Mazarin's rash treasurer, Fouquet. This prodigal was ill-advised enough to attempt to compete in splendor with the King, the source of whose funds he alone best knew. Yet, without ever suspecting he was playing directly into the hands of Colbert, Mazarin's successor, he asked Louis to his palace, which at this time rivaled Versailles. The fêtes he gave precipitated his downfall. Fouquet was too quick to flatter a royal interest in the theater. Molière, working to order, produced a three-act verse comedy in two weeks which was a coherent pretext for those dances, considered a formal necessity.

It was all simple enough; a young lover tries to have a quiet talk with his mistress, and their every attempt to be alone is interrupted by a succession of bores, each of whom, by various little plots and by-play, distracts the attention of the lady, or prevents the young man from having her to himself. Molière assumed the rôle of a different sort of bore in each act, to display his own virtuosity. Even in the intervals, the lovers had no peace, for then entered dancers as gardeners, as cobblers, as bowlers, and all the ballets emphasized the social satire, for Molière was mocking court pretensions, to amuse its courtiers. All the speech, the miming, the dancing was neatly calculated to catalogue familiar bores.

Lully at once realized the part of a witty musician like himself could play in developing the *Comédie Ballet* in its own right. His collaboration with Molière started on the stage of the Palais Royal in 1664 with the production of *Le Marriage Forcé*. In *Les Fâcheux,* the *récits* of the old *ballet de cour* had been omitted, but now they were replaced by Lully's songs, performed by professional singers. Lully himself danced, although the *premier danseur* was the great Beauchamps. This professional was paid fifty gold louis, by the treasurer of Molière's company, for arranging the ballets. Their success was followed by many more; but the dialogue of Molière was nearly forgotten in the enthusiasm for Lully's entries, and the comedy, as such, was almost swamped by danced interludes.

Molière, from following a troupe of strolling popular comedians in his youth, was master of stage tricks, whose technique he had wholly assimilated from contact with the *Commedia del' Arte.* This was the popular Italian comedy, or more exactly the native farces of Italian towns, out of whose each particular locale emerged a comic figure, until a whole roster of classic personalities was brilliantly formulated, to replace the lost Roman *Fabulæ Atellanæ,* which had a similar arising. The Italians were inborn artists in the use of mimicry and earthy humor. The masks they invented for Harlequin, Colombine, Pantaloon, Scapin, the Captain and Punch in his various forms were as immediately popular in Paris as they had been in Bergamo, as they would be in London or Vienna. A famous company of these comedians, the *Gelosi,* created a furore in Paris as early as 1571. Their plays were not written, but improvised spontaneously by the actors, upon a repertory of a hundred familiar intrigues, filled with salty local allusions and decorated with *lazzi,* contrived clowning, acrobatic tricks or broad slapstick which the spectator grew to love as the very badge of the *Commedia.*

And Molière, adapting their popular figures to the French people, used them again and again in his own plays. The vitality, precision and wit of the popular comics was an inexhaustible mine of devices for such a genial technician of farce as Molière. Similarly, Lully put into his music a stylization, even that distortion, which was the *Commedia's* burlesque of ordinary movement, no matter of what class or profession. In writing dances for Harlequin in the costume of Louis Quatorze, as André Levinson said, Lully was a real *comediante;* the dances he inspired, designed on the deliberate mockery of his careful tunes called for a sequent choreography, whose patterns could be designed by whatever master cared to use the style, but whose gesture was founded on the improvisation, the conventionalized grotesquery of the Italians. For each mask, Polichinelle, Scapin or Scaramouche had his particular set of hand and arm movements, or methods of holding his body. Just as Molière could manipulate their whole vocabulary of entrances, conflicts and exits, so Lully learned to handle the acrobatic, lecherous, silly or cruel characters and situations, indicating music which presupposed their behavior on the stage.

Molière's *Le Bourgois Gentilhomme* carefully multiplied the occasions which demanded dances. In it he satirically wrote:

> All the ills of mankind, all the tragic misfortunes that fill the history books, all political blunder, all the failures of great commanders, have arisen merely from lack of skill in dancing....
>
> When a man has been guilty of a mistake, either in ordering his own affairs, or in directing those of the State, or in commanding an army, do we not always say: So and so has made a false step in this affair...?
>
> And can making a false step derive from anything but lack of skill in dancing?

Too often today, when this play is produced, the scenes are run together without benefit of the ballets which were designed as integral part of its comedy. Just as the eighteenth century would be seized by taste in the 'Chinese' manner; the nineteenth by the 'Gothick' and the twentieth, or at least part of it, by 'Egyptian,' 'Russian' or 'East-Indian,' so Lully's epoch suffered a crisis of Turkishness. Molière was swift to burlesque this fol-de-rol in a grand Turk ceremony, where Monsieur Jourdain is ordained as an apocryphal *Mamamouchie,* by the Grand Mufti, which rôle was mimed by Lully on its première, with extravagant success.

Up to the end of his life, the French considered Lully primarily as a composer of ballet music. Dances took up about a quarter of his lyric tragedies, and such was his effect that by the time of Rameau the proportion increased to a third. Yet, Lully, dominated by his ideal of synthesis, understood the element of the ballet, if it was only a divertissement, as extraneous. Again and again he attempted to integrate ballets with the body of his work, by writing melodies which gave determining expressive character to their movement. By this he greatly accelerated the growth of dramatic pantomime. In his classic ballets, he preferred melodies of an alert, even angular character, using the old dance rhythms of *gigues, canaries, passepieds* or *bourées*. His entries were framed in characterized thematic material, appropriate to the plot. 'The fortunate shades of *Proserpine* move in a pale and fluid melody. The nymphs of *Attys* are wrapped in soft sonorous scarves. It is scarcely fair for us to complain, when we hear the music now, it can often seem monotonous, faded, almost uniformly immobile, for we can see none of the dancing which was its chief reason for being.

The establishment of a department of Dance in the Royal Academy of Music, was not among the least of Lully's innovations. As early as 1661, a group of dancing masters had applied to the King for permission to establish an authorized Academy, and he gave them a room in the Louvre for their business.

> Although the art of dancing has always been recognized as one of the most honorable, and the most necessary for the training of the body, to give it the first and most natural foundations for all kinds of exercises and amongst others to those of arms; and as it is, consequently, one of the most useful to our nobility and others who have the honor of approaching us, not only in times of war in our armies, but also in times of peace, in the performances of our ballets, nevertheless, during the disorder of the last wars, there have been introduced into the said art, as in all others, a great number of abuses likely to bring them to irretrievable ruin.
> Many ignorant people have tried to disfigure the dance and to spoil it, as exhibited in the personal appearance of the majority of people of quality; so that we see few among those of our Court and suite who would be able to take part in our ballets, whatever scheme we drew up to attract them thereto. It being necessary, therefore, to provide for this, and wishing to reëstablish the said art in its perfection, and to increase it as much as possible, we deemed it opportune to establish in our good town of Paris a Royal Academy of Dancing....

These gentlemen preferred to meet for a pipe and a glass at the sign of the Wooden Sword rather than in their salon in the Palace. Their researches were not very significant. But when Lully assumed his control, he asked the advice of Pierre Beauchamps, their dean and the King's dancing-master, an able choreographer; perhaps the first great French dancer. His exact work is almost a myth to us, transmitted at second or third hand by pupils who were not writers at the start of the next century. But he, and after him Pécourt and Feuillet were to lay down a solid basis for virtuoso technique, founded on the experiments and habits of professional dancers of their epoch. Noverre, with his revolutionary dogmatism, would poke preposterous fun at their old-fashioned noble dances. "That dance, which they call *noble* was denuded of expression and sentiment." To him, perhaps: but to the audience of Lully it was as serious an innovation as Noverre's own reforms seemed, when methods of improved execution would finally triumph over the 'figures' which the Milanese had established in the middle of the sixteenth century.

It is very possible that if we should now see a ballet of Lully's as mounted in his time it would rather resemble a good deal of elegant marching about than what we are accustomed to recognize as stage-dancing. Developments are slow in one sense, amazingly fast in another. We must not forget that theaters which held raised stages, stages which divided the audience from the dancers by a proscenium-arch were not yet half a century old. Richelieu had built in his grand Palais Cardinal a new stage which enabled dancers in the patriotic ballet of the *Prospérité sur les Armes de France* of 1641 to make their evolutions without descending into the hall. The effect of this architectural feature was significant, for ballet, which for a long time had lost its dramatic character, now took on an undeniable theatricality. Prunières particularly stresses a point, not easily settled, and which is denied by many previous historians. He insists that neither the libretti of the poets, nor the memoirs of the period, prove that social-dances were used as a choreographic base except when special exigencies demanded. The ballets proper whether they were "serious" or "comic" had nothing to do with social-dances, and were composed professionally by the choreographers of the *Ballet de la Maison*. Fifteen days were allowed for the rehearsal of a *grand* ballet, eight for a *petit,* and it was no small task to teach the courtiers what they must do.

The choreographic principle with which Beauchamps had to start was *horizontality,* what the Jew of Pesaro called *partire del terreno,* or judicious maintenance of the floor plane. The *géométrie inventive* of Beaujoyeulx, however complex and involuted the figures on the ground-pattern, would have been more interesting to see from the ceiling than from the eye-level of the floor. Naturally, for the audience did not sit at one end of the hall, but on three, or sometimes four sides of it, all around the dancing-place. This kind of ballet, Levinson compares to chessboard movement, great military parades or big equestrian carousel-tournaments of Louis Fourteenth and the Tuscan Grand Dukes. All floor dancing, of which the *Basse Danse* was typical, following whatever wavy designs, were traced on the rectangle of a ballroom.

With the opera-ballet of Lully, there opened up the possibility of *verticality* and an ensuing use of arms, the whole body, and also of elevation. A dancer could now also inhabit the vertical province of air, using his legs to aid him leave the ground. The creation of the *danse de l'élevation* would take two hundred years to develop. Indeed it is by no means static today, and we cannot underestimate the root contribution of Beauchamps' generation, primitive as it was. It oriented ballet towards the conquest of space.

The important principle of being *turned-out;* the frontal plane of the dancer's body facing his audience in its maximum silhouette, was established. Rules for the maintenance of this *en dehors* position, turned out buttocks, knees and feet to control and develop the dancer's greatest equilibrium. Earlier opera-ballets were severely restricted by long heavy court uniforms of the dancers, and it was almost impossible to move with any degree of freedom, till Noverre destroyed this precedent. Nevertheless, under Beauchamps, the gradual emergence of the figures of *ballet de cour* into the technical nuances of the *danse d'école* commenced, and the system he formulated on existing traditions of society dances has an unbroken descent down through Camargo, Vestris, Taglioni and Anna Pavlova.

The effect of the French Academy on European dancing cannot be over-estimated. The very names for the positions in the vocabulary of the classic dance are learned in French, from the time when Feuillet, grammarian of Beauchamps' school Frenchified them, whether the school is situated in Paris, or Moscow, Milan or New York. *La danse d'école* is the best understanding of the choreographic idiom and it is useless to try to translate *croisée, effacée, attitude,* or *arabesque* into Italian, Russian or English. French *is* the lingua franca of the great tradition, and time has long passed when its frank use can be considered an affectation.

In spite of its national priority, France continued to absorb influences from other countries. There was a constant exchange of artists between France and England, France and Italy. An academician, André Lorin, the real promoter of choreography (at first understood as only the *writing-down* of dances) went to Britain to perfect himself in his art. There he learned the *contre* (country) *danse;* which when imported into Paris would be so popular the French considered it their own invention. On the other hand, a Frenchwoman, Mademoiselle Subligny, danced the *gigue* in London. It was a French or Italian (*giga*) folk-dance, but the English confused it with such forms as Kemp's "jig" or an Irish jog-trot, though it resembled them not at all. Both sides of the channel shared an enthusiasm for the innovation of Spanish national dances, in the *entrée Espagnole,* based on Moorish or ancient Iberian forms.

Beauchamps, who had designed dances for court fêtes for twenty-one years, and who had been Lully's *maître de ballet* since the opera's inception in 1671, retired in 1687. When some one complimented him on the ceaseless "variety" of his *entrées,* he always said that he learned "from the pigeons in his dove-cote. He himself cast their grain to them, and the birds ran for it in different groups and these gave him the ideas for composing his dances." We can see, that, if he looked down on his doves from above, what sort of patterns he would arrange for his dancers. Beauchamps was not supposed to have a "very good *manière* (style) as a dancer, but he was full of fire and vigor. No one danced better *en tourbillon* (turning); no one knew better how to invent." The technical vocabulary of the dance was very limited, and it was not lack of training alone that separated the nobility from professional dancers. However, the division was quick to come, and by the first decade of the eighteenth century, Feuillet will give minute rules for innumerable methods of pirouetting.

Lully's connection with his Academy was severed the same year as his ballet master's. He hurt his leg with the big stick by which he stamped the tempo for his orchestra, and died of the results of an infection. The *Opéra* was almost entirely his work, and in the *Opéra* we can fairly include Ballet for he wholly revitalized dancing with his *pas d'expression*. A man of superior judgment, he brooked no advice even from his equals; and only on rare occasions, from the King. When *Cadmus et Hermione* was produced Louis came up from the country especially to hear it. He could discuss with scene-designer or librettist the fine points of their craft, and what was most important, he knew how to make out of the Royal Academy of Music a great school where instrumentalists, singers and dancers were bred.

He taught his well-trained singers the secret of a declamation modeled on accents of normal speech. "This manner of *récitatif;* lively without being bizarre." He himself paid a dancing-master to instruct a good bass with a bad stance. A contemporary said:

> From that moment when a singer whose voice pleased him, fell into his hands, he at once started to mold him with marvelous affection. He himself taught them how to enter, to walk on the stage, to give them grace in gesture and movement. When he charged them with a new and difficult rôle he commenced to show them in his own room, before the regular rehearsals.

It was the same with soprani, machines, or arrangement of the repertory. The opera played regularly on Tuesday, Friday and Sunday. Thursday was the night for novelties and long lines of coaches blocked the Rue Saint-Honoré. Advertisements were on yellow placards as they are on opera-kiosks to this day. Performances started at five o'clock with the stroke of a baton, still heard from behind the curtain. The overture of strings alone, frequently massing those of the Royal Chamber, Chapel and Equerry, uncoiled its rich vapors of sonority. The prologue commenced before the painting of a pastoral landscape. It was always the same extravagant flattery of the King, comparing him (to his favor) with Apollo, Mars or Jove, and alluding to his battles in terms of Greece or Rome. Then the curtain revealed a scene of splendor, from the designs of the decorator Bérain. This brilliant artist stands in much the same position to Italy as Inigo Jones. He refined the promiscuous exuberance of Parigi and Torelli, by that compact French taste which makes their sense of theatrical tact preëminent in the lyric, if not in the tragic genres.

With the introduction of the Baroque, its violent, lush manner invaded the stage, for it was far easier to realize architecture of advanced fantasy in canvas or paint than in marble or plaster. To say that perspectives were madly overexaggerated, that proportions were inflated to gigantic orders is to indicate only a trace of truth. Nothing was impossible or forbidden. Vitruvius was pushed to the point of megalomania. Cupids swung garlands from columns quartered and laminated. Lolling entablatures and pendent pediments precipitated a dizzy mania of architectural aberration.

Bérain, however, restricted the heaps of trophies, toned down the fanlike vistas, suppressed the sub-tropical growth on Corinthian capitals. The Italian strove for marvels, for miracles to make audiences gasp trying to figure out the tricks. The French aimed only at enveloping atmospheres of a mysterious and poetic wonder whether they were black awful caverns, flowery golden halls, or armed encampments. Grave, deliberate, intensely theatrical (if to us heavy and ostentatious), of an unsurpassed elegance in refinement of detail and execution, Bérain's costumes and scenery were the perfect setting for the songs and dances of Lully, and would continue to be the dominant influence in the decoration of the operas until 1770, a century later.

Lully was cursed with such bad sight he could not tell five feet away whether or not a woman had a lovely face. Although for a long time noble ladies had danced in the *ballets de cour,* it was considered bad form to allow professional women to perform. Their rôles had always been played by boys, masked, *en travestis.* In 1681, with *Le Triomphe de l'Amour,* came the first of the ballerinas, Mademoiselle La Fontaine. Soon she was followed by Subligny and the Maupin, who would serve as the heroine of Gautier's romance. Lully was very severe with his artists, fair but not familiar, even to their morals. He never permitted himself the choice of a mistress from his troupe, which was considered exceptional. "I can tell you that under the reign of Lully the singers didn't have rheumatism six months in the year and the men weren't drunk four times a week." The Academy was a model institution, due to his discipline, and a shrine, where all Europe was pleased to pay the homage of grateful memories. As soon as he died, decadence started in, but even so, with his impetus, it remained the capital of musical and choreographic creation till the French Revolution, after which his principles were better realized in Milan, Petersburg or Berlin than ever again in Paris. But in his lifetime he had the satisfaction of seeing opera-houses opened at Marseilles and Lyons, and shortly afterward at Rouen, Rennes, Bordeaux, Dijon, Brussels and The Hague.

Lully's direction was really, after all, toward music. He incorporated into his ballets whole scenes of recitative. He developed the importance of symphonic interludes to the detriment of pantomime. Soon it all oddly resembled the Italian opera that Mazarin patronized. By forging the instrument of recitative he made music-drama possible, and all this time, songs and dances were crowded out, for incidental or almost conventional use in moments of joy or sorrow. As Prunières concludes in his brilliant article,* Lully was not content

* *Lully et l'Opéra Français: Numéro Spécial de la Revue Musicale.*

merely to create masterpieces. He revived, and made triumphant, in competition with Italian opera, a certain musico-dramatic ideal, and at the same time, a new vocal and instrumental style of execution. His practical labors with orchestras, dancers, singers and with his Academy were no less admirable than his creative life. And what is more, he had the rare satisfaction of knowing the full value of his work and enjoying its appreciation by the French court and the French people. There was the famous anecdote of his stopping his coach on the rise of the Pont-Neuf, to give the correct pitch to a street violinist playing one of his tunes; and the *récit* of *Amadis,* "Love, what wouldst with me?" was sung by all the cooks in France.

The seventeenth century, so rich in occidental innovations, also includes a semi-oriental beginning which is of utmost importance. While Renaissance had been merging into Reformation, while France was taking the place of Italy in Western culture, there began in Russia an activity which decade by decade increased in power, up to the present day, when the schools of Leningrad and Moscow produce the finest dancing technicians in the world.

Unquestionably there must have been some infiltration of ancient traditions from the Eastern Roman Empire or Byzantium up into the Crimea and South Russia. There are mural decorations of Byzantine mimes in the Church at Khiev. But this influence is negligible compared to the national dances of the Slavonic races inhabiting the vast domain of Tartars, Mongols or European Slavs. Among the initial references to Russian dances in modern history is the mention of one Ivan Loduigi who performed on a tight-rope and gave lessons in drum-beating and dancing in the reign of the first Romanov, Michael Fedorovitch (1613-1645). Before that time the Court of Muscovy was famous for its barbaric and extravagantly oriental splendors. Great families kept slave-girls as professional dancers, for private amusement, but it was scarcely in the nature of spectacle. The Tsardom of Muscovy was the whole of the Russian Empire. Compared to Western Europe the nation was in a primitive state of culture. Women were confined to their *terems* and only permitted to emerge when their masters wished to display them. The natural barbarism of the folk was complemented by the bigotry of the Greek Orthodox Church. A chronicle of the period stated: "When dancing and the strife of fiddles begin, the good angels flee away as bees before smoke, and the Devil and his angels rejoice." In 1649 the Patriarch Joseph had all the musical instruments in Moscow burnt, except those of the Tsar's personal band.

From the foreign quarter of the capital, an interest in the dramatic arts was gradually articulated, and Russian Ambassadors to Europe were ordered to report on all spectacles to which they were invited and to send home the cleverest trumpeters who could best play dance-tunes. Naturally the tales of the tournaments of the Grand Dukes of Tuscany seemed particularly brilliant to the Boyards. After importing some foreign talent in the way of comedians and musicians, in 1673, a German Lutheran, Pastor Gregory, instructed twenty-six Russian boys as "The Comedians of His Majesty the Tsar."

Around the same date the danced *divertissement* made itself known in these barbarous parts. It was prologue to a drama, and was called 'Orpheus.' A special theater was constructed for the occasion, with the Tsar's chair in the middle, a latticed gallery for the Tsaritsa and their children. 'Orpheus' was an imitation of a German marriage fête, and there was a *pas de trois,* executed by the heavenly musician and two pirates. After which Orpheus reappeared, superbly dressed, and throwing aside all European pretensions, executed some brilliant national dances, which, we may imagine, were a good deal more to the court's taste.

Now the Tsar's Minister Matveyev was ordered to select a group of likely children from the bourgeoisie to be sent to Germany for instruction in acting. A theatrical school was founded, and a Hall of Comedy installed in the Kremlin, in which, from time to time, performances were given, though dancing languished until the turn of the century. But the history of dancing in Russia, as with so much else, starts with Peter the Great, and it is to him and great Catherine that the schools and the theaters owe the encouragement which enabled them to be what they are today.

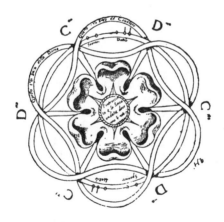

THE 'CONTREPASO'   *Caroso:* 1581

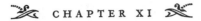

CHAPTER XI

Rameau and Noverre: OPÉRA-BALLET *and* BALLET D'ACTION

THERE are two main sources from which methods of theatrical dancing have resulted in tradition. They are inseparable, but fairly definite in essence. The accumulation of technical knowledge, of information regarding the efficient means of executing a step, or a series of steps in combination, gradually becomes codified into dogmatic rules, without which pupils are deemed incapable of learning their métier. This is the academic line. It is useful insomuch as it presents in an economical form all existing methods for performance, accumulated since the art's beginnings. This academic line tends to become rigid, unresponsive and restricting. Then, it is either broken, or at least interrupted by individual artists of advanced ideas or individual technique, who make new additions to the rules which at first seem in violent opposition to everything previously considered correct, but which tend to become a valued part of the school. This is the line of personal innovation. To understand fully not only the development of the *danse d'école* but of our contemporary ballet, one must have at least a rudimentary knowledge of these two interacting forces.

Lully died but his Academy, though deprived of his genius and solicitude, survived. Through its influence in theaters throughout France and Europe it was maintained as a world standard for technical execution and artistic excellence. Soon a succession of the best dancers, even before their dancing days were over, turned into teachers, and a pedagogical system evolved. Their practical experience was handed down by personal demonstration and word of mouth to be adapted and amplified from generation to generation in an unbroken, hereditary descent. Lully's *maître de ballet* was Beauchamps. In 1687, his pupil, Pécourt, followed him, 'handsome and well-made, and dancing with all possible *noblesse.*' This man is the accredited author of the *Chorègraphie,* or the art of writing dancing by signs. There is a question whether that widely translated and popular work, edited by Feuillet, is actually his invention. In itself, it is as remarkably ingenious as it is difficult to read. We remember William's, the Jew of Pesaro, exhortation about the necessity for *Memoria.* The greatest waste in dancing is the loss of creative work, because of composers' and dancers' inability to recall combinations of steps. The *Chorègraphie* proposed a system of signs, by which one is enabled to read steps just as if they were notes on a staff of music, assuming the feat can be accomplished. This is more difficult than would first appear, since frequently only the *ground* plan is indicated; that is, the floor pattern traced by the dancer's feet. The arms have only the roughest indications; as for the carriage of the whole body in relation to music, we must wait for cinematic-recordings. Nevertheless, Pécourt's reputation was venerated for his contribution to the dance, insomuch as he at least thought the work was not of an ephemeral nature, that it deserved preservation for future audiences. At intervals over the next two hundred years, new methods of steno-choreography will be presented, with the same disappointing conclusions. It is almost more difficult to learn to read the signs than to retain the dances in one's memory.

The first English edition of Feuillet's 'Choregraphy, or the Art of Writing Dancing' appeared in 1706. In the *Tatler* (no. 88) Addison reports a very British idea of the French dance and of French dancing science:

> I was this morning awakened by a sudden shake of the house, and as soon as I had got a little out of my consternation I felt another, which was followed by two or three repetitions of the same convulsion. I got up as fast as possible, girt on my rapier, and snatched up my hat, when my landlady came up to me and told me "that the gentlewoman of the next house begged me to step thither, for that a lodger she had taken in was run mad, and she desired my advice," as indeed everybody in the whole lane does upon important occasions. I am not like some artists, saucy, because I can be beneficial, but went immediately. Our neighbor told us "she had the day before let her second floor to a very genteel youngish man, who told her he kept extraordinarily good hours, and was generally home most part of the morning and evening at study; but that this morning he had for an hour together made this extravagant noise which we then heard." I went up stairs with my hand upon the hilt of my rapier, and approached this new lodger's door.
> I looked in at the keyhole, and there I saw a well-made man look with great attention on a book, and on a sudden jump into the air so high, that his head almost touched the ceiling. He came down safe on his right foot, and again flew up, alighting on his left; then looked again at his book, and holding out his right leg, put it into such a quivering motion, that I thought he would have shaked it off. He then used the left after the same manner, when on a sudden, to my great surprise, he stooped himself incredibly low, and turned gently on his toes. After this circular motion, he continued bent in that humble posture for some time, looking on his book. After this, he recovered himself with a sudden spring, and flew round the room in all the violence and disorder imaginable, until he made a full pause for want of breath.
> In this *interim,* my women asked "what I thought." I whispered, "that I thought this learned person an enthusiast, who possibly had his first education in the Peripatetic way, which was a sect of Philosophers, who always studied when walking." But observing him much out of breath, I thought it the best time to master him if he were disordered and knocked at his door. I was surprised to find him open it, and say with great civility and good mien, "that he hoped he had not disturbed us." I believed him in a lucid interval, and desired "he would please to let me see his book." He did so, smiling. I could not make anything of it, and therefore asked "in what language it was *writ.*" He said, "it was one he studied with great application; that it was his profession to teach it."

Arbeau, in his 'Orchesography' over a century before, had suggested a rough idea by using letters of the alphabet for dancing positions. Just as his book is the standard for our knowledge of dancing of the sixteenth century in France, so is Rameau's *Maître à Danser* (The Dancing Master) our best guide to the eighteenth, not only in France, but in all Europe since the French kingly idea has become a model for every royal follower of Louis Quatorze.

Of Rameau nothing is known except that he was the official dancing teacher of the pages of Her Most Catholic Spanish Majesty. His book was published first in Paris in 1725, and it bore the printed approval of Louis Pécourt:

> I have read, by order of the Keeper of the Seals, a Manuscript bearing the title *Le Maître à Danser* (8vo.). I have found in this work all the precepts of dancing set forth precisely and clearly. The engraved plates which represent the various postures of the body will render the execution easier and I believe that this book will be of no less service to the student desirous of learning dancing, than it will lighten the labors of those who teach.

"The Dancing Master" is primarily a guide to social-dances, just as were William's and Arbeau's treatises. But these had considerable effect on theatrical dance of their epochs, and Rameau's has even a closer connection, since in his descriptions of actually *how* to do a menuet we can clearly visualize the dancing manners, the essential *style* of the period, which must have been apparent on the stage as well. Also, Rameau has the advantage over his predecessors, insomuch as there existed for him a considerable body of reference, to which he could point, and in every case he refers to a great *stage* dancer as the standard for whatever type of social-dancing is to be undertaken. Naturally the book would have meant more to readers who had actually seen Pécourt or Balon or Subligny, but even so we can derive much from a thorough reading.

We must be careful not to confuse his terminology with indications for our contemporary positions employing the same names. In the long evolution of the *danse d'école,* terms remain conservatively the same, just as French has been kept its universal language. But under the blanket of the names, steps and gestures, the enlarged vocabulary of the developed classic dance has grown.

Rameau says his views on dancing have 'been acquired not so much from personal experience, as from the practices of the great masters with whom I have had the fortune to associate.' By this we may infer he was more of an observer than a technician, but nevertheless a professional, belonging to a profession of honor which has long outgrown the class of accident or dilettantism. He tells us although he has spent his life in the study and teaching of dancing, he will not give a long dissertation on the history of the ancient art (like Lucian or Arbeau), but will leave that to historians.

> Yet the reader would have cause to complain if, at a time when dancing has achieved the highest degree of perfection, I said nothing of the progress it had

made towards the end of the last century, a progress which increases daily owing to the rivalry aroused by the performances given at the Academie Royale de Musique. For dancing must not be regarded as an exercise designed solely for pleasure. I certainly think that the joy and vivacity attendant on banquets and festivals led to its birth, but it is with dancing as with acting, men have sought to turn to useful account what was originally intended as a diversion. If dancing were confined to the theater, it would provide occupation for a few people only; but it may be said that it merits the attention of almost every one, even if they be destined to make use of it from their earliest years. Dancing adds graces to the gifts which nature has bestowed upon us, by regulating the movements of the body and setting it in its proper positions. And, if it do not completely eradicate the defects with which we are born, it mitigates or conceals them. This single instance will suffice to explain its utility and to excite a desire to be skilled in it.

He then gives a résumé of the glorious history of Lully's Academy and the brilliance of French dancers. His attitude is extremely close to our own. While he realizes that dancing is both enjoyable and useful to every one (he makes several references to its therapeutic properties) nevertheless, his interests are professional; his words are intended for others who desire similar accomplishments, which, after all, take considerable application and time. He commences by a discussion of the correct way to hold the body:

> The head must be held erect without any suggestion of stiffness, the shoulders pressed well back, for this expands the chest and affords more grace to the body. The arms should hang at the sides, the hands be neither quite open nor quite closed, the waist steady, the legs straight and feet turned outwards.

The feet turned *outwards*. The rest of his rules are simple enough and accorded with the most dignified carriage of the upright human. But the feet, *turned out,* is a formalization, an extension of a natural position for purposes of greater steadiness, freedom in shifting position, and general kinetic precision. The establishment of the five absolute 'positions' of the feet, he attributes to Beauchamps, although in Arbeau there are woodcuts showing similar ones.

> What is termed a position is nothing more than a separation or bringing together of the feet according to a fixed distance, while the body is maintained upright and in equilibrium without any appearance of constraint, whether one walks, dances, or comes to a stop.

The *first* position of Rameau shows the two feet heel to heel, at an angle of probably a little more than forty-five degrees. The contemporary Russian-American 'first position' is a ninety degree angle, the two feet heel to heel in a straight line, which insures a maximum effect of legs and thighs turned-out for supple though solid support of the torso above. Similarly in the other of Rameau's directions, a difference in the extremes is visible between 1725, 1830 (Carlo Blasis), and 1934 (Vaganova).

The *second* position has the same line-up of the feet, now *apart*

> but there should not be more than the space of a foot between them, which is the correct proportion of the step and the true position of the body supported on both legs, which is shown by the shoulders being at the same height. That is the reason why the body can easily be supported on either leg without any forced movement.

The *third* position (*emboîture:* boxed-in, enclosed) has the legs and feet extended and close together

> so that no light can be seen between them, and they join like the sides of a box.... The body is placed erect on both feet, the left in front but crossed before the heel of the right at the ankle, as shown in the figure. This position is one most necessary to good dancing; it teaches the dancer to stand firm, to straighten the knees, and constrain him to that regularity which is the beauty of this art.

The *fourth* position regulates changes of step, back or front, giving them the correct distance for walk or dance. The left foot is in front. The right, apart from it, behind. Rameau discusses the necessity of walking elegantly. Such dances as the menuet consisted chiefly of a conventionalized walk. It was hardly a fluid movement which we could call dancing.

The *fifth* position (in Rameau's time) has the feet one behind the other fairly close together. It is used for crossed steps; for moving sideways. In our day the two feet are tight together, the toes in opposite directions. These five positions are absolute for excellent reasons. They are the residual bases for feet movement in every direction, presupposing either a single partner, or the collective partner of the audience. Knees, spine and arms combine to produce the greatest frontal silhouette: the body must seem as *front* as it can be, for inclinations to either side pare off the façade and tend towards a visual malformation. Distances between legs and feet in the five positions are not capriciously determined, but give the greatest breadth and meaning to the air which frames them, showing that in no matter what relation, they are separate supports for the trunk, capable of alliance, balance and spread.

> In all these positions I have shown the body supported equally on both legs, which, by the distance observed, proves that one foot may be raised, while the body rests on the other, without any strained movement. I shall not speak of the false positions, because they seem to me useless for young persons to learn, but leave their explanation to the discretion of those masters who care to teach them to their pupils. However, they are rarely encountered, save in turning steps, or in *pas de ballet*.

That is to say, in ballet, violations of the five positions are countenanced, in fact demanded. *Anything* is possible at all times, depending on the exigency of the occasion. The five positions, however, always remain in a dancer's mind, indeed a sense of them becomes instinctive, not only as a structural underlying base from which all other steps spring, but also as a magnetic anchorage to which all steps, however eccentric, return.

All balls at court, or in princely houses, reflected the manners of the King. Louis Fourteenth cultivated personal dignity to the point of public grandeur. The Sun King was first dancer as well as first gentleman of France. Court etiquette developed a ceremonial of extreme, often grotesque and inhuman complexity. There is Saint-Simon's famous description of a crisis precipitated by the unforeseen absence of one of the gentlemen of the King's bedchamber, charged with the daily presentation of the royal hose. No one else had authority to assist with his socks and for a while it seemed as if the King would never again be fully clothed. After the death of Louis, his heirs consciously imitated this court behavior, their entourage following suit, down into the rising pretensions of the bourgeoisie. Court functions were interminably tedious. A small basswood plate called a *moniteur* would be strapped to the back beneath one's clothes to relieve spinal strains, for very often the only seats were thrones provided for royal family or royal favorites.

It is unlikely that the *moniteur* directly affected Rameau's ideas on the correct carriage of the body. But a certain stiffness was deemed elegant, and also an erect stance tended to tire less quickly than a slouch. Rameau has a long section on 'honors,' the correct ways for ladies and gentlemen conventionally to 'revere' one another; to bow, to curtsey. Rules are given for approved manner of taking off one's hat, proper means of curving the elbow, or holding the fingers. In all such uncoverings, the five positions are held. Then the curtseys of ladies are discussed, the deportment of their hands and fans, their entering or leaving a salon.

Rameau's description of the King's grand ball reads like the libretto for a ballet, whose plot is the platonic essence of eighteenth-century principles of loyalty, aristocratic behavior, the social amenities of courts and their dependents. He says the King's functions should be a model for all private balls 'in regard to the order of the proceedings, and the respect and politeness to be observed thereat.' After every one is seated, according to their rank, the King, princes and princesses of the blood royal, dukes and peers of France, duchesses and other lords and dames of the court, His Majesty rises, opening the ball, and every one else does likewise.

> The King takes up his position at that end of the room where the dancing is to begin, which is near the musicians. In the time of the late King, the Queen danced with him, or, in her absence, the first Princess of the Blood, and placed themselves first. Then the company took up their station behind them, two by two, according to their rank. That is to say: *Monseigneur* (the King's eldest son) and *Madame la Dauphine* (the title of the wife of the King's eldest son), *Monsieur* (the title of the King's brother), and *Madame* (the wife of the King's brother), then the other Princes and Lords. The Lords stood on the left side, the Ladies on the right. Retaining this order, they made their bows in turn. Afterwards the King and Queen led the *Branle* with

which all Court Balls opened, and all the Lords and Ladies followed Their Majesties, each on their own side. At the conclusion of the strain, the King and Queen went to the end of the line, then the next couple led the *Branle* in their turn, after which they took up their position behind Their Majesties. This continued until all the couples had danced and the King and Queen were at the head again.

After which comes the *Gavotte,* followed by paired dances, a series of *Menuet,* the first of which the King dances, while every one stands. After he is seated, the Prince who follows makes him a profound bow, bows to the Queen, to Princesses of the Blood Royal; dances and then bows all over again. We can imagine what leeway for sarcasm, irony, petulance and insolence all this bowing allowed. Protected by a careful execution of ordained honors, a man of spirit could, by an infinity of subtle nuance, express a clear idea of his state of mind, his feelings for royalty, or perhaps his milder, more personal emotion towards his partner.

The Court disposed of, Rameau continues with the most important part of his book; a discussion of movement and the manner in which the steps and measures are performed.

> There are three movements from the waist to the feet; that of the hip, knee and instep; all the different *pas* in dancing are formed from these principal movements. But they cannot attain perfection until the joints have made their bendings and returned to their original (five) positions; that is to say, until the leg is straight. I shall begin then by explaining the action of the instep, which can move in two ways; that is, tension and extension, to use the terms of anatomy, which is what we call raising the toe and lowering it.

He explains the uses of the *demi-coupé* (half-cut) and in excellent detail the full nature of the menuet. He makes a great point of the necessity for dancing it with preconceived uniformity, allowing no slipshod improvisation (nor, we must admit, any spontaneity), to mar the brittle beauty of its symmetrical exchange. His suggestions are always towards a canon of conscious behavior, based not only on the mutual consideration of the sexes, but on means by which men and women will seem most gracious to each other, while at the same time, reflecting the focal grace of the sovereign whose courtiers they are; their dancing is mimed homage to him.

Rameau speaks of changes time has wrought with the older dances, described by Arbeau, and of the grave dances enjoyed by the late King, Louis Quatorze, who:

> despite the weighty affairs which continually occupied the mighty conqueror, he never failed to set aside some hours each day for the practice of the *courante,* throughout all the twenty-two years that Monsieur Beauchamps had the honor to instruct him in his noble exercise.

When we read over Rameau's rules for the execution of various steps, even though it is difficult to obtain a clear picture of them, without music or dancers, we realize the movements of limbs and torso are very complex in themselves, and not, as in Arbeau, merely complex in floor-pattern. Each part of the body, (though with particular emphasis on propelling and supporting feet at the expense of expressive arms), receives consideration as to the orbit of its correct, potential activity. If this is not stage-dancing it is very much dancing for show, with its function as a form of social intercourse greatly diminished. Rameau, probably upon the base of the dancers of Lully's Academy, creates the possibility for a progressive technique, and eighteenth-century dancers were the first modern artists who could lay claims to what, by our own terms, can be called brilliance. This is not to infer that in comparison to our extraordinary technical endowment, Rameau's contemporaries would not seem extremely naïve and restricted to us, particularly regarding turns and elevation.

"The Dancing Master" does describe the pirouette. It is, to be sure, a complete pivotal turn on one or both feet. But any one could do it with a few tries, which is by no means the case with the contemporary dancer's turn, which is multiple, and except for the ultimate restrictions of lungs and the skull's semi-circular canal, can be prolonged with skill almost indefinitely. The modern male pirouette is executed upon a half-toe held as high as can be, and this is only possible with a "classic-ballet" shoe. We must not forget that eighteenth century dancers still wore leather-soled shoes, with painted heels, and this, to a very large degree, conditioned their foot-action.

Rameau describes the *Balancé,* a dipping knee-shift; the *Sisonne,* a manner of a hop, bend and recovering; *Jetés* or jumps, and many other terms, which today keep their same names, but the interim has altered their execution by filling them with new variants and activities. He tells how to keep the legs open, how to do beats, including *Entrechats,* when feet cross, beating the air. This famous step, canonized by the Russian acrobatic school, is not difficult to execute simply, but when multiplied past four beats it is rarely cleanly performed. Nijinsky is said to have twice done ten, back and forth, not on the stage, but in his classroom. Few living dancers can do eight.

The whole second part of Rameau's treatise is occupied with the arms, "of the importance of knowing how to move them gracefully." He again refers to Beauchamps as having been among the first to lay down rules for their control, and many engravings illustrate exactly their circulatory wrist movings, fingers always natural, hands never stiff. He states a very important principle which the Italian sculptors of the late renaissance and baroque had popularized. This they called *Controposto* and we, *Opposition.* It is the emphasis of the plasticity of the human body as an erect column in space, capable of accentuating its tri-dimensionality by the opposition of arms and legs. This contrast of the upper and lower parts of the body, stressing the free-moving high-relief of arms and legs contributes enormously to making the static symmetrical human silhouette, two legs supporting a trunk; two arms capped by a head, an interesting, varied and asymmetrical outline. It can be observed in the swing of opposite arm and leg in walking, but the normal movement can be altered as opposition to its very opposition. There are numerous changes which can be rung on the basic idea, involving balance and a visual equilibrium of hand and leg from the audience's sight, as well as a physical equilibrium enabling the performer to keep erect while moving.

By 1725, the tradition of the Renaissance *Basse Danse* was not dead. Although infrequently performed, it nevertheless served as an unconscious restriction against high leaps. Besides, 'good manners' would scarcely permit violent physical display. Hence, instead of jumping to express exuberance, a dancer requiring the expenditure of energetic measures, took them out in quick steps or running cadences rather than in high steps or crashing chords. Sharply marked, broken rhythm or accented syncopation were impossible. Beside viols there were only those instruments which would develop into the pianoforte. At this period, music written for them had to have shortish intervals between notes to sustain their limited range of vibration, by being repeatedly struck or plucked.

The shadow cast by Sun King and his Academy may have testified to the grandeur of his epoch, but it was not an incentive to much creative activity after the epoch was over. The end of his reign was far less brilliant than its beginning. His wars and fêtes were eventually reckoned in terms of a national debt. France would never again see such mythical extravagance. This can in no way be regretted. Now, instead of having all the entertainment and talents of France at court, smaller fêtes were arranged by provincial princes, less grand yet more exquisitely conceived in their detail than at Versailles. A whole new class of patrons who could be relied on to commission music and decor, arose in place of a unique royal Mæcenas. These were the ascendant bourgeois merchants and bankers of the towns, and they developed more and more a mode conceived in the freedom of Parisian society, released from palace discipline. It was for the first time public taste, not royal caprice, which gave artists their pitch. The *grand goût* of Louis Quatorze, *Les Plaisirs des Iles Enchantées,* the age of Lebrun and Lully, gave way to *Les Fêtes Galantes* of Watteau and the musician Rameau.

The transformation undergone by opera and ballet may be less apparent to us than it was to audiences who had been born and grown up in the seventeenth century, only to be affronted by an eighteenth century novelty whose outrage we can only with difficulty comprehend. The element of novelty is extremely important in the progress of ballet. The 'new,' in this sense is difficult to define. A list of sensations, or innovations of the last three hundred years surprises one by their essential similarity. The 'new' consists of adaptation, revival, or rediscovery of factors which will please the intelligent minority of an audience, tired of academic repetition which inertly performs previous novelties without development. We must always try to pretend in reading of the eighteenth century that there was no thought of a nineteenth or an early twentieth. Novelty was a shock to them in forms which we do not even recall in their subsequent academic clichés. But novelty and the violent reaction it arouses is an impetus of the first order.

After Lully, during the long interregnum until the arrival of Rameau, poetic and dramatic elements passed into a decidedly secondary importance. Music took first place, and this change was largely achieved by the influences of Italian composers and instrumentalists who in creating lyric tragedy, developed both musicians and music comprehension in their audience. A real passion for dancing was characteristic of the period, and provoked in the opera an often unbridled choreographic invention at the expense of song and drama. The rupture of equilibrium between poetry, music and dance was responsible for the formation of a new genre, more pleasing to present than past taste, and which would dispute for public favor with the old lyric tragedy.

This was the *Opéra-Ballet* of the first half of the eighteenth century. It was in fact, a sort of opera, where dancing and orchestral-music predominated. It comprised under a single title, not only one subject, but as many different subjects as there were acts. A very vague idea might relate them, such as the Four Seasons, the Ages of Man, the Cosmic Elements, the Parts of the World. Each act was divided into a little opera, sufficient to itself. Dramatic action was reduced to a minimum. Plot becomes mere pretext for music, and above all, for dancing. Everything tends toward ballet. It is, as Masson says, the ballet which gives birth to that simulacrum of opera, destined to frame it.

As always the new direction had been carefully prepared for a long time. Its ancestry was inherent in Lully's lyric drama which it came to replace. A taste for pastoral scenes, delights of the country, bucolic farmers and adorable shepherdesses had been readapted from the antique, modernized by Italians in France, and became increasingly popular down to the Revolution. Its most lasting definition is the dairy-hamlet Marie Antoinette had herself designed, a little way back in her palace woods. The literary type of pastoral after 1630, disappeared to take refuge with tragedy and comedy in Opera. Lully restored the pastoral in his *Fêtes de L'Amour et de Bacchus*, in 1672. The *Fêtes* were merely a series of ballet entries. The Florentine had an affection for the gay and peaceful and sensed that his audiences were increasingly more interested in dancing and light music than in pathetic or heroic dialogues, however expressive.

In Lully's lyric dramas, though the dances might have slowed up the action, they were never separate from it. Unlike Italian opera of the same period, ballets were not independent *intermedii* or entr'actes. Now, however, the fine unity of lyric tragedy was destroyed. The first proof was the production of *L'Europe Galante* in 1697, by an Italianate composer, Campra. It was a veritable *ballet d'entrées,* the one previous form to survive the arrival of opera-ballet. In *L'Europe Galante* it became a series of ballet entrances corresponding to the scene and act divisions of a dramatic poem. The general drift tended definitely away from drama. The French public could never seem to support a sustained danced action. They preferred short, simple plots, which would furnish a sequence of agreeable interludes without much logic. This fragmentary form quickly defined itself in the term applied to a composite spectacle embracing scenes from wholly different operas: *Fragments de Lully: Fragments Modernes.* The independence of each act allowed for a renewal of interest. The division of five acts was replaced by three, and later, by a single act, the *acte de ballet.* In this reduced form Louis Quinze was to know the opera and dance. It was the most typical music expression from 1700 to 1750.

Casanova, about 1745, saw Dupré, the successor of Beauchamps, in *Les Fêtes Vénétiennes,* an opera the title of which, as he said, was of great interest to him. When the curtain rose, the scene represented Saint Mark's Square in Venice, taken from the Island of Saint George: he was shocked to see the ducal palace on his left and the campanile to his right. The scene designer had not known enough to reverse the perspective from the engraving he had copied of the Piazza San Marco.

> The action of the opera was limited to a day in the Carnival, when the Venetians are in the habit of promenading masked in Saint Mark's Square. The stage was animated by gallants, procuresses, and women amusing themselves with all sorts of intrigues; the costumes were whimsical and erroneous, but the whole was amusing. I laughed very heartily, and it was truly a curious sight for a Venetian, when I saw the Doge followed by twelve councilors appear on the stage, all dressed in the most ludicrous style, and dancing a *pas d'ensemble.* Suddenly the whole of the pit burst into loud applause at the appearance of a tall, well-made dancer, wearing a mask and an enormous black wig, the hair of which went half-way down his back, and dressed in a robe open in front and reaching to his heels. Patu (Casanova's companion) said, almost reverently, 'It is the inimitable Duprès.' I had heard of him before and became attentive. I saw that fine figure coming forward with measured steps, and when the dancer had arrived in front of the stage, he raised slowly his rounded arms, stretched them gracefully backward and forward, moved his feet with precision and lightness, took a few small steps, made some battements and pirouettes and disappeared like a butterfly. The whole had not lasted half a minute. The applause burst from every part of the house; I was astonished, and asked my friend the cause of all these bravos.
> 'We applaud the grace of *Duprès* and the divine harmony of his movements. He is now sixty years of age, and those who saw him forty years ago say that he is always the same.'
> 'What! Has he never danced in a different style?'
> 'He could not have danced in a better one, for his style is perfect, and what can you want above perfection?'

But now emerges a mysterious figure, who, asserting his belief in the principles of Lully, precipitated a revolution among Lully's heirs. The début of a musician of fifty, previously unknown to the official academy, was in itself a scandal. For Jean-Philippe Rameau had been born in Dijon in 1683, the son of petty bourgeoisie. His father was an organist and no relation to Rameau, the dancing-master. As a boy of twenty he had been sent to Italy, possibly to forget a grand passion, but the musical influence of this tour was negligible. On his return to France he gained a meager livelihood as a traveling church-organist. He married, living a life of irreproachable moderation, which had so little interest to his contemporaries that almost no documents survive. But he wrote an extremely important theoretical treatise on harmony, which did not cause at once the great effect it should have, probably because he was a provincial, not a Parisian. A remarkable improviser on the organ, his technical training was of such a sturdy work-a-day nature as to stand him in better stead later than he probably imagined at the time. At forty he had only written a few clavichord pieces, some cantatas and the book which never helped his fame. It is a curious contrast to Lully, violin-virtuoso and youthful dancer of his King's youth, or to Mozart, the prodigy of eight, the genius of eighteen.

Upon the publication of a second treatise Rameau's reputation began finally to increase. He had good positions and pupils but the official Opéra remained stubbornly shut. Vainly he tried to find a poet of sufficient academic standing whom he could use as librettist to advance his cause. Through the offices of a rich pupil he met Voltaire, who proposed to write for him a *Samson,* a 'tragedy to be put into music,' but nothing came of it. Finally, he obtained from an abbé who had some experience in opera, the book of *Hippolyte et Aricie,* an imitation of Racine's great tragedy *Phèdre.* During its rehearsal Rameau had considerable trouble with singers who complained his music was too learned, too theoretical; unsingable in fact. Rameau loved the baroque figuration of Italian singing, and as an excellent technician, courted difficulty. His opera was a success, but he disavowed launching a new taste, as if it were any conscious plan on his part. He had no choice but to write as he did.

Nevertheless the Lullists formed a strong opposition, and there was a concentrated effort to discredit the tall, thin, stoop-shouldered provincial. The Ramists (there were soon two violent factions) were seduced by the richness of his music, the force of his impulse, the extreme refinement of his writing. The Lullists were disconcerted by this very abundance, and by the complexity of orchestration, which they said was mere 'science' lacking in 'expression.' Their one agreement was on the novelty of his conceptions.

In 1735 he attempted the *Opéra-Ballet,* which he preceded by an *Avertisse-ment,* calculated to cover him from all sides, enrolling him as it did under the correct standard.

> Forever occupied with fine declamation and the lovely melodic line which reigned in the recitatifs of the great Lully, I attempt to imitate him, not as servile copyist, but availing myself, as did he, of fair and simple nature as my model.

As his biographer de la Laurencie explains, his policy was double-barreled. On the one hand Rameau recommends himself to Lully; on the other, by exalting nature and imagination he parried the thrusts directed against him as mere theoretician or savant.

The libretto of *Les Indes Galantes* is not only a perfect example of the genre of a semi-political opera-ballet but also of the geographical mode of a Europe newly aware of our globe's size. Renaissance discoveries had finally penetrated into the mind of the whole world.

In the prologue, the youth of the four allies, France, Spain, Italy and Poland, are practiced in the arts of war by Bellona, abandoning the joys they tasted under the rule of Hebe and Amor. The Loves, then Europe herself, quit them to emigrate into distant lands.

The First Entry: *The Generous Turk:* (Turks, Incas, Persians are all Indians, of the Indies). Osman, Turkish pasha of an isle in the Indian Sea, loves his Provençal slave Emilie who has been captured by a pirate from her fiancé Valère, a naval officer. A tempest hurls on their coast a vessel carrying him. He also becomes the slave of Osman, finding again his Emilie. Osman, after a moment of simulated rage, renounces his love and joins the lovers. Rejoicings of African slaves and Provençal sailors.

Second Entry: *The Incas of Peru:* In a desert of the Peruvian mountains terminated by a volcano, Don Carlos, a Spanish officer, loves a young native princess, Phani. The Inca, Huascar, commands the Feast of the Sun, to separate her from her lover, by artificially provoking the eruption of the volcano. But Carlos survives, saves Phani, while the criminal Indian, mad with rage, jumps into the fire.

Third Entry: *The Flowers: a Persian Fête:* On the day of the Feast of Flowers, Tacmas, Persian Prince and King of the Indies, comes disguised as a slave-merchant, into the gardens of Ali, his favorite. For he loves the slave of Ali, one Zaire, 'an ex-Circassian Princess,' and he disdains his own slave, the Georgian Fatima, who is infatuated with Ali. She follows, disguised as a Polish slave. In this disguise, Tacmas takes her for a rival and draws his sword. But all ends happily. Tacmas and Ali change slaves, and the quartet figures in the Flower Feast, of 'amiable odalisques of divers Asiatic nations.'

Fourth Entry (added the next year as a kind of after-thought): *The Savages.* In an American forest, neighboring on French and Spanish colonies, warriors of the savage nation, commanded by Adario, draw near to celebrate peace with their European conquerors. A French officer, Damon, and a Spaniard, Don Alvar, dispute the hand of Zima, a chief's daughter. One shows his infidelity, the other his jealousy. But she wishes a mate *ni jaloux, ni volage;* and following her 'innocent nature,' she gives herself to Adario, who has been waiting, hidden during the previous scene. Damon calms with philosophy, the fury of Don Alvar. Peace is celebrated by the *Danse du Grand Calumet.*

Rameau worked hard not only for ballets exalting the noble savage, but for his theoretical ideas upon the supremacy of a dramatic form, the necessity for expressive diction, in spite of spectacle. He had a measure of success, and became a focus for intrigue and controversy. But he abandoned this side of his talent, and became a court-musician, an official composer. His music assumed a consequent lightness, diminishing in dignity.

In 1745, on the occasion of the marriage of the Dauphin with the Infanta Maria-Theresa, Rameau and Voltaire triumphed in their collaboration of *La Princesse de Navarre,* a comedy-ballet, after which the composer enjoyed a royal subsidy. A lyric comedy, sung from beginning to end, very like a Lullist lyric-tragedy except for the subject, it was wholly different, however, from Molière's comedy-ballet, that juxtaposition of spoken comedy with interludes of music and dancing, more or less tenuous and not specifically linked to the action. In each of the three acts of *La Princesse,* there were *divertissements de ballet,* caused by logical demands of the plot. In the first act, a dance of warriors and gypsies, in the second of loves and graces, in the third a Franco-Spanish entry—inspired by the wedding at Versailles. A little later, Jean-Jacques Rousseau collaborated with Rameau in uniting the three ballets in one consecutive entertainment, *Les Fêtes de Ramire.*

Each act of the opera-ballet was wholly disparate with very weak libretti. But there was a shift in the interests of the librettists. Quinault, and the poets for Lully, had always drawn on pathetics from antique tragedy or marvels in the epics of Tasso or Ariosto. Actors were all gods, goddesses, demi-gods or heroes, who mixed in the affairs of men, behaving in a highly conventionalized, preconceived manner, displaying the grandeurs of their divinity. In Rameau's time, exuberance of the marvelous gave way to exoticism; a more or less exact evocation of national characteristics of distant places or peoples. The *ballets géographiques* were not unknown to the seventeenth century, but in the eighteenth, China, Persia, India and Mexico were as popular, and more piquant than Greece or Rome. Magic (if with a more oriental tinge) was still a standby. The quarrel of Lullists and Ramists also extended to the decor which framed the action. The Age of Reason was at its start. The encyclopædists were launching their rational, anti-theological explanation of all natural phenomena. The attitude of the *philosophes* (lovers of wisdom) was defined by Diderot, who, in attacking the principle of the *deus ex machina* and the clouds (*gloires*) the seas, the machinery, said, "The enchanted world may serve to amuse children. The *real* world alone pleases the mind." There was an increasing desire to discover 'human' sentiments, 'human' relationships, as opposed to the capricious, arbitrary action of the gods. Prompted by contemporary Italian lyric tragedy they were interested in more psychological excuses for behavior.

In fact, with Rameau the use of the miraculous was such a weakness it became exaggerated. Often stage artists, like Wagner and Meyerhold, have insisted on the necessity of removing audiences from mere corroborative naturalism. But with Rameau, his formulated, mannered system, whether it employed Pashas, Spanish princesses, or Castor and Pollux, tended to exclude all normal or recognizable emotion, making his sentiment chilly, however charming. But one could hardly expect much interest in a conflict of emotion when most of the emphasis was on dancing.

The music for it, the *symphonies de danse,* or as they were currently known, the *airs de danse,* held a place about as important as the *symphonies dramatiques,* from the time of Lully on. This was the logical effect of its double origin: the Italian lyric-tragedy or *opéra* and the French *Ballet de Cour.* The danced divertissement itself only developed since the death of Lully, favored as it was by the evolution of eighteenth century manners and taste. Even in the most moving of the *tragédies-lyriques,* dancing was always welcome, and audiences asked only that it should have some slight connection with the plot.

France provided dance-music for the continent, which was the western world, and a good part of the airs were written by Rameau. They would often be inserted, taken out of context, as interludes in the widely performed Italian opera patronized from Madrid to Saint Petersburg. The simple dance, without any definite dramatic program, had above all a decorative rôle, as was often the case with the singing chorus. It completed the endowment of the scene's atmosphere by costumes, movement and sound. Often it was only an *entrée,* an animated cortège or procession, usually joyful. In these instances the librettists would merely indicate: *On danse:* 'here should be dancing.' The nature of it was left to musicians and dancers. The dancing was not only superficially allied to the action; it was in itself an action more or less promoting the drama. Sometimes there were precise indications by the poet for pantomime, called *danse en action* or *ballets figurés,* which are the immediate predecessors of Noverre's far more expressive *ballet d'action.*

The *maîtres des ballets* who collaborated with Rameau, tried to avoid old-fashioned, arbitrary dancing and strove for as much genuine expression as they understood. Mechanical movement, composed of regularized, gracious gesture, like those codified by Rameau the dancing-master, were only an amplification of ordinary ballroom-dancing, and held a revered, hence necessary place on the opera stage. Their dramatic significance, except in rare exceptions, was the simplest expression of group rejoicing or grief. There was little choral use of local color until Noverre. Individual dancers could and did add steps and gestures. They influenced each other and were imitated by their followers, becoming thus a part of dancing tradition. But more often as far as *corps de ballet* went, its chief use was to provide a symmetrical plastic harmony.

Nevertheless, during the epoch of Rameau, the whole technique of stage dancing was modified, and although the modifications were chiefly personal and could not be synthesized for integrated use by a whole troupe until Noverre, they are nevertheless important contributions in themselves.

Around 1730, the so-called *danse haute* (high-dance) began to be preferred to the old *danse basse,* or more accurately, the *danse terre à terre,* (close-to-earth). The ballets of the Renaissance, even despite the rapid measures of Lully, were conceived entirely on a horizontal plane. This planimetric choreography, describing a surface pattern for the feet was more of a predetermined promenade than a dance. But with the strict separation of ballroom and opera-stage, the *vertical* dance started to emerge under the regency of Louis Quinze, and above all, permitted the aerial displacement of the body in space and height.

The Lullists, accustomed to the comfortable "nobility" of traditional dances were scandalized. "Once there were dances: now, only jumps." This criticism coincided with the quarrel over Rameau's musical idea. He could pretend he followed Lully's precepts. But the high leaps, and nimble entrechats of his dancers could not be disguised. The Ramists and the young lined up with the *danse verticale;* they were opposed by the Lullists and defenders of the *danse noble.*

As in all feuds, partisans on both sides created their scandals, precipitating duels and broken heads. All the excitement, however, had a salutary effect for it popularized dancing with the great public who had previously considered it the court's special plaything. Now it became the property of the people. The two sides had their champions, and followers of Rameau swarmed to the banner of La Camargo.

Marie Anne de Cupis was born in Brussels in 1710. She took the name of her Spanish mother's family. From the Camargo strain came her fire. During her youth she was patronized by court ladies and enabled at an early age to be instructed by Mlle. Prévost, *première danseuse* of the Academy. Her young pupil made such progress that the older woman grew jealous. Camargo appeared at the Brussels Opéra and finally made her Parisian début in 1726. The ballet was a series of short divertissements, enabling a virtuoso to display herself in period dances and in pantomime. The reviewer in the official gazette, *Mercure de France,* said:

> Mlle. Camargo, a dancer from the Brussels Opera, who has not previously been seen here, danced *Les Caractères de la Danse* with all the liveliness and intelligence that could possibly be expected from a young person aged fifteen to sixteen....Her *cabrioles* and *entrechats* were effortless, and although she has still many perfections to acquire before she can venture comparison with her illustrious teacher, she is considered to be one of the most brilliant dancers to be seen, in particular for her sensitive ear for music, her airiness, and her strength.

Soon she became a favorite and dresses, hats, slippers, coiffures, received the accolade, *à la Camargo.* She seems to have been, for her day at least, a 'brilliant' technician. Though her elevation, which was limited by heeled shoes, would scarcely seem noteworthy to us, she is credited with having first executed the *entrechat quatre.* But what is far more important, by shortening her skirt a few inches she opened up unimagined vistas of technical possibility.

Costume plays a very important part in the development of the dancer's technique. The most perfect costume for a fine body is its own nakedness, an unadorned silhouette; but social customs have clad the nude with all sorts of appurtenances which emphasize in turn buttocks, shoulders, legs or arms. The ponderous clothing of French opera had hardly changed since Lully's day, when his costumer, Bérain, adapted antique detail to Louis Quatorze court-dress. While it surpassed Europe in richness and elegance it was not suitable for dancing. Any attempt at realism or local color was considered in bad taste. It was not until Noverre's reform that dancers' bodies were liberated. With all the talk of grace no one thought of using simple draperies on Greek statuary to robe Dianas and Junos, who infallibly supported great panniered skirts, with such perfunctory classic accessories as gilt bows and quivers, or silver-crescent bandeaux. The panniers, or as we call them, hoop-skirts, were of English origin, first appearing on the French stage in 1716. Some two years later they were adopted by French society, not to be taken off until the eve of the Revolution. Male dancers wore equivalent if shorter *tonnelets,* stiff bouffant skirts, from under which emerged their thighs in tight breeches, gartered at the knee. In Grimm's *Correspondance Littéraire,* the Baron wrote:

> Camargo was the first who ventured to shorten her skirts. This useful invention, which afforded connoisseurs an opportunity of passing judgment upon the lower limbs of a *danseuse,* has since been generally adopted, although, at the time, it promised to occasion a very dangerous schism. The Jansenists in the pit cried out heresy and scandal, and refused to tolerate the shortened skirts. The Molinists, on the other hand, maintained that this innovation was more in accordance with the spirit of the primitive Church, which objected to *pirouettes* and *gargouillades* being hampered by the length of petticoats.

Once more, as in the old days, dancers seem to have precipitated theological controversy. By lopping off a modest few inches, not for coquetry but merely in order to permit her legs increased liberality of action, Camargo opened a way for *allegro,* the rapid, brilliant category of classic ballet technique. She also was supposed to have introduced *caleçons de précaution,* or tight-fitting drawers, which enabled her to bound about without any danger to her or the audience's modesty. But in the notice of her death we find:

> Adopting the principles of executing all her steps under her, she always dispensed with that modesty garment worn by *danseuses* to avoid any offense against decency, notwithstanding the height of her cabrioles, entrechat, and *jetés battus en l'air.*

Her leaps were not very high and really belonged to the old-fashioned *danse mécanique,* but she was vastly popular with the public, introducing a new element of expressive, active gayety. Thanks to her Spanish inheritance the antique *danse heroique* received a little of the variety of character or folk dancing, and the *basse danse,* for all intents and purposes, was dead.

"Ah! Camargo. How brilliant you are!" ran Voltaire's madrigal, though he added, "But, great gods, how ravishing is also Sallé." Marie Sallé, the "muse of gracious, modest gesture" was the pride of the Lullists, the preference of the Royal Family. Her father was a tumbler in a company of strolling comedians. Born in Paris in 1714, she appeared at the Opéra seven years later when Mlle. Prévost was suddenly ill. The audience took her for a girl of ten or eleven. She was a success. She performed in England as well, with rising popularity, and her gifts were continually contrasted with Camargo's. While the latter was considered preëminent in "technique" Sallé was unrivaled in "expression."

In 1734, in London, she presented an entirely new ballet-pantomime arranged for herself, by herself. The plot was the story of Pygmalion, which we may peruse with profit, both because of its suggestion of an accumulating interest in mime, and because of its scandal. The London correspondent of the *Mercure de France* sent back to Paris the following report:

> For nearly two months *Pygmalion* has been given without any signs of failing interest. This is the theme: Pygmalion enters his studio accompanied by his sculptors, who execute a characteristic dance, mallet and chisel in hand. Pygmalion bids them throw open the back of the studio which, like the forepart, is adorned with statues. One in the middle stands out above all the others and attracts the admiration of every one. Pygmalion examines it, considers it, and sighs. He puts his hands on the feet, then on the body; he examines all the contours, likewise the arms, which he adorns with precious bracelets. He places a rich necklace about the neck and kisses the hands of his beloved statue. At last he becomes enraptured with it; he displays signs of unrest and falls into a reverie, then prays to Venus and beseeches her to endow the marble with life.
>
> Venus heeds his prayer; three rays of light appear, and, to the surprise of Pygmalion and his followers, the statue, to suitable music, gradually emerges from its insensibility; she expresses astonishment at her new existence and at all the objects which surround her.
>
> Pygmalion, amazed and transported, holds out his hand for her to step from her position; she tests the ground, as it were, and gradually steps into the most elegant poses that a sculptor could desire. Pygmalion dances in front of her as if to teach her to dance. She repeats after him the simplest as well as the most difficult and complicated steps; he endeavors to inspire her with the love which he feels and succeeds.
>
> You can imagine, Sir, what the different stages of such an action can become when mimed and danced with the refined and delicate grace of Mlle. Sallé. She has dared to appear in this *entrée* without pannier, skirt, or bodice, and with her hair down; she did not wear a single ornament on her head. Apart from her corset and petticoat she wore only a simple dress of muslin draped about her in the manner of a Greek statue.

There was a delicious scandal, and the forces of progress triumphed. Now there was precedent for dancing not merely in the fashionable mode *à l'antique,* but in the archeological style or more accurately, *à la grecque.*

Marie Sallé instituted a number of reforms which anticipated Noverre. Not only her skirt and bodice were loose but her whole body had a new freedom. Her ideas were scarcely received with general approval, and she went back and forth between Paris and London in search of an understanding audience. Although there were many demands from her followers, and what is more, Camargo had retired, she made little attempt to appear at the Opéra. But just at this time Rameau had completed *Les Indes Galantes,* and the combination of this happy event with the assurance of a proper salary induced her to return to the stage.

She appeared as "The Rose" in the third entry, the Persian festival. An eye witness recalled,

> La Sallé danced like a bird in foiling the zephyr who woos her. She has learned in England not to put too much voluptuousness in her dancing, which is all for the better.

She excelled in giving new interest to the simplest dances, and imagined, with creative gesture and without any indication from the libretto, touching pantomimes, wholly in key with a given situation. Cahusac, the pedantic author of *La Danse Ancienne et Moderne* writes of a revival of Campra's *L'Europe Galante,* in 1736:

> That dancer (Sallé) appeared in the midst of her rivals with the graces and desires of a young *odalisque* who has designs on her lord's heart. Her dance was formed of all the pretty poses which such a passion can express. She developed it by degrees; one read in her expression a whole range of emotions; one saw her hesitating between fear and hope; but, at the moment when the Sultan gives the handkerchief to his favorite wife, her whole being quickly underwent a change. She tore herself away from the stage with that degree of despair, characteristic of tender and passionate beings, which is expressed only in moments of utter dejection.

Sallé was to perform in several of Rameau's ballets and she achieved a notable success in the rôle of Terpsichore, Goddess of Dancing, in his *Fêtes d'Hebé ou Les Talens Lyriques.* Rameau's music was a very satisfactory background for an artist of her caliber. The audible soul of the dance of his time, distinguished by its exact yet varied adaptation to dramatic movement and mimicry, it explained the action, characterizing its sequences. It was a new type of musical realization. The motifs were personally felt, the melody incisively articulated, the rhythms, precise, audacious, seeming almost to lead dancers by the hand. Rameau had a sure dramatic instinct and a sound plastic sense, tracing in advance patterns for possible choreography. The tunes describing shepherds or sailors, priests or warriors, gentlemen or savages, ghosts or demons, each has its quality for particular movement. Masson, in his monumental study of Rameau's opera, describes how

> In the fifth scene of *Zéphyre,* upon a *grand air de danse* with two reprises, the Zephyrs are opposed to the flight of the Nymphs. The various parts of

the melody are preceded by the letters F, O, or E, which correspond to the following choreographic movements: *Flight, Opposition* or *Ensemble*. Towards the end of the same scene, one finds at the head of a 'sarabande' (*Pas d'un Zéphyr et d'une Nymphe*) this curious direction: 'Flutes, with which Zephyr runs to the Nymph.' For the more complex pantomimes of which the program is furnished by the librettist, it is easy to distinguish, in the course of the musical development, descriptive elements more or less analogous.

Rameau's position in the history of music has been compared to Descartes in philosophy. "Music," he said, "is a science which should have definite rules, —a physico-mathematical science." His theoretical achievements are objectively more important than his work as a composer, in which he seems more the follower of Lully than a parent to Mozart. But, from our point of view, he made important contributions to dramatic expression in dancing. While his basic conceptions may have been unchanged from Lully's day the proportion of the various elements alters. His often mediocre libretti are sacrificed to dance and music. Also, Rameau's melodies, clothed a form Lully never knew; —the *opéra-ballet* La Motte and Campra conceived at the end of the preceding century. With its fragmentary unsustained action broken up into acts, music took a new freedom which had its dangers in the abundance of its divertissement. But Rameau anticipated Gluck, Wagner and Stravinsky, and provided usages unknown before him.

After Rameau opera-ballet suffered the crystallization of formula and academic inertia. This is the unfortunate side of traditionalism. So often when a line is refreshed by an innovating energy, the very strength needed to assimilate new blood seems almost to exhaust the organism, so that it coasts along until another revitalizing shock. Noverre angrily wrote:

> Let us see what the *maître de ballet* usually does at this spectacle, and let us examine the work he is given to do. He is presented with a prompt copy: he opens it and reads: PROLOGUE: *passepied* for the dancers representing Games and Pleasures; *gavotte* for the Laughs, and *rigaudon* for the Pleasant Dreams. FIRST ACT: march for the Warriors, second air for the same, *musette* for the Priestesses. SECOND ACT: *loure* for the People, *tambourin* and *rigaudon* for the Sailors. THIRD ACT: march for the Demons, lively air for the same. FOURTH ACT: entry of Greeks and *chaconne,* without counting Winds, Tritons, Naiads, Hours, Signs of the Zodiac, Bacchantes, Zephyrs, Shades and Fatal Dreams—because there is no end to them. See how well the *maître de ballet* is instructed! Witness him entrusted with the execution of a truly magnificent and ingenious plan! What does the poet demand? Simply that the members of the ballet dance and are made to dance; from this abuse are born ridiculous claims.

The story no longer determined the dances, the best performers were saved till the end; there was no integration of mise en scène, and poet, *maître de ballet,* musician and scenic artist scarcely ever coöperated, each working by himself without mutual regard for a unified work.

There were new dance-forms, their names taken from social dances but theatricalized by the choreographers. Without giving musical quotations, all of which can easily be found in Masson, we list the most used, going from the slower to the quicker. The *Gavotte* was slowest of the *danse à deux temps*. It started on its second beat, and had a 'sweet, active gayety': The *Bourée* was more rapid, giving its name later to a toe-step. The *Rigaudon* had only appeared at the end of the seventeenth century with Lully. But it was very fashionable under Louis Quinze and expressed "pure celestial joy." The *Tambourin,* was of Provençal origin, quicker than the *Bourée.* Its bass repeats the same note imitating a rapped tambourine. The *Contredanse* was the basis for the later *Quadrille.* On the stage it served for popular rejoicings or finales. It had a simple repetitious melody and had been brought from England around 1690. In the *Loure,* a form unknown to Lully, the tempo slows down toward the end rather than accelerates. The *Forlane* was similar to it, of Italian origin, but more rapid. The *Gigue* had enjoyed an English adaptation and was very chic under the Regency of Louis Fifteenth.

Among the *danses à trois temps* was the *Sarabande,* a kind of slow menuet forming the grave largos and adagios of classical symphonies. It was elegiac, meditative and noble, full of the possibilities for nuances of pantomime, and was probably of Spanish origin, perhaps linked to the *Canaries,* described in Arbeau. The *Chaconne* was taken a little faster and the *Passecaille* (Italian, *passacaglia*) was a slow chaconne. It was used as an orchestral underwriting to important dramatic scenes, rather prolonged, to fill up time. The name had a Basque origin. The *Menuet* was rapid and had been introduced around 1670. It originated in the province of Poitou and was first used theatrically by Lully. It was a simple, polite measure affording numerous chances for an exchange of courtly, elegant gesture, bows and curtseys. The *Passepied* was a fast menuet and Rameau used it more often than its slower form. In addition to these were the *Airs.* The *Musette* was a pastoral "symphony," imitating at least in part that rural pipe, and was not necessarily a dance. The *Marche* was a dramatic symphony used to sustain large group movements, arrivals, processions, ceremonials and departures. Each of these traditional dances had a general character suitable for fitting situations or characters, which needed underlining or explanation, although naturally more would be left to the artistic taste of the composer,.than his reliance on the forms themselves.

The *Académie Royal de Musique et Danse* had become a public institution and enjoyed a popularity as focus both of art, manners and politics, increasingly apart from the court. In 1716, opera balls were established in form of masquerades.and social gatherings which came to be supported by the rising bourgeoisie as well as the aristocracy. In 1715, on the morrow of Louis Fourteenth's death, letters patent were drawn up at Vincennes, entrusting the control of the opera to the Duc d'Antin. At the start of the Regency there were loud cries of *'Vive le Regent,* who prefers the Opéra to the Mass!' Constant fights occurred in the precincts of the theater. There were duels in dressing-rooms and armed guards were posted to keep nobles from the stage boards. The influence of the dancers themselves as mistresses of influential men, was not to be laughed at. A pasquinade signed "Mariette," proclaimed in print what every one already knew, the formation of a powerful ministry.

> The ladies of the opera have shared the Government among them. One has the war office, and another the department of finance, a third Public Worship (what had the Church come to, now?) and a fourth, the management of foreign affairs.

From Lully's day Fridays remained the fashionable night. The principal artists appeared then, while Sunday and Tuesday programs were left to chance. At the start of a new century, the orchestra vaunted but one double-bass, intended to sustain the chorus. This monstrous fiddle was played on Fridays alone lest it wear out. The opera was one of the town's chief sights to show off to any foreign embassy. The most famous was the Siamese visit of 1686.

> The Ambassador was taken to the opera one evening that they were playing *Armide,* and had the whole piece told him, its every detail explained. Seeing the enchantment Armida had recourse to, to gain Rinaldo's heart, he enquired if she was a Frenchwoman; and when they answered no, that she was the niece of Hidrast, King of Damascus: 'Just so,' he replied, 'if she had been a Frenchwoman, she would have had no need of magic to get herself beloved; for Frenchwomen have charms enough in themselves.'

Indeed the Academy of Music itself was something of an asylum for French women, young girls, unhappy wives and lonely widows who wanted to escape from family troubles. 'Such has been the decision of His Gracious Majesty.' They needed only to be entered officially on the rolls as *filles du magasin,* (music or dancing students), and whether or not they finished their studies, or even never appeared on the stage, they could enlist and be forever free to lead whatever lives they wished, independent of any one, save, we can imagine, the protectors who found them at the doors of their dancing-school or behind the scenes at the opera. From Rameau's time and even before, the wings of the Paris Opéra have been considerably more interesting as insight into the manners of their visitors, than any revelation of ballet-technique or ballet-composition. With few exceptions there have been no first-rate French dancers. When they do appear in the nineteenth century, they were more appreciated abroad than at home. The great stars of the French opera, even to this day, have been Italian, Russian or of mixed ancestry. The Diaghileff Company had not a single French dancer, although filled with English, Scandinavians and different types of Slavs. The greatest name in French ballet was not native, but Swiss, possibly of Swedish ancestry, and he found everywhere but in Paris a receptive direction, if not a receptive public.

In the history of classic theatrical dancing, considerably less than in other arts, it is difficult to point to masterpieces, to master-performers. There is no

Parthenon, however ruined; no tomb of Pope Julius, however dispersed; no Last-Supper, however faded. There is no Hamlet, no Emperor Concerto. Nor would it be difficult to prove that since there are no such residual crystals left, the art itself is not grand. Proof is already conceded by people whom dancing does not affect. For those whom it does, there need be no defense. Dancing exists in time to a far greater degree than music, not only because it has no convenient method for being recorded or transmitted. A dance more than any other form demanding a performer, is a *personal* performance. Choreographers work with dancers they know. Their very costumes, scenery, ideas, are an expression of individuals in a certain time. When the time passes, an important factor of freshness is lost. Revivals have always a faded air unless it be revivification, casting all archeological exactness aside. Ballets are created for their own time, to be enjoyed with an intensity not even shared by music. This very intensity may exhaust their interest. A piece of music can delight generations after its composers; then, why not dancing? In music the sound is released onto an air to which it gives all color, light and warmth. The importance is in the hearing. In ballet it is seeing. The hearing is a base. Good ballet music can always serve afterwards. But there is, they say, no Dante, no Homer, no Shakespeare of the ballet. To many people the performance of Nijinsky in *Les Sylphides* has meant an equivalent grandeur, if one must have these categorical standards. As for there being no Shakespeare of the dance, there seems to have been at least one, or so David Garrick thought, and he had acquaintance with Hamlet.

The life of Jean Georges Noverre, like many great artists, was, in its human scale, a long desperate struggle against official inertia and reactionary influences, which however superannuated, managed in their rigid stagnation to keep him from achieving what must have been his greatest work. His effect was posthumous. His pupils realized his principles, not in France but in Italy and Russia. His monument is not his dancing but his writing, the brilliant, angry *Lettres sur la Danse,* which are still the best introduction to a critical conception of theatrical dance. The more one reads them, the more one feels that perhaps they are the *only* criticism of theatrical dancing. Indeed no one who has not danced, at least enough to know the limits and possibilities of his own body, can possibly write about others.

His father was a Swiss Aide-de-Camp to the Swedish King, Charles the Twelfth. Of his mother little is known. He was born in 1727, and was destined for a military career; but in his early adolescence he came to be a pupil of Louis Dupré, (*le grand Dupré* whom Casanova saw). He made his début at Fontainebleau at sixteen but enjoyed such a mediocre success that he left, invited to Potsdam by Henry of Prussia. He shortly quit this skinflint prince for Paris. The Director of the Opéra Comique hired him as *maître de ballet*. He had already appeared at a less important Parisian theater in a parody of Rameau's *Les Indes Galantes*. Now he achieved a considerable success in a new ballet, first produced in 1754. Noverre considered it a futile and freakish concession to a passing fad, the vogue for the Chinese, but the painter Boucher designed its enchanting scenery, and the best French costumer since Bérain, René-Louis Bouquet, did the dresses. The *Nouveau Calendrier des Spectacles de Paris* said of *Les Fêtes Chinoises:*

> This ballet had already been performed at Lyons, Marseilles, and Strasburg. The scene represents at first an avenue ending in terraces and in a flight of steps leading to a palace situated on a height. This first set changes, and shows a public square, decorated for a festival; at the back is an amphitheater, on which sixteen Chinamen are seated. By a quick change of scene, 32 Chinamen appear instead of 16, and go through a pantomimic performance on the steps. As they descend, 16 other Chinamen, mandarins and slaves, come out of their houses and take their places on the steps. All these persons form eight ranks of dancers, who, by bending down and rising up in succession, give a fair imitation of the waves of a stormy sea. When all the Chinese have come down they begin a characteristic march. In this is to be seen a mandarin, carried in a rich palanquin by six white slaves, while two negroes drag a car in which a young Chinese woman is seated. They are both preceded and followed by a crowd of Chinamen, who play divers instruments of music in use in their country. When this procession is finished the ballet begins, and leaves nothing to be desired, neither for the variety nor for the neatness of the figures. It ends by a round-dance, in which there are 32 persons; their movements form a prodigious quantity of new and perfectly planned figures, which are linked and unlinked with the greatest ease. At the end of this round-dance the Chinamen take up their places anew on the amphitheater, which changes into a porcelain shop. Thirty-two vases rise up, and hide from the audience the 32 Chinese. M. Monnet has spared nothing that could possibly assist M. Noverre's rich imagination.

Its success was so great that Garrick, the great actor-manager, invited Noverre to London with his designers, engineers and dancers. But unfortunately, its opening coincided with the start of the Seven Years' War, and it was useless for Garrick to insist Noverre was Swiss and his *corps de ballet* was two-thirds British. Even the presence of the King could not prevent a patriotic demonstration turning into a bloody fight in which all the stage effects were destroyed. Nevertheless, his association with Garrick was one of the most valued in his life.

> Mr. Garrick, the celebrated English actor, is the model I wish to put forward. Not only is he the most handsome, the most perfect and the most worthy of admiration of all actors, he may be regarded as the Proteus of our own time; because he understood all styles and presented them with a perfection and truth which aroused not only the applause and praise of his countrymen, but also excited the admiration and encomiums of all foreigners. He was so natural, his expression was so lifelike, his gestures, features and glances were so eloquent and so convincing, that he made the action clear even to those who did not understand a word of English. It was easy to follow his meaning; his pathos was touching; in tragedy he terrified with the successive move-

ments with which he represented the most violent passions. And, if I may so express myself, he lacerated the spectator's feelings, tore his heart, pierced his soul, and made him shed tears of blood.

When Noverre returned to Paris, where his reputation was already made, he naturally tried to enter the Opéra, immeasurably the first theater in Europe both in mechanical efficiency and prestige. But in spite of the official intervention of the Pompadour (or perhaps on account of it), the direction would have no traffic with such a potentially dangerous rival. So, in 1758, having nothing better to do, he accepted an engagement at the provincial capital of Lyons, and, we can imagine, irritated to the point of exasperation by his inability to affect the Academy, pondered his notions on his art, ordering them in a series of epistles, as was the eighteenth-century formula. His *Lettres* are his testament of faith, his practical rules for choreographic procedure. When they burst like an explosion of compressed fresh air, he had already left France, called to be ballet-master for Charles-Eugène, the lavish Duke of Württemberg. France had just paid this prince enormous subsidies for the loan of six thousand mercenary soldiers, and he spent a good part of it on theatricals in Stuttgart. The indefatigible Casanova reported that his army was justly prized

> but his chief expense was the large salaries he paid his theaters, and above all his mistresses. He had a French play, an Italian opera, grand and comic, and twenty Italian dancers all of whom had been principal dancers in Italian theaters. His director of Ballets was Novers (sic), and sometimes 500 dancers appeared at once. A clever machinist (the fine engineer and designer, Servandoni) and the best scene-painters did their best to make the audience believe in magic. All the ballet-girls were pretty, and all of them boasted of having been enjoyed at least once by my lord (Charles-Eugène).

Jérôme Servandoni invented miraculous dioramas and transformation scenes. His *gloires* surpassed any clouds Inigo Jones or Torelli had made; Brunelleschi would have embraced the man who pushed his *nuvole* to such extremities. Bouquet was the costumer, a man of great taste, and Jomelli led the violins. Stuttgart would later be rocked by inevitable financial scandals, but for a time Noverre enjoyed a freedom, and mechanical possibility unknown in Paris. In 1760, at the head of the Ballet of Opera and Comedy, he made his début in *Amor et Psyche*. His fortunes seemed assured and he was well paid. Stuttgart, though a petty capital, became a real center for any one interested in the new choreographic principles, and many visited Württemberg.

Among others came Gaetan-Appolon Balthazar, magnificent Vestris, the first academic dancer in Europe, a pupil of Dupré, and ballet-master of the Academie Royale. He was also a Florentine and possessed of remarkable pretensions. When his son was sent to prison for one of the continued revolts against the Opéra direction, "Go, *mon fils!*" he superbly said. "This is the most glorious moment of your career. Take my carriage, and ask for the cell which was occupied by my friend, the King of Poland." *Le 'Diou' de la*

Danse bitterly added this was the first time in history when there had been "any difference of opinion between the House of Bourbon, and the House of Vestris." Gaetan, in talking of his boy, allowed "Auguste is cleverer than I, as is natural enough; he has Gaetan Vestris for a father, an advantage nature denied me."

The House of Vestris was a dynasty. Dancing families are a tradition in the profession. There are the Taglionis, the Karsavins, the Petipas, the Nijinskys. The elder Vestris, from all reports, must have been one of the finest male dancers the world has seen. He was the unique standard for his epoch, and like all such executants, greatly increased the vocabulary of the *danse d'école*. In his vacation, he went down to Stuttgart, to argue with Noverre and was amazed and delighted with the "new" forms of his *ballets d'action*. Noverre made as profound an impression upon Vestris as Garrick upon Noverre. In 1770 he took the 'Jason and Medea' of the unacknowledged master back to Paris, and himself mimed the rôle of Jason. He revealed, prompted by Noverre, an unsuspected talent for pathetic gesture and facial expression, for he dared to discard for the first time the absurd leather-mask, that mask which was supposed to draw Paris closer to Athens, and which all French dancers were forced to wear.

> The particular merit of Vestris was his grace, his elegance, his delicacy. All his *pas* had a purity, a finish of which one can have no idea today, and it was not without reason that they compared his talent to that of Racine's.

So wrote an eye-witness of *Jason et Medée,* but however brilliant the success of Vestris, Noverre was no nearer Paris. It was the Opéra that he longed for all his life. He was master everywhere, but it was Parisian justification, its official vindication, he longed for. Now, he was to work in Vienna for seven years. The Austrian capital was renowned for its ballet girls. Casanova wrote of one Juliette:

> Expulsion from Vienna, for this class of women, had become a title to fashionable favor, and when there was a wish to depreciate a singer or a dancer, it was said of her that she had not been sufficiently prized to be expelled from Vienna.

Here Noverre allied himself with Christoph Willibald Gluck, a musician greater than Rameau, another foreigner who in the field of lyric drama effected the same revision of values and creation of new standard as Noverre's in the dance. In 1767, he dedicated his *Alceste* to the Grand Duke of Tuscany, with words Noverre might have used:

> I shall try to reduce music to its real function, that of seconding poetry by intensifying the expression of sentiments and the interest of situations without interrupting the action by needless ornament. I have accordingly taken care not to interrupt the singer in the heat of dialogue to wait for a tedious *ritournel,* nor do I allow him to stop on a sonorous vowel, in the middle of

a phrase, in order to show the nimbleness of a beautiful voice in a long cadenza.

The collaboration with Gluck would bear later fruit, but the appointment to Paris, an appointment which carried the prestige enabling his productions to be imitated from Madrid to Moscow, seemed no nearer, even though he offered his services free. In 1774 he worked in Milan, Naples, Turin, accomplishing wonders with inferior talents, always sharpening his instruments toward an ultimate lyric synthesis.

Finally in 1776, Marie-Antoinette, whom he had once instructed in Vienna, named him upon the resignation of Vestris to the position he had so long desired. The Queen's caprice detonated the Academy, full of indignation at Noverre's commission over the heads of an hereditary official succession. His quarrel with the dancer Gardel, whom he had replaced, was not resolved for three years which did little to reduce the natural antipathy Parisians felt for the usurper. Noverre made an equivocal début in two tedious ballets, but it was generally understood that their execution was left in the hands of his avowed adversaries. Gardel, it was true, was one of the finest technicians in Europe and one of the boldest actors, yet, "he would rather have renounced kingdoms of the world than his *entrechats*." Even if Noverre did not have the success promised by his great reputation, all sensitive people agreed no one knew better the resources of the dance.

Meanwhile, Noverre prepared *The Horatii,* on the Roman legend, "Where the theatrical action, the mute declamation, the pantomime competed with dancing and music to create the spectacle." The critics charged that he dared to equal, or what is worse, to change Corneille. *"Les Horaces* is only Corneille *en pantomime."* Noverre, so long used to Parisian complaints, began to have his own doubts as to the wisdom of his innovations. The public attitude upset him. He was almost ready to make changes.

Marie-Antoinette also patronized Gluck. She liked his music, but there was also their common Viennese origin. The burning of the Opéra in 1763 had delayed his arrival, but when finally he came, it was as if another thunderbolt had come to destroy its foundations. No one had taken the place of Rameau. Gluck decided to do Racine's *Iphigénie* as a lyric tragedy. Noverre had just completed it as a *ballet d'action.* Now they worked together in the closest of beneficial collaboration; the choreographer of the 'Greek Games' entirely dominated the musician, in their expression of a theme based on antique sport:

> Since then, before selecting melodies to which I could adapt steps, before studying steps to make them into what was then known as ballet, I sought subjects either in mythology, history or my own imagination which not only afforded opportunity for the introduction of dances and festivals, but which in the course of the development of the theme, offered a graduated action and interest. My poem once conceived, I studied all the gestures, movements

and expressions which could render the passions and sentiments arising from my theme. Only after concluding this labor did I summon music to my aid. Having explained to the composer the different details of the picture which I had just sketched out, I then asked him for music adapted to each situation and to each feeling. In place of writing steps to written airs, as couplets are set to known melodies, I composed, if I may so express myself, the dialogue to my ballet and then I had music written to fit each phrase and each thought. Thus I had explained to Gluck the characteristic air of the ballet of the savages in *Iphigénie en Tauride:* the steps, gestures, attitudes and expressions of the different characters which I outlined to him, gave to this celebrated composer the theme for that fine piece of music.

Noverre was an excellent musician, as all good inventors of dances must be. He proposed the subject of Alexander and Roxana to young Mozart. There was some correspondence about it. Wolfgang received prudent advice from his father in Salzburg as to how he should proceed with official commissions to further his career. Mozart, on speculation, did compose the short ballet of *Les Petits Riens,* as part of an entertainment composed by several others. He hoped something would come of it, that Noverre might order another ballet. Unfortunately, there was no further work between them.

In 1780, there was a revival of *Jason et Medée,* which Vestris had brought back as a novelty from Stuttgart nine years before. Now, the audience saw it in a new light, with the advantage of its creator's supervision. They conceded that

> Vestris had not observed something essential in the music. It is in Noverre's ballet that the dance and the cadenced walk are very distinctly separated. They dance only in the large passionate, decisive moments. In the *scènes* they move strictly to measure, but without dancing. Dancing for the sake of dance has no place until the end of the piece.

There was a differentiation between the danced *air,* and the danced *recitatif,* an idea which had been dear to the Encyclopædist, Diderot. Noverre always appealed to the intellectuals but never to a general public. As André Levinson says in his fine edition of the "Letters," Noverre, as an innovator, had come too late into a world already modified by his influence, which, popularized by others, preceded him to Paris. The immediate, but not the basic occasion for his downfall, was the opposition to him of a cabal headed by the famous ballerina, Madeleine Guimard, who hated him with personal rancor. Guimard, who through her third lover, the Bishop of Orleans, controlled the church patronage lists, and through her second, the Prince de Soubise, the Royal Hunt, maintained Noverre was wildly extravagant in executing his (by now) faintly old-fashioned ideas. Her personal reasons for feeling the necessity for economy were plenty.

Guimard was a thin, sallow small woman, but a brilliant artist. Her hôtel in the Chausée d'Antin or her charming country house at Pantin were constant scenes of three official weekly suppers, the first for great nobles, the second for artists and writers, the third for her theatrical friends and the more fashionable whores. Both in town and country she kept private theaters managed by the financier De la Borde, where it amused her to produce risqué farces. She knew well how to seduce the corrupt court society, and had wire screened boxes built in one of her theaters where ladies could come, without danger of recognition. She was the real Queen of the Opéra. Her power was impregnable. Little wonder that Noverre, a man absorbed not in the world, but in his work, was no match for her machinations.

He retired to Clermont Ferrand, where the revolution took him off his guard. Although he had not worked for six years, he had been receiving a substantial pension. For Citizen Noverre it was drastically reduced. Also, he had been a little too friendly with the Queen; so, fearing denunciation, he fled to London, which he had not seen for thirty-eight years. He produced a ballet, *Adéle de Ponthieu,* which his disciples were often to revive into the nineteenth century. The libretto was dedicated to the influential Duchess of Devonshire. In January, 1793, as Louis Sixteenth was being guillotined, Noverre capped his life with a brilliant epilogue, 'The Lovers of Tempe.' He returned to France and under the patronage of Josephine Bonaparte, edited a final, authoritative edition of his letters and libretti, and in his modest retreat at Saint Germain, died in 1809.

In his white rages he had indicated the positions he wished his dancers to assume, by jetting saliva onto the stage floor. Arrogant, quick to anger, his epistles are charged with the venom of hurt pride. It was the accumulating resentment of a long life, full of every reason for success, yet almost always failing. For thirty years he had been kept from the one theater he felt would have made him. He was always *Le Petit Noverre,* a provincial artist, to be tolerated, to be imitated, never to be allowed command. Although Diderot loved him and Voltaire said of him, "You are a Prometheus, you must mold men and move them," he was treated as an outsider and fed his fiercest energies with a decade of articulate anger. His ferocity of style, his violence of self-confidence led to the formulation of some of the most virile words a dancer ever wrote.

Dancing needs only a fine model, a man of genius, and ballets will change their character. Let this restorer of the true dance appear, this reformer of bad taste and of the vicious customs that have impoverished the art; but he must appear in the capital. If he would persuade, let him open the eyes of our young dancers and say to them:—'Children of Terpsichore, renounce *cabrioles, entrechats* and over-complicated steps; abandon grimaces to study sentiments, artless graces and expression; study how to make your gestures noble, never forget that is the life-blood of dancing; put judgment and sense into your *pas de deux;* let will-power order their course and good taste preside over all situations; away with those lifeless masks but feeble copies of nature; they hide your features, they stifle, so to speak, your emotions and thus deprive you of your most important means of expression; take off those

enormous wigs and those gigantic head-dresses which destroy the true proportions of the head with the body; discard the use of those stiff and cumber-
some hoops which detract from the beauties of execution, which disfigure
the elegance of your attitudes and mar the beauties of contour which the bust
should exhibit in its different positions.'

These words are the essence of Noverre's reforms. His letters are but a
detailed expansion of them. People today who assume Noverre aimed to
destroy the *danse d'école* should read his letters carefully, not superficially.
His letters do not corroborate any votary of "free" expression, "spontaneous"
movement, or "spatio-dynamic" relations. Just as he believed in the focal importance of the position of Paris as capital, so did he believe in the institution
of the *pas de deux* and the vocabulary of the classic dance. He wished to destroy
nothing, except inertia. He wished to use, to its best advantage, all previous
researches, and everything that could in any way further the precise indication, the directed, considered expressiveness of dancing.

When Noverre came to the theater, the formula for stage dancing seemed
completely set, unchanged for half a century, since the foundation of the
Academy. Rameau in no real way altered possibilities laid down by Lully. This
authority Noverre did not revere. He also deplored the weakness of the
librettists and longed for a poet like Quinault, Lully's collaborator, whose
verses are no longer read, but who seemed then, in comparison to eighteenth
century poetasters, a veritable genius.

> There is no question of the advantage that would have been gained, not only
> by the dance but by all the other arts which contribute to the charm and per-
> fection of opera, could the celebrated Rameau (without offending the sages of
> the century and that crowd of people who can conceive nothing superior to
> Lully) have set to music the masterpieces of the father and creator of lyric
> poetry....
> Even if my opinion bring down upon me the wrath of a multitude of old
> people, I shall assert that Lully's dance music is cold, tedious and devoid of
> character. It is true that it was composed at a time when dancing was re-
> strained and the executants totally ignored expression. Everything then was
> wonderful, the music was composed for the dance and *vice versa*. But what
> was compatible then is no longer so; the steps are multiplied, the movements
> are quick and follow each other in rapid succession, there are an infinity of
> *enchainements* and variations of time; the difficulties, the sparkle, the speed,
> the indecisions, the attitudes, the diverse positions—all this, I say, cannot be
> harmonized with the grave music and uniform intonation which are the
> characteristics of the works of the old composers.

The *Philosophes*, encyclopædists and rationalists, castigated French music for weakening the structure of the classic dance. They condemned 'pure'
dancing for its lack of instruction or of moral subject-matter. This quarrel is
a perennial debate, from century to century down to our own decade. Which
is the correct path for the dancer:—dance or meaningful gesture,—abstract

movement or pure expression? This inherent dualism in the art is at the root of all choreographic discussion, and can never seem to be resolved even by judicious combination.

Rousseau, the romanticist, complained that dances interrupted the action at the moment when interest had been roused to its greatest pitch. Others insisted upon the superiority of pantomime which appealed to the 'sympathies,' while ballet affected only their 'eyes.' The theory of danced spectacle, elaborated by Lully and his school, linking a number of entries had only, as Rousseau ironically remarked, "a metaphysical rapport."

Already there had been some progress made in the personal costume reforms of Sallé and Camargo. But a greater intellectual force, a more authoritative propagandist was needed to dislodge the idea that French dancers had achieved a summit of technical perfection, that the French school could admit no esthetic improvement. There was some loose talk, in the old manner of antique comparisons, which vaguely contrasted the 'strength' of Roman pantomime with the 'weakness' of French Ballet. But as Diderot wrote, "Dance is to pantomime, as poetry is to prose, or rather, as song is to natural declamation." In order to create the *ballet d'action,* an autonomous medium, a choreographer and a thinker were needed. Noverre formulated ideas already in the air, and broadcast laws for their methodical practice.

> A well-composed ballet is a living picture of the passions, manners, habits, ceremonies and customs of all nations of the globe, consequently, it must be expressive in all its details and speak to the soul through the eyes; if it be devoid of expression, of striking pictures, or strong situations, it becomes a cold and dreary spectacle. This form of art will not admit of mediocrity; like the art of painting, it exacts a perfection the more difficult to acquire in that it is dependent on the faithful imitation of nature; and it is by no means easy, if not almost impossible, to seize on that kind of seductive truth which, masking illusion from the spectator, transports him in a moment to the spot where the action has taken place and fills him with the same thoughts that he would experience were he to witness in reality the incident which art has presented to him in counterfeit.

The apogée of the *ballet d'action* was in the tragic subject, plots that were close to Racine or Euripides, but any exotic material would be plausible if it underwent the theatrical alchemy of French taste. The correct expressive method for ballet-pantomime, mere technical mastery of steps being no longer enough, was gesture, not conventionalized, but prompted by 'deep sentiment' to create emotion. The sequence of entries was replaced by the flow of action fitting the plot and persons involved. The *corps de ballet* ceased to be a mechanical background, and participated individually in the action. As a living chorus it could be sacrificed to purely symmetrical, automatic balance. The costumes of court or civil dress, blown up to staginess, were replaced by clothes of appropriate simplicity, whose colors carefully contrasted, harmonized with scenery which was more an atmospheric frame than a grandiose architectural distraction. Noverre insisted on the rejection of masks, counting much on the significant play of dancers controlled facial expression. He considered no part of the body dead to dancing. If he proclaimed it was of great use to know the five absolute positions, he added it was worth more to forget them. Culture has been well defined as the sum of what an educated man forgets. He carefully studied all the anatomical and habitual faults of the conformation of a dancer's anatomy, and invented means to combat and correct them. He reiterated the Mosaic law of the classic dance: *the feet must be turned-out.* However much he disdained the execution of his contemporaries, he rehabilitated the classic technique. He hated those "who moved without principle, leaping more than dancing."

Towards the end of his life, he became pitifully doctrinaire, establishing an absolute canon for the *ballet d'action.* He would permit the distance between the two feet to be no greater than eighteen inches. No stage should accommodate more than thirty-two dancers. No music previously composed should possibly be employed by a sensitive choreographer. A singing, long-sustained melody is to be preferred to bursts of harmonic chords. While he demanded an archeological accuracy in costume (as far as the knowledge of the times allowed), the purist in him revolted against the transparency of costumes purely *à la grecque.* He had his rights to dogma, if fifty years of heroic work in the dance means anything. It was natural that the passionate revolutionist of his youth should turn into a petulant defender of his own innovation. He threw strong doubts on the academic prestige of Roman pantomime as having ignored the dance to create a merely manual virtuosity, in itself probably as highly conventionalized as the *danse d'école.* He made a qualitative distinction between dancing proper, the form of ballet, and the language of pantomime.

Dance is the art of steps employing gracious movements and lovely attitudes. *Ballet,* of which dance is an adornment, consists of design in related figures. *Pantomime* is the explanation of emotion by gesture, which "passion" should determine, while "good-taste" orders dance and ballet. If Noverre liberated dancing by his *ballet d'action,* and his 'Letters,' he indicated a strong direction towards pantomime. While he did not consider technical perfection any end in itself, he surely recognized it as a necessary means for expression.

> I think, Sir, that this art has remained in its infancy only because its effects have been limited, like those of fireworks designed simply to gratify the eyes; although this art shares with the best plays the advantage of inspiring, moving and captivating the spectator by the charm of its interest and illusion. No one has suspected its power of speaking to the heart.
>
> If our ballets be feeble, monotonous and dull, if they be devoid of ideas, meaning, expression and character, it is less, I repeat, the fault of the art than that of the artist.

In his life, Noverre failed, but within his living memory, his ideas triumphed. His influence on Salvatore Vigano, Carlo Blasis, Philippe Taglioni,

Saint-Léon, Le Picq, Perrot, Petipa and Michel Fokine combine to make him a world-influence on the dance. "The man whose works have effected, in dancing, a revolution as marked and even more widespread than Gluck's in music; whose productions served and still serve as models for those who persecuted him." He was, as Levinson sums up, the creator of the *independent* spectacle of the dance; a self-sufficient, synthetic, integrated form, rejecting lyric declamation in favor of developing to their fullest, those elements which were most profoundly choreographic. In his life he worked enormously, creating more than a hundred and fifty ballets. His pride was monstrous, his vigor unmatched, his cupidity, brutality and despotism enabled him to defend himself against enemies, willfully blinded to the light he shed.

The Paris Opéra was destroyed in the great fire of 1781. Dauberval, Noverre's chief pupil, and one of the first-dancers, had the presence of mind to lower the curtain, and save the audience, if not some of his *corps de ballet.* Guimard herself was discovered in a loge, clad only in her chemise, and was rescued by a stage-hand. After Louis Capet had fled to Varennes, it was no longer *L'Académie Royale de Musique,* but simply, the Opéra. It continued unabated during the Terror, the proclamation of the Republic, the rise of the Directory, but it had little if any artistic interest. The same was true in London, only there were native shows of scenic splendor using British forms from the Italian popular comedy as their protagonists. Dancing was a part of the "Pantomime," and an increasingly popular part.

The Italian comedians had a considerable effect on English stage dancing. By 1715, Pulchinello (Punch), Scaramouche and particularly Harlequin, were so popular that ordinary plays began to be followed by danced scenes, in which these traditional maskers performed. An actor-manager, John Rich, was the first to produce "pantomime" on a sound basis. In 1717, he announces "Harlequin Executed: A new Italian mimic scene between a Scaramouche, a Harlequin, a Country Farmer, his Wife and Others." Rich's pantomime was generally divided into two parts: one serious, the other comic.

> By the help of gay scenes, fine habits, grand dances, appropriate music, and other decorations, he exhibited a story from Ovid's Metamorphoses, or some other fabulous writer. Between the pauses or acts of this serious representation he interwove a comic fable, consisting chiefly of the courtship of Harlequin and Columbine, with a variety of surprising adventures and tricks, which were produced by the magic wand of Harlequin; such as the sudden transformation of palaces and temples to huts and cottages; of men and women into wheel-barrows and joint-stools; of trees turned to houses; colonnades to beds of tulips; and mechanic shops into serpents and ostriches.

Rich himself danced Harlequin, and had a great reputation as a mime. In Cyril Beaumont's fascinating 'History of Harlequin' there is a contemporary account of him in 'Harlequin Sorcerer,' where he is hatched by the sun's rays from an egg:

From the first chipping of the egg, his receiving motion, his feeling the ground, his standing upright, to his quick *Harlequin* trip round the empty shell, through the whole progression, every limb had its tongue, and every motion a voice, which 'spoke with most miraculous organ to the understandings and sensations of the observers.' He was famed also for his trick of scratching his ear like a dog. Some idea of his agility may be gained from the account of a certain dance he performed, in which he is said to have executed three hundred steps in a rapid advance of three yards only. He seems to have exercised great care in the selection of the music to accompany his mimed scenes, for a contemporary writer declares that 'every action was executed to different agreeable music, so properly adapted that it properly expresses what is going forward.' Despite his success as Harlequin he never conquered his personal belief that he was a great tragic actor, and declared to a friend that he would rather act tragedy to half-a-dozen people in the pit than play Harlequin to a crowded house.

Another famous Harlequin was Henry Woodward, a contemporary of Rich, who elevated the genre to a position frequently compared to the Roman mimes. He was extremely graceful, and his scene with the currants was famous.

Soft music was played: he came on, sat at a table (on which there was placed *nothing*), and made pretense of taking up the stalk of a bunch of currants. Then, holding high his hand, with the points of finger and thumb compressed, he seemed to shake the stalk, and to strip off the currants with his mouth. In like manner he would appear to hold up a cherry by the stalk, and, after eating it, to spurt the stone from his lips. Eating a gooseberry, paring an apple, sucking an orange or peach—all were simulated in the same marvelous fashion. In short, the audience perfectly knew what fruit he seemed to be eating by the highly ingenious deception of his acting.

But neither were there widely important artist-dancers emerging from its insular forms, nor did England herself affect the history of stage-dancing to any large extent, although pantomimes kept a vital interest in the dance alive in a country, which only up to the present has had no national ballet comparable to Italy, France, Russia, or even Germany.

The French Revolution inspired two mass fêtes, under the supervision of the state; one of the Supreme Being (in place of God and the Saints); the other of Reason enthroned on a cathedral altar. Dancing was a part of these. But Noverre had caused a revolution in the dance far greater than the year 1793. The history of French or English dancing will not occupy us again, though both Paris and London will often be theaters of important manifestations. It is to Russia we must turn to find the flowering of ideas that Western Europe refused fully to employ.

After Peter had crushed the rebellion of his standing-army, he introduced western Assemblies or court dances, forcing open the doors of the *terems,* commanding the women to appear, with their husbands, both in European dress. He had seen ballets abroad, loved dancing in masquerades. "He made

such *caprioles,*" said a contemporary, "that any dancing master might envy."
He is credited with having introduced into Russia the courante, menuet and
pavane. In 1703, the first Russian theater was built near the Kremlin, in Moscow. It was wooden, and burned four years later. Peter was surrounded by a
fantastic suite of Dutch admirals, negro princes, hunchbacks and midgets.
He gave balls for dwarves, dressed in the uniform of Versailles, ordered the
boyards to shave their ancestral beards, had women dragged to balls by
guardsmen, when gentler invitation failed.

In 1721, after the Swedish peace of Nystad, there was a great *bal masqué,*
lasting five days, and a parade of sixty sleighs, of which the smallest was har-
nessed to six steeds. Swedish prisoners are thought to have been among the
first dancing-masters from the West. The nobles, tired of their endless pretexts
for avoiding the Assemblies, made a show of dancing, however boorishly; but
the Tsar, and his wife Catherine, astonished every one with their neat steps.
Peter's balls, however, resembled the pleasures of the field, rather than the
graces of a court. His friends cursed and drank: played cards and rattled dice.
Dancing continued till midnight on an open pavilion overlooking the Neva,
and concluded usually with a pyrotechnical display.

The first ballets given in Russian were performed in Saint Petersburg in
1727, by Russian dancers, the volunteer pupils of a German. They were called
"The Fabulous Comedy: with dances in the German, French, English and
Polish Manner," and "Bright Falcon's Feather: A Comedy with Songs and
Dances." When the Princess Anna Ivanovna had been elected Empress, the
Court took on a positively European luxury. At her wedding feast Great Peter
had two huge pasties set before the royal pair, from each of which popped a
richly clad dwarf, who danced a menuet together on the table. In 1731, the
ladies of her court danced *Baba Yaga,* a Russian fairy story, and one of the
earliest ballets to use a native theme.

In 1735, occurred an important event. The Empress ordered an official of
the Infantry School for the Education of Officers' children, one Christian
Friedrich Wellman, to teach all her cadets to dance, in order to supplant
imported Italian artists. Thus began the great Russian Academy. Wellman
was replaced by a Frenchman, Landé, who soon said "one must go to the
Court of Russia to see the menuet properly performed." His students were poor
children, sons and daughters of court valets and choir-singers. He worked
unceasingly to produce a *corps de ballet,* and soloists, receiving considerable
aid from Biron, the Queen's lover. Under Landé, the Russians began to prove
themselves in every way the peers of the aliens. Lady Rondeau, the wife of the
English resident, described a royal marriage of 1739:

> On Friday there was a masquerade; there were four quadrilles, as they are
> called, consisting of twelve ladies each, besides the leader of each quadrille.
> The first was led by the bride and bridegroom, who were dressed in orange
> colored dominos, and little caps of the same with a silver cockade, and a little
> laced ruff round the neck, tied with the same ribbon; and their twelve couples

were all dressed the same, among whom all the foreign ministers and their wives were placed, whose masters were related either to the Prince or Princess. The second was led by the Princess Elizabeth and Prince Peter, in green dominos and gold cockades, and their twelve couples the same. The third by the Duchess of Courland and Count Soltikoff (a relation of the Empress), in blue dominos and pink and silver cockades. The fourth by her daughter and youngest son, in pink dominos and green and silver cockades. There was a supper for the four quadrilles only, in the long gallery; the table had benches round it, so placed as to look like a turf bank, and the table the same; the table and benches were covered with moss and flowers, stuck in as if growing, and the supper, though very magnificent, was served to look like a rural entertainment.

Naturally, court festivities and royal theatricals aped Paris or Berlin. Naples, Milan, Stuttgart and Marseilles would send dancers and teachers to provide a necessary background for the great Russian school. Russia was medieval when Peter came to the throne. It skipped a Renaissance and had no Reformation. Echoes of Marley at Oranienberg, of Versailles at Tsarskoë-Selo served to give a Western cultural tradition to a land whose own was Oriental. That Russia, even with the aid of foreign virtuosi, could create a school of her own, is another proof of the remarkable suppleness, stamina, imagination and persistence of the Slavs, who are today the ablest dancers in the world. The same enthusiasm naturally extended to the ball-room. Casanova, whose father was a dancer, attended a ball under Anna Ivanovna.

> The ball began with a polonaise. I was a stranger, with introductions, so the duchess asked me to open the ball with her. I did not know the dance, but I managed to acquit myself honorably in it, as the steps are simple and lend themselves to the fancy of the dancer.
>
> After the polonaise we danced menuets and a somewhat elderly lady asked me if I could dance 'The King-Conqueror,' so I proceeded to execute it with her. It had gone out of fashion since the time of the regency, but my companion may have shone in those days. It was followed by a square dance.

Catherine the Great's ties with France were closer than any of her predecessors'. She wrote comedies in her adopted tongue, imitating Molière. At the age of four, while an obscure little German princess,—a French master came to Stettin to teach her to dance. "This was money thrown away," she wrote years later. But the ballet under Catherine greatly developed. At her coronation in 1763, there was a spectacle employing four thousand people and two hundred triumphal cars.

> This month, from ten o'clock in the morning until the afternoon, there will be a grand masquerade procession entitled *Minerva Triumphant,* in which the Abomination of Vice and the Glory of Virtue will be shown. After the return of the procession to the Ice Mountain, the members of it will toboggan and perform different dances, puppet comedies, tricks and so on, at a specially constructed theater. The artists will be awarded prizes for their talent.

There will be riding also. People of every denomination may attend there if they wish, and toboggan the whole week from morning to night, with or without a mask, as may be thought convenient.

Among her *maîtres de ballets* were Angiolini, Hilferding and Charles le Picq. Angiolini had preceded and replaced Noverre at the Royal Opera in Vienna. The Italian had an extensive quarrel with him, and insisted *his* master, Hilferding, had invented the *ballet d'action,* around 1742, twenty years before the Swiss. But Hilferding is only a name, Angiolini a footnote, yet the world knows Noverre. Baron Grimm described his pupil, Le Picq:

> Charming features, the most slender body, the easiest and lightest movements, the purest, most spirited and most natural precision, such are the qualities which distinguish Lepic (sic). If he does not dance like God the Father, at least he dances like the King of Sylphs. He has elasticity and brilliance. His grace and airiness triumph above all in demi-caractère dancing.

He was considered the equal of Vestris or Dauberval, and arranged in 1791 ballets for Potemkin's fabulous party in the Tauride Palace, which cost half a million roubles. His Italian wife achieved a great success in *Adèle de Ponthieu,* that ballet Noverre dedicated to the Duchess of Devonshire. The principles of the *ballet d'action* were presupposed in Petersburg, while they were still being attacked in Paris. Le Picq produced his version of the master's *Jason et Medée* towards the end of the century, just as Dauberval, returning from Stuttgart, had set it at the French opera in 1771. Under Catherine, performances were given by the Smolney Institute, a fashionable young ladies' school. Dancing seemed to have escaped the censure of the Greek Orthodox Church. Provincial nobles commenced to have *corps de ballet* composed of serfs from their properties. The girls were strictly ordered, and generally speaking badly treated. Count Araktcheiv, favorite of the first Alexander, met one of them traveling in the country. This was Pauline Kovalevsky, who, having been trained by the best masters, made her triumphant début in 'Inez de Castro' (1790) and became one of the first grand ballerinas. She called herself "Fine Pearl" and wore a collar worth one hundred thousand roubles. Catherine congratulated her on her performance in a *ballet-féerie,* "The Marriage of Samnith," little realizing that the dancer would put an end to her intention of marrying her grand-daughter Alexandra to Chermetiev, the Empress' choice. The connection of Ballet and Court, artistic and political power, was intimate from the beginning. Catherine the Great, not as dancer but as Empress, was the model for more than one ballerina who aspired to a larger stage than the opera's.

CHAPTER XII

Vigano and Blasis: CHORÉODRAME *and* BALLET ROMANTIQUE

WE have now reached a point in our history which includes persons and events almost within the memory of living men. Memoirs, letters and programs of the nineteenth century rustle with a vivid recollection. The epoch gave to the world, not to Europe alone, but to a new continent, a symbol for classic ballet which persists into the popular conception of our time. The long white tarlatan skirt, the tight white bodice, the sylph wings, create a uniform immediately recognizable as the ballet-dancer's, from Moscow to San Francisco, from Tokio to Barcelona. So much so, in fact, that we may forget that the contribution of the last century had much more significance than the canonization of a single one of its many aspects, not only on personal grounds but on technical and theoretical as well.

The emphasis leaves France. Paris now becomes for us only a theater and a *foyer de danse.* Perhaps the two greatest names of the hundred years are Italian, one in the field of realized esthetic, the other, in the descent of realized technic. The first was Salvatore Vigano, of whom, of his contemporaries still known to us, the novelist Stendhal has left the best record. He was, however, almost forgotten until recently, when by researches of Henry Prunières and André Levinson he has finally taken an indisputable place with Noverre and Fokine.

He was born in Naples in 1769, where his parents happened to be dancing. As often happens with such men, he came of a large, talented family of ballet-masters and ballerinas. His father was one of the best *maître de ballet* of his day, his uncles were almost equally accomplished. His mother, a well-known dancer, was the sister of the composer Boccherini. Salvatore received a professional education, very much on the model indicated in Noverre's Letters. He read omnivorously and had a fine memory. Of music, he made a special study, almost as if he wished to compose, which on occasion he did. He honestly knew the imaginative processes of poet, painter and musician. His esthetic was founded on a most intimate liaison between plastic gesture, which he understood as "statuesque," and fundamental musical rhythm.

Having made his début in Rome, he left for Madrid to perform in festivities attendant upon a coronation. There he married a beautiful Spanish dancer —and what is perhaps more important to us, there he also met the famous technician and *maître de ballet,* Dauberval.

The French had not been slow to abuse their reputation for virtuosity. They automatically exercised their bodies, developing lightness and suppleness, but emotionally they were wooden. Noverre tried reforms, but to a large extent they went unheeded. Dauberval was one of the few who actually attempted to put Noverre's ideas of unity and expression into practice. He attached a great importance to pantomime. "It expresses with rapidity the movement of the soul: it is the language of all peoples, of all ages and times. It depicts better than words extremes of joy or sorrow. . . . It is not sufficient for me to please the eyes. I wish to involve the heart." His designs were always expressive, yet eminently danceable. There was a famous *pas de deux* in 'Silvia' in which a nymph and a faun mimed a whole amorous intrigue while dancing. Dauberval, struck by young Vigano's talent, proposed to take him to England, where he had been engaged, and there to teach him the whole inheritance of French theatrical dancing which he knew as tempered by the critical and creative attitude of Noverre. Hence, from the mouth of Dauberval, Vigano heard the words of the master.

He returned to Venice in 1790. His father controlled the San Samuele Theater, where Salvatore displayed all the graces of his newly acquired French technique. There he produced his first ballet, under the influence of Dauberval, and shortly after, frankly avowing admiration for his teacher, produced *La Fille Mal Gardée,* perhaps the only ballet of the Frenchman which is still on occasion performed. It was a great favorite in Russia at the turn of the century.

In 1793 Vigano left for Vienna. His wife, the beautiful Spaniard, was adored by the town. He contrived a dance in which she appeared all but naked, under transparent veils, in a series of plastic positions taken from "Greek" sculpture. Her voluptuousness more probably resembled a chaste pastiche of Canova, but the Viennese were enchanted. Indeed the Emperor was so affected that the Empress became jealous, and the court could not frequent the theater. The public, however, continued to pack it.

They had an enormous success. Young Beethoven composed, on a theme from one of their ballets, a menuet *à la Vigano*. There were the usual hair-dresses, clothes, social-dances, bonbons, all in the Vigano mode. When Maria became pregnant, Viennese society ladies tied on small false stomachers, *à la Vigano*. The Prime Minister, Schloisnigg, contracted them for two solid years, but Maria Vigano involved him in intrigues too close to the crown and he was disgraced. Yet they continued to live in Vienna until the end of their contract. Salvatore arranged a *Richard Cœur de Lion,* in which there was a procession, so well conceived that even the horses' hoofs struck the stage in musical cadences. The Viennese particularly admired an expressive pantomime of the heroine, when, anguished by a dream, she beheld visions; and another, in which guards, dashing from all sides into the night, made picturesque, monumental groups with lanterns and cast shadows.

After traveling extensively in Central Europe, Germany and Italy, they returned to Vienna where they produced 'The Creatures of Prometheus,' not an impressive achievement, except that Beethoven wrote its score. Nevertheless, ideas in it served Vigano importantly later. Up to now, in fact, there had been nothing really original in his effort. He had done mythical or allegorical ballets in the French taste. The action in them, however, had always been danced, differing from various historical ballets then in fashion, in which pantomime was "walked-through," without any regard to music. Vigano's particular genius lay in his perfect correlation, his minute interest in details, his incomparable talent for groups and mass-formation, and he was so recognized by even his early contemporaries.

He made his début at Milan in 1804. In the ballet of 'Coriolanus,' to a large degree he sacrificed dance proper to dumb show. The Roman's mute oration was understood by the whole audience, even by those who had not read the libretto, without which it had been impossible to follow the plots of his predecessors. During all this time Vigano spent months in serious reflection, with great difficulty attempting to discover his own personal direction. In Venice, during 1809, he set out on a new path, with 'The Streletski.' The Streletz were those armed guards of Peter the Great, whose rebellion the young Tsar suppressed with savage cruelty. Up till then, Vigano had been content enough to try to reconcile his ably conceived action with the pantomime of French and Italian ballet-masters, learned from Dauberval. But now he decided it was pointless to mime a tragedy, instead of declaiming its verses. Ballet had something better to do than merely, by virtuoso tricks, to imitate spoken words. In ballet, he had plenty of means of expression, and laws useful to the form, the first of which was that he must always depend primarily on *dance*. Vigano understood by "dance" not only the French scientific virtuoso technique, but an expressive gesticulation, rigorously cadenced to music. He could not, naturally, in a single work, free himelf of *ballabile* (complex group-finales), or episodic *pas d'ensembles,* or inevitable *pas de deux* or solos to which his audiences were accustomed, and which managers demanded, but he did reduce their importance, justifying his interruption of the ballet by the demands of the story, while waiting an opportunity to suppress all convention. In 'The Streletski' he began to achieve his personal ideas towards dramatic choreography. The scene of the conspirators in their barracks, swearing their oath, was the occasion for plastic, sculptural groups and evolutions which struck his audience with unforeseen novelty. A hint of what it must have looked like we reproduce in an engraving of his fine scenic collaborator, Sanquirico. Prunières suggests, that in recalling these gestures submitted to the imperious necessities of the music's rhythm, one can find traces similar to the researches of Nijinsky and Jacques-Dalcroze.

Vigano gave up dancing himself, remaining in Milan from 1812. A happy combination of events would permit him to create his best work in an atmosphere of security and technical excellence. The vast stage of the Scala Opera House could support an army of dancers and supernumeraries. His money worries were over, for his father, whom he had for long supported, died, and a rich female admirer left him her fortune. The Milanese impresarios paid well. He worked in peace and had every reason to be completely happy, except that the flagrant infidelities of his wife whom he adored caused him constant anguish.

Now consecrating himself entirely to choreography, he worked methodically, without haste, toward the realization of an absolute ideal, what he came to call the *choreodrame*. He rehearsed one ballet for months at a time. The anxiety of the impresarios left him cold. They were lucky if a *première* intended for Spring managed to come off by Fall. Often, in the midst of rehearsing, he would be struck by an idea. Everything stopped; the artists could wait hours until the maestro was pleased to indicate the next scene. Stendhal saw him rehearsing, "surrounded by eighty dancers on the Scala stage, having at his feet ten musicians. He composed, and would make them recommence without pity." He would spend a whole forenoon on ten measures of a ballet, if he thought it lacked something. Savagely strict about rehearsals, he would not permit the company to rehearse a ballet of Philippe Taglioni's while working on one of his. The exasperated directors were continually threatening him with jail for unfulfilled contracts, but *lento e freddo* (slow, cold) Vigano did not even worry.

Before his time, plastic groupings were unknown or ignored. In France and Italy, the *corps de ballet,* it is true, used expressive mime, but dancers and supers were trained to make the same gestures in choral unison. Sometimes they might be split into separate bands, each executing a variant of the group-movement, but with Vigano every dancer preserved his or her personal individuality in the ensemble. Prunières imagines how difficult it must have been for the choreographer to realize such a scene as the reception of Othello by the Venetian Senate. Each person in the crowd was to act on his own in forming with the others harmonious, expressive groups. The difficulty was rendered greater insomuch as he never composed mere *tableaux vivants,* but always aimed for continuous orchestral mobility, where every figure moved in accord with the music. As often with vaunted novelty or greatness, gestures which Stendhal felt so vital, seem to us, at least from engravings, stylized or unreal. Vigano was very much a man of his epoch. Antiquity persisted, a powerful ghost. His dancers, whether they wore the fur-edged cloaks of Peter's guard, Roman togas, or the robes of a Venetian senator, were haunted by attitudes also shared by gods and heroes on antique vases and sarcophagi. Nevertheless, his work was not a servile copy, but rather a transformation of it, however stylized, to fit the special conditions of his theater.

Here it is possible to give only a few clues as to the nature of a Vigano ballet set on a stage. Prunières' excellent article * quotes extensively from Carlo Ritorni, the official biographer, and those interested will derive much factual information from the two sources. In the Spring of 1813 was produced 'Prometheus,' perhaps the first work displaying everything Vigano had to offer. Now he abandoned historical anecdote and amorous myth, rediscovering an old legend, to depict primitive humanity and the origins of civilization. The first scene demonstrated his powerful originality. It was a big contrast from the Louis Seize loves of Apollo and Daphne among the hedges of Versailles, for it

* *Revue Musicale: Numéro special: Le Ballet au XIXième Siècle.*

showed a savage landscape, covered with rocks. Beings with human faces, but who could only with difficulty be recognized as men, stumbled around in bestial or stupid attitudes, or wandered, seeming to ignore one another. In the background, on a rock, was Prometheus, with his chorus of Arts and Muses. One saw the fruitless effort of the Titan to teach men to build shelter or cultivate their earth. An apple given by him, was the occasion for an angry quarrel among the aborigines.

> The apple passed from hand to hand, always seized by the strongest. One could see as in the palæstra, a thousand varied attitudes of these savage athletes, the interlacings, the numerous contrasts.... At each measure the picture shifted and the same elements competed to compose an entirely new painting.

Prunières compares this scene with one in Fokine's *Daphnis et Chloé,* where pirates are terror-struck to a rhythmic pantomime. A hundred years before the Russian ballet, Vigano was putting into practice Noverre's ideas of a realistic mise en scène, a genuine pantomime, ideas which the reformer himself had never the chance to integrate. There were not merely wild Greeks whom Vigano motivated, but ferocious beasts who fought with teeth and nails, destroying the weakest, whether they were their babes or women. At the end of the scene, one of them, using a tree-trunk as weapon, smashed a fellow who seemed to eat the apple.

The second scene was in the vast stretches of heaven. Prometheus and Minerva rode past on their chariot, in the midst of starry constellations, to Händel's music for the "Creation." Prometheus lit his torch on the Sun, fell back to earth, and in the third scene presented the immortal fire to man. From the sparks of his torch little Loves sprang up, who immediately leaped about, like birds filling the branches of a tree. They descended to a melody, and followed the mortals, who now, for the first time, commenced to be conscious of their wretchedness and nature's beauty. Affection and gratitude began to warm their hearts. Men gathered around the liberating Titan in grateful homage. This free adaptation of a familiar myth had some interest, but its three following acts were obscure. Vigano said he had no wish to compose a regular drama, but rather six vast pictures. "Without doubt," wrote Stendhal, "there were preposterous parts in 'Prometheus.' But at the end of ten years, my remembrance of it is still fresh, as the first day, and it still astonishes me." From the point of view of choreography, it was a perfect synchronization of crowds, the cadenced figuration of the several plastic groups. This was Vigano's special talent and secret, a secret which on the authority of his contemporaries, died with him.

In *Otello* he offered a different kind of dramatic ballet. It started with a fête, an original idea (instead of ending with it), which Stendhal praised for its boldness. One saw Othello's triumph as conqueror, his solemn reception by the Venetian Senate, amid the multitude's rejoicings, which served as an excellent background for a *forlana,* a native dance often described by Casanova. But then, at once, all the action centered around Othello, Desdemona and Iago, with infrequent interruption by episodic characters. Stendhal said his imagination was as "strong as the most atrocious Shakespeare." Vigano's theatrical direction preceded the great film directors, Griffith, Eisenstein and Pudovkin. He could express the pathos of silence in action. To be sure he had fine pantomimic executants, trained to transmit his directions, regulated by the music down to a last flickering eyelash.

La Vestale was perhaps his most perfect work, though it seems less original than the rest. Vigano, on the soil of Italy, had the advantage of archeological research, precipitated by Winckelman, Piranesi and the Napoleonic scientists. During the first act, one was seated at the Circus-Games. On the grand-stands, a mob of togaed supers were packed together in picturesque positions; on a perspective track, a real chariot-race with horses on a treadway, the ancestor of "Ben Hur." After the race, vestal virgins entered upon "a rhythm of appealing gravity," bearing the winner's crown. Their dance consisted of "poses and attitudes recalling carved Victories on Roman triumphal arches. They seemed to float in air, lifting their wreaths to heaven." During the sacrifice which followed, young Decius, a consul's son, winner of the race, caught sight of Emilia, a vestal. Both were much moved, but none observed them. The act ended with a sacred bacchanal of mænads, satyrs and young bacchants. Vigano contrived a happy mélange of contemporary ballet with antique gesture. (The only criticism was that Decius, as a consul's son, would not have been allowed to race in the games.)

In the second act, Decius, lovelorn, sulks without pleasure at a feast tendered him by his friend, Murena. He watches the dance of two Greek slaves. Here, Vigano introduced a traditional *pas de deux,* demanded by the Scala's balletomanes. An unfortunate accession to public taste, it spoiled the harmony of his choreodrama. After the guests are gone, Decius confesses to Murena his guilty passion, and a plan to penetrate into the Vestal's convent. He convinces his friend, not without some persuasion, to accompany him on this mad enterprise. (The Milanese critics solemnly blamed Vigano for an immoral show of one friend seducing another into evil.) There were three more acts and a tragic ending.

In this work Vigano used none of the conventionalized gesture taught in the ballet of his time. The movement was "natural," full of meaning, yet without any doubt must have had its own quality of stylization stemming from antique marbles. Vigano's actor-dancers were also instructed to use their faces. Contemporary descriptions indicated the very moment when the vestal "altered her glance," blushed or blenched, showed love or terror. Better than any pantomime we could now see, a memory of acting in early silent films gives us an approximation of Vigano's pantomime. Prunières accurately suggests that in confronting a film even five years old, one feels a certain quaintness or drollness in its gestures. Only, it is necessary to remember in any attempt to revive in our minds Vigano's style, the synchronization of movement with the tempi of orchestral accompaniment.

His last great effort was 'The Titans' of 1819. Here he permitted himself no concession to public taste. The entire action was in his brand of rhythmic pantomime. There was an enormous advance interest stimulated and when the curtain rose, Ritorni wrote:

> It was in truth a very beautiful painting by Albani (a baroque painter) which greeted our eyes, the celestial prospect of the Golden Age. Children, maidens, adolescents, formed harmonious groups, amused themselves with domestic animals, gathered fruits and flowers, played, and gamboled, representing wholly naturally everything of the most seductive that a painter's mind could imagine of so happy an age.

A short dramatic action unrolled in the long scene, of which the composition continually varied. Thia, of the race of Titans, bade farewell to Hyperion, her husband. He was about to visit his brother, hurled by Jupiter into Tartarus. In the next act, one distinguished among shadows the monstrous forms of vanquished Titans. Here, Vigano was inspired by the Michelangelesque frescoes of Giulio Romano. The Titans sent back to their still mortal sister three metal urns, which they wished to present to men. In the third act Thia opens the first vase. A thick vapor issues from it, putting an end to eternal spring. Heaven covers with clouds. Trees lose leaves and fruit. Love came to the aid of men menaced by death and hunger, showing them how they could be taught by the god Pan to work fields and forests. The second urn, accidentally upset, provoked a new cataclysm. The age of silver was followed by the bronze age. Men, dressed in furs to keep them from the cold, became hard and selfish. They refused all aid to old Hyperion, who dies in the snow. We see the influence of his early 'Prometheus,' but here Vigano reverses the plot.

The fourth act passes in the depths of a cave. An infant opens, in pure curiosity, the last of the vases, which were hidden there by prudent Thia. Inside are bracelets. She puts them on. Every one admires, but a jealous woman asks her lover to find her jewels like these. He searches in the fatal urn and draws forth a sword and diadem. All fear him. He cuts the child's throat to gain the baubles. Begins the age of iron. Strong massacre the weak; theft, violence, despotism. The Titans themselves surge up from the bowels of earth to war against gods. From here on, the interest lagged. It took all the splendor of glorious clouds (a long way from the *nuvole*) to keep the audience happy. In the end Titans are confounded, Jupiter triumphs.

The underlying idea was the same as Richard Wagner's in his "Ring of the Niebelungen"; evil corrupting humanity from the possession of gold. There are so many parallels that one might almost think, although there are no documents to support it, that Wagner had somehow chanced to read an obscure Italian libretto. In his day, Vigano's name would mean little. Yet he had worked in Berlin.

He died in Milan in 1819, and his solemn obsequies were memorialized by all the poets of Italy. Physically vigorous, he was small but well-made. An agreeable face, with intelligent eyes, he had a pleasant expression of goodness and a sweet nature, with an equal, unexcitable temper. His slowness, no less than his patience, proverbial. He was seldom angry, loved to be idle, but no doubt his long reposes were full of creative thinking. He would spend the nights talking with friends and did not sleep till dawn. His large house was full of dependent relations and his good humor was not impaired towards the end of his life when he became deaf. He would start a ballet by showing each dancer separately his or her rôle. Then every group worked, one after the other, and when time came to rehearse the whole together, every one was surprised that everything coincided in such a sensible design. One of the strangest things about his work was the fact that he left hardly one disciple nor an imitator. When he died his principles perished for the rest of the century, almost without trace.

His single greatest characteristic was his use of rhythmic pantomime halfway between normal imitative gesture and traditional dancing, with a complete subordination of both to the music. His own musical compositions were considerably superior to many of his contemporaries. They sound German, owing much to Haydn and Mozart.

During his life, his critics not only complained of unprecedented liberties he took with honored legends, but there were those who saw the art of dancing itself, sacrificed. They feared an end of the marvelous French technique in which the professional amateurs found their exclusive satisfaction. One evening, Rossini complained to Stendhal, "the trouble with Vigano is, he has too much pantomime and not enough dancing." Many felt the same, who preferred the simplicities of the *danse d'école* to the dumb-show tragedies of the great Italian. Both had their rights. It was merely another chapter in the interminable record of quarrels between "expressiveness" and "pure-dance" which roused Ramists and Lullists a century before, and which would irritate lovers of "the ballet" as against "the modern dance," a century later. There is no absolute dichotomy. The best dancers are also often the best mimes. The *ballet d'action* can always support the intrusion of *ballet classique*. All contemporary choreographers, Fokine, the Nijinskys, Massine and Balanchine presuppose an attitude which Vigano was perhaps the first to realize consciously, in terms we can still understand; the ancient, yet ever-to-be achieved synthetic perfection of dance, mime, and music.

While Vigano himself had no heir, the contribution of Italy to the nineteenth century theatrical dance was doubled by the work of Carlo Blasis, who was only eighteen when the creator of choreodrame died. Born in Naples in 1803, of a supposedly noble family, at the age of two he was taken to Marseilles where he received the best possible education in his time for a ballet master. He followed the precepts of Noverre and Vigano, learned the classics, frequented studios of the best painters and sculptors and studied music. Each of

his family achieved distinction in his chosen art,—Teresa upon the pianoforte, Virginie as first dancer of the Paris Italian Opera. Carlo, himself, might
have become a practitioner of any of the mediums in which he was thoroughly
trained, but he chose choreography as best suited to combine his talents. Also it
paid about three times as well as any other single art. He seldom labored less
than fifteen hours a day, working also in mathematics and anatomy. All his
miscellaneous information was useful when he started to compose dances.
His library of music from the time of Palestrina, his editions of Greek and
Roman writers, his collections of prints, engravings, and musical instruments
were a constant source of his researches.

Having made his début in Marseilles and the provinces, he was asked to
Paris where he appeared with success, but because of the usual cabals and
intrigues with which that empty citadel protected itself against new life,
Blasis accepted a post at Milan, where he stayed for fourteen years as dancer
and composer of ballets. At Bordeaux, he had once studied under Dauberval,
and was then exposed to the direct influence of Noverre, who though long
dead, probably affected him more profoundly than Vigano, in spite of their
common ancestry and work on the same stage. From his writing he strikes us
as being more academic in borrowing from antiquity than Vigano, with a
closer eye to the accumulation of archeological detail for its own sake. Of this
we cannot be sure, but his writings are full of such paragraphs as this:

> It is in the best productions of painting and sculpture that the dancer may
> study with profit how to display his figure with taste and elegance. They are
> a fountain of beauties, to which all those should repair who wish to distin-
> guish themselves for the correctness and purity of their performances. In the
> Bacchanalian groups which I have composed, I have successfully introduced
> various attitudes, arabesques and groupings, the original idea of which was
> suggested to me, during my journey to Naples and through *Magna Gracia,*
> on viewing the paintings, bronzes and sculptures rescued from the ruins of
> Herculaneum.

He appeared with a partner, in a series of celebrated *pas de deux* in which
they were entwined in roseate veils, not unlike, from all appearance, Mordkin's and Pavlova's 'Autumn Bacchanal.' But his dancing days cut short by a
mysterious leg injury, he decided to retire from active work to become entirely
a choreographer and theoretician. In 1830 he published his "Code of Terpsichore," upon which rests his principal fame. Translated into all European
languages, it became the standard of ballet instruction not only in Italy, France
and England, but also to an even greater degree in Russia. His method, however modified to suit local schools, is still the backbone of the purest traditions
of the *danse d'école.*

An English edition appeared in London in 1830. It was subtitled "The
Art of Dancing, comprising its theory and practice and a history of its rise
and progress from earliest times: intended as well for the instruction of
amateurs as the use of professional persons." Its frontispiece is a clean line-

engraving of the Greek dancing muse, after Canova's frigid carving. The first part is an orthodox historical survey, but it is more than ordinarily full of literary allusions to both classic and contemporary writers, testifying to the extent of his erudition. He explains that Terpsichore means "delight in dance," and he also says that the Iroquois and even the Hurons have their dances, quoting a notice from the *Mercure de France* of 1725, which reported the performance of two savages from Louisiana. There was no anthropological method in Blasis' time to illuminate for him, as Fraser has for us, the origin of rite and dance, but we can see by his citation of savage sources, that anything remotely to do with dancing was alien to his interest. He gives the names and origins of numerous folk and national dances; tarantella, fandango, bolero and the many others.

> I shall now conclude by remarking that dancing, besides the amusement it affords, serves to improve our physical, and even to animate our moral powers; gives relief in certain diseases, affords a cure in others, promotes the harmony of society, and is a most requisite accomplishment for all who have the happiness to possess a good education.

In Part Two, he gives his theory of theatrical dancing. His "general instruction to pupils" are full of salutary moral precepts. He insists upon the necessity for constant and frequent practice, but he also cites dangers in overwork.

> Be temperate and sober if you desire to become a finished dancer. To render yourself capable of sacrificing before the shrine of Terpsichore, partially renounce every pleasure but that which the goddess affords. Let no other exercise be intermingled with dancing: horsemanship, fencing, running, &c. are all powerful enemies to the learner's advancement.

Every student must listen attentively to the music, must look long at paintings, must study proportions of the best sculpture. Dancing, ideally for him also, is synthesis.

> Particularly attend to the carriage of your body and arms. Let their motions be easy, graceful, and always in accordance with those of the legs. Display your form with taste and elegance; but beware of affectation. In the *leçon* and *exercices* pay an equal regard to both legs, lest the execution of the one surpass that of the other. I have seen many dance with one leg only; these I compare to painters that can draw figures but on one side. Dancers and painters of such limited talent are certainly not to be considered as good artists.
>
> Take especial care to acquire perpendicularity and an exact equilibrium. In your performance be correct, and very precise; in your steps, brilliant and light; in every attitude, natural and elegant. A good dancer ought always to serve for a model to the sculptor and painter. This is perhaps the acme of perfection and the goal that all should endeavor to reach. Throw a sort of *abandon* into your positions, groups and *arabesques;* let your countenance be animated and expressive.

He proceeds, then, to study with solicitude the body, in each of its parts. He shows not only a theoretical knowledge of the underlying organic structure of human anatomy, but also a practical dancer's information, of what is possible to be done with the instrument of the dancer's body. He continues the process of "turning-out" hips and feet upon principles long ago articulated by Thoinot Arbeau.

> In the management of your legs, endeavor chiefly to acquire a facility of turning them completely. To this end make yourself easy about your hips, that your thighs may move with freedom, and your knees turn well outwards. All the openings of your legs are thus rendered easy and graceful. By dint of practice and attention, you will be able to accomplish this without any painful efforts.

Part of Blasis' importance is his realistic attitude towards that body with which a dancer is born. He realizes that some people have not been endowed with a pleasing physique, some have arms too long or legs inclined to be bowed. He gives rules for overcoming every disadvantage with which an artist may be cursed. His basic canons are not far from Rameau's, the Dancing Master. But Blasis is writing in the epoch of a developed *danse d'élévation* and perpendicularity aids his leaps:

> Let your body be, in general, erect and perpendicular on your legs, except in certain attitudes, and especially in *arabesques,* when it must lean forwards or backwards according to the position you adopt. Keep it always equally poised upon your thighs. Throw your breast out and hold your waist in as much as you can. In your performance preserve continually a slight bend, and much firmness about your loins. Let your shoulders be low, your head high, and your countenance animated and expressive.

The "slight bend" is the *plié,* resilient knees which in good dancers becomes second nature, permitting him easily to shift from a high to a low, a right or a left position with maximum spring and minimum effort. Indicating the best position of the head, he advises against allowing an absolute, perpendicular balance on the neck, straight up and down, which tends to look wooden and inexpressively stiff. Rather incline it slightly to right or left. He discusses a dancer's center of gravity and his counterpoise.

> A person that carries a burthen placed out of the central line of his body, must necessarily add, from his own weight, a balance sufficient to counterpoise it on the opposite side, and thus form a true equilibrium round the perpendicular of gravity.

He describes the pirouette, no longer the simple turn of the eighteenth century, in considerable detail. Since the death of Noverre it has become a multiple twirl, executed as high as possible on the half-toe. Very often the step is abused, as a means of eliciting surprise by a dancer's remarkable ability to turn continuously without reason, to show a trick. Ideally speaking and particularly in the class of the slow pirouettes (which are incidentally a great deal more difficult to perform than the fast), it displays in simultaneous plasticity all aspects of the turning column of a dancer's body. It is an ultimate emphasis of its tri-dimensionality. An audience cannot encircle the dancer; hence, the dancer revolves, presenting himself in completeness to his audience. Blasis attributes its development particularly to Gardel and Vestris. He speaks of a pirouette of three or four turns in "second" position, to be stopped in the same, as the greatest proof of a dancer's uprightness. The *stopping* is as important as the start. It must be a knife-edge, clean arrest to contrast in sudden immobility to the dizzy whirl of its preceding movement. The Russo-Italian school provides a modern dancer with eight in a single spot; more, if moving diagonally across the stage.

> Pirouettes require considerable exercise and study. He whom nature hath favored with pliancy and agility, is always able to perform them gracefully; but he that is tight about the hips, whose legs are not sufficiently lithesome as to open with ease, and who, therefore, cannot turn well but on his instep, never meets with more than a partial success. Such a dancer should abandon all thoughts of distinguishing himself in the higher kind of pirouettes. It is the same with respect to bow-legged dancers, and those who are of too vigorous a construction: the strength of their muscles deprives them of flexibility and softness, and their bodies are ever wavering as it turns round. Slender and close-legged dancers are far better adapted to it than the last mentioned; their limbs are softer, more pliant, and, in general, turned more outwards; three essential qualities to perform a good pirouette.

Blasis speaks of three distinct types of artist, each endowed by nature for a particular genre. The most difficult in which to excel is the serious (*'tragic'*) dance. Persons essaying it must be majestic, elegant, of noble carriage most nearly approaching "the statues of Apollo or of Antinous, and of the Troadian Venus." This serious dancer reigns in the province of *adagio,* the slow, sustained movements, which also supports a female partner. *Adagio,* Blasis considers "the *ne plus ultra* of our art; and I look on it as the touchstone of the dancer."

Next, are the dancers of *demi-caractère* ('satiric'-dance). They should be of middle height. Their work is a mixture of all styles. Last, the *comic* dances, for rural or pastoral subjects, are suitable for thick-set, small or vigorous statures. Blasis here raises folk or character-dancing to an importance equal to the more august tragic and comic styles.

> In my opinion, the very type of this branch consists in the imitation of all those natural motions which have been denominated dances in every age, and amongst every people. To offer a true picture of pastoral life, the dancer, in his performance, must copy and mimic the steps, attitudes, simplicity of manner, and sometimes even those frolicsome and rude motions of the villager, who, inspired by the sound of his rustic instruments, and animated by

the society and liveliness of his cherished companion, or beloved mistress, gives his whole soul up, without restraint, to the pleasures of dancing.

In presenting a methodology for instruction, Blasis insists that only first-rate dancers make first-rate teachers, and it would be folly for any serious artist to base his style on anything less than perfection. He analyzes the underlying angularity of the body; obliques, right and acute angles as the basis for dancing movement, exhorting students to comprehend the profound geometrical logic of ballet design. He provides a careful series of progressive exercises which will enable a young dancer to gain an accurate, brilliant technique.

The Third Section of his study is devoted to pantomime, "the very soul and support of ballet." His analysis of gesture and movement is extremely acute, and in spite of the researches of Charles Darwin and later scientific observers can still be read for interest and use. He divides gestures into the "natural" and the "artificial," discusses the necessity of artificial conventionalization or stylization enabling them to carry across footlights. He also observes the contributions of the Commedia dell' Arte and the inherent Latin gift for mimicry. He understands that pantomime, like dancing itself, has a grammar, vocabulary, and idiom, possessed of a superior logic, in no way accidental, which must be mastered by any serious dancer. Although he cites as authority a second-rate diluter of Vigano, there is no mention, among all the other names and quotations, of the creator of 'The Titans,' himself.

Blasis lived at a time which had at least a century of accumulative background for theatrical dance. The eighteenth century had begun to formulate its own theories on the arts without an overwhelming influence of remote antiquity. Aristotle was no less valid. Only, his analysis took on contemporary examples, his rules had modern application, after all the pedantic and often illusory scholasticism of the Renaissance. The esthetic of the early nineteenth century has a curious stiffness, a careful rigidity, which however practical (and it was eminently practical) lacks a spontaneity bred of its being an initial formulation. As time goes on, practitioners grow more secure, their canons enlarge, leaving more to the discretion of individual artists. Blasis analyzes the composition of dance-drama with the conscience of his time. There should be an exposition, which is the introduction or statement of theme and which, concisely and clearly should "awaken interest." Plot is the creation of emotion by incident, excitement of curiosity, maintenance of the interest awakened. Catastrophe (*dénouement*); the unraveling. This, Blasis feels, is the most difficult to resolve. "Shakespeare is often very defective in his catastrophes; the conclusion of Othello is void of all good sense, and produces nothing but horror." In other words, intensity of emotion is, for him, not enough. He explains that while he does not subscribe to the unities of time, place or action, nevertheless it must all be *consistent*. Blasis is the soul of consistency. He is the synthetic principle in its middle level. Noverre's or Vigano's violence and experiment would have seemed to him in bad taste. He provides a measured method, preventing excess in any field.

His esthetic may have been conditioned by his epoch's or his own personal, academic taste. His technic is one of the soundest articulation of ballet idiom that we have. When we study the careful engravings of positions and movement, contained in this book, we are forcibly struck with a clean purity in the human silhouette; in its best sense, classic.* In 1830, an Italian of predominantly French background and tradition, has a style of physical expression, already brilliant (even by our terms); suave, yet generous; energetic, but noble. After him, the Italians would degrade it into a frog-like acrobatic of distended buttocks and preposterous theatricality, and the French into stagy graciousness, reeking with affectation. The Russian School alone understood the purity of Blasis. He is still a barometer for the *danse d'école*.

The classic dance will be exploited throughout the rest of the century by great dancers, each of whom will affect it by his personal style. Each adds to its vocabulary, new means of more economically executing old steps, while creating new ones. There is the greatest importance in some details which may strike one at first as unimportant. In Blasis, finally, the feet in first and fifth position, are in an absolutely straight or parallel line. The angle of forty-five degrees has been pushed to its ultimate ninety. The exuberance of the Romantic Ballet, from 1830 to 1850 accelerated enormously the *danse d'élevation*. In Blasis, the path is prepared for the greatest possible extension of legs, arms and torso. Previously the air was more a province for male dancers than the ballerina. Now, fulfilling a preparatory process of fifty years, she rises on her toes. Her feet, as Levinson said, refused any longer to stay on the floor. With the aid of reënforced shoes, somewhere around 1830, toe-dancing began. It was a final realization of the body's inherent verticality.

In 1837, Carlo Blasis was appointed by the Italian Government as Director of the Imperial Academy of Dancing and Pantomime, in Milan. The reforms he instituted made the Milanese School the world's finest and most influential. In Paris dancing was at a lower ebb than it is even now. Russia to a large extent was still enjoying French taste of a previous epoch. Italians trained under the guidance of Blasis' school, spread its principles all over Europe. The system of hours of practice, bar-work, the exercises, an equalized training in character-dancing, pantomime and adagio, the discipline and self-respect of the modern school are due in great measure to him.

Italy, however, was not the only locality which affected the classic dance. After the passing of Noverre, ballet in France ceded to Vienna a priority it would never recapture. We have seen that the Viganos enjoyed a considerable popularity there. And, at the Viennese Opera, after almost two decades of absence, Italians would return, to implant themselves, first expressing the classic Italian tradition, which was evolving towards the efflorescence of

* The Front Endpapers of this book show Blasis' positions: See Notes on Illustrations.

Romantic Ballet. Their immediate success was due to the influence of their compatriot, Rossini. His compositions, full of a variety of technical effects, languorous, melodic with an intoxicating sensuality, indicated a corresponding choreography from the ballet masters who used his scores. Wenzel Robert, Count Gallenberg, a pupil of Rossini's, was his spokesman to the Viennese. As a musician he may have been inferior even to Vigano,—but he understood Vigano's choreodramatic principles and showed the Viennese an 'Alfred the Great,' in 1820. It was full of rural feasts, feudal ceremonies, fights to military music and a battle on a bridge. It may not have been such a work of genius which the Milanese already knew, but it achieved a considerable local triumph. Philippe Taglioni, a native of Milan, who had been *maître de ballet* in Stockholm where he married, came to Vienna, and was a popular master. Under his auspices, his great daughter Maria made her début in an "anacreontic" ballet.

With the advent of Taglioni, we will presuppose for the rest of our history technical considerations. The dancer's technique was to develop enormously into an expression she never knew but along the lines she certainly used. For us, perhaps, the most important aspect of nineteenth-century ballet after Blasis is the contribution of great dancing personalities, who always, from the days of Sallé and Camargo, polarize around their characters the predominant conflicts of tradition. Maria Taglioni, Fanny Elssler, Cerito, Grisi, Grahn: a golden age of virtuosi who defined in their dancing *Le Ballet Romantique.*

We must understand the word "Romantic," for the Romantic ballet of the eighteen-forties means "Classic" ballets today. By Romanticism, we understand the violence of Delacroix, Victor Hugo's tragedies and the taste for the Gothic inaugurated by Horace Walpole and universalized by Walter Scott. Classicism was the style of the Directory, of Napoleon's vision of himself as Cæsar, although no nostalgia is devoid of romantic elements. But Romantic ballet can best be recognized by contrasting it with the chilly mythological divertissements of the late eighteenth century. *Les Sylphides* of 1909 means 'classic' ballet to us. Its origin was in the very sources of nineteenth-century romanticism. *La Sylphide,* the crown of Marie Taglioni's fame and the symbol of the romantic dance was first revealed to the public on the night of March 12, 1832, at the Paris Opéra. By this time *Opéra* must read often as 'theater for *Ballet.'*

The Sylphide, an ethereal creature, winged and clad in her imperishable long tulle skirts, first designed here by the painter Eugène Lamy, kneels beside James, a Scottish youth, asleep in an arm-chair. He is awakened by the brush of a "kiss from ideal lips," and at once her visionary presence fades. James is betrothed to Effie, a dark peasant lass. At their marriage-ball, in the midst of highland-reels, the Sylph reappears from the very embers of the fire-place, or floats momentarily upon a window-sill. But all the first act is only mimed *pas d'action,* setting an atmosphere for dancing.

The second scene reveals a mysterious glade. An unearthly flight of Sylphides, their wings shimmering in pink and blue sequins, flutter through the gnarled limbs of forest oaks. The sorority of virgin fays shimmer in timid vibration about the white holiness of their prime sister. A few of them toss scarves onto trees, swinging themselves with willowy bends. Others clasp the low branches and let the boughs, on the rise, carry them into air. There was the famous *entrée* of quadrilles by fours, two and two, meeting at the back of the stage, coming forward, often subsequently imitated (notably in *Lac des Cygnes*). In front of the shadowy, rhymed activity of white fairies, Taglioni and her partner, commence their *pas de deux*. It is a lyric sport of blind-man's buff, shifting among shadowy boughs and ominous branches. James pursues his unreal inamorata. Almost within his anguished arms, she always leaves them empty.

Taglioni! How did she dance? How, indeed? Amid the mass of pictures and panegyric, there remains scarcely an accurate objective hint of how her dancing looked. All we know is what she meant to those who saw her. Her critics compete with each other in extravagant hymns; but surrounded by praise, the Sylphide, maintaining her rôle, eludes us. She "glides over the flowers without bending them." In one print she bounds in high *jetés,* full face toward the footlights. Such a wraith was undreamed of before. Every one agrees upon her gliding lightness, the frail imponderable weight which slight limbs could never support except for their pact with ether. Her toes have 'points.' Her body is veiled diaphanously in misty muslin. Under the vague outline of skirt and bodice there is pure strength; geometry the base of every arabesque.

But the tragic sense in romance must be fulfilled. The enchantress' scarf about her shoulders falls to earth, and with it her delicate wings (for "which she had no use") bruised as a broken butterfly's. She expires in the arms of the poor Scotch lad, his strong body shaken with a bird's weight. Sylphides hover nearby. Veiling their faded sister's face with her fatal scarf, they bear her into the night. Sylphlets support the burden, caressing her floating feet. They ascend, twelve of them, carefully hauled up by a tangle of wires.

Its success was stupendous. There was a new verb at once: *taglioniser.* *Sylphide* was the adjective of the hour. Victor Hugo dedicates a book *A vos pieds, à vos ailes* (To your feet, to your wings). Success was stupendous, but not unprepared. A triumph that depends on novelty depends for its shattering, breath-taking exhilaration on decades of accumulative ennui. Novelty is not essentially new. It is a final definition of some of the elements in the world of ideas, always ready for another assemblage. Their previous articulation, even in fragments, sows the soil for a new acceptance when that artist appears who will gather those that fit his uses, to stamp them with his mark.

Yet everything about the Sylphide seemed new. Her costume, that modest, long, white maiden's dress, more robe for saint than dancer, its great skirt, unribbed with hoops or whale-bones, permitted the easiest foot-movement beneath. Its billows in flight emphasized the leaps. Inverted lily, or swinging bell, it hung from a tight bodice which molded the decent plasticity of a female bosom. Arms and neck alone were bare, for all touching display of expression, of longing, sympathy or resignation. The *tutus* were the uniform of the *ballet-blanc*. Before then, David, the painter with an official eye on the chill stones of Rome, designed a conventional tunic for all dancers which would not be used again till Duncan's day. Now, after Taglioni, his chiton seemed grotesque, almost improper. The innovation of gas-lighting, with its uneven, throbbing warmth, pooling the revolving white calyx of dancers' skirts with round dark shadows, making its tarlatan edges incandescent from beneath, had also its part in the romantic revolution, aiding the spectral, the nostalgic, the magic atmosphere.

And the ballet itself, the whole Sylphide was novel. Under the Empire, choreography had been a series of divertissements tacked onto a myth. In Italy it had become a *drame-passionel,* mimed to music. Now with *La Sylphide,* dancing was used to express the aspirations of its epoch. In fact, ballet was but another channel by which the predominantly Germanic ideas affected the period. Levinson points out the significance of Scandinavian blood in Marie Taglioni's veins for she "danced what Kant purely thought," what Novalis, of the blue flower sang, what Hoffman and Lenau nocturnally imagined. Everything in her expression had an inherent duality; the real world, immediate and everyday, juxtaposed to an ideal, higher plane of essential reality. Thus, the ballet also proved the vanity in appearances, the truth of dreams. Everywhere a transcendental fiction gave a deeper significance to actual existence. The poets the period loved, Byron, Keats, Shelley, Heine, Poushkin, Lamartine, Chatterton, Hölderlin, were either phthisic or dead young. The dreamy spirituality of violence exhausted always determined the tragic climax in danced drama. When the ethereal Sylphide, loving a mortal, loses her wings she dies, as Théophile Gautier noticed, like virgin ants which lose theirs after the first aërial loving.

In all *ballets-blancs,* the mechanism of choreography, the character of movement, the quality of gesture is determined by the romantic conception of ruined towers, of unachieved yet aspiring desires. The decisive arrival of toe-dancing, the victory of the *danse d'élevation* is only another facet of its thesis. In every one of the famous ballets, the winged ballerina links her supernatural origin (Sylphide, Ondine, Peri, Ghost or Spectre) with a terrestrial destiny. The dancing, which we now call *classic,* was in the *ballet romantique* a suave, yet acrobatic style, satisfying the epoch's insistent longing for symmetrical action. Toe-dancing became the speech of the inexpressible. Its gliding movement was raised to a symbol, *the* symbol of imaginary worlds made real. The dancer, now rising on her toes, firmly supported on a rigid arch, neither walks nor runs, but flows. Here *is* novelty, a form of human mobility hitherto unknown. It freed the dancer's body, to a great extent, from the laws of gravity and from mechanical habits of everyday motion, which not even theatrical stylization had saved from banality.

Twelve years after the Sylphide's début, Taglioni revived her greatest triumph. Théophile Gautier, clearest of his period's critics, in spite of poetic indulgence, leaves us what is almost an epitaph, comparing her to another Maria,—Malibran, the great singer.

> For us, Taglioni was already what Terpsichore was in the days of the Empire —a madrigal in a word. Taglioni, the Sylphide! All this began to become an idealized form, a poetic personification, an opalescent mist seen against the green obscurity of an enchanted forest. Taglioni was Dancing, just as Malibran was Music; one with a smile on her lips, her arms outstretched in harmony, the tip of her toe poised on the calix of a flower; the other, a flowing wave of black hair, one pale cheek supported against an alabaster hand, a vibrating harp, a shining eye glossed with tears; two fairies whom we invoke to inspire us, we romantics who do not believe in the Muses.

Taglioni inaugurated the brilliant, dangerous tradition of modern virtuosity. Year by year, more and more is expected of a dancer. She must not only presuppose all the technique of her predecessors, but she must also have a personal brilliance in addition to charm, or expressive talent with which nature endowed her. Taglioni developed a new style of *danse noble,* only in the days of romanticism, it was rather *la danse transcendentale.* Transcendence, however, is only one side of the portrait of Romantic Ballet; its heavenly aspect. The earthly energy is typified by Fanny Elssler, a young Viennese who aroused not only in Berlin and Paris, in London and Saint Petersburg, but also in New Orleans and Philadelphia, a fame even surpassing the Sylphide's.

In her early career, her name had been judiciously linked with the unhappy Duc de Reichstadt's. Perhaps L'Aiglon loved her. In any case the rumor did her no harm. Elssler precipitated a passion for character-dancing. Her stage was not set with cardboard donjons or transparency moonlights, nor was her *corps de ballet* strung up on wires when the ascension mechanism refused to work. She danced in the broad sunlight of Granada to the clapper-clapper of castanets. Fanny in her *cachucha* was that aspect of romanticism exemplified also in Gautier's Spanish stories, in the Hungarian folk-tales which inspired Lenau and Hoffman, in the Moroccan harems of Delacroix. Elssler borrowed extensively from ethnographic sources. If her Spanish, her Polish or her Magyar numbers were not absolutely correct, nevertheless she transposed their fire, essentially undiluted, to the stage of the Opéra. Fanny used her whole body, and, with a knowledge of folk-dance and her own indomitable temperament, she split the public, heretofore votaries of the Sylphide alone. "The others," said Gautier, not daring to say *"the* other," "are nothing but a pair of legs struggling beneath a motionless body," and more fairly,

> Fanny Elssler's dancing is quite different from the academic idea, it has a particular character which sets her apart from all other dancers; it is not the

aërial and virginal grace of Taglioni, it is something more human, more appealing to the senses. Mlle. Taglioni is a Christian dancer, if one may make use of such an expression in regard to an art proscribed by the Catholic faith: she flies like a spirit in the midst of the transparent clouds of white muslin with which she loves to surround herself, she resembles a happy angel who scarcely bends the petals of celestial flowers with the tips of her pink toes. Fanny is a quite pagan dancer; she reminds one of the muse Terpsichore, tambourine in hand, her tunic, exposing her thigh, caught up with a golden clasp; when she bends freely from her hips, throwing back her swooning, voluptuous arms, we seem to see one of those beautiful figures from Herculaneum or Pompeii which stand out in white relief against a black background, marking their steps with resounding cymbals.

The competition between Taglioni and Elssler was more intense than that of Camargo and Sallé. Fanny was a good business woman, always taking into consideration her rival's fears of being superannuated. Nevertheless before seeing Taglioni, Elssler thought she herself had reached technical perfection. One view of the Sylphide terrified her into three months' arduous study with the younger Vestris (no longer young). Her Paris début was cleverly contrived. Preceded by months of whispering, semi-secret publicity, she was finally allowed to appear before Parisian audiences, at that time wholly under the sway of Taglioni, mysteriously veiled. Elssler overcame all her natural nervousness in competing with such a favorite. What she could not rely on, but what enormously aided her, was the natural fickleness of a public palling under the pale beauties of a Sylph. Gautier wrote of the rivalry in a ballet called 'The Tempest' (a "ballet, the best of which can be said of it is that it is a ballet"):

> Undoubtedly, spiritualism is a thing to be respected; but, as regards dancing, we can quite well make some concessions to materialism. After all, dancing consists of nothing more than the art of displaying beautiful shapes in graceful positions and the development from them of lines agreeable to the eye; it is mute rhythm, music that is seen. Dancing is little adapted to render metaphysical themes; it only expresses the passions; love, desire with all its attendant coquetry; the male who attacks and the female who feebly defends herself is the basis of all primitive dances.

At all events, Elssler went from continent to continent, prepaid in gold before she danced. In Havana she received seven thousand dollars for one performance. Nicolas the First, learning of her unofficial arrival in Saint Petersburg, invited her to dance at the small court theater at Tsarsköe-Selo. Followers of Taglioni, piqued by Elssler's rise, invented all sorts of ways to honor their goddess. They persuaded Vestris, once their model, now their idol, to leave retirement for a single menuet, as her partner. The idea was, that at the end of the performance, the *Dieu de la Danse* would crown her *Deésse de la Danse*. After their menuet, when the ensemble had withdrawn to the sides, for the coronation, the orchestra spoiled everything by playing the

Grand March too soon. Vestris fled the scene. Taglioni dissolved into tears. Who gave the *chef d'orchèstre* his miscue? Unquestionably, if not Ellsler, some one close to her.

Elssler with her Cachucha, her Tarantella, her *Cracovienne;* Taglioni with her purity and supernatural fluency revitalized the whole idiom of ballet which had been starving on the thin fare of the French and Italian Academies. This revivification amounted to revolution, and in the revolt Théophile Gautier, the exquisite author of *Emaux et Camées* was intimately involved, not only as propagandist and critic, but as librettist. He understood and consciously defined the Romantic Ballet under its two standards of Elssler and Taglioni, of folk-dance and *ballet-blanc*. He almost anticipated a synthesis of the two styles in a single person. When Carlotta Grisi appeared, he would write the book of 'Giselle' for her. With it and Grisi's entry into glory, the Romantic Ballet was given its finest choreographic work, perhaps its only ballet which still survives (at least in Paris, Leningrad and Moscow) after nearly a century of constant use. "Giselle" is for the dancer what Hamlet is for an actor, "Don Giovanni" for a singer. Gautier, as a real poet, assimilated the pathos of his period so perfectly that it still seems in spite of quaintness and the nostalgia of distance, pathetic to us.

We know almost everything there is to know about 'Giselle,' except the actual dancing. Gautier, in 1841, wrote to his great German friend,

> My dear Heinrich Heine, when reviewing, a few weeks ago, your fine book, *De L'Allemagne,* I came across a charming passage—one has only to open the book at random—the place where you speak of elves in white dresses, whose hems are always damp, of nixes who display their little satin feet on the ceiling of the nuptial chamber; of snow-colored *Wilis* who waltz pitilessly, and of all those delicious apparitions you have encountered in the Harz mountains and on the banks of the Ilse, in a mist softened by German moonlight; and I involuntarily said to myself: "Wouldn't this make a pretty ballet?"

The scene is set in a "vague country, in Silesia, in Thuringia, even in one of the Bohemian sea-ports Shakespeare loved." But let Gautier tell us what he best knew.

> Hillocks weighed down with russet vines, yellowish, warmed and sweetened by the autumn sun; those beautiful vines from which hang the amber-colored grapes which produce Rhine wine, form the background; at the summit of a gray and bare rock, so precipitous that the vine tendrils have been unable to climb it, stands, perched like an eagle's nest, one of those castles so common in Germany, with its battlemented walls, its pepper-box turrets, and its feudal weathercocks; it is the abode of Albrecht, the young Duke of Silesia. That thatched cottage to the left, cool, clean, coquettish, half-buried among the leaves, is Giselle's cottage. The hut facing it is occupied by Loys. Who is Giselle? Giselle is Carlotta Grisi, a charming girl with blue eyes, a refined and artless smile, and an alert bearing; an Italian who tries to be taken for

a German, just as Fanny (Elssler) the German, tried to be taken for an Andalusian from Seville. Her position is the simplest in the world; she loves Loys and she loves dancing. As for Loys, played by Petipa, there are a hundred reasons for suspecting him. Just now, a handsome esquire, adorned with gold lace, speaks to him in a low voice, standing cap in hand and maintaining a submissive and respectful attitude. What! A servant of a great house, as the esquire appears to be, fails to lord it over the humble rustic to whom he speaks! Then, Loys *is not what he appears to be* (ballet style), *but we shall see later.*

But do not think that although Gautier so clearly understood the essence of its style, almost to a point of parody, that he was making fun of it. Giselle loves a Prince, disguised as a country-boy. When she finds out the truth, she loses her mind. She repeats insanely the very dance she did with her lover, and staggers to fall upon his dagger. The first act is full of Gothic décor, *à la* Viollet-le-Duc and pantomime of the tenderest order, relieved by adaptations of folk-dances and festivities of a central-European vineyard town. The second, completes the romantic synthesis:

> The stage represents a forest on the banks of a pool; you see tall pale trees, whose roots spring from the grass and the rushes; the water-lily spreads its broad leaves on the surface of the placid water, which the moon silvers here and there with a trail of white spangle. Reeds with their brown velvet sheaths shiver and palpitate beneath the intermittent night breeze. The flowers open languorously and exhale a giddy perfume like those broad flowers of Java which madden whoever inhales their scent. I cannot say what burning and sensuous atmosphere flows about this humid and leafy obscurity. At the foot of a willow, asleep and concealed beneath the flowers, lies poor Giselle. From the marble cross which indicates her grave is suspended, still quite fresh, the garland of vine branches with which she had been crowned at the harvest festival.

Hunters come, in spite of the fact that the sinister place is haunted by the *Wilis* "and nocturnal dancers, no more forgiving than living women are to a tired waltzer." Myrtha, the Wilis Queen appears, to summon her unearthly minions. It is a *ballet-blanc*. The fairies are to admit a new sister that very night, Giselle, but recently a mortal maid. This girl emerges from the damp of her fresh-filled tomb, wondering, looks about, to discover her own name on its cross. Suddenly she sprouts two wings, under the Queen's wand. Inevitably, Loys or Albrecht comes to the spot, drawn by remorse. Giselle, in spite of her fairy troth, tries to warn him of his hideous fate. She knows full well the doom awaiting. He will be *danced to death!* To prove her mettle, it even must fall on Giselle herself to entice him to his ruin. She signs him to embrace the Cross of her tomb, not to leave it what may e'er betide. The Cross, at least, is sanctuary. But the Wilis Queen

> resorts to an infernal and feminine device. She forces Giselle, who in her capacity of subject, must obey, to execute the most seductive and most grace-

ful poses. At first, Giselle dances timidly and reluctantly; then she is carried away by her instinct as a woman and a *Wili;* she bounds lightly and dances with so seductive a grace, such overpowering fascination, that the imprudent Albrecht leaves the protecting cross and goes towards her with outstretched arms, his eyes burning with desire and love. The fatal madness takes hold of him, he pirouettes, bounds, follows Giselle in her most hazardous leaps; the frenzy to which he gives way reveals a secret desire to die with his mistress and to follow the beloved shade to her tomb; but four o'clock strikes, a pale streak shows on the edge of the horizon. Dawn has come and with it the sun bringing deliverance and salvation. Flee, visions of the night; vanish, pale phantoms! A celestial joy gleams in Giselle's eyes: her lover will not die, the hour has passed. The beautiful Myrtha reënters her water-lily. The *Wilis* fade away, melt into the ground, and disappear. Giselle herself is drawn towards her tomb by an invisible power. Albrecht, distracted, clasps her in his arms, carries her, and covering her with kisses, places her upon a flowered mound; but the earth will not relinquish its prey, the ground opens, the flowers bend over.... The hunting-horn resounds; Wilfrid anxiously seeks for his master. He walks a little in front of the Prince of Courland and Bathilde. However, the flowers cover Giselle, nothing can be seen but her little transparent hand...this too disappears, all is over!—never again will Albrecht and Giselle see each other in this world.... The young man kneels by the mound, plucks a few flowers, and clasps them to his breast, then withdraws, his head resting on the shoulder of the beautiful Bathilde, who forgives and consoles him.

So ends 'Giselle,' the triumph of Grisi and Perrot, of Nijinsky and Karsavina, of Pavlova and Pierre Vladimiroff, of Spessivtzeva and Serge Lifar, and "so, my dear Heine, your German *Wilis* have succeeded completely at the French Opéra."

The French Opéra was remarkable as a social institution. The period of 1830 to the battle of Sedan, even in spite of 1848, was an uninterrupted epoch of extreme brilliance, particularly in foyer, boxes and the wings. But on the stage, if there was anything of interest, we may be sure it was not French. The great names associated with it, the Duc de Morny, Paul Daru, Ludovic Halévy, Rossini, Meyerbeer, Scribe and Auber, established a continual communication between public and the stars. It was like an imperial court with rigidly established hierarchies, etiquette and precedents for the descent of power.

In the "first" class there were one, two or three stars, hired not for life but by the season, or even the performance. In the "second," there were ten *premiers sujets*. The notices they received enabled them to get engagements in Europe and America. In the "third," there were twenty-two *second-sujets*. The pay they received was augmented by the material aid of "platonic" admirers. There were three divisions of *coryphées,* each containing two sections of six, and one of eight, ballerinas. There were two "quadrilles" each divided into two, and these were generally kept by men-about-town. Finally, there were the *petites classes,* or the *marcheuses,* energetic, hard-working, ambitious, tough and pretty, the hope of their teachers, the source of new stars. Badly paid and always tired, they could amidst considerable competition raise their level.

There was ceaseless gossip about the imminent arrival of novelties upon the opera stage or amorous crises behind its scenes. Two exceedingly clever directors, the Doctor Véron and Nestor Roqueplan, knew how to create a busy atmosphere of glamour and charm which attracted many rich men to the opera, whose milieu, few of them had previously considered to be their own. There was much to amuse them, particularly at champagne suppers after theater, or in loges during intermissions. The royal box was on the fore-stage to the left. Facing it, was the Marquis Aquados's, always filled with pretty women from the Spanish colony. The *Grande Baignoire* at the left of the first floor was called the *Loge Infernale,* since its occupants were the most devilish members of *Le Jockey-Club.* The house detonated when they released bravos or hisses.

In 1837, when they heard of the approaching departure of Taglioni, her partisans issued a solemn manifesto demanding the head of Duponchel, that frightful director who dared permit their goddess to depart. The *Loge Infernale* planned to hurl his luckless skull (in *papier-mâché*) onto the stage. The house was packed, even the Royal Family being present for the Sylphide's farewell. All Elsslerites noisily rejoiced. Before *Le Jockey* had time to make its symbolic gesture, an aide-de-camp of the King entered their loge, and begged them, in the Queen's name, to renounce the macabre jest. The regicide, Meunier, was to have been guillotined on the morrow. Marie-Amélie was horrified at the idea of seeing even an imitation of a severed head roll on the ground. The gentlemen of the jockey made the Queen's wish their law, and in the morning the King signed Meunier's pardon.

Under the first empire, the *Foyer-de-Danse* played rather a minor rôle. Bonaparte, however, had included a troupe of ballet dancers among the provisions for his Egyptian campaign. Later, Napoleon had said to his Minister of Fine Arts, "Tell those young ladies to behave themselves, or I'll give them a general for director, and he'll make them march like soldiers." Its unimportance extended into the Restoration, due largely to the naïveté of Sosthenes de la Rouchefoucauld, Intendant of the Royal Theaters. He built two staircases up to the dressing rooms which he hopefully expected to be restricted to the separate sexes. "Do you wish to please me?" he asked his girls. "Yes? Then wide pantaloons, please, and good morals." The young ladies had a fair idea of how to take care of themselves. The French ballerina, later to be immortalized by Edgar Degas, was a stock type of shrewdness. One sobbing mamma was supposed to have come to her daughter with the news of father's death. The child is candid. Suppressing a sigh, she remarks, "Why tell me that now? It will spoil my *mastic.*" The *mastic,* a thick white liquid enamel, took a long time to apply over face, neck and arms. Then, a bit of cold-cream, mascara, rouge and teeth-whitener. A girl's training occupied from eight to ten years. She knew, perhaps, in addition to their steps, a smattering of music. The men were in a very poor position. Male dancing under Vestris, Dauberval and Gardel had meant something. Now, even as partners the men were effaced. All solos were ceded to the ballerina, and male-dancers were little better than a support in the classic style, or in character-dancing a background for the girl. To be sure there were the high pirouettes of Auguste Vestris, and the brilliant work of Perrot and Saint-Lèon. These were exceptions; their best work was achieved not in France, but in Russia.

For, to a predominant degree, the rest of the history of ballet will be Russian. It is the Russian School which will take the French and Italian Academy and make of it something Paris or Milan never knew, and probably never will know. The Slav material itself was superb, and had been developing for a century, independent of Western Europe except for the direction of alien ballet-masters. Now the heirs of Noverre and Vestris, from Denmark and Sweden, from Austria and Germany, from Italy and France converged on Russia to produce the greatest school, the greatest technicians and the greatest choreographers of traditional theatrical dancing.

Catherine the Great's son, Paul, was mad. He had an aversion to round hats and proscribed them. He appropriated green, dark blue, white, red and strawberry as his personal hues; no one else could wear them. At court balls the dancers were forced to twist themselves about in every conceivable position so their backs would never be turned on their Czar. He forbade the *Valse,* since he felt it was immodest, though when he fell in love with Princess Gagarina, at her whim, rescinded the ban. But under him Noverre's disciple, Charles Le Picq, produced *Jason et Medée* as well as *Adèle de Ponthieu,* and there were numerous good dancers, both French and Russian. Nevertheless, it was hardly easy for a *maître de ballet* to work for such a master. He hated male dancers, and ordered that their rôles be assumed by women. (Catherine and Elizabeth, on the other hand, always had men at masquerades disguised as girls.) In the year 1800 the Czar ordered all performances to start at five in the afternoon, to end by eight. Besides the regular staff, the children employed at the tapestry-works danced in big ballets, dressed as cupids. A year later, conspirators, among them his minister, Count Pahlen, found the Czar hidden behind a screen in his bedroom and strangled him.

Nevertheless he had caused the ballet-master, Charles Louis Didelot, to be engaged. The history of Russian theatrical dancing falls into two periods: before, and after Didelot. His work continued into the epoch of Alexander the First. The new King was an enormous relief after the insanity and insecurity of his predecessor, and much occupied with theater, which he personally encouraged, Russia achieved a renaissance of her own, not only in the dance, but in architecture, music and poetry.

Didelot had been born in Stockholm in 1767, the son of a French first-dancer at the Royal Theater. His son was short, bright and well-built, but he contracted smallpox at the age of six and Didelot *père* considered his career ended. But, as luck would have it, the Swedish King misplaced his marmot, with which he wished to appear in a masquerade, so the little boy was stuffed into squirrel skin, had a marmot's head squeezed over his own, and "made an excellent impression."

The King sent him to Paris to study with Dauberval, and later he worked under Auguste Vestris. Noverre contracted him for London where the youth put on a ballet inspired by the master's ideas. 'Richard Cœur de Lion,' a favorite patriotic theme. Didelot had the advantages of the best training the culminating schools of the eighteenth century afforded. Beauchamps, Pécourt, Dupré, Vestris *père et fils,* Noverre; the link from Didelot to our own day is made by Christian Johannsen, Marius Petipa, Platon Karsavin, the brothers Legat, who taught Nijinsky. In all some dozen names, in an unbroken line, from Lully to the present, a dozen men who receive, like runners their wands, the purest technical principles, the cleanest dancing style.

Didelot had appeared as Guimard's partner on the boards of the Paris Opéra, so he came well breveted to Saint Petersburg. He was an excellent teacher, as well as an interesting choreographer and a good dancer. His ballets, though they were not expensive to produce, proved popular. His own appearance, from a contemporary report, was odd enough. He was

> as thin as a skeleton, had a very long red nose, wore (as Apollo) a light red wig and a laurel wreath on his head, and danced with a lyre in his hand, with great success. But he evoked a caricature rather than the sun-god.

His *corps de ballet* were talented and trained to a considerable perfection. Their flying was particularly famous, and they could soar back and forwards, stopping on the very brink of the footlights. Outside the theater, he was kindness itself to his pupils. But inside it was otherwise.

> It was very amusing to see Didelot behind the scenes watching his pupils. Sometimes he swayed from side to side, smiled, and took mincing steps and stamped his foot. But when the little pupils danced he shook his fist at them, and, if they missed the figures, he made their lives a misery. He pounced on them like a hawk, pulled their hair or ears, and if any ran away he gave them a kick which sent them flying. Even the solo dancers suffered from him. Being applauded, a dancer went behind the scenes, when Didelot seized her by the shoulders, shook her with all his might, and having given her a punch in the back, pushed her on to the stage as if she were recalled.

He preferred to return to Russia in 1815 than to work at the Paris Opéra, under the jealous eye of Gardel. His contract makes indicative reading. It was valid for six years, after which he would retire on a pension. He and his wife received sixteen thousand rubles a year. Each was to have one benefit a year during the best season, with all expenses paid by the state. When on duty he had the use of a carriage, and what was quite as important, he was to have a yearly allowance of twenty cords of wood, to keep him warm.

After 1816, he produced more than twenty ballets. The names of some of them tell the taste of the period. There was 'Theseus and Ariadne' (1817), 'A Hunting Adventure' (1818), of which the Flemish scene in the second act was reproduced from a painting by Teniers. There was 'The Caliph of Bagdad, A Youthful Adventure of Haroun al Raschid,' which brings the precedent for Bakst-Fokine's *Scheherezade* curiously close to home.

Afterwards came *Raoul de Crequis, or The Return from the Crusades,* a grand Pantomimic Ballet in five acts by Didelot, music by Cavos and Sushkov, scenery by Kondratiev and Dranchet, final scene by Conoppi, fights by Gomburov, machines by Burset, costumes by Babini. Principal dancers, Mlle. Kolosova and MM. C. Didelot and Auguste.

His was the period immediately preceding Romantic Ballet. His plots were always strong in dramatic sequence, while as a direct result of his teaching a considerable number of fine Russian dancers were trained. Among the most famous was Marie Danilova, whose work he particularly cherished. He sent her to the best teachers of pantomime, and only at rare intervals would permit her to appear. Her début was an instantaneous success, but true to her virginal beauty, she refused to be turned from her career by love affairs. "I am not free," he had taught her to answer. "I belong to my art." But tragically ignorant of its result, Didelot invited an excellent French dancer to Russia, Duport, who arrived with his mistress, a famous actress. Her funds were low, and her lover took her diamonds as security.

Duport first appeared with Danilova in 'Cupid and Psyche.' He managed to seduce her, being skilled in ways the natives did not know, and abandoned his Frenchwoman. But not for long. His engagement over, he made peace with her and quit Russia without so much as a word to poor Danilova who adored him. She fell ill, crushed, and quite as in a *romance* of Poushkin, died, at the age of seventeen, of a broken heart.

The Russians became *balletomanes,* even more ardent than the French, and more critical, since, though it was the woman that attracted them, it was always the dancer that held them. In 'Eugène Onegin,' which he dedicated to her, Poushkin wrote of Istomina, a dark-haired ballerina, who captivated not only the pit, but the salons of Petersburg.

The house is crammed. A thousand lamps
On pit, stalls, boxes, brightly blaze,
Impatiently the gallery stamps,
The curtain now they slowly raise.
Obedient to the magic strings,
Brilliant, ethereal, there springs
Forth from the crowd of nymphs surrounding
Istomina the nimbly-bounding.
With one foot resting on its tip
Slow circling round its fellow swings
And now she skips and now she springs

Like down from Ælous's lip,
Now her lithe form she arches o'er
And beats with rapid foot the floor.

Social-dances had become a serious part of ordinary academic routine. For cadets in the Higher Military School, there were voluntary as well as compulsory classes. Polonaises and quadrilles were popular, with the waltz, mazurka and cracoviack. At public halls there were also the *ecossaisse,* the four-coupled mazurka, the French quadrille.

The Ballet School was well established along lines set by Didelot, but nothing of much artistic interest happened until 1837, when Taglioni arrived to set Russia some new standards. She was preceded by publicity, delays and setbacks. But when she finally appeared there was no disappointment. Even Nicolas the First, that implacable Emperor, melted under her serenity; her contract was four times renewed, and the Russians saw her some two hundred times. A former pupil of the Theatrical Academy left a souvenir of her visit to the School:

> The most celebrated dancer Taglioni arrived at St. Petersburg with her father and came to our school to do her exercises. The director and officials treated her with every courtesy. Taglioni was a very plain, excessively thin woman with a small, yellowish and very wrinkled face. I felt quite ashamed because the pupils after the class surrounded Taglioni, and, with a charming note in their voices, said in Russian: "What an ugly mug you've got! How wrinkled you are!" Taglioni, not knowing the language and thinking compliments were being paid to her, smiled and replied in French: "Thank you, dear children."

Her father designed a new ballet for her called *L'Ombre.* There was a famous *pas* in which she danced with her own shadow. She performed with Russian artists and became a great favorite with Petersburg's public. Moscow courted her in vain. That is, they could not guarantee the three thousand roubles a performance she demanded. When she finally left, after eighteen curtain calls, she made one of her rare lapses into public speech: "Eternally, you are written in my heart; if I bid Russia farewell, believe me, it is not forever." A pair of her ballet shoes supposedly sold for two hundred roubles. Cooked, with a delicious sauce, they were piously eaten at a memorial dinner of fanatical *balletomanes.*

Taglioni had a quickening influence on the Russian School. After her departure, several native ballerinas essayed her most difficult rôles, and with success. Russia was still a provincial kingdom and the Narishkin's and Dolgo-rukoi's who went to Paris for the season naturally brought back a snobbish critical attitude about home-talent. Elena Ivanovna Andreyanova was accused of competing with the Sylphide, when she was merely testifying to Russian stamina. It was she who first danced *Giselle* in Petersburg. She later (1845) appeared with success in Paris, one of the first Slavs to appear in Western Europe.

In 1847 Marius Ivanovitch Petipa arrived in Petersburg. The reign of Petipa extended into the twentieth century and is remembered with affectionate homage by every one of the best living choreographers. The school of Petipa precipitated the revolution of Fokine. They were the virtual Renaissance and Reformation of the Russian Ballet. With Petipa's arrival, Petersburg was not only the capital of the world's dancing technicians but of ballet composition as well.

The Petipas were a dancing family and Jean, father of Marius, had already taught at the Imperial Russian School. Marius was asked to Petersburg by Titus, a rather uninspired composer. Only twenty-five and not famous, he had an extensive experience, particularly in Spanish dancing, and had performed the Fandango amidst the cheers of a *feria* at San Lucar. His experience in Spain he was to draw on continually for character dances, for divertissement in 'Carmen,' and for the 'Don Quixote' of Minkous, a ballet entirely in the Spanish manner. He had even danced in America. His arrival in Russia coincided with a Romantic revival. The white heat of the thirties had cooled. The Classic ballet had become rigid again, incorporating complacent adaptations from the folk of Hungary, Italy or Spain. Petipa took this fused idiom, and with the aid of his accomplished lieutenant, Ivanov, practically single-handed created the repertory of the Russian Ballet, a repertory which is even today popular at the Marinsky Theater in Leningrad, and at the Bolshoi in Moscow. For twenty years he worked parallel to Perrot, and Arthur Saint-Lèon, the dancer-violinist, two men of great talent both as dancers and choreographers. From 1870 till 1905 he was uniquely in command. He served under four Tsars, under eight directors, for nearly sixty years. He himself invented fifty-seven new ballets, revived seventeen with additions from his hand, and composed, besides, dances for thirty-four operas. Marius Petipa who was the 'Phoebus' to Fanny Elssler's 'Esmeralda' (of Victor Hugo's *Nôtre Dame*) gave Anna Pavlova her first rôle as *prima ballerina*.

To us, his compositions seem the essence of 'old-fashioned'; Fokine has taught us to laugh at them as he did in his youth. He had more right to laugh in 1905 than we have in 1935. Petipa's energy, his strong sense of symmetrical composition, his orderly variety, his inexhaustible invention have no parallel in the history of theatrical dance. To be sure, he grew doctrinaire and unresilient. Yet he admired young Fokine's radical activity, he believed in the Muscovite Gorski, he felt the promise of the twentieth century, even though he had grown too feeble to partake of another Romantic revolution. We remember how démodé the music of Tschaikovsky seemed until who but Stravinsky championed it just after the war. Now we realize that perhaps the two greatest sustained scores ever written for dancers are *La Belle au Bois Dormant* and *Petróuchka*. It was for Petipa (and Ivanov) that Tschaikovsky wrote 'Swan Lake' and 'The Nut-Cracker.' The choreography, the pantomime is a perfect counterpart for those magical, faded and disconnected melodies. An analysis of the 'classic'-Russo-Italian pantomime which Petipa used in the 'Swan

Lake' and which is typical of all his dramatic recitative, Adrian Stokes well defines in his "Russian Ballets":

> The mimed action that follows the meeting of swan-princess and prince should be carefully noted because it provides a most exquisite example of that old-fashioned mime which once was almost as complete (and conventionalized) a language as deaf and dumb signs. "Mother," for instance, should be indicated by arms crossed over the breast and hands reaching up to the shoulders. An index finger held upward and outward means "but," held upward and inward means "one." A "wicked man" is indicated by the raising of clenched fists to the sky.
>
> After the first questions the swan-princess says in effect: "I am queen of the swans." (She points to her crown and performs the flying motions with her arms.) "You see here a lake" (swimming motion). "My mother wept so much because one wicked man me a swan did make: but if one person will love and marry me the spell will be lifted and I a swan shall be no more."

In 1862, Petipa inspired by Théophile Gautier's 'Tale of a Mummy,' and by the collection of Egyptian Antiquities in the Kaiser Friedrich's Museum in Berlin, produced 'The Daughter of Pharaoh.' Years later Fokine would point to its preposterous tutus, papyrus-pattern brashly appliquéd onto tarlatans, its English explorers from Shephard's Hotel, as a conventional monstrosity of incorrect archeology. Yet Fokine produced *Une Nuit d'Egypte* (or *Cléopatre*). What is more droll today than watching the miming of 1910, the stale eroticism once warmed by Ida Rubenstein's statuesque presence, unfold in sorry parade? No one would wish to denigrate the Noverre of the twentieth century, who has given us not only *Les Sylphides* but *Prince Igor*. Nevertheless, Ivanov's *pas de quatre* of cygnets in *Lac des Cygnes,* the grand adagio of 'The Sleeping Beauty,' (still to be seen as 'Aurora's Wedding') have a quality of solid construction, coherent form and splendid accent that have never been surpassed.

André Levinson, the most erudite, perhaps the only contemporary critic of dancing after Gautier most of us can read (since Volyinsky, Lopoukhov and Vaganova are still untranslated), has analyzed past paraphrase the essence of the style and structure of the ballet, a ballet which, Romantic or Classic, in spite of the definitions of the decades 1830, 1850, 1870, Petipa canonized as the *classic* ballet.

> The "ancient ballet" consists essentially of a series of dances bound together and coördinated by dramatic action. This dramatic action is expressed by means of pantomime with conventional gestures, and it is joined to the music only by the dynamic links of the emotion expressed. But this inherent dualism of pure pantomime and abstract movements of dancing is modified by a process, the *pas d'action,* wherein every movement of the dance is dictated by the dramatic situation and linked to it by the actions, mimicry or gesticulations that interpret the feelings of the actors. The dance itself is amplified; the so-called character-dance reverts to the true fountain-head, its popular source,

the local motif being adapted within the boundaries provided by the "classical" education.

The classical dance can be succinctly characterized by the use of beats on the points and beats of *elevation*. It contains the traditional, symmetrical forms of the *pas de deux,* a choreographical poem in three verses in a rigid frame-work: —the *adagio,* which is a chain of movements and pirouettes by the ballerina supported by the dancer; the two *variations,* that of the ballerina and that of the dancer, whose more restricted art is confined to leaps, the *entrechat* and series of pirouettes; lastly the *coda,* in which the dancer alternates with the ballerina in a succession of accelerated measures that mount up to the presto and ends in a whirlwind of movements and dizzy complicated turns, crossing the stage diagonally.

At other times the diverse and complicated dance of the ballerina is accompanied by uniform and powerful movements of the whole *corps de ballet.* In Russia the latter is by no means reduced to playing the subordinate and purely decorative part of a mute chorus. In the *ballabili* it goes through its evolutions to the rhythm of a waltz or march, a complex organism moved by a single will. *Soli* detach themselves from this living orchestra, standing out vigorously against the compact background and then sinking back into the ensemble.

It would be vain to say that even a tenth of Petipa's vast output was worth saving. For one thing, hack musicians like Minkous or Pugni were scarcely an inspiration to any one but the leader of a regimental-band. Nor was Petipa unmusical, but he worked constantly under pressure. It was easier to regulate dances to the rhythms of mechanical tempi and simple accent than to try to parallel complex, subtle melodies of the composer of the 'Serenade for Strings,' or of "Eugène Onegin." Later, Tschaikovsky enthusiastically studied the difficult problems of dance-music. He understood that the cadences for a symphonic poem are not necessarily those which determine the symphonic combinations of a *corps de ballet.* He adapted himself to the rhythm of the human body's mobility, regulated as they were by the law of *danse d'école.* The liberty he abandoned as an independent composer, the limits he assumed in agreeing to invent dance-tunes, measure by measure, and pantomime, gesture by gesture, were more than compensated for by a triumphant collaboration. He provided Petipa with the best music which would ever prompt him. He indicated a new direction for all dance-composition, from which we still can draw.

When Petipa composed he called for absolute silence. Then, referring to notes he had already prepared, he proceeded methodically to the arrangement of groups. Many of these he had previously studied at home, working them out like figures on a chessboard, copying into a notebook the patterns he chose to keep. They inclined to be static and disparate, perhaps due to this preconception, not spontaneously fluent like Vigano or Fokine. Individual number, solos and *pas de deux* he invented on the floor of the rehearsal hall. He composed superbly for women, rarely giving difficult steps, but mainly those calculated to demonstrate the beauty of line and plastic silhouette. For men, he was not so satisfactory. Very often male dancers would have to adapt what he gave them to what they thought suited them, in reference to their partners. For this they often asked the aid of Johannsen.

Christian Johannsen's teaching was in every way the equal of Petipa's choreography. Between them they created the Russian school we know. This Swede had been trained by the Franco-Dane, Auguste Bournonville, a famous pupil of Vestris. Unfortunately, we have no space here even to hint of schools in Berlin, Warsaw or Copenhagen. But these smaller academies, through their best dancers, modified the course of theatrical-dancing almost to the extent of their more famous contemporaries. Johannsen's pedagogical style is still a model for the Soviet State schools, and it was to a large extent his understanding of style, which became the Russian style, today *the* natural good manners of classic dance. Such a statement may superficially sound prejudiced or snobbish, since its proof depends on personal taste alone. But of the three schools, the French have produced not one able male dancer in the century and their women are inferior even to the English. The Italian style, popularized by Enrico Cecchetti, in England (Nijinsky, contrary to his wife's book, owed little to him as far as dancing-style went), is so full of disagreeable stage-play, *cabotinage* and affectation, as to be not from a social but from a purely theatrical attitude, extremely ill-bred. As for the Russian style, the style of Perrot, Saint-Léon, Petipa, Nijinsky, Vladimiroff, Viltzac, and Messerer (to limit it now only to men), let us have the testimony of Nicolas Legat, one of Johannsen's most famous pupils and a real preceptor of Vaslav Nijinsky:

> Without embarking in this limited space on an analysis of the two systems, it may be said briefly that the differences lie, firstly in principle, and secondly in taste. One of the principles of the Russian school is that of balanced training; the Italians, on the contrary, permitted a great deal of one-sidedness for the sake of superficial effect. Enrico Cecchetti, for example, though a brilliant pirouettist, could only do pirouettes and *tours en l'air* in one direction. We used sometimes to tease him into trying the other direction, and this would make him angry. A series of double *tours* in alternate directions, often done by our dancers, was beyond him. Our dancers eventually did seven or eight pirouettes habitually in their solos, but they did them in either direction at will. Whether they outdid others in this or not was merely incidental, it was the principle of balanced training that was at stake. We rejected a number of easy effects obtained at the cost of beauty and grace, and we avoided those faults of *épaulement* and carriage which are always marked in the Italian school. To the untrained eye these differences may appear insignificant. But it was our refusal to sacrifice esthetics to effect, combined with our success in adopting and adapting Italian technique, that enabled us in the generation that followed the arrival of the Italians in Russia to produce the greatest dancers of the past four decades.

The question of a classic dancer's style is as important as a bull-fighter's, a boxer's or a professional diver's. But while, with sportsmen personal taste is conditioned by a consciously controlled acrobatic, in dancing the executant's individual esthetic controls his technical expression. When one comes to its highest exponents, the style itself becomes a kind of sixth sense, almost more important than plot, mime or music. Pavlova's *mise en scène* was shoddy, her music trivial, but the style bred between Petipa and Johannsen, became on each seeing more crystalline, more scintillating, more pure, and in a profound sense, more tragic. The possession of a noble style compensates for all technical incapacities and the ravages of time. It was not Pavlova's technique but her manner which was memorable. Style means mastery presupposed, authority unquestioned, an expression which is the exact equivalent of the artist's considered, gracious intent. It is economical, intensely personal, however chilly, remote, artificial even, when it remains in the grand tradition. It is the single element which heats the quality of an ordinary technician into that of a great artist.

The ideas that were becoming, after they had created some masterpieces, increasingly inert in Russia, were theatrical ideas, insomuch as the dance is but one province of theater. But they were ideas too limited to the single province, having no reference even to another form, close to ballet,—the Opera Ballet. In Russia, as in France, it was a frankly inserted divertissement, and could be counted on, when all voices and tragics failed, as a drawing-card. In Dresden, however, and later at Bayreuth, Richard Wagner proposed ideas which, having their immediate effect on opera stagecraft would influence every other allied theatrical realm, including declamation, stage-architecture, lighting, mise en scène and the dance.

It has been said that music as such did not primarily interest him, except as an accidental approach to an ideal synthesis. He learned composition, overcoming the handicap of a lack of any natural musical predisposition. His entire effort was towards *Gesamtkunstwerk,* a collective art-form, in which music, to be sure, would play an important part, though only a part. His actor-singers had to move and act. Yet how? He must have known that the work he gave a singer to execute to the best of his vocal ability would preclude his moving with much expressiveness. Ideally speaking, music-drama must have a double cast, singers and dancers. As for 'dance,' Wagner hated it, insomuch as he thought it meant opera-house dancing. The only dance he considered worthy of the name (useful to him) was mimicry. That at least did not consist merely of arm and leg movements, but was a vital expression of the whole body. "Mime is the immediate expression of the inner life, and it is not only the sensual rhythm of sound, but the spiritual rhythm of the word which gives its law. . . . The harmonized dance is the base of the richest masterpieces of modern symphonics." Wagner insisted that an artist must be at once dancer, poet, and musician. But in spite of his intellectual comprehension of the place of dance, and even his written indications, he never developed a method for a new dance, suitable to his music-drama. Dance meant to him only bad ballet. The "Ring of the Nibelungs," as has often been noticed, was conceived in reverse. *Götterdämmerung* was first thought of in 1848 when he was full of French grand opera, with its silly divertissements and irritating pageantry.

Wagner remembered seeing one evening at the Scala a ballet pantomime of 'Antony and Cleopatra.' The climax was the interment of the Queen's mummy, a pretext for an extensive evolution of the *corps de ballet* in all its conventional glory. Vigano had been too long dead. The Italian public received it with a warmth which shocked the German, and he took it as a sign of the audience's general demoralization. Only color and movement of costumes and dancing permitted a long-suffering public to support three hours of vile music. Wagner's hatred of the classic ballet amounted to a passion. He never mentioned a dancer's name, not even Noverre's, whose ideas were not so far from his own; nor, of course, Vigano's. As for Gluck, of whom he often talked with admiration and who Isadora Duncan said wrote better dance-music than any one, he does not seem to have noticed that Gluck (with Noverre) reformed the dance of his epoch. He particularly hated French dancing and French dance-music, as being *contre-danse de salon* swollen up to opera-sized scale.

In his *Rienzi,* based on Bulwer-Lytton's "Last of the Romans," Wagner himself had written just such a ballet for a *Grand Opéra Tragique*. This meager scene was the only one which remotely pleased the King of Prussia, and when the piece was mounted at Darmstadt numerous cuts were made in the score to give more emphasis to the dances. Half a century later this still made Wagner nervous. He had wanted to continue the course of the action, even though Rienzi must give a fête to the people, by having as pretext for the feast a mimed episode of ancient tyranny, Tarquin's rape of Lucrece. But with his usual bad luck it was replaced by an ordinary ballet. Dresden, where it was first produced, had few choreographic resources. Wagner contented himself as best he could with two little *danseuses* "who executed a certain number of *pas"*; after which entered a dreary handful of soldiers, impersonating with shields above their heads an 'antique Roman' phalanx. Finally, the *maître de ballet* and his acolyte, in pink skin-tights, leaped up on the shields where they exhausted themselves in cabrioles and pirouettes, which was their idea of a gladiatorial combat. "It was at this moment," Wagner bitterly writes, "that the theater always burst into roars of applause."

Tannhäuser was first produced in Germany in 1845. When it was to be done at Paris in 1861 (Paris was for Wagner the focus, as it had been, in the same way, for Noverre), the director of the Opéra informed him that if it was to succeed in *his* city, it must be equipped with a second act ballet. Wagner, exasperated, was able at least to insert it in the first act. He realized it would otherwise completely destroy the coherence of action. "Why the second act? Why, indeed? Because the gentlemen of the Jockey Club never come in for the first."

We have seen how *Le Jockey* behaved over Duponchel's head. They arrived in plenty of time for the second act of *Tannhäuser*. Prompted at court, for political reasons, the royalist snobs formed a savage claque. They interrupted the performance with dog-whistles and hissing. After three presentations it was taken off. Wagner was heart-broken. But he left considerable directions for future regisseurs as to the nature of dances accompanying the Bacchanal ("My *Palais-Royal* Venus"). It was to be no ordinary ballet-ballet.

> What I see, is on the contrary, to put into practice all the resources of the mimed dance: A savage and seductive chaos of groups and movements, of softness and languor, up to the very explosions of unlimited delight. The problem, indeed, is not easy to resolve, and the drastic impression that I desire can only be obtained at the price of the most minute study of all the smallest details. On the orchestral score, the course of this savage scene is precisely indicated in its essentials, and I must beg (the *maître de ballet*) to observe them exactly, in spite of all liberties of interpretation that I leave to him.

He followed by describing just what sort of scenery and effects he wanted. When he came to *Parsifal* there were more difficulties about costumes and gestures for the Flower Maidens in Klingsor's Castle. What he actually wished, seems to us naïvely "naturalistic," rather in the style of Tiffany pen-wipers, or the *Art Nouveau*. Yet he thought it "repudiated the whole convention of opera." But in spite of his excellent stage sense, there are portions all through his music-dramas which emphasize, either by procession, spectacle, scene-transformation, or orchestral display, one important element at the expense of his ever-to-be achieved synthesis. Again it was not so much the execution, as the ideas that were impressive.

The real dance, Wagner repeated, would be in his lyric-drama, a dramatic action, just as the music of popular dancing becomes the minuet (or scherzo) of a symphony. André Cœuroy ingeniously suggests that real dances do exist in Wagnerian operas, but one must discover where they are hidden. Often they are in a simple gesture, underwriting a brandished sword, a lifted cup, a trembled veil. Often they sustain silence, when singers hold their peace; when Mime scowls, when Hans Sachs dreams, when Sigmund approaches Sieglinde. Choreography linked to action is always a sound ideal, but Wagner proposed no method for its achievement. The mise en scène at Bayreuth, in spite of Isadora Duncan's inspiration from Wahnfried, or Laban's restudying of the scores, is still grotesque. Only the synchronization of the cinema can make a real Wagnerian synthesis. With the camera, dancing could be marvelously, magically, lyrically used. The Rhine Maidens could actually dance in water, not hang like bait from the flies. Valkyrs could really ride to Valhal, without having to be little ballet-girls strapped to hobby-horses, jerked up into a canvas sunset. Sometimes later, Berlioz understood very well the Wagnerian genre of "hypocritical pantomime," a strict correspondence between music and the artist's body, where orchestration gives its sound to physical movement, where gesture is strait-jacketed into song. Vigano, unremembered, had proclaimed from his own wide experience, the uselessness of merely miming tragedies rather than declaiming them. Wagner, since music was for him but an end to a means, conceived of it as serving outside its own province an end of whose use he had no clear conception. His vague, powerful dogmas are the root of three-quarters of the misconceptions inherent in contemporary antipathy to the *danse d'école*. His idea of music serving motion is still valid. But his interpretation proclaimed that virtuosity in any element (save the orchestral, which he controlled) was wrong. It was he who precipitated the first attacks against virtuosity, since virtuosi are the highest examples of their school. In Vienna, in Dresden, in Berlin, fifty years after his death, his "disciples" were inventing, in opposition to ballet, not only a *non*-synthetic idea of dance for the sake of dance (although Art-for-Art's sake died with the nineties), but they also proposed an accompaniment for this sterile motion, entirely amelodic, consisting of percussive instruments alone. Just as Schoenberg was made inevitable by Wagner, so is Wigman. One can only blame Wagner insomuch as he did not occupy himself with practical questions of realization, of method. He was content to articulate dogma, and his pupils, developing the single element he left unachieved, seriously betrayed him. They have made the *Tanz als Tanz*, dance as dance, which is no *Gesamtkunstwerk*, nor is it in any sense, whatever else it may or may not be, theatrical dancing.

CHOREOGRAPHIC DESIGN   *Zorn:* 1857

CHAPTER XIII

The Early Twentieth Century: Duncan and the Russians

BUT a third over, this twentieth is already the richest of any century in wealth of documentation. Theatrical dancing no longer is the property of a single class or a special place. It is popular among all peoples of the Western hemisphere. In our epoch it is not so much the development of forms or techniques that will interest us, but rather, the expression of ideas demonstrated also by music, poetry, painting and architecture. The instrument of the *danse d'école* has been forged for three centuries. It still evolves in an almost daily development. But now we are occupied with the uses of this instrument, rather than its further tempering.

In the last thirty years, the lines of traditional descent and of personal innovation became almost indistinguishable in the closeness of their reciprocal effect. The method of classic stage-dancing has become so highly developed that it can not only withstand any outside shock, but in its best realization can also absorb into its fabric the most useful theories and inventions of those who invent beyond its limits. There are two perfect champions of the initial contribution of our century: the American, Isadora Duncan, and Michel Fokine, the Russian.

Duncan stands for the new West. A Californian, she always felt the great moments of her life would be linked to vast spaces of the sea. Her declaration of freedom was a real act of revolution, though like many revolutionaries she left behind her a school of weak betrayers. Fokine recreated the Russian Orient and the cream of Europe, selected by a Slavic culture neither exhausted in its own efforts towards civilization, nor satiated by Western Europe. Cradled in tradition, he evolved from a rigid chrysalis to make ballet what it had never been before. Between Duncan and Fokine, the classic theatrical dance established itself as one of the preëminent contributions of modern creative endeavor, an expression of poetic truth as powerful as rhythm in paint, verse or music itself. There is nothing in the contemporary 'modern (concert) dance' which does not stem from one or the other.

No one who has ever read "My Life" can doubt the greatness of Isadora's spirit. All the sensitive people who saw her dance in her best days, testify to the powerful emotion she evoked as a dancer. This history has tried to limit itself as strictly as possible to the forms of classic theatrical dancing, and one could construe the effect of Duncan upon a rigid definition of it, as negligible. That is, unlike the reforms of Sallé or Camargo, she contributed almost nothing to its vocabulary, in new steps, technical tricks or even a type of gesture. She did have a powerful influence on the reform of theatrical costume. Towards the end of her life she used to say all she actually accomplished was a change for the better in women's civil-dress. After Isadora, corsets could never again seem a necessity. A rigid constructionist could even eliminate her effect on stage-dress, pointing out many dancers who liberated their bodies from official uniforms long before she was born, which is true, but irrelevant. By the greatness of her living, Duncan established a kind of symbolic reference. She shone, a constant evocation of possibility. Anything, everything was possible, is possible, will forever be possible. It is her affirmation, her positive declared independence to which dancers must be grateful, even more than her ideas or her dancing itself.

The epigraph to her memoirs, she took from Nietzsche:

If my virtue be a dancer's virtue, and if I have often sprung with both feet into golden-emerald rapture, and if it be my Alpha and Omega that everything heavy shall become light, every body a dancer and every spirit a bird verily that is my Alpha and Omega.

She was born in San Francisco, the child of Irish parents. Her mother taught music to wealthy families; from her Isadora derived her sensitive understanding of a relationship between music and physical motion. They were very poor, but somehow Isadora danced herself into a precarious place in various productions of Shakespeace, or performed in restaurants. Her memoirs give no indication that she was ever in doubt of her ultimate success. She read considerably. Without any formal education, she was nevertheless by her associations and curiosity an extremely intelligent woman. She told Augustin Daly, the first American theatrical manager of his time, "I have discovered the dance that is worthy of the poems of Walt Whitman. I am indeed the spiritual daughter of Walt Whitman." Just as Whitman so often means America to Europeans, although Whitman's America never realized itself, so Isadora typified a similar breathless, expansive, divine new continent, which existed only in their hopes for it. Dancing as the First Fairy in Daly's 'Midsummer Night's Dream,' she could be found behind-scenes reading Marcus Aurelius, developing her own philosophy of stoic, blissful optimism which would make the whole world know her. Mrs. Astor invited her to dance at Newport before 'rows of Vanderbilts, Belmonts, Fishes, etc.' However, 'these ladies were so economical of their *cachets* that we hardly made enough to pay our trip and our board.' At this time she composed a dance to the entire poem of Omar Khayyám. Sometimes her brother, sometimes her sister read it aloud as she danced. They went to London. They were marvelously hungry for Europe; unappeasable, naïve and healthy. But it was by no means easy. They spent hours in all the museums.

And then one day we returned from the National Gallery where we had been hearing a most interesting lecture on the Venus and Adonis of Correggio to find the door slammed in our faces and the little baggage we had, inside, while we ourselves were on the doorstep.

But she managed to dance for the best British families, arousing the passionate enthusiasm of many of London's illustrious painters and men of letters. In Paris, there was the Louvre. Her brother started to copy 'all' the Greek vases. Isadora particularly loved the group of dancers by Carpeaux in front of Charles Garnier's Opéra, free figures so exuberantly different from the ballet-girls inside. Sadi Yacca, the great Japanese tragic dancer, made a profound impression on her in the International Exposition of 1900; and there were Rodin, and Versailles, and the grandiose city of Paris, itself, Isadora was so fortunate. She had not been spoiled by travel-lectures, by college-courses, by a pre-digested assimilation of culture's cream. She was not raised in the tradition of any school. No dogma held her down. She was as eager as a virgin for the miraculous impact of Europe at the turn of the nineteenth, into the twentieth century. We are inclined to think it was only Greece that molded her. On the contrary, it was Greece, Rome, Italian Renaissance and German Reformation; every age which left a monument of distinction to enrich our world's treasure. She educated herself to be a dancer, discovering a method which best suited her unique expression.

> I spent long days and nights in the studio seeking that dance which might be the divine expression of the human spirit through the medium of the body's movements. For hours I would stand quite still, my two hands folded between my breasts, covering the solar plexus. My mother often became alarmed to see me remain for such long intervals quite motionless as if in a trance—but I was seeking and finally discovered the central spring of all movement, the crater of motor power, the unity from which all diversities of movements are born, the mirror of vision for the creation of the dance—it was from this discovery that was born the theory on which I founded my school. The ballet school taught the pupils that this spring was found in the center of the back at the base of the spine. From this axis, says the ballet master, arms, legs, and trunk must move freely, giving the result of an articulated puppet. This method produces an artificial mechanical movement not worthy of the soul. I, on the contrary, sought the source of the spiritual expression to flow into the channels of the body filling it with vibrating light—the centrifugal force reflecting the spirit's vision. After many months, when I had learned to concentrate all my force to this one Center I found that thereafter when I listened to music the rays and vibrations of the music streamed to this one fount of light within me—there they reflected themselves in Spiritual Vision not the brain's mirror, but the soul's, and from this vision I could express them in Dance.

Isadora's discovery had much in common with oriental dancing. Levinson, in his analysis of the classic spirit in theatrical dancing, makes a useful differentiation. Western dancing is centripetal; Eastern, centrifugal. That is, the West accentuates the extended silhouette, since it is primarily for display, and *to be seen,* at a distance. The East, emphasizing the visceral centers of movement as circular, moves within the enclosed orbit of the body's comparative restriction. It is *to be done,* or felt, rather than to be shown. Isadora's understanding of our organism's psychic and physical center, largely ignored up to her time by ballet-masters, indirectly enabled the *danse d'école* to extend itself, (although along its own direction,) with increased strength and expressiveness.

> I also then dreamed of finding a first movement from which would be born a series of movements without my volition, but as the unconscious reaction of the primary movement. I had developed this movement in a series of different variations on several themes,—such as the first movement of fear followed by the natural reactions born of the primary emotion of Sorrow from which would flow a dance of lamentation or a love movement from the unfolding of which like the petals of a flower the dancer would stream as a perfume.

Few people have thought or felt as profoundly as Duncan on the sources and uses of lyric movement. It is all the more remarkable that she should be so methodically curious, young as she was, free from any academic standard, lacking in practical background. Noverre and Vigano, she never knew. Their stages were the theaters of Europe. Hers was the wide world's horizon, with stars as lamps; the universe, not only as audience but as actor-dancer too. Her vision was no less vast for its being supported by a sweet sense of immediacy, however vague. She freely took and generously gave. Her whole presence, not only her dancing life, was open to activity. The capitals of Europe patronized her but never spoiled her. Lovers were merely another aspect of her education. She was at heart always, what she said of Walt Whitman, (though both suffered sensationalist attacks,)—New England Puritans.

She read omnivorously in the archives of the Paris Opéra, filling notebooks with her researches. What other great woman dancer, (and here is no wish to dim the fame of Taglioni or Pavlova,) has ever been so well informed? Which of them ever doubted their teacher so profoundly, on such excellent basis? "I realized that the only dance-masters I could have were Jean-Jacques Rousseau (*Emile*), Walt Whitman and Nietzsche."

A manager from Berlin came to offer her a thousand marks a night. She would be magnificently presented; *Die Erste Barfuss Tänzerin:* The world's first barefoot dancer. To his amazement she flatly refused under any such billing. As he left, she added:

> I will come to Berlin one day. I will dance for the country-men of Goethe and Wagner, but in a theater that will be worthy of them, and probably for more than a thousand marks.

Her prophecy was fulfilled. Munich had been waiting for Isadora. The lovely provincial capital with its marbles from Ægina, its gates and museums designed by votaries of Olympia and Florence, home of the *Secession* whose models were realistic fauns and human centaurs, adored her. The Grand Duke Ferdinand said: *"Ach wie schön ist diese Duncan!* . . . Springtide is not so fair as she," when she inaugurated that bathing costume which since became a universal dress for swimmers. She composed the tragic story of Iphigenia, "her farewell to Life on the altar of Death." Always she worked and observed, and worked her observation into dancing.

At that Villa in Abbazia there was a palm tree before our windows. It was the first time I had seen a palm tree growing in a temperate climate. I used to notice its leaves trembling in the early morning breeze, and from them I created in my dance that light fluttering of the arms, hands and fingers, which has been so much abused by my imitators; for they forget to go to the original source and contemplate the movements of the palm trees, to receive them inwardly before giving them outwardly.

Whether it was the 'Primavera' of Botticelli, in front of which she sat for hours to make a dance, the tragic acting of Mounet-Sully in *Œdipe,* listening to Gluck in Paris, or hearing a *viola d'amore* play Monteverde in a Florentine Palazzo, Isadora's direction lay towards Greece. Hellas was the source, an ultimate life-spring of her dance. And if Duncan did not understand Greece, as we think we understand it, what with the benefit of research, the uncovering of archaic periods with which we have replaced the age of Phidias, nevertheless she meant and still means Greece to the people of her generation. She was more vitally Greek than crumbling Parthenon or the shattered gods in the Elgin Chamber. She was Samothrace in the flesh; a sudden, long-desired yet unexpected apparition of an ideal, affirmed since the Renaissance, yet never so revivified, so made new as now.

Again, the question of novelty. Was Duncan after all so new? Once Goethe was a guest at the British Ambassador's in Italy. At his Villa in Caserta a beautiful young Englishwoman danced and posed with extraordinary grace. Emma, Lady Hamilton, had seen antique marbles in Naples. As she moved, she draped two gossamer shawls about her, calling her husband to hold candles behind her, so that she seemed a goddess dancing in a windy halo. Sallé was once Galatea. Loie Fuller, a Chicago girl, intoxicated with the marvels of electricity turned Edison's genius towards stage-illumination. No accomplished dancer, she nevertheless swathed herself in yards of luminous veils. Lights thrown on them created snakes of brilliant motion. Her 'Serpentine Dance' with its diaphanous, ethereal rainbows, astonished Europe. Years later, the Irish poet Yeats remembered

> When Loie Fuller's Chinese dancers enwound
> A shining web, a floating ribbon of cloth
> It seemed that a dragon of air
> Had fallen among dancers, had whirled them round
> Or hurried them off on its own furious path.

Isadora met her in Berlin. She wrote a charming, generous, comic description of *La Loïe,* and her troupe of 'beautiful but demented ladies.' But she was quite clear as to Fuller's contribution:

Before our very eyes she turned to many colored, shining orchids, to a wavering, flowing sea flower, and at length to a spiral-like lily, all magic of Merlin, the sorcery of light, color, flowing form. What an extraordinary genius! No imitator of Loie Fuller has ever been able even to hint at her genius! I was entranced, but I realized that this was a sudden ebullition of nature which could never be repeated.

In a very great measure Isadora was an original artist; her own work benefited and suffered from the very isolation of its originality. Loie Fuller may have impressed Duncan, who had already draped herself and her stage in simple folds of light or heavy stuffs, but there was no direct 'influence' as such. Similarly, the nineteenth century had been excited by various pedants and earnest amateurs, like Maurice Emmanuel or Mrs. Richard Hovey. By careful reconstruction from vases or reliefs, by comparison with ballet and with nineteenth-century Attic or Albanian folk-dancing, they comforted themselves by imagining they actually discovered the lost Greek dance. Isadora read everything. She was not ignorant of their efforts. But her way was not through archæology but in the air of Athens, among ochre pillars of broken sanctuaries, packed dancing-floors which were once threshing-floors.

> The sun was rising from behind Mount Pentelicus, revealing her marvelous clearness and the splendor of her marble sides sparkling in the sunlight. We mounted the last step of the Propylaea and gazed on the Temple shining in the morning light. With one accord we remained silent. We separated slightly from one another; for here was Beauty too sacred for words. It struck strange terror into our hearts. No cries or embraces now. We each found our vantage point of worship and remained for hours in an ecstasy of meditation which left us weak and shaken.

After Greece, Isadora returned to Europe and could name where, when and for how much she would dance. She brought ten little Greek choir boys whose singing of the hymns of the Byzantine Church she felt to be in the pure antique mode. Before their voices had changed so much that she had to ship them back, they sang a chorus from 'The Suppliant Women.' Vienna, to her sorrow, received them coolly. But when she danced *Die Schöne Blaue Donau,* they sprang out of their seats with joy. She was so in love with hope, expectancy, a brimming relief in herself and in her audiences that she scarcely noticed it was not Greece they adored her for, but her waltzing vision of *Alt Wien*. If it was wonderful to have watched her, think how much more marvelous it would have been had we seen what she saw when she danced.

> I so ardently hoped to create an orchestra of dancers that, in my imagination, they already existed, and in the golden lights of 'the stage I saw the white supple forms of my companions; sinewy arms, tossing heads, vibrant bodies, swift limbs environed me. At the end of 'Iphigenia' the maids of Tauris dance in Bacchanalian joy for the rescue of Orestes. As I danced these delirious rondos, I felt their willing hands in mine; the pull and swing of their little bodies as the rondos grew faster and madder. When I finally fell, in a paroxysm of joyous abandon, I saw them
>
> > *Drunken with wine, amid the sighing of flutes*
> > *Hunting desire thru woodland shades alone.*

Cosima Wagner asked her to dance in the Venusberg Bacchanal, and Duncan shared Wagner's hatred of the classic ballet. She realized it would be preposterous for a soloist to attempt it, surrounded, as usual, by girls in short tutus. She needed a school. She needed pupils to be trained in her method. But she went to Bayreuth. She studied *Tannhäuser's* score. She realized the orgy was *cérèbrale,* that it took place only in the imagination of the Wanderer. She wrote her excellent analysis for a proposed choreography. It was not easy to work in the sacrosanct atmosphere of Festspielhaus or Villa Wahnfried. There were theological discussions as to what the Master really meant. Duncan danced. Cosima pale, almost convinced, was ready to consign to Isadora all dancing at the festivals. But Isadora was in the throes of one of her more cataclysmic love-affairs, which instead of destroying her creation, liberated every personal impulse.

> My soul was like a battlefield where Apollo, Dionysos, Christ, Nietzsche and Richard Wagner disputed the ground. At Bayreuth I was buffeted between Venusberg and the Grail.

One day, at luncheon, Isadora Duncan, the American dancer, the real source of much in one "modern" school, calmly announced: "The Master has made a mistake, however great was his genius." Cosima Wagner froze. "Yes," the new Venus continued, "the great Master has made a great error. *Der Musik Drama* is indeed nonsense." Duncan knew. Music-drama cannot be. That is, not as vaguely indicated by Wagner or as crassly executed by his pious heirs. But she articulated or at least implied a philosophy no less disastrous to the 'modern' dance, the policy of *Tanz als Tanz*.

> "Yes," I continued, "Man must speak, then sing, then dance. But the speaking is the brain, the thinking man. The singing is the emotion. The dancing is the Dionysian ecstasy which carries away all. It is impossible to mix in any way, one with the other. *Musik-Drama kann nie sein.*"

She arrived in St. Petersburg the day after the massacre precipitated by the priest-provocateur Gapon. Nijinsky's wife tells us that on January 9, 1905, young Vaslav had been walking home from school and ran into the massacre. A Cossack gashed his forehead with a knout. Isadora came into the black Russian dawn to be met by an interminable procession of coffins, victims buried in the dark so as not to provoke any further revolutionary sympathy. "If the train had not been twelve hours late, I would never have seen this.... I vowed myself and my forces to the service of the people and the downtrodden. Ah, how small and useless now seemed all my personal desires and sufferings." Sixteen years afterwards she would be asked back to create a school of her own. But now in sandals and a white tunic she danced in the *Salle des Nobles,* before a simple blue curtain, in front of all the nobility and balletomanes of the capital. Her music was Chopin. There was but a single piano, and the young soloist, untrained to do a single pirouette.

Yet even for the first dance there was a storm of applause. My soul that yearned and suffered the tragic notes of the Preludes; my soul that aspired and revolted to the thunder of the Polonaises; my soul that wept with righteous anger, thinking of the martyrs of that funeral procession of the dawn; this soul awakened in that wealthy, spoilt and aristocratic audience a response of stirring applause. How curious!

Although she was, as she said, the 'declared enemy' of ballet, she could not help admiring Mathilde Kschesinskaya, "more like a lovely bird or butterfly than a human being." She was given a box to watch Pavlova "in the ravishing ballet of *Giselle*." She applauded the exquisite apparition, "although the movement of those dances was against every artistic and human feeling." She met Diaghileff with whom she argued, defending her new dance, *the* new dance; while he, traditional ballet, to whose theater he was attached in an official capacity. Bakst read her hand, foretelling her children's death.

She could never understand ballet, even if she had wanted to. It seemed hideous, crippling torture. Pavlova's hours of exercise, the mechanic routine, the artificial idiom were foreign and hateful to her expansive, democratic, grand, vague nature. She felt

> The whole tendency of this training seems to be to separate the gymnastic movements of the body completely from the mind. The mind, on the contrary, can only suffer in aloofness from this rigorous muscular discipline. This is just the opposite from all the theories on which I founded my school, by which the body becomes transparent and is a medium for the mind and spirit.

Duncan was right. But she had no means by which she could directly affect stage-dancing except with the sunny instinctive wisdom of her personality. After the long scarf had strangled her at Nice, after she had achieved her ultimate *gloire,* and even before the end of her life, her work was only a memory. In the American Middle West, pitiful, aspiring devotees would try to recapture her spirit by teaching "esthetic" dancing. The schools of her pupils in Germany, in Russia, in New York, would give recitals which were only shadows of her violent impulse. Her autobiography is her best memorial, with the photographs taken by Steichen and Genthe. Did Duncan directly affect dancing? She surely affected the theatre. She sponsored Gordon Craig. Settings for his *Rösmersholm,* with Duse, launched this artist on his career of potent influence. She made dancers think carefully about the music they used. Not directly but indirectly, she shifted the course of ballet. Her indirect effect, however, had a positive, not negative result. She did not destroy the *danse d'école.* She corroborated its reintegrators.

If she failed to found a school, if she left no method for future development, it was because an academy, a system were in the nature of her gifts, inapplicable to her creation. She loved, felt it and danced, not only men, but the acts of men, their moral pattern and political will. It is not her fault that her visions, "I See America Dancing," of thousands moving to the finale of

Beethoven's Ninth, fostered swarms of dilettantes. But there were others, bolstered by the ancient means, who knew better than she the limits of ballet, since they were trained in it. And as much as she, they wished to revivify dancing. For them, Duncan was an heartening sign. But for Michel Fokine she was neither a source of ideas nor an immediate influence.

The condition of Russian theatrical dancing, when Fokine achieved his first efforts, was not so degenerate as it was static. Petipa but recently had completed *La Belle au Bois Dormant,* his greatest masterpiece. But it was a synthesia of the best in nineteenth-century choreography rather than a sign-post towards the new century.

When Isadora first came to the Ballet School of the Marinsky Theater, Fokine was twenty-five years old. In 1898 he had graduated and was an outstanding male dancer in a company full of able technicians, an expressive mime where the Italian canons had deadened his less imaginative colleagues. His masters were Platon Karsavin (father of Tamara, author of *Theatre Street*), Volkov, Gerdt, Christian Johannsen, now an old man but a living encyclopedia of the academic dance. Fokine inherited the best of the traditional past; by theory, from his instructors; by practice, from performing important rôles in the ballets of Petipa, Saint-Léon, Coralli and the rest of the nineteenth-century repertory.

Next to performance the most instructive process for a dancer is teaching. Inventing daily combinations of various routine exercises provides practice as useful as finger-exercises for a pianist, or counter-point problems for a composer of music. Fokine in 1902 started to teach classic ballet technique to the junior class of girls in the Saint Petersburg School. Still a great teacher, he is less known as a great dancer. Yet he surpassed even Nijinsky in certain parts which he created for himself, but which the Pole made famous in Western Europe. Fokine was one of Anna Pavlova's first partners. He gave to the genre of the male dance something positive, virile, the peer of the feminine, a position it had not enjoyed since the days of Vestris.

It would have been enough for Fokine to have taught, danced, received considerable local fame and retired. This was the normal course indicated for an artist of his gifts and background. But he had a different nature and another destiny. He was inquisitive, philosophical, well-educated in fields other than the dance and had ideas of his own. The contemporary state of Russian theatrical dancing disturbed him as much as it did Duncan; if not more so, at least differently. He was a Russian, a master of the *danse d'école,* a theatrical artist, occupied with a theatrical art. Duncan's interest in theater was incidental. It was merely a frame for the expression of her attitude towards life in general. Fokine, on the other hand, worked daily in the small, intense, official, musty world of the Imperial Theaters, which was under the personal subvention of the Tsar's privy-purse, under the personal jurisdiction of an Intendant close to the *Ministère de la Cour.* The position of a first dancer in the Marinsky Theater before the war (just as in the Bolshoi now), was an almost diplomatic though non-official position. But in 1904, Fokine was preparing to thrust cobwebs aside.

"Why," he asked, "in an Egyptian ballet were the dancers in ballet costume and the supers in the dress of the period? Why did a certain dancer execute such and such difficult steps, what were they intended to express, for surely if dancing were not expressive it became acrobatic, mechanical, and meaningless? Why in ballet was a psychological feeling always expressed by a fixed gesture or a series of gestures which neither described nor symbolized anything? Why must the arms be always rounded, the elbows always held sideways parallel to the audience, the back straight, and the feet always turned out with the heels to the front? Why was ballet technique limited to the movements of the lower limbs and a few conventional positions of the arms, when the whole body should be expressive to the last muscle? Why did a dancer rise *sur les pointes* not to convey the impression that she was rising from the ground, but in order to astonish the audience with her strength and endurance? Why was the style of a dance always inharmonious with that of the theme, its costume, and its period?" But to each question he received the stereotyped answer: "Because it is tradition."

Every question, every implied reply, might have been proposed and answered by Isadora Duncan, with this difference. Duncan *felt* the staleness of the schools. Fokine *knew* wherein that staleness lay, and how to effect a change through existing channels. Duncan, in attempting to destroy all tradition at one glorious blow, proposed not method but emotion to take its place. Fokine, using given instruments of excellent material, put them to uses for which they were well-fitted, but for which they had never been employed. In his historic letter to the Director of the Imperial Theaters, appended to a ballet libretto based on Longus' 'Daphnis and Chloë,' Fokine enunciated his principles, demands for reform which, at first ignored, were within five years to triumph from Petersburg to Paris.

The new Noverre stated and had shown that it was impossible any longer to form automatic combinations of ready-made steps. One must create a real expression to fit a given libretto's subject. No longer could one put together a string of *pirouettes,* a series of *fouettés, glissades* to right and left, ending with a *tour en l'air* or an *entrechat six* and call it anything but an exercise, or a brilliant fragment without meaning. In other words, every new ballet demanded a new technique, conditioned by its *style,* music and meaning.

Nor does dancing or any kind of mimetic gesture have any significance, except to describe dramatic action. Gestures could not longer be used as a mechanical handshake or a mechanical bow, the formalization of empty stage usage or theatrical habit.

Conventionalized gesture can be used only when the *style* of the ballet demands it. No longer can movement of the best alone do service for the immobility of the rest of the figure. The whole body from head to toes is a dancer's instrument.

Groups and dancers in ensemble must be used expressively as a whole and not merely as a symmetrical decorative screen for three soloists. When a *pas de trois,* for example, was about to begin, the rest of the *corps de ballet* formerly bustled brashly off the stage, leaving it free for the bland emphasis on one, two or three technicians. Fokine insisted on a participant troupe.

Finally, there must be an unbroken alliance between dancing and the allied arts in music and painting. Special ballet-music, which measure for measure follows the beats of the feet is not necessary. Music of any fluency, if suitable, is useful. And, as for costumes, no longer can a strip of tartan across a tutu, or a thistle behind one ear be sufficient to represent a Scotch peasant girl. Archeological sources must be respected as the only sources for the *style* of a ballet.

Fokine was not to be *maître de ballet* of the Marinsky Theater until Diaghileff's great Paris seasons established his fame even beyond doubts inspired by official jealousy in Petersburg. But he continually composed ballets, if not for the large theater, at least for pupils in the schools, or for charity performances, employing his fellow-artists in the Imperial company. Although his first real work was set on a stage two months after Duncan's apparition in the *Salle des Nobles,* although its subject *Acis et Galatée* was Greek, there is no reason to assume they shared a common attitude about Hellas. To Duncan, Greece was day-spring. To Fokine it was a *style* to be mastered, an epoch to be reinterpreted, in contrast to the silly conventions of Petipa's Greek-keyed tutus. Fokine went to the library; he studied Schliemann and German "reconstructions" of Troy, Athens and Mycenæ. The Greece of Alma-Tadema, of Sienkiewicz's "Quo Vadis," of Bulwer-Lytton's "Last Days of Pompeii" or Frederick Leighton's "Homer" was, at the root of it, his Greece. Perhaps we think him naïve to have depended so touchingly on his own epoch's archeology. But remember, he was destroying a century of inadequate, icy inertia. The 'scientific' approach to antiquity, however debased Græco-Roman or Hellenistic hang-overs were, was a powerful weapon. T. S. Eliot says that any dramatic revival of a past period tells us more of the times in which they are produced than the time which they attempt to reproduce. Fokine, in the body of thirty years of constant work has never invented a single ballet with a contemporary subject. Does he disdain the present? Is it an 'escape' into the past? Not exactly; Fokine was brought up in a period (from 1900 to 1914) when the 'past' was more actual, more keenly felt than everyday events in Petersburg, London, or Paris. His past was Persia, India, Egypt, "Old" Russia, Georgia, the Venice of Veronese: Viennese Biedermeier or Le Nôtre's Versailles. In this he was enormously aided by collaboration with Leon Bakst. Nowadays, it is fashionable to ignore Bakst, or to treat him as a rather quaint vulgarian, an attitude resulting partly from the propaganda by art-dealers and painters of the School of Paris. Later, Diaghileff would use easel-painters as stage-decorators. They were the best of their day and, to be sure, Bakst was a bad enough easel-painter. But he was a stage artist whose sense of theater places him with

Lully's Bérain, the Bibienas and Noverre's Bouquet. At the time of Bakst's death, Paul Morand wrote of his work in the light of later, non-Bakstian ballets, which in 1925 seemed more impressive than they do in 1935.

> It is true that his art is too often vulgar, barbaric, effective only as a blow between the eyes; but such as it is, it has now become an historical city, books, and music.... It has been said that it was a Jewish art, with its emphasis upon raw tones, its passion for gold and precious metals, its dearth of line, its nomadic origins, its Oriental sensuality, its contempt for architectural construction. Bakst was, in fact, a Jew; and it was the great Israelite audiences that established the success of the Russian Ballet, that first great international success, marked by the boldness of the audience's dress, its immodesties, extravagant coiffures, depilated bodies, cosmetics, by that mixture of all modes to the point where one could not always distinguish between the house and the stage.

If it was Bakst's violent color, it was also Fokine's violent motion. There is no need to rehearse the plots of his familiar ballets. Generally speaking, they can be divided into four categories, all *ballets d'époque;* Greek, oriental, Russian, and a hybrid style of the Franco-Viennese from 1750 to 1830. There have been others. Lately he has essayed the periods of François Premier, the Aztecs, Spain and China, but with less of his former choreographic invention. The particular quality of his sensuality, his feverish (if to us literary) 'passion' has most flourished on the Arabian Nights, Greek or Slavic legends. He repeated his success in dilute version time and again, for twenty years. "Carnaval" weakened to "Papillons" and "The Affairs of Harlequin," "Scheherezade" faded to "Islamey"; "Cleopatre" was a gaudier parade, but less consistent than "Thamar,"—another legend of the *femme fatale, Le Pavillon d' Armide,* served for the short *La Rêve de la Marquise.* After *Acis et Galatée, Eunice* and *Narcisse* comes *Daphnis et Chloé* with Ravel's music, the best of his Greek series.

It may be useful to know what contemporary audiences thought of the different types of Fokine's ballets, not only in themselves, but as background for choreographers who followed him. He was the first to whom every historic style seemed an opportunity for dancing. The *ballet d'époque* was primarily a decorative, if accurate as possible, resurrection of a time past. Their dramatic intrigues of love and death were almost as conventional as the noble intrigues of eighteenth-century gods. In Noverre's days it was chiefly the conflict of 'passions' that was important. With Bakst and Fokine, the conflict of color,— the contrasting palettes were rendered more intense by whatever the plot happened to be. Disassociated from their chronology, their original scenery, from the first shocked audiences, lacking Fokine, Karsavina, Bolm, Nijinsky or Vladimiroff, Fokine's ballets seem tame enough now. But by every indication, *Daphnis* was a remarkable work divested of any heat of sensationalism. The rhythmic patterns were fluent and varied, some in a complex of $\frac{5}{8}$ tempo. Fokine's patterns were extremely ingenious matching Ravel's counterpoint with a mobile, asymmetrical complexity, unknown since Vigano. The première of *Daphnis* was obscured, even defeated by Nijinsky's scandal over his 'Faun.' Of all Fokine's forgotten work it should most surely be revived. It was a tribute to Greece not as a denial of Petipa, or a manifesto in favor of bare-foot dancing, but rather as a deep understanding of the bucolic lyric atmosphere which the tale of Longus still holds. It was Fokine's final definition after three previous essays. His sketches, *Acis, Eunice, Narcisse,* were forgotten. *Daphnis* was an independent evocation. The critic Robert Brussel said:

> I do not know whether *Daphnis et Chloë* is what is termed a "manifestation," that is to say, whether it reverses present opinion, or reveals a depth of humanity hitherto unknown. I only know that it is, or at least I believe it to be, a marvelously gifted and tender work full of suggestion; it presents the most agreeable scenes and incidents which evoke deep feeling, for the ballet is the work of a poet and an artist. This gives the whole an exceptional character, rather than any surprising detail, which doubtless would not fail to arouse ecstasy. Thus its title *"symphonie chorégraphique"* need not astonish us nor cause us to misinterpret its purpose. *Daphnis et Chloë* is a ballet and in according it this title I have no wish to offend its authors or lessen their merit. To renew a form which has served as a model, to infuse new life into material about to perish, is a more difficult, a more useful work, than to aspire to the exceptional with mediocre means and to create a fashion rather than solve an artistic difficulty.

It will be a long time again before dance composers are safe to ransack the orient. Fokine's 'Scheherezade' bred so many bastards in films and vulgar extravaganzas that it is now almost impossible to understand the astonishment of the first Paris audience. To a public accustomed to the pallid eroticism of romantic French orientalists, safely insulated in novels, the fresh vision of Fokine's half-naked slaves and almées seemed only pornographic. Nijinsky was a prune-colored savage animal; Rubenstein white, plastic flesh, Cecchetti's half-obscene miming as the Eunuch, the frank abandon of the orgy, not on toe-shoes, nor in corsets, had a reality, an immediacy more exciting than as a photograph. Now, when we see it there is little to admire except the oddly symmetrical (to us) movements of circle against circle. Fokine could not control his imitators, but so many of his 1750 or 1840 *ballets d'époque* were essentially of *his* epoch; 1910, 1912, 1914. In 1935 they mean little save as illustrations for a history of women's fashion, which was continually affected by Bakst's designs.

The Polovetsky Dances for Borodin's *Prince Igor* are another matter. Because part of his work has faded past recognition, no one can ignore the range of Fokine's invention. His choreography for 'Igor,' with its remarkable balance of masculine and feminine choral elements in the dancing to balance the two voices in the music, is still (when well-danced) strong and challenging. Fokine created the Tatar war-dances out of whole cloth. There was no precedent for such monumental virility, such sensitive acrobatics. In 'Thamar' the character dances from the Caucasian provinces are not as thrilling and less well integrated into the dramatic action. Just as Fokine drew on every historic period, so he could conceive in every idiom of the dance. Duncan was illiterate in the folk-expression of Spain, Italy, Georgia or Hungary. It did not occupy her, for she was not primarily a theatrical artist. Fokine was equipped with a basic knowledge of what hard or soft soil, what syncopated or broken melody, determined by geography and social background constructed the dances of the world's people. No modern choreographer can afford to know less, yet there are only a half dozen who know as much. Fokine was accused of reducing the male dancer to the position of an hermaphrodite, a superficial criticism. Nijinsky's Rose Specter became a symbol for the 'Russian Ballet,' but it was not typical. *Les Sylphides* used only one man, frankly androgynous, but the *style* required it. Incidentally, *Les Sylphides* shows, on consideration, more the *effect* (not the *influence*) of Duncan than a mere pastiche reminiscence of Taglioni or Grisi. Watch the Duncanesque arm-movements, so beautiful in Fokine's feminine partitions, so wooden in most of his predecessors. Fokine composed equally well for men and women. Among his greatest rôles,—the Polovetsky Chief, the Comte de Beaugency in *Armide,* the Slave in "Scheherezade," Harlequin, Petrouchka, all are male.

In "Petrouchka" the chosen epoch was nearest his own time and people. For all intents and purposes it might be our present. As a matter of fact, it is Admiralty Square in Moscow or Petersburg, in the 'Butter Week' of 1830. The collaborating painter is not Bakst, but Benois, a Russian of predominantly nineteenth century French taste. The subject is close to the tragic farces of the Commedia dell' Arte. Already Fokine had invented 'Carnaval' (in which Nijinsky became famous as a Biedermeier Harlequin). Even in their own youths, Benois, Fokine and Stravinsky had seen street-fairs with show-booths framing the familiar Punch and Judy figures of Petrouchka, Ballerina and Blackamoor. Petrouchka is Russia's scapegoat, a sacred fool, who is also the wisest man, her Pierrot, Puck, Kasperle or Tyl Eulenspiegel. He is the ridiculous, hapless butt of the nation's typical bullies, the spirit of innocence and childish disaster. A Russian legend capable even of Marxian interpretation, it is an international myth as well. Momentarily, Benois forsook his Versailles, and Fokine, his Greece and Persia. Stravinsky, at the start of a career inextricably linked to the ballet, imagined

> A puppet suddenly released, who by cascades of diabolic arpeggios, exasperates the patience of the orchestra, which, in its turn answers him by menacing fanfares. There follows a frightful racket, which, coming to its paroxysm, ends by the sad, plaintive fading-away of the unfortunate doll.

It was specifically ballet-music not program-music like Strauss' "Tyl," but a dramatic score as important as its choreography in a complete performance. The world created was that Russia which the ballet's initial audiences loved best,—an immediate past, almost their own or their parents' childhood, an atmosphere of gypsies, organ-grinders, moujiks in from the provinces, uniformed coachmen of the Muscovite bourgeoisie, nurse-maids, drunken nobles, street crowds all sharing a tacit if fairytale democracy under the falling snow. It was almost a Slav challenge to the previous Hellenism and Orientalism of Bakst. It would precipitate him, and his followers, into a more Nationalist expression.

When we see "Petrouchka" now it is *not* the "Petrouchka" of Fokine except by the remotest courtesy. As done by such a company as the Monte Carlo's, the street crowd is recruited the day before its troupe hits a new town; without rehearsal, merely rudimentary directions are given how to cross and recross the stage. The dances were originally created, like costumes fitted, for Nijinsky, Karsavina and Bolm. If dancers today can execute the steps, we are grateful. As for acting the subtle, complex rôles, expressing the nuances of meaning, there is scarcely a mime in the West who is up to it. Far better to restudy "Petrouchka" for a small company, a small crowd, than to pare it down past recognition just as Stravinsky's music is spoiled by being played by shabby, undermanned, overworked orchestras. Similarly, remember that "Scheherezade" and "Thamar," even "Les Sylphides" of the Basil Company, is *'after'* Michel Fokine. It is Massine's or Grigorieff's readaptation, as far as the limits of their memories go. No ballet can be imagined as accurately presented unless its choreographer is also a *maître de ballet* of its dancers.

In essence, and if well-danced, "Petrouchka" is not only Fokine's masterpiece, but with its strong plot, a consummate ingenuity in combining the classic idiom *sur les pointes,* character-dancing, mass-movement and pantomime, coherently employed in a synthesis, is a standard for dance-drama in our time. The bustle in the orchestra before the curtain rises is the reflection of the shifting crowd when the fair is revealed. We do not see dancers, but only people in the streets. Yet, it is not long before we realize these folk could only be dancers. Fokine invented an orderly hurly-burly, an underlying, invisible pattern of pushing and shoving, interrupted by fragmentary *entrées* of nurses, coachmen or gypsies. The old Charlatan, before his show-booth, points ominously to the pendent dolls, and with his sinister wand taps them into life. The virtuosity of that first trio, soloists supported by their arms in air was a courageous use of acrobatics ten years before the music-halls of Paris, London or New York affected the ballet as we know it. Red and tinsel Moor, symbol of luck and the South, who prays in toy-homage to his coconut god; flirting ballerina, a cruel trumpeter; above all, misformed, ugly, straw-stuffed Petrouchka, changeling of the North, fool of the world's Charlatan, of all handsome men and lovely ladies, are characterizations which give the richest rewards to their ablest interpreting artists. Of the choreography, André Levinson wrote best, when he saw a revival of it, ten years after its Paris début:

The first, the grand manner of Fokine has been the *parody* in and of (classic) choreography. Those dances which we were shown in the rustic dances of the first scene, and then of the puppet-ballerina, are an ironic deformation of ballet steps—while nurses, postillions or maskers gain by grotesque exaggeration, imposed by the master, on the movements of folk dances.

For the dolls, in the interior scenes, the method is different. Petrouchka is a puppet constrained by a mechanical, limited angular movement. But Petrouchka loves. This makes him almost human; he tries to express himself. This determines his sorry sport on the stage. In vain the soul flutters against an armature which imprisons it, unable to free itself; the fervent gestures come to naught, and fades again into the automatism of a doll. And this *dualism* in the movement, poignant and abrupt, controls the breath of a whole audience. Finally, there's the crowd of Fair folk which revivify the old Saint Petersburg. This crowd wanders *freely,* grouping itself according to the accident of the action without occupying itself too much with the musical rhythm: The sonorous fresco of Stravinsky serves it simply as a background. But suddenly the danced episodes break in, designing themselves and then losing themselves in the gay bustle.

"Petrouchka" was composed in 1911. What has Fokine done since 1914 to add anything to his stature? He has lived in America sixteen years. Italian nepotism at the New York Metropolitan Opera kept him from being its *maître de ballet,* surely his due. He was asked to return to Russia, but had his own reasons for not going. Fokine's style, his most famous ballets, were formulated before his association with Diaghileff. Yet when he left the atmosphere generated by that great catalyst, he failed to find a more nourishing one. To be sure he was busy. In Russia, before 1917, he worked with Meyerhold on a production of Gluck's "Orpheus." He created several new ballets. He taught many American dancers. He made seasons for Ida Rubenstein in Paris. Fokine's greatest labors were achieved before the war, in a period of his almost imperialist assimilation of historic styles. His *ballets d'époque* made what almost amounted to a new technique, necessary for the adaptation of every period. Knowing the classic theatrical dance so well, he could best afford to be cavalier with its treatment when needful. This he has always been. Dancer, reformer, choreographer, the Russian Ballet could not have existed without him.

Nor could it have existed, in an entirely different way, but for Serge de Diaghileff. Since his work was correlation, discovery, presentation and propaganda, since he was neither painter, poet, musician nor dancer, his exact position during his lifetime was often obscure, and since his death it has tended to become mythical. Diaghileff was such a complex personality that it will need the accumulative testimony of all his collaborators before a final estimate is achieved. He affected through the medium of ballet, every field of art in his time, including painting, architecture, interior decoration, clothes and literature. Without his back-drops, the School of Paris might have always remained the obscure local movement into which it is rapidly relapsing. But what did he do, specifically, for theatrical dancing? Two things, among many others. He provided a hotbed of collaboration for the most distinguished energies of his epoch. He gave a form to the one-act danced dramatic-poem which for lack of a better term can be called the *ballet-ballet*.

Petipa's ballets were three acts and many scenes long. They occupied a whole evening. When Diaghileff first took the Imperial Russian troupes to Paris, there were on the program none of the full-length works from the Marinsky repertory. "Igor," for example, was the danced scene from Borodin's long opera: "Sadko" was the under-sea scene from one of Rimsky-Korsakoff's. "Carnaval," *Spectre,* "Sylphides," were divertissements previously arranged for special occasions. Even in the times of Rameau or Lully we have seen how unwilling the French were (and French taste can be considered Western European taste) to sustain dancing unrelieved by frequent breaks. Diaghileff rather catered to the French predilection for vaudeville. Also a short form was both economical, easy to mount, and enabled him to build a variable repertory in a short time. Nowadays, with our habit of underestimating Diaghileff's contribution, we should like to watch at least two acts of a consecutive subject. In Russia, even with their most recent choreography, they still demand at least three more acts. Diaghileff's cutting tended towards a treatment which in its best uses was compact, but in its most frequent, trivial. There was literally not time enough given for the development of a grand theme. A "long" ballet, like "Petrouchka," is only some forty-five minutes. We recall the *Ballet Comique de la Reine* lasted five hours. We have no wish to revive it. But nevertheless, no intelligent audience needs a talk every twenty-five minutes. Diaghileff would have answered: That depends on the audience. He was a master, among his other provinces, of audiences. The audience of the Russian ballet in Western Europe was one of its most indicative marginal phenomena.

In the beginning there was the court, the *haute bourgeoisie* and diplomatic corps, habitués of the Marinsky Theatre. This was a discriminating, if over-familiar training-field. The Russian ballet that we know was never seen by Leningrad or Moscow after 1914. As early as 1900 Diaghileff's name was not heard kindly in official theatrical circles, for he was a menace to the bureaucracy. He soon realized his activities would have to be acclaimed abroad before they could be appreciated at home. While he was still abroad, the war came, and he never returned. The Soviets invited him to come back in a good position, but he feared he would be unable to leave Russia again, once within her borders. The Franco-Russian Entente arranged between Poincaré and Isvolsky unquestionably aided Diaghileff to show the Russian ballet to France in 1909 as a propaganda gesture of good-will. Backed at first by the government, he was later supported by his audiences, or rather by those wealthy few who could afford the pleasure of patronizing such a man. We can imagine that even if *Le Dieu Bleu,* the Cocteau-Fokine-

Reynaldo Hahn ballet on a Hindu pretext was not ordered by the Aga Khan, it at least was intended to please him. But do not think Diaghileff inclined to simple flattery. It was not necessary. Such disinterested rich men as Dimitri Gunsbourg preferred to lavish their money on the ballet. When Diaghileff took in two million gold francs in a single season, he spent three, if not on present expenses, then on future prospects.

Audiences before and after the war were different. Emphasis shifted from Paris to London. The premières had to be in Paris, but England supported the company. Similarly the troupe changed. Fokine, Nijinsky, Bolm, the great generation bred at the Marinsky, passed. The creative interest shifted from the choreographers to painters and musicians, since Diaghileff had no school to give him new dancing technicians. He was greatly responsible for the Ecole de Paris, *after* it was well launched by the initial efforts of Picasso, Matisse, Derain and Braque. In the beginning, from 1912 to 1914, he ignored Montparnasse. There could have been, by later standards a Rousseau *le Douanier* or a Modigliani ballet but then, as far as decor went, it was entirely Bakst or Benois, till the 'Russian' revival began with the collaboration of Roerich, Larionov and Gontcharova. The Russian ballet ceased being Russian, and became international, with the arrival of the Picasso-Cocteau-Satie *Parade* and the Paris painters. But their paint was rather a compensation for lack of better dancers. At the end, his company was inferior, though he had brilliant choreographers. His later ballet-masters were seriously affected by having to work with inadequate material. Music, Diaghileff particularly loved. His initial success in Paris, even before the ballet, was producing the great Russian music dramas "Boris" and "Ivan the Terrible" for the first time in the West. Towards the end of his life, he was reviving the operas of Gounod and Cimarosa. He kept to ballet since he was famous for it, and since it displayed young men whom he admired, more than for any essential belief in the dancing. How could he, with half a dozen exceptions, believe in the dancing? He had known the greatest possible dancing. He had made of its preëminent figures his personal company. Now since they were gone, and he was separated from the source of new material, the situation had altered. When there was no longer the fascination of superb individual or ensemble performances, there was his particular invention of interesting collaboration. The right painter, Juan Gris, or Marie Laurencin; Braque or Matisse; the right musicians, Stravinsky or Poulenc; Prokoviev or Auric; the right costumes, Chanel or Schervachidze were exposed to each other with his tact or his caprice, and the results were, more often than not, sensational.

His younger collaborators, since his death, accuse him of every conceivable betrayal. He sacrificed dancing, they say, with some truth, to paint or music. He encouraged weak talents, giving them an importance by contact with his prestige which they could not survive. It is true of every strong character that they are often a solvent. Minor talents he projected were at least given a chance. It was not his fault if isolated they failed. His audiences became more and more androgynous, impatient and insufferable. But the end of his life coincided with a post-war crop of British and French ambiguous, perennially adolescent enthusiasts. He polarized their enthusiasm, to be sure, but he was not responsible for their manners. Towards the end he was ill and tired but his dominant energy, his essential aristocracy, his profound distinction and human generosity warmed every one who had any contact with him. The present writer never did, but on many occasions some dozen of his collaborators have imitated him, not together, but singly. Each time, the imitation is identical; a surly grandeur, the magnificent snarl, the staggering, penetrating, shrewd instinct. Some of them, for their own reasons, even hate his memory, but in their creative lives, they are never free of his shadow. If he had gone back to Russia perhaps he would have accelerated sooner the inevitable Soviet progress. It is unimportant. For the West, he was the benevolent despot of an artistic empire, under whose auspices, from 1909 to 1929, the best, almost the only classic theatrical dancing was achieved.

Diaghileff came increasingly to be known as a purveyor of novelty, a presenter of the extraordinary. In the beginning the very transporting of Russian dancers to French theaters was in itself a sensation. Later, it became necessary to invent sensations of his own, or rather to electrify the surrounding air sufficiently so that artists breathing it became dynamized. The first great sensation which had its immediate origin away from Russian soil was the choreographic experimentation of Vaslav Nijinsky. There is neither necessity nor place here to expatiate on Nijinsky's qualities as a dancer. His wife's book is full of marvels, about his personality, his accomplishments as a performer, his tragedy. As a great dancer, perhaps the greatest Western dancer who ever lived, he might have added some new expressions to the idiom of ballet, and it would have been enough. But his contribution was far more. It is in the realm of choreography, in the theory of dancing that he should particularly interest us.

His contribution is hard to define with certainty. Its sources are mysterious. Yearly, memoirs appear which serve to deepen rather than to clarify an already confusing picture. His wife, in spite of her seriously discredited accuracy, more clearly understood the nature of his attempts than any one else. In his four ballets, something entered dancing which was not there before, which has never left it since. If, as Stravinsky, Ansermet and Fokine tell us, there was little originality in his composition, why was the quality which appeared in his work not manifested by them, either separately or in collaboration, before or afterwards?

Nijinsky quickly went mad. He was a Pole, not a Russian, and although he spoke Russian from birth, he always had difficulty expressing himself. His wife could not have had more than a couple of years of actual talk with him, since his French and Hungarian were inadequate. When he was with Diaghileff, the intellectual weight of the older man completely over-balanced whatever attempts at verbal formulation he might have essayed. It is convenient for many reasons for Cocteau (who knows perhaps more than any one), even for Fokine, for his other colleagues, dancers and musicians, to keep either a deprecatory silence about his creative expression (apart from his dancing) or to flatly run it down. Also, none of it is left to be seen, except in photographic fragments.

Nevertheless, the present writer, after some study of availing remains, after discussions not only with his detractors but with people who knew and loved him, firmly believes that great as he was in the province of the per-forming dancer, he was far greater as a practicing choreographer, in which function he either demonstrated or implied theories as profound as have ever been articulated about the classic theatrical dance. Not only was he a pro-vocative philosopher of the dance but he was also an immediate source of a kind of gesture, which for twenty years, disguised under dubious and numer-ous aspects, is increasingly known as "modern" or "concert" dancing.

His first essay at choreography was a short danced poem on Debussy's "The Afternoon of a Faun." Stravinsky, in his memoirs, implies Nijinsky was wholly unmusical, and could scarcely tell one note from another. It is natural, that in comparison to the greatest musician of our day, even the greatest dancer might seem so. The orchestral conductor, Ansermet, corroborates this. Stravinsky credits Leon Bakst, who designed the decor and costumes for 'Faun,' with indicating "even the slightest gesture," of the quality of its movement. Bakst had been to Greece and Nijinsky had not. He had executed a large canvas called *Terror Antiquus;* in it he placed an *archaic* stone figure like one of the enigmatic sixth-century Apollos found under the Athenian Acropolis which was almost a manifesto intended to replace the Alma-Tadema vision. The favorite Greek epoch of Fokine's *Narcisse,* or *Daphnis* (like the Greece of Walter Pater) was Phidian or Hellenistic, and, generally speaking, in a late nineteenth-century attitude. Now 'Faun,' considered as a *ballet d'époque,* was archaic Greek. The gestures were neither soft nor fluid, but abrupt, angular and monumental as in Sixth Century kraters and vases. 'Faun' can be interpreted as a conscious or an unconscious negation of all previous ideas of Greece, including Ravel's, Bakst's and Fokine's *Daphnis,* produced (and slighted in favor of it) in the same year. But the most imme-diately impressive thing about 'Faun' was its *not* being a *ballet d'époque,* or if so, only incidentally. It was an essay in a different type of movement, newly conceived and executed.

Even in "Petrouchka" dances were *inserted* however ingeniously when-ever called for by the decorative plot. The dances, of gypsies, grooms, or nursemaids, were linked by pantomime, expressive and natural, but never-theless, they were "entries" and "variations." 'Faun' was no ballet by these standards. Rather, a series of related plastic poses, on a single plane, like an animated bas-relief, no movement was made which was not significant for its absolute kinetic succession. There was no *pretext* for dancing. It was all a coherent fluid activity built logically within its own terms, a denial of everything in ballet-idiom. But more remarkable, since Fokine had already used gestures against ballet-idiom, was the new consistent quality and employment of gesture, neither imitating Persian, French nor Russian "styles," as in Fokine's denials, but synthetic and coherent in itself. To be sure, archaic Greek vase-painting and reliefs may have been a source, as far as Bakst went. But its result was not by any means motivated *tableaux vivants*. Nijinsky understood even its *style* better than Bakst. His back-drop was painted with a vague, splotchy, impressionist landscape, which confused the brusque profiles of Nijinsky's movement. As to allegations that Nijinsky was unmusical, he bitterly complained of the liquescent sonorities of Debussy, alien to the crisp angularity of 'Faun's' poses. Nijinsky left Bakst, Debussy and Greece behind. He conceived a poem in movement, in the best sense abstract and lyrical. His gesture intensified the given atmosphere (early Greece, adolescence, the human-animal or whatever) by designs specifically conceived for the given problem, without consideration of traditional ballet technique or historic style, which even if unfamiliar, as the Greek sixth-century was to 1913, nevertheless was in the course of theatrical tradition.

Fokine said Nijinsky took this type of movement from his own satyrs in a *Tannhäuser* "Bacchanal" previously done for the Marinsky Theatre. Fokine's fauns do move with a similar bouncy step and in profile. But this is not a profound criticism, granted a common Greek source. Before Nijinsky, no one, neither Fokine, Duncan nor Noverre, had conceived of movement simply as movement. Even Duncan thought of it as expressing Duncan. Pantomime, we have been told, should respect its "natural" manual origin. But movement was considered as a kind of plastic cement, in which 'dance' and "pantomime" could be inlaid. Now movement with 'Faun' was used for the sake of its own interest alone. This was a huge affirmation. Yet for Nijinsky it was only an initial step. Unfortunately for his later imitators and diluters, who never realized he was the root of it, movement for the sake of movement became a kind of fetish. Nijinsky used it to cleanse his tradition which had become lush and over-decorative. From this necessary catharsis, he, not they, progressed.

Nijinsky had been the Spectre of the Rose. His personification of luxurious "grace" and easy "beauty," his final miraculous leap had become as famous and irritating to him as the first great accidental flight of an aviator. It was not only the "beauty" in *Spectre* that was oppressive, but its whole lineage of suave, honeyed gesture from which theatrical dancing could not seem to free itself, even by exposure to the ruins of Athens, Egypt, Persia or Rome. Cocteau, with his usual lucidity, remembers Nijinsky at the time of the creation of *Sacre*.

When he is at home—that is to say in the Palace Hotels where he bivouacks—this young Ariel frowningly examines folios, and revolutionizes the grammar of gesture. Badly informed, his modern models are not of the best; he makes use of the *"Salon d'Automne."* Too familiar with the triumph of grace, he rejects it. He seeks systematically the opposite to which he owes his fame; in order to escape from old formulæ, he hems himself in with new ones. But Nijinsky is a moujik, a Raspoutine; he carries in him that fluid which stirs crowds, and he despises the public (whom, however, he does not refuse to gratify). Like Stravinsky, he metamorphoses into strength the weakness of whatever he derives his inspiration from; by means of these atavisms, this absence of culture, this meanness, this *humanity,* he escapes the German danger, the system which desiccates a Reinhardt.

It was not a *new* style he sought, but a new *means* for any style, of which he might afterwards make use. Convenient as it would be for us to assume his clear comprehension of the cleansing process he undertook, all reports seem to show that, at most, he was little more than half conscious of its significance. For him, the doing was sufficient. For us, after it has been done, it is of the greatest importance to realize exactly wherein lay the revolution he wrought.

To discover any absolute truth about innovation in the field of ballet is as difficult as penetrating into some secret shrine. Not only are subsequent choreographers envious and jealous, but they themselves forget, if indeed they ever knew, what is their borrowing, what their invention. They are surrounded with dancers who created famous rôles, and each feels a proprietary, almost a protective interest in their sources. They subconsciously feel (even if they know the truth), that there must be no betrayal even to a disinterested historian, and perhaps it is no more than an academic question. But take the case of the influence of the ideas of Jacques-Dalcroze on modern ballet. There was a definite influence. It deeply affected Nijinsky. Yet although Romola Nijinsky wrote it into her husband's biography, it was excised by her English editors. In Haskell's life of Diaghileff, the facts, as if shameful, are still omitted.

Emile Jacques-Dalcroze is a Swiss. He was born in Vienna in 1865. At the age of eight he came to Geneva where he later studied music at the Conservatory. In Paris he worked under Delibes; in Vienna under Brückner. He was a practicing teacher, composer and critic of music, and in 1892 became Professor of Harmony at Geneva. He was seriously disturbed, as Fokine had been in his field, over the deadly inertia which crippled musical appreciation and musical education. In the nineteenth century, music assumed, with Beethoven, Wagner, Brahms and the rest, an almost holy aspect. Its prestige commanded the authority of money and influence. But to an increasingly predominant degree musical 'appreciation' was mechanical, false, in that deepest sense, unmusical.

The students were taught to play instruments, to sing songs, but without any thought of such work becoming a means of self-expression, and so it was found to deal with the simplest problems in rhythm and that their sense for pitch, relative or absolute, was most defective; that, while able to read accurately or to play pieces memorized, they had not the slightest power of giving musical expression to their simplest thoughts or feelings, in fact were like people who possess the vocabulary of a language and are able to read what others have written, yet are unable to put their own simple thoughts and impressions into words.

Jacques-Dalcroze created a method by which these abuses could be partially corrected. This is not the place for an exposition of his method, but it exists, still to be learned. From 1905 on, recognition of his labors became more and more widespread. Wolkonsky, Intendant of the Russian Imperial Theatres, was enthusiastic about the Dalcroze principles, but his dancers, regarding them as dilettantism, were not affected. Similarly, Anna Pavlova employed a Dalcroze instructress, who was unable to impress her company as she had the great ballerina herself.

Dalcroze, with remarkable intuition, felt that the rhythm in hearing, or in creating harmonies was not separate from, but rather intimately linked to, rhythm in seeing and in moving. He created bodily exercises which intensified a basic appreciation of musical rhythm by physical movement. The professors of the Classic dance assumed he was attempting to invent a new school of dancing, which he was not. Incidentally, some of his gestures may have been beautiful to watch, but they were not primarily intended as theatrical. However, if correctly understood they were most sensibly applicable to the science and craft of theatrical dancing, particularly in relation to choreography.

In 1910, Dalcroze was invited by the wealthy brothers Dohrn, to Dresden, where in Hellerau, a garden-suburb, he was built a beautfiul and complete college for the instruction of his method. In the year 1912-13 over six hundred children and adults, representing sixteen nations, were studying there. In this year, Diaghileff came to Hellerau, with his artistic collaborators and Nijinsky. They saw demonstrations of the system and were impressed. For his school festival of June, 1913, Dalcroze was preparing Gluck's 'Orpheus,' with a "rhythmic"-movement chorus. It was the first attempt to apply his theories to a lyric stage, and when achieved, created intense interest and speculation. Dalcroze was an admirer of the ballet, but he wrote of it:

> Their wonderful leaps and voltes, their impetuous gestures, their fantastic evolutions amid dazzling stage effects and flashing lights—all this gives extraordinary brilliance to their interpretations. But just as, in order not to spoil the effects of the painted scenery, their illumination is frequently compelled to dispense with the art of nuance, so—for lack of having studied those which rhythm sets up between the different degrees of energy—the Russians as a rule only interpret perfectly the violent or fantastic passages of the music

they have to express, and not the parts that indicate restrained tenderness and poignant intimacy.

Diaghileff asked Dalcroze to recommend one of his best pupils to instruct his company of Russian-trained dancers. So Miriam Rambach, a very intelligent young Polish Jewess, accompanied the troupe for their preparatory season at Monte Carlo, where 'The Rites of Spring' and *Jeux* were being composed and rehearsed. Rambach was to give instruction to the *corps de ballet* in the Eurythmic exercises of her master, which she attempted to do. The Russians, however, with an understandable, if ridiculous attitude, rebelled. They were graduates of the Imperial Academy and this presumptuous young female could not turn one pirouette. They omitted the fact that they often ignored the music to which they danced, that their sense of timing, when it was not instinctive, was often inaccurate; that their realization of the underlying rhythmic pattern was superficial. Instead, they called Miriam Rambach *Rythmitchka*. They taunted her, and flatly told Diaghileff they would not dance if she was their teacher.

Rambach and Nijinsky were both Poles. There were few people with whom the boy could talk about professional or technical problems in his creative life, upon which he was just commencing. Diaghileff understood him emotionally, but he had the great business of the whole ballet organization for which to care. Nijinsky appreciated whatever he could learn from Rambach about Dalcroze. Such a system for absolute comprehension of rhythmic principle filled a large gap in his frugal musical education.

Vigano had been famous for the closeness with which he adapted his gesture to music. He knew, however, there was no use miming tragedies instead of declaiming them. When he died, his secret (if 'secret' it was) disappeared because he had no system which survived after him, by which his method could have been transmitted. Dalcroze, a musician with the full technical information of nineteenth-century polyphony at his disposal, absorbed music wholly, creating an exact means by which others also could. It was *not* a method for literally transposing into gesture what each instrument in the orchestra played. It gave dancer and choreographer an absolute, instead of an accidental sense of rhythmic and harmonic structure. How much of the actual Dalcroze dialectic Nijinsky was able to understand in terms of theory is open to question. But he certainly understood the general complexity of implications inherent in it. As for its "Eurythmics," Levinson wrote:

> It is interesting to see what Nijinsky made of this music, defying as it does all attempts at plastic transcription. The sole aim of the dance movements he originated for the production was the realization of the rhythm. He thought of this rhythm as a gigantic force, the only thing capable of dominating the primitive soul of man. The dancers, by very simple means, became an incarnation of the various elements of the music, the respective duration and force of the sound, its quality and quantity, the speeding up and slowing down of the pace. They bent at the knees and straightened up, lifted their heads and let

them fall, stamped with their feet, insistently marking the accented notes. ...But just when this barbaric frenzy, full of the ferments and awakening passions of Spring, the intoxication of community with the divine presence in nature, was at its height, it shifted to a demonstration of eurythmics. The illusion was gone, submerged in academic dullness.

The performance, however, continued in a second scene, an episode of lyric grace. Young girls, shoulder to shoulder, dance an old round with the angelic affectation of Byzantine saints. They single out and greet the virgin, chosen to be the victim of the holy rite. The ancients surround her and invest her with sacrificial robes. Then in this magic circle, the victim, until that moment motionless, wan under her white fillet, begins the death dance. And I recall Marie Piltz, facing calmly a hooting audience, whose violence completely drowned out the orchestra. She seemed to dream, her knees turned inward, the heels pointing out,—inert. A sudden spasm shook her body out of its corpse-like rigor. At the fierce onward thrust of the rhythm, she trembled in ecstatic, irregular jerks. This primitive hysteria, terribly burlesque as it was, completely caught and overwhelmed the spectator.

His new ballet had for its score Stravinsky's "Rites of Spring." This orchestral partition which precipitated a revolution in the field of music as important as Nijinsky's in the field of dance was, for its time (and still is) of the utmost rhythmic subtlety. The suavities of Tschaikovsky and Petipa no more applied to what was here indicated than brick bearing walls to a steel skeletoned sky-scraper. A new dancing language was needed. Directly or indirectly, Dalcroze gave Nijinsky a weapon without which he could not have achieved his masterpiece. The reasons for the deliberate omission of Rambach's historic service in the published books are hard to guess. With the commencement of the War, Miriam Rambach changed her name to Marie Rambert. Over the last fifteen years she has done fine work fostering a national English Ballet. She adopted the *danse d'école* whole-heartedly, and some of the best English dancers have been her pupils, among others, Nijinsky's eldest daughter.

As for the epoch, in which the "Rites of Spring" was set, this also was a definite break. Bagdad, Versailles would soon be rejected for Russian fairy tales. But as yet, it was not ikons or the bulbous domes of Saint Basil's. It was Nicolas Roerich's researches into the remote past of the Slavic race, before the Balts or Tatars came. Anthropology, not archeology, provided this atmosphere. In the 'Afternoon of the Faun' Nijinsky indicated a naïve, archaic, pre-legendary mood by a sophistication of movement, restricted to a single mobile plane. In *Sacre* he used not one plane but the whole dimensional pattern of the stage surface, to demonstrate the birth of human activity, by instinctive rituals inherent in primitive tribes. His wife tells us:

> The dancers shiver, tremble, and vibrate at the entrance of the Seer. Later come emotional values in the movements of the dance of the Chosen Maiden. Her leaps, her jerks, are the ultra-modern descendant of pirouettes and *entrechats*

of the classical school, and their choreographic value is the same. Nijinsky contradicts the classical position by making all steps and gestures turn inward. The choreography was the most amazing and correct visualization of the score. Each rhythm was danced, the counterpoints were built up choreographically in the groups. It is through rhythm, and rhythm only, that the dance identified itself with the music. The rhythmical counterpoint is employed in the choral movements. When the orchestra plays a trill on the flutes, movements thin out, and so do the dancers. Then the tune begins on woodwinds two octaves apart, and on the stage two groups of three dancers each detach themselves from the lines and dance, corresponding to the tune. The mouse-like shuffling of the Sorceress, the rapid steps of the young men, correspond to the musical expression of the movement as the intricate rhythms of the joyful dance of the Chosen Maiden. At the end of the first tableau great circles (women dressed in scarlet) run wildly, while shifting masses within are ceaselessly splitting up into tiny groups revolving on eccentric axes.

In one sense, Nijinsky reaffirmed the classic *danse d'école* by annihilating it. Whenever a violent revolt is precipitated against traditional form, the result is more often an opposite, rather than a basically different phenomenon. When one throws a coin into the air, heads up, it comes down, tails up; there may be a new face, but it is the same coin. The symphonic design of the *corps de ballet* in *Sacre* had been prefigured by Noverre, Vigano and Fokine. But now, instead of tension, extension, elevation, feet turned-out, Nijinsky used relaxation, hugged-in shivers, jerky shakes, sub-human vibrations and feet turned-in. Just as Fokine took the credit for the quality of the Faun's angularity, maintaining it imitated his satyrs in the *Tannhäuser* Bacchanal, so after *Sacre,* he saw in its abrupt, broken, spasmodic movement an echo of Petrouchka's puppet-life, jerked on invisible wires. Perhaps Nijinsky, like every other genius, did use whatever he saw. The new freedom of his rôle in 'Petrouchka' may have corroborated his instinctive direction towards released movement. But it was more than an imitation of a puppet that evolved into the activity of *Sacre's* tribal ancestors. It was Nijinsky's new understanding and use of elements even though they may have been already at hand. The grotesque, ugly, brutal and the strong he wielded like a weapon, not to destroy the past, but to open up through thickets of inertia, a new landscape of future possibility. It was even more than a destructive or even a creative impulse that aided him, however necessary and forceful they may have been. He presupposed, as well, all the technique of theatrical effect inherent in the Classic ballet.

We have seen such "modernization" for twenty years, in fact ever since Nijinsky's *Jeux.* But not before. Search through the repertory of the Marinsky Theatre, scarcely one ballet can be found even with a basically contemporary mood, to say nothing of gesture or style. To be sure we can find a few odd exceptions, where "modern" explorers *à la* Puccini discovers Egyptian mummies (come to life), or where ballet-girls with tunics taken from the Preobrajensky regimental uniform, 'evolute' in their short tutus with military formations.

But a ballet seemed to demand removal from the world inhabited by their audiences outside the theaters. The stage was affected by the society of its time, but at one remove. Now, Nijinsky took in *Jeux* a frank departure, not into the temporal past or geographic distance, but into immediacy. *Jeux* was called a "tennis-ballet." His only partners, Karsavina and Schollar, wore sport jumpers from Paquin, he, himself, a soft white shirt, tie, and flannel trousers, buttoned at the calf, not our tennis-slacks but an adaptation of the classic-ballet-practice uniform. The tennis-racket he held at his entrance, the tennis-ball tossed onto the stage at the curtain's rise and fall tended to confuse the issue again. The English, sticklers for sport, took it all with a stubborn outrage. A tennis-game could not be violated so abstractly, merely as pretext for dancing. As for Nijinsky, it could have been golf, swimming or polo as far as the pure element of *la vie sportive* went. Tennis, to him, was merely a symbol of the contemporary playful attitude in manners and society, towards personal relations. It was no longer a harem-queen stabbing herself over the body of a smothered slave. It was youth, and two young girls, "a plastic vindication of the man of 1913," in an emotional trio of every possible combination or cat's-cradle of flirtation.

> The scene is a garden, at dusk; a tennis ball has been lost; a young man and two girls are searching for it. The artificial light of the big electric lamps that shed fantastic rays about them, suggest the idea of some childish game; they sulk without cause. The night is warm, the sky is bathed in a pale light; they embrace. But the spell is broken by another tennis ball which is mischievously thrown in by an unknown hand. Surprised and alarmed, the young man and girls disappear into the nocturnal depths of the garden.

As for the dancing:

> The choreographic movements in *Jeux* were stylized, and were on the same principle as *Faune*, only in this network the frieze was alive and moved in space, the gestures were split up so that it would give the impression of many small movements consecutively following each other as they logically developed, and through this it gave the impression, as some called it, of a *ballet cinematographique*. Each limb made a different movement and followed a different rhythm.

The atmosphere evoked in *Jeux* was not exotic, but emotional. It was not remote but immediate. Debussy's music, written for the occasion, was paralleled by gesture which bore the imprint of Dalcroze. Debussy as a master-musician was as contemptuous of Dalcroze's musical ideas as the Russian dancers had been of his choreographic ones. Both treated Dalcroze as a competitor, which was beside the point. Nijinsky either understood (or instinctively felt) his principles far better than his own colleagues or the composer of *Pelleas* who wrote to his friend Jacques-Durand on September 12, 1912, that the end of *Jeux* was very difficult to get right, for the music has to convey a rather *risqué* situation. But of course, in a ballet, any hint of immorality escapes through the feet of the danseuse and ends in a pirouette.

Debussy was still thinking of *ballet* in terms of the nineteenth century, while Nijinsky created in the twentieth. Yet Debussy's orchestral score was completely in harmony with Nijinsky's ideas. The music critic Vuillermoz wrote of the orchestral partition of *Jeux:*

> This supple music, always prepared for sudden movements, is extraordinarily nimble. It is constantly on the alert like the tennis players it describes. Every few bars, its movement and color changes. It quickly abandons a design, a timbre, an impulse, and rushes off in another direction. Presently, the melody is returned with a skillful back-hand stroke; the theme, dextrously taken, is sent to and fro in volleys or half-volleys, now taken on the rebound, like a cut ball.

In photographs, at least, his gestures resemble action sketches drawn by Paul Thevanaz to illustrate Dalcroze's theoretical texts. But where Dalcroze was inventing exercises to educate the whole being of the ordinary sensitive person, Nijinsky on this base, invented gestures, steps, combinations only possible for a highly trained theatrical artist, grounded in the *danse d'école*. *Jeux* was angular, more so even than in 'Faun.' But it was not a denial of the classic ballet. In fact Nijinsky attempted to dance on his toes in it, gaining by this greater extension an accentuation of its underlying geometry. Toe-dancing for men is rarely successful, although possible. Nijinsky rejected it for himself in rehearsal, since he found he could realize the same effects better on flat-feet, without it seeming an effeminate overtone. Nevertheless, here we find Nijinsky in the midst of creating a 'modern' vocabulary, perfectly willing to use in an unfamiliar manner, the essence of the traditional school. Like all genius, he was intensely conservative. That is, he wished to preserve from the best of the past everything applicable to his present. He wasted nothing. He condemned nothing in the enthusiasm of ignorance, which at first sight might seem intrinsically bad, but which, more profoundly understood could be realized as merely badly used. It was not Dalcroze alone, which made *Jeux*. Nor Nijinsky alone, nor Nijinsky the classic dancer of *Spectre* or *Giselle,* but every one of these components. Duncan's triumph was, in its esthetic negation, a personal affirmation. Nijinsky's esthetic and personal affirmation presupposed a technique shared only by those who are ready to submit to that most rigid discipline, the *danse d'école*. Before he went insane he had planned a ballet to the music of Bach, which was not to be a costumed evocation of *Le Grand Siècle,* like Fokine's *Pavillon d'Armide,* except incidentally. By its rhythmic comprehension it would have independently erected the atmosphere of grandeur, authority and nobility, clothing the music of the splendid period in which it was written. Nijinsky's vision was essential and lyric, never stylistic or decorative. He soon tired of the angularity of 'Faun,' of *Sacre* and *Jeux*. He proposed another kind of move-ment, endlessly circular. Even the proscenium arch was to be round: the stage curved, the motion fluent, infinite, unbroken; no beginning, no end, only the flux of kinetic forces, visually, theatrically imagined.

Nijinsky believed that the permanence of his reputation would rest not upon his fame as dancer, or even as choreographer. Photographs still show him to us in a way which we can never recall Vestris or Taglioni. His ballets are forgotten. We are told authoritatively they were so confusing even to the dancers that after half a dozen performances they again became almost improvisations. Stravinsky, in rather an excess of pleading, assures us that the choreography of *Sacre* was not at all what he wanted. But Nijinsky wrote a book, primarily a system of simplified choreographic notation, which he felt would make his name forever living to dancers centuries after him. Since the time of Arbeau, Beauchamps and Feuillet, dancers had been occupied with trying to devise means whereby their steps would not be lost. In the nineteenth century the Franco-Russians, Saint-Léon and Stepanov, the German, Zorn, had conceived various systems of *Stenochorégraphie,* but the signs could not be generally read. It was still primarily a question of the use of visual memory.

Nijinsky proposed a system which could be, ideally, as easily read as music. That is, a ballet would be preserved, similar to an orchestral score. Steps were on staves, like musical notes, each one referring to a master-key. The master-key was a ball divided into segments. Taking the human body at its greatest extension, he described a network of circles, tangent to stretched arms and legs, which became in three dimensions an imaginary sphere tight-massed with every possibility of movement within its extremities. He col-laborated with a physician in order to make it anatomically feasible. Not only dance-movement, but motions for sport, industrial activity, physical ex-ercise, could be simply recorded. He worked on it before any possibility of widespread recording by a motion-picture camera was promised. It has never been published. When it is finally edited perhaps it will seem as obscure as Feuillet or the rest. But from its formulation can be derived canons and theories of movement which are more revealing than any conceived, up to the present. Since dancing is a visual (and aural) art, it is impossible to de-scribe it in flat words. When critics describe a dancer they find themselves speaking not directly but in images, parallels as close as possible to the vision itself, without being identified with the vision. In musical criticism, quotations from the score, or marked phonograph recordings may be used to show dif-ferences and similarities. In dancing we only have emotional reactions, anec-dotes, or decorative paragraphs, most fallacious and useless of analysis; at best photographs, good enough for style,—but for motion, wholly static. Per-haps through Nijinsky's system, a new attempt can be made to provide ob-servers with a method for clarifying to a large public, the real nature of dancing, to destroy for example the widely spread error that dancers actually improvise their movements as they go along.

At all events, even if no stenographic means of notation is ever made practical, we are indebted to Nijinsky for his attempt. Confused perhaps, often vague, surrounded by a tangle of strong influences which he had little or no experience in assimilating, even insane, he nevertheless was possessed of an articulate curiosity about the roots of human physical activity in its theatrical uses, not shared before him either by scientists, dancers or choreographers. Nijinsky did not destroy the *danse d'école* even when he invented exercises Petipa would consider crippling. He did not eliminate the possibility of the *ballet d'époque,* though the style of *Sacre* as "style" was wholly inimical to Fokine. As Isadora had in her amateur way made every possibility an ideal if unrealized standard, he as a professional creator in tradition, made it an absolute, methodical realization.

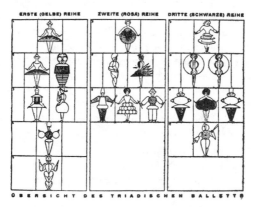

THE TRIADIC BALLET   *Schlemmer:* 1923

The Contemporary Classic Dance

THE influence of the war of 1914 on classic theatrical dancing is important but not easy to determine on account of its paradoxical effect. The War precipitated the Russian revolution, yet traditions of the Marinsky Theatre in renamed Leningrad, or the Bolshoi in Moscow, the old capital made the new, were not destroyed. But, by a series of inevitable historical accidents, the war caused a suspension of dominant creative energy in the Russian dance, which only now, after nearly twenty years, is beginning to reassert itself. The Russians in Western Europe, under Diaghileff ceased being Slav to become international; or rather, with Paris as their headquarters, the Russian dancers expressed ideas of the western world through painters, poets and musicians there resident. In Russia, the new government continued ancient policies which led to a constant supply of excellent classic technicians. Diaghileff, never having time or money to found a school of his own, and therefore lacking a troupe of great executants, called on the talents of collaborators in the allied arts beyond the strict realms of dance to eke out this lack. Ballet in Russia, maintaining a pre-war proficiency in remounting the established repertory, was not basically affected by the revolutionary changes in her destiny, to such a degree, for example, as her moving-pictures. Yet the Diaghileff ballet, by no means so proficient as the Soviet's, reflected immediately from year to year the society which supported it. The situation in Russia was logical, healthy and comparatively uninteresting to any one but a balletomane. The displays in London and Paris were brilliant, fragmentary, and doomed only to an immediate interest. The past was still useful to them and could be refurbished for twenty years more. But for Paris there was to be no limitless future, the way indicated in Russia and America.

Diaghileff's great company recruited from the classes of 1909, 1910, 1911 and 1912 from the Imperial Petersburg and Moscow schools fell away around 1916, as far as a working entity went. Many who sailed with Nijinsky to America stayed, to teach or dance alone. Others were in Russia, unable to rejoin the company after war had been declared. Diaghileff took refuge in' Italy and Spain, with a skeleton company, waiting for the war to end. He was not idle.

The history of the classic dance from 1900 to 1917 is to be found in a succession of choreographers, rather than, as in the nineteenth, the careers of individual dancers. In Russia, after the death of Petipa, there was only Fokine at the Marinsky Theatre, and Gorski in Moscow. Unfortunately the latter was destined to a purely local fame. Fokine created heroically for Diaghileff for five years, returning to Russia in 1914. He was replaced by Nijinsky, who on his own, wholly without Diaghileff, invented Strauss' "Tyl Eulenspiegel" for New York, with the fine designs of the single American to collaborate with the Russians, Robert Edmond Jones. It was as if some of Diaghileff's talent for divination descended on to Nijinsky, fresh from his terrible experiences of Hungarian internment. Jones, however, young and inexperienced at the time, was the one designer in America worthy of Nijinsky's partnership. There was also an unproduced ballet which they did between them, Liszt's "Mephisto Valse." Too many Europeans, particularly the English who are entirely uninformed as to this incident, are willing to assume there was little of interest in "Tyl"; that it was a failure. This was not by any means the case. In it Nijinsky indicated a new direction, not only in motion but in social ideas, of which those who followed him have never taken sufficient advantage. If it recalled, in a way, the individual tragedy of Fokine's "Petrouchka,"—in "Tyl," Nijinsky created a more volatile and human characterization. The story of it all is told in his wife's biography. The American tour of the Russian dancers was a failure, financially, but this was not due to Nijinsky as Haskell's "Diaghileff" states. It was due to the almost deliberate sabotage of the tour's arrangement inspired by an Italian bureaucracy at the New York City Metropolitan Opera House, which feared public enthusiasm for the Diaghileff-Nijinsky combination. The Russian dancers were the first interesting attraction to fill the house in ten years. Yet they need not have feared it. No combination between the two was possible again, for the most tragic of reasons. However, the Italians in New York, holding lazily to the dead traditions of the Scala, were responsible for the inexcusably low state of the classic dance in America. Even when they mounted Stravinsky's *Petrouchka* they did not permit Fokine to direct his own masterpiece. Bronislava Nijinska was in Russia, busily continuing her brother's creative researches, independent of his collaboration. With the war in full horror, Fokine in Russia, about to leave for America, Nijinska not yet accessible, her brother mad,—what did Diaghileff do for ballet-master?

His choice of Leonide Massine might at first have almost seemed petulant or accidental. To pick a seventeen-year old boy, however strikingly handsome, not from Petersburg but from Moscow, not from an orthodox Imperial company, but primarily from a Dramatic School, was the kind of genius stroke of which only Diaghileff was capable. To be sure, Massine had danced a little but he could hardly have been included in the *corps de ballet* of the company of 1909. Now, he was trained by Enrico Cecchetti, the Italian, which was not to his advantage, if he had had the choice to hope for a pure classic style. His schooling was neither under Johannsen, Legat nor Fokine. In the beginning he was predominantly a character-dancer. Happening to be in Spain with Diaghileff he took advantage of a complete absorption in the rich school of the Iberian peninsula's native classic genre. The Moslem invasion and supremacy, propinquity to Africa, the gifts of the indigenous folk produced a Spanish dance of remarkable if limited style and brilliance. Massine mastered the Spanish school as few Spaniards know it. While such a native as Escudero has perhaps more brilliant footwork, he is only impressive in the intimacy of a small room. In the dances for the Picasso-deFalla "Three Cornered Hat," Massine translated the Spanish idiom, with amplifications, to a large stage. The type of gesture in the early Massine ballet, whether they were Russian fairy-stories, Spanish fables or Venetian comedies, show the weight of his instruction in the abrupt, angular, percussive Spanish school with overtones of Russian folk-movement. Cecchetti also taught him the antique Italian panto-mime which he has used again and again, mostly as a grotesque parody on its base. Often unsympathetic to those who prize musical lyricism as the highest quality in the classic dance, he has nevertheless an intelligence, a premedi-tated, conscious, intellectual appreciation of motion which however hard, is usually interesting. And as a dancer, he has an individual style of grandeur, which is his personal comment on the *danse d'école*.

The application of the intellect as such had not loomed large in the Diaghileff cabinet up to this point. Instinct and enthusiasm, the use of materials already at hand, or ideas already in the air, of collaborations long indicated, marked the period from 1909 to 1917. Perhaps "intellect" is the wrong word. Both Fokine and Nijinsky were actively intelligent, one well-educated, the other inherently intellectual. But with Massine, (if not directly through him, then by his aid,) a new element of poetic innovation enters choreographic conception. Before, it was chiefly the combination of dance, music, and color which made a ballet. Nijinsky commenced to direct the dancers towards ideas. With Massine and Cocteau, a new element of poetic atmosphere arrives. It is no longer story, plot or literary pretext which ties the action together; it is the lyric quality of a mood evoked, the projection of a type of atmosphere suitable to clothe ideas with which, for one reason or another, the given collaborators are occupied. To be sure the *ballets d'époques* of Fokine evoked the airs of Versailles, of Bagdad, or old Russia, but his was a more decorative, superimposed evocation. The ballets of the nineteen-twenties, increasingly *ballets d'atmosphère*, would be set in the immediate present, precipitated by the ambiguous tennis-players of Nijinsky's *Jeux*. Their evoca-tion would be achieved with the philosophical means advocated by Cocteau: "the rehabilitation of the commonplace."

Since it is still impossible in any real sense to present to a person who has not seen a particular ballet any clear idea of its synchronized color, motion or music, even with the aid of piano, photographs or old programs, the next best method is to resurrect underlying ideas prompting a production. The poet, Jean Cocteau, is the best barometer for most of the notions which inter-ested Diaghileff's audiences. As a young man in the earliest seasons Cocteau had written a brochure for Diaghileff, drawn posters of Nijinsky and Karsa-vina, spreading useful salon propaganda for the imminent Russian invasion. He collaborated with Fokine, Bakst and Reynaldo Hahn on a Hindu ballet, *Le Dieu Bleu,* not an unqualified success. Cocteau has an extraordinary gift as a writer of memoirs. Even as events happen, one can feel him instantaneously formulating them for future reference. His writing has an epigrammatic lucidity, a clean, incisive reportage which makes his testimony of historic occasions unique in the history of the arts of his epoch. Cocteau is not merely the incidental historian of the Diaghileff period. As a man of letters, as a poet living in Paris both directly and by the violent opposition he inspired, his influence on the ideas of Diaghileff's circle was large.

French audiences, since they are so long accustomed to an everyday familiarity with the arts of music, poetry and painting, since the artistic expression of their tastes has always been closer to their political lives than England's or America's, comprise a public always susceptible to manifestoes. A clique or a party will by some overt act demonstrate in favor of or against some other clique, party or principle. Nijinsky's 'Faun' precipitated a scandal which was not only a statement of new choreographic ideas, but the daily papers used it as pretext for a political fight on the Franco-Russian alliance. 'The Rites of Spring' caused a riot predominantly artistic, and later Diaghileff consciously designed the launching of such scandals as efficient advertising.

When theatrical artists work together it is extremely stimulating for them to feel the production upon which they are engaged uses material so inflammable that merely its tactful employment will detonate instantaneous and shattering explosions of ideas or influences. In his best achievements, from 1917 to 1929, Diaghileff managed to detonate several. He had prepared audiences for ten years to be accustomed to novelty. The first novelty deliberately conceived as a manifesto against the usual novelties was Jean Cocteau's, Erik Satie's and Léonide Massine's *Parade*.

Parade was first produced in 1917. On its subsequent revivals it did not seem extremely impressive. Indeed it was one of the first victims of the very school that it launched,—the cult of the contemporaneous. But any student of poetry or theater will find in this brief work many elements of contemporary stagecraft and dramatic device, here used for the first time. By 1935 they are presupposed, and yet even the most recent 'modern' manifestoes from Russia, Germany and the United States were all defined in *Parade*.

In *Petrouchka* the orchestra made noises like a hurdy-gurdy, though what it played was tunes. In the *Sacre* there was also a deliberate and full melodic content, but with a difference. It was more in the separate uses of all musical elements,—rhythm, harmony, melody—in their disjunction—that lay the novelty of *Sacre*. Nijinsky chose deliberately to accentuate the rhythmic pattern in its disparateness above any other interpretive idea. For *Parade,* Cocteau's collaborator, the composer Erik Satie, striving consciously for simplicity, tried to strip his score down to its dramatic essentials, after all the 'horrors' of Teutonic over-orchestration. He 'meant to supply a musical background to suggestive noises; e.g., of sirens, typewriters, aeroplanes and dynamos.' In the actual performance, the typewriters could not be heard.

Cocteau, aided by Satie and Pablo Picasso, wished to present a poem of ordinaries, of such usual types that only by selection, isolation and caricature are they surprised out of banality. In their escape from cliché lies our interest. The mood of *Parade* was one of the outside platforms of a side-show, portrayed also so beautifully in the canvas of Seurat, the harangue of the dime-museum barker to get the crowds to go in, the initial "Ladees and Gentle-men, I am happy to present," of the circus ringmaster. It is the mood of the worn-out repetition of all spiels, specious but tacitly specious. The audience as well as the actors are conscious of the deception, and willing to pay to be duped.

> *For Reality alone, even when well concealed, has power to arouse emotion.* The Chinaman pulls an egg from his pigtail, eats and digests it, finds it again in the toe of his shoe, spits fire, burns himself, stamps to put out the sparks, etc....
>
> The little girl mounts a race-horse, rides a bicycle, quivers like pictures on the screen, imitates Charlie Chaplin, chases a thief with a revolver, boxes, dances a rag-time, goes to sleep, is shipwrecked, rolls on the grass on an April morning, buys a kodak, etc.
>
> As for the acrobats ... the poor stupid agile acrobats—we tried to invest them with the melancholy of a Sunday evening after the circus when the sounding of *Lights Out* obliges the children to put on their overcoats again, while casting a last glance at the "ring."
>
> Erik Satie's orchestra abjures the vague and the indistinct. It yields all their grace, without pedals. It is like an inspired village band.
>
> I composed, said Satie modestly, a background for certain noises which Cocteau considers indispensable in order to fix the atmosphere of his characters.*

Cocteau had his first idea for *Parade* when he was on leave from the French Army in 1915. He heard Satie play his piano "Piece in Form of a Pear." 'A kind of telepathy' inspired them simultaneously to collaborate. Notes and sketches evolved. Gradually a score resulted. The first idea was to have each music hall turn (or in ballet terms, solo *entrée* or *variation*) introduced by an anonymous voice from a megaphone, each singing a *leit-motif* to describe the different characters.

> I then conceived the "Managers," wild, uncultured, vulgar and noisy, who would injure whatever they praised and arouse (as actually happened), the hatred, laughter and scorn of the crowd by the strangeness of their looks and manners.

It is hard to say after a work of art emerges from the collaboration of a number of minds how much was accidental, how much conscious intention during the creation. It may even seem a great deal has been here read into very little. This is possible. But even so, whatever we read into it, even in retrospect, had a determining effect on imitations and adaptations which dadaists, and later surrealists worked into their ballets.

> Subsequently in Rome, where I went with Picasso to join Leonide Massine, in order to unite scenery, costumes and choreography, I perceived that one

* The Collaboration of *Parade* from "Cock and Harlequin" by Jean Cocteau.

voice alone, to represent each of Picasso's Managers, even though reënforced, jarred and constituted an intolerable error of equilibrium. We should have had to have three timbres for each manager, and that would have led us far from our principle of simplicity. It was then that I substituted for the voices the rhythm of footsteps in the silence. Nothing satisfied me so much as this silence and these stampings. Our mannikins quickly resembled those insects whose ferocious habits are exposed on the film. Their dance was an organized accident, false steps which are prolonged and interchanged with the strictness of a fugue. The awkwardness of movement underneath those wooden frames, far from hampering the choreographer, obliged him to break with ancient formulæ and to seek his inspiration, not in things that move, but in things that round which we move, and which move according to the rhythm of our steps.

The new ballet was not well received. Many thought Diaghileff was desperate for novelty, even lowering himself so far as to play a thin practical joke on that public he used to feed so sumptuously. "In *Parade,* the public thought that the transposition of music-hall (to the ballet-stage) was a bad kind of music-hall." So people today often complain that trained theatrical dancers are "not as good as" eccentric vaudeville artists who have sacrificed every trace of expression, style or imagination to the tricky perfection of one difficult turn. *Parade* did not try to reproduce the vulgarities of a music-hall. It used its vulgar styles as part of a cumulative effect. "The Chinaman, the little American girl, and the acrobats, represent varieties of nostalgia hitherto unknown." Instead of trying to recapture the remote past, here was caught a recent past, the past of one's childhood, which, since it is still carried in one's memory, is almost a present. Marcel Proust, the greatest specialist of a past recaptured, thought the two blue acrobats of *Parade* resembled the brothers Dioscuri.

Suggestive and atmospheric in its impact rather than choreographic, *Parade* had perhaps more to do with the poetic heritage of Guillaume Appollinaire, than with dancing. It was nevertheless, in its own scale, a synthesis whose esthetic, if not whose execution, was close to the principles of Noverre and Vigano. Here was no quaintness, no archaic or exotic attractions. Instead, there was an individualized nostalgia, almost as warming. The quality of strangeness here, its particular exoticism, was a love and loathing for the immediacy of the passing moment. *Parade* anticipated the newsreel. It was based on the achieved epoch of telegraph, daily-papers and all modern conveniences. In its first performance, all the component parts seemed so diffuse as to be almost incomprehensible. The general lyric impact, however, was intense. Though dancing had been allowed to disintegrate into shuffling, painting into an artificed cubist chaos, music into carefully negligible noise, nevertheless by this very degringolade it destroyed the comfortable, overstuffed, familiar lushness of Bakst and Benois. In its exquisite snobbery, its almost ecstatic preciousness, its clever eclecticism, it presupposed the origin, rise, peak and disintegration of whole traditions in every art,—painting, music and the dance, to give accent and pathos to their perversion here. It used the factors of Realism in a hyper-, or super-real method. Though it did not draw on the war itself its disintegrated elements reflected the general break-up.

As for consequent contemporaneity, Bronislava Nijinska invented *Les Biches,* with Poulenc's music and Marie Laurencin's costumes and scenery. This was a house-party of 1924, no longer parodied as in *Parade* of seven years before, but seized in its own context, intensified in its own sophistication, to be, as Cocteau wrote, the *Fêtes Galantes* of its epoch.

> How right Stendhal is in his use of the word 'sublime'! The entry of Nemtchinova is, in the true sense of the word, sublime (no Wagnerite will be able to understand what I mean). When this little lady issues forth from the wings on her toes, in an excessively short jerkin, with her long legs, and her right hand in its white glove raised to her cheek as if in a military salute, my heart beats faster, or stops beating altogether. And then, with unfailing taste, she presents us with a combination of classical steps and quite new gestures. The most difficult sums solve themselves all alone on this slate, with the aid of the pupils' colored chalk (costumes)—white, blue, and pink....
> Next the two doves make their appearance. Two young girls in gray, side by side, but facing one another. One holds the other by the neck; the other places her companion's hand on her own heart. They are profoundly actuated by a singular friendship. They perform their disdainful dance. To the accompaniment of a stormy roll of drums and swallow-like twitterings, the dance increases in intensity, and finally leaves them crossed one behind the other, like a pair of steel scissors, and then they part—but not without exchanging, as they go off, one on the left and one on the right, a brief glance—proud, full of complicity, and unforgettable; the glance of the young girls in Proust.

The music with its rag-time parody of César Franck, boys in sashed blue bathing-suits, ladies in pink, gray and blue afternoon-dresses, all in a faded myopic feminine key combined in one of the happiest of all the ballets. It was, at least in the first season of its life, an unforgettable, however transitory, definition of the charm of contemporaneity with the contrast of tradition. The use of the grammar of the *danse d'école* in contrast and in opposition to the argot of musical-comedy dancing first achieved in *Parade,* was a formula frequently used from that time to date. Like any other attractive innovation it tended to become tediously over-employed. It served for Massine's *Matelots* in 1925, amid sweet memories of summers at Villefranche, Nice and along the Mediterranean coast. In 1933 Massine invented "Beach" with more sailors, (this time American) and more chic bathing-suits. Nijinska's *Le Train Bleu* of 1924 was the first of that special genre of Vacation specials. The tap-dancing of artists trained in ballet is no more effective than the constricted *jetés* of a vaudeville artist. The combination of the two styles requires more tact than is usually expended on it.

Diaghileff cultivated the contemporary scene and restudied the past in its terms. Archeology was deserted. Now it became amusing to revive ancient Greece through the double exposure of the twentieth century Riviera. A legend of Apollo's birth was imagined in the classic severity of Taglioni, combination of a ballet-blanc and a naïviste bow to provincial French painting of the School of the *Douanier* Rousseau. Prokoviev even contributed a twenty-one gun salute in the general direction of Soviet Russia, for Massine's *Pas d'Acier*. It had constructivist sets, electro-welding lights, komsomols, and trip-hammers. Essentially it was as much a *ballet d'époque* (1927) as Fokine's *Pavillon d'Armide* (1909-1700).

The music used by Diaghileff became increasingly trivial, the scenery prettier, the dancing more and more capricious and fragmentary. The circle of Cocteau's aides and satellites alternately turned on Diaghileff for his "vulgarity" or created for him thrilling surprises equipped with personal symbolism fresh from their private lives, fascinatingly vicious to themselves and the season's audience, but scarcely interesting for the next season or to us. In Vincent Sheean's "Personal History," a type young man of the epoch, fresh from revolutionary China, Soviet Russia, and from French imperialist war in Morocco, returns to Western Europe and finds the ballets of Diaghileff "the most contemporary expressive efforts of the age."

> They were contemporary above all in their determination to be contemporary —in their fluttering from novelty, and, when novelty failed, from pastiche to pastiche, in the consistent self-conscious assertion that this was 1924 (or 1926 or whatever year it might be).... But his (Diaghileff's) most loyal ally, in the years of this frantic effort to be contemporary, was his audience. Both in Paris and London it was a hysterically devoted audience, made up of fashionable ladies, ambitious artists or musicians, esthetic young men and others who, for whatever reason, wished to signalize their consciousness of a break with the past. It was not the largest public (it was never big enough to give the ballets a financial success) but it was the most conspicuous and the most self-conscious public then visible in either of the capitals. And on a Diaghileff first night, what with the excited recognitions and salutes, the scents and jewels, the chatter and affectations of the peacock people, you certainly get a sort of cinematographic impression of the semi-Bohemian-semi-fashionable bourgeoisie in its period of luxurious decay.

Decadent, corrupt, perhaps, yet it was an active, not a stagnant or dusty decay, nearing the end of an epoch which exhausted itself. It had been a remarkably productive epoch, judged either by Puritan ethic or historical fact. Also, Diaghileff harbored within his own circle certain young men who were on the verge of their own species of Manifesto *against* Cocteau (while owing much to him): *against* the *musiquettes:* fashionable, jazzed, parodies of *Les Six* (Milhaud, Poulenc, Auric and the rest): *against* triviality: *against* the increasingly untheatrical tendency of the Diaghileff repertory. Indeed the last two seasons of 1928 and 1929 gave notable hints of what might well have been a reintegration, towards a new synthesis, had not Diaghileff himself died.

Such a manifestation, of more interest again, perhaps, in its ideas than in its execution, was *Ode* of Nicholas Nabokoff, Pavel Tchelitcheff and

Léonide Massine (1928) *Ode,* among many other things can be interpreted as a Russian nationalist polemic against the School of Paris. The collaboration of *Ode* was not a successful juxtaposition of talents which resulted in a masterpiece, like *Petrouchka.* But Stravinsky's work as a masterpiece, stood alone, self-sufficient,—to breed no heritage but dilutions of it. *Ode,* on the other hand, in its very failure, due to personal disagreements, technical limitations and individual confusion, indicated a direction in theatrical dancing which is still useful to follow.

The musician Nicolas Nabokoff had the germ of *Ode* long before meeting Diaghileff. He originally wished to write a pure cantata or oratorio on the words of the eighteenth century Russian, Lomonosoff. This poet-peasant-scientist, a type similar to Goethe, had written an "Ode: Meditation on the Majesty of God on the Occasion of an Apparition of the Aurora Borealis." Russian musical literature has little secular choral music. Nabokoff wished to write a Russian cantata-oratorio in a specifically Russian form, just as Tschaikovsky had constructed operas on native *Romances* or *lieder.* This was a purely musical idea of an artist primarily occupied with music.

When the musician met Diaghileff, and his project for *Ode* had been explained, it was decided to theatricalize the whole thing into spectacle. Diaghileff, due to his early background, was attracted to eighteenth century Russian allusions implicit in a not exactly obscure, but nevertheless (to Paris) unfamiliar atmosphere. This was the source of initial confusion. The young collaborators, Nabokoff and the painter, Tchelitcheff, had no desire to create a *ballet d'époque* even with the benefit of a chorus.

What Nabokoff did wish to do was to create a new form of Russian cantata based on the traditional *Romance,* to provide a lyric musical score which was sincerely and seriously emotional, however consciously polemical against *Les Six,* against the *gai* or *drolle* spirit from 1923 to 1928. In the realm of theater, Tchelitcheff wished to invent a spectacle, not specifically *ballet-ballet,* but a more synthetic form capable of profounder meaning, which would combine an Aristotelian conception of pantomime, melody and dance. As a painter (and a Russian painter) Tchelitcheff's particular polemic was directed against the easel-painters of the School of Paris. He was irritated by the Diaghileff habit of commissioning designs by artists not specifically stage-decorators, to have their sketches blown up to stage-measure, preserving the too-charming quality of an accidental *croquis.* Tchelitcheff did not wish to use static paint, but instead mobile light and shadow, the cinema, fluid cloths, plastic stuffs, nets, ropes, curtains, hung dolls which merged into live dancers, and dancers who were white silhouettes in transparent suggestions of classic robes. His approach was more a sculptor's than a painter's. His color was pure, his intention deliberate and grand, rather than a parody. Decor was to move as much as music or dances. As for the choreography it was to be integrated with the scenery, not to stand out as *entrées* or individual variations. Nabokoff did not write a single dance, as such, for the original score. But Diaghileff insisted upon a last minute addition of three danced numbers, which the musician felt weakened the whole. We remember Wagner's anger at the insertion of dances into *Rienzi* and *Tannhäuser*. Tchelitcheff's, Massine's and Nabokoff's ideal was to fuse dance, orchestra, song and light, in a lyric, noble flux. All through *Ode* there was to be no single movement, melody, rhythm or plastic form suggesting "ballet-dancing," though it was all mounted in the idiom of the *danse d'école*. Nevertheless it was a theatrical definition, a dramatic convergence and contrast of figures, personified ideas, a conception (in its broadest sense),—poetical.

It is impossible for us to recapture the immediate vision of *Parade* or *Ode*. The authors of the two works would themselves protest against any attempts to revive them. They are, however, both land-marks in the history of our theatrical dance. *Parade* in spirit was a realistic or more accurately a *super*-realistic mirror of its time, insomuch as it borrowed from the objective contemporary world sights, sounds and figures which were its most apparent symbols. Police regulations forbade some of the important light effects, yet *Ode* however aborted in production, was in principle *conceived* towards a romantic, generous spirit of the best of the eighteenth, nineteenth and twentieth centuries, against the sophisticated diminishment, the self-satisfied indulgent international snobbery of the nineteen-twenties.

Though it was the most important agency for the development of theatrical dancing in Western Europe, Diaghileff's ballet was not the only one. There was considerable activity in Soviet Russia and Germany. The work of Rudolph von Laban in Berlin, particularly through his most famous pupil, Mary Wigman, unquestionably affected the tradition of classic theatrical dancing, more directly even than such a personal innovator as Isadora Duncan. That is, gestures, types of movement and grouping inaugurated by Laban and Wigman, have been freely borrowed by ballet-masters trained in the contemporary *danse d'école* and have contributed to its development. Nevertheless, since it is the opinion of this writer that Wigman is not a theatrical artist, that her school and those who, outside the ballet, are directly or indirectly affected by her, are not in the descent of the classic dance as here outlined,—it will be necessary to investigate her position as a force behind the so-called "modern" dance, only in a very cursory way.

Mary Wigman was born some forty years ago in the town of Hanover. Unlike Isadora Duncan, her greater counterpart on the left, or Anna Pavlova, on the right, she did not start dancing till comparatively late. She was primarily impelled by seeing, on a visit to Amsterdam, a performance of Dalcroze's pupils. Three leaping girls interpreted, according to his Eurythmic system, Weber's 'Invitation to the Waltz,' which also served as accompaniment for the Fokine-Nijinsky *Spectre de la Rose*. Shortly after, in Hanover, she saw Grete Wiesenthal, one of the famous Viennese sisters who in "concert" form expressed "the soul of the Strauss waltzes." The Wiesenthals before the war had been trained dancers attached to the Royal Opera Ballet. They introduced programs in smaller theaters, without a large supporting corps or orchestra. They were, however, well-trained artists, unlike a whole flock of other concert artists, (for example the Sakharoffs). Mary Wigman felt Grete Wiesenthal was the "expression of the natural lyric flow of gesture, a joy in movement *for its own sake*." Very early in her career her impulse was formulated towards *Tanz als Tanz*.

She entered the Dalcroze School at Hellerau with an earnest desire to learn everything he had to offer. However, she quickly found herself confused by inner convictions. The priority of the musical elements in Dalcroze's system oppressed her. She felt his movements were restricted by too dogmatic submission to given melodies. This was undoubtedly true. She was developing towards the *absolute* dance, and her ideas of possible movement had gone far beyond the limits of Dalcroze's simple gestures and combinations. Unfortunately for herself, however, the rejection of *all* musical support would seriously cripple her.

Breaking with Dalcroze, she worked by herself. She had a *Wanderjahr* in Italy and was deeply affected by "the powerful plasticity of the Roman landscape." The abstract fluidity of the Campagna is a new element to affect a dancer. But its rolling, monotonous, slightly varied curves remained in her consciousness. In 1913, through the wife of the painter, Emil Nolde, Wigman met Rudolph von Laban, where he worked with his pupils at Ascona, on Lago Maggiore. Laban was a powerful confused individualist dance-composer. He was a Nietzschean theorist, a Wagnerian innovator, dedicated to quasi-mystical attempts to enforce the unique supremacy of movement as movement. His researches toward the direction of movement he called "Eukinetik," indicating a preoccupation with *motion* as against Dalcroze's "Eurythmic."

Laban in his vague violence was more sympathetic to Mary Wigman than Dalcroze's learned, systematic academy. She exposed herself to his dominant energy "which fluctuated between poles of impassioned theory and uncharted creative desires,—both involved in continuous alternation, both striving for victory, yet embraced in a death-grasp." Wigman's own personality managed to survive Laban as she had Dalcroze and in late fall of 1913 she composed her first *Hexentanz* (Witch-Dance). It was a "primitive outbreak of almost raging, overflowing force, which, however, was governed by deep instinct for form and contour." It was danced without music, to accentuate all possible interest on its movement.

At the same time, Paris and London were recovering from the effects of the Stravinsky-Nijinsky 'Rites of Spring.' However confused his activity may have been, Nijinsky's choreographic invention was not a subjective declaration, nor an individual vindication. He was working with spectacular elements to evolve a theatrical poem *against,* but *within* that huge technical idiom of which he was a master. It is significant that in *Sacre* Nijinsky himself did not dance.

Mary Wigman, in Zurich, on the other hand, during the War, where she went to be Laban's assistant, dedicated herself to discovering, or rather, inventing an entirely "new" language of gesture. By a concentration on movement for its own sake, she felt she could intensify the emotional aspects of dance to an unlimited degree. She strove with persistence against considerable economic and emotional odds.

> Fatigue and exhaustion were stages through which I continually passed. Exaltation and depression gradually became alternating rhythms of my work. The most difficult thing of all was to acquire patience and to wait, year after year, without losing one's strength. Incessant experimentation...

In fact, she worked herself into a nervous breakdown. In 1918, while recovering in the Engadine, she completed in manuscript form (Laban had invented an ingenious system of stenochoregraphy) her first group composition, 'The Seven Dances of Life.' It was the beginning of her public career.

It is difficult for an individual to buck academic inertia as Fokine did, but results he achieved against tradition are partially efficient through his complete knowledge of the tradition itself. For a lonely woman like Wigman, unblessed with either conventional good looks, or any real technical background, impelled only by a dæmonic will, it was almost impossible. The results of her personal labor were entirely determined by accidental conditions of her education and self-training. Wigman did create a school of her own. Whether it was from contact with the pedagogues Dalcroze or Laban, from hints in seeing the Wiesenthals or the Sakharoffs, she understood the necessity of a systematic series of exercise. Her method was far more deliberately conceived than Duncan's. It could be taught and learned.

Her fame increased in Germany and in 1920, during the unsuccessful Kapp insurrection, she was offered the post of ballet mistress at the Dresden Opera House. The first production under her intendancy was to have been Gluck's *Orpheus,* which had been a keystone on Dalcroze's fame and which Fokine arranged for Meyerhold in 1916. But disagreements arose with the management and she never assumed her position. It is the opinion of this writer that Mary Wigman never was, and by her own nature, never could have been considered as a theatrical dancer, whatever else she had a right to be called.

When a person creates not against, but in spite of and outside tradition, there is an almost infallible risk of erecting idiosyncrasies into a system whose logic attempts to compensate for numerous lacks of information, competence or accomplishment. Unconsciously personal faults are made a virtue, considering what cannot be done as better not done at all. Personal incompetence is used as a criticism of academic proficiency, canonizing an individual brand of "Freedom" from traditional methods, so that it quickly becomes a rigid school of formulated dilettantism.

Mary Wigman doubtless invented a new type of gesture. That is, she evolved a particular quality of spasmic alternative of tension and relaxation, of thrust and pull out of the combined influences of Nietzsche and semi-oriental philosophy, the cult of madness and post-war German starvation. The Schools of Munich and Dresden both in music, painting or poetry, had always been susceptible to a certain kind of comfortable well-fed decadence partly borrowed from Aubrey Beardsley, Felicién Rops, as well as French and English poets of the eighteen-nineties. This combined with a literal, archaicistic pornography, stemming from the unachieved left-overs of Nietzsche's and Wagner's vaguer, more cosmic notions. But a new type of gesture is no more remarkable than a private choice of colors by a painter, a series of harmonies preferred by a musician, or a style or decorative detail employed by an architect. The quality of gesture is based on the idiosyncrasies of its creator. With Wigman, no matter whether it was a "mystic ceremonial," a "Hungarian," or a "Russian dance," it was first and last a frame for expressing herself. She was not expressing ceremony, Hungary or Russia. She was presenting Mary Wigman in any setting which she thought became her. Isadora Duncan was brought up in a more peaceful time, but she had also a more generous spirit. Hence her idiosyncrasy was less offensive. It was more Greek, or rather, more flowingly vital than, as it might have been, pure Californiac or American girly-girly. Anna Pavlova toured the world continually with an inferior company, no 'taste,' unworthy music, and inconsequent choreography. But somehow, neither carelessness, nor vulgarity tainted her. She was the last of the *primi ballerini assoluti*. She was the living definition of a certain genre of theatricality. She represented an artificial perfection so personally intense in reliance on tradition that her work became, even against odds, a new and remarkable force in itself. But Mary Wigman, in spite of her energy, or perhaps on account of its blind drive, always remained Mary Wigman, the German blue-stocking with a female virginal egotism which could not be masked by soul-immersion in Nietzsche, dim readings of the Bhagavad-Gita or in her half-controlled self-hypnotized projections of grief, passion, ecstasy or boredom. In spite of her insistence on 'form,' her famous compositions like 'Monotony' or 'Swinging Landscape' were without choreographic structure. They had neither beginning, middle, nor end. Similarly her prejudice against melodic accompaniment did not demonstrate any great understanding of *rhythm,* but merely a very ordinary sense of regularity. Her dances were unsustained formless fragments which depended for their effect on to whatever degree her audiences managed to identify her visceral pleasures with their own. There are always people who go to *Parsifal* or *Tristan,* delighted to emerge after the hours of sound bath 'like a limp rag,' the general effect being that of an esthetic laxative.

Her system taught a series of basic, semi-acrobatic movements for a certain period. Then pupils would be released together in a large room; percussive instruments indicated a beat and the dancers improvised on a ground work of their exercises. They could express joy, terror, grief, or whatever she suggested by simultaneous emotional telepathy. From the point of view of psychic self-indulgence, it had its dangers as well as its advantages. But unlike the *danse d'école,* it was neither brilliant, precise nor capable of repetition. It occupied sufficient muscular expenditure to rouse a satisfactory sweat. It fitted in with the epoch's loose thinking on "progressive" education and "self-expression." Since adolescents have little to express that is new, they were delighted to be given a method of systematically expressing the soul of perennial adolescence.

On the "concert" stage, Mary Wigman had success for a few seasons. Her every attempt to achieve a sustained theatrical spectacle failed. She planned a vast memorial to the war dead in *Totenmal,* (Munich, 1929), but its performance was unachieved. Wigman is not by any means unoriginal, nor incapable of being instructive in one department of dance. But for those people who are primarily interested in theatrical dancing, or artists who wish the discipline of objective lyric expression, to demonstrate dramatic ideas larger than their own frustration, she has little to offer. This little is in the personal palette of her created movements. Leonide Massine, in his *Présages* and *Choreartium* (1933) skimmed the cream off it, putting it to theatrical, that is, legible use. After all is said and done about such enthusiasts as Wigman, however difficult, complex or individually rewarding their work may be for a student to *do,* it cannot be *seen.* Visibility is still the prime standard of theatrical dancing.

The influence of Mary Wigman on contemporary dancers has been powerful, due in some degree to a much wider and more articulate public occupied with dance as an art form, than, as for example, in Duncan's day. Wigman's (and to a greater degree, Laban's) effect on male dancing is uniquely demonstrated by the supple plastic miming of Harald Kreutzberg. Wigman had as little interest in the male dancer either as partner or a supporter, as in music, where she suppressed melody for percussion. Her girl pupils modeled themselves on her to such a degree that they seemed merely younger replicas, hair, clothes and all. She could brook neither the aid, nor competition of an equal. It is significant that Wigman is one of the few first rank artists to be consolidated into the Nazi régime. Her Apologia, announced as "The Path of a Dancer," was finally published under the title of "The German Dance."

At the *Bauhaus* in Weimar, under the Republic, there was considerable activity in theatrical experiment. The painter, Oscar Schlemmer, conceived his 'Triadic' Ballet, a curiosity of the period's (ca. 1925) faith in absolute abstraction, again *Tanz als Tanz.* Photographs still give us a sense of careful considerations in the costumes. Schlemmer attempted to use the principle of the face-mask applied to the whole human body. The dancer's only function was to give motion to costumes which they supported. These were globed surfaces, springs, straight bars or hoops. They expressly denied the human aspect of the body's silhouette in a desire to achieve abstract "purity." The "purer" that is, the more lacking in side-references or allusion dance, music or paint had become, the greater contentment of these individual abstractionists. Purity as a principle was quickly exhausted since it had little interest except to the inventors of whatever ingenious expression it happened to take, other than in being pure.

The 'Triadic' Ballet was a group of twelve "abstract" dances, separated into threes. The triad colors were yellow, pink and black, corresponding to a trilogy of moods; gay, majestic or fantastic, which the motion indicated. Schlemmer reduced human expression to nullity; costume to a geometrical formula. Yet three of his costumes unmistakably are only stylized *tutus*. His chief interest was in textural contrast of shiny or mat surfaces on moving rhomboids, spheres or spirals. Dance was entirely subordinated. This is a variation, or inversion, rung on the Wagnerian heritage, a new mysticism attempting to probe a 'spatio-mathematical' realm. However sterile the actual production, due to the impact of the renaissance of the *Neue Sachlichkeit* (new-functionalism), Schlemmer nevertheless understood theater in a way Wigman never could. His address at the dedication of the new *Bauhaus* theater in 1927 strangely enough makes an admirable preamble to a reaffirmation of faith in the classic theatrical dance. He describes, no longer the entry of a machine or an intellectualized abstraction, but the reëntrance of man on the stage. In principle, it is close to the esthetic of *Parade,* and against such manifestoes as his own *Triadisches Ballet.*

> We shall perceive the appearance of the human being as an event, so that the moment the figure becomes part of the scene, it becomes a 'space-enchanted' creature. Every moment, every gesture becomes automatically of great importance. The figure of the performer stands in an empty space unclothed or dressed in white tights. In front of him is the public, watching eagerly his every movement and action; behind him is the safe background of a curtain; on both sides are entrances and exits. This same situation may be created by any one who places himself in front of a group in order to 'put himself across.' It is the situation which created the old peep-show, and it is also the probable origin of every theatrical production.

Experiment, research, innovation are enriching factors, but over the last twenty years they followed each other with such headlong rapidity that many of them, which did not die a quick natural death, were never permitted the full extent of their possibility. This was true primarily since they were outside a theatrical frame which might have made them clear to a large public. Experimentation and novelty almost precluded the creation of works which had individual importance, forbidding a repetition even one year after their début. So much energy went into declarations against tradition that we almost forgot uses to which the classic dance itself has been actually put in our own time. Yet both in Russia, Western Europe and in America, audiences are increasingly interested in ballet; yearly new developments are being made.

The contemporary period of any general history is, of all sections, the hardest to write. The wealth of documentation is embarrassing. An historian must have had actual contact with many of the described works as well as their creators. He is open to every criticism of personal prejudice. This writer is glad to be considered the partisan of one man who in himself, more than any other, unites contemporary Russia, Western Europe and America. He is largely undocumented in comparison with his three other colleagues under Diaghileff. Details in a short summary of his career are also significant illustrations in the history of stage-dancing for the last fifteen years.

George Balanchine is now *maître de ballet* of the American Ballet Company and of the Metropolitan Opera Association in New York City. He was born Georgei Melitonovitch Balanchivadze in Saint Petersburg in 1904. His father, a well known composer, has been called the Georgian Glinka, on account of his collection of Caucasian folk-tunes. Balanchine's musical background is extremely important. When he collaborated with Stravinsky, remounting 'The Nightingale' or creating 'Apollo, Leader of the Muses,' the composer could not say of him as he did of Nijinsky, that the young dancer did not know one note from another. The impulse of all Balanchine's choreography is primarily musical. If he had not been a dancer he would have been a musician.

Yet it was by accident that he came to dance. On account of an excellent physique his family, on his mother's side predominantly military, proposed him for the army. She, however, had always wanted a daughter to dance. Once, while waiting for her at the ballet-school, one of the Governors suggested the boy enter it. If he didn't advance he could always be a cadet, later. He was admitted out of one hundred and fifty applicants, with some seven or eight others of his age. It was August 1914.

At first he hated it; ran away, was returned by an aunt. He was not attractive. His schoolmates called him "Rat." No one thought he had any chance for a future career except the great ballerina, Preobrajenska, and his own master, Andreanov. The routine was similar to that Nijinsky knew, with daily lessons in classic ballet, in character dancing, French, arithmetic, Russian grammar, etc. At the end of a year he was formally assumed as a government charge.

In 1915, among the youngest boys he was chosen to dance at the Marinsky Theatre, in a performance of Petipa's *Belle au Bois Dormant*. Members of the school appeared with the *corps de ballet* who held flowery garlands while the children danced beneath. They were transported from their home in Theatre Street to the stage door by court carriages, two horses for every six children, with a footman in front and in back. When 'The Sleeping Beauty' was given there was a cavalcade of ten carriages. Ballet evenings were always, and only, twice a week, Wednesdays and Saturdays. After the performance lasting from eight to twelve, the children were fed.

As soon as he danced on the stage, Balanchine began to like school. His favorite master was Samuel Constantinovitch Andreanov, an excellent dancer and pedagogue, who had graduated with Karsavina. From him, he learned adagio and classic technique. Paul Andrevitch Gerdt, one of Fokine's masters, taught him the Italian alphabet of gesture and pantomime. He appeared as a child in the established nineteenth century repertory of the Imperial Theatres; *Esmeralda, Don Quixote, Paquita,* 'The Nutcracker,' 'The Hunchbacked Horse,' and other Petipa compositions. He was always poor at lessons, excelling only in music and religion. But it was the stage he loved the best and in one of the new ballets, Fokine's *Jota Aragonese* (1916) there was difficult Spanish character dancing to be learned. The ballet-school children were also loaned to the Dramatic Theatres for the Fokine-Meyerhold *Orpheus* and 'A Midsummer Night's Dream.' Balanchine's particular admirations as a child (which he has always kept) were the great artists Thamar Karsavina, who became a star also of the Diaghileff company, and Pierre Vladimiroff, who when Nijinsky left the Imperial Theatres in 1911, assumed his rôles, and who is today among the noblest living exponents of pure classic style.

War had little effect on the schools, except on certain days sugar was not used, for collection to be sent to the Front. In March 1917, Nicolas Romanov abdicated. Sailors came into the dormitories looking for counter-revolutionaries. The school was closed for a year, but for one year only. In the midst of revolution and civil war, ballet and opera were regularly given. A friend of Kerensky, standing on the Troitsky Bridge, amid the November cannonading of the Winter Palace, which marked the fall of the provisional government and the triumph of the Soviets, was told by passers-by that Chaliapin that night at the Marinsky, had been incomparable in 'Don Carlos.'

During the year the ballet-school was shut, Balanchine worked as a bank-messenger and a saddler's apprentice. Soon one of the former officials, Excusovitch, a Communist, was appointed head of the Academy. He was a friend of Lunacharsky, Lenin's Minister of Public Instruction. He had loved the ballet, and when he learned the theaters were to be closed, begged to have them kept open. Every day students would gather in front of the building in Theatre Street, trying to find out how soon they would be reopened. When the children finally returned to their bars and mirrors, the younger boys found little difference. Revolution seemed very interesting but they understood scarcely anything of what had happened. The most important changes they noticed were that their practice floors had to be scraped, since for a year they'd been trodden by soldiers' boots. There was also a new professor of Marxian history. And from the balcony of Kschesinskaya's palace Vladimir Ilitch had addressed the people. The place of the Imperial ballerina became the first headquarters for the dictatorship of the proletariat.

In 1918, theaters were open, and ballet performances given twice a week as usual. The school was miserably cold. There was little to eat. The government gave permission for the destruction of some wooden houses to provide fuel, and the students of the ballet-school went to wreck them, with great excitement. Schatilov, another former *valet de chambre,* also devoted to the ballet, requested the use of the old imperial carriages, so the children no longer had to walk to the theater. The stage was freezing, musicians played with their coats on, and the audience was in furs. Dancers on the stage, however, wore only their proper costumes, about as much protection from winter weather as bathing-suits. Everybody worked gladly for nothing, though it was a rare and wonderful day when they had the lungs, neck and heart of a horse for "black-stew." In 1920 Lunacharsky himself appeared and took the ballet-children to see Griffith's film 'Intolerance,' explaining its social significance. They still wore the old imperial uniforms, with two silver lyres on the stand-up velvet collars, however worn and full of holes they had become.

In the summer, a former palace of the Yusoupoffs at Tsarkoë-Selo was placed at their disposal. Nearly fifty children practiced there, for performances given for the charity benefits for Pioneer Children. Balanchine graduated in 1921. He passed his finals with honor and immediately entered the company of the Marinsky Ballet. The rules had been changed after the Revolution; now, not every one graduating from the school was automatically admitted to the State Company. At the same time, he entered the Conservatory of Music, where he studied piano and theory for three years, wishing to become a concert pianist even more, perhaps, than a dancer.

At this time Russia was almost completely separated from Western Europe, as far as the arts went. Except, that if Parisian cubism of 1917 was not immediately transmitted to Petrograd, the Russians themselves had their own independent "modernist" tendencies. Stravinsky and Diaghileff left before the war. Mary Wigman and Laban were unknown. But as far as choreography went, Moscow had a powerful experimentalist in Goleizovsky.

Kazian Yaroslavlevich Goleizovsky was born in 1892. At the age of eight he entered the Moscow school, three years later changing to Saint Petersburg's from which he graduated. He returned to Moscow as soloist, performing the famous 'Blue-Bird' variation in Petipa's 'Sleeping Beauty,' as well as the rest of the classic repertory. But he was primarily occupied with choreography. He composed a ballet on Poe's "Masque of the Red Death," and made attempts at breaking up the official inertia which existed in Moscow. Fokine's influence was felt less here than even in Petersburg. His ideas on the dance were revolutionary, and at first seemed to coincide with the political revolution. In 1919 he was permitted to form the Moscow Kamerny ballet in which dancers from the Bolshoi Theatre appeared. It existed till 1923. His personal system, in spirit was plastic, emotional; conspicuously erotic. Historically as far as innovations in gesture applied, he was ahead of his time (that is arriving first and independently before similar researches of the Central Europeans), but he was not an easy person with whom to work however brilliant his ideas. He wore long hair in the fashion of the romantic poets, with heavy finger- and ear-rings, and was highly temperamental. In 1921 he came to give a concert in (what was not yet) Leningrad. Balanchine saw the performance in the old Dverenskayi Sobrani (The Hall of Nobles). His program consisted of his own compositions based on Debussy's 'Faun' (Nijinsky's has not yet been seen in Russia), and on pieces after Scriabine, Ravel, Medtner and Strauss' 'Salomé.' His dancers were almost naked, and created a scandal. Balanchine was much impressed. He met the Muscovite after his concert, almost the only one to congratulate him. He wished to open a school with Goleizovsky to teach his 'New' Dance, but nothing came of it.

Already Balanchine had composed an 'erotic' ballet of his own to music from Rubenstein's *La Nuit*. In those days *erotic* was synonymous with *modernistic*. The students who danced it were not upset by its 'eroticism,' but one of the lady inspectresses was so horrified she tried to have him expelled from the school.

In 1923, with his friend Dimitriew, an excellent scenic artist, Balanchine started their "Evenings of the Young Ballet." They gathered together a company of some fifteen dancers, students of their own age. Their first performance was held in the wooden amphitheater of the old Duma. The audience sat on benches once occupied by former Constitutional Assemblies. The dancers moved in the hemicycle below, as in the orchestra of an antique Greek theater. Posters in the street announced the event, which according to the spirit of the times was 'historical' in concept. Three parts demonstrated the evolution of contemporary theatrical dancing from Petipa, through Fokine, to Balanchivadze. The young artists of the theater enthusiastically received it, but the older dancers were unanimously in opposition. They told their students to choose between dancing at the Marinsky Theatre or with Balanchine. His company was ruined.

Nevertheless he continually composed. He arranged dances for Ernst Toller's 'Broken-Brow' at the Milhailovsky Theater. For Shaw's 'Cæsar and Cleopatra,' he invented an Egyptian cabaret scene. In the meantime he was constantly dancing at the Marinsky Theater, whose repertory was ten years behind Western Europe's. Only now did they begin to present 'The Fire Bird' or 'Petrouchka.' Rehearsing and performing in the *corps de ballet,* Balanchine was constantly hoping to form a company of his own, though there seemed little enough chance for it. Some modern French music managed to filter into Russia. He mounted the Milhaud-Cocteau *Boeuf sur le Toit* at the Art Institute, more as pantomime than a ballet. Every one was interested to hear new scores. He commenced to work on Stravinsky's *Pulcinella,* which Massine had mounted with Picasso for Diaghileff in 1920.

In the same amphitheater of the old Duma, Balanchine finally managed to arrange a "Second Evening of the Young Ballet." Kaltzov, a very old, very Russian poet, had the idea of presenting Alexander Blok's poem, "The Twelve," as spectacle, with a rhythmic spoken chorus made up of students from the dramatic school, complemented by mimed action. Balanchine inventing this mobile accompaniment, again suffered from academic disapproval. But he became well-known, arranged dances for artists' clubs and special performances in nearby towns.

In February 1924, a tenor of the Marinsky Opera, Vladimir Dimitriew was asked by some of his friends to back a tour for his fellow artists, throughout Russia. This did not interest Dimitriew as much as presenting a series of recitals of "The Young Ballet." He was one person who realized not only the worth of Balanchine's choreography, but also the excellence of dancers connected with him, numbering among them Alexandra Danilova, now prima ballerina of the Monte Carlo Company, and Tamara (Gever)-Geva. They were tired of Leningrad, and wished to spend their vacation dancing in the provinces, perhaps in Siberia or even as far East as China. But there was difficulty with passports and when they finally received permission to leave the State theaters in order to spread Russian art, there was not enough time to go far away. Finally this company of "Soviet State Dancers" reached Germany for a tour which was not even arranged. Their average age was eighteen. Their costumes had been made by themselves, all choreography was arranged by Balanchivadze, either his own compositions, or taken from the classic repertory of the Marinsky Theatre. They could not speak any European language. Their street clothes seemed wholly outlandish. Dimitriew, however, by heroic manipulation, managed a surprisingly successful tour, among the German watering-places. It was summer; Berlin and the large towns were empty. In Paris, Dimitriew obtained an audition with Serge de Diaghileff who promptly absorbed the whole troupe of "Soviet State Dancers" into his own company. The Georgian name, Balanchivadze, difficult to pronounce, was changed by Diaghileff to Balanchine. At the age of twenty, a boy fresh from Soviet Russia found himself ballet-master of the remains of the old Imperial Company which was making theatrical history even in its decline.

It was not easy for Balanchine. The troupe disliked him for his youth and because he replaced Bronislava Nijinska, an accredited and talented choreographer. On his part, he had little respect for the proficiency of Diaghileff's company. Members of the *corps de ballet* of the Leningrad theaters were infinitely superior to many of these soloists. But working and traveling with Diaghileff was a liberal education in itself. At this epoch, there was more freedom for a progressive ballet-master in Western Europe than in Russia. Lenin said that the art form most useful to affect the masses was the film, and he was right. No choreographers at this time could emerge who had the stimulation of an Eisenstein or a Pudovkin audience. This is no criticism of choreography as a creative instrument or of Marxian artistic policy, but simply an historical fact. Even in 1935, Goliezovsky achieves his best works apart from the official Bolshoi Theater, though such separation is less significant now than it would have been ten years ago. The Russian classic theatrical dance is safe for its own great future. Its inevitable renaissance is a question of time alone. Perhaps at this moment a Mohammedan boy from Tadjikistan, or a Mongol from Central Asia is training himself to continue the line of Petipa and Fokine.

In the four years Balanchine acted as *maître de ballet* for Diaghileff he created ten works, besides mounting dances in opera seasons at Monte Carlo.

It would be interesting to relate in even greater detail than the early Diaghileff seasons have already been chronicled here, the story of his last years in order to analyze to something more than a superficial degree the range of Bronislava Nijinska, Leonide Massine and George Balanchine. Such a record would tell more of the creative processes in the arts of these ten years than any other single interpretation. It was an epoch full of brilliant deaths and dubious births; old ideas exhausted themselves in the trappings of the newest vogue, while new ones appeared, confused and hidden under the weight of ancient influence or historic allusion. Ballets added to the Diaghileff repertory were more remarkable from a single aspect of their collaboration (painted decor, music or solo dancing), than from any coherent or fused achievement. By achievement, one means a finished production, which however novel or cleverly sketched-out, was actually presented on the stage, after all preparations and rehearsals, with a completeness approximating the authors' original intentions. Factors against successful achievement, aside from the general triviality of the subject-matter, were the disparate, uncoördinated impulses behind nearly every collaboration. Many of the painters had undeniable talent. The musicians were not ungifted. The dancing troupe, if not brilliant, at least numbered some excellent artists, such as Felia Doubrovska, Alexandra Danilova, Leon Woizikovsky and Serge Lifar. The choreography was ingenious, in fragments subtle; occasionally independently lovely. But as a whole, five or ten years after, all that remains in the memory of those whose whole intellectual and artistic excitement derived yearly from the ballet a richness found in no college nor in any reading,—is the faded fragrance of anticipation, whispers of what one might hope for, the breathless moments before the conductor tapped his baton, and footlights turned up.

As a typical "late" Diaghileff ballet, let us examine the libretto of *La Pastorale;* book by Boris Kochno (Diaghileff's secretary); music by Georges Auric (one of *Les Six*); costumes and scenery by Pruna (a pupil of Picasso's); choreography by George Balanchine; the scenery executed by the master-craftsman Schervachidze; Bicycle by courtesy of the 'Olympique' Company: Makers.

> 1. Prelude: The curtain rises. 2. Entry of the Telegraph-Boy (Serge Lifar) on his bicycle. He stops, sees a river, dives in to bathe. 3. Entry and divertissement of young girls. One of them, in love with the Telegraph-Boy, discovers him bathing, and flees with her friends. 4. He comes out of the water, goes to sleep behind a rock, in the middle of the prairie. 5. Entry of a motion-picture company; the Star (Felia Doubrovska), Director, Operators. They install their apparatus and scenery, not noticing the Telegraph-Boy. Solo of the motion-picture director (Woizikovsky) in which he indicates the work he wants done. *Pause Musicale.* The operators fix their projectors. 8. They start to shoot the film. *Pas de Trois,* the Star and Two Actors (in Spanish renaissance *costumes de ballet*). The Star receives a letter, while the actors sing. She sends them away. Alone, she tears the letter. 9. Awakening of the Telegraph-Boy. His

emotion finding himself in the midst of movie-scenery, close to this unknown woman. 10. *Pas de Deux:* The Star and Telegraph-Boy: Astonishment, interest, dance, and exit of couple. (Here Balanchine invented an extremely curious classical duet). 11. Scandal. Operators, actors, director, furious, rush in all directions, trying to find the star. 12. Dénouement; finale. The Telegraph-Boy remembers his fiancée and his bicycle.

Nevertheless, Balanchine, among his ten ballets for Diaghileff, designed at least three which were achieved, to such a degree that a revival of them would still interest us. 'The Triumph of Neptune' was an elaborate Victorian spectacle, a compliment to England, whose audiences came to love the ballet more than any on the continent. Lord Berners, the composer and Sacheverell Sitwell had showed Diaghileff some cut-out toy theaters, designed in the nineteenth century by the naïviste artist, Pollock. A ballet was formulated in the spirit of an old English Christmas "Pantomime," with reminiscences of Cruikshank's illustrations for Dickens' novels: Thackeray's 'Rose and the Ring,'—early bound volumes of *Punch.* "The puerile romanticism of a race of grown-up, laughing children" wrote Levinson. Balanchine designed a bustling Sunday morning crowd on Fleet Street, full of sea-faring men from all over the world, and at the end, an apotheosis of Britannia and the sailor, home from the sea.

In 1921 Diaghileff had made an heroic attempt to interest European audiences in a single ballet as a full evening's entertainment. With great outlay of money and talent, the best dancers from the Russian theaters, many excellent soloists, Bakst's sumptuous settings, he reviewed the Petipa-Tschaikovsky *Belle au Bois Dormant.* Its failure was due more to bad luck, confusion in the scenic arrangements at the *première,* than to any lack of interest in the choreography. Although in 1921 Tschaikovsky was still considered a purely sentimental musician, and the war had destroyed much interest in the grandiose, Diaghileff's impulse, as usual, was correct, even though he had perhaps miscalculated his chronology. 'The Sleeping Beauty' would have been a triumph ten years later; after the creation, for example, of the Balanchine-Stravinsky "Apollo, Leader of the Muses."

Stravinsky had been responsible for a musical reintegration when he destroyed by his *Sacre* the suave, gracious sonorities of his predecessors. In a similar way Nijinsky had criticized gesture. But in the fifteen years since *Sacre,* both ballet-music and choreography were given a strong nostalgia for the consciously trivial, the modish and the gay. Nevertheless, it had always been an exception when Stravinsky contributed a new score. He collaborated with Bronislava Nijinska on 'The Village Wedding' (*Les Noces:* 1923) developing to a perfection and in a wholly personal form the line of Fokine's *Petrouchka* and her brother's 'Rites of Spring.' In a way it ultimately and victoriously exhausted the line of ballets stemming from the Russian folk-song tradition which included 'The Fire Bird,' *Les Contes Russes* (Skazki), 'The Midnight Sun,' *Chout,* and the *Coq d'Or.* It had a splendid choral accompaniment, and was set on a completely bare stage hung in gray, blue and white. The painters Gontcharova and Larionov gave it the clean accents of four shining black grand-pianos which were a part of its score, and a small window cut in the backdrop. The dancers wore the simplest of costumes abstracted from peasant-clothes.

Nijinska was fresh from Russia. She wished to essentialize the roots of the Slav race, not through a distant pre-historic past as Nicolas Roerich and Vaslav Nijinsky had done, but more lyrically. It was a remote village-wedding that she made spectacular, but through her own brutal choreography, not in any borrowings from peasant-dances in the style of the *Chauve Souris*. As André Levinson, who was not wholly sympathetic to its achievement, while admiring its intention, wrote:

> Every detail of this page of Russian folk-lore is transfigured by an ineffable emotion. The same rays of light gleam upon the glass of vodka, given to the old neighbor at the wedding feast as illuminate the cup of the Holy Grail. The lively movement of the games and the wedding songs comes straight from the soil of Russia. In the whole history of art it would be hard to find anything more poignant than the mother's lamentation on bidding her daughter farewell.

> To this score, so full of vitality and direct power, with its alternating ecstasies and primitive brutalities, Mlle. Nijinska brought a hollow image of life, mechanical and bloodless, through her choreography, that reminded one of nothing so much as the athletic stadium or the drill grounds. The executants were arranged in columns or in symmetrical figures, dressed exactly alike in brown and white. These groups alternated, taking each other's places and reproducing the rhythm, going through the identical movements at the same instant. Or else they were arranged in double files, like the soldiers of a firing squad, the first with their palms supported on their bent knees, their bodies leaning forward, while the second placed their elbows on the shoulders of the first group. In this position, the dancers advanced in strict time, serving as a moving background to the isolated protagonist. In due course, the fiancée leaned against this living pedestal. In the end Mlle. Nijinska herded her cowed company into an immobile group in three tiers—a sort of practicable stage property constructed of flesh and blood or an apotheosis of exhibition gymnastics.

Stark, uncompromising, bold and noble, it achieved a *succès d'estime,* only a little more warm than the revival of 'The Sleeping Beauty,' and for the same reason. The public was not ready for it. The more intelligent ones confused it with *Sacre*. Cocteau did not like it. It was not, strictly speaking, of 1923. But Vasily, the moujik man-of-all work in the Diaghileff company, who had been with Nijinsky in the beginning, who had seen ballets come and go, fail and succeed, be remounted and sent to the storehouse, told Bronislava Nijinska: "Don't worry. There is one ballet which doesn't need to be sent to the *garde meuble*." It has since been revived by her with considerable success in Europe and particularly in South America. In 1928 after a sufficient passage of time it was the triumph of the international seasons, considered the master-piece of the "Russian" Stravinsky.

Now, Stravinsky, as well as Diaghileff, was irritated with all the young diluters of his revolution. And with a complete turn-about face of which only he and Picasso are perhaps capable, he wrote *Apollon Musagète,* with its homage to Delibes, Tschaikovsky and Bach, containing some of the most beautiful melodies, string-writing and musical fluency of our time.

For 'Apollo,' Balanchine composed a "strictly-classic" choreography. Or rather it was perhaps the first positive affirmation of the *developed* classic theatrical dance. Nijinsky, Nijinska, Massine had been almost too busy paring down the *danse d'école* to its essentials, or enriching it by eccentricities or acrobatics to consider the pure tradition of Taglioni and Pavlova, which had rested more or less inviolate since *Les Sylphides.* Now, all the strength of its clean geometry could support the most surprising novelties. Instead of using a large *corps de ballets* as a background for soloists, Diaghileff (who was also poor), Stravinsky, and Balanchine employed only four Muses and the God (Lifar). This was more an advantage than a restriction. The rôles of the Muses were for soloists and each could only have been danced by a *prima ballerina.* Their brilliant variations were not any more a "resurrection" of Petipa or Ivanov than Stravinsky's music was a "resurrection" of Tschaikovsky or Minkous. Spurning modishness in favor of nobility, "Apollo" was a part of a rather stumbling attempt at a genuine classic reintegration of the epoch. Picasso's sheep-eyed Zeus, Athena or *Mercure,* Cocteau's *Oedipe* and *Orphée* drew their breath from that ancient Mediterranean which also lapped the coast of Greece, but the classicism of the nineteen-twenties had far more the air of the bay of Villefranche than the wine-dark Ægean.

Variations given to Lifar were athletic and brusque, no longer playful. The figures were surprisingly ingenious, yet strangely familiar. Although obeisance to the classic idiom was presupposed, Balanchine employed it with such a masterly extension of allusion, fact and phrasing, that it was parallel to a poet's extension of language, hitherto believed formulated forever. At the end, there was an apotheosis; Apollo ascended to the clouds; a naïvely painted antique chariot came down to take him. Even now the *gloire,* the *nuvole,* symbol of aspiration as traditional and true as toe-shoes, reasserted itself. It is significant that the finer the music, the finer Balanchine's choreography.

'The Prodigal Son,' music by Sergei Prokoviev, scenery and costumes by Georges Rouault, was presented in the final Diaghileff season, 1929. It was a genuinely achieved ballet, a final, fortunate resumption of the great impresario's genius for divination. The Bible story was suggested by a nine-teenth-century engraving, illustrating a poem of Poushkin on the ancient parable. Perhaps the Russians were most right when nearest home, or at least the lyric quality of it. Rouault is one of the few great painting imaginations of our time. His religious ferocity, his burning stained-glass colors are consummately fitted for the stage. Yet he was not a stage-decorator. Diaghileff had him come to rehearsals, gave him a chair, told him to paint,—not costumes, but whatever he wished. Rouault produced heaps of water-colors, none of them possible as guides to an ordinary costumer. Yet Schervachidze was no ordinary scene-painter or costumer. Under his guidance Rouault's designs were seen on the stage in a brilliance, a somber velvet grandeur of bottle-green, crimson, black and white, a heavy orientalism unrecalled since the days of Bakst. Balanchine's choreography was its kinetic equivalent. The present writer may be forgiven quoting from a notebook recording its London *première,* climax to that last unforgettable season.

> It was the Bible story they danced. In the gravity of the free action of the dancers, the parable took on overtones, almost of an ecclesiastical pantomime. It was not Oriental, nor Byzantine. Rather in the painted velvet tunics on the dancers, with the anatomy boldly described in heavy brushstrokes, under breasts, and over buttocks—it seemed as if the characters stepped from a stained-glass window or a Limoges enamel—only their articulation was never stiff. Gestures flowed smoothly, richly into one another like honey into a jar. Velvet whites and black in combination, bottle-green and glass-blue clothed the Prodigal Son and his young friends. He bade his father farewell; knelt to receive a blessing, his big yellow straw hat hung on his back. Two black-haired sisters in purple and green with wide sweeping gestures begged him to stay. His temptress floated in on her extended toe-points with outstretched arm and half-averted head. Her crimson cape floated across the length of the stage. His companions became a boat to row him to further excesses. The temptress leant forward and back to form the ship's figurehead. Her great cape flew in its wake, the ship's velvet sail—and so on through a hundred adventures which was also an Hebraic recital of continuous lyric narrative. The men had shaven heads; a curious inhuman, almost eunuch quality clung to them. The Prodigal Son rushed up on the peak of a platform his companions held,—half kneeling with one arm flung out, the other clutching his throat; from then his descent into poverty, his degradation, his return. The father stood at his house-door with his two daughters, awaiting, but not expecting his son's return. His boy crawls in the dust, on hands and knees, gradually gaining the gate of his old home. His back to the audience, his arms raised, his head fallen back, with ...a gesture of exquisite tenderness the bearded father places his own arms under his son, drawing him up with the support of his own body, and his cloak falls to cover them both.

After Diaghileff died, his company dispersed. Massine went to work in New York City at the thankless task of designing weekly 'presentations' for a moving-picture palace. Nevertheless he also presented his version of 'The Rites of Spring,' using the gifted American dancer, Martha Graham, as the Chosen Maiden. The performance, for many reasons, was not a success, but it was part of necessary waste always needed, however regrettably, before the establishment in a new country of a solid foundation for such an expression as the ballet. America had no good school for theatrical dancing at the time. Dancers were recruited from wherever they could be found. Neither the equipment at the old Metropolitan Opera, nor its management had as yet enjoyed house cleaning it had so long needed.

Balanchine went to Copenhagen as *maître de ballet* of the Royal Opera house. It was a provincial milieu in every sense, after Diaghileff, but it afforded interesting possibilities. Nijinska produced on her own, and for the Teatro Colon in Buenos Aires. Serge Lifar, Diaghileff's *jeune prémier,* became first dancer and choreographer of the Paris Opéra. His early career showed promise. His middle period, when he found himself no longer adolescent, was disappointing. But recently he has given evidences of considerable choreographic talent. As a classic mime, for example in *Giselle,* he is unsurpassed.

In Russia the ballet school for the Marinsky Theater in Leningrad, the Bolshoi in Moscow, are known as "Choreographic Technicums." Though Kasian Goleizovsky produced his 'Joseph the Fair' (music by Vasilenko, decor by Erdman), and a football ballet, he has not been a positive force. Duncan and Fokine might almost have worked in vain. The first important development in Russian dancing since the Revolution, as far as a large public went, was Tikhomirov's lavish revival of *Esmeralda* in 1926. This was a Petipa ballet based on Hugo's *Nôtre Dame de Paris,* and his original choreography was scarcely touched. A year later came the first ballet with a consciously "revolutionary" subject, 'The Red Poppy,' a tale of Communist love, intrigue and tragic triumph in the Orient. Tikhomirov came from Leningrad to the Bolshoi to produce the second act, as well as the classic dances; while the first and third acts, the Chinese, Russian and sailor numbers, were invented by Laschillin, a native Muscovite. The *prima ballerina* was Ekaterina Geltzer. In 1934, this historic artist celebrated her fortieth anniversary jubilee. She made her début in 1894, in the legendary days of the great Italians, Legnani of the original thirty-two *fouettés,* and Zucchi. Geltzer is almost a Queen Victoria of the classic dance. Another admirable production is the Petipa-Tschaikovsky *Lac des Cygnes.* The great pedagogue and artist, Vaganova, whose illustrated hand-book on the classic-dance, published in 1934, is a succinct and valued work, frequently shines as its *première.* Among the best of the Soviet technicians are Ulianova, Kamenskaya, Bank, Vecheslova and Vachtang Chabukiani, Asaf Messerer, Sergeiev and the young choreographer Moiseyev, whose pantomime-ballet 'Three Fat Men' was a feature of the 1935 theatrical festival.

The greatness of the Russian Theater is exemplified by its tacit treatment of dancing, of movement as part of dramatic action, though frequently as only a part. Modern Russian stage-craft has no peer. Meyerhold, Nemirovitch-Dantchenko, Taïrov, Vachtangov and Stanislavsky have always understood the necessity of plastic motion in relation to drama. Their plays are produced almost as danced action, in a careful design and consciously patterned rhythm. Principles learned with difficulty by Western dancers are presupposed by the best Russian actors. Not only must a Soviet actor sing and dance, but he must be master of dumb-show, acrobatics, fencing, make-up and dialect. Meyerhold says:

> ...You know the essential thing is rhythm...how the actor breathes, how he walks, how he combines with the rhythm of other bodies and other movements on the stage...how he embodies the rhythm of the play. There exists a subject—between it and its theatrical presentation exists the same relation as between the harmony and the melody of a piece (of music)...music does not illustrate, it articulates, it coördinates the movements of the disciplined players ...movement gives speech to emotion...on the stage there are problems which are *ipso facto* musical problems...they demand the melody of movement—or its discord—for their solution.

Meyerhold productions of Shakespeare or the Russian classics are in fact at present more interesting to an American or European balletomane than the classic choreographic repertory itself. But this is a temporary condition giving every indication of change.

In 1932 was founded the *Ballet Russe de Monte Carlo* by René Blum, a director of the Monte Carlo Opera, and a Russian emigré theatrical agent called de Basil. This company is now known as the de Basil Ballet Russe. Balanchine was employed as ballet-master. He insisted on choosing an entirely new troupe but there were disagreements and de Basil combined some of the old Diaghileff stars with a number of promising young dancers, mostly children of White Russians, raised in Paris, trained by the former Imperial ballerinas, Egorova, Kschesinskaya, Preobrajenska, Trefilova, and selected by Balanchine. Massine also was asked to collaborate and the first season excited bright hopes for a continuation of the tradition of Russian Ballet in Western Europe.

Massine composed his *Jeux d'Enfants,* with scenery and costumes by Joan Miro. It had an abrupt freshness, clear color, delicious invention, combining 'sport' motives and classic dancing, yet sweetly, without any post-Cocteau smirks. There was a revival of *Les Sylphides,* tactfully set in a Corot background. Balanchine contributed *La Concurrence,* a burlesque with music by Auric and a dazzling parade of André Derain's 1900 provincial French clothes. Derain, years before had given Diaghileff *La Boutique Fantasque* in the spirit of 1870. Balanchine also produced *Cotillon,* with a red, white and gold marbleized decor by Christian Bérard. This ballet is still in de Basil's repertory. It has no longer the freshness of its first season, since its underlying choreographic design is intensely musical, needing constant correction by its composer, who alone remembers it, or if even he also forgets, can at least invent equivalent patterns. *Cotillon* is a beautiful work; a *ballet d'atmosphère,* whose climate could scarcely be considered novel if we recall Nijinska's *Les Biches,* or even Balanchine's own *Bal* (Chirico: Rieti: 1929). Yet *Cotillon* had something none of the late Diaghileff ballets contained; frank youthfulness, gayety divorced from drollness; a tragic deliberation distinct from melodrama. If Balanchine never read Proust, it is of no importance. He absorbed from Chabrier's brilliant music the acrid perfume of adolescence; divinity felt by young dancers at their first ball, heady with their own youth, shyness and insecurity, masking it all in false boredom, and the frightened indifference of aching wall-flowers at a heart-break ball. Perhaps also, its extreme and real sophistication might seem trifling; that is, another *ballet-ballet* with entries and odd occurrences. But we cannot afford to be so hasty in our judgment. Not only in its remarkable use of a new type of gesture based on contemporary and aging social dances, but on the intensity of its sincere emotional temperature *Cotillon* was a thrilling work. Balanchine is always first motivated by his music; then by the individual dancers with whom he has to work. He is an instinctive composer, as opposed to an intellectual composer like Massine. He never preconsiders a design until that moment in rehearsal-halls when he sees those very dancers who will execute his designs in relation to his chosen music. If Tamara Toumanova, Tatiana Riaboushinska and Irina Baronova had not, in 1932, their individual quality of emerging adolescence, of partial shyness, even of a charming awkwardness, *Cotillon* might have been otherwise, but not possibly the same masterpiece it is.

Balanchine, unlike Fokine or Nijinsky, has asserted no principles against the established academies, at least since his school-days. He has not been responsible for any new genre of ballet. His youth was chaotic, full of diverse influences; he is still a young man. He has employed every "style" from Etruscan, through *Fêtes Galantes* to the Jazz-Age, every type of gesture, stemming from Petipa through Duncan to adaptations of Goleizovsky. The only factor which remains constant in his mercurial, flowering talent, is his devotion to and profound comprehension of the spirit of the music he employs. Yet there is something about a Balanchine ballet, even in fragments, though frequently in complete and achieved work such as *Cotillon,* 'Mozartiana' or 'Serenade' which, defying analysis, nevertheless is at once apparent; pungent as a clean vegetable scent, calendula or lemon-verbena: sharp as certain metallic bird-notes; tragic as the haunting end of some German Lied or Russian peasant song. To Balanchine the nineteenth century, the epoch of Poushkin, Gontcharov, Chopin, Glinka, Byron and Heine, represents what ancient Greece and Rome must have meant to Noverre and Vigano,—not a decorative, nostalgic past—but since it has been selected by the passage of time, becomes an epoch familiar but grand; if lost, nevertheless as real in memory as to-morrow is in fantasy. His personal experience has tended to make him a philosophical anarchist. The only order in his creative life has been accidental, its only logic, chance encounters with music, with a painter, or a dancer. He has been criticized for a lack of continuous principle, an absence of interest even in his own career's consecutive development. He is not given to talking, writing, thinking, or in any way expressing himself, except by the dancing he directs for the theater which is his world.

In 1933, Massine composed his first two symphonic ballets, *Les Présages* (Destiny), to Tschaikovsky's Fifth Symphony, and *Choreartium* (The Art of Dance) to Brahms' Fourth. Whatever one may think of the advisability of using large symphonic music, played by a small pick-up orchestra as accompaniment for dancing (this writer feels it ill-advised), however hideous the costumes and scenery for both these works, their choreography had a cold lavishness of invention, singular and stimulating. Massine was attacked for having employed tricks learned in his exile to the music-halls. Balanchine also did similar work. In both cases it enriched their theatricality without vulgarizing their capacity for design. Massine's use of spectacular adagio, in *Les Présages,* the catapulting of girls like sky-rockets into the air, is, when well-performed, breath-taking. Trained as a character-dancer, in the folk-expression of Spain and Russia, having felt the impact of Nijinsky, Laban and Wigman, Massine nevertheless returned to the developed *danse d'école,* to the pure classic idiom, for his strongest expression. The variation of "Action" at the end of the first movement of *Présages;* the adagio of "Mirth" and the "Hero," the wonderful entrance of "Fate," even in bastard bat-wings, are in their very special quality, remarkable achievements. *Présages* could never have been tolerated by Diaghileff. It would not have been that he would have objected to Tschaikovsky's music, as many do, but only to its use as dance music to underscoring a quasi-philosophical libretto. Nevertheless, this break with the Diaghileff formula was a healthy sign, which unfortunately was not continued.

Massine's *Choreartium,* originally composed in 1933 is a work which demands the clearest analysis, the closest attention. It is even now (1935) in process of change and it can still stand correction. In essence it is a series of abstract, related dance patterns founded on Brahm's Fourth Symphony. The music, somehow, fades away, serving only as rhythmic substructure for choreography. Massine has been found guilty by numerous critics of Fokine's famous accusation: "This is not a *new* style, but only Laban (or Wigman) *sur les pointes."* "Only" is a very large word. For in *Choreartium* Massine embroiders on a ground-work of the *danse d'école* a great deal of plastic, Middle-European gesture, but he has theatricalized this to such a degree that it is always genuinely spectacular. All the self-indulgence and self-love of the "concert-dancers" has been ironed out. A cold majesty of fluent forces animates the figures, not only on a floor-plane, but constantly in the air;—the male leaps and aërial turns, with the combined tapestries of grand adagios. Some geniuses have such a prodigality of talent that their gifts spatter the field of their labors like fountains. Others create up to the very limit of their power, and the result is no less imperfect for it being, in a way, exhausted. There is little prodigality of choreographic invention in *Choreartium* less even than in *Présages,* which served almost as its dress-rehearsal, or in Balanchine's 'Serenade' (1934) or 'Cotillon' (1932). But the spiritual evocation is grander, on a nobler scale. Its faults are heroic errors, its achievement, in spite of a very weak third movement, is a triumphant affirmation of the possibilities of classic theatrical dancing developed for our time. *Choreartium* is a transitional work indicating new openings. One hopes Massine will not feel the necessity of always employing the "great" symphonies, because unquestionably their "greatness" will recede when placed in conjunction to his dancing. Also, a literary plot, or a more coherent context would not mar the intensity of his pure design.

The Diaghileff formula,—three short ballets in an evening, a choice of surprising collaborations, a new personality or mood for a given season, was even in Diaghileff's own day exhausted. The Monte Carlo Ballet, with the exception of the above-mentioned works or artists, has not developed as a creative organism, choreographically or as far as individual dancers go. It now relies entirely on revivals from the old Diaghileff repertory, or on new ballets such as 'Beach' (which has precedents in *Les Biches, Le Train Bleu,* and *Les Matelots*), or *Scuola di Ballo* (which recalled 'The Good-Humored Ladies,' and *Lés Fâcheux*), amounting to the same thing. Even the recent addition of Nijinska as choreographer does not indicate an open future. Although they have brilliant technicians, notably Yurek Shabelevsky, Toumanova, Baronova, and Riaboushinska, they must rely for new dancers on accidental recruits picked up on tour, none of whom are equipped with more than an adequate style or a consistent technique. More serious, the director of this company is no artist with a courageous, inspired sense of divination as was Diaghileff, but merely a commercial agent with an ordinary sense of business organization. What policy he has, wanly continues the old Diaghileff idea. Revivals of old ballets are faded and shoddy, lacking not only original dancers, but their choreography and even scenery and dresses as well. The younger dancers just as they are about to mature find themselves worked into a state near to collapse by a crippling year-around schedule. No new choreographer seems on the horizon. Nevertheless, this company does valuable spadework, particularly in its tours of North America, where a form of art, like ballet, is forced almost to have European sanction before it is accepted as native possibility. Any one interested in the history of stage-dancing over the last thirty years must see their work, however fragmentary or disappointing it may be on an ideal basis.

There is a generation's difference between Massine and Balanchine. The latter spent only half as much time with Diaghileff as the former. After the first Monte Carlo season, together with Vladimir Dimitriew, with whom he left Russia nine years before, Balanchine founded *Les Ballets 1933,* in a sense defiantly, a declaration of independence from the Diaghileff inheritance. The younger artists, painters, musicians and dancers showed their creations at the Champs Elysées Theatre, the older succession at the Châtelet. The season was not without its recriminations, rivalries, and genuine excitements. Out of seven of the *1933* ballets produced, three, *Errante,* 'Dreams,' and 'Mozartiana' are still to be seen in the repertory of the American Ballet. A fourth, 'The Seven Capital Sins,' was probably the season's most important contribution, less significant than either *Parade* or *Ode,* yet in their line. If we understand a little of what lay behind *Les Sept Péchés Capitaux,* we will realize a few of the basic problems for the future of theatrical dancing.

This work was a Marxian morality-play by Bert Brecht, a German Communist poet, and Kurt Weill, a German Jewish composer. They had already become famous for their play and film, *Die Drei Gröschen Oper,* a readaptation of John Gay's 'Beggar's Opera,' set not in the gaols of the eighteenth century, but in the slums of the early twentieth. 'The Seven Capital Sins' told the story of Anna-Anna, a double character portrayed by a singer and a dancer. One Anna chanted the story, the other Anna danced it. Anna, to find food for her starving family, went into the world, committing in turn each cardinal sin. Her family in front of an enlarged photo of them, sang a thank-you chorus. The decorations, designed by Caspar Neher, did not mask the ordinary stage ropes or machinery. Lamps, like those of a cheap public-dance hall, illuminated an open space, around which were seven doors, screened in paper, marked Lust, Avarice, Gluttony, Pride, Envy, Hate and Idleness. As each crime was committed, a door was shattered. At one side, on a small platform, was the gas-lit home of Anna-Anna. While the songs unrolled themselves in a dreary succession of dehydrated jazz tunes, describing *Mein Schwester An-na's* adventures in Philadelphia, Boston, Louisiana, and her return *zu Hause bei der Mississippi Flüss,* a pungent, cigarette-smoke-filled beer-lees atmosphere of Kürfürstendam before Hitler, was evoked; sawdust on the floor, sordid, wryly sentimental, monotonous and tragic. At the *première* there were hisses because it was German, Jewish, and Communist.

It was all three. Yet it was not a full achievement. The people who backed *Les Ballets 1933* were rich, basically Diaghileff's audience. The star of the *Sept Péchés* was a German dancer, trained in the 'modern' school, not in the *danse d'école,* though in one sense she danced on her toes. The choreography was conceived more as ballet than as it maybe should have been, pure pantomime. Perhaps it was Piscator that Brecht and Weill needed more than Balanchine. Nevertheless, its production was a definite break with the Diaghileff formula.

In the same year, the Swedish dance-lover, Rolf de Maré, who in the early nineteen-twenties produced his 'Swedish Ballets' with the dancer Jean Börlin, founded in Paris an International Archives for the Dance. This bibliographical service was of even greater importance than his presentation of *Les Ballets Suédois,* which in spite of interesting collaborations, were never as impressive as Diaghileff's. Under the A.I.D., a competition was held for the most original 'new-dance' compositions. It was won by the company of Kurt Jooss, a pupil of Laban's, in a ballet-pantomime, 'The Green Table.' The subject matter Jooss chose was more impressive and immediate than any attempted by the orthodox ballet. It showed a Dance of Death having its inception not in medieval churchyards, but across the baize-covered tables of Geneva or Versailles. Goggling diplomats set off the irrelevant guns that destroy our world. The figure of Death was strongly mimed by Jooss, not a trained dancer, but a conscientious, imaginative young man who had been exiled from Germany with his colleagues, on account of their race. Their performances were strikingly sincere, simple, unpretentious. But their occupation with the immediacy of the world's disaster struck a responsive echo in their audiences, not enjoyed by the more accomplished artists in ballet proper.

Nevertheless, for many reasons the Jooss ballets were unachieved even in their own genre, while Jooss tended to formulate their lacks and limits into a kind of credo. Without well-trained professionals Jooss conceived a dancing language combining the 'modern' German dance with simpler elements from the *danse d'école*. His poetic impulse, rather than his choreographic execution was impressive. The intimacy, directness and sensibility he showed were all admirable. But his weak musical accompaniments (not necessarily his use of two pianos), his restricted executants, his limited theatricality make him less interesting potentially, even if more immediately, than such a manifestation as 'The Seven Capital Sins.' But Jooss, unlike Wigman, has always insisted on a direction towards theater, rather than on dance for its own sake.

As time went on, it became increasingly apparent that Western Europe had less and less to offer a young choreographer who, after leaving Russia had known Diaghileff. Italy and Germany were hopeless, due to their Fascist State. France, or rather Paris, was a home for left-overs, intrigue, and dregs from the days of Diaghileff. In England there was, to be sure, a rising native ballet and a good ballet public; but it was also (even posthumously) a Diaghileff province.

Just as Balanchine had left Russia in 1924, with his friend Vladimir Dimitriew, so together they left Europe in 1933, for America. They had been invited by Edward M. M. Warburg and this writer to found the School of American Ballet, which was to be ideally, a basis for an academy similar to the best of the Russian Imperial and State schools. Just as a Frenchman Didelot, had been asked to Russia in the eighteenth century, to aid in establishing the classic style at the root of Russian tradition, so Balanchine, Dimitriew, and their colleague, the great dancer Pierre Vladimiroff, came to America to launch a similar consistent discipline for the native American stock. To some degree, this has been already done.

It is too soon to speak of the American Ballet Company, trained in the School of the American Ballet, with choreography so far by George Balanchine. Any interested American theater-goer is the best judge of their efforts. Suffice it to say it is still in an early stage; its great possibilities are its gravest responsibilities.

More important than the actual production of ballets danced or designed by Americans to date, is the existence of a school which in succeeding years can train class after class of accomplished technicians, in the purest idiom of the developed *danse d'école*. It is on these emerging artists that the future of classic theatrical dancing on the American continent depends. There are those who reject the traditional idiom on a number of grounds. Perhaps the most frequently proposed is an assertion that every epoch has its art- (dance-) form; hence "ballet" is superannuated, without reference to the twentieth century. There is the inference that ballet reached its peak (at any date which one may give) between 1750 and 1914. Similarly, one could say the symphonic form in music which also developed between those years, was exhausted after Mozart, by Beethoven, again by Brahms, by Richard Strauss or by Debussy. Stravinsky has written no symphonies: mainly operas or orchestral poems to be danced, but he does not say the symphonic form is exhausted. The best ballets we see danced today, in the idiom of the developed *danse d'école,* would seem more foreign to Noverre or Vigano than dances of Bali or Cambodia are to us. The classic dance is an infinitely to-be-amplified theatrical instrument. If theatrical music (not necessarily the first act of *Tannhäuser*) is true to us today, so is theatrical dancing (though not necessarily the first act of *Lac des Cygnes*).

A number of young dancers of the 'modern' school protest against ballet because its dancers still use toe-shoes, pirouettes and *batterie.* The remarks above referring to Isadora Duncan, Mary Wigman, and those others who attempt to create in spite of the descent of the classic dance, instead of within, (however against it), apply also to the entire sect of American 'concert-dancers.' Their historical, philosophical or rather,—ethical objections to the *danse d'école* seem inconsequential when compared with the one unfortunate fact that America has no state-endowed dancing schools, and the 'modern' dance is the only training of which they have been able to avail themselves.

A more serious objection is leveled against ballet by critics on the left. They tell us ballet is a bourgeois form; having no significance to the conditions of our moral and economic insecurity, nor will it be any aid towards achieving a secure state or steady life. The musical analogy holds. Chamber-music is an aristocratic form in so much as it was developed by the patronage of European principalities. But vast radio audiences today enjoy the same music. Stalin is rarely absent from a performance of 'Raymonda' or 'Swan-Lake,' though a Tsar once occupied his same stage-box. It is not even regrettable that the Soviet ballet today mainly displays a pre-war repertory. Comparatively few workers or peasants had ever been in the Imperial Theaters before 1925. Ballet is not a style or a dialect; it is a vocabulary of gesture, collectively accrued for four hundred years. Its uses depend on choreographers who not only understand its language, but in a profounder sense, who comprehend the emotional and moral idiom of the times in which they live. The use to which they put ballet is a reflection of their present; the closer the reflection the greater the reference, and impact of their art. In America, just as there are great symphony orchestras in every large town, so in time there may be ballet companies. Some people believe music developed only when it was liberated from the words of song; and now, that dancing may be freed only when it breaks its alliance with music (as Wigman has done), or severs its relation with human dramatic action (as in the 'Triadic' Ballet). But our decades are not propitious for such remote purification. Dancing that will move crowds to act on their present insecurity towards a better existence, must not merely be rewarding for dancers to *do.* It must be precise, brilliant, pulse quickening, exciting to *see.* If ballet-masters abuse their instrument by over-employing acrobatics, it is also because their audiences are as yet undeveloped and respond most easily to physical show. If a lyric, essentialized expression such as classic adagio in the *danse d'école* seems artificial, or old-fashioned, a worn-out sexual allusion to a past epoch, either the audience is as yet unfamiliar with its expression or unaccustomed to the best uses of its convention. The useful, necessary limits of classic theatrical dancing are no more constricting than whatever blank-verse good modern poets have devised between the metric of Shakespeare, his heirs, and our everyday speech in a city street. Poetry, from the point of view of an abstract logophile; realism, from the attitude of an indiscriminate 'liberal' documentor; romanticism, as understood by static nostalgists for their own youth, have no place in the theatrical expression of our inflammable epoch. The developed classic ballet is a powerful modern weapon articulated by its amplification of an ancient language. It has a profounder and more elastic truth than a rigid, philosophical purity of Dance as Dance. Rather, it possesses as so few other forms the ore of immediate lyric truth. It has a superior realism to any remounting of historic incident,—the visual actuality of physical impact. And it has the only valid romanticism possible,—the presentation of the body of a human being in an heightened, *super*-human capability, a poetic standard for every man and woman's ideal capacity. The *danse d'école* is not French, nor Italian; Russian nor American. It is not alone of the seventeenth, eighteenth, nineteenth or twentieth centuries. As Russia is a collective expression of Asia and the East, so is America a collective expression of Europe and the West. Their theatrical dance is an inscription of their life that has been, that is and as it must be.

Dancing in North America: 1519–1942

For Cyril Beaumont: *Gibbon of Ballet*

IT IS now seven years since this book was issued. It is wartime, no time to make new plates, wholesale corrections or refinements of judgment, and all the luxurious improvements an easier age demands. But a popular reprint does permit itself a brief postscript on a vast subject, the book's most salient omission. Only two Americans, those who perhaps most closely affected the international dance as a movement, have so far been described: Loie Fuller and Isadora Duncan. Very quickly, let us survey the crowded chronology of dancing in our country. We may be surprised to find how much there has been, how constantly since the first discoveries has dance activity been connected with our national history and western Europe.

Before Columbus came, there was dancing. Bernal Diaz del Castillo, chronicler of the conquest of Mexico (1519), tells us when Montezuma dined, the Emperor's corps of women dancers performed. His tumblers were trained to tricks unsurpassed in China or India. In the codices, we find pictures of dancing strongly reminiscent of court ballets in Bali and Cambodia. Cortés sent two Aztec mountebanks to entertain Clement the Seventh. The palace dancers dwelt in a separate section of the capital, allotted to them.

Xochipili-Macuilxochitl was god of music, blossoms, love, and the dance. Aztec musical culture was highly developed. They used a variety of percussive and wind instruments which has been the subject of recent intensive research by Mexican musicologists. But already in 1613, Father Juan de Torquemada, in his *Monarquia India,* gave an observant missionary's view:

> One of the principal things which they had in all this land was Songs and Dances, as much to solemnify the Fiestas of their demons as to honor gods. ... For this reason ... each gentleman in his house had a Band of Musicians, with its Singers, its Composers of Dances and Songs.... Ordinarily they sang and danced ... every twenty days. The Dances of most importance were in the Plazas, other times in the house of the most important Gentleman, in his patio.*

The elements involved were religious, social, and spectacular. From these documents we deduce Aztec dancing was as lively as Egyptian or Greek.

Early settlers, far to the north, also observed the aborigines. In 1585, Thomas Harriot described the dances of the Virginian savages, and John With (White) detailed them in loving water colors. His drawings, treasures of the

---

* *Catalogue of Mexican Music Directed by Carlos Chavez for the Museum of Modern Art.* New York: 1940.

British Museum, were splendidly engraved by Theodore de Bry. In the eighteenth plate of Harriot's *Description of the Marvelous and Entirely Accurate Account of the Manners and Costumes of the Virginian Natives,* we have a splendid picture of a ceremony where, between tree trunks carved with heads resembling veiled nuns, men and women dance, holding symbols, perhaps local signs of the Zodiac, skipping around three maidens, their arms interlaced like three antique graces. All this at dusk to avoid the day's heat. When the dancers tired, they rested, gave place to others; the dancing went on a long time, followed by a banquet.

De Bry also engraved drawings by Jacques le Moyne illustrating three voyages to Florida (1562 to 1567), of dances he himself saw. In the thirty-eighth plate we watch a solemn reception for the King and Queen of a part of Florida, where more than a dozen girls dance in a circle, each maintaining at all times a different position. When a leader moved, the others followed. They were beautifully ornamented with inflated fish skins, their hair loose about their bare bodies, and a large belt, dangling with gold and silver pendants, hid their secret organs.

The Plymouth Colony founded in 1620, was followed ten years later by Massachusetts Bay which was to embrace Salem and Boston. The Puritan settlements for three hundred years endured a calumny of the historian's perversion, subscribed to by Hawthorne, Matthew Arnold, and other nineteenth-century chroniclers. It was not until 1934 that Percy A. Scholes's omniscient study of *The Puritans and Music* appeared, to set everything aright. For the first time, he conclusively proved that the Puritans neither hated all music save psalm singing and all dancing whatsoever, nor proscribed either. Rather they helped both and, quoting Scripture, defended these arts against evil-minded neurotics. The three greatest Puritan models, Oliver Cromwell, John Milton, and John Bunyan were, as Scholes takes great care to illustrate, ardent lovers of music. In 1651, at the height of the political power of the English Puritan party, appeared the first of eighteen editions of John Playford's *"English Dancing Master;* plaine and easie rules for the teaching of Country Dances, with the tune to each Dance,"* subsequently to become vastly influential. Its author's wife kept a school where "young gentlewomen might be instructed in dancing."

A good deal of the popular misconception, romantic or political, about Puritan fun, can be traced to Hawthorne's story, "The Maypole of Merry-mount," published in *Twice Told Tales (ca.* 1825). He tells us:

> There is an admirable foundation for a philosophic romance in the curious history of the early settlement of Mount Wollaston, or Merry Mount. In the slight sketch here attempted, the facts, recorded on the grave pages of our New England annalists, have wrought themselves, almost spontaneously, into a sort of allegory. The masques, mummeries, and festive customs, described in the text, are in accordance with the manners of the age. Authority on these points may be found in Strutt's Book of English Sports and Pastimes.

That is, he gives as historic basis Strutt, who is occupied only with British customs, and he assumes they must have been the same for Kingdom and Colony. Oddly enough, Scholes never mentions Strutt's name. But he explains how the festivities at Merry Mount were not condemned because they were gay, but because they were based on *pagan* games, on the Roman Floralia, and because they tended to corrupt natives as well as Colonials. William Bradford's *History of Plymouth Plantation* (edit. 1856) gives us the real story, here in modernized spelling.

> After this they fell to great licentiousness, and led a dissolute life, pouring out themselves into all profaneness. And Morton became lord of misrule, and maintained (as it were) a school of Atheism. And after they had got some goods into their hands, and got much by trading with the Indians, they spent it as vainly, in quaffing and drinking both wine and strong waters in great excess, and, as some reported, ten shillings worth in a morning. They also set up a May-pole, drinking and dancing about it many days together, inviting the Indian women, for their consorts, dancing and frisking together (like so many fairies, or furies rather), and worse practices. As if they had anew revived and celebrated the feast of the Roman goddess Flora, or the beastly practices of the mad Bacchanalians.

As far as the New England colony went, a dancing school had been opened and shut by 1673, but a man called Enstone kept another in Boston by 1716. While dancing has a long line of enemies against it as an inciter of the flesh from the time of the fathers—Chrysostom, Ambrose, and Augustine—the Bible itself differentiated between dances Miriam did, the dance with which the woman celebrated the slaying of Saul's thousands and David's ten thousands, and the dance with which Salome paid for the Baptist's head. The Reverend John Cotton, dean of the early theocrats, wrote in answer to a troubled query of 1625:

> Dancing (yea though mixt) I would not simply condemn. For I see two sorts . . . in the Old Testament . . . the one religious . . . the other civil. Only lascivious dancing to wanton ditties and in amorous gestures and wanton dalliances, especially after great feasts, I would bear witness against.

We know what sort of dancing this was in New England from a reference in William Prynne's *Histriomastix* (1633), a huge compendium of quotations demonstrating the horrors of the stage and all its attributes:

> It is known from their own Confessions that among the *Indians* in this *America,* oftentimes at their *Dances,* the Devil appears in bodily shape, and takes away one of them alive. In some places of this Wilderness there are great heaps of Stones, which the Indians have laid together, as an horrid Remembrance of so hideous a fruit of their *Satanical Dances.*

But even Prynne was not opposed to decent recreation of body and spirit. The virile games of the bumpkin he recommended to replace the soft indulgences of the dandy. Prynne was a primitive anthropologist, resembling those other scrupulous missionaries who minutely detailed the Indian dances they sought to destroy.

In 1685 there was scandal over a dancing master, one Francis Stepney who tried to set up a school of "mixt dancing," unreasonably enough on Sunday. He was a blasphemer besides, and finally fled his debts. It is Scholes's shrewd guess that he precipitated the famous tract, "An Arrow against Profane and Promiscuous Dancing, drawne out of the Quiver of the Scriptures. By the Ministers of Christ at Boston in New England" (1686). While the "Arrow" has often been taken, unread, to serve as a wholesale condemnation, actually it is sensible enough, condemning only that which leads to sexual excess, yet always admitting that "Dancing or leaping is a natural expression of joy, so that there is no more Sin in it than in laughter, or any outward expression of inward rejoicing."

The metaphysical poet, Thomas Traherne, educated in Puritan Oxford in 1657, wrote,

> All Musick, Sawces, Feasts, Delights and Pleasures,
> Games, Dancing, Arts, consist in *govern'd measures*.

The Puritans could accept dancing as a means to teach children good behavior and decent carriage, *if* they practiced it without promiscuity and without mixing the sexes. H. B. Parkes, biographer of Jonathan Edwards, the Fiery Puritan, admits that by 1700 there were few official prohibitions against dancing, that when Edwards himself was ordained at Windsor Farmes, Connecticut, in 1694, he held a dance in his own house. Certain later ordinances against dancing in taverns or public houses seem to have been prompted by the noise that kept neighbors awake. In a funeral sermon preached in 1708, Cotton Mather, speaking on the need of educating American children, did not condemn dancing instruction out of hand, but only its exaggeration. As late as 1849, Nathaniel Hawthorne's sister-in-law, Elizabeth Peabody, edited a volume of *Aesthetic Papers*. The editor's contribution urged cultivation of the body through music and dancing, although even in transcendentalist times, as F. O. Matthiessen points out in his superb *American Renaissance,* this was a radical doctrine.

It all comes down to the traditional Puritan prejudice that theater, as an *institution,* is evil, although perhaps not Shakespeare's plays; that the *profession* of actor is wicked, although maybe not amateur appearance in a Christmas play or an Easter pageant. The professionalism seems to hold the sin. As far as any professional theater went, there was none in seventeenth-century New England. The snobbery of the amateur is a curious phenomenon and requires analysis. In early colonial days, the universal resourcefulness of a ubiquitous jack-of-all-trades was a matter of pioneer pride among the first settlers, who were to constitute the new aristocracy. A professional artist somehow smacked of the gaming tables, a card sharp, short-changer, or sleight-of-handsman. The only precedent of professionalism was the fact that players, dancers, and entertainers of antiquity were slaves, while the services of their bodies were always the properties of their masters.

In 1750, the General Court of Boston passed legislation against public stage plays, as much for their outrageous expense, and probably the consequent unpaid bills of theatrical managers, as for their immorality, impiety, or contempt of religion. The Colony was still poor, living under the shadow of the early famines, and now came questions of taxation. In 1778, the Congress was to proscribe lavish entertainment, public or private, for the duration of the Revolutionary War. We recall the ostentation of Major André's brilliant "Meschianza" in Philadelphia, where at a splendid party he revived the glories of Jacobean court mummery and disguisings, while Washington's men froze at near-by Valley Forge.

Thomas Jefferson, writing to his daughter Patsy from Annapolis in 1783, gave her a schedule for her studies. From 8 to 10 she was to practice her music, from 10 to 1, she was to dance one day and draw another. From Paris in 1785, he wrote his other child, Polly, telling her she must come to Paris, "to play on the harpsichord, to draw, to dance."

As for the Revolutionary fathers, we have records of Washington dancing. Later we find the young John Quincy Adams in 1788, dancing late, twice in a week at Sawyer's Tavern, and complaining a few days later:

> The ballrooms were too small—not one-quarter of the ladies could dance at a time. I danced enough myself, and made out to affront three or four ladies; which is much in my favor.

William Maclay, a cynical observer of the ceremonies in New York in 1789, initiating our Federal government, disgusted with snobbish wrangling over protocol, wrote, "I sincerely, for my part, wished all set ceremony in the hands of the dancing-masters."

Although the Puritan prejudice has hung on well into the twentieth century and provincial pastors still claim that dancing, as such, may be abstractedly considered innocent but that mixed dancing is certainly dangerous, it is interesting to wonder why Morris dancing and the singing games of the English countryside never took much hold, either in the North or even in Virginia, as ballads surely did. There the feudal system and separation of classes was a close parallel to England. We find little American dance music composed anywhere, North or South, until the end of the eighteenth century, few dance forms original with the colonists, few dances borrowed from the Negro until after the first quarter of the nineteenth century, and hardly any transposition of the traditional English Court Masque to fit new conditions.

The chief reason for the lack of early theatrical entertainment was physical. There were no theaters, and shows consisted of some simple celebration to mark a specific occasion. At Tlaxcala, in Mexico, in 1538, the monk,

Toribeo de Benevente mounted several sacred representations. In 1566, a pageant celebrated the baptism of twin daughters to the Marqués del Valle, Hernán Cortés's heir. What is taken to be the first piece of secular drama performed on the North American continent occurred on April 30, 1598, when the Spanish explorer, Onate, reaching the banks of the Rio Grande, took possession of the adjoining land for the King of Spain. Mass was celebrated, a sermon said, and in the evening an original comedy was enacted on a subject connected with the conquest of New Mexico, written by a Captain Far Fán. These performances were all in the open air.

The first dramatic show north of the Spanish colonies, performed in 1606, took place on the shores and in the bay proper of Port Royal, in Acadia of New France. Marc Lescarbot, a young Parisian lawyer, composed the rhymes of his *Theatre of Neptune* to welcome the leader of the second expedition sent to Acadia, on his return from a disappointing voyage down the coast, attempting to discover a warmer site for the colony. The Commander was met on the water by Neptune, in his royal barque, attended by six Tritons, all of whom recited heroic tirades in the manner of Benserade. On the sandy shores, in tribal regalia, gathered the people of the hundred-year-old Chief, Membertou. Lescarbot had his eye on the distant court of Henri of Navarre and was careful to include verse compliments which were reprinted in Paris three years later.

In 1640, the Jesuit, Paul le Jeune, reported from Quebec the performance of a tragicomedy, in honor of the Dauphin's birth. This magnificent production contained scenes where "The Soul of the unbeliever was pursued by two demons who finally hurled it into a hell that vomited forth flames." Corneille's *Le Cid* was offered in 1646, and in the same year Father Lalemant reported to the Jesuit Journal that "the social event of the summer was the marriage of Montpellier, who was both soldier and cobbler, to the daughter of Sylvestre." At the ball, a kind of ballet was performed by five of his comrades, but the Jesuit fathers expressed their disapproval. They approved of ethical classic drama such as Racine's *Mithridate,* but frowned on Molière, and *Tartuffe* had to be cleaned up before presentation. They also did not sanction the Shrovetide ballet of 1647 given at the Stores of Les Cents Associés, the great commercial company, and chastized one of their young pupils who disobediently attended. However, Governor Frontenac encouraged spectacles. In 1667, the Civil and Criminal Lieutenant of the Province gave a ball, supposedly the first of an official nature in Canada. In 1730 there were elaborate fetes for the birth of a new Dauphin.

What is taken to be the first English play in our states was *The Beare and the Cubbe,* performed by "amateurs" of Accomac County on the Virginian eastern shore, in 1665. In 1702, a pastoral colloquy was presented by students of the College of William and Mary, and our first theater building was erected some time in the seventeen-twenties in Williamsburg. In 1709, the Governor's Council of the Virginia Colony forbade "play-acting and prize-fighting." In New York, Anthony Aston, a questionable character, presented *"The Fool's Opera,* or the Taste of the Age," in the season of 1703-04. The usual dates of the earliest recorded dramatic performances are 1736 for Charleston, South Carolina (Otway's *The Orphan*), 1749 for the Murray-Kean Company's debut in Philadelphia, and 1750 for a performance of *Richard the Third* in New York, which was not a success.

And what part did dancing play in such spectacles? In Charles Town, as it was then known, dancing was continually taught from 1734. Then it was Henry Holt, advertising himself as the pupil of the best English dancing masters, who opened his school and danced publicly at the "Play-House." On February 18, 1735, was presented the "Opera" of "Flora, or Hob in the Well," which contained "the dance of two Pierrots and the pantomime of Harlequin and Scaramouche." The early playgoers took a lot for their money. The "heavy play" of an evening was usually followed by a farce or burlesque, while in between came jigs, hornpipes, and other dances.

Charles Durang, author of one of the earliest of our theatrical histories, that of Philadelphia, credits the dance with inaugurating our stage tradition. Actually, it must have been more acrobatic than terpsichorean, for, in 1734, we have a newspaper announcement that:

> By permission of his Excellency Sir William Keith, Bart.:
>
> 1st, a little boy of seven years who dances and capers on the strait Roap to the wonder of all spectators.
>
> 2nd, a woman who dances a Corant and a jig upon the Roap, which she performs as well as any Dancing master upon the ground.
>
> 3rd, she dances with baskets upon her feet and iron Fetters upon her legs.

While Shakespeare was only then beginning, due to the performances of Garrick, to enjoy his ultimate prestige, such pieces as *Romeo and Juliet* offered pretexts for dancing. The masked ball in the house of Capulet could be interpreted as a harlequinade straight out of a London pantomime.

In 1752, the late Frederick A. King tells us, in his as yet unpublished "Pageant of the Dance in America," with the arrival of Hallam's dramatic troupe, our legitimate stage story may be said to have commenced. But shortly before this, Anthony Joseph Dugee, "late Apprentice to the Grand Turk Mahomet Caratha," assisted by an Indian and a young Negro, danced, booted and spurred on a rope, concluding with a Sailor's Hornpipe.

> After rolling the Negro boy in a wheelbarrow over the wire, his Indian associate ate his supper standing on his head poised on the nob of a chair. The place of honor was again assigned to the dancer and this feature was called "The Drunken Sailor.". . .

In New York, *The Beggar's Opera* was presented in 1751 by the Murray-Kean Company, "with entertainments between the acts, viz. a Harlequin's dance, a Pierrot dance, and the Drunken Peasant, all by a gentleman late from London." In Hallam's first company, Mr. Hullet, the ballet master, doubled as fiddler.

The harlequinade, the English descendant of the *commedia dell' arte,* was a particularly popular form in early America. In 1767, *Harlequin's Vagaries* was given in New York "by command of His Excellence the Governor, for the entertainment of Ten Indian Warriors that arrived here ... from South Carolina." From 1782 on, a series of "pantomimes," extravaganzas with frequent songs and dance numbers, was the rage. In Baltimore, a Monsieur Roussel danced *Harlequin Landlord.* In 1783, New York saw *"The Witches,* or Birth, Vagaries and Death of Harlequin," concluding with a grand "Dance of Shepherds and Shepherdesses," and in the same year *"Columbus,* or the Discovery of America, with Harlequin's Revels," concluding with a double hornpipe by Messrs Roussel and Patterson. As M. H. Winter says in her pioneer article on our stage dancing before 1800,* this represents a new manifestation—pantomime with national themes—which was later to embody our heroes, from Pocahontas and the Indian Sachem, Tammany, to Fulminifer, the Spirit of Benjamin Franklin.

A Jesuit missionary, Nicolas Ignace de Beaubois, after five years in Louisiana and up the Mississippi, returned to France in 1725. He took with him Osage and Otoplata chiefs and an Indian girl known only as La Belle Sauvage. They danced for Louis Quinze, then twenty-two years old, in the palace of Fontainebleau. Some Cherokee chiefs and warriors, lately returned from the Mohawk Country, were entertained in April of 1768 by a performance of "The Constant Couple." In order to express their appreciation to the people of New York they staged an authentic war dance. In 1845, George Catlin, the limner of our redskins, conducted delegations of Ojibbeway and Ioway Indians through England, France, and Belgium. They performed a war dance in full regalia before Queen Victoria at Windsor Castle, and an Eagle dance in a London park. At St. Cloud, they danced before Louis Philippe, his Queen, and the Royal Belgian family.

The first native American dancer of whom we have much record was born in Lancaster, Pennsylvania, in 1768. This was John Durang, who made his first appearance on any stage in 1785 at the old South Street Theatre in Philadelphia. He danced, sang, acted in small roles, and died in Philadelphia in 1822, bequeathing an honored name to an Augustus, a Catherine, a Charlotte, a Ferdinand, and a Mr. and Mrs. Charles Durang, all of whom are duly noted in Brown's *History of the American Stage* (1870). Charles was a well-known teacher and published numerous pocket guides to the social dance.

Charleston, South Carolina, saw much activity. In 1786, Mr. Godwin opened his famous school in King Street, where he taught fencing, too. On opening Harmony Hall, he felt obliged to disguise his performances as "Concerts" or "Recitations": "After the third Act of the Concert: A Hornpipe

* *The Musical Quarterly:* Vol. 24, pp. 58-73. January, 1938.

... to Conclude with a Pantomimical Dance, called L'Amour du Vin. Italian Shepherd, by Mr. Godwin; Peasant by Mons. Corre."

In 1791, Alexandre Placide arrived with his company of actors, acrobats and rope dancers, in flight from Santo Domingo after the disaster and race riots. Along with him came Pierre Tastel, an accomplished French dancing master, who kept his "long-rooms" where the still renowned St. Cecilia Society used to give its concerts. Placide had a handsome wife, and they presented pantomimes, operettas, and ballets with such marked success that he was soon invited to Hallam's playhouse in New York City. He performed in Philadelphia in 1792. In addition to tightrope and acrobatic specialty acts, he mounted pastoral ballets in the French taste, to music of the fashionable opera composers, Monsigny and Philidor. He particularly insisted on the beauty of his *corps de ballet,* establishing a precedent for the subsequent splendors of *The Black Crook* and the Ziegfeld chorus. He is quoted as saying: "Give me de pretty vimmens; I don't care, den, for de talent."

There was naturally little activity in the American theater of a spectacular nature during the revolution of 1775-1786. But after the war came a wave of patriotic spectacles in which dancing was more or less important. In New York was seen *"The Patriot, or Liberty Asserted"* (1794), and in Baltimore, *"The Patriot, or Liberty Obtained"* (1796). There was *"The American Heroine* ... Grand Historic and Military Pantomime ornamented with Military Evolutions and Fights" as well as *"The Independence of America, or, the ever memorable Fourth of July 1776,* with a pastoral dance and verses sacred to Liberty," "St. Tammany's Festival in the Temple of Liberty" with Indian Dances, and "The Warrior's Welcome Home (Liberty, Independence, Washington, Wayne and the Western Army, complete with ballet-*divertissement."* These recall the grandiose fêtes designed for Louis, the Sun King, to celebrate his successive imperial triumphs.

Miss Winter tells us that Placide's Charleston company offered the finest one of all in 1798—*Americania and Elutheria.* The libretto is extant:

> Hybla, a mountain nymph, desirous to see a mortal, implores Offa, a satyr, to procure that pleasure. Offa deludes an old hermit up to the summit of the Allegani Mts. to a great rock, inhabited by Genii, or aerial spirits, the chief of whom, called Americania, understanding that the old hermit is ignorant of the American Revolution, commands her domestics to perform an allegorical masque for his information.

> In Act First.... A Grand Dance of nymphs and satyrs, who will form a groupe of the most whimsical kind.

> In Act Second.... A meeting taking place between Elutheria, the Goddess of Liberty, and Americania, who descend on clouds on opposite sides.

> A pas de deux, between the satyr Horbla and the nymph Hybla, the whole to conclude with a general dance of the nymphs and satyrs, a pas de deux by a young master and lady; and a pas de trois, by Mrs. Placide, Mr. Placide, and Mr. Tubbs.

The masque within the masque shows the defeat of Tyranny by the chief of the American armed forces assisted by twin Spirits of France and Benjamin Franklin, with his electric rod.

Judged by present standards, perhaps the dances in these shows were naïve, but scarcely less so than equivalents at Sadler's Wells, the Porte St. Martin, or the Fenice, at the same period. Since many of the ballet masters taught social dancing, their choreographic patterns for the stage were frequently theatricalized social dances, just as the costumes of the Romanized heroines were much more in the style of the waistline of the 1786 grand season as dictated by Paris *haute couture,* than of any recently unearthed Roman remains. There were few dance books published in the seventeenth or eighteenth century in America, aside from engraved sheet music for the ballroom, and most of the ideas were piratings from foreign authors.

Certain European books were known in America. Rameau's *Maître à Danser* (1725), or one of its early English translations, was in many Virginian libraries and probably in New England ones as well. Giovanni Andrea Gallini's *Critical Observations on the Art of Dancing* (London: 1770) was widely quoted. T. W. Wilson's numerous guides to and analysis of Country (contra) dancing, which appeared in dozens of editions from 1808 to 1822, were unquestionably popular.

Perhaps the first detailed book on dancing to appear in English in North America was:

> Elements and Principles of the Art of Dancing, as used in the polite and fashionable circles; also rules of deportment, and descriptions of manners of civility appertaining to that art. From the French of J. H. G., Professor of dancing in Paris by V. G., Professor of dancing in Philadelphia, 1817.

V. G. was Victor Guillou, one of the Santo Domingo refugees, coming to Philadelphia to give lessons in French and fencing. For many years he taught dancing, until 1827 when he retired to a planter's life in Cuba. J. H. G. was that Gourdoux who had published in Paris six years before his *Principes et notions élémentaires sur l'art de la danse de la ville.* Guillou translated it without comment, although he gave its author at least the courtesy of naming his initials, a formality frequently dispensed with. The London edition of Carlo Blasis' *Code of Terpsichore* (1830), was widely pirated. *Terpsichore* came to be a synonym for a pocket guide to dancing. Henry Whale's tiny, pretty *Hommage à Taglioni,* (Philadelphia: 1836), has as frontispiece a steel engraving, pirating one of the smaller Chalon Taglioni lithographs of 1831. Count Alfred D'Orsay's *"Etiquette; or a guide to the usage of society with a glance at bad habits, to which is added the true theory of the Rhenish or Spanish (sic) waltz, and of the German waltz a deux temps analyzed for the first time,"* was published in New York in 1845, two years after it appeared in London. Durang's *Terpsichore or Ball Room Guide* (Philadelphia: 1847) copies in naïve woodcuts Gavarni's beautiful engravings for Cellarius's *La Danse des Salons,* which appeared in both

London and Paris that same year. Durang's miniature guide was reprinted from these same plates as late as 1856. Anaïs Colin's large beautiful colored lithographs, *Le Maître à Danser* (London: 1844), were repeatedly stolen for American sheet-music covers for the next twenty years.

Native books of interest were D. L. Carpenter's *The Amateur's Precepts on Dancing and Etiquette* (Philadelphia: 1854), Elias Howe's *Complete Ball-Room Handbook* (Boston: 1858), which contained charming and expressive woodcuts, as did also Thomas Hillgrove's *A Complete Practical Guide to the Art of Dancing,* (New York: 1863). Later on in the century there were innumerable manuals on how to call quadrilles, all types of square dances, how to lead the german, the cotillion, what favors to have, in fact, how to turn a ballroom into a domestic ballet.

But social or theatrical, most Americans loved dancing. In the first half of the nineteenth century we find, aside from the epic visit of Fanny Elssler, a full roster of French, Italian, and English dancers swarming to these shores, many of whom were to retire here and teach genteel society as well as budding professionals. Most interesting will be the increasing role assumed by our native dancers.

Among the French induced to appear in America (exclusive of Havana and creole Nouvelle Orléans), was Mlle. Louise, *première danseuse* of the Porte St. Martin, who made a New York debut in 1828, and in the same year Estelle Benardin, *première* of the French Opera of Brussels. Madame Augusta came in 1836, two years later showing Philadelphia Taglioni's role in *La Bayadère.* Blangy performed *Giselle* in 1846. Madame Celeste, perhaps the most famous of all these early Parisians, was a pupil of the Académie Royale de la Danse. However, she made her first appearance on any stage at the Bowery in New York in 1827, at the age of fourteen. Her Philadelphia debut was a solo arranged by a Monsieur Barbière in Turkish costume. She married well, exhausted her husband's fortune, enjoyed English triumphs, and made her Philadelphia farewell in 1836 as Fenella, *The Dumb Girl of Portici* (Masaniello).

M. and Mme. Ronzi-Vestris, vaguely attached to the clan of the great Gaetan *"diou de la danse"* (see page 216), appeared in 1828 at the New Bowery Theatre, in a program of solos and duets without the benefit of corps de ballet. But their *pas de deux* created a sensation. Mr. King tells us, quoting Charles Durang,

> Their European fame had preceded them, and their performances fully satisfied anticipation, in fact "they entirely eclipsed all contemporary competition. ... The novelty of the style of the dancers and their elegance conquered fastidiousness. A Vestris mania resulted, pervading all orders of society, filling the theatre nightly.". . .

The most popular French dancers of all were the Ravel family, arriving in 1832. At that time, they numbered ten artists. Some were born Ravels: Jean, his wife and small daughter, the two Gabriels, Jerome, Antoine, and

François. The others were to marry into the family or had already done so. They were rope dancers as well as acrobats, and acted pantomime ballets in four parts in which young Gabriel starred. The troupe toured the United States, France, England, Cuba, Peru, and Brazil. In 1866, they retired to their native land after an extraordinarily active career.

After the tide of French, the Italians. Signora Ciocca, first dancer of the Imperial Conservatory in Milan (La Scala), with her partner, Morra, appeared in 1847 as Diana, in *Diana and Endymion*. Domenico Ronzani, born in Italy in 1800, arrived in New York in 1857 with his ballet troupe including Signor Filippo Baratti, the Pratesi family, and the Cecchettis. This last named covered generations of Italian and Russian dancers. Enrico Cecchetti was the instructor of Vaslav Nijinsky and Leonide Massine. He died in London in 1929. The Ronzani troupe performed *Faust* as their debut in Philadelphia. The Italian ballerinas of *The Black Crook* companies will be mentioned later.

An earlier company enjoying a vast popularity were the Viennese children. These forty-eight well-trained Austrian infants, under the strict discipline of a Madame Weiss, had enjoyed a previous European success. Their dances are extensively documented on lithographic music covers of 1845. They performed a "Pas de Guirlandes," involving forty-two of the company, a "Peasant Polka" with twenty-four, and a "Pas Oriental" for the entire troupe. A large native Spanish troupe traveled the country in 1855, performing among other *divertissements, The Vintage of Xeres*.

There were also the English. Mr. and Mrs. E. Conway appeared in New York in 1825. On his retirement he kept a dancing academy in New York. It may have been Mr. Conway who was also responsible for

> *Le Maitre de Danse,* or the art of dancing cotillions, by which everyone may learn to dance them without a master, having the figures displayed in drawings for that purpose. Also a vocabulary explaining all the French terms used in cotillions; with their signification. By Edward Henricus Conway.

The only copy of this book available, a second edition dated 1827, is now in the New York Public Library. Mr. Chekini, London-born, made his American debut in *The Maid of Cashmere*. Leon Espinosa, of the famous English dancing family, first appeared in New York in 1850 in *Le Diable à Quatre*.

As for Russians, there were few. A. M. Tophoff came to America in 1860 with Mme. Galleti. A. M. Zavistowski, possibly a Pole, married to an Englishwoman, arrived in 1848 to appear in a "grand Cossack dance."

Perhaps the best known of our native American-born dancers of this epoch was Augusta Maywood, not to be confused with Mme. Augusta. Born in Philadelphia in 1825, her real name was Williams. She made her debut at the Chestnut Street Theatre for her mother's benefit in 1837, as Zelica in *The Maid of Cashmere*. In 1839 she was the first American to be admitted to the Académie Royale de la Danse, and in the same year actually appeared with Fanny Elssler in *La Tarentule*. She eloped with a musician, lived and danced in Florence, her fame reaching home. Only less well known was Julia Turnbull of New York, who made her debut as a child actress in 1826, to turn dancer and pantomimist. There were numerous child performers, few of whom seemed to survive as adult artists. La Petite Celeste, appearing in 1837 in Philadelphia, was "the smallest child to dance with such perfection ever seen on the stage."

Our first dancer to derive a national fame strictly from the practice of traditional ballet was Mary Ann Lee. She was born in Philadelphia, around 1823, performed as a child actor around the city and made her debut as Fatima in *The Maid of Cashmere,* the same performance in which Augusta Maywood first danced in public, as noted above. Both she and her slightly younger rival were pupils of a French dancing master, P. H. Hazard, once a member of the *corps* of the Paris Opéra. She appeared, as Lillian Moore tells us in her unique study, as a rival of Augusta in a *pas de deux* and, although less strong technically, pleased at once. In March 1838, she appeared in *La Sylphide,* a mongrel sired by the great romantic ballet and a popular opera, *The Mountain Sylph*. She observed the Paul Taglioni's performances in New York, in 1839 learned Elssler's "Cachucha," from Fanny's partner, Sylvain, and even dared to compete with her in another theater during her New York triumph. She also performed Taglioni's *Tyrolienne* (acquired from Paul) all over this country. In 1844 she went to Paris to learn from Jean Coralli, choreographer of the original *Giselle,* which she danced in America in 1846, two months after Mme. Augusta (the French dancer, not Augusta Maywood) had first performed it.

American dancers came not only from New York and Philadelphia. Augusta Lamoureux, born in New Orleans in 1845, joined the Ronzani Troupe in 1857. Señorita Marie (née Davis) from San Francisco, seems to have made her debut outside of California, at the age of eight in New Orleans. Miss Marietta made her Indianapolis debut in 1853. The first Latin American ballerina seems to have been Marie Zoé, born in Havana in 1840, where she appeared at the age of fourteen in the Tacon Theatre before local gentry and the Governor-General. She was in Philadelphia a year later, and in 1863 first dancer with the St. Denis-Ravel Troupe, which opened Laura Keene's theater in New York. These faded names may signify little to us now, but they prove that the North Americans were coming of dancing age.

There were, however, two Americans who achieved, mostly through mediums other than that of Terpsichore, international reputations, and who were even better known abroad than at home. Adah Isaacs Menken was born in a small village outside of New Orleans in 1835. Not a Jewess, she married a Jewish musician in Galveston in 1856, and with her sister made her debut as *danseuse* in the New Orleans Opera. Adah learned French and Spanish, appeared with success in Havana, Mexico, and throughout the

United States. Her chief fame derived from appearances in *Mazeppa,* during which she was bound to a wild horse, opening to $1640, in the San Francisco opera house, a record for the epoch. She was later strapped to local livery hacks all over Europe and America, and died in Paris in 1868.

Lola Montez was not strictly an American. She was born in Limerick and arrived here on the same boat as the Hungarian exile-hero, Louis Kossuth, in the revolutionary year of 1848. She danced a little, but was more of an actress. Her relations with European aristocracy were more spectacular than her stage appearances. She enjoyed the intimacy of mad Ludwig of Bavaria and was recently portrayed in the Massine-Dali *Bacchanale* (1939) in crinoline bloomers, garlanded with false teeth.

Famous European ballets were presented within a very short time after their original creation, considering the difficulties of communication and the fact that our young country, before the industrial revolution or the Gold Rush, was scarcely an inducement to risk Atlantic breezes or contracts signed on spec. But, for example, *Masaniello, or The Dumb Girl of Portici,* Auber's famous opera, whose heroine was a mute ballet girl, created at the Opéra by Mlle. Noblet in 1828, ten years later serving as the great role for Cerrito, was danced in Philadelphia in 1836. In the next year, in the same town, was presented *La Bayadère.* This opera-ballet on Goethe's ballad, created originally by Filippo Taglioni in 1830 as *Le Dieu et La Bayadère* for the greatest star of the Romantic epoch, was presented three years later in London as *The Maid of Cashmere.* Mme. Augusta, the French dancer, was Fatima. In 1838, she appeared in the same work as Zoloe, in Philadelphia. *La Sylphide* was first presented in Paris in 1832, and in Philadelphia by 1840. *Giselle* was first seen at the Opéra in 1841, and five years later at the Arch Street Theatre with Mlle. Blangy as "Gizelle, or the Miller." The *Diable à Quatre,* with its apotheosis of the Polish Mazourka, by Mazilier and Adam was created for the Opéra in 1845, and given in New York in 1850. *Faust,* which the Ronzani troupe offered for their 1857 debut here, had been done by Perrot for the Scala in Milan seven years before. The American cast included Gasparre Pratesi who had danced its Italian debut.

It was not until nearly halfway through the century, however, that the United States made its first great contribution of an indigenous stage type, to stand in history beside Italian Scaramouche, French Pierrot, or English Harlequin. This character was peculiar. As reflection of popular myth he was hardly less familiar than the exotic native Indian, Yankee Tar, or Pioneer. But Indian dances somehow did not theatricalize easily; the hornpipe was also a popular English dance, while the barn dance of New England transported into Ohio and our new frontier was a group number, no frame for a hero. In any case, the American stage character par excellence was the negro minstrel.

And he was usually white, a disguised paleface, hero and comic only by virtue of burnt cork. In blackface he was representative of a legend, a white superior becoming a black zany, by choice. The negro-born professional entertainer was not widely popular until after Emancipation. To be sure, there was quite a precedent for the stage darky. Sixteen ninety-four is the first date given for *Othello*. Ninety years later came Thomas Southerne's *Oroonoko*. In 1768, *The Padlock,* a comic opera by Bickerstaffe and Dibdin, celebrated the oddities of a negro actually observed in the Bahamas. Charles Dibdin sang and danced its chief role of Mungo at Drury Lane, while the young Hallam, Lewis, played it in New York a year later. The pantomime of *Robinson Crusoe,* attributed to Richard Brinsley Sheridan, (Drury Lane, 1781) with Man Friday as a blackface clown in coffee-colored fleshings, was reproduced elaborately in New York in 1785.

A troupe of negro amateurs, calling themselves "The African Company," appeared in the North, the season of 1820-21. They presented *"Tom and Jerry, or Life in London,* a Musical extravaganza, concluding with a scene from the Charleston Slave Market," anticipating Gershwin's *Porgy and Bess* of 1935. This African Company performed "in the course of the evening a variety of songs and dances." Even in the last years of the eighteenth century there had been negro ballad singers, some appearing as far afield as England.

The Bonja Song, which survives in sheet music, was popular in New York around 1820. Bonja was the rudimentary banjo, a hollow gourd slack-strung, making an agreeable sound without sharpness or resonance. With tambourine, ivory or wood "bone" clappers, and the accordion, the developed banjo became a badge of negro minstrelsy. George Washington Dixon, a well-known early minstrel immortalized "Coal Black Rose" and "My Long Tail Blue," about 1827. The tune of "Old Zip Coon" was "Turkey in the Straw," and "Jim Along Josey" of a slightly later date developed into a party game or square dance, something our Middle-Westerners call a play-party game.

Often the ballads had meaningless syllables as a refrain, supposedly parodies of African jungle- or plantation-talk, serving as accompaniment for dance steps, after the sung verse. "Ching a Ring Chaw" of 1838 was inspired by abolitionist hopes for the Republic of Haiti as final solution for our negro problem:

> (In Haiti) Dar we hab parties big, dar dance an play de fiddle
> Dar waltz an hab de jig, cast off an down de middle.

Edwin Forrest, born in Philadelphia in 1806 became, after the younger Booth, America's greatest tragedian. In Louisville he enacted Othello, as well as a negro dandy. "He was the first *actor* who ever represented on the stage the southern plantation negro with all his peculiarities of dress, gait, accent, dialect and manner." In Cincinnati, at the Globe Theatre in 1823, Forrest sang and danced a negro in *The Tailor in Distress.* Ira Aldridge (1804-1866), who happened to have been born at Edwin Booth's birthplace, Bel

Air, Maryland, was a full-blooded negro tragedian who played Othello as well as Dibdin's Mungo in a single evening.

But the traditional source of organized Ethiopian minstrelsy was Thomas Dartmouth (Daddy) Rice. Stories surrounding his start are in the grand tradition of racial myth. Born in New York in 1808, he was apprenticed to a wood carver. In the season of 1828-29, at the Columbia Street Theatre in Cincinnati, Ohio, he was observed doing "negro bits." Back in Louisville, as the story goes, Rice had seen a slave attached to a livery stable owned by a man called Crow. The stable was behind the theater, and the negro, Jim, had assumed his master's name, as was the custom. Jim Crow was a deformed, half-paralyzed old man, his right shoulder drawn up high, his left leg stiff and crooked at the knee. Walking with an odd limp, he cackled an old tune, to which he made up words as he went along, rocking on heels, flat in his worn-out shoes, marking the end of each verse. "Jump Jim Crow" became the theme song of the day and points down the years to "Old Black Joe" and "That's How Darkies Were Born." Generations of adapters of Daddy Rice's famous act have aped the poor old man, with little idea that it was a particular person rather than a quaint characteristic of his race or class as a whole, who was their model.

Rice also created for himself several variants of the Dandy Darky, "Dandy Jim of Caroline" and "Spruce Pink." He went to England in 1836 to make a fortune, flattered by a swarm of imitators. Already, in 1833, a Mr. Blakely at the Park Theatre in New York had sung a "comic extravaganza of Jim Crow," preceding the play. On the same bill was Signora Adelaide Ferrero in a new "ballet dance" entitled *The Festival of Bacchus.*

The first minstrel troupe, as such, was accidentally evolved in a New York boardinghouse in 1842. "Dan" Emmett played the fiddle and banjo, by now a properly strung instrument, "Frank" Brower manipulated the bones, and there was "Billy" Whilock and "Dick" Pelham who happened in that afternoon, too. They all started improvising, making spontaneous arrangements of tunes they knew well, then on everybody's lips. The minstrel troupe originated from something like a jam session, entirely in the spirit of workouts which contemporary dance bands indulge in, after hours, for their own pleasure.

First they played in a billiard hall, then gave a benefit at the Chatham Theatre, in February 1843. The minstrels sang songs, danced jigs, accompanied themselves with free cadenzas on tambourine and bones, to evolve a three-cornered dramatic form which would include primitive jokes as well as more elaborate dramatic sketches or burlesques. The master of ceremonies was Mr. Interlocutor, the men on the end seats, Messrs Bones and Sambo. The costumes were theatricalized variants of the epoch's long tailcoat, with spectacular lapels and shiny revers, perhaps based on the costume worn by an old circus tumbler, or the "Long Tail Blue" of Old Zip Coon. This first troupe of Virginia Minstrels was so popular that soon followed "The Ethiopian Operatic Brothers," "The Sable Sisters and Ethiopian Minstrels," and so on for seventy-five years. The parade, headed by a local band advertising the arrival of minstrels, was an indelible memory for most small-town boys of our grandfathers' youth.

The world-famous company founded by Edwin P. Christy started in 1846, although his posters boasted a date four years earlier. His company (without him) trouped England, and a large number of British pamphlets give evidence of local success. As early as 1845, Liverpool saw "Old Joe Sweeney," Father of the Banjo, a nigger dancer. Stephen Foster produced many of his loveliest songs for the Christy troupe. Some minstrel artists had individual specialty acts, songs and dances for which they became personally famous, and thus evolved our rich tradition of vaudeville, which served as the training ground for the best actors in Hollywood today, from Charles Chaplin and George M. Cohan (whose father, Jerry, was a blackface dancer) to James Cagney and Mickey (Yule) Rooney. The clog dancers, the soft-shoe, buck-and-wing, the sand, stair, and pedestal dancers look forward to tap masters like Fred Astaire, Paul Draper, and, greatest of all, the born blackface, Bill "Bojangles" Robinson.

The iconography of the minstrels is extraordinarily rich. Visually, the shows were superbly dressed, and wood cuts and posters, now in the Museum of Modern Art Dance Archives in New York City, indicate their splendor. But perhaps the most touching representations of our Negro lyric tradition can be found in the paintings of William Sydney Mount (1807-1868). Mount also painted barn dances beautifully, but among the best of the work of this admirable artist are moving portraits (1856) of Negro (not blackface) minstrels, with their bones and banjo.

Negroes themselves imitated white men in blackface. Only they used burnt cork, too, in order to approximate a uniform skin tone. Other racial characters emerged in white face: the comic Dutchman; the Irish Mick, with jig and shillelagh; the German immigrant. Even ladies used blackface. Lotta Crabtree, as a girl in 1863, danced in a minstrel troupe in Virginia City, California. So did Trixie Friganza, later. There were dozens of black and whiteface female impersonators, great-grandaunts of Julian Eltinge, Bert Savoy, and Barbette. G. N. "Christy," E. P's successor (whose real name was Harrington) is remembered by a lithograph portrait in a cachucha à la Elssler, in complete ballet costume. "The only" Leon appears on point as a ballerina in an 1860 print. Eugene d'Ameli, who made a New York debut in 1855, appeared in Berlin, where they *swore* he was a woman. We recall that in our own day many insisted La Argentina was actually a man. There were also innumerable "brother," "sister," and "family" acts as well as infant prodigies of all brands.

William Herndon, the outspoken law partner of Abraham Lincoln, recalls him on the Illinois circuit:

Amid such surroundings, a leading figure in such society, alternately reciting the latest effusion of the bar-room or mimicking the clownish antics of the negro minstrel, he who was destined to be an immortal emancipator, was steadily and unconsciously nearing the great trial of his life.

But it is significant that the single rôle assigned to the Negro type was that of clown, and that few Negroes themselves have attempted to broaden the character established by the black-faced whites.

The astonishing richness of the minstrel tradition, extending in a lively echo to the present, may easiest be indicated by a recital of names of men or teams who either were minstrels or connected with minstrelsy: Montgomery and Stone, Raymond Hitchcock, Chauncey Olcott, Billy Jerome, James J. Corbett, Nat Goodwin, Eddie Foy, DeWolfe Hopper, Maclyn Arbuckle, Lew Dockstader, Harrigan and Hart, George Primrose, Bert Williams, Daniel and Charles Frohman, Willie Collier, Otis Skinner, Billy B. Van, Jefferson d'Angelis, Denman Thompson, Weber and Fields, David Belasco. The golden dusk of the minstrels was in the spectacular tours of Cohan and Harris's imperial troupes, about 1906-10. They were killed by a rise of railroad rates at the outbreak of the first World War. Transporting upward of one hundred men and baggage from one small town to another no longer paid. The *coup de grâce* was administered by the entrance of nickelodeon and dime movies, and also to some degree by two-a-day vaudeville, as manipulated through the vast circuits controlled by B. F. Keith and F. H. Proctor.

A spectacle that revolutionized theatrical dancing and established a number of ancestral precedents in the line of ballet for America was the production in 1866 of *The Black Crook*. The entrepreneurs, Jarrett and Palmer, had brought over to New York from Paris a vast amount of costumes and 'stage equipment for a projected staging of *La Biche au Bois*. This was to have been for the Academy of Music, which burned. *La Biche au Bois* was a perennial extravaganza success of the Porte St. Martin since 1845, and elaborate ballets were included. These were inserted into *The Black Crook*. Charles M. Barras produced a new libretto, useful in its outlandish pretexts since anything might happen in it, and usually did. A large number of excellent Italian-trained dancers appeared as soloists, among them Maria Bonfanti, Rita Sangalli, the Rigl Sisters, and Rose Delval. The stage of Niblo's Garden was entirely reconstructed for its *première,* and thirty thousand dollars were spent before the curtain rose. David Costa was choreographer. It was all of a lavishness beautiful beyond belief. The New York *Tribune* said in particular after the first night:

A vast grotto ... extending into an almost measureless perspective. Stalactites depend from the arched roof. A tranquil and lovely lake reflects the golden glories that span it like a vast sky. In every direction one sees the bright sheen or the dull richness of massy gold. Beautiful fairies, too, are herein assembled, the sprites of the Ballet. ... The last scene ... however, will dazzle and impress to even a greater degree, by its lavish richness and barbaric splendor. All that gold, and silver, and gems, and light, and woman's beauty can contribute to fascinate the eye and charm the senses is gathered up in this gorgeous spectacle.... One by one curtains of mist ascend and drift away. Silver couches, on which the fairies loll in negligent grace, ascend and descend amid a silver rain. Columns of living splendor whirl, and dazzle as they whirl. From the clouds droop gilded chariots and the white forms of angels.

The Black Crook seems to have combined features from Weber's *Der Freischütz* as well as *The Naiad Queen, Lurline,* and *Undine.* It ran 475 nights, a record in that time, made $600,000 for its producers, $60,000 for Barrow, the author, and was continually revived throughout the century. In 1929, it was reproduced in Hoboken, the dances by Agnes de Mille based on original documents, of which there are many extant.

Later in its first season it was much refurbished and a swarm of new ballerinas added: Mlle. Pagani from La Scala; Mlle. Setti from the San Carlo, Naples; the sisters Riemelsberg from the Berlin Opera; Mlle. Kurtz from Hamburg; Mlles. Rose, Berthe, Gabrielle, Lotti, Leoni, and Artois from the Porte St. Martin; and a dozen more English ladies from Covent Garden.

The Black Crook got all the breaks, enjoying denunciations by the *Police Gazette,* and many more respectable journals, but more importantly from the Reverend Charles B. Smyth, who hired the Cooper Institute and harangued three thousand people for a whole afternoon on the sins of the show:

The first thing that strikes the eye [gloated the Reverend] is the immodest dress of the girls, the short skirts and undergarments of thin gauze-like material allowing the form of the figures to be discernible through it, *in some instances;* the flesh-colored tights, imitating nature so well that the illusion is complete; with the exceeding short drawers, also of thin material, almost tight-fitting, extending little below the hip; arms and necks *apparently* bare and bodices so fitted as to show off every inch and outline of the body above the waist.

What more could a press agent want? James Gordon Bennett involved himself in a feud over a lease with P. T. Barnum, who had an interest in Niblo's at the time, and delivered a regular biweekly castigation: "Nothing, as we said, has been witnessed in a theater in modern times so indecent as this spectacle." Little wonder that *Black Crook* productions appeared like wildfire all over the map.

In 1868, when *The Crook* finally shut, *The White Fawn* took its place, and although it ran 150 performances this was considered a failure. It closely followed the Porte St. Martin *Biche au Bois ou Le Royaume des Fées* with its Fish Dance, its Vegetable number, and ballet of Fireflies. Its animal and food numbers may have been inspired by the wonderful drawings of Grandville, later transposed by John Tenniel for his illustrations to the *Alice* books.

On its first night in New York, at ten minutes to two A.M., the final transformation scene defeated eighty stage carpenters and twenty gas men, who could just not get it on. The impresario appeared to apologize to his public, "who dispersed quietly." On the last night of its run, at a benefit, the large *corps de ballet* danced Beethoven's Pastoral Symphony, the rivulet scene turned into a *pas de deux.* This anticipated Isadora dancing the Seventh, and Walt Disney's Pastoral in *Fantasia.* *"La Biche au Bois* or the Enchanted Fawn" (introducing De Pol's European Ballet) was presented in Cincinnati that same year. The dancing of Mlle. Blasina was especially noted. Born in Trieste in 1848, she was a pupil of Carlo Blasis, and in Boston created a furore in "De Pol's American Can Can."

Various burlesques, a growing genre, were turned out—*The White Crook* and *The Wite* (sic) *Fawn.* A ballet organization appeared in *Undine,* which introduced "some effects" from *The Black Crook* and *The White Fawn.* In 1868, *"The Crimson Shield,* or the Nymphs of the Rainbow" was presented at the Bowery, one more variant on a seemingly inexhaustible pattern. *The Black Crook*'s universal success raised traditional ballet, as such, to a new level of independent importance, although to be sure it also included elements of music hall and burlesque.

In earlier days, burlesque was indeed a theatrical parody of something else, classic and serious. *The Bohemian Girl* was flattered by "The Bohea Man's Girl," *Hernani* by "Her Nanny," *Der Freischütz* by "Fried Shots." This naïve genre was slain by the arrival of Lydia Thompson and her British Blondes, in 1868. Parodying an antique myth (as Offenbach had in *Orphée aux Enfers*), "Ixion, or the Man at the Wheel" introduced plaster-cast characters out of the "Age of Fable," as well as a Mob of *Red* and *Unread* Republicans. The British Blondes were hefty, sexy, and drew exploitable howls from press and pulpit. The New York *Clipper* allowed:

> ... to represent Minerva with a whiskey flask, Jupiter as a jig-dancer, Venus with a taste for the can can, is all done, we suppose, in a laudable spirit of burlesque, but we could almost hate Miss Thompson and her assistants for spoiling a pretty story.

The British Blondes launched a line of fleshy, upholstered dancers which was to culminate in Billy Watson's "Beef Trust," and ultimately in the striptease. Mazeppa, in flesh tights, bound to her Byronic stallion, was prophetic of Gypsy Rose Lee and Ann Corio.

New characteristics emerged. The first Hootchy-Kootchy was an aftermath of the Philadelphia Centennial of 1876. Three male musicians armed with an Armenian pipe, a fiddle, and a small drum or tabor, made music for two women, who wore short skirts and tight breastbands, their middles quite exposed. They were intended for a "Turkish Theatre" at the Exposition Midway, but it failed. The cancan and other pantie dances were hot stuff, and their sex appeal drew church lightning. "Little Egypt" and the cooch and belly dances of the Chicago World's Fair of 1893, confirmed the dance as deviltry to the visiting provincial public.

Vaudeville or the variety show contained mixtures of minstrelsy and burleycue. Its dances involved all manner of technical innovation; ninety per cent of the two-a-day performers danced. Charlie Dimond did his soft-shoe number while he played the harp. Fine sand was spread on a stage and the dancer, in 4-4 "ballroom schottische" tempo, traced a pattern in it with thin hard soles, sliding and shuffling, to accent an accompaniment with double or triple taps. Douglas Gilbert in his compendious *American Vaudeville; its Life and Times* (1941), tells us that Kitty O'Neill was the outstanding sand-jigger during the seventies and eighties. In the egg dance, a dozen raw eggs were deftly avoided. In the spade dance, the shovel was used like a pogo stick. Bottles and lighted candles served as hurdles, and here dancing overlapped into circus. The "mirror" dance was good for a sister act, the "cane" dance was natural for a dandy or city slicker, and later on came roller skates and stilts.

Pat Rooney, the founder of three generations bearing his name, was seen in "a cutaway coat with tight sleeves, fancy waistcoat, pants with large plaid checks, a plug hat of quaint model, and all-round whiskers called 'Galway sluggers.'" He rendered, among other ballads, his hit, "Biddy the Ballet Girl."

Vaudeville finally canonized a mythical hierarchy conceived in the younger days of minstrelsy. The Nigger, the Jew, the Irish paddy, Max and Moritz, and, most acrobatic of all, the Tramp, all had specialty acts. The film comic, W. C. Fields, in his youth was a hobo juggler, and Nat C. Will's famous bum number was billed as "The Happy Tramp."

On a more pretentious plane, the tradition of spectacle in the line of *The Black Crook* persisted. Two Hungarian brothers, Imre and Bolossy Kiralfy arrived in New York, and in 1869 produced *Hiccory Dickory Dock*, employing Costa, *The Black Crook*'s choreographer as well as Rita Sangalli, one of its chief ballerinas. The Kiralfys were billed as a troupe of Hungarian dancers. The brothers, assisted by their sister, Haniola, and company, appeared in The Palace of Dazzling Light, to dance a Magyar Czardas.

Imre Kiralfy directed the ballet of *The Bridal Beauty* in 1870 and a year later, *The Pearl of Tokay*. In an 1873 revival of *The Black Crook* he mounted the new dances. The brothers staged three Jules Verne romances, long staple of le Théâtre du Châtelet: *Around the World in Eighty Days* in 1875, *A Trip to the Moon* in 1877, and *Michael Strogoff* in 1881. In 1883 they were responsible for the very influential ballet-spectacle, *Excelsior*.

Luigi Manzotti, the famous *maître de ballet* of the Scala, had produced this for the first time in Milan, 1881. It chronicled the triumph of electric light over darkness. Volta and Civilization, besides a corps of French and Italian Engineers and Fireman-Miners were personified, aided by Navvies, Telegraph-messengers, Science, Agriculture, Glory, and Invention. In Part

II, the Brooklyn Viaduct was disclosed, also Volta's laboratory at Lake Como and Telegraph Square in Washington, D. C. In the London production of 1885, Enrico Cecchetti "fairly astounded by his wonderous pirouetting." *Sieba and the Seven Ravens,* another Manzotti piece (1876), inspired by the music-dramas of Richard Wagner, was produced in New York in 1884. Cyril Beaumont tells us in his invaluable *Complete Book of Ballets* that,

> Manzotti's ballets were not ballets in the present understanding of the term, but a succession of related episodes expressed in mime, varied with simple but effective *ensembles* by dancers, and striking processions by well-drilled supers.

The Kiralfy brothers' *Excelsior,* closely following Manzotti, even in small details, successfully brought high-grade extravaganza before an eager public as a spectacle in which dance predominated, with real dignity. "*Nero,* or the Fall of Rome," came in 1888. For the Columbian Exhibition of 1892-93, they produced *Christopher Columbus* and in the Chicago Auditorium, the great pageant, *America.* Manzotti's spectacles had frequently been propagandist. This brings us by an odd, yet strictly logical, road through minstrelsy, vaudeville, and transplanted Milanese spectacle, to one of the most influential figures in the American theater, Ruth St. Denis.

Ruthie Denis was the cheerful offspring of an unconvinced atheist and a devout Methodist. Her deepest impulses have, throughout her long career, assumed religious expression. An eclectic in creation, she has continued to praise God and Man through her dance, aided by Christian Science, Buddhism, Mithraism, and the Christian and Hebrew books, with side glances at Islam and a plunge into Greece. She tells in her *Unfinished Life* (1939) —which, with Isadora's *My Life,* forms the cornerstone to American dance literature—that she early came into contact with local heirs of Delsarte. There were numerous American manuals of the Delsartean dispensation for relaxation and posture. François Delsarte (1811-1871) was a radical analyzer of gesture and basic movement. An American, Steele MacKaye, attended his pantomime classes in Paris and hoped to bring him to the United States, but he died and MacKaye was left to spread his gospel. These teachings, in one form or another, served as philosophical and even physical basis for generations of fairly well-educated dance students of the *fin de siècle,* who grew up before Duncan and St. Denis made a dancer's career honorable for a well-bred girl.

In a circus side show, little Ruth saw the spectacle of *The Burning of Rome.* We recall the Kiralfy *Fall of Rome* of 1888.

> As a grand finale a ballet of a hundred angels floated about on the stage, dressed in costumes made of ribbons.... The first thing I did when I got to the farm was to go into the garret and slash up a pair of Mother's old curtains to create my first dancing costume.

Instruction from Karl Marwig, a fashionable Swiss social dancing and "deportment" teacher in New York, did little to satisfy her eagerness. She was packed off to Dwight L. Moody's Seminary in Northfield, but quickly escaped to appear in church vestry theatricals. But Methodism was no atmosphere for a young devotee of Delsarte. At the Palisades Amusement Park, she watched a "Toe-Ballet" in *Egypt through the Centuries,* mounted by Imre Kiralfy. "The choreography and the costumes were totally unsuited to the theme ... but to me it contained such magic that for months I dreamed of it."

From Genevieve Stebbins, an independent precursor of Isadora, working with ideals of unfettered, improvised body expression, she learned even more. At her rare private performances given before friends, Stebbins stood for what was most vital in creative dance, the opposite of the dead tradition of classic ballet as maintained by teachers at the academic Metropolitan Opera House. Nevertheless, Ruth studied briefly with Mme. Bonfanti, Italian ballerina of *The Black Crook,* and, indeed, her first solo dramatic appearance was in *The Ballet Girl,* as a little blue Pierrot. Imitating Bessie Clayton and Mabel Clarke, famous toe dancers of the time, she never felt easy on her points.

Ruth St. Denis, from her beginnings, impressed many by her simple religious faith in herself as dancer. Stanford White, the architect, and David Belasco, the producer, backed her at this time, although she had scarcely danced a step. She acted a dancing girl in Belasco's *Zaza,* starring Mrs. Leslie Carter, and had five apprentice years in theaters all over England and America.

At the Paris Universal Exposition of 1900, she was amazed by Loie Fuller and deeply impressed by Sadi Yaco's troupe of Japanese actor-dancers. As Isadora had felt the magnet of Greece, with St. Denis it was always to be a deep attraction for the Orient. Her first creation was inspired by an advertisement for Egyptian cigarettes. How she fought for her talent, how she finally interested commercial managers, how she brought *Radha* onto the stage is a story of touching heroism. Her transcendent optimism, the ubiquitous confidence of the self-taught, brought her influential patrons and assured her an early, overwhelming success.

Mrs. Jack Gardiner in Boston, Mrs. Otto Kahn and Mrs. W. K. Vanderbilt in New York; later, Count Kessler and Hugo von Hofmannstahl in Berlin, Rodin in Paris, Alma-Tadema and G. B. Shaw in London propelled her on tours of the western world which were no less spectacular than Isadora's.

What did she dance? It is hard for us to imagine today, when *Scheherezade,* badly done with only a faint echo of its meretricious pornography, is all that's left of the novel orientalism of that epoch. But St. Denis's early dances, even as she does them now, have a naïve theatrical structure, backed always by the idea of extra- or superhuman elements, which the ancient human disciplines of the East keep alive. Her *Radha,* her *Cobra,* her *Yogi,* and her *Egypta* might seem odder to us today than even *The Black Crook*. Historically, they mark the first time a cultivated American exploited the material of Lafcadio Hearn, Denman Ross, Tagore, and Coomaraswamy—the decorative patterns of China, Japan, and East India—as art for the theater. It was a wholly fresh visual world for the West, which was partially prepared by Whistler's "Japanese" arrangements. St. Denis was more "oriental" for the fact she had never been East. The Athenaeum and public library, cigarette cards, and travel photographs taught her as much as she needed.

And, even so, she was primarily an American dancer. Although her German successes made her feel that here was a second home, although they offered to build her a personal theater and give her a school, nevertheless she chose, in spite of devout adulation, to return to the land of vaudeville and burlesque. And, on her return in 1910, she found her country had, to some degree, come of dancing age. During her first New York season, Isadora was dancing with Walter Damrosch's orchestra, Loie Fuller's company was at the Metropolitan, Adeline Genée was at the New Amsterdam. Anna Pavlova and Maud Allan were soon to arrive.

Ruth St. Denis is in the grand line of our great protestant artists, the dynasty of Margaret Fuller, Julia Ward Howe, Harriet Beecher Stowe, and Emily Dickinson. Incapable of dissimulation, hot with ecstasy, primarily intellectual, she is one of our romantic Puritans. Her essential contribution she best describes herself:

> I brought a very meager technical equipment to assist me in the expression of these ideas. I say meager equipment only in comparison with the virtuosity of the ballet girl or the acrobatic dancer, but I sensed at that time what I later knew—that any technique is sufficient which adequately expresses and reveals the thought intended by the artist. With this in mind my medium of expression was more than adequate to my needs at that time. I had a naturally supple body, well proportioned, very strong, and extremely responsive to the mind.*
>
> The ballet represented aestheticism, whereas both consciously and unconsciously Duncan and I were attempting to fuse certain elements of life and movement into a deeper identification with the natural expressions of being than had been attempted since the golden age of the dance. I knew at that time, as I know now, that both she and I must rise and fall by that. Her weakness lay in the fact that her technical equipment was meager, but her power lay in an ideal which she gave to the entire world of the dance. My strength and my weakness lay in the choice of media. Had I put as much talent and energy into interpreting Christianity as I had into interpreting the Orient, I would today be an established institution, with my temple and school. But the end of the story is not yet, and I have swung slowly around

---

* Ruth St. Denis, *An Unfinished Life*. An Autobiography. P. 56. (New York and London: Harper & Brothers, 1939.)

to becoming an instrument for our Christian realizations to be manifested in terms of the dance.**

In 1914, in New York, Ruth St. Denis met Ted Shawn. She has so beautifully told her story of their remarkable meeting, marriage, life together, and their separation, that there is no need to repeat it. Briefly, Edwin M. Shawn was born in Kansas City in 1891. His father's people had come over from Germany during the Revolution of 1848, his mother's were connected with Edwin Booth. In Denver, Ted, as he has called himself since, preparing for the ministry, became paralyzed from the serum that cured him of diphtheria. He became interested in exercises that developed into his life work. In 1913, in Los Angeles, with Norma Gould, a well-known teacher and dancer, he made an historic dance film for Edison—"A Dance of the Ages: Recording the dances from the Stone Age to Present Ballroom Dancing." The ballroom dancing of the time was ending its first sweep of Latin American music, the maxixe and the tango.

"I should only believe in a God that would know how to dance. Many years ago in my first reading of *Thus Spake Zarathustra,* my whole being leaped to an ecstatic agreement with this credo of Nietzsche's." Whitman, Nietzsche, Buddha, and Havelock Ellis served for his philosophical basis. From Shawn came the plans and finally the realization of the Denishawn idea. He aided in Miss Ruth's Egyptian pieces, and much later they toured the whole Far East together, learning native dances from authentic sources. They pilfered the world's religions and decorative arts for ballets, showing them all over America, in one-night stands, on arduous vaudeville tours, to get money to build Denishawn House, the extraordinary school with its branches all over the country, where for the first time young Americans could obtain the best there was of available techniques, from Japanese sword rituals to Mary Wigman, taught not by diluters but from the source itself.

But apart from their borrowings from Persia and Morocco, from Australia and Japan, from the court of Josephine and Crete, Shawn had always had a bent for indigenous expression. He actually first employed the term "American Ballet" and created works to give it distinction. In 1920, he mounted *Xochitl: a Toltec Drama,* for a vaudeville tour. His partner was a violent young girl called Martha Graham. In 1922 his American Sketches included *Crapshooter* (Charles Weidman), *Cowboy,* and *Boston Fancy.* In 1930 he used revival hymns, negro spirituals, and a barn dance. He adapted Hopi, Osage, Pawnee, and Zuni ceremonials from the originals, and produced *Jurgen,* a ballet after James Branch Cabell's book, to music by Deems Taylor.

Shawn's musical interest was considerably more distinguished than many other recitalists before or after. In 1917, he was using J. S. Bach Fugues and Inventions, and in 1919 danced Erik Satie's *Gnossienne.* He made experiments such as the *Geometric Dance* to music by Max Reger, and

** *Ibid.,* p. 92.

Musical Visualizations to Brahms, in which the dancers personified musical material. He danced to Griffes, Holst, Vaughn Williams, and Respighi, earlier than far more acknowledged European choreographers. In this work, Louis Horst, the pianist and composer, unquestionably aided the Denishawn companies.

But perhaps Ted Shawn's greatest independent service to the dance was achieved alone, in creating a company of male dancers, and starting in 1932 to tour America and Europe for the next eight years. He taught dancing for students at the Young Men's Christian Association Training College in Springfield, Massachusetts. The subsequent performances of his young athletes did much to destroy our prejudice against the male dancer. Shawn was an evangelist. He still is. He created and offered Church Services in Dance Form, and by his lectures, demonstrations, books, and performances gave continual acts of faith in his America, dancing.

It was inevitable that such strong characters, who had worked so hard against difficulties of time as well as of circumstance, should consider themselves apart, almost ancestral authorities—the beloved Miss Ruth and Papa Shawn. And it was inevitable that their conflicting, although essentially loving personalities, should split first with each other and then with their most devoted disciples. Each assertion of independence is in a sense a betrayal. The young traitors, in the long run are forgiven, when the teachers realize that each pupil, by the painful break, becomes himself.

There is no place here to trace all the varying forms that went into the origins of the so-called "Modern" or concert dance. Duncan and Denishawn, Wigman, Gordon Craig, Appia, Nijinsky, Whitman, Nietzsche, George Washington, Dalcroze and Delsarte all have a responsibility. So has Bird Larson and her valuable effect on the instruction in physical training through our whole school and college system. Miss Larson died in 1927, but her researches in the field of orthopedics affected her own pupils, and indirectly a whole subsequent generation. She taught physical education at Barnard College of Columbia University, at a time when the whole science was emerging from the chrysalis of "Swedish" or Central-European gymnastics. In Wisconsin Margaret H'Doubler had been (and still is) occupied with similar ideas. Miss Larson was a technician in body mechanics. She, as apart from other colleagues such as Mensendieck and Gertrude Colby, turned toward the professional dancer, and away from the purely educational field. Isadora, as John Martin has shown in his fine study in "Duncan and Basic Dance," * had no real system to her free flowing impulse, save the impulse determining extensions from the normal human hop, skip, run and jump. But Bird Larson's "Natural Rhythmic Expression" included three lines of instruction. First to be learned were the possibilities of natural body movement, then other movements could be assimilated "of purely gymnastic ori-

* Project for a Textbook. Dance Index: 1942.

gin"; finally, controlled movements combined with musical feeling and form were used in the expression of an idea.

We recall how Isadora insisted on the solar plexus as the source of her "System" (p. 266). The search for the Duncan "crater of movement" is the continual grail of all innovators in dance. Mr. Martin says of Bird Larson:

> She was one of the first to emphasize the importance of the torso as an originating center of movement. The spine was used as a supple stem through which movement flowed to the extremities creating a continuous flow. Sometimes, to those who were unable to see the source of a particular movement, this led to the impression that the dancer was lagging behind the musical beat. "During the last years of her teaching," says Miss Hewlett (her pupil), "she developed the backward and forward, sideward and rotary movement of the pelvis. This gave to her work a greater force and a more 'earthy' feeling, and also brought about the use of angles and distortion of line." To actual physical distortion she was vigorously opposed, and insisted that all technical movement be anatomically correct and do no injury to the body. For this reason, she disapproved of extreme back bends and turned-out positions of the legs and feet.

This last is, of course, against the basis of the classic traditional dance. But Bird Larson did not fully realize that the ballet offers a training which can accept the most radical ideas, and which always has done so, or it could no longer exist.

We are too close to this heroic Iron Age of American Ballet to do more than acknowledge its historic founders. From Denishawn emerged Doris Humphrey, Charles Weidman, and Martha Graham, all that is most native in our dance today. The summer seasons at Bennington College in Vermont, from 1934 on, have provided a place to create a repertory which represents all that is best in the Modern Dance. This "Modern" or free technique was idiosyncratic, antitraditional, and—above all—against the ballet.

Miss Ruth wrote about their early training at Denishawn House:

> We had not included the dance on the point, or the traditional ballet, not because of any barriers between what we considered the truly American development and the old traditional forms, but because we felt that we could not assume the organization of a complete ballet department. Yet we always taught the fundamentals of bar work which would allow a girl to become a ballerina with very little adjustment. We believed that, as the American dance developed, all forms, old and modern, would have to be represented.*

The young revolters against Denishawn were not so frank. They asserted the ballet was dead, that to touch it spelled the death of the dance. But, understood in historical perspective, we realize that much of their own immediate inheritance was cloying, indiscriminate, and superficial. Like Blake, they felt they must create their own system or be enslaved by another

* *Ibid.*, p. 244.

man's. But after the long decade of experiment (1930-40), we find the modern dancers eager to assimilate the bar work of traditional ballet. Martha Graham's partner, Erick Hawkins, is an outgrowth of ballet training. Graham herself recognizes what is complementary in ballet's centripetal brilliance to her own powerfully centrifugal control.

And Martha Graham from year to year stands as a monument to the pioneer strength of the American Dance. Her *Frontier* (1935) is a kinetic statement of Whitman's essence, and her *Letter to the World* (1941) gives us Emily Dickinson in a most precious lyric portrait. Graham has also been occupied with her spiritual sisters, Duncan and St. Denis, with spiritual problems, even at the expense of theater and the sacrifice of spectacle. Now her expression is no longer naïve. Her work is as simple as Shaker furniture and the crucifixes of the New Mexican pueblos, and as rugged as a clipper ship's figurehead. She is the center of the American dance.

Gertrude Hoffman, an American-born dancer, created something of a sensation in 1908, when she danced for Oscar Hammerstein in his famous production of Richard Strauss's *Salome*. Her dance of "The Seven Veils," ended with her fondling the prophet's head, and she landed in court on a charge of indecent exposure. Miss Hoffman, in later years, attributed it more to a Tammany plot than to either a publicity trick or the nature of her dance. "Big Tim" Sullivan owned part of another theater and didn't want business taken away from it.

Through 1910 and the spring of 1911, the directors of the Metropolitan Opera House had been considering inviting the Diaghilev ballet (p. 294) to appear on their New York stage. In the meantime, Miss Hoffman slipped abroad with her husband and took the initiative out of their hands. She contrived to obtain the services of the dancer, Theodore Kosloff, soloist in the original Russian company, and brought him back to America with such other of his colleagues as Maria Baldina, the mime Alexis Bulgakov, the dancers Tarasov and Zwerev. Rehearsing quietly in Brooklyn for some weeks, remembering as much as they could of the Fokine choreography and the Bakst decor, suddenly the impresarios Morris Gest and F. Ray Comstock produced in September, 1911, *La Saison des Ballets Russes* at the Winter Garden. *Cleopatre, Les Sylphides, Scheherezade, Carnival, Prince Igor* and *The Fire-Bird* were offered without acknowledgment to Fokine, Diaghilev or Bakst. We remember that Fokine describes *Les Sylphides,* his monument to the romantic epoch, as a "romantic revery in one act." Here is the program-note for the Winter Garden:

> Les Sylphides is well described as a "romantic revelry" (*sic*), and reveals yet a third phase of the Ballet Russe. The scene, hardly to be adequately described, is a vision of love and forest revelry—in itself a poem and a rhapsody. There are wood nymphs (*sic*), wild and shrieking, in some pagan saturnalia, the magic of music and rhythm, the sheer made beauty of grace and motion, a vision of charm never to be forgotten.

Miss Hoffman, at the least, was a pioneer. The Metropolitan abandoned the idea of bringing the bona fide Russians over until 1916, nearly five years later, and while *Coq d'Or* was later produced (1917) with the Diaghilev *mise en scène,* Bolm, not Fokine, was asked to stage it. Fokine should have been ballet-master there, but the Metropolitan Opera direction has never wanted an excellent ballet.

Increasingly, after the first World War, American dancers had been to Europe to be touched by the sunset, decadent fragrance and excitement of the late Diaghilev seasons. Ever since the arrival of his company in 1916, artists trained in the academies of Petersburg and Moscow had stayed in America to found their own schools. Fokine and Mordkin in New York, Bolm in Chicago and California, Paveley and Oukrainsky, Kosloff, Kotchetovski, Tarasoff, Gavrilov, Bekeffi; later Vladimiroff, Oboukhoff, Shollar, Vilzac, Swoboda, and Nijinska gave performances and raised two generations of native American dancers in the classic traditional theatrical dance, according to venerable international usage. These pupils called into being a native repertory.

In 1915, as John Martin tells us in his "America Dancing" (1936), shortly before the Denishawn School commenced in Los Angeles, the Neighborhood Playhouse opened its beautiful small theater on Grand Street, in lower New York City. It was an outgrowth of the Henry Street Settlement, but it went far beyond the scope of ordinary social-service activities. Although it was a repertory theater among other things, and gave notable performances of advance-guard plays of all kinds, dancing was always a most important part of its functions. Irene Lewisohn, a pupil of that influential student of Delsarte, Genevieve Stebbins, was particularly interested in calling into being a definitely theatrical dance. Mr. Martin describes her vision.

> It is characteristic of Miss Lewisohn's approach that the type of movement upon which she built her concept of dance was also that upon which she built her concept of theatre. It was not the sheer representationalism which is generally associated with the actor's pantomime, neither was it an arbitrary code of attitudes and geometrical abstractions; it was rather a creative, expressional medium closely akin to Isadora's.

But Miss Lewisohn was not basing her spectacles on improvisation, but rather on a general attitude of universal symbols deriving from folk cultures. While the Denishawn oriental works were frequently superficial and purely decorative, the Hebraic, Balinese, and East Indian dances from the Neighborhood Playhouse showed a more serious compression of the underlying ethnic ideas, whose correspondences in every culture approach a mystical, Whitmanesque unity.

Until 1927, when the Playhouse was reorganized, many ballets were produced, among them Stravinsky's *Petrouchka,* Prokoviev's *Chout,* the Rossini-Respighi *Boutique Fantasque,* a Noh drama produced by Michio Ito, a

Chinese opera, a Commedia dell'Arte, a Hungarian folk-festival to Bela Bartok, and the annual delicious "Grand Street Follies," which contained many dance numbers, from oriental to jazz. In an eighteenth century minuet, a young hoofer called James Cagney made his debut.

Mr. Martin analyzes the great contribution of Miss Lewisohn:

> Such an approach is in effect an effort to lift the theatre into the more elevated stratum of the dance without sacrificing any of those vivifying forces which belong exclusively to the theatre. Where, for example, Denishawn may be said to have put the dance into the theatre, the Neighborhood Playhouse has striven rather to put the theatre into the dance.

Ruth Page in Chicago, Catherine Littlefield in Philadelphia, William Christensen in San Francisco evolved companies to give seasons all over this continent. Page danced with Diaghilev in Monte Carlo, and commissioned works from first-rate American composers on folk themes. Littlefield carried her ballet abroad. Hers was the first American ballet to appear in France and England, although, of course, Duncan and Denishawn had preceded her with a different kind of work.

George Balanchine's activity in the United States since his arrival in 1933, has been varied and full, ranging from the creation of films, *The Goldwyn Follies* (1938), to musical comedies, *On Your Toes* (1940) and *Louisiana Purchase* (1941), and to a repertory for his "American Ballet" which has traveled in this country and throughout the length of South America (1941).

As an outgrowth of Balanchine's company, the present writer founded the Ballet Caravan in 1936, which created a repertory of classic and character pieces by three young dancers trained in the School of American Ballet. Lew Christensen (*Filling Station,* 1937), Eugene Loring (*Billy the Kid,* 1938), and William Dollar (*Juke Box,* 1941) give promise for good future work. Elements of the "modern" or free dance have enriched their choreography, but they utilize as basis the assimilated academic classic form.

In the meantime, Russian companies, employing the direct heirs of Diaghilev (d. 1929), continue to tour the country with the repertory he created in the years 1909-1929, as well as new works which show an increasing dilution of his taste, and a total lack of his gift for discovery. The commercialization, the glamorization of Russian ballet in the United States, its tie-up with cosmetic advertising and cheap films, have been detrimental to it. Certain interesting international painters of the neo-romantic or surrealist school have provided occasional beautiful scenery, but there have been few interesting new productions. However, there were some striking performances by Danilova, Tamara Toumanova, Frederic Franklin, and Alicia Markova. *St. Francis* (1939), had a fine score by Paul Hindemith and beautiful decor by Pavel Tchelitchew. Massine's dances gave him his most effective recent role. Neither De Basil's company nor Massine's has otherwise shown much initiative.

The Ballet Theatre emerged from a company directed by Michael Mordkin with American talent. It has evolved into an orthodox international troupe, with ranking Russian soloists. Its chief contributions are in the gifts of Antony Tudor (b. 1909), an Englishman. His *Jardin aux Lilas* (1936), *Dark Elegies* (1937), *Gala Performance* (1938), and *Judgment of Paris* (1938), all first given in London, were vital additions to a thin repertory.

With the war many things change. Dancers become soldiers, yet the dance survives. We are trembling on the verge of a new repertory and on the appearance of a new generation of our own first dancers. In any case, there is an audience here for dancing, talent among dancers, and great subjects from which to draw for music, painting, and movement. In spite of terrible threats to all of us, we can honestly say there has never been a time in history when lyric spectacle is more needed or more possible.

There have been as many influences at work in our dancing as in the rest of our national life, of which it is a part. But out of them all comes a curious, definitely strong stylistic flavor, something one can call an *American* dance, just as one knows the Russian or Italian. In a very remarkable recent article on "Conducting Modern Music," Mr. Virgil Thomson, the New York *Herald Tribune's* brilliant critic, analyzed the essential musical base.

> The basis of American musical thought is a special approach to rhythm. Underneath everything is a continuity of short quantities all equal in length and in percussive articulation. These are not always articulated, but they must always be understood. If for any expressive reason one alters the flow of them temporarily, they must start up again exactly as before, once the expressive alteration is terminated. In order to make the whole thing clear, all instruments, string and wind, must play with a clean, slightly percussive attack. This attack must never be sacrificed for the sake of a beautiful tone or even for pitch accuracy, because it is more important than either. Besides, once a steady rhythm is established, the music plays itself, pitch and sonorities adjust themselves automatically, as in a good jazz band the whole takes on an air of completeness.

BIBLIOGRAPHY OF SOURCE MATERIAL

CHAPTER I: (Primitive dance and general history)

Expressions of the Emotions in Man and Animals, by Charles Darwin (Curious and rewarding)
Ancient Art and Ritual, by Jane Harrison (Brief but indispensable)
Tribal Dancing and Social Development, by W. D. Hambly (Facts)
The Drama of Savage People, by Loomis Havemeyer
Africa Dances, by Geoffrey Gorer (The best description of dances. Localized to West Africa)
Patterns of Culture, by Ruth Benedict (American; and excellent)
The Dance of Life, by Havelock Ellis
Qu'est ce que c'est La Danse? Jean d'Udine (pseud. Albert Cozanet)
Danse, by Francis de Miomandre (cheap, with good pictures)
Der Tanz, by Oscar Bie (general)
Welt Geschichte des Tanzes, by Curt Sachs (general)

CHAPTER II: (Egypt)

The Golden Bough, by James Fraser (indispensable)
Every Day Life in Egypt, by S. R. K. Glanville
Egypt, by Wallis Budge
Dramas and Dramatic Dances of non-European Races, by Ridgeway (Very valuable)
The Sacred Dance, by W. O. E. Oesterly (Used also for Greece, Rome and Christianity)
Egyptian Festivals, by Flinders Petrie
Egypt: Lepsius (Old-fashioned but full of facts and cuts)

CHAPTER III: (Greece)

The Poetics: Aristotle
The Bacchæ: Euripides (Use Loeb Library rather than Gilbert Murray)
La Danse Grecque Antique: Louis Sechan (Better than Emmanuel: section on Dalcroze also)
Der Tanz in der Antike: Fritz Weege (splendid plates of Egypt, Greece, Rome)
Themis: Jane Harrison (The best in English for ritual)
A Prolegomena to the Study of Greek Religion: Jane Harrison (Indispensable)
The Attic Stage: A. H. Haigh (most useful)
The Mænads: Lillian B. Lawler (Memoirs of the American Academy in Rome, Vol. VI, 1927, pp. 69-112. Ingenious and good pictures)
A History of Theatrical Art: Karl Mantzius (general)
The Musical Basis of Verse: Dabney

CHAPTER IV: (Rome)

On Pantomime: Lucian of Samosa
Roman Life and Manners under the Early Empire: Ludwig Friedländer (complete)
Lives of the Twelve Cæsars: Suetonius
The Golden Ass: Apulieus
Lives (Sulla): Plutarch
Sexual Life in Ancient Rome: Otto Kiefer (Full of good gossip)

CHAPTER V: (The Christian Church)

Masks, Mimes and Miracles: Alardyce Nicoll (indispensable)
The City of God, and Confessions: Augustine (Loeb Library)
Liturgy and Worship: Clarke and Harris (detailed practical information)
Concerning Spectacles: Tertullian
The Ritual 'Reason Why': Walker and Bell
Liturgical Prayer Book: Don F. Cabrol (editor: indispensable)
The Catholic Dictionary (Edition in French)
The Christian Eucharist and Pagan Cults: W. M. Groton
The Drama and the Medieval Church: Karl Young (indispensable)
The Christ Myth: Arthur Drews
Dramatic Traditions of the Dark Ages: J. B. Tunison (outdated but interesting)

CHAPTER VI: (The Middle Ages)

The Mediæval Mind: H. O. Taylor (absolutely indispensable)
The Mediæval Stage: E. K. Chambers (absolutely indispensable)
The Troubadors at Home: J. H. Smith (gossip)
Trouvères and Troubadors: Pierre Aubry (good for music)
Troubadors and Courts of Love: J. F. Rowbotham
Sports and Pastimes of the People of England: Joseph Strutt (outdated but good)
The Spirit of Romance: Ezra Pound (excellent for poetry)
The Origins and Sources of the Courts of Love: W. A. Nielson (Literature)
The Dance of Death: Florence Warren (indispensable)
The Physician of the Dance of Death: A. S. Warthin (splendid pictures)
The Romaunt of the Rose: Geoffrey Chaucer

CHAPTER VII: (Feudalism)

English Pageantry: Robert Withington (indispensable)
The Chronicler of European Chivalry (Froissart): G. G. Coulton (Fine pictures)
Modes and Manners: Max von Boehn (vol. I) (Gossip)
Popular Entertainments Through the Ages: Samuel McKechnie
Les Noëls de France: Maurice Vloberg (Fine pictures)

Social England: Knill and Mann (vols. I and II)
Dancing: Mrs. Lilly Grove (and other writers)
Das Mittel Alterliche Hausbuch: Bossert and Storck (Fine pictures)

CHAPTER VIII: (The Renaissance)

The Renaissance in Italy: J. A. Symonds (complete 2 vols. Modern Library)
The Medici: G. F. Young (complete 1 vol. Modern Library)
The Courtier: Castiglione
A Jewish Dancing Master of the Renaissance: Otto Kinkeldey (indispensable)
Lives of the Gallant Ladies: Brantôme
The Italian Theater: Kennard
Modes and Manners: Max von Boehn (vol. II) (gossip)
Lives of the Illustrious Painters: Vasari

CHAPTER IX: (The Early Ballet)

Les Origines de l'Opéra: Ludovic Cellar (indispensable)
Le Ballet de Cour en France avant Lully: Henry Prunières (indispensable)
The Court Masque: Enid Welsford (The best book on the period in English)
Orchesography: Thoinot Arbeau
Foundations of English Opera: E. J. Dent
How to Dance the Revived Ancient Dances: Ardern Holt (with music)

CHAPTER X: (*Ballet de Cour*) The English Masque

L'Opéra Italien: Henry Prunières (between 1630 and 1650)
Lully: Henry Prunières (French. Short, with good pictures)
Lully: Numéro Spécial de la Revue Musicale (Full of good pictures and articles)
Molière: A. Tilley
Les Fâcheux: J. B. P. Molière
France under Mazarin: James B. Perkins (Vol. II)
Designs by Inigo Jones: The Walpole Society (The best pictures)
The Restoration Theater: Montagu Somers
The Puritans and Music
English Music. Edited by F. J. Crowest

CHAPTER XI: (Eighteenth Century)

The Dancing Master: P. Rameau
L'Opéra de Rameau: Paul-Marie Masson (indispensable)
Rameau: Lionel de la Laurencie (French, short, with good pictures)
Letters on the Dance: Noverre
Noverre: (introduction to the French edition: André Levinson)
L'Opéra avant la Revolution: Adophe Jullien
The History of Music: Cecil Gray (general)
The Pageant of Ballet: Mark Perugini (Vestris)
Three French Dancers of the Eighteenth Century: Cyril W. Beaumont (short and good)
A History of Pantomime: R. J. Broadbent

A History of Harlequin: Cyril W. Beaumont (fine text and plates)
Modes and Manners in the 18th Century: Max von Boehn
English Men and Manners of the 18th Century: A. S. Turberville
Mémoires: Le Duc de Saint-Simon
Memoirs: Jacques Casanova de Seignalt (Machen Translation)
A History of Ballet in Russia: Cyril W. Beaumont

CHAPTER XII: (Nineteenth Century)

Salvatore Vigano: Carlo Ritorni (in Italian)
The Art of Terpsichore: Carlo Blasis
Meister des Ballets: André Levinson (German)
Taglioni: André Levinson
The Romantic Ballet: Théophile Gautier
The Sleeping Beauty: André Levinson (for the Bakst 1921 revival)
My Life: Richard Wagner
Wagner en Caricature: John Grand-Carteret
Le Ballet au 19ième Siècle: (*Numéro Spéciale de la Revue Musicale*) Full of
splendid articles by Levinson, Prunières, Cœuroy
Nash Balet: Pleschaev (in Russian: curious pictures)
The Annals of the Imperial Theatres (Russian: 1891 yearly to 1915: Pictures
and fine articles)

CHAPTER XIII: (Early Twentieth Century)

My Life: Isadora Duncan
Modern Dancing and Dancers: J. E. Crawford Flitch
Michel Fokine and his Ballets: Cyril W. Beaumont
Fokine: Lincoln Kirstein
Nijinsky: Romola Nijinsky
The Eurythmics of Jacques Dalcroze: M. E. Sadler
Eurythmics, Art and Education: E. Jacques Dalcroze
Le Ballet Contemporain: Valerian Svetloff (fine plates)
Diaghileff: Arnold Haskell
The Dance: Ivan Narodney
Pavilion des Fantômes: Gabriel Astruc (good memoirs)
Commedia Illustre (magazine: fine pictures)
The Story of the Russian School: Nicolas Legat
The Russian Ballet in Western Europe: W. A. Propert (letters and plates)
Claude Debussy: Leon Vallas
Music at Midnight: Muriel Draper (Diaghileff)
Musician's Gallery: M. D. Calvocaressi (memoirs)
Theater Street: Thamar Karsavina
Russian Ballets: Adrian Stokes (good summaries)

CHAPTER XIV: (The Present)

A Call to Order: Jean Cocteau (The collaboration of *Parade*)
La Danse au Théatre: André Levinson (collected reviews)

La Danse d'Aujourd'hui: André Levinson (fine pictures)
Visages sur la Danse: André Levinson (his last reviews)
Lifar: Destin d'un Danseur: André Levinson (good pictures)
Das Mary Wigman Werk: Rudolph Bach (pictures)
Deutsche Tanz Kunst: Mary Wigman (pictures)
Balletomania: Arnold Haskell (gossip)
The Russian Ballet: 1921-1929: W. A. Propert (good plates)
Chroniques de Ma Vie: Igor Stravinsky (important memoirs)
A Textbook of the Classic Dance: Vaganova (in Russian)
The Modern Dance: John Martin
Tonight the Ballet: Adrian Stokes (Excellent introduction)

POSTSCRIPT: (Dancing in North America: 1519-1942)

Mexico Before Cortez: J. Eric Thompson
Catalogue of Mexican Music Directed by Carlos Chavez for the Museum of Modern Art. 1940
The Puritans and Music: Percy A. Scholes
The English Dancing Master: John Playford
Histriomastix: William Prynne
"An arrow against Profane and Promiscuous Dancing, drawne out of the Quiver of the Scriptures, By the Ministers of Christ at Boston in New England."
Jonathan Edwards: H. B. Parkes
Aesthetic Papers: Elizabeth Peabody
Twice Told Tales: Nathaniel Hawthorne
History of Plymouth Plantation: William Bradford
American Renaissance: F. O. Mathiessen
Memoirs of a Life Chiefly Passed in Philadelphia: Alexander Graydon
History of the American Stage: Brown
American Stage Dancing 1750-1800: Marian Hannah Winter, The Musical Quarterly, Vol. 24, pp. 58-73, Jan., 1938
Terpsichore or Ball Room Guide: Charles Durang
Pageant of the Dance in America: Frederick A. King (unpub.)
Critical Observations on the Art of Dancing: Giovanni Andrea Gallini
Principes et notions élémentaires sur l'art de la danse de la ville: J. H. Gourdoux
Hommage à Taglioni: Henry Whale
Etiquette, or a guide to the usage of society with a glance at bad habits, to which is added the true theory of the Rhenish or Spanish (*sic*) waltz, and of the German waltz a deux temps analyzed for the first time: Count Alfred D'Orsay
Le Maître à Danser: Anais Colin
The Amateur's Precepts on Dancing and Etiquette: D. L. Carpenter
Complete Ballroom Handbook: Elias Howe
A Complete Practical Guide to the Art of Dancing: Thomas Hillgrove
A few Reflections upon the Fancy Ball, otherwise known as the city's dancing assembly, by a Representative of thousands.

Uncle Sam Ward and his Circle: Maud Howe Elliott
Autobiography of America: Edited by Mark Van Doren
Le Maître de Danse, or the art of dancing cotillons: E. Conway
Our Old Feuillage: Walt Whitman
American Vaudeville; its Life and Times: Douglas Gilbert
Complete Book of Ballets: Cyril Beaumont
An Unfinished Life: Ruth St. Denis
Project for a Textbook: John Martin
America Dancing: John Martin
Blast at Ballet: Lincoln Kirstein
Songs of the Cattle Trail and Cow Camp: John A. Lomax

SUPPLEMENTARY:

The Dancing Times: London: Edited by Philip J. S. Richardson (good articles)
The Theater Arts Monthly: New York: Edited by Edith J. R. Isaacs (excellent articles and plates)
The American Dancer: New York City
Dance Index: New York City
Dance Observer: New York City
Educational Dance: Los Angeles, California

NOTES ON ILLUSTRATIONS

FRONTISPIECE:

From "The Code of Terpsichore" by Carlo Blasis: London 1830. These figures are perhaps the cleanest record of the unadorned classic *danse d'école* which is to be found. Contemporary theatrical dancing has enormously developed a decorative idiom on this grammatical base.

1. First position. 7. Second position. 3. Third position. 6. Fourth position. 4. Fifth position. 5, 8, 9. Various positions in *plié*. 9. Method of holding one's self in practicing. 15, 14. Close-legged and bow-legged pupils. 33, 34, 35, 36. Various attitudes and derivatives. 37. Giovanni de Bologna's "Mercury." 3 and 4. *Epaulement,* "opposition" of the body. 52. *Entrechat.* 53, 54, 55, 56. Various steps used in *elevation.* 31. Start of *pirouette.* 47. Arabesque.

1. Primitive Dance from the Caroline Islands: Early nineteenth-century engraving, based on sketches or descriptions brought back by explorers. A round-dance, similar to those of almost every other primitive people.

2. New Guinea Tribal Dance: Costumes designed to accentuate motion in dancing. Dance pattern more or less regular, for display.

3, 4, 5. Egyptian Dancers: Seated musicians accompany two dancers who mark their own time with clapping. An acrobatic dancer executing the position known as 'The Bridge.' Chorus-girls as high-kickers showing considerable extension of arms and feet; toes pointed, not 'natural.'

6. Archaic Greek Haymakers returning from work to quartet accompaniment. An agricultural procession, with song and dance of a type which would develop into dithyramb.

7. Greek Theater at Epidauros cut into a hillside: Circular orchestra or dancing floor: ruins of *Skene.*

8. Attic Comedians: Masked, with artificial comic appendages: A masked actor-dancer accompanying himself on a tambourine.

9. A choros of juggling satyrs probably based on acrobatic movements of a satyr-play. Tails, horns, etc., strapped on.

10. Drunken Mænads. Close in spirit to the choros of 'The Bacchæ' of Euripides. They bear bacchic symbols of goats and branches. One dancer holds castanets similar to Egyptian ones. (Compare no. 4)

11. Dancers draped in veils, with which they cover or reveal their moving bodies.

12. Etruscan wall painting at Corneto: A funeral dance. The dark man is conventionally red, his girl-partner paler, from less exposure to the sun, as in Egypt. (Compare no. 3)

13. War Dance: Campagna Relief. Similar to dances of the Salii. This illustrates the legend of Jove (Zeus) and the Kuretes. The infant god on the ground is protected by their clashed weapons.

14. Roman Burlesque Dancers: hold castanets, are either masked or are dwarfs. (Compare no. 8)

15. Nereids: This late, naïve relief, shows naked veil-dancers similar to those described in circus-shows.

16. Ivory Diptych of Anastasius: A.D. 517. In the lower portions, scenes from the amphitheater, indicated by semi-circular molding in left-hand panel. Lower right-hand panel shows Mimi. The three to the right and the second on the left, in tragic costume. The rest are comedians. Possibly a mimic burlesque scene of the healing of the blind. See Alardyce Nicoll: "Masks, Mimes and Miracles," pp. 143, 144.

17. Ivory Dipytch of St. Etienne of Bourges: Top rank, the Greek Muse Melpomene, with the tragic mask. Leda and the Swan; Lowest rank, Dionysiac (?) dance. (Compare no. 10)

18. David and Solomon with Six Choirs: This miniature is from a sixth-century Byzantine manuscript now in the Vatican Library (Greek, Ms. 699). It illustrates the gnostic romance of Cosmas, Traveler to India. The two scarf-dancers can be compared with nos. 11 and 15.

19. The Women of Israel greeting David with song and music, on his triumph over Goliath. The choir of women and the instruments used must be similar to those in thirteenth-century pageants. Below, to the left, Saul tries to slay his minstrel (troubador David).

20. Church of Santa Sabina: Rome. Early Christian Basilica with Imperial Roman columns. At the far end, altar slightly raised. Chancel-rail in marble. Mosaic dome.

21. Bishop and Worshipers. Tympanum of Sant' Ambrogio; Milan. Conventionalized ritual gestures made more rigid in the sculpture than in life.

22. Crucifixion Group: Tivoli, Twelfth Century. Illustrates such a *Planctus Mariæ* as that of Cividale del Friuli. Note Christ being deposed (taken down); His hands released from the nails.

23. Porch at Rouen: Salome dances on her hands. The relief shows a simultaneous stage-set with banquet, dance, execution, presentation of the Baptist's head, and Baptist in his prison, similar to mystery plays, staged (possibly) before these very doors. (Compare Salome with no. 4)

24. The Masque of Wild Men: Miniature in a manuscript of Froissart, painted ca. 1470. The incident of the ball in which costumes took fire occurred in 1393. Hence, costumes and accessories are of a court-mask of the later date, typical of medieval entertainment.

25. Salome: engraving by Israhel van Meckenem. The Bible story, a mere pretext, is relegated to the background. The fore-scene is a medieval German social (processional) dance.

26, 27, 28. Medieval Dancers: Stone reliefs on the Inn of the *Goldene Dachel,* Innsbruck; for Maximilian's Entry in 1500. The King and Queen watch professional dancers from their box. To the King's left is a Fool with cap and bells. Dancers are accompanied by a tabor (small drum). An hermaphrodite with long hair, wears morris bells on wrists and ankles. An acrobat in a back bend, is seconded by a dancing dog. The head of one of the dancers is shaved, badge of a *jongleur.*

29. German Spectacular Tournament with specially designed costumes, horse-trappings, etc. A knight rides up to the Tribune (compare with no. 26) to dedicate his spear to his lady.

30. Emperor Maximilian, calling himself the "Young White King," loving chivalric conceits, greets an entry of mummers to his banquet. They are dressed as Saracens, masked like birds, preceded by torch-bearers.

31. Lorenzo di Medici as one of the Three Wise Men of the East. An allegorical compliment to the House of Medici. Benozzo Gozzoli makes the young heir not an attendant upon the Wise Men, but one of the Magi themselves.

32. Allegory of the Return of Spring. Botticelli was inspired by court allegorical shows. The three dancing Graces based on a recently discovered antique marble. Persons of the Medici family are idealized with antique literary allusions of the Renaissance.

33. English Morris Dancers: Six Morris dancers, a maypole, a musician, a fool with cap and bells, a "King" riding a hobby-horse, a "Queen" holding a mayflower, and a Friar with a May-wreath. The last three are probably Robin Hood, Maid Marian and Friar Tuck.

34. Florentine Round-Dance, similar to those described in Boccaccio, and enjoyed by the early Medici. Accompaniment of Horns. ca. 1460.

35. Country Dances: paired dancers turning with high steps.

36. Court Dance, possibly a Pavane, or some other *basse danse.*

37. Ball of the Duc de Joyeuse: The Medicis, become French, in 1581, arrange court dances accompanied by a stringed orchestra. Greatest nobles dancing first, indicate a precedent for 17th and 18th century balls.

38 and 39. Dancing positions from Cesare Negri's *Nuove Invenzione di Balli,* published in Milan in 1604 and typical of the theoretical works of the Milanese dancing masters which would influence French social-dancing, and then French ballet of the seventeenth century. Negri's book was an amplification of Caroso's *Il Ballarino* of 1581.

40. Equestrian ballet-entrance at the Florentine Festivities of 1616, given in the Piazza Santa Croce, in honor of the Duke of Urbino. Giulio Parigi designed

the costumes and arrangements. This plate is one of a series of four engraved by Jacques Callot. The ground-plan of this fête or triumph is determined entirely from the air, or rather from the top-rank of seats in the especially constructed grandstand or *Teatro* made only for the occasion. The city soldiers, men-at-arms, police, etc., were used as "supers."

41. *Ballet Comique de la Reine:* disposition of the hall: with dispersed decor: The grove of Pan; Circe's Palace; the Golden Vault. This plate shows the start of the spectacle: *Le Récit du Gentilhomme Fugitif.*

42. *La Liberazione di Terreno,* a Florentine *Veglia* (vigil) or combined ballet and masked-ball. The stage is at one end of a ballroom. Scenery is localized, not dispersed (as in no. 41). Dancers descend onto the ballroom floor for grand evolutions of the ballet, and at its end will join with spectators in social dances.

43, 44. Fantastic ballet entries. Civil-dress of the epoch made theatrically grotesque. Compare the maskers of no. 44 with no. 30, a century before.

45. An orchestra; lutanists costumed as antique Romans. The forest and perspective stage-set show influences of Serlio's stage designs based on Vitruvius; (his 'Satiric' and 'Tragic' scenes).

46. Dancers in a lively measure of a definitely theatrical (as opposed to social) nature.

47. Inigo Jones costumes for two fantastic figures in an anti-masque. They are masked, wear medieval tabards and slashed sleeves. On their feet, birds' talons. Their movement suggests a rout.

48. 'Ballet' at the end of Milton's *Comus* showing a nocturnal illumination of the castle hall, a round-dance, and costumes based on antique models.

49. *Les Festes de L'Amour et Bacchus:* Comedy with music (and dances) given in the *Petit Parc* at Versailles, July 1668. Pastoral by Lully after Italian models, presented magnificently before Louis XIV. Note orchestra of strings and wood-wind in the trees; ballet entry of Satyrs. Compare with no. 45.

50. *Le Temple de la Paix:* Ballet by Quinault and Lully, Fontainebleau, September 1685. A garden theater with the Insignia above of the Royal Academy of Music. Note heavy ballet dresses *à la Berain:* (theatricalized civil-dress).

51. French and Italian Comedians in Paris, ca. 1670. The various masks; Scapin, Harlequin, Scaramouch, Pantaloon, in a perspective stage set, no longer inspired by the antique, but taken from the streets of Paris. Note stage illumination by candelabra (perhaps Cyrano's *Hôtel de Bourgogne*).

52. Coviello, a Neapolitan stock character from the *Commedia*. This is a nineteenth-century redrawing of a seventeenth-century wood-cut. Coviello appears around 1550. His stylized posture almost suggests a ballet position.

53. From Gregorio Lambranzi's "New and Curious School of Theatrical Dancing," printed in German and Italian, 1716. The dancing figures are out of the *Commedia*. The positions are highly stylized for the stage.

54. Initial positions from Rameau's 'Dancing Master': Paris and London: 1725.

55. Menuet: Engraved with its music, and a floor pattern in Feuillet's choreographic notation. Note the fluency of line, continuously indicated in the arms of the lady and gentleman; his feet are *turned out.*

56. Allegory of the Heavens: Agostino Caracci. If this was not taken from an actual ballet-opera, it might have been. The clouds, once *nuvole,* now *gloires,* are similar to machines invented by engineers of Lully and Rameau, to descend and ascend, carrying whole choirs of singers and dancers.

57. Early Russian Masquerade ca. 1735. Note figures of Harlequin and comic German soldiers. This kind of entertainment, imitated from Western Europe, shows a native, provincial heaviness and lack of sophistication.

58. Marie-Anne de Cupis de Camargo: A painter's idealization of the epoch's typical opera, ca. 1740. The ballet-costume, however long it may seem to us, was strikingly short for the period, displaying a bit of leg above the ankles.

59. Lady Hamilton (?) as a Bacchant (ca. 1800). Not an absolutely certain representation of Nelson's mistress in a "Greek" pose; if not, it is in her identical spirit. Her costume is a literal adaptation of the antique. On her tambourine is a similar figure. Her attitude, however 'free,' is nevertheless affected by ballet positions of the period. (Compare no. 10.)

60. Ariane Hugon, dancer of the Paris Opera (ca. 1820). Though photographed in the open air, she is shown in her interpretation of Berlioz' ballet of Sylphs in the Damnation of Faust.

61. *La Princesse de Navarre:* 1745: Ballet-opera collaboration of Rameau and Voltaire. Drawing by Cochin for a detail of the large engraving. It shows a typical theatrical dance borrowed from social *contre-danses* of the period. Note spectators sitting on the stage.

62. The Generous Turk: First *entrée* of Rameau's *Les Indes Galantes* as given in Vienna the 26th of April 1758. Vienna had not so long ago been besieged by the Turks, hence Osman the Pasha is wearing fairly accurate Moslem robes. His harem are dressed like the court-ladies of Maria Theresa. Note the stage-boxes, the crystal lusters, main source of illumination and the strings and horns in the pit. The engraver of this fine plate was Bernardo Belotto.

63. Ballet decor and costume by Bouquet, ca. 1765, typical of the new delicacy and refinement; contrast with the heavy sumptuousness of the 17th century (no. 50). Here is tacit acceptance of artificial convention. Architecture no longer imitates "Roman" buildings. It is frankly theatrical scenery.

64. The Three Graces: Ballet costumes by Bouquet. Very little footwork could be visible in these garments. (Compare Botticelli's Three Graces in no. 32.)

65. A Chinese Dance by Boucher: If not patterned actually on Noverre's *Fêtes Chinoises,* it must have been strikingly like it. Note contemporary French adaptations of Chinese costume. Baggy trousers of the male dancers are more Turkish than Chinese; but they seemed at least, "oriental."

66. *Jason et Medée:* English caricature of a local version of Noverre's ballet. The dancers seem not to have benefited much from his attempted costume reforms as yet. However, the 'passion' in the gestures give some idea of its dramatic intensity.

67. 'The Streletzki' choreodrame by Salvatore Vigano: Scenery by Sanquirico shows traces of Piranesi's Prison engravings. The actor-dancers, though in Russian costume, move in poses reminiscent of classic sculpture. Early use of psychological stage lighting.

68. *Le Rossignol:* with Carlotta Grisi and Jules Perrot. Typical early 19th Century ballet using elements from peasant dances (a village band, tavern, etc.). A group in classic *adagio* is in the center. The whole scene could be based on an opening dance or a finale.

69. Perrot, an excellent male dancer of the period. He wears traditional ballet slippers, and is costumed as a Tyrolean "peasant."

70. Grisi in 'Giselle'; her costume taken from folk sources, has been made as demure as possible. The sleeves and bodice, however, show gothic influence. The wand in her hand is an accessory in a wine-festival, and is none other than a romantic adaptation of the Bacchic thyrsos. (Compare nos. 10 and 68.)

71. Idealized *Pas de Trois* showing three great ballerinas in characteristic costumes: Taglioni as the Sylph, Elssler in Spanish dress (the *Cachucha*), Cerito as Diana, the Huntress.

72. Taglioni's greatest rôle: Sylphide costume designed in tarlatan by Eugène Lamy is here idealized into a satin bouffant skirt. In her hair and on her breast are morning-glories (soon to fade).

73. *Ballet de l'Opéra,* ca. 1850. This lithograph suggests *Giselle,* although it is a late amalgamation of several similar dream-ballets. Here white ballet-skirts are three tiered, appliquéd with ribbons and blossoms.

74. *Foyer de Danse,* ca. 1850; a ballet-master is exercising a few dancers, while the dandy is arranging an after-the-theater rendezvous.

75. Finale from *Katerina,* ballet with choreography originally by Perrot, remounted for the repertory of the Marinsky Theatre.

76. Group from *Melusine,* choreography by Valtz (an assistant of Petipa's). The scene is an artist's studio. The girls in ballet-skirts are models.

77. Group from Petipa's 'Victims of Amor: or the Joys of Love': This group is an 1893 idea of the 18th Century. Legat, the young male lead, represents Cupid: he wears flesh-colored tights. (Compare with no. 63.)

78. Isadora Duncan, fresh from California: New York 1898. Her costume, perhaps specially conceived for her photographer, seems to have been made from a "lace" window-curtain. But her arms are more open, her head more expressive than most nineteenth century ballerinas. On her feet, however, are classical ballet-shoes, not with hard toes, but with the double ribbon.

Caroline Islands

New Guinea

3. Abd-El-Kurna

4. The Bridge   (1580-1350 B.C.)

5. Sakkara

6. Haymakers Returning From Work

Epidauros

8. Attic Comedians   (Fourth Century B.C.)

9. Dancing Satyrs

Drunken Maenads

11. Tanagra Veil-Dancers

12. Etruscan Funeral Game

13. Kuretes

14. Roman Pantomimes

15. Circus Veil-Dancers   (Fifth Century A.D.)

18. David and Solomon   (Sixth Century)

19. David and Saul
(Thirteenth Century) Morgan Library Ms. 728

20. Roman Basilica   (Santa Sabina)

21. Bishop and Worshippers   (S. Ambrogio: Milan)

22. **Crucifixion**   (Twelfth Century)

23. **Salome Dances: Rouen**

24. Masque of Wild Men   Ca. 1470

25. The Ball of Salome   Ca. 1475 Van Meckenham

26.

27.

28. Inn of The *Goldene Dachel:* Innsbruck   1500   R. Müller

29. Tournament: Wittenberg   1508 Cranach

30. Banquet and Mommerie   Ca. 1500 Burgkmair

31. Florentine Pageant   Ca. 1459 Gozzoli

32. Primavera   Ca. 1477 Botticelli

MORRIS·DANCERS.

From an Ancient Window in the House of GEORGE TOLLET Esqr. at BETLEY in STAFFORDSHIRE.

33. English Morris Dancers

Florentine Round Dance   Ca. 1460 Crivelli

36. Court and Country Dances   Ca. 1570 De Bry

Ball of the Duc De Joyeuse   1581 Clouet

38. and 39. Positions of Milanese Dances   1604 Negri

40. Florentine Spectacle   1616 Callot

42. *Liberazioni di Tirreno:* Florence   1617 Callot

41. *Ballet Comique de la Reine*· Paris   1581

43. French Ballet Entry   Ca. 1606

44. French Ballet Entries   1617

45. Orchestra and Recitatif : Paris   1617

46. Ballet of Demons : Paris   1617

47. Anti-Masque: "Chloridia": London
1631 Jones (Copyright By The Duke Of Devonshire)

48. Final Ballet: Milton's "Comus" 1634

Le Vilis S. L'Amen it de Guerlad Comide en Musique
represente dans le peut Parc de Versailles

Venus Cupidinis et Bacchi, Comædia ad perpetuam rerum
et tibiarum cantum uda in Hortis Versailiani

49. Ballet of Lully: Versailles 1678 Le Pautre

50. Ballet of Quinault and Lully:

Fontainbleau 1685

51. French and Italian Comedians: Paris   Ca. 1670

52. Coviello   Ca. 1550 Sand

53. Dancing Comedians   1716 Lambranzi

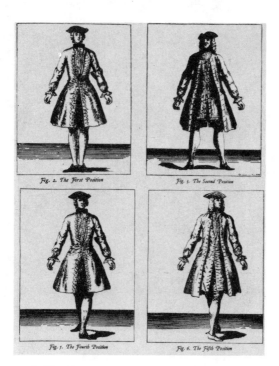

Fig. 2. The First Position   Fig. 3. The Second Position

Fig. 5. The Fourth Position   Fig. 6. The Fifth Position

54. The Dancing Master   Ca. 1725 Rameau

55. Menuet   Vanhaecken

56. Heaven   Caracci

57. Masquerade: Russian   Ca. 1735

58. Camargo   Lancret

. **Lady Hamilton**   Ca. 1800 Townay (?)

60. Ariane Hugon   Ca. 1920 Boissonas

61. *La Princesse de Navarre:* Versailles   1745 Cochin

62. *Les Indes Galantes:* Vienna   1758 Belotto

63. Ballet Decor: French   Ca. 1765 Bouquet

64. Ballet Costume: French   Ca. 1765 Bouquet

65. *Les Fêtes Chinoises*   Ca. 1755 Boucher

66. *Jason et Medée:* London   Ca. 1790

67. "The Streletzki": Milan   1812 Sanquirico

68. "The Nightingale": London   1836

69. Perrot: Paris Ca. 1835

70. Grisi: "Giselle": Paris 1844

71. *Pas de Trois*: Paris Ca. 1845

72. Taglioni: *"La Sylphide"*: Paris

73. *Ballet de L'Opèra:* Paris   Ca. 1850

74. *Les Rats* Rehearsing: Paris   Ca. 1850

75. *Katerina:* St. Petersburg   Ca. 1895

76. *Melusine:* St. Petersburg   Ca. 1895

77. "Victims Of Amor": St. Petersburg   1893

Isadora Duncan: New York City   1898

79. Loie Fuller: New York City   1901

80. Duncan: London   1910

81. Pavlova (Bacchanale): Paris Ca. 1913

82. & 83. Caricatures By Nicolai And Sergei Legat: St. Petersburg   Ca. 1904

84. "Carnaval": Paris   1910

85. "Fire-Bird": Paris   1910

86. *"Les Sylphides": Paris* (Fokine) 1909   Commedia

87. *Le Pavilion D'Armide: Paris* (Fokine) 1909

88. *Schèherezade:* Paris (Fokine) 1910

89. Petrouchka: Paris (Fokine) 1911

0. *Daphnis et Chloè:* Paris   (Fokine) 1912

91. "Joy"; "Mourning"   (Jacques Dalcroze) Boissonas

92. *Daphnis et Chloè:* Paris   (Fokine) 1912

93. Nijinsky: Petrouchka 1911

94.

95. Nijinsky-Karsavina: Giselle 1909

96. Nijinsky: *Dieu-Bleu* (Fokine)

Dionysos: Exekias   Sixth Century B.C.)

98. Orfeus: Florence   1608 Parigi

tele of an Athenian

(Sixth Century B.C.)

100. "Afternoon Of A Faun"

(Nijinsky) 1912 De Meyer

101. "Afternoon Of A Faun": Paris (Nijinsky) 1912 De M

102. *Jeux:* Paris (Nijinsky) 1913

4. The Rites of Spring: Paris   (Nijinsky) 1913

. The Village Wedding: Paris
(Nijinska) 1923

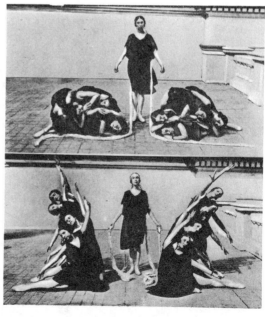

106. The Village Wedding: Paris   (Nijinska) 1923

107. Tyl Eulenspiegel:

    New York: (Nijinsky) 1916

108.

109. Tyl Eulenspiegel.

    Costumes by R. E. Jones 1916

110. Vaslav Nijinsky: New York

11. 112.

113.

Parade: Paris: (Massine) A Manager; The Horse; The American Girl. 1917

14. *Les Biches:* Paris   (Nijinska) 1924

115. *Ode:* Paris   (Massine) 1928

Lipnitzk

116. *Apollon Musagète:* Paris   (Balanchine) 1928

117. "The Prodigal Son": Paris (Balanchine) 1929 Sascha

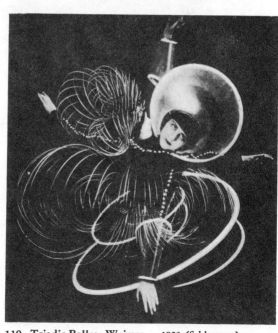

. Mary Wigman:
   Dresden 1924

119. Triadic Ballet: Weimar 1923 (Schlemmer)

120. Rehearsal: "The Sleeping Beauty" Moscow   1932 (Petipa)

121. "Transcendence": Hartford: (Balanchine) 1934   Newell

122. The School of American Ballet. 1935

123.   Newell

79. Loie Fuller: New York 1901. Her arms support poles which carry butterfly wings. In motion, they float about, illuminated by electric lights casting multi-colored shadows. (Compare with no. 11.)

80. Isadora Duncan: London 1910. In the height of her early successes, she is shown in a quiet pose reminiscent of Græco-Roman figures on the Borghese vase. Her feet are bare, her costume is based on the antique.

81. Anna Pavlova as a Bacchant: Paris ca. 1912 or later. Typical of the Dionysiac spirit in Fokine's work. Her position is precisely taken, however free the gesture. Hands, naturally relaxed, nevertheless hold her fingers as in such a ballet as *Les Sylphides.*

82. The Brothers (Nicolai and Sergei) Legat, with the aid of Igor Stravinsky's father, published a remarkable portfolio of caricatures of artists associated with dancing at the Imperial Theatres; not only dancers, but wig-makers, musicians, gendarmes, stage hands. The drawings show an amazing ana-tomical documentation of the styles of individual dancers. Sergei Legat him-self, at the upper left, is about to step off into a classic *variation.* Enrico Cechetti, the famous Italian dancing mime, is shown, with a violin which he used for practice-exercises (instead of a piano), hopping like a green grasshopper. Michel Fokine, the new Mercury, holds his caduceus. He is dressed like a Greek god. Marius Petipa, in dress-clothes, too old to dance, still supports the banner of *Ballet.*

83. Preobrajenska, a butterfly, glistens with jewels: Mathilde Kshessinska, from whose palace balcony Lenin proclaimed the Soviets, leads her goat in 'Es-meralda.' Trefilova is "in preparation" for a turn, and Anna Pavlova, thin to a degree, dances with a veil.

84. Fokine and Fokina in 'Carnival.' Witty characterizations in Fokine's stylized adaptations in Italian pantomime, with his own brand of fluent mimicry, set in the Viennese Biedermeier, and interspersed with brilliant classic dancing. Compare with no. 51.

85. Fokine and Fokina in Stravinsky's Fire-Bird: the *pas de deux* in the first scene; at the time, it seemed very new; to us, an ordinary classic duet. How-ever, the ballerina is dressed by a good designer. She wears no tutus; her costume is an example of orientalism in early Diaghileff ballets.

86. *Les Sylphides:* A group from Fokine's 'Romantic Revery in One Act,' used as an automobile-advertisement of the epoch (1910), "What every one must do! See the Russian Ballet and buy a 'Panhard' car." Compare arm gesture of the dancer on the extreme right with no. 81.

87. The start of the *pas de deux* (Fokine and Karsavina) from *Le Pavillion d'Armide.* Spectacular ballet, style of the epoch of *Le Grand Monarque.* Compare with nos. 50, 61 and 77.

88. Finale of 'Scheherezade.' Lacking the garish brilliance of Bakst's coral, green and purple hangings, nevertheless some idea of the miming can be obtained

from noticing positions of the Shah throttling his faithless wife. A henchman spurns the dead slave (Nijinsky) with his foot.

89. *The Death of Petrouchka:* The Moor (Bolm) is about to deliver a *coup de grâce*. Nijinsky pleads; Karsavina, the ballerina, averts her face. Notice various Russian types in the crowd at the fair. The show-booth is in the background, beneath the ferris-wheel.

90 and 92. Poses from *Daphne et Chloë:* (Fokine and Fokina). Sensitive absorption of Greek stylization from sarcophagi and vase-painting. The Ballerina is barefoot; the male dancer in antique sandals; Bakst's costumes are pleated as on the old vases. Compare with nos. 10 and 12. Bakst's scenery not realistic but executed as *painted* surfaces.

91. Rhythmic compositions by Jacques Dalcroze: Compare with nos. 11 and 8. The spontaneous freedom, lack of precision or style is an interesting contrast with no. 90.

93 and 94. Two positions in Fokine's *Petrouchka* (Nijinsky). Brusque angularity and extreme rigidity of movement. (The background is a photographer's.)

95. Nijinsky and Karsavina in a *pas de deux* from *Giselle*. Shows admirably the elegance of nineteenth century classic dancing; tender balance in the support, sureness of the male partner. Notice Karsavina's bent-back hand, to emphasize the plasticity of the plane of her arm.

96. Poses from Fokine's 'Blue God' (Nijinsky). Influence of Mughal miniatures, cave-painting at Ajanta, etc. Another example of technical stylization to fit a given epoch (here not Greek but East Indian). The precision and absoluteness in gesture presupposes a basis of the *danse d'école*.

97. Bacchos-Dionysos in his ship: Greek black-figured vase painting by Exekias. His boat is a stylized Dolphin. From the mast sprouts grapes and vine-leaves.

98. A Renaissance pageant ship for a Florentine festival on the Arno. This is an adaptation from *purely literary* sources, largely Græco-Roman (Lucretius, Lucian, etc.) of the antique (no. 97). It is Orfeus, playing the lyre (violin) on the ship of Bacchus, designed by Giulio Parigi for the naval fête of 1608. This was the barque of Messer Niccolo Berardi. Notice Renaissance adaptation and accumulation of "Roman" decorative detail.

99. Funeral stele of a soldier: (Athens: 6th Century): The delicacy of the archaic stylization of a dead hero in a semi-ritualized kneeling position. The bas-relief uses the convention of the 'significant profile.' Compare with no. 90.

100. Nijinsky: 'Afternoon of a Faun': Plastic appropriation, not of literary remains as in 98, but of an *exact document* such as 99. Notice sandals, profile, and Bakst's make-up, not on face alone, but on the whole torso. Compare with Fokine's painted mask, no. 85.

101. 'Afternoon of a Faun': Nijinsky: A Frieze of Maidens. Notice the vague impressionism of the painting in Bakst's background, contrasted with strong angles of the dancers' arm movements.

102 and 103. *Jeux:* Flannel tennis-jumpers, style of 1913. Note toe-shoes on Karsavina and Schollar.

104. Group from 'The Rites of Spring': Nijinsky, 1913: Primitive Russian Earth Ceremonial imaginatively stylized from Roerich's designs and Stravinsky's music.

105 and 106. Groups from *Les Noçes Villageoises,* 1923: Choreography by Bronislava Nijinska (Vaslav's sister): Photographs taken on the roof of a theater in practice-clothes. The central female dancer is Felia Doubrovska. Use of abstract, stylized movement in the precision of ballet technique.

107 and 108. Vaslav Nijinsky in 'Tyl Eulenspiegel': Ballet Pantomime based on medieval Flemish and German Gothic paintings and sculpture. (Compare nos. 26, 27, 28.)

109. Use of "Expressionist" costumes and scenery. Desertion of archeology for the intensification of lyric atmosphere by selection, distortion and emphasis. These costumes, in motion, accentuated the strangeness of the gestures of the bodies beneath. (Compare with no. 25.)

110. Nijinsky in New York, 1916. The perfect security and balance of a trained dancer's body in repose. While he is obviously posing for his photograph, the unerring, conscious yet unaffected elegance is the mark of the best traditions in the *danse d'école.*

111, 112, 113. *Parade,* 1917: Picasso's Cubist "Theatrical Manager." The ferocious horse. Compare the American Girl with nos. 102 and 103.

114. The Houseparty: 1923. Nijinska's amplification of *Jeux* (nos. 102, 103). The dancer in black tunic, on points, with white gloves, is Nemtchinova. Her partner in the bathing suit is Serge Lifar.

115. *Ode:* 1928: Massine—Tchelitcheff—Nabokoff. The use of extra-choreographic material, ropes, nets, etc., to enhance a musical choreo-dramatic synthesis.

116. 'Apollo, Leader of the Muses': 1928: Balanchine—Beauchant—Stravinsky. Reintegration of the classic ballet. Photographs taken on the stage.

117. Ballet pantomime at its best. Excellent combination of all contributing factors; paint, music, dance. Chief dancers: Serge Lifar, Felia Doubrovska, Leon Woizikovsky, Anton Dolin. Decor by Georges Rouault.

118. Mary Wigman: Subjective, personal, non-theatrical dance. Compare with nos. 77 and 79.

119. One of the mobile costumes in Schlemmer's 'Triadic' ballet. This double exposure shows essential dehumanization of the dancer, emphasis on costume, or rather abstract forms supported by the dancer's body.

120. A Rehearsal (1932) of a children's scene from Petipa's 'Sleeping Beauty' in the Soviet State School, Moscow. Notice insistence on the classic theatrical dancing manner.

121. 'Transcendence': 1935: (Liszt). Choreography by George Balanchine, decorations by Franklin Watkins. Stage photograph of adagio scene from the initial repertory of the American Ballet.

122 and 123. Scene in the classroom: School of the American Ballet: Adagio dancers are Holly Howard, William Dollar, Charles Laskay and Katherine Mullowney: *tour en l'air* by Paul Haakon.

ACKNOWLEDGMENTS

This book, in more ways than one, is a collective effort. Not only am I indebted to numerous authors living and dead on whose works I have drawn, but also to many friends who have been generous with their time and ideas, in three categories of principles, facts and bibliography.

First of all I wish to thank A. Hyatt Mayo, once my co-editor of "Hound & Horn," now of the Metropolitan Museum Print Room in New York City, for putting at my disposition all books and engravings with which his museum is endowed. Conversations with F. A. Brinser of 'Every Week,' aided my historical and political formulation. I wish particularly to thank Martin Mower of the Department of Fine Arts, Harvard College, for whatever correlation of styles and epochs I appreciate. Payson Loomis illuminated for me principles of dancing beyond the limits of the Western classic school, not only in Islam, but also in Spain and Asia.

A book about dancing relies on the aid of dancers. George Balanchine, whose name appears in this story, has told me much of a practical nature about Russia, Diaghileff, and choreography. Agnes de Mille and Roger Pryor Dodge have aided me in understanding the styles of antiquity and the essence of the contemporary.

I am indebted to Michel Fokine, to Bronislava Nijinska, to Romola Nijinsky, and to Anatole Bourman, Vaslav Nijinsky's classmate and author of an important, as yet unpublished biography of his friend, for information which they alone can impart.

Paul Magriel has compiled an astonishing bibliography of all books relating to the dance, in American libraries. He permitted me to use the results of his monumental labor before its imminent publication. Eugene Bonner of the Music Division of the New York Public Library has done a similar inestimable service for magazine articles and information *not* in books specifically about dancing. Robert Pitney played and analyzed for me almost every piece of ballet music mentioned. Frederick A. King has been so generous with books, prints and information from his unique collection that this book would not have been possible without them. His book on dancing in America, when published, will supplement a portion of contemporary history not touched on here.

Muriel Draper has told me everything about the Soviet Ballet. Nicolas Nabokoff, composer of "Union Pacific" and *Ode,* has given me the invaluable benefit of his information as well as artistic and personal advice. Pavel Tchelitcheff, designer of *Ode* and *Errante,* explained to me the essence of the Diaghileff period from a social and philosophical point of view. Monroe Wheeler and Glenway Wescott have told me much about their friend Isadora Duncan. I am indebted to Carl van Vechten for his description of early Diaghileff seasons. Edna Ocko and Jane Dudley of *New Theater* did their best to make me like the "modern dance." Arnold Haskell, dance critic of the

London *Daily Telegraph,* and John Martin of *The New York Times,* aided my formulation of a critical attitude. Harry Dunham described for me the methods of his teacher, Mary Wigman. Erick Hawkins taught me most of what I know about the practical technique of classic ballet, through our common master and model, Pierre Vladimiroff. Paul Boepple, Director of the Dalcroze School of Music, provided me with ideas and information, not alone on Dalcroze. Priscilla Fairchild of *Time* aided my researches in the Eighteenth Century. Much of it, unfortunately, had to be cut for lack of space. H. S. Ede of the Tate Gallery, London, enabled me to meet people connected with Diaghileff in England. The late T. E. Lawrence wrote me a description of Nijinsky modifying my idea of a dancer I never saw, and which I hope to employ further in another study. I am indebted to M. Pierre Tugal of the *Archives Internationales de la Danse* for facts gathered from his review, the best periodical on dancing published today; and to Mrs. Edith J. R. Isaacs of *Theatre Arts Monthly,* for advice, bibliographical information, and permission to quote the remarks of Oscar Schlemmer.

I wish to thank the publishers who have permitted me to quote from their publications. First of all, Cyril Beaumont of London, whose original work and reprints provide an almost complete historical bibliography of the classic dance. I have used his "Marie Taglioni" by André Levinson, "The Romantic Ballet" by Théophile Gautier, "The Dancing Master," by P. Rameau, "Letters on Dancing and Ballets," by Jean Georges Noverre, "Orchesography," by Thoinot Arbeau; and from Cyril Beaumont's own "History of Ballet in Russia (1631–1881)," "The History of Harlequin," and "Three French Dancers of the 18th Century." To Macmillan and The Cambridge University Press, for H. O. Taylor's "The Mediæval Mind," Enid Welsford's "The Court Masque," and the Collected Poems of William Butler Yeats. To Houghton Mifflin for "Patterns of Culture," by Ruth Benedict. To the Oxford University Press for Fowler's translation of Lucian, for Sir E. K. Chambers' "The Mediæval Stage," and for Karl Young's "The Drama in the Mediæval Church." To the Liveright Publishing Corporation for "The Book of the Courtier," by Count Baldesar Castiglione, translated by Leonard Eckstein Opdycke, c/r 1929, Liveright. This is a different translation from the Tudor Classics. To Doubleday Doran for Vincent Sheehan's "Personal History." To Harcourt Brace for Alardyce Nicoll's "Masks, Mimes and Miracles" and "The Development of the Theater." To Faber and Faber (London) for "Russian Ballets," by Adrian Stokes. To the British Continental Press for "The Story of the Russian School," by Nicolas Legat. To Alfred A. Knopf for D. H. Lawrence's "Mornings in Mexico." And to Dr. Otto Kinkeldey, of Cornell University, for "A Jewish Dancing Master of the Renaissance."

I also wish to thank Mr. Bruce Rogers for his kindness in permitting me to quote from Colonel T. E. Lawrence's translation of The Odyssey.

I am indebted for the use of photographs to His Grace the Duke of Devonshire (Inigo Jones' Antimasque); to Baron Gayne de Meyer (Nijinsky); to Sascha of London; to Lipnitzki of Paris; to Fred Boissonas of Paris (Dalcroze); to the Pierpont Morgan Library for permission to reprint a plate from their manuscript (No. 728).

I am under great obligation to the kindness and untiring service of the staff of the Metropolitan Museum Print Room in New York City, to the Frick Reference Library, to the Morgan Library and Miss Helen Frank; to the New York Public Library (Music Division), Dr. Carleton Smith and Miss Pratt, to the Congressional Library in Washington (Music Division) and Mr. Rodionoff; and to the Smith College Library.

Two persons are almost equally responsible for this book. My friend and secretary, Doris Levine, undertook all the drearier tasks connected with its consistency. Mrs. Harry Curtiss of Chapel Brook, Ashfield, Massachusetts, allowed me to work in such ideal conditions for which few authors or brothers are permitted to be grateful. Thanks of a different nature are also due to Rima, Josephine, Garbo, Muffin, as well as Master Boodle Curtiss.

Lincoln Kirstein.

QUOTATIONS FROM WORKS OR TRANSLATIONS BY CYRIL W. BEAUMONT OCCURRING IN "DANCE"

IMPORTANT EVENTS IN
THEATRICAL DANCE

6th Century, B.C.

"Thespis," described by Aristotle as a dancer, taught the Bacchic choros.

535 First competition for choral declamation at the Feast of Dionysos Eleutheros: Athens.

499 Wooden theater replaced by stone: Athens.

405 The *Bacchæ* of Euripides produced in Athens after his death. The finest type of Greek dance drama.

390 Under the Consulate of Sulpicius Peticus scenic games were invented to appease the gods and distract plague-stricken Rome.

329 Stalls erected for circus chariots and horses by Tarquin the Younger. Foundations of the Circus Maximus.

240 Livius Andronicus, an "actor" supposed to have invented mime.

211 Establishment of *Ludi Apollinares,* annual theatrical games.

154 Stone theater destroyed as unsuitable by Roman Senate.

129 Birth of Quintus Roscius, the great Roman Mime.

68 A law of the tribune L. Roscius Otho fixed places in theater for the various classes.

55 First permanent Roman theater erected, largely of wood, under Pompey.

55 A.D. First stone theater in Rome erected under Tiberius.

ca. 100 Rivalry of the mimes Pylades and Bathyllus.

ca. 150 Lucian, author of the dialogue on "Pantomime," the best picture of Roman mimes.

ca. 160 Apocryphal (gnostic) gospel of "The Acts of John," portraying Christ as dancer.

ca. 200 Tertullian, the Christian, anathematized without differentiation (*De Spectaculis*) all dramatic performances.

300 Council of Elvira rules players, dancers and mimes be denied the Christian Sacrament.

410 Rome sacked by Alaric.

426 Augustine's "City of God," blaming the scenic games.

544 Childebert, King of the Franks, proscribes dancing in all his lands.

ca. 550 The last spectacle in Rome under the East Goths (Theodoric).

604 Dancing in certain English churches.

ca. 650 Complete fall of Roman stage.

692 Council of Trullanum forbids all stage-dancing: Constantinople.

692 Edict of Council of Constantinople: For fear lest ecclesiastical dogma might hide under oriental symbolism the essential human-

ity of Christ, ordered the Redeemer should be shown *humana forma* (in human form).

744   Pope Zacharias forbids all dancing.

ca. 850   Development of symbolic ecclesiastical costume: alb, dalmatic, stole, etc., in Eastern and Western churches, as projection of civil garb.

ca. 935   Birth of Hrswitha of Gandersheim.

ca. 970   *Quem Queritis* playlet in St. Ethelwold's (English) code for Easter celebrations, with miming indicated.

ca. 973   Use of the *Palmesel:* wooden figure of Christ on the Ass, used at Augsburg at Easter.

ca. 1000   Rise of wandering minstrels and jongleurs: Provence.

1087–1127   Life of Guilhem IX, Seventh Count of Poitiers; The First Troubadour.

ca. 1110   Dunstable play of St. Catherine: Early religious drama. Birth of Provençal dance-songs.

ca. 1200   Cathedrals develop as symbolistic theaters for performance of the Mass, parallel to the development of the cult of the Virgin.

ca. 1200   Emergence of *Sacre Rapprazentazioni,* in which vulgar Italian (not Latin) is exclusively used.

1226   The English ms. of dancers' tune "Summer is a'cummen in."

1235   The Albigensian Crusade: End of Provençal culture.

1258   Ranieri Fusani of Perugia organizes the *Disciplinati di Gesu Cristo:* Their *Laudi* from which simple dramatic forms arose, and later Renaissance drama and opera.

1260   The *Carole* danced in Sweden.

1263   Mumming forbidden in an edict of Troyes.

1273   Guiraut de Riquier's 'Supplicatio' to Alfonso X of Castile, stating categories of troubadour and joglar.

1312   First painting of the Dance of Death; Klingenthal, Little Basle, Switzerland.

1347   Edward III of England holds a Christmas Mask at Guildford. Dancing mania at Aix-la-Chapelle.

1350   *Devozioni* of Holy Thursday and Good Friday, Florence: Sacred dramas given in church.

1373   The Black Death: Popularity of representations of the Dance of Death.

1374   Dancing mania strikes Cologne.

1377   The Commons of London compliment Richard II in mummer's disguises.

1389   Isabella, Queen of France, enters Paris. All gates adorned with "pageants."

1393   The Masque of Wild Men (Wodehouses) or *Bal des Ardents;* Hall of St. Pol, Paris.

1424 Famous Mural of the Dance of Death in Church of the Holy Innocents: Paris.

1429 Discovery (in Germany) of ms. with twelve new comedies of Plautus, the classic Roman Comedian.

ca. 1431–1500

Activity of Antonio Cornazano of Piacenza: Master of William the Jew of Pesaro.

1431 Henry VI enters Paris: Met by pageants, mimes and 'mysteries.'

1444 Foundation of the Medici Library: Florence.

1450 Feo Belcari's: *Abraham and Isaac.* Earliest formalized *Sacre Rapprazantazione.*

1452 The architect Alberti's theater for Pope Nicholas V.

1453 The Fall of Constantinople scatters Hellenic learning westward. The story of Jason and the Golden Fleece enacted as a mimed mystery at the Court of Burgundy. Actors did not keep time with the music.

Allegorical representations at Reggio Emilio for the entrance of Borso d'Este.

1457 Reception at the Court of Charles VII of France to the Hungarian Embassy. The *Moresque* danced.

ca. 1460 French *entremets* and Italian *intermedii* very similar: Entertainments at banquets.

1463 Date of Paris ms. of *De Arte Seu Tripudii,* text-book of William the Jew of Pesaro.

1468 Marriage of Charles the Bold and Marguerite of York: Dramatization of the Tournament.

1469 Betrothal of Lorenzo di Medici and Clarice Orsini: The pageants painted by Benozzo Gozzoli in the Ricardi Chapel.

1471 The *Orfeo* of Angelo Poliziano: a pastoral at the Gonzaga Court at Mantua.

1475 Giuliano di Medici's Pageants: painted by Sandro Botticelli in his *Primavera.*

1486 A theater in Ferrara for Latin comedy.

1487 Duke Ercole d'Este of Ferrara produces *The Fable of Cephalus,* a pastoral play based on Politian's *Orpheus.*

1489 Bergonzio de Botta's Banquet.

1490 Feast of Fools in Rheims Cathedral.
Milan: The Sforza Court: Bernardo Bellincioni's *Il Paradiso.*

1493 Pavia: Production of Leonardo da Vinci's *Paradiso* with seven gyrating planets.

1494 Charles VIII of France invades Italy.

1507 'Dance of the Seven Deadly Sins,' poem describing a Scotch Shrovetide revel, by William Dunbar.

1509   Coronation of Henry VIII: Magnificent tournament at Westminster: a pageant with Pallas and Diana, etc.

1512   Henry VIII introduces into the English Court the forms of the Italian masquerades.

1519   Rafael Sanzio's designs for the pastoral drama, the *Suppositi* of Ariosto.

1527   The Bourbon Sack of Rome. End of the Italian Renaissance.

1533   Catherine de Medici lands at Marseilles: The show to greet her marks official beginning of Italian influence in French pageantry.

1539   Francis the First, having invited the Italian painters forming the School of Fontainebleau, gives masquerades in the Italian manner.

ca. 1540   Cosimo di Medici introduces chariot races into Florence.

1548   Entry of Catherine de Medici to Paris: one of the oldest examples of the distribution of verses after the masquerades. Prototype of form of court ballet.

1551   Serlio's *Architettura,* great reëditing of Roman architect, Vitruvius.

ca. 1555   The Milanese dancing masters, Pompeo Diabono and Cesare Negri leave for the French Court.

after ca. 1552

Numerous princely Italian theaters built.

1558   Entry of Henry II into Paris. Jodelle, inspired by the Italian *trionfi* has Orpheus praise the King.

1559–60   Masques at the Court of Queen Elizabeth.

1563   Pageants at the proclamation of the Edict of Amboise: The end of the first French religious wars.

1565   Carnaval at Fontainebleau with one of Ariosto's comedies given. Interview of Catherine de Medici and her daughter, the wife of Philip II of Spain. Masquerade with rhymed compliments—perhaps the first dramatic ballet.

1569   First Company of the *Gelosi:* troupe performing the Popular Italian Comedy.

1571   de Baïf's Academy of Music and Poetry founded. Great influence on future of French dancing and music.

1573   Catherine de Medici's reception to the Polish Ambassadors. Triumph in France of the Italian Figured Dance.
Torquato Tasso's *Aminta.* A pastoral with huge influence all over Europe.

1580   Palladio's Olympian theater at Vicenza, a model for two hundred years.

1581   *Ballet Comique de la Reine* of Beaujoyeulx: the first modern ballet linked with sustained mood in action, verse, music and decoration.

1588 The "Orchesography" of Thoinot Arbeau (Jean Tabouret), published at Langres. First modern technical work on dancing embodying vocabulary of subsequent ballet terms.

ca. 1590 Society of Florentine Gentlemen interested in music: The *Camerata* precedent for Academies for music.

1592 *Ballet de Chevaliers François et Béarnais,* allegorical and patriotic *dramatic* ballet.

1594 Masque of 'Proteus and the Adamantine Rock' at Shrovetide. The prototype of the Jonsonian masque.

1596 Sir John Davies' "Orchestra: a poeme on dancing." London.

1597 *Daphne,* opera by Jacopo Peri: Florence.

1599 Archange Tuccaro's book: "Three Dialogues on the exercise of leaping and turning in the air": Paris; Technical discourse on acrobatics.

1603 Ben Jonson's appointment as poet of the revels at the Court of Elizabeth.

1605 The Twelfth Night Masque: Collaboration of Ben Jonson and the architect Inigo Jones. *The Masque of Blacknesse.*

1608 Wedding of Cosimo de Medici and Maria Maddelena, Archduchess of Austria: Important influence on the English Mask. *Veglia:* (vigil), 'The Night of Love.'
Naval-battles (*fêtes*) in the river Arno at Florence, designed by Alfonso and Giulio Parigi for the marriage of the Prince of Tuscany.
Orfeo: opera by Monteverdi: Mantua.

1609 Twelfth Night Masque. Queen Elizabeth takes part. The antimasque becomes integrated into the action.

1610 Ballet of *Alcine;* adroit use of "burlesque" entries of *ballet-mascarade,* with "noble" entries of *ballets-comiques.*

1615 The War of Love: Fête of the Grand Duke of Tuscany Cosimo di Medici: Florence.

1617 *Délivérance de Renaud:* Final type of *ballet melo-dramatique;* i.e., with predominantly musical interest.

1618 The Farnese Theater at Parma.

1619 "Adventures of Tancred," French dramatic Ballet in three almost equal acts.

1621 *Ballet d'Apollon:* from now on, until Lully, the genre regresses in dramatic interest.

1634 *Comus,* a mask by John Milton, performed at Ludlow Castle. Music by Henry Lawes.

1638 Twelfth Night Masque at Whitehall. *Britannia Triumphant* of Inigo Jones and William Davenant. Strong influence of the Florentine *intermedii.*

1641 Richelieu's Ballet: *Prosperity of the Arms of France.*

1645-46-47 Cardinal Mazarin's Italian opera presented at Carnival time.

1647 *Orfeo:* Luigi Rossi's opera mounted magnificently with machines of Jacopo Torelli: Prototype of French opera production.

1645-47 First visit of Giuseppi Bianchi's troupe of Italian popular comedians to Paris. Influence on Molière of *Commedia del' Arte.*

1647 The *Cid* of Corneille, translated into Italian. The French stage of the epoch of Louis XIV, the model for all Europe.

ca. 1650 Constant use of elaborate theatrical machinery spreads from Italy to France.

1651 Louis XIV, aged 13, makes début as dancer in *Cassandre* (Benserade).
Playford's English "Dancing Master."

1653 *Ballet de la Nuit:* Representation of the *Cour des Miracles* with acrobatics and clowning.

1661 Louis XIV founds a Dancing Academy in a room in the Louvre.

1662 Louis XIV's *Fête des Bagues: Carrousel:* Equestrian Ballet.

1664 Louis XIV's *Plaisirs des Iles Enchantéés:* Versailles.

1669 28th June: Perrin obtains letters patent to found Academy of Music.
Louis XIV retires from the ballet stage in "Flora."

1670 23rd October: First performance of Molière's *comédie-ballet: Le Bourgois Gentilhomme.*

1671 March 3rd French *Opéra* opens.
Psyche: opera-ballet by Molière, Corneille, Lully and Quinault.

1672 Lully takes over the opera: a pastorale, *Festes de l'Amour et de Bacchus.*

1673 Beauchamps made *Maître de Ballet* of the *Académie Royale de Musique et de danse,* by Lully.

1681 First appearance of female professional dancers on the French stage: "The Triumph of Love."

1687 The death of Jean Baptiste Lully, leaving the French opera ballet formulated.

1695 *Ballet des Saisons:* by Colasse: Prototype of opera-ballet for first half of the 17th Century.

1697 *L'Europe Gallante,* ballet of entries by La Motte and Campra.

1701 R. A. Feuillet's "Choreography, or the Art of Writing Dance Steps," issued in Paris.

1703 First public theater constructed in Moscow.

1708 The Duchesse du Maine gives the fourth act of Corneille's *Horace* as pantomime, mimed by two dancers, at Sceaux, in imitation of Roman mimes.

1716 Establishment of Opera Balls by the Regent in the minority of Louis XV.

1725   P. Rameau's *The Dancing Master:* Codification of the five absolute ballet positions.

1726   Début of Camargo: Her skirts shortened; she introduced many innovations in ballet technique.

1727   Birth of Noverre.

ca. 1730   Controversy over *perpendicular* versus *horizontal* dancing in Paris: The Lullists against the Ramists.

1735   Empress Anna Ivanovna of Russia establishes a State dancing school directed by Landé, a Frenchman.
        Les Indes Galantes, opera-ballet of Rameau, in the third entry of which Mlle. Sallé makes her appearance.

1745   Rameau's Comédie-Ballet *Le Princesse de Navarre:* lyric comedy sung and danced, with words by Voltaire.

1758   Noverre at the Court of Stuttgart undertakes reforms in ballet.

1759   Publication of Noverre's "Letters on Dancing."

1762   *Orpheus,* by Christoph Willibald Gluck: Opera equals for music Noverre's reforms in dancing.

1766   Anne Heinel of Stuttgart invents the *pirouette à la seconde.*

1770   Noverre in Vienna, dancing master to Marie-Antoinette.

1773   Abolition of dancers' masks at the Paris opera (Performance of Rameau's *Castor et Pollux*).

1775   Noverre's great *ballet d'action, Jason et Medée,* performed in Paris.

1794   Paris: The revolutionary, ambulatory ballet-spectacle, *La Fête à l'Etre Suprème.*

ca. 1795   Le Picq, Noverre's pupil, produces his master's ballet 'Jason and Medea' in Russia.

1800   Gardel's ballet *La Danseomanie* introduces the waltz of the *Opéra.*

1801   Didelot, French ballet-master, goes to Russia to develop native talent in the classic school.

1809   Death of Noverre at St. Germain.

1812   Salvatore Vigano establishes himself at Milan and achieves in his 'Choreodrame' or *ballets d'action* a realization of Noverre's reforms.

1815   The Bourbon Restoration reopens the Academy of Dancing: Paris.

1820   Publication of Carlo Blasis' *Treatise on the Dance,* the canon of modern classic dancing.

1822   Marie Taglioni makes her début in Vienna.

1832   March 12: Taglioni's *La Sylphide:* triumph of the Romantic Ballet.

1836   Fanny Elssler appears in *Le Diable Boiteux.*

1837   Carlo Blasis becomes Director of Imperial Academy of Dancing and Pantomime at Scala Theater, Milan.

1840   Auguste Bournonville, *maître de ballet* and first dancer at the Royal Theater, Copenhagen.

1841   Carlotta Grisi appears in *Giselle*.

1845   The *pas de quatre:* London: Taglioni, Grisi, Cerito and Grahn.

1847   Marius Petipa of Marseilles arrives in Russia as first dancer at the Imperial Theater.

1858   Marius Petipa appointed *maître de ballet* in St. Petersburg.

1861–64   Auguste Bournonville director and intendant of ballet and opera in Stockholm.

1862   Première of Petipa's *Fille de Pharaon*.

1866   'The Black Crook' at Niblo's Garden, New York City, Maria Bonfanti, *première danseuse*.

1872   Birth of Sergei Pavlovitch Diaghileff.

1873   German Academy for the Art of Teaching Dancing founded in Berlin by the ballet masters of Berlin, Koenigsberg, Hamburg and Leipsic.

1889   Michel Fokine enters the Imperial ballet school.

1894   Fokine's letter to Directors of Imperial Theaters, embodying basic ideas for reform.

1897   Serge Diaghileff edits Annuals of Imperial Theaters.

1898   Diaghileff founds and edits *Mir Iskoustvo* (The World of Art).

1899   Anna Pavlova's début: Marinsky Theatre.

1900   Vaslav Nijinsky enters Imperial Dancing School.

1905   Fokine's Greek ballet *Acis et Galatée*.
       Isadora Duncan dances and lectures in Russia.

1906   Fokine's *Chopiniana* and *Sylphides*.

1908   Vaslav Nijinsky graduates from the Imperial School; his début.
       Diaghileff takes the Russian Opera to Paris.

1909   Serge de Diaghileff forms company of Russian dancers.
       Fokine's dances for Borodin's *Prince Igor*.
       First season of Russian Ballet in Western Europe.

1910   Fokine: 'The Fire Bird' (Stravinsky).
       Death of Marius Petipa.

1911   *Petrouchka:* (Fokine, Nijinsky, Stravinsky, Benois). The finest achievement of dance-drama as danced before the war.

1912   Nijinsky's "Afternoon of the Faun."

1913   Mary Wigman at Ascona (Italy) with Rudolph von Laban.
       Nijinsky's *Jeux* and 'The Rites of Spring.'

1914   Festival at Geneva demonstrating the Eurythmics of Jacques Dalcroze.

1915–16   The Diaghileff Company tours North and South America.

1917   The Russian Revolution: Soviet Government through Lunacharsky continues to maintain ballet schools and theaters.
       Parade: Cocteau: Satie: Massine: The Cubists enter the Russian

Ballet which is no longer Russian. Bronislava Nijinska in Kiev continues her brother's researches.

1920–24 The Swedish Ballet under Rolf de Maré and Jean Börlin.

1922 Boris Romanoff's *Ballets Romantiques*.

1923 The 'Triadic' Ballet: *Bauhaus* Theater, Weimar, under Oscar Schlemmer.

1929 Death of Serge de Diaghileff: Venice.

1930 Mary Wigman's mass dance spectacle, *Totenmal:* Munich.

1931 Death of Anna Pavlova.

1932 Founding of de Basil's Monte Carlo Ballet Company: George Balanchine and Leonid Massine, choreographers.

1933 Foundation of the International Archives of the Dance, by Rolf de Maré: Paris.
Emergence of Kurt Joos Ballet: *The Green Table* takes the prize at the A. I. D. competition: Paris.
Production of Kurt Weill's 'Seven Capital Sins,' ballet-recitative: Neher: Balanchine. *Les Ballets 1933:* Paris.
Massine's *Présages* and *Choreartium*.

1934 The School of American Ballet founded: New York City.
Vaganova's "Handbook to the Classic Ballet" published: Moscow.
'Three Saints in Four Acts': Virgil Thomson: Frederick Ashton.
Season of the Vic-Wells Ballet Company: London.

1935 Martha Graham's composition for Panic, by A. MacLeish.
First season of the American Ballet.
Jubilee of the Moscow Ballet celebrated by the U. S. S. R.

INDEX

389